AF560241

Crusader Extraordinary

Krishna Menon and the India League 1932-1936

Suhash Chakravarty

India Research Press

India Research Press
B-4/22, Safdarjung Enclave,
New Delhi – 110 029.
Ph.: 24694610; Fax : 24618637
www.indiaresearchpress.com
contact@indiaresearchpress.com ; bahrisons@vsnl.com

2006

ISBN : 81-87943-57-2

Cataloguing in Publication Data
Suhash Chakravarty

Crusader Extraordinary
Includes Biographical Index, Bibliography, References and Index.

1. India 2. Krishna Menon 3. India League
4 . United Nation 5. Freedom Movement
i. Author ii. Title

Printed at Focus Impressions, New Delhi – 110 003.

Contents

Dedicated to
the memory of my parents

Preface

Our investigation in this volume begins in 1932 when Krishna Menon along with Ellen Wilkinson, Monica Whately and Leonard Matters were commissioned by the India League to proceed to India. The group was entrusted with a mission to study in depth the nature of the authoritarian regime initiated by Wedgwood Benn and carried out in cold blood by the combined efforts of Samuel Hoare and Willingdon. From London, Menon had been watching closely the failure of the western democracies to contain the sinister advent of fascism. With his immense insight into the existing political and economic systems, Menon had galvanized the India League into an effective platform for struggle. By 1932 the League committed itself to *Swaraj*. It had become an uncomfortable organization for the Conservatives and the Theosophists who deserted it and the League affiliated itself to the mass movement in India.

The publication of the *Condition of India* in 1934 was a momentous occasion for the League. Officially discouraged in Britain and proscribed in India, the delegation's report on India captured vividly the operation of the civil disobedience movement and intensity of official reaction. In sum, the report of the League's delegation stated candidly a simple but unassailable position: The people of India had been a subject people. Their government, culture, education and economy had been dominated, directed and restricted by an alien rule. To remain subservient willingly to a foreign power any longer would be to submit to their moral and spiritual degeneration as a people. It was added that the Indian people had been awakened to the grave danger of the continuation of the ruthless imperial rule, and, as a consequence, their movement for self-determination had been transformed into a unique struggle for human freedom.

By then, Menon had realized that behind Britain's love of freedom, her sensitivity to beauty, her *joie de vivre* and optimism, there was an unhappy growth that glorified the inhuman. It set up a standard image of India which was worked out without warmth, without tolerance and without respect for human beings who were of a different cultural, social and intellectual inheritance. Over the years, the imperial perception of India had been internalized by Britain's core culture cutting across party affiliations. Economic power, military authority and diplomatic ascendancy of the empire were sustained by the centrality of *Raj* in British imperial sensitivity. Evidently, British policy with regard to the Indian empire displayed an arrogant and an authoritarian programme in contrast to the fraternal fellow-feelings which were shown to Australia, Canada, New Zealand, South Africa and Rhodesia. Despite tactical differences, there was a strategic consensus that upheld imperial perception. An overwhelming majority of the Indian people, it was resolutely maintained, were committed to the uninterrupted continuity of British rule. The so-called problems of self-determination, it was added, had been contrived and manipulated by a clamorous minority unconcerned with the interests of the inarticulate masses. It seemed that even a genuine liberal opinion was obliged to sympathize with the tragic dilemma of the 'over-worked' and 'grossly misunderstood' civil servants operating in an ungrateful and turbulent land.

The *Raj* projected a complex 'imperial fellowship' that was replete with its own tensions, arrogance, ambiguities and tortured sensibilities along with the shattered self-images of 'paternalistic' district officers, inconsistent self-justifications of ideologues, inexorable idealistic suppositions of scholars and continual self-doubts of internal critics against the backdrop of an elaborate European mission. There was no sustained attempt to comprehend the aspirations of New India in rational democratic terms. There was no concerted effort to conciliate the dominant voice of an awakened civilization. The image presented by imperial perception continued to be that of an ostentatious imperial collage and of a nostalgic potpourri tenaciously upheld despite perceptible decline in imperial self-confidence. Call it in terms of 'reluctant' imperialism or in its 'constructive', variation, or project it under the cover of 'pragmatic compromises' or offer it in eugenic conceptions, or dress it in the restless endeavour of a creative minority seeking cross-cultural understanding, if you please. But from the vantage point of Menon, Shelvankar, Platts-Mills, Leonard Matters, Monica Whately and most of the activists of the India League, the discourses and initiatives of imperialism offered the spectacle of a garish and sentimental kitsche. In the course of an intense political struggle and an animated public debate, and in opposition to a vitriolic anti-Indian campaign, Menon's kindergarten often tended to overlook the 'obvious and real' limits imposed by imperialism on the evolution of British public opinion towards India. Yet it cannot be denied that they made their best efforts to summon all those positive and creative sentiments and initiatives that were articulated outside the essential imperial limits. They were, however, invariably confronted by the impact of British political chemistry. In fact, the general consensus was that the solution to the Indian problem would be found only in Westminster's constitutional confectionery in cooperation with Indian moderates such as Sapru, Sastri and Jayakar and against Gandhi and the Congress. The growing animosity between Jinnah and the Congress hardened this imperial conviction.

Among Menon's intelligent audience, some were sincere socialists with an international outlook then confronted with a perplexing intellectual problem in comprehending the claims of Indian nationalism in class categories. Some others were bourgeois liberals who often used the Marxian idioms to plead for a progressive capitalism and to conjure up the vision of a liberal imperial commonwealth. Some others were willing to promote socialism at home in sheer indifference to the aspirations of the colonial peoples. Yet there were some others who were entrenched in the Fabian illusion of gradualness. There were also some to whom the elementary struggle for bread and butter and against unemployment was more than enough to have either the opportunity or the inclination to strive for an imperial salvation. The problem was that Menon had no party in British parliamentary life working for India's freedom with coherence and with a striking power. The strength of Menon and the India League was that they successfully identified themselves with an England of labour, of cooperative endeavour, of the struggle for human freedom and of the great ideals of international solidarity against an England inebriated with imperial pride and prejudices. India League's popularity with the liberal democratic public opinion in Britain was enhanced as the decade unfolded itself. It was the principal anti-imperialist platform in Britain that swerved overwhelmingly to the Left and converged with the global anti-fascist mobilization. In its turn, the India League found its crucial empathy and support from the international Left. Despite the sharp divergences in perspectives, Menon found his speeches at different meetings cheered by bands of enthusiastic communist workers who were more actively committed to India's independence than any other political force in England. In fact, communists were in the forefront of all radical movements of the day. They had a decisive international outlook. More than any other theory of knowledge, Marxism offered a comprehensive and interconnected perspective of the fragmented realities of life and experience. A substantial section of trade union militants in the CP had been gradually moving away from the 'class against class' thesis and CP, in the course of its struggle developed ample space for cooperation with the India League. Hunger marchers were out in England; the unemployed were reading the *Daily Worker*; there was the clamour of social justice; social existence was being widely viewed in terms of class struggle; there was a lively boom in anti-war activities; articles were written about 'the next war', both rearmament and disarmament were being discussed; Gandhi's non-violent struggle against British imperialism had become a talking point of both the right and the left wings of the British political spectrum and the steady advance of Nehru as the successor of the Mahatma stirred the imagination of many. The overriding consideration that constituted the underpinning of the new awakening was the retreat of democracy in the face of the ascendancy of fascism and militarism.

Propaganda was a complicated affair and Menon, with all his intensity, had made India work quite arduous. It had fairly advanced outlets to various fronts: the parliamentary committee, the labour committee, the women's committee, the executive committee, the committee in charge of the *India Review,* the committee looking after the League's publications including bulletins, pamphlets, books and talking points, the affiliating committee and the general body. It was also imperative to nurse about 2,000 organizations having fraternal and affiliating relationships with the League requiring considerable information and ideological input. Arrangement of periodical meetings, delegate conferences and public meetings on political and social issues confronting the India policy of the day and the current public debates could not have been passed over. In fact, contact with India was in itself a time-consuming affair and the section of the Strand office dealing with the newspaper cuttings involved a good deal of unpaid labour donated voluntarily by a fairly large body of students who constituted Menon's cheerful kindergarten. He saw to it that the timetable of the League was closely followed, the meetings were well advertised, an attentive audience was mobilized, intelligent questions were posed that inspired new interest in India, caused doubts and introspection and invariably created significant ripples in local public opinion duly recognized by the press. British rule came to be analyzed with an element of scepticism. The hiatus between British profession of liberalism at home and imperialism in India came under careful and scientific scrutiny and a section of public opinion began to appreciate, albeit hesitatingly, the difference between the advertised official projections and the realities of life in India.

The impact of daily controversies and noisy disturbances at public meetings sharpened Menon's repartee and verbal counter-offensives. Increasingly, he became allergic to mediocrity and hostile procrastination. Yet his tactlessness was compensated by his alert instincts and his finely-tuned fund of principles, theories and perceptions and his endless hunger for knowledge. A hard task master and a perfectionist, Menon became early in his life a remarkable loner even amidst a dedicated following. Somewhat susceptible to a touch of adulation, Menon had been trying hard to cultivate compassion and the spirit of conciliation and to distinguish between the essentials and non-essentials. He was in touch with the leading journalists and publicists. He had established an easy and comfortable access to the official and unofficial circles of the British power-elite. He had also worked for himself a special position in the political moots all over the country and carefully cultivated lively contacts with political groups and associations concerned with India and the India policy. London society had come to acknowledge this *rara avis,* an Indian nationalist *pur sang,* given to propaganda.

All these years Menon carefully analyzed the League's appeal on English public opinion. The old England of traditional life had virtually nothing in common with the India League and its concerns. The remnant of the nineteenth century industrial England had a tremendous attraction for the League's essay to tie up colonial discontent with social miseries of the urban underclass in Britain. But it was the dynamics of contemporary world forces of the inter-war period that demanded the League's comprehensive appreciation. Mond-Turnerism, the growing respectability of the Labour Party, unemployment, the rise of authoritarianism, the militant labour movement, the prolonged discussion in London over the proposed Indian reforms, the left wing swing in British political and intellectual life typified by the King and Country debate, the united front thesis of Georgie Dimitrov and the Unity Campaign, the rise of the die-hard conservatism, the entropy of the labour movement under an unimaginative leadership, the advancement of socialist thought in India, the formation of the Congress Socialist Party, the ascendancy of Nehruvian nationalism and the rising communal tension in India were some of the diacritical marks of the contemporary world. The success of Menon in projecting through the League's programme a coherent and integrated response to the world crisis underlined the rich texture of the Indian national struggle. The result was astounding. It drew sympathy from various sections of enlightened opinion as Menon went ahead to rope in several intellectuals, authors, playwrights, journalists and leading personalities at different levels of affiliation with the League. The Scotland Yard observed, with a good deal of uneasiness, that Menon's outstanding intellectual qualities, attractive personality and his ready wit, repartee and aphorisms placed him in an intriguingly conspicuous position in the left-wing circles. In fact, as he went ahead to add Abyssinia, Spain, China and the Unity Movement within the ambit of the League's propaganda, Menon began to be viewed as the marked man of the British empire and the most malignant contact of Jawaharlal Nehru. Despite considerable backbiting and intrigues manipulated by the intelligence department, the dingy little room in the Strand became the principal centre from where the nationalist perception of the Indian struggle was disseminated, all imperial distortions were challenged and official misrepresentations were questioned. The interactions between the India League and various organized bodies such as the Labour Party, the ILP, the Communist Party and the Conservative Party and their front organizations have been examined. Personalities such as George Lansbury, Horace Alexander, Agatha Harrison, H.S.L. Polak, Fenner Brockway, James Maxton, Wedgwood Benn, Lord Zetland, Louis Stuart, Lawrence Housman, Francis Horrabin, Aneurin Bevan, Michael Foot, Barbara Castle, Shapurji Saklatvala, Harry Pollitt, James Klugmann, R. Palme Dutt, J.F.F. Platts-Mills, R.H. Sorensen, Monica Whately, Ellen Wilkinson, Bertrand Russell and many others have found their appropriate places in this historical narration. So have the Indian Empire Society, the Defence of India League, the Union of Democratic Control, the League of Nations Associations, the Cooperative Guilds, India Conciliation Group and the Friends of India. Having established contacts with sympathetic bodies in Germany, France, the United States and Geneva, Menon fashioned a remarkable intellectual fraternity with Jawaharlal Nehru. The relationship between an enthusiastic, optimistic and popular Nehru and a somewhat sceptical, caustic and introverted Menon grew very intimate over the years. Despite misgivings, intrigues, manoeuvres and desertions, the League forged ahead and Menon found himself, at the end of the period, at the centre of the India lobby both within and without the parliament.

The work has been made possible by the access given to me by the late Indira Gandhi to the large collection of Menon's papers at the Nehru Memorial Museum and Library in New

Delhi. I have supplemented the Menon Papers with substantial research at other centres in India, Germany and Britain. I am indebted to the staff of a number of libraries and archives who made their facilities available to me. They have been duly acknowledged in the notes and references as well as in the bibliography. The research project was initiated by a grant from the Krishna Menon Memorial Society whose liberal assistance helped me undertake a field trip to England for this volume. The field research was also supported by the Indian Council of Historical Research, the University of Delhi and the Vasant Valley Centre. A Nehru fellowship offered by the Jawaharlal Nehru Memorial Fund in 1991 enabled me to entrench myself firmly in this multi-volume project.

Many people shared with me their experience in the India League and their precious reminiscences and recollections with Menon thus enabling me to formulate my own sense of direction. I would like to record my gratitude and thanks for what I have learnt from extensive interviews with some of them. In particular, I am grateful to Sri Jyoti Basu, Justice V.R. Krishna Iyer, Sri Mulk Raj Anand, Mr Michael Foot, Prof. Manmohan Singh, Prof. Margaret Chatterjee, Ms Pamella Cullen, Sri T.N. Chaturvedi, Sri Vasant Sathe, Mr. A.B. Bardhan, Sri George Fernandes, Dr B.R. Nanda, Sri Ram Niwas Mirdha, Rev. John Sweet, Prof. Irfan Habib, Prof. Lotika Sarkar, Mr S.F. Bolt, Prof. Paul Ries, Dr Martin Yuille, Sri V. K. Madhavan Kutty, Sri Subrata Banerjee, Mr. Subhash Chakravarty, Prof. G.K. Chadha and Prof. Indira Goswami. Among friends and colleagues, I would like to mention Dr Gordon Johnson, Prof. Ashwini Roy, Dr. Nikhilesh Banerjee, Prof. Matin Zuberi, Prof. Nandalal Gupta, Prof. Sukhomay Ganguli, Sri Nirmal Roy, Prof. V.R. Mehta, Prof. Rakesh Gupta, Dr. V.C. Bhutani, Ms Jehanara Wasi, Prof. Vepa Rao, Mr Inder Malhotra, Mr N. Ram, Mr Sumit Chakravartty, Mr Hardeep

Puri, Mr Arun Kapur, Mr. Alok Sen Gupta, Mr Sham Sher Sheriff, Prof. Roger Louis, Dr Nicholas Owen, Prof Subrata Mukherjee, Prof. Manoranjan Mohanti, Sri Janardan Dwivedi, Prof. D.K. Bhattacharya, Mr Ravi Vyas, Dr Amar Farooqui, Dr Shama Mitra Chenoi, Dr Anil Kumar, Dr Ajit Jha and Dr Amrit Basra, Dr D.N. Gupta, Dr Ratan Singh, Dr Kabita Sharma, Mrs Suchitra Gupta, and Dr Rajendra Prasad. Regretfully, some of my guides and advisers such as Emily Polak, Krishna Shelvankar, J.F.F. Platts-Mills, Julius Silverman, Muquiuddin Farooqi, S.K. Ananth, Raghav Menon, P.N. Haksar, Sheila Uttam Singh, Sisir Das and Mohit Sen are no more. The exciting discussions that I had with them left an indelible imprint on my perceptions and sensibilities. Their incisive comments on the volume would have certainly enriched my insight.

I am also indebted to the stimulation, encouragements and intellectual generosity extended to me by Dr Karan Singh, Justice V.R. Krishna Iyer, Sri K. Natwar Singh, Srimati Shiela Dixit and Sri A.K. Damodaran all through my engagement with Krishna Menon and his League. As I have stated in an earlier volume, often even a simple flash of fading memory of an episode or something expressed casually in a conversation might have turned out to be a useful indicator of a specific investigation. In fact, it is not possible to acknowledge all those from whom I have had the occasion to derive benefit or information or whose brain I happened to pick. I buttonholed many of my bright students and acquaintances while I was writing the volume and was occasionally benefited by their perceptive comments and suggestions. Some of those who deserved to be mentioned are B. Raja Rajan, Bhuban Jha, Annie Mathew, Manoj Sharma, Rajen Saikia, Vikram Diesh, Cynthia Masih, Madhu Sharma, Santhosh Rai, Manorama Masih, Aprana Vaidik, Shaleen Jain and Kamal Kumar Mishra.

The volume took its final shape in the picturesque environment of the historic city of Tashkent, thanks to the vibrant academic atmosphere generated by some sedate and inspiring scholars and a number of enterprising students in the classrooms and seminars. I should like to remember the extensive dialogue I had with Academician, S.F. Tusrsunmuhammedev, Prof. A.A. Fayzullaev, Dr. Surat Mirkasimov, Prof. Kh. G. Gulyamov, Prof. Azad Shamatov, Dr Bakhtiyar Abidov, Prof. Dinora Azimova, Prof. Timur Giyasov, Mr Botir Ochilov Mr. Nigai Stanislav Lvovich and Dr Muzrab S. Tashmuhamedov.

The stimulating discussions with some of my students such as Kakhramon Asronov, Saiyora Ismailova, Saidolimhon Gaziyev, Zaynab Muhammad Dost, Sukhrob Khalilov, Alisher Kasimov, Rashidkhan Aripov Khayrullakhanovich and Sirajuddin Nurmatov helped me in making the writing of the volume a gratifying experience.

Parts of the work were discussed at various presentations in the India Club (Birmingham), the India International Centre (New Delhi), Zamorin College (Kozikode), the Department of Political Science (University of Delhi), Maulana Azad Institute of Asian Studies (Kolkata), the Indian Society of International Law (New Delhi) and the Nehru Memorial Fund (New Delhi). I thank all those who cared to make comments and suggestions on those occasions.

I also take the opportunity to thank Sri Vijay Ahuja (Delhi) for having typed and re-typed the various incarnations of the manuscript with ungrudging forbearance and Sri Manohar Lal (Tashkent) for his helpful disposition.

Finally, I owe much to my wife, Shachi, for her smiling face, both in hard times and smooth, and for blending her intelligent criticisms with witty comments and liberal appreciation and to my son, Surajit, for his infinite patience and timely editorial suggestions. I alone am responsible for the views expressed in the book with all its inadequacies.

Suhash Chakravarty
25 December, 2005

CHAPTER I

PASSAGE TO INDIA

A firm stand in India had become the general tenor of British policy since the inauguration of the civil disobedience movement in 1930. Menon had been watching a tragic metamorphosis of the Labour Party, which over the years internalized imperial sensibilities of the Conservatives. Wedgwood Benn, in charge of the India Office, made it abundantly clear that the significant demands of the nationalists with regard to full responsible government as the basis of the RTC would not be touched by the government even with a bargepole. With regard to the question of withdrawal of repressive measures and release of political prisoners, popularized by the India League, as condition precedent for normalizing the Indian situation, Benn was equally candid. He maintained that the government had a judicious policy seeking a constitutional settlement of the Indian problem acceptable to all parties and the RTC had been summoned to that end. The vast masses of the Indian population were law-abiding people who wished to pursue their vocations in peace and tranquillity and were committed to ensure their political destiny by constitutional means. Benn was irked to note that unfortunately a section of the Indian people led by Gandhi had been consistent in their effort to coerce the government by methods which might be in intention non-violent, but which would inevitably lead to unbridled violence. He held that government had a definite obligation to enable the ordinary machinery of administration and business to proceed and when faced with civil disobedience it had no option but to call into play measures adequate to secure this. Benn insisted that any government would have done the same and such actions were bound to be the 'butt of wild rumours and misrepresentations'. Appreciating the 'remarkable moderation' of the police action in combating that 'very insidious movement' known as *satyagraha*, Benn applauded the equanimity with which public opinion in India accepted the necessity of stern action taken by the authorities. Although the administration was not as yet out of the woods, Benn insisted that the country was generally tired of civil disobedience and dislocation of daily routine and there were signs of improvement in the conditions of life in India. In its annual conferences the Labour Party was given to use the strongest card in the government's armoury in the form of initiatives taken by Tej Bahadur Sapru and M.R. Jayakar towards a peaceful settlement. The responsibility for the state of affairs in India lay with the leaders of a wicked movement organized by the 'crafty Gandhi' and the government was certainly unable to offer a policy of conciliation to soften the blows of that 'increasingly hostile and unrepentant leader'.[1]

Under Samuel Hoare and Lord Willingdon the perspective turned more onerous and the official response more aggressive. They, in tandem, sharpened the policy and, in consequence, considerably narrowed the scope for flexibility and adjustment. Along with the harsh ordinance rule, strict censorship was systematically clamped down.[2] On 4 May 1932, for example, Menon brought to the notice of George Lansbury a special case in which the *Indian Review* was involved. A paper by Lansbury on the Delhi events and the repression in India, published in the *Review* of 30 April 1932, was cabled by Menon to the *Hindustan Times* together with summaries of the views of Harold Laski and Tom Williams. The Imperial and International Communications, a cable company, sent a representative to meet Menon as they had instructions to communicate information to him verbally. The representative, unwilling to put down anything in writing, intimated that the cable was not delivered as the Indian administration refused to hand over the message. The company also informed Menon that they would no longer accept telegrams from him since if the telegrams were not passed on they would not be able to charge the *Hindustan Times*.[3] This regulated flow of information was backed by the official bulletins aimed at weaving a well-knit blanket of disinformation. An impression was sought to be fostered in Britain that civil disobedience meant violent terrorist onslaught on lives and property, that timely intervention by the state machinery had retrieved the situation to some extent, that the continuation of the ordinances in some form was desirable as the minimum condition of law, order and civilized existence, that the government was alive to its responsibilities and did not desire to continue the operation of ordinances and emergency measures longer than was absolutely necessary and that there was a growing awareness in India in sympathy with the government and its unenviable position.[4]

As against this intricate official propaganda, Menon emphasized repeatedly that the political situation was more serious than ever before as Hoare was determined to crush the Congress at all costs. Hoare's resolve was so firm and inflexible that Menon thought that it was needless to say any more on the subject.[5] The situation in India was sized up by Mirabehn immediately upon Gandhi's arrest and in one of her despatches to Tom Williams she pleaded that a deputation of public men including a few MPs should be encouraged to visit India in order to carry home first-hand information about the nature of the ordinance rule.[6] The proposal was attractive and gained currency and the League discussed the suggestion in its various meetings, in the executive, with friends outside the immediate circles. In India, Madan Mohan Malaviya's response to the proposal was positive and spontaneous and he even offered to raise financial assistance in India for the project.[7]

Contact with Malaviya had been maintained ever since the RTC days. Malaviya had been one of the patrons of the *Review,* periodically sent newsletters from India, helped streamline Menon's journalistic engagements, especially with the *Hindustan Times* and on more occasions than one stood by the *Review* during its perennial financial crisis.[8] The *Review* had caught the imagination of a class of perceptive public opinion and by mid-1932 Menon could report enthusiastically that he had been getting a much better lot of contributions and a wider interest for the journal. But as a financial proposition it would at least be another half a year before it would even pay any appreciable part of the expenses.[9] About the same time a distressed Menon wrote to Malaviya: 'I am obliged to cable to you again today for money. May I request you to let me know immediately — even airmail will be of no use — what arrangement are you making with regard to the appeal for funds that we have made.'[10] He entreated Govind Malaviya that unless Panditji sent some money 'We shall have stopped by the time you will receive this letter, which is a great tragedy indeed'.[11] On 2 July 1932 Menon returned to the theme. Together with James Francis Horrabin he had been pinning his faith on the prospect of receiving a remittance from Malaviya. 'We are hemmed in from all sides', Menon wrote, and in spite of every effort 'we not only cannot carry on but are even unable to meet the obligations we have incurred.'[12] He thought that it would be unwise to discuss the situation in greater detail. He clarified that if in the course of the week no money was received from India for the *India Review*, 'I dare not contemplate what the position would be.' If the delegation as contemplated materialized, Menon hoped to see the Malaviyas in India before long.[13]

The *Review* had been struggling ever since its inception and all of Menon's associates in the League were concerned about the difficulties faced by it.[14] Horrabin had worked out that the actual cost of production of the journal was to be £400. But the *Review* met greater opposition than they had anticipated and it had been very difficult to keep it going. Even its distribution had been very expensive.[15] Although Menon had always been definite in stating that the League had no direct responsibility for the paper, everyone was aware that it was the most potent means of propaganda that the League had; the necessity of carrying it on and enlarging its sphere of influence was of vital importance to the India work undertaken in Britain. Menon was, therefore, assured by Horrabin and other members of the executive committee that, if need be, they would do their best to keep the journal alive as they keenly felt a moral responsibility for it. They all realized that there was immense difficulty in raising money in England, especially in the existing situation in Britain and as the public knew very little of what was going on in India. After a good deal of discussion it was concluded that the only way out of the deadlock was to seek funds in India.[16] Menon was requested to emphasize to everyone who mattered in Indian national life the need for some substantial means for reaching out to a wider public in England. The League felt that the *Review* 'fills this need as nothing else can'.[17] Menon was expected to use all his powers of persuasion to convince the leading nationalist leaders then outside prison and make them appreciate the urgency of a continued campaign for India in Britain. By then, the counter-offensive against the League had become biting, tart and acrimonious. All endeavours of the League and the National Congress were dismissed as an exercise in futility based on a morbid hostility organized 'by a self-centred Brahmin oligarchy' towards the historic British mission in India. The business of government was to govern and any attempt at subversion ought to be countered by a modicum of 'controlled ruthlessness'.[18] The general impression that was sought to be created was that the condition of India had been steadily returning to normalcy and no effective or constructive purpose would be served by making a mountain of a molehill.[19] Opposition to the League's proposed delegation to India found several proponents.

By July 1932 Menon was somewhat disconcerted by the prolonged silence from India. He had been anxiously waiting to hear from Malaviya in reply to several cables that had been sent to him during the preceding two weeks. Menon was uncertain if the cables had been directed to Malaviya by the post office at all or if they were intercepted *en route* by the government.[20] By then, so far as the India League was concerned, the decision to send the deputation along with other preparatory measures had been almost finalized. The proposal attracted a good deal of attention in the intellectual and political circles and some of them toyed with the idea if one of the Laskis could be persuaded to participate in the investigation.[21] Ellen Wilkinson was inclined to accompany him and all those who visited the Strand office agreed that Wilkinson's personal acquaintance with the governor of Bengal and quite a few highly placed civil servants would be of great value to the team.[22] It was also desired that Lord Snell, formerly under-secretary of state for India, should be invited, and, what was more, he was not averse to accompanying the delegation.[23] Menon, however, was not inclined to discuss these matters as a practical proposition because it meant additional costs while he managed with merely scrapings from the bottom of the barrel. Somewhat harassed, Menon meekly reminded Govind Malaviya that the entire arrangement including lengthy negotiations had been carried out on the strength of Panditji's cable and he hoped that there would be no hitch at that stage. An urgent cable had been sent out because it was particularly necessary to seek an appointment with Hoare before the adjournment of the House.

Menon cheerily added that both Laski and Brailsford had been taking greater interest in India than before the arrest of Gandhi and the meetings of Laski were extremely well attended by a large number of people who were new recruits of the League campaign. He was also glad to inform that the League had been able to harness a team of young workers and that they were mostly drawn from the British university students who were thoroughly familiar with Laski's point of view.[24] A passionate authority on libertarianism and individual expression, Laski was not merely a megaphone for the Left. He was an international inspiration who offered to many remarkable intellectual excitement. Menon thought that with the knowledge that the deputation would be able to bring, the League should be able to inaugurate and carry on an intensive campaign all over the country towards the end of the year and in spring before the legislation came before parliament. With uncertainties emanating from Malaviya's eerie silence, there was still some doubt and hesitation about the departure of the delegation.[25]

On 9 July 1932 Menon appeared to be in a more spirited frame of mind. Erulkar had instructions to hand over to Menon a sum of £200 as advised by Birla. Menon felt relieved: 'May I say how grateful I am to you, for this timely assistance, as we were literally unable to meet our past obligations on the *India Review*.'[26] A letter from Govind Malaviya cleared all doubts about the reception of the delegates in India and the *India Review* got another shot in the arm.[27] Some significant changes were made in the composition of the delegation. Owing to the emergency session of parliament it would be impossible to take anyone from the House of Commons. The League thought it judicious to discuss the matter with Andrews and Laski and the names which were discussed were those of Harry Snell and Emmanuel Shinwell. Snell could not make the long journey unless his doctors cleared him. Morgan Jones was also disallowed by physicians. If it was humanly possible for Snell to come, Menon felt, it would be done. As a former Under-Secretary of State and a man of moderate views he had a value outside Labour ranks which would be of assistance to the League. Shinwell would also be useful as he was an ex-minister and likely to get into the House of Commons again at a by-election.[28] Meanwhile, a vigorous campaign had been started by the India League to prepare public opinion for use when the delegation returned. Menon also suggested to Malaviya that it would be inadvisable to make the remittance through David Erulkar or any other friend in England as it might lead to some delicate complications. The best plan would be to cable it to Lloyds Bank asking them to advise the League of its arrival.[29]

Following the completion of the crucial financial settlement with Malaviya, Menon was able to work out the panel of names from which the final selection would be made. From the House of Commons it would, in all probability, be either Morgan Jones or Tom Williams. Menon believed that Williams had an edge over Jones as he was more energetic and more inclined to speak his mind. He was well-known and well received on all sides of the House while Jones had the advantage of being junior member of government. The Executive Committee had also been making efforts to obtain some others who might pay their own expenses. It was also decided that at least two ladies would join the team and the persons then considered were Monica Whately and Ellen Wilkinson. Whately was the granddaughter of an archbishop and belonged to what might be called the British ruling class. She was a very effective speaker and one of the foremost women in the militant suffragette movement and had been in prison on several occasions. She was strongly recommended by Mrs Pethick-Lawrence, unquestionably the most prominent leader of the Women's Freedom League. Whately had lately thrown herself with enthusiasm into the India League and had been doing her assignment very well. She was also a Labour candidate for parliament with a sporting chance of winning the next time and was the vice-chairperson of the Labour Candidates' Association.[30] The position of Ellen Wilkinson was extremely difficult although she was anxious to assist. As a salaried officer of her union she could not dispose of her time as she liked. After negotiations, however, the union officials allowed her to take leave without pay. She was an extraordinary Labour candidate of left-wing vintage. A sharp orator, a trade union organizer, an international propagandist and an ubiquitous crusader, she was thorough in politics and a committed India League spokesperson. 'The majority of our people here think', Menon wrote, 'it would be a great advantage to send her out as she has *entrée* into the press here and in America and has the capacity of making herself heard.' The most prized possession of the League, Wilkinson, in her early thirties had already made an indelible impression on the mind of the British left. Personally, Menon thought that she was a celebrity and worth 'any three or four people whom we might send'.[31]

With regard to planning out the delegation it was arranged that the body of people would go out from the India League as an accredited group of observers making investigations on the spot. The League considered it vital that the party should be sent as a deputation from Britain and be independent in character. The procedure of work was then under consideration. But it had been decided that the deputation should leave Venice on 5 August 1932 and arrive in Bombay on 17 August and return, leaving Bombay on 7 November and arriving at Genoa on 17 November. This would give them nearly eleven weeks in India and also enable the deputation to be back in time for the parliament session.[32] It was useful if the proposed constitutional bill was presented in the winter session. It would be essential to make the fullest use of every day of the visit considering the short period of stay of the delegation. It was suggested that the party should go directly north from Bombay so as to avoid the rigours of climate in the early autumn.[33] It would also appear to be essential for the team to have reliable and important persons in each of the places to be visited. Horrabin emphasized in no uncertain terms that it would be unfortunate if lack of organization made the visit not as rewarding as it could have been.[34]

Malaviya was informed that Menon had been asked to accompany the deputation as secretary in view of his being an Indian and knowing all the people intimately. His presence in the team fashioned a greater degree of cohesion and willingness to go out as they all felt that they were being accompanied by someone belonging to the country.[35] It was also decided that the party would make no speeches and take no part whatever in political work as it would be against the interest of everyone concerned. The League thought it expedient to get in touch with Samuel Hoare as early as possible and apprise him of the League's intentions. The League had no desire in any way to embarrass authorities in India, their task being one of obtaining information for the education of British public and parliamentary opinion.[36] With regard to finance, the delegation was prepared to travel economically, and from all enquiries

Menon understood that £200 per head would be the bare minimum expenditure and a party of four was then the League's computation.[37] Although attempts were being made to garner sufficient funds in England it was almost certain that it would be an uphill task, especially as they had only three or four weeks before the departure. Besides, most of what little might be raised would have to be left behind to carry on while Menon was away.[38] Malaviya had already been informed by cable that preliminary arrangements had been completed and further steps could only be taken after the funds were guaranteed from the Indian side.[39]

Malaviya was requested to refer to the assistance from India as a donation to the League and there was no need to explain the touchy decision and its sensitive implications. Emphasizing the urgency of the delegation, Menon wrote to Govind Malaviya that everyone concerned with the League delegation had pulled their weight and put on one side most of their own work to get the delegation through and they would spare no effort to make it a success.[40] To the delegates a letter under the signatures of Horrabin and Marley examined in detail the terms of reference of the deputation. The tour itinerary and other details relating to the work of the delegation were largely left to the collective judgement of the delegation. It was, however, desired that the executive committee should communicate to the members of the team its conception of the task of the delegation, its scope and limitations. The delegation was being sent for the purpose of collecting firsthand information about the state of affairs in India and trends of opinion there and to make a report on its return. It was hoped that the report would serve as a basis for a more intensive education of public opinion in Britain. In the event of any statement having to be made to the Indian press or journalists, such a statement should be of a joint character and be issued in the name of the delegation by the secretary. The committee, however, assured the delegation that it had confidence both in its judgement and discretion, as well as in its initiative and sense of responsibility.

Despite a free hand given to the delegation with regard to the collection of information, the members were reminded that certain essentials should not be overlooked. They were to investigate the nature of the police and its functioning, prison conditions, opinion of men and women of all parties including officials and non-officials, Indians and British, Congress, moderates, conservatives, Hindus, Muslims, etc. They were to ascertain the sections which would stand by the proposed constitution and what section would willy-nilly line up with it, the actual position of Muslim opinion, the impact of a policy of no-return to the RTC method on the cooperators and if the return to the method would improve the quality of public temper. Other areas of the proposed inquiry would be to assess the attitudes of the cooperating Hindus and Muslims and the nature of Indian poverty, both agricultural and industrial, the existence of national feelings in rural India, the general strength of the trade unions, official and non-official British feelings, etc. Besides, the delegation was urged to make a reasonable endeavour to raise funds in India for work in Britain.[41]

By then, the India League had emerged, by all reckoning, as the acknowledged, though as yet unofficial, representative of Indian nationalism in Britain. Under Horrabin's editorship and with Menon's inspiration the *Plebs* had taken upon itself the responsibility of pushing India's case in the Labour's educational programme.[42] In an article, "India and the Round Table", Ernest Thurtle argued that the least that would satisfy India was the concession of dominion status.[43] It meant immediate acknowledgement of India's right to the status. With this just claim conceded, he added, negotiations for its application could proceed and they would present no insuperable difficulties and a few years might be fixed as the transition stage. The Congress might have declared a complete severance of the British connection but Thurtle thought that it was doubtful if that national party would opt to fight for a 'somewhat academic distinction' between dominion status and complete independence. Indian leaders, he was convinced, knew well enough that British dominions were, in all essentials independent, self-governing states and, as a dominion, India would enjoy all that might be summed up as the substance of independence. There was no unimaginative reactionary in Britain so remote from reality, Thurtle wrote, as to dream of coercing a self-governing dominion to keep within the Commonwealth. Thurtle was quite uninhibited about the political situation and asserted that 'India asks for bread these days and cannot be fobbed off with a few official husks'.[44]

In an attempt to analyze the reasons for British determination to retain India under domination, Horrabin made a significant statement.[45] Britain wanted to hold India primarily to continue intensive exploitation of the country. India was still very much the greatest overseas consumer of British goods. A large proportion of total trading, banking and shipping business of Britain directly depended upon her connection with India. But that trade had already been shaken owing to the growing nationalist demand. Besides, the British governing class wished to retain its hold on India because of thousands of jobs, military and administrative, which India's government machinery provided for its sons and cousins. A third of the British army was trained and maintained by her, thus considerably relieving the British taxpayer. The Indian army, one of the largest standing armies in the world, was controlled and directed by Britons and it guarded strategic areas including the West Asian oilfields and Malayan rubber belts. A third of Britain's overseas trade from Egypt to North China was militarily supervised by the *Raj*. Many members of the British Parliament had family connections with the Indian army or civil service. India's geographical position invested her with a striking military importance in a transcontinental front stretching from Libya to Singapore. The defence of India was much more than a local issue: it was recognized as a part of imperial high policy.

It was true that in Indian conditions the quest for freedom could only be articulated by an educated minority. But the significant fact was that, of late, the nationalist demands attracted considerable support from the agriculturists of rural India. Evidently, the Congress had been turning into a mass movement. It was true that neither self-government nor dominion status would improve the lot of the Indian cultivators or factory labour overnight. But once foreign rule was cleared out, the masses would have a greater opportunity to wage a war against class exploitation.[46] In another article, Fenner Brockway maintained that the existing situation would never have arisen if the Labour government had been prepared to implement the declared policy of the party.[47] It was the refusal to accept the basis of self-government, to release the imprisoned political 'offenders' and to promise adequate representation of the Congress at RTC that led to the commencement of the civil disobedience campaign. Again, when the Congress agreed to participate in the conference on five reasonable conditions, which were adopted by the CIL, the government refused to budge although they were in accord with the Labour Party policy. Written before the RTC II the article asserted that in the judgement of all progressive and democratic opinion in the world the India policy of the Labour Government was bringing disgrace upon the British labour movement. 'Our honour as Socialists is involved', Brockway affirmed. 'We cannot be silent.'[48]

One thing that struck the editor of the *Plebs* was that in view of the plethora of books and articles that had been written on India from different angles during recent years, the insensitivity of the British public as a whole on the Indian questions was quite extraordinary.[49] The general lack of interest in Indian affairs was prevalent among a fairly large section of the working class. Lester Hutchinson, in an informative article written primarily for the working class, felt that the British worker was inclined to think that he had enough on his plate with the threat of unemployment, wage cuts and daily increasing difficulties of his life under capitalism to think about what goes on thousands of miles away.[50] Because of this incomprehension he was inclined to become easy prey to capitalist ballyhoo. Combating the public propaganda carried out by Winston Churchill, Lord Beaverbrook, Lord Melchett and other 'instruments of fascist imperialism', Hutchinson sought to analyze the nature of the crisis in Lancashire.

The publicity that was carried out among the textile workers was to the effect that unemployment and short-term work were due to the trade depression caused by Japanese and Indian competition on the Indian market. The inevitable suggestion was that the only way out of the crisis was to reduce English wages nearer to the Indian and Japanese standards thereby reducing the price of English cotton goods in the Indian market. Hutchinson maintained that it was true that competitive industry was being developed in India in spite of imperialist opposition and the cost of production of Indian goods was lower than the Lancashire products. But Indian industry was as yet too small and had been suffering under too many restrictions to compete seriously with Lancashire in an enormous Indian market especially because every attempt of the Indian working class to organize itself into effective trade unions was met by the whole force of imperialist repression. The real reason of unemployment and distress in British industry lay in the nature of capitalism itself. The distinguishing feature of modern capitalism was the export of capital, originally accumulated by prosperous industries, to colonies and backward countries thus draining large yearly tribute in the form of interest and profit. This export of capital, though initially profitable, was ultimately disastrous to home capitalists.

The constant drain of wealth, Hutchinson explained, impoverished the Indian peasantry whose purchasing power was so depleted that it constituted the main cause of trade depression and working class distress in Lancashire. The importance of an adequate assessment of Indian realities by the British working class could not be overestimated. The lifestyle of the British workers, Hutchinson explained, depended on the condition of the Indian workers and peasants and as long as the Indians remained on the verge of starvation, the standard of life of the British working class would deteriorate. The Indian peasantry would never be able to recover its prosperity under imperialism. It followed, therefore, that the only hope of the British industrial workers lay in an India free from imperialist exploitation which could only be attained by the liquidation of imperialism and all that it stood for.[51] Recommending John Beauchamps' *British Imperialism in India* and Freda Utley's *Lancashire and the Far East*, Hutchinson made a passionate appeal to the British working class to make a correct assessment of the impact of British rule in India. It was in this context, Horrabin claimed in one of his presentations, that the synchronized cry for rationalization in the British empire, initiated by James Garvin, Lord Beaverbrook and Lord Melchett, crusading for Empire Development, Imperial

Economic Unity, Empire Free Trade and so forth, must be analyzed.[52] The conglomeration of self-governing dominions, colonies and protectorates which had grown up in the traditional British capitalist fashion were sought to be organized into a symmetrical pattern. The idea was to bind together the whole of it by economic arrangements and counter-arrangements designed to keep out foreign competition and refurbish British capitalism with greater honour and profit. It was more than evident that British capitalism would attempt to proceed on some such lines. Horrabin doubted if the attempted unification of the British empire would ever be possible.[53]

R. Coppeck joined the *Plebs* symposium in a reasoned article pointing out that the British worker must realize that whether he was employed or unemployed, the great economic changes then going on in the name of rationalization affected and would continue to affect his very livelihood and he must direct his thoughts and organizational activities not towards 'a vain hunting after still vainer palliatives', but towards the creation of a world opinion of the working class that would make possible drastic changes in the whole social system.[54]

Emphasizing the need of a counter order of thoughts and ideas as an instrument of struggle against capitalism and imperialism, J.P.M. Millar stressed that the school system constituted one of the most effective organs of state power in civilized communities. Time and again, he claimed, education has been used as a means of empire building. A conquering nation, he wrote, repeatedly used education to force upon the defeated the language of the conquerors with a view to ensuring stability by spreading among the colonized the culture, habits and thoughts of the colonials. The author underlined that the Indian government had been developing a campaign for a wide and vigorous anti-Congress propaganda and to this end they pressed into service district boards and education committees and even village school teachers.[55] The official argument for such an organized effort was that the 'subversive campaign of the Congress was not so much political as anti-social and that it is therefore the duty of all good citizens to take part in fighting and suppressing it'. One of the purposes of the educational system was to build a sort of an 'intellectual rampart' to keep out those forces which seek to 'destroy the existing social order' irrespective of whether those forces were, from the point of view of history, rational or retrograde.[56] The *Plebs* declared that the working class was a historic force whose purpose was to destroy the existing inequitous society. The editor felt that education was being used to counter the development of international socialism as much as to thwart the aspirations of Indian nationalism. The *Plebs* seemed to argue in its columns that the struggle against imperialism in India was integral to the concerns of international socialist conscience.

One of the major organizational problems for the League was caused by the alienation and estrangement of the left-wing of the League and its impact on the activities of the Bristol branch. Gandhi's incarceration, ordinance rule and the brazen defence of government policy by Samuel Hoare in parliament seemed to confirm the conviction of the left activists that imperialism must be faced squarely. Developments in India, they thought, could no longer be allowed to drift and a temporizing policy at that stage would be but suicidal.[57] Eileen Merrie, the ebullient secretary of the Bristol chapter, felt that Menon was probably being compelled by some odd circumstances to line up with Gandhi and moderate Congressmen. She had hoped that the year 1932 would witness a resolute fight for freedom in India and the League would go for an all out endeavour for freedom and self-determination. The year, Merrie wrote in one of her communications to Menon in early 1932, was 'certainly starting well - it looks as though the world is really going to see the display of the beast in the Briton'.[58] Merrie was disposed to agree with Menon that 'as much as we attacked the L.P. (Labour Party) it did function as some sort of a bulwark against the right-reaction'.[59] But there was no room for complacency and Merrie argued very vehemently if there was any adequate reason to put off the 'bitter day' after all. She prayed with all her heart that 'it is going to be the real fight this time and there are enough K.M.s in India to see it through the end'.[60]

A letter of protest had been sent by the Bristol Chapter to the Prime Minister but Merrie, who had scarcely any faith in him, felt despondent as the protest was simply ignored. Both she and George Hennessey were convinced that since the new government had come in, MacDonald's political stance on domestic and imperial issues had completely swerved.[61] It was common knowledge that Stafford Cripps had met the attorney about the question of Bengal ordinance and although the attorney shared Cripps' opinion as regards the necessity of amending the ordinance to provide for an 'appeal' and annulling the provision of fining of villages as unfair, he did not hold out any prospect of being able to influence the Prime Minister on these scores. In fact, Cripps confided to Hennesey that we 'cannot hope to place any reliance on him any longer' and that persuasion would no longer be at all effective.[62] Lansbury was also equally ineffectual. Merrie was inclined to believe that in Britain, India 'seems to have suffered a total eclipse' and the government was 'really in a nice mess all round'. Things, she thought, seemed to be 'taking a headlong plunge towards war and makes one as pessimistic as a thundercloud'.[63] Merrie had been working for the League for nearly five years and was instrumental in transforming the lackadaisical theosophical outfit of the CIL into a fighting machine, and through the years of slump and unemployment, participated in hunger marches, organized enthusiastic meetings and demonstrations on India, issued statements, wrote pamphlets for the League and had been close to Menon during Gandhi's participation in the RTC. She had first-hand knowledge as an animateur of the League of the 'duplicity and guile' of the Labour Party leaders and officials and the 'dilatory and equivocal' disposition of the Labour government.[64]

Fascism was on the ascendant in the continent and politics in Britain was taking an unqualified right-wing swing. 'Yes, I am still under the Red Flag,' Merrie declared in one of her letters to Menon, 'and have not regretted it, for one minute.'[65] It seemed that Merrie was then quite anxious to walk out of the League. In fact, the Bristol branch, as a whole, was dispirited by the League's attitudes and was not interested in keeping company 'of a lot of wavering Labour men'.[66] 'Is your position still the same?' Menon was asked by a restless Merrie, 'Do you still feel inclined to support Gandhi and Joshi?'[67] Menon was busy organizing the delegation and its investigative tour of India. He could, however, still filch an hour from his 'stuffy Strand office' for 'a chat' with Merrie *entre nous* trying to convince her of the League's proposed course of action, the importance of the mission to India and its extraordinary propaganda value. But then, it was difficult to get away from office for long and to wrangle with the high-spirited lady determined not to shift her position.[68]

In August the party left for India. In early October, Barbara Macnamara, a bright student of LSE then in charge of the League's office in the absence of Menon, received a cryptic note from Bristol: 'I am sorry not to have replied before. If Mr Menon had told me that you would be managing H.Q. in his absence, I would have informed you before this of the position in Bristol. The branch here has been disbanded. My own political views have changed considerably, and this I discussed with Mr Menon before he sailed. I can no longer associate myself with the League which I consider very opportunist and far too closely in sympathy with the National Congress and its amorphous composition. I have no confidence in its leadership for Indian freedom. It refuses to recognize the class struggle in Indian society and only misleads the masses. Gandhi's last manoeuvre is no victory at all; it only shows his acquiescence in the new constitution. So with regard to arranging a meeting here for the delegation, there is no branch and I am afraid I cannot undertake it.'[69] With this, Merrie snapped her connection with the India League. Over the last few months Menon had been apprehensive of this unfortunate finale of a high profile Bristol connection.

The attitude of the Bristol branch was symptomatic of the perception of the Communist Party on the Indian question and it was largely conditioned by the proceedings of the so-called Meerut conspiracy case. Of the accused, three were Englishmen and the other twenty-eight were Indians. Five of these were at the time of their arrest members of the executive committee of the All India Trade Union Congress. It was during Baldwin's premiership that the accused were arrested on specially framed charges of conspiracy and 'waging war against the king'.[70] Their trial was the greatest state trial ever held in India and was remarkable in many respects. Charges of conspiracy, as D.N. Pritt put it, were among the oldest devices of oppressive governments to secure convictions when they could not prove any positive actions by their victims.[71] Although all the Meerut prisoners were charged with the same offence, they were differently treated as regards admission to bail. For a period correspondence with some of the prisoners was censored and the Government of India prevented funds subscribed for the defence from reaching the prisoners. The very place, Meerut, chosen for trial illustrated the determination of the government to preclude a trial by jury. All arrangements in Meerut were of a primitive Nature. The false statement about the long delays brought about by the prisoners themselves in protracting their defence over so many months was repeated by the secretary of state, time and again, despite denial of the judge himself. It had been pleaded by the Labour government that the responsibility for the trial and for procedure rested with the Baldwin government.[72] The British people, Reginald Bridgeman, Menon's close associate, alleged, were given to understand that the brutal regime over the colonial people would cease with the assumption of office by a Labour government in 1929. Yet the prosecution continued. In the Meerut 'frame up' was reflected, Bridgeman wrote, in the anti-combination spirit of the Trades Disputes Act of 1927, and its retension in 1931 and in the suppression of the Pan-Pacific Trade Union in Shanghai.[73]

The real significance of the Meerut trial could be gathered from the opening speech of the Crown counsel, Lanford James, which was a violent diatribe directed not so much against the accused as against the Soviet government.[74] Bridgeman maintained that the Labour government could not deny equal responsibility with the Tory government in the prosecution of the working class leaders whose activities had been devoted to building the working class organization in India.[75] He urged the delegates to the Scarborough conference of the Labour Party in October 1931 to demand that the government should unconditionally release all the Meerut prisoners, who, after two and half years' of imprisonment, had nothing proved against them. Quoting Abdul Majid, one of the Meerut prisoners, Bridgeman affirmed that a revolution in India would not be due to the efforts and activities of the communists, but would be due to the oppression and terrorism of British imperialism as well as to the poverty and helplessness in India.[76]

The report of the Whitley Commission, Bridgeman added, on the condition of labour in India was a sufficient condemnation of British rule in India. It exposed the appalling conditions under which millions of human beings remained diseased, hungry and illiterate until death relieved them of their sufferings.[77] Menon joined his voice to the general condemnation of the trial and the decision of the Labour government 'not to hinder the processes of law'.[78] He quoted Jawaharlal Nehru, chairman of AITUC, that the condemnation of the Meerut prisoners would mean the break-up of the organized labour movement in India. Besides, an impression was fostered by the government counsel that the proceedings were directed not so much against the accused as against the Russian revolution, the Soviet government, the Communist International and the whole gamut of theories of Marxism and Leninism.[79] The death of Jatin Das in prison after 63 days of hunger strike on 13 September 1930 and the execution of other three Lahore prisoners, Bhagat Singh, Raj Guru and Sukhdev following another trial without jury on 23 March 1931, was linked up with the prosecution of the Meerut prisoners. Menon held that all of them were presented in quick succession in the collective perception of the Indian people as martyrs for the cause of justice and freedom. The case of the Meerut prisoners constituted a travesty of justice and Menon declared that the prosecution needed overhauling, that the connection between the executive and the judiciary was too close in India and the machinery of British justice in India found itself being driven along a circuitous, tedious and expensive road. The ultra-left of the CPGB, however, decided to remain unconvinced of Menon's position as spokesman of a 'temporising' Congress and its uncertain leadership and they were particularly nettled by what they thought to be the mystical formulations of Gandhi.[80]

Eileen Merrie and the Bristol branch had been basically operating in an atmosphere of doubt and suspicion very ingeniously engineered by contemporary communist tracts and strategies. The CPGB had been over time making an invigorated reappraisal of the British position in the strategy and tactics of the international communist movement. R.P. Dutt, the undisputed theoretician of the communist movement in Britain, presented his thesis in 1928 on the need for a careful consideration of the priorities of the Labour movement.[81] The central idea of the debate that was initiated by Dutt was that the general character of the international situation was acutely reflected in Britain and was distinguished by sharpening of contradictions within the process of stabilization of capitalism and reawakening of the working class despite past defeats and combined capitalist and reformist repression. It would have been a fantastic exaggeration, Dutt wrote to Harry Pollitt, to imply from this formulation that the Communist Party had concluded that the mass of the workers were completely disillusioned with the Labour Party and were ripe for revolutionary leadership, etc.[82] On the contrary, Dutt maintained that the Communist Party was convinced that the mass of the workers were not as yet disillusioned although there was a significant awakening of working class consciousness in response to the concerted capitalist assault on them. It was argued that it was the job of the party to stimulate class consciousness by its independent initiative and struggle, to drive home the spirit of disillusionment and utilize the exposure that had taken place. Unless the party carried through that fight, the disillusionment and revolutionary advance would not take place and it would only signify the growing stagnation and decay of the movement. The party felt that the general character of the Labour Party in Britain had introduced a new angle of vision in the whole debate.

The Labour Party, an important section of the communist leadership held, had developed a special character. It was both an instrument of the reformist bureaucracy moving fast towards the extreme right as well as a crafty operator with its diabolical ideological platform holding the mass of the workers in its grip by its control over the labour organizations and trade unions. The new phase of the British labour movement was a sequel to the victory of the bourgeoisie over the General Strike, and the miners' struggle, their successful imposition of the Trade Union Act to consolidate their control over the working class and their rewarding intervention in China and break with the Soviet Union. The crux of the proposed initiative was that the Communist Party had then acquired an adequate measure of real and potential support within the working class and achieved a remarkable experience in militant struggle through the process of the MacDonald government, Red Friday, the General Strike, the miners' struggle, the existing repression and the exposure of the reformist leadership.

The totality of revolutionary experience had moved far enough to warrant a qualitative transformation of Communist strategy involving a definitive step forward. It was conceded that the proposed strategy might be misunderstood and even criticized by a large body of 'more backward workers'.[83] But it was nevertheless concluded that it was the task of 'revolutionary leadership, while maintaining contact in every possible way with the backward workers and making clear our policy, not to determine our policy by the level of understanding they have reached ... but to determine our policy by the whole political situation and the true interests of the working class, and then to make clear the reasons of our policy and bring it home to the widest possible body of workers.... We cannot weaken our fight against the social democratic leaders for fear of misunderstanding by a section of the workers of such a policy as a splitting of workers' forces against capitalism; but we seek at the same time to dispel those misunderstandings by our readiness to enter a united working class front in any struggle against capitalism...'.[84] It was assumed that the interests and perceptions of MacDonalds and Thomases were 'identical with capitalism, differing in practically no fundamental issues from Baldwin and Lloyd George' and, therefore, even registering a minority revolutionary vote against them should be viewed as 'the strongest possible blow against capitalism'. The principal idea was that the British working class movement had been entering a critical stage; that such a move forward had been conditioned by the development of the objective conditions; that the failure to rise to the occasion would inaugurate a wretched period of disintegration, decay and reaction and the responsibility for the required initiative in the new situation was to be undertaken by the CPGB.[85]

It is in this context that one might assess the policy of the Communist Party and its ardent sympathizers towards Indian nationalism and the leadership of Gandhi. The conclusion of the Gandhi-Irwin pact was announced in the Soviet press in the most laconic manner. It was observed by the British embassy in Moscow that Gandhi's name had provoked for some time a more or less steady flow of abuse in the Soviet press. Gandhi was presented as an agent of British imperialism and a traitor to the broad masses whom he professed to represent.[86] In an article entitled 'Anglo-Indian Peace', published in a obscure journal of the Soviet Union, *Krnasnava-Zvezda*, an expert on India dealt at length with the significance of the pact. It appeared that the pact was in the nature of a compromise and was based on an understanding of mutual retreat.[87] In reality, however, the pact represented a complete capitulation of the nationalist reformists in India who abandoned their weapon of civil disobedience without taking a firm stand on any of their original demands. The more level-headed bourgeois press in Britain such as the *Times* and the *Daily Telegraph* realized that it would be worth their while to override recognized procedure in order to reap their victory over India. In fact, Indian reformists had never lost hope of coming to some sort of a peaceful negotiated settlement with Britain even when they had been compelled by the militant masses to organize civil disobedience. They had been waiting for months, the Soviet expert maintained, to commit skilfully an act of treachery against the Indian people. The expert affirmed that neither the proposals of MacDonald at the RTC nor the agreement in Delhi would decide the question of Indo-British relations or liquidate a single one of those contradictions which brought about the campaign of civil disobedience.[88] Even if the new constitution of India became an accomplished fact, British rule would still remain untouched.

The new Indian parliament composed of one-third of the Indian princes, creatures of imperialism, would be a toy in the hands of the latter; eighty per cent of the budget would remain outside the control of the Indians while army and finance, two of the most decisive levers of British power in India, would still be commanded by the British. Industry would still lack the necessary customs protection; the colossal system of taxation would remain unchanged; India would continue to bear her external debts as well as the grandiose salaries and pensions to the 'English satraps' and a huge expenditure for the construction of strategic railways.[89] It appeared to the Soviet expert that even from the vantage point of the diffident Indian bourgeoisie, the agreement would merely be a short-term armistice. What the English imperialists feared were the toiling Indian masses who had been groaning under the heavy burden of taxes, rent and moneylenders' interest. 'Having forced the Indian Kerenskys to a full and complete capitulation', the communist analyst wrote, 'English imperialism has done its cause a great harm as the capitulation of Gandhi and Gandhites is at the same time a self-revelation and in this connection has a first-class revolutionary meaning.'[90] In the very near future, it was asserted with confidence, the Gandhi-Irwin peace would release forces for the development of a revolutionary mass movement in India. The analysis had an artificial ring about it.

Shapurji Saklatvala, the legendary figure in the British working class movement and the prime mover of the Workers'

Welfare League, examined the implication of the new orientation of the communist strategy in the context of the Indian policy of the Labour Party. In an article meant for circulation through communist journals throughout the colonial world, Saklatvala examined, with remarkable authenticity, the nature of British imperialism as a dangerous threat to world peace.[91] He maintained that the development of imperial power provided Britain with a 'dishonourable excuse for maintaining large and mobile forces firmly planted in all the four corners of the world'.[92] The world had become, as a consequence, a huge military camp absorbing about 60 per cent of industrial human energy for its upkeep utilizing practically the entire development of physical and chemical sciences to the baser use of terrorism and destruction. In that phase of world history, therefore, it was necessary to impress upon the Indian nationalists the need to work out India's emancipation along entirely new lines.

The problem of the struggle against imperialism had become, in communist discourse, clearly a problem of class struggle in which the toiling masses and peasants would be involved not only against foreign rule on sentimental grounds of national pride, but in which the whole of their militant efforts would be organized to overthrow the British imperial exploiters and their henchmen. The organized workers of India could alone win India's emancipation. The Labour Party and the ILP had been able to comprehend the significance of the struggle and, therefore, they had been trying to create an impression that there was still some hope in the two Labour parties who respected India's cause of self-determination. The second programme of the Labour parties was to put aside their political and parliamentary mask and put on their trade union cloak, to create a deliberate split between the labour and nationalist movements in India and isolate Indian workers from other revolutionary groups in the world. The Indian masses were called upon by Saklatvala to appreciate the sinister motives of the Labour Party and the ILP and allow themselves to be guided by the revolutionary movement of the Indian working class away from the pernicious influence of the National Congress and its seductive leadership armed with a semi-spiritual programme.[93] This formed the perspective of Eileen Merrie and the erstwhile Bristol branch and all those who were clearly influenced by the communist perception of Indian nationalism. To many it seemed that the communist prognostication probably had elements of fundamental truth and the rule of the ordinances in India would have an uninhibited sway for long with the unlimited support of the British bourgeoisie and its belligerent media despite token resistance offered by Gandhi and his civil disobedience.

Reports on the proposed visit of the delegation to India caused much flutter in official circles. The Government of India was visibly upset by the disquieting prospects of a few political luminaries of Britain perambulating all over India to collect unpleasant information which might damage the government's sense of righteousness, so carefully nurtured by the official media. It might lift the curtain of ignorance, once and for all in Britain and present a scurrilous portrayal of the Indian realities and sustain it with an unmistakable array of facts.[94] The Government of India had learnt from an intercepted letter of Govind Malaviya to C.F. Andrews that a commission of three or four prominent persons including a few members of parliament and 'an influential lady', all having marked pro-Indian sympathies, would visit India. It was feared that if the services of Harold Laski, 'whose extreme views are well known', were requisitioned by the League, the report of the delegation could spark off a good deal of embarrassment for the Indian administration. It might even offer a fresh spurt of life to the dying agitation. The sticky situation in India might then become even more intricate and perplexing by any act of indiscretion on the part of the delegation.[95]

The administration was conscious of the fact that the delegation could not possibly be blocked off or thwarted. But in view of a vague suggestion that the delegation could partially be funded by the National Congress, government thought it necessary to stress the unpropitious implications of the visitation.[96] It was keen that the home government should be thoroughly briefed about the impairment that the proceedings and the reports of the commission could cause to the law and order situation in India.

Early in July 1932, when the composition of the team and its terms of reference were still conjectural and uncertain, Maurice G. Hallett, secretary of the home department, cautioned Samuel Findlater Stuart, Under-Secretary of State for India, about the harm that could be done by the League's team.[97] He pleaded that the Government of India would be grateful for any information regarding the members of the team and about their previous histories, if they were not well-known people. Before long, more letters were intercepted. From a letter from Horrabin to Madan Mohan Malaviya it was learnt that the delegation would be sent out by the India League and it would not be affiliated to the Congress or any other political party. It was also clear that members of the delegation would not make any speech or participate in political activities while in India. Hallett noted with satisfaction that the League had been living through pecuniary difficulties and that the deputation scheduled for India, as a result, might not even take off. An appeal for an emergency fund of £1,000 for the delegation had been made by the India League, but Horrabin was inclined to believe that the solicitation would, in all probability, attract a doubtful response from the public. Hallett gleefully reported that there was a desperate attempt to exhort Malaviya to raise suitable financial assistance in India. He would not, however, fail to take advantage of the League's acute indigence and began to insist regularly that the delegation was being sent out in response to an invitation of the Congress.[98] Every effort was being made, Hallett stressed, to conceal the fact that the deputation was in fact sponsored and funded by the Congress. In all essentials it was, according to him, a deputation designed in India and occasioned and financed by the Congress.[99]

The administration was unaware that Madan Mohan Malaviya had been taking a special interest in the League's deputation. Since his return from the RTC, he had been adopting an advanced position in politics.[100] He addressed a strong letter to the Viceroy against the reversal of the policy of Irwin, authored a series of memoranda on the notorious ordinances and sent them out to the India League and Tom Williams for wide publicity and had been working for rounding up support for an enormous manifesto from the liberals and constitutionalists of all political persuasions. He had initiated the process of working on the minds of a 'reasonable' Rajendra Prasad and 'moderately minded' Muslims through Saifuddin Kitchlew and M.A. Ansari. The management of the *Hindustan Times* had been handed over to 'an advanced nationalist' in the person of Potham Joseph and a decision had been taken to the effect that the policy of the paper would be so guided as to give 'a kindly lead to the lib-lab'.[101] There was perfect unanimity about the need for greater coordination and frequent consultation between these forces. It was assumed by the Indian administration that these developments had prompted Malaviya to take a special interest in the League's deputation which was viewed as an important event and the Pandit undertook to raise a tidy sum of £1,000 for the project. Assessing Malaviya's position and interest, the administration took for granted that the Pandit considered publicity in the west a matter of supreme importance and his close identification with the proposed delegation would serve as a sure and certain conduit to the British political stage. Though still sceptical of the outcome of the League's endeavour, Hallett adopted an uncompromising position. He held that the independent and impartial stance of the League in promoting the delegation was a smokescreen. In his circular to all the local governments and their agents he warned against the deputation which, he alleged, was surreptitiously sponsored by the Congress and assisted by funds supplied by Malaviya.[102]

By August 1932 the full list of the delegation had been prepared. For reasons of political convenience, lingering illness and health hazards, both Tom Williams and Morgan Jones were unable to accept the invitation to tour India.[103] Leonard Matters was to join Monica Whately and Ellen Wilkinson in the team with Menon as secretary.[104] Before long, the Government of India procured more comprehensive information about the League's delegation. During a frank discussion with the deputation of the League, Lord Lothian explained to Whately that it was inadmissible for the India office to give the delegation a letter of introduction enabling them to go wherever they liked placing them beyond the authority and control of various administrations in India. Whately was cautioned against the danger of being compromised by 'their Congress friends' which might lead them into an offence against the law.[105] He urged the desirability of the party keeping in close touch with the officials and promised all assistance. He volunteered to write to all prominent persons, outside Congress circles, whom it would be worth their while to meet. A letter was written by Lothian on these lines to various notables giving a brief account of the members of the delegation and the objects of the mission as approved by government appending a cautious warning against its possible adverse impact.[106]

The India office felt that the League's delegation was conscious of the delicacy of its position and would avoid all possible confrontation with the Indian government. Members of the delegation apparently agreed to make no speech, raise no impediment and cause no crisis, and Lothian concluded that at least the ladies might be relied upon to behave sensibly.[107] The Government of India was advised to note the antecedents of the members of the delegation.[108] Monica Whately was introduced as one with a suffragette past, an active member of the Labour Party and socially a well-connected person. Leonard Matters, Labour MP (1929-31), had been a freelance journalist who was believed to have contributed to the *Moscow Daily News* and lectured extensively on the Soviet Union. It was added that Matters' nomination was only a last minute addition to the party and 'probably a *pis aller*'. He was regarded as 'rather a suspicious character' although 'there was nothing very conclusive against him'.[109] The officials considered it rather a great pity that a person of his vintage should have been accommodated in the party. The only area of satisfaction was that Matters was a person of little importance and it might safely be assumed that he would remain by and large 'under female thumbs'. The local governments in India were warned against him for his 'somewhat fishy reputation'.[110] Menon, secretary to the delegation, was referred to as 'a journalist in Britain of somewhat extreme political tendencies'. He was secretary of the India League and although quite presentable, was a 'fellow traveller' of the communists, indulging in diabolical political positions on Indian and international politics.[111]

The officials were also told that all information would be sent directly to them by the secretary of state. In any case, officials should appreciate the need for circumspection, close watchfulness and intelligent coordination. The delegation was especially anxious to visit jails and meet political prisoners: no such permission should be extended to them. The India Office had already advised members of the delegation to keep in close touch with officials and if they showed any inclination to do that, it should be convenient to give them an opportunity of acquiring correct information and being animated by a broad official perspective.[112] In fact, at the London end, the India Office found itself in a *cul-de-sac*. It was aware of the delegation's potential to cause mischief. But it was equally convinced that the very inclusion of persons like Wilkinson and Whately had rendered the prevention of the visit quite impossible.[113] The itinerary of the delegation was hectic and the schedule included among other places Bombay, Poona, Madras, Calcutta, Shantiniketan, Dacca, Rajshahi, Chittagong, Manipur, Patna, Cuttack, Banaras, Allahabad, Kanpur, Delhi, Agra, Meerut, Simla, Lahore, Peshawar, Karachi and Ahmedabad.[114] The India Office suggested that the best policy would be to treat the party with every consideration and courtesy, to accede to requests for interviews with officials and put them in touch with 'reliable people' who would be encouraged to counter the Congress point of view.[115] No special facilities deemed to be undesirable were to be given to them and one was never to overlook the close rapport between the Congress and the delegation. No effort was to be spared to emphasize the fact that the Congress Party was primarily responsible for providing financial assistance to the delegation and Malaviya himself to a great extent had been running the show at that end.[116]

Apart from Hallett at the centre there were other observers having direct contact with the secretary of state. Thus C.H. Everett in Delhi, C.B.S. Clee in Bombay, G.T.H. Bracken in Madras, and B.N. Reid in Calcutta occupied commanding positions in the official network that was devised specially to deal with the delegation.[117] In official communications it was firmly stated that members of the delegation were prominent members of the Labour Party operating on behalf of the India League and although its ostensible purpose seemed innocuous, it had far deeper and devious designs.[118] Peel made it unambiguous that despite the apparent slogans of impartiality and firm public pronouncements against being spoon-fed, members shared a natural political inclination towards the extreme left. There were reasons to believe, Peel portended, that if the delegation was not judiciously managed, the government might find itself in a delicate situation. The Government of India was, therefore, urged to be circumspect and to avoid the adverse political fallout resulting from any serious contention with the delegation.[119] It was further decided that the department of information should send periodical reports to the provincial police regarding the movements of the delegation. The India Office added that it was quite probable that the delegation would produce a report of some kind in November 1932 on their return to provide effective ammunition for parliamentary questions.[120] It would, therefore, be desirable and even imperative to obtain from the Indian government adequate information as to the kind of line which the secretary of state might be expected to take.[121]

In the absence of Menon in India, Horrabin's responsibility multiplied enormously. Fortunately, the office was managed by one of Menon's close associates, Barbara Macnamara. Propaganda was a complicated affair and Menon with all his intensity had made India work quite arduous. It had fairly advanced outlets to various fronts: the parliamentary committee, the labour committee, the women's committee, the executive committee, the committee in charge of *India Review*, the committee looking after the League's publications including bulletins, pamphlets, books and talking points, the affiliating committee, and the general body. Besides, interaction had to be sustained with various branches for coordinating programmes. It was also imperative to nurse about 2,000 organizations having fraternal and affiliating relationships with the League requiring considerable information and ideological input. To add to this, there was an exhausting responsibility to maintain live contacts with the major newspapers and journals and political parties and organizations in Britain. Menon would not withdraw the League's interests even in the most conservative and imperialistic bodies. Arrangement of periodical meetings, delegate conferences and public meetings on political and social issues confronting the India policy of the day and the current public debates could not have been passed over.[122] In fact, contact with India was, in itself, a time-consuming affair and the section of the Strand office dealing with newspaper cuttings involved a good deal of unpaid labour donated voluntarily by a fairly large body of students who constituted Menon's cheerful kindergarten.[123] At one corner of the office, a copper kettle on a heater boiled water without interruption and tea was available all the time. At another corner, an over-used Remington typewriter typed away. Invariably, Menon found himself early in the morning at the India League's office at the Strand and he worked sometimes with his folks and often all alone, all through the day into the evening and even at night.[124] At times he was fortunate to have a secretary to assist him. Often the secretary was to become a member of the League's optimistic family living on tea and sympathy.

Menon had become for many an addiction. His was an irresistible company with all his wit, humour, encyclopedic mind, an amazingly integrated theory of knowledge and his remarkable sense of obligation. His loyalty to his own values and ideas and to the services of all who worked for him and India was firm and inflexible. Unmindful of the jealousies of others he was always keen to meet misfortunes and setbacks with fortitude.[125] Probably, he was egged on by his formidable spirit which made him feel that dedication to a given work was more important than the worker himself. Commitment to his own ideals and to those who looked up to him was the essence of his integrity. A hard taskmaster and a perfectionist, Menon became early in his life a remarkable loner even amidst a predominantly dedicated following. He avoided malicious gossip. Somewhat susceptible to a touch of adulation, Menon had been trying hard to cultivate compassion and the spirit of conciliation and to sharpen his ability to distinguish between essentials and non-essentials.[126]

Ever since his arrival in England, Menon had been witnessing a sea change in life and society around him. Over the last few years he had been travelling around the countryside and urban centres holding meetings, schools and conferences on India. He had carefully analyzed the appeal of the League on what J.B. Priestley called the 'three Englands'.[127] The old England of cathedrals, ministers, manor houses and inns with piquantly old-fashioned roads and lanes retaining parts of traditional life, both in form and in spirit, had virtually nothing in common with the League and its concern.[128] The remnants of the nineteenth century England, the industrial England of coal, iron, steel, cotton, wool, railways, town halls, literary and philosophical societies, liberal associations, slums, dismal towns and grim cities, fried-fish shops, etc. had a tremendous attraction for the League's essay to tie up colonial discontent with social miseries of the urban underclass in Britain.[129] It was the arterial and by-pass roads, filling stations, giant cinema houses, dance halls, cafes, Woolworths and chain stores, buses, wireless, typing, the metamorphosis of tophats and tailcoats into the lounge suits, fashionable girls in mass-produced attractive clothes and short boyish hair, growing gender equality, the Mond-Turnerism, gradual but perceptible respectability of the Labour Party, unemployment, means test, rationalization, snooty class consciousness, print culture, vast monopolized mass media and listening posts were some of the signposts of the Third England. Besides, there an awareness of international politics, and an aggressive and militant labour movement, renewal of socialism, an articulate peace movement and paradoxically, the rise of authoritarianism, the Soviet planning process, the right to work and leisure and what appeared to be an intriguing short-circuit of history, Germany and its preoccupation in the European mind and the endemic colonial insurgency and struggles for freedom. In addition, the culture of the crowd and the ascendency of the masses, the presence of a host of working women who unlike their mothers ceased to have bosoms; instead, they had legs, as the skirt rose above the knee, constituted the rich texture of the fabric of that England which demanded a comprehensive appreciation of the dynamics of the contemporary world forces.[130]

Kingsley Martin came to the Strand office with a bagful of ideas: ideas as a solvent of the establishment, ideas to debunk and ideas to corrode the established order. His weekly seminars, 'for that was what the *New Statesman* amounted to', glorified the virtues of rationality, honesty, sympathy and freedom in public life.[131] Academic, journalist and labour activist, Kingsley Martin was a relentless campaigner and a persuasive polemicist, and for the next few decades was to remain a dominant left-wing personality and a valuable patron of pressure groups such as the Union of Democratic Control, the National Council of Civil Liberties and the India League. He almost intuitively anticipated and articulated the ideas and ideals of liberal minded middle-class opinions in Britain. It seemed that Kingsley Martin had been attempting at times to add socialism to his inborn liberalism. He, like many of his generation, was sceptical of all political dogmas. They, Martin quipped, were probably the 'comfortable beneficiaries' of the system they had promised to change. They advocated changes whose implications they could probably only view with horror.[132] For the India League Martin was a valuable asset. His presentations, known for 'a persistent standard of readability', invariably touched India with profound sympathy.

The National government had been at the service of the industrial and financial interests. The Labour Party, having experienced the morbid fear of social turmoil during the General Strike, decided to opt for industrial peace. Unemployment and malnutrition were widespread in Britain.[133] Japan had already entered Manchuria with little intention to quit. Hitler made the necessary arrangements to grab power in Germany; its implications were well-known all over Europe. Hunger marches had been confronting the privileged young men and women in the universities with a novel experience of the organized working class taking a lead in social action.[134] Young communist volunteers were creating tasks for themselves and carrying them out with the assistance of the workers. The minority government of the Labour Party of 1929-31 seemed incapable of resolving the capitalist dilemma and they were divided between what bankers and investors demanded and what some of their fellow party men thought prudent to leave to the Tories.[135] The traumatic impact of the events of July and August 1931 on the British left was stupefying for many: quite a few of them made a sizeable lurch to the Marxian left. Despite sectarian excesses of 'class versus class', many communists had been participating along with the Labour unions in struggles for daily needs at local levels. Marxist texts became popular reading material for all those who stood at the left end of British politics.[136] Germany attracted attention: continental news was intently followed while the policies and moves of the British government were scanned and analyzed closely.

The cumulative impact of social and political animation of the period was that the significant element of pacifism of the Left was overwhelmed by political realism and one could not help picking up the human and intellectual excitement in the air. Theory was crying out for self-expression in the course of the political experiences of the day.[137] It was more than evident to all who were perceptive that 'capitalist civilization', as Trotsky put it, was 'disgorging undigested barbarity' in the form of Nazism.[138] In Germany, the lower middle class and its *lumpenproletarian* fringe, inflamed by the rhetoric of Hitler, were being drawn like the 'human dust' by the 'magnet of power'.[139] In the grip of their pathological anti-communist bitterness, the social democrats, having abdicated their responsibility and initiative, continued to preach moderation and expediency especially when as political formulations these cliches had become dangerously counterproductive. The communists decided to cling to ultra-radicalism and declined to accept the difference between bourgeois democracy and fascism.[140] British media were aware of the brutal police rule in India since the arrest of Gandhi; there were protests from various platforms spearheaded by the India League but the government maintained without batting an eyelid that things were returning fast to normalcy.[141]

Michael Foot was available at the Strand office as a young student from Oxford. He was still upholding liberal politics although some of his intimate friends and intellectual companions were members of the Labour Club and the Socialist Society. Apparently he was steadily moving towards socialism under Menon's care and compassion.[142] Menon was in charge of a large number of young people who were recruited by the Labour Party and sent over to the India League for an in-depth exposure to socialism as an intellectual discipline and as a way of life.[143] Henry Noel Brailsford moved in and out of the Strand office as an easy insider, always ready for a discussion on the traditions of Marx and historical materialism.[144] Brailsford combined in himself a non-conformist conscience, an English radicalism and Marxist imagination. His interpretation of Marxism in the British context was read by that generation with rapt attention. Having had a successful stint with the *New Leader* and then as a regular writer for the *New Statesman*, Brailsford had devoted himself to the analysis of capitalism and its close relationship with imperialism and war.[145] John Faithful, Fortescue, Platts-Mills and Tiny Rowland were among the many who joined the League with youthful sincerity for the cause of human freedom. They were the ebullient 'Bevan boys' and were associated with left-wing Labour activists such as Geoffrey Bing, Donald Bruce, Harold Davies, Jennie Lee, Leslie Hale, Fred Lee, Benn W. Levy, R.W.G. Mackay, Ernest R. Millington, Stephen Swingler, etc.[146] They were sceptical of the Labour leadership's wholehearted inclination to endorse the legitimacy of intense economic tensions threatening the peace of the world.

Ernest Bevin, the Labour leader, argued for the party that it was the search for raw material in exchange of manufactured goods that had been the basis of Britain's international trade. It was for this reason, he wrote, that Britain developed a colonial empire, built up the most lucrative foreign trade ever known, constructed the world's greatest mercantile marine, and maintained the largest navy. It was held that new industrial countries, such as Germany, France, USA and Japan, seeking a similar destiny, intensified tension and competition. The goal of the Labour policy was to bring about rapid productive efficiency. It was asserted that the problem of the market was also the problem of supply and they could no longer be separated, and in international competition, finance in many cases was the dominating factor. 'Modern international power is economic', wrote Bevin for the Trades Union Congress General Council. He stated, 'The nation which conrols oil and other raw materials, foreign markets and credits will rule the world.' It meant, so far as the Labour leadership was concerned, unhindered use of diplomacy, cartels under international supervision, economic groupings, rationalization and industrial peace.[147] The radical Young Turks of the party, on the other hand, were keen to ensure that the Labour Party should not commit itself to a the 'people's capitalism' or to offering a less glossy version of Tory policies. They felt that the Labour Party was used to fighting skirmishes while avoiding pitched battles and had been suffering from acute anaemia. Many of Menon's kindergarten spent a good deal of their time at the Strand office attending and addressing meetings on India, arranging newspaper material, editing pamphlets and articles, typing out letters and putting them in addressed envelopes. Menon had generated an atmosphere of fraternal creativity, cooperation and goodwill within the League.[148] Intellectually, the company of kindred souls was receptive to all rational arguments for peace and against war. The India League was not less eager than any other association in the thirties such as the Union of Democratic Control, the League of Nations Union, the Peace Council and the like to argue for a living space and better life for all irrespective of race, nationality and religion. No less than any other body, it was open to all who would have liked to help extend humanism to every area of social conflict. It was sensitive to the miseries attending human exploitation. In a sense, the India League was increasingly turning into an association devoted to the liberation of the imperial world from bondage and subjugation.

Krishnrao Shivarao Shelvankar had met Menon at Adyar where Menon, on his bicycle used to visit regularly to give, a series of lectures on constitutional development in India way back in the early 1920s. In those closely argued lectures, Menon's political development in future was not reflected. He was a somewhat dedicated scout master, and a law student having attained a Master's degree and was full of problems of social service and the awakening of India. In Britain, Shelvankar met Menon with a distinct and a totally different outlook. Suave, gentle, persuasive and erudite, Shelvankar was a devoted scholar of the development of modern political thought, not in an abstract form, but in terms of historical and sociological manifestation of human experiences. His study in the development of the idea of equality as a Western political phenomenon and a philosophical ideal having deep historical roots was a novel enquiry and his commitment to freedom and equality as mutually complementary positions made him closer to Menon and his intellectual development.[149] Redfern was unwilling to rejoin this intense group with its ever expansive area of interests. He, and many of the theosophists, developed a deep antipathy towards the trends of the League's objectives and found for themselves a safe refuge amidst the passive ambience fashioned by the Friends of India.

The India League was Menon. It appeared to many that Menon's methods as secretary of the India League, always financially insolvent and, paradoxically, always rich in ideas, were idiosyncratic and egocentric. He appeared to an outsider somewhat inept at organizing his plans and work, and somewhat inebriated by his own attractive flights of imagination.[150] Menon seemed to exploit his friends shamelessly but he did not scruple to exploit himself to the hilt either.[151] There was no doubt, however, even in the minds of his many critics that he could find in his mess and disorder a distinct pattern. The League that had been stumbling along for some time had a firm sense of purpose. If many left its office at regular intervals never to return, many more entered the Strand office to add their cheery energy to the demands of this man of extraordinary paradoxes and intensity and yet having a remarkable unity of purpose.[152] To many it was more than perplexing to comprehend his intricate but cosmopolitan *weltanschauung*. His doggedness invoked strong reactions. He was either loved or loathed. But few could overlook the fact that Menon was the one who could see the woods for the trees, separate the grains from the chaff, take major political and other decisions unruffled by impediments, and then go along with his mission undaunted by temporary setbacks or unqualified critical evaluations.[153] An undefined personal ambition, a unique organizing ability, an overpowering energy and drive and a marked tendency towards self-absorption made him a difficult person to live with. He was somewhat over-cautious and thrived on adversity. He was not gregarious but a fairly good mixer in social gatherings. And yet he was endowed with a strong melancholic temperament.[154]

Janaki Amma in Calicut was one of the few recipients of Menon's letters. His theme was the urgency of cooperative endeavours for social change in India.[155] He would argue for the upliftment of individual conscience with a healthy commitment to social service. He did not see any limit to effective social action for the removal of the dirt, filth and evils of society. Menon would not endorse any procrastination in the promotion of education and eradication of all forms of cruelty and superstition such as untouchability, feudal extortion, communal disharmony and a self-centred exclusiveness. All reformers of modern India, he thought, stressed these imperatives for the revitalization of the social fabric. It was axiomatic that all forms of enterprise should be encouraged to open fresh vistas for social action. It did not matter much if the prescriptions of 'Krishnaji' (J. Krishnamurti) or the theosophical order fell short of expectations and did not accommodate a whole range of human services to mankind.[156] Menon was not inclined to circumscribe his vision by the directions of a particular discourse or a dogma. He was concerned about urgent social actions for a better life for all, constant comparative endeavours and a steady creative social performance unhindered by prejudices or a set of inflexible injunctions.

For Macnamara and many of her contemporaries at the LSE and London University, Menon was a staggering phenomenon, a whiff of fresh air. His anti-imperialism was unhedged and unambiguous. His appreciation of British liberal tradition was equally unmitigated.[157] His commitment to rend the curtain of ignorance and duplicity, carefully raised by the compulsions of imperial politics, was also fundamental. His determination to work for the termination of British rule and to witness the struggle for socialism in India constituted a resolute paradigm that was placed beyond the makeshift compromises of politics. By then, Menon was convinced of the righteousness of mass action and mass movement.[158] He no longer entertained any scruple in acknowledging the efficacy of Gandhi. For him adherence to non-violence was, however, still a tactical requirement and not a permanent philosophical engagement.[159] Marxism was a credible construct to analyze social developments but democratic values could not be wished away. He was aware of the growing opposition towards him in England, especially from circles where India meant something.[160] Over the years, many young minds were drawn towards him. His attraction was primarily intellectual. His decision to stay on at that alien and unexplored outpost of Indian nationalism as a solitary sentinel was personal and decisive. He wrote to his father repeatedly about the morbid loneliness of life in London, a city with extraordinary contradictions.[161] Probably, his interest in others was limited by his own instinct of self-preservation. He could love individuals passionately but he needed to be assured that he was passionately loved by them in return. Once satisfied, he adored many of them. Many women, who desired to be the objects of his devotion, were touched and then embarrassed at finding themselves adulated as the personification of all that was pure and spiritually ennobling by this apparently stern personality.[162]

In fact by then, Menon's personality and general

demeanour had become fascinating. His eyes had become more searching and piercing. There were some faint lines on his face indicating the footprints of a tough life on the left in Britain. A thin touch of grey added to his irresistible intellectual magnetism. He was more analytical than ever. He tended to become more logical and less sentimental in his public addresses. Facts, figures and cold statistics buttressed his arguments. He took note of the various comparative indicators as well. At meetings and public presentations he had become an unmistakable draw.[163] But seldom could he find time to spare for a cup of tea and a few potato chops with Macnamara at London's left-wing *demi-monde,* a seedy Soho establishment called the 1917 Club or for a walk around the Old Curiosity Shop or even for a meal at a cheap joint at Waterloo across the river.[164] Even so, like all his commitments, Menon's attachment to Barbara Macnamara grew gradually and very conspicuously and what was more important, she reciprocated warmly.

Menon's absence from England meant an opportunity for Macnamara to prove her mettle; she was determined to carry forward the task left behind by Menon; she was eager to assist Horrabin in every way possible to raise funds, organize the preliminaries for an India campaign following the submission of the delegation's report and energize the League in various ways.[165] In fact, Menon had become to the Strand kindergarten a sort of an embodiment of a fearless mission for freedom, and for Barbara Macnamara, he was also the incarnation of sincere, raw, rugged humanity. She was awaiting his return from India with all her desire to sit with him and to go on an endless excursion on matters concerning India, Menon's family at home, and Kerala. She had been trying to encompass within herself her vibrant emotions and shape herself for her new home in Malabar.[166] A letter from Menon posted at Port Said arrived in time to overwhelm Macnamara,[167] a somewhat shy, introvert, comely, moody, attractive and a dedicated scholar, of a robust

Krishna Menon in Tellicherry in about 1916. Menon Papers.

Komath Krishna Karup, Krishna Menon's father. Menon papers

Postcard depicding the presentation of the Commonwealth of India Bill to the British Parliament in 1925. Annie Besant papers.

Krishna Menon as Scoutmaster.
Menon Papers

With a friend in 1917.
Menon Papers

The British delegation to the International Congress against Colonial Oppression and Imperialism at Brussels in February 1927, attented by Jawaharlal Nehru. Saklatvala Papers.

A Home rule League rally at Adyar, 1916. Annie Basant Papers

Scottish family.[168] She was a sensitive observer of human behaviour. She was never superficial. A vague sense of a lurking danger, however, enveloped her days and nights although her fears were well covered by her infectious sense of humour. She had a vulnerable heart and highly tender feelings and she often sought peace in solitude and introspection. She had a bright face, a pair of sparkling eyes always amused by a sort of mischievous intent and a set of prominent teeth, irregular in some ways. Her frail frame held aloft an inquisitive mind that continually gathered, absorbed and reflected.[169] Intuitively, she sided with the cause of India's freedom. Instinctively, she grasped Menon's confidence and his effusive love.

There was perfect harmony of purpose between the two of them. Macnamara realized that Menon's belief in public duty went together with academic growth, aesthetic values, intellectual curiosity and a messianic zeal for India work. She was convinced that Menon must continue with his quest. He must complete his studies. His work on the process of reasoning should be published and Menon should then be encouraged to undertake his research on the psychology of theatre and Paul Rotha might be egged on to persuade Menon to take up his project in right earnest.[170] But he must take care. Menon had a weak constitution and Barbara knew that life was not easy for this man of firm convictions and resolution and an almost ascetic food habit. She wondered if Menon would have anyone in India to keep the collar of his shirt clean, a strange fascination for a man used only to scarcity, and she also worried about the worn-out ends of his jacket and trousers since her mother would not be available in India to mend them.[171]

In a circular under the signature of Macnamara and addressed to influential members and sympathizers of the League, the executive committee explained the objective of the delegation and its possible political output.[172] Macnamara stated that the object of the team was to investigate existing conditions in India, to see at first hand the effects of ordinance rule and to ascertain the extent of the support that the government had in its methods and intentions. It was believed that members would interact with all classes and try to obtain the points of view of as many representatives as possible. They would take into account all shades of opinion and hope to discuss the question with Hindus and Muslims, officials and non-officials, their intention being to visit not only all the main towns but as many villages as possible. They would have about three months in India during which they would travel all over the country. The mission would be one of investigation and the members would take no part whatever in politics or propaganda. The India office was informed of the project and an assurance was given that no obstacle would be put in the way of the delegation and all possible help would be given. On their return, the delegates would issue a report which might be published and circulated widely. Other activities would be conferences and public meetings all over the country by means of which truth about the situation would be spread.

The League, therefore, wished to organize a campaign of intensive propaganda with the object of reaching as wide a public as possible in England, on the continent and in America as well. The cost of the delegation was extremely heavy. They were short of the sum decided upon as necessary by a considerable amount. The entire amount raised in England was largely obtained by small donations given specifically for the purpose. The amount given, while barely enough to seed the delegation, was not enough to enable the League to carry on its work and prepare for a campaign on its return. It was acknowledged by all that the League would be unable to make the fullest and the best use of the work accomplished in India if it could not continue with the preparation to that end. It was with this end in view that the League thought it judicious to offer the last penny to fund the delegation and the two men of the team were obliged to go third class under disagreeable conditions.

The whole project had been discussed extensively with such celebrities as Lansbury, Laski, Brailsford and Andrews and the details of the *modus operandi* had been worked out. The League laid special stress on the non-party character of the delegation and emphasized that an investigation of great value could be carried out in India in spite of the disturbed state of the country. It was maintained that the party would return towards the end of November to undertake parliamentary work as well as other public activities. The League, therefore, appealed to all friends and sympathizers and also to those who were interested in India's freedom to come forward and contribute generously to its fighting funds.[173]

The position was also made unambiguous to Malaviya at the India end. Malaviya was told on the arrival of the deputation in India that the investigation and observations of the delegates would be of great assistance in 'furthering our mutual cause'.[174] At the Strand, Horrabin maintained, the absence of 'our hard-working' secretary, with his wide knowledge of Indian affairs and his varied experience in the methods of propaganda, was very seriously felt. The League, however, had been working hard and kept the 'flag flying in England'.[175] It succeeded in obtaining a large amount of voluntary help which made the burden of work less heavy. The departure of the delegation had created a new interest in Indian affairs in Britain and elsewhere and the League had taken advantage of those extensive and intensive activities. Frantic queries about the deposition of the delegation came even from the USA and Switzerland. The League had already initiated preliminary spadework for a country-wide campaign so as to give the widest possible publicity to the observations immediately on their return.

Finalizing a meeting for Menon organized by the Eastbourne ILP, Macnamara asked concerned institutions and individuals to be generous enough to respond 'to our request as we are in urgent need'. 'We are not in the habit of charging a fee for such lectures,' she wrote, 'and only ask for travelling expenses and hospitality. Should your branch, however, feel disposed to give the League a small donation, it would be gratefully accepted as we are finding it hard to get sufficient financial support.'[176] While thanking Malaviya for the generous assistance which made the delegation possible, Horrabin stated that the existing resources of the League and even prospective help would not ensure the publicity which the report would deserve. The outcome of a half-hearted attempt would be disastrous and unless assistance could be secured in India, justice could not be done to the work at hard and the great sacrifices already made would be useless. Emphasizing the urgency of assistance, Horrabin made a special appeal: 'Knowing the keen interest that you have taken in the matter and how necessary it is to educate British opinion (a point of view which is not as widely held amongst Indians as one would like) we feel sure that our appeal will not fall on deaf ears and that everything which one man can do will be done.'[177] Horrabin thought it necessary to add that he decided to write to Malaviya after serious consideration and having taken into account Malaviya's grave responsibilities in those trying times. Horrabin wrote earnestly that to no one else could the League have thought of writing so frankly and he trusted that 'our anxiety to do our best may be taken as our only excuse for troubling you still further'.[178]

Meanwhile, Macnamara took a bold stand in publicizing the letters and communications from India for publication in the *India Review*.[179] One piece from Gangavihari L. Mehta made a good impact. Mehta, an honourable gentleman of substance, wrote in a sharp acerbic vein on the impact of the ordinance rule on trade and commerce, which even the leading nationalist dailies in Calcutta did not venture to publish without drastic modifications.[180] With the ordinances in force the Indian press was unable to publish even criticism of individual officials except at considerable risk. Freedom of trade, Mehta maintained, was the official ground of the ordinances and the principal justification for suppressing the Congress movement. The public and especially the commercial community, it appeared, had been moaning under the tyranny of the Congress which had been interfering in every possible way with the normal and even course of trade and industry. It had also been maintained that trade depression was partly due to what was called world factors beyond the control of the government and partly owing to 'the mischievous activities of a section of Indians, organized under the Congress, who despite the fact that they were in a minority, could, by some sort of magic, coerce traders and hamper trade'.[181] Suddenly, therefore, in the month of January 1932, Mehta wrote, the champions of freedom in the home department of the Government of India 'woke up to this fact and decided to free the country once and for all from this Congress oppression by suspending the ordinary law of the land and promulgating a series of Ordinances'.[182] No stronger action, Mehta wrote tongue-in-cheek, in the cause of freedom had been taken 'since Abraham Lincoln made war on the Southern States of America for freeing the slaves'. The commercial community was thus, he added, slowly recovering its lost freedom to trade 'owing to the noble war on the Congress, and the freedom which had been usurped by the Congress is being re-conquered from it by our trustees'. Giving details of the impact of the ordinances in Madras, Bombay, Kanpur, Delhi and Calcutta, Mehta wrote in sheer anguish: 'Not even the most unimaginative die-hard can agree that arrests, *lathi* charges, forcible opening of shops, ban on *hartals* and such other measures are likely to increase a feeling of goodwill — unless human nature in India and in the East is the reverse of normal. Only bitterness and resentment will be the legacies of such a policy.'[183]

On board the *S.S. Gange* on their way to India, the delegation did not feel very comfortable as the future was engulfed in somewhat baffling contingencies. 'What the result of this undertaking will be', Menon wrote to his friend at Birmingham from the boat in the Mediterranean, 'God alone knows. We are in such a difficult business without solid backing or foundations anywhere, the fate of all those who are not fanatics or purists. I shall however do my best and I think the rest of the party also will do the same.'[184]

Within a week of its arrival in India the League's delegation was to land in rough weather. Wilkinson and Whately pressed hard to see Sarojini Naidu, who had been confined to Yeravda jail, on the ground that Naidu was a personal friend. The governor of Bombay was inclined to think that the concession could be granted as an exceptional case. Under the existing rules, A class prisoners might have one interview a fortnight, although the conversation should be limited to private and domestic matters, discussions on political affairs not being allowed. The Bombay government was, therefore, prepared to allow the interview as an exceptional privilege and would take care to see that the conversation should be confined to private and domestic issues.[185] But the home secretary would not have it. He maintained that the interview was obviously sought for political purposes. The delegation had come out under the auspices of and financed by the Congress. This fact was unalterable and no stipulation that the government might make would alter the fact, notwithstanding the interpretation that might be put upon it by the Indian public. 'I am afraid if an exception is made in this case,' Hallett gave his considered opinion, 'it will form the basis for further applications by members of the delegation who, we know, were specifically anxious to see political prisoners and a relaxation of our general rules about interviews with the prisoners.'[186]

In a note dated 31 October 1932, Hallett gave his reflections on the attitudes of the delegation.[187] Reviewing his extensive discussions with Menon and Wilkinson, he observed that although Menon did not talk much, his pertinent interventions at crucial points showed his incisive comprehension of the situation and that he, more than anyone else, provided the typical Congress background and orientation to the whole operation. Menon was sharp in detecting the nuances of a situation and prompt in locating all points of departure in a fairly long and rambling discussion. His intelligence and grasp made him not very agreeable company to all his adversaries, especially in the officialdom. The home secretary found in Wilkinson a more moderate and reasonable figure. She had assured the home secretary that she was sincerely anxious to ascertain the facts of the situation and that she was conscious that possibilities of misapprehension had arisen in the official mind from her close Congress, connection. Menon qualified the position by readily adding that the delegation was not exclusively in touch with the Congress but with Indians and non-Indians of all political persuasions and social complexions. The home secretary felt that while Wilkinson was genuine in her concern, it was Menon who had been commanding the proceedings of the delegation. Hallett believed that Wilkinson showed, definite interest in meeting officials wherever she went and that her general attitude was quite different from that of Whately. Hallett specifically mentioned that Whately had refused to listen to what the officials told her or even to visit villages other than those selected for her by her Congress friends. The home secretary was convinced that Wilkinson was somewhat embarrassed by this extraordinary phenomenon and she made it a point to get in touch with the officials wherever she went and listened with an open mind to what they had to say. It was evident to Hallett that her attitude was quite open and unprejudiced in contrast to those of the other members of the team. She was uninhibited, open and accessible. At least on one occasion Whately's extrovert leaning towards the Congress was sought to be explained away by an abashed Wilkinson. Another significant point that struck Hallett was that Wilkinson was the only member who was prepared to make allowances for the impediments and discomfitures faced by a harassed administration and a vexed police force in dealing with an essentially unlawful movement.[188]

Authorities were comforted to find that they could engage Wilkinson in a good deal of discussion about the land tenure system.[189] Wilkinson raised the issue that the system of tenancy constituted a harsh institution of the government. Hallett thought it necessary to explain that the government could not be blamed as the system was inherited by the British administration, which relaxed considerably its original severity by introducing the rules of suspensions and remissions.[190] As regards the prices realized, the home secretary tried to convince Wilkinson that they had been obtained in an open market and if any one considered them to be low he could have offered a higher bid.[191] In fact, a good deal of care was taken to influence Wilkinson. Initially, it was presumed by the officials that Wilkinson was fed up with the Congress attitude of presenting facts in a perverse manner with a view to misleading the team.[192] The home secretary tried hard to persuade her to ponder over the dangers of accepting everything mentioned by the Congress without verification.[193] But he was rattled to find that ultimately Wilkinson put up a stout resistance to official persuasion. Perhaps Hallett felt let down as she was somewhat disinclined to accept any version except the one 'dished out by the Congress' and 'glibly accepted such general statement as police *joolum*'.[194] In the face of what appeared to the officials to be the delegation's ostensibly pro-Congress consciousness, the administration had but little opportunity other than repeating *ad nauseam* its pet nostrums on the remarkable restraint exhibited by the police, in spite of its extensive powers under the ordinances, faced as they were, by the excessive provocations of the Gandhian *satyagrahis.*[195]

At Bardoli in Gujarat, Menon showed, it was reported, 'a sort of haughty impatience' and objected to the official attempt to present the administration as faultless and aggrieved.[196] By and large, the officials were convinced that the delegation was prejudiced and they 'did not want to be convinced'.[197] It was also taken for granted that the delegation had kept up 'an appearance of impartiality by interviewing officials in most places'.[198] But they 'lived in an atmosphere of civil disobedience' throughout their stay in India and it would be preposterous to expect that their views had not been coloured accordingly.[199] The reports maintained that the matters in which the team displayed the greatest interest were labour conditions, especially wages and housing, repression with special reference to police excesses, jail conditions and the general atmosphere of the country as affected by the ordinance rule with regard to the ensuing political reconstructions.[200] It was held that the views of the party on labour questions were identical to those which could have been expected from a Labour delegation.[201] It appeared that both Wilkinson and Menon were eloquent on the subjects of poverty and housing conditions. Wilkinson addressed labour gatherings on these topics and also urged the need to strengthen the trade union movement in order to improve the lot of the working classes.[202]

The police reports were full of apprehensions about the impact of the visits of the members to the slum dwellers and villages. From the stray conversations with the depressed classes, the delegation seemed to have gathered the impression that Gandhi was regarded, almost without exception, as their leader and was held in esteem as a demi-god.[203] It was suspected that various classes and sections gave expression to some well-rehearsed lines. Police thought it amazing that the delegation everywhere has confronted with stories of police excesses and various persons were produced before them as victims of police brutality.[204] Some of these persons, it was alleged, showed old scars which were the result of *lathi* blows although the police contended that the scars were due to some other causes.[205] It was maintained that at certain places where members of the delegation visited, Congress organizers, acting under detailed instructions from headquarters, made strenuous endeavours to organize 'lawless demonstrations and acts of defiance of authority calculated to bring the populace into conflict with police'.[206] The administration felt encouraged to assert that the history of the preceding two and a half years clearly illustrated that the task of maintaining law and order in a vast subcontinent containing 350 million people, the vast majority of whom were illiterate and ignorant, was one of extreme difficulty and although there had been remarkable success in that undertaking, occasional unfortunate incidents could not be avoided. The official position, it was added, ought to be viewed in the context of inadequacy of the police force and the strains and provocations to which its members had so far been exposed.[207] It was a *déja vu* condition with which the administration had been familiar.

In her conversation with Harry Haig, Wilkinson maintained that she was amazed by the uncivilized act of the forcible breaking up of peaceful processions by the police and that it had become a daily routine in India. Wilkinson drew the attention of the home member to an incident in Gujarat which she had herself witnessed. The procession included women and children and was attacked ruthlessly by police with *lathis*. She also complained that once the police realized that the brutal action was being noticed, they stopped the charge and began arresting the processionists.[208] Menon narrated a similar incident at length where the Redshirts were most mercilessly beaten by the frontier police at Mardan. Menon and his associates were told that the procession had been stage-managed for the benefit of the delegation and the assaulting policemen were in fact the Redshirts volunteers dressed in police uniforms, the whole episode being prearranged in order to create an impression on the delegates about the so-called police *joolum.*[209] The story was discounted by the delegation as fantastic and they were bemused when they found that the authorities showed no intention to maintain it when pressed and challenged by Menon.[210] The home member felt disconcerted and concluded that it must have been a bad case of unnecessary cruelty.[211] In his confidential note he was shocked by the lack of basic common sense in the police force and was apprehensive that many such stories of police high-handedness would be found in the delegation's report. 'It was obvious', he wrote in sheer frustration, 'that if they themselves had witnessed any really unjustifiable beatings, as they alleged, this would enormously strengthen their conviction in the general allegation of police brutality in India.'[212]

Another issue raised by Wilkinson related to a general complaint of beating of undertrial prisoners. Questioned by the home member, it appeared that she had been referring to torture in police lock-ups.[213] Wilkinson put her accusing finger to the fact that, in many cases, Congressmen were arrested, kept for a few hours in police lock-ups, mercilessly beaten and then released.[214] She was shocked by the fact that in many villages the police really acted in an arbitrary and overbearing manner without any effective political or administrative control.[215] One of the main complaints was that the ordinances conferred extraordinary powers on the police which had been exercised with very little supervision.[216] Officials were distressed to find that Wilkinson was not inclined to be persuaded by the police implorations that the civil disobedience movement did not touch rural life and, therefore, there was hardly any occasion to exhibit police power in the villages.[217] It seemed to Hallett that Wilkinson would carry with her a firm impression that the police in India had been empowered with great authority which was being used indiscriminately, unscrupulously and, of course, with impunity.[218] Even the home secretary in his pensive moments must have pondered over the fact that police autocracy in India formed a general background of complaints even in ordinary times.[219]

The weekly confidential report from the district magistrate of the Kanarese area of Bombay Presidency reported on the visit of Leonard Matters to Siddapur on 1 September 1932.[220] He interviewed both officials and non-officials. His principal area of inquiry included such issues as the alleged prohibition of relief work by the government, attachment of property for the recovery of land revenue, police assistance for conducting the work of attachment, deteriorating economic conditions and depopulation in the *taluk*. He also made searching enquiries about police excesses. Both at Siddapur and Sisri in Kanwar district he witnessed police action against processions in support of civil disobedience and discounted the official description of these demonstrations as stage-managed. The official report squarely blamed Matters for being partial and for not accepting police allegations. It was also reported that the unexpected visit of Matters at Tyagli, Kansur, Ankola and some other places in Kanara district gave a lot of trouble to the local authorities in checking 'the Congress shows secretly arranged by agitators in defiance of law and order'.[221]

On 19 October 1932 Hallett reiterated his position that the delegation was really occasioned and financed by the Congress through Madan Mohan Malaviya.[222] Despite all forms of civility and cooperation extended to the delegation, he complained, 'Wilkinson and Co.' confined themselves to the formalities of discussion with the officials at different levels but they continued to work on lines outlined by the Congress and, as a result, investigations at different places had been conducted on the preconceived Congress allegations.[223] By that date parts of the Madras Presidency, Bombay Presidency, and Bihar and Orissa had been covered by the delegation.[224] It was striking, Hallett maintained, that at all the places that they visited demonstrations were organized by local Congress leaders for the observation of the delegates and often they provoked police action. Demonstrations took the form of processions, flag salutations, sale of unauthorized and proscribed Congress bulletins, picketing and fake attempts to raid notified Congress buildings forcing police action to disperse crowds and arrest leaders.[225] Some of the delegates discussed the situation with officials and non-officials and although they did not express their opinion categorically, the tenor of their inquiry, Hallett wrote, amply exhibited their predilections in favour of the Congress line.

During the stay of the delegation in the Madras Presidency from 25 August to 7 September 1932, the delegates split up into batches and visited several districts. Congress workers and sympathizers, Hallett noted, acted as guides and interpreters and arranged what they were to see and whom they were to talk to.[226] The whole tour in South India was masterminded by C. Rajagopalachari, acting president of the Congress.[227] As the administration was conscious of the Congress strategy, they showed a good deal of self-restraint and, more often than not, could manage to avoid unpleasant incidents. In Rajamundri, Hallett continued, the delegation was induced to attend the funeral of a prominent civil disobedience agitator whose death, it was generally believed, was hastened by his treatment at the hands of the police. Hallett was convinced that by that time the delegation had already been prejudiced and it was quite prepared to accept any story, however improbable, provided it was unfavourable to the police, and disregarded any suggestion from official quarters.[228] The 'incidents' had been fabricated or exaggerated by the Congress for the purpose of propaganda. Facts and figures placed by the officers before them, Hallett complained, did not appear to have made any impression on their minds.[229] It seemed that the delegation had apparently heard, Hallett complained, lurid accounts of prison conditions prevailing in India, but they were unable to conceal their astonishment at the general cleanliness and good order of the three typical jails they were allowed to visit. Hallett must have chuckled when he wrote that Wilkinson was reported to have compared the conditions of Dartmoor with those of the Cannanore jail, much in favour of the latter.[230] To stress his point Hallett wrote that the delegation was inclined to be critical of the classification of civil disobedience prisoners and to be distrustful of the treatment of B class prisoners irrespective of the situation and facts.[231] He also maintained that on the general political situation the delegation professed to reserve judgement. But although their public utterances were guarded, judged by private conversation it appeared that Congress leaders had already created a strong impression on their minds that the whole country had been seething with discontent at the policy of repression and that the administration of the ordinances had created a universal spirit of bitterness.[232] Hallett was eager to establish that the committee's attempts to wear a mask of impartiality was fairly transparent and the longer they stayed, the more difficult it would be for them to maintain the veneer of objectivity. They were constantly associated with the organizers of the civil disobedience movement and, as a consequence, the report the delegation was to produce on return to England was not likely to be anything but one-sided and prejudiced.[233]

From the official point of view it seemed that the impressions left behind by the delegation were fairly depressing and they were monotonously similar. The impact of its visit to Cuttack on 8 September 1932 and some other districts of Bihar and Orissa from 20 to 25 September 1932 was no better.[234] They watched picketing of cloth and excise shops at Cuttack and discussed with local lawyers the communal award and the conduct of the police. They also visited some collieries at Dhanbad and made inquiries into labour conditions.[235]

Reporting that the delegation moved around Patna in Hasan Imam's company and surrounded by Congressmen who 'regaled them with stories of police excesses', Hallett made a special mention of Whately's firm prejudice against government, her constant harangue to the officials regarding police atrocities, her advice to the Congress leaders not to relent in their policy and await the arrival of the new government in England, her promise to see to it that existing officers trained in inhuman methods would be wiped off the board, her frank admission to the district magistrate at Monghyr that she would not hear anything against the Congress and that she would believe anything that had been told by her Congress friends.[236] Hallett emphasized once again that the definite impression of the officials was that the delegation was not prepared to hear the other side of the case.[237]

Forwarding the report of Monica Whately's visit to Monghyr, the commissioner of Bhagalpur division thought that the account was both amusing and irritating.[238] It appeared to him that the delegation was busy preparing a brief against the British government in India and was not honestly searching for information. The commissioner felt that it would be injudicious to allow the delegation to continue as it had been consciously abusing the opportunity given to them. The district magistrate of Monghyr held that Whately was prejudiced against the government.[239] The magistrate, used to unbridled authority, was struck by the audacious Whately's claim that every 'Congressman was a devoted patriot who had sacrificed his all for the country'. She had no confidence in the claims of the district magistrate and believed that there was no flaw in any of the Congress actions even when she was told of specific instances. The officials discounted her comprehension of the Indian realities as 'some erratic antics' indulged in by 'an unsuccessful candidate of the Labour Party at the last British election'.[240] On her part, the conscientious lady must have found that the officials were bent upon derailing her line of investigation. She was presented as a cantankerous and suspicious woman given to fanciful thoughts. The population of India, she allegedly held, mainly consisted of pleaders and doctors professing Congress politics. She was firmly convinced, the district magistrate reported, that she knew much more about this district after a few hours experience 'than any of the rest of us who have been here for years'. She believed in everything that she was told by Congressmen who acted as her interpreters.[241] The district magistrate thought that the lady personified Rudyard Kipling's Mr Paget MP and had been wandering around with a remarkably closed mind. Repudiating the charges of police torture, the magistrate wrote back: 'You will probably not believe me, but it is a fact, that the Congress organization in this district regularly publishes false and malicious stories about government servants in the secretly cyclostyled Congress bulletin. That is the local idea of the way to conduct a campaign of civil disobedience. It is easy to throw mud anonymously at government servants who are not in a position to defend themselves, but, as they say in England, it is not cricket.'[242]

In fact, the officials felt that there was a concerted effort to project a well- synchronized parody of investigation carried on by the party. In the official report it was emphasized that Whately arrived from Patna in the company of a provincial leader of the Congress and was welcomed at the railway station by a body of Congress stalwarts of the area who accompanied Whately throughout her stay. Her car sported a small Congress flag, Congress crowd followed her shouting Congress slogans and her Congress companions participated both in the shouting as well as in her investigations and prompted by her to cross-question the officials.[243] An excited crowd was encouraged by her to shout that in the event of *swaraj* they would prefer Gandhi as the ruler and not the king-emperor and that there was no prejudice in India against the untouchables who were united with the caste Hindus. False cases of police atrocities, it was alleged, were entertained and accepted. The officials were irked to see that one Badri Narayan Singh provided an elephant on which Whately made a local tour of inspection of the places of police action, while about 2,000 people followed her and the *mahout* carried a Congress flag.[244] Whately refused to be exhorted, when, at an exclusive tea-party the leading officials along with the manager of a major tobacco factory persuaded her to believe the claims of the officials and ignore the apocryphal stories floated by the Congress. She definitely indicated, the official report commented, that 'she distrusted everything we said, but believed everything that had been told by the Congress' and relied on the Congress interpreters.[245] The district magistrate dismissed the trip of Bihar by Whately 'as a big *tamasha*'.[246]

The district officer of Muzaffarpur reported that Matters covered about 100 villages in the district in about seven days. In a meeting attended at the town hall, Muzaffarpur, presided over by the local MLC, Matters thanked the people for their hospitality and courtesy. He reaffirmed the resolve of the delegates that they would be able to inform the British people about the condition of India. He insisted that public opinion in England was ignorant of the situation in India and with a good deal of political acumen the delegation was sure to grasp the essential drift of India's feelings despite considerable intricacies of life and conditions in India.[247]

Although Congressmen exhibited a remarkable spirit of cooperation, the national party was not as yet fully convinced of the efficacy of the delegation or its unbiased perception. It was sceptical of the outcome and preferred to keep its fingers crossed. The Congress bulletin of 13 August 1932, issued from Bombay, spelt out its attitude towards the delegation in some detail and the authorities took note of the trends of Indian thought.[248] Welcoming the mission of the delegation, it maintained there was a sizeable section of people in England which was far from satisfied with the kind of news they happened to get from India and the manner in which it was served in that country. The Congress was aware that this enlightened section of British public opinion was not prepared to accept Samuel Hoare's uncorroborated statements *ex cathedra* as the truth about the Indian situation. The Congress held that whenever intelligent and fair-minded Englishmen were in a position to check the official version of events in India from reliable sources of their own, they were disturbed to see through the garbled official opinion. The British Labour Party, for instance, was far from impressed by the unreliable nature of the India office account and its grossly undesirable fallout. From their personal experience it was apparent that both the Indian administration and the Conservative Party were given to wilful distortion of facts. The testimony of a trusted observer, H.N. Brailsford, and the account of his own experience of the first phase of the civil disobedience movement of 1930 was in itself an eye-opener. It was firmly maintained that the delegation had been working on its own and the Congress had neither sponsored nor financed it. Madan Mohan Malaviya's pecuniary assistance was his personal initiative, unrelated to any Congress pressure or initiative. The Congress welcomed the investigation and held out no special offer to it and it only presaged some of the probable conclusions of the investigation.

It was presumed that perhaps the delegation, owing specially to the paucity of time, would come to some superficial conclusions overwhelmed by a large country of subcontinental dimension having, as the imperial propaganda maintained, 350 million inhabitants, seventeen hundred religions, nine thousand sects and countless languages and dialects. Thus it would be compelled to confirm that although there was suffering and repression at places, it was difficult to judge the issues and their intensity amidst a jungle of conflicting information and tense political atmosphere. It might also maintain, the Congress bulletin argued, that terrorism in Bengal was most unfortunate and was bound to retard the political progress of the country. The Congress was certain that the delegation would rightly find the industrial condition of India very backward and the roots of the political unrest would primarily be seen to lie in economic distress. The delegation might thus offer a not very satisfactory report concluding that the very complex drift of the Indian situation had rendered the Indian question intricate and placed the government in an unenviable position. The Congress was convinced that the delegation would feel obliged to recommend moderation to the government and reasonableness to the Congress and would expect a meaningful dialogue between the two adversaries leading to a 'satisfactory' settlement of the problem. It was hoped that by judicious handling of the situation both the contenders could bridge the gulf between them.

The Congress announced boldly that it would not agree to any recommendation of conciliation that was sure to underlie the delegation's report. On the contrary, the Congress was keen to announce that it had nothing to do with such a concoction or prescription. 'We believe in our creed', wrote the Congress bulletin, 'that India must and will free herself by her own unaided efforts. We firmly believe that it would be criminal stupidity on the part of any Indian to rely on the help of British socialists or British communists or of any Britisher or foreigner for the freedom of this country.'[249] The bulletin stressed that the prosperity of Britain was too closely bound up with the exploitation of India to leave any ground for doubt that no political party in Britain would lightly let go its hold of India. 'British delegations may come and go as often as they like. The work of the Congress will go on unrestrained and with unabated vigour.'[250] The officials were inclined to attach significant importance to the sarcastic prognostications of the Congress on the delegation's report; some of them thought it prudent to bring the bulletin to the notice of Wilkinson and others.[251]

By October 1932, the attitude of the Congress became clearer. In a press release by C. Rajagopalachari, president of the Tamil Nadu Congress committee, the impression of the Congress on the India League delegation was unambiguously spelt out. The Congress appreciated their earnestness of purpose, ability and freedom from prejudice. The delegation, it was recorded, fully realized that India must help herself in her quest for freedom and that British friends could be of no avail in the struggle against imperialism beyond certain limits and what could save her was the sacrifices of her men and women in India. Their real work, the press release added, was to set right England's name, which could be done not by disguising uncomfortable facts and whitewashing disquieting realities but by confession and repentance. It was for this purpose they had been collecting facts and working out a rational plan to create a healthy public opinion on their return home. The members of the delegation appeared to be very different from the usual tourist sympathizers. They were impressed more deeply with the substantial convergence of all shades of opinion in India instead of being confused or misled by apparent differences on the surface. Rajagopalachari argued that while most friends of India appeared to be dazed into despair by the overwhelming Conservative majority in the parliament and its disastrous policy in regard to India, the tenor of the investigation of the delegation is fairly optimistic. The delegates had taken into account the nature and intensity of the struggle, then being carried out by India, and they felt that the struggle had 'thrown a fresh ray of light into the dark corner of political defeat'. Rajagopalachari maintained that '*satyagraha* shows a way out of the impotence of political minorities as well as a way out of the impotence of a disarmed subject nation. It has a validity in England as well as in India.' It was hoped that the delegation on its return home in November 1932 would be able to fight 'the intoxicated majority in the House' in new ways than the parliament had hitherto known.[252]

Both Wilkinson and Whately decided to turn a deaf ear to all official promptings against the Congress. On the other hand, they were inquisitive about the whipping penalty. On their persistent enquiry about the extent to which the penalty was employed in India, the head of the Bombay police explained that it was resorted to as per court sentence, that it was more frequently inflicted in jails for offences against jail discipline and that the European Association had urged the administration to recommend whipping for picketing, communal violence and active civil disobedience. It was assumed that there was little likelihood that the Government of India would finally disagree with a recommendation advocating extension of the whipping penalty.[253]

Hostility was the keynote of the official reports on the activities of the delegation in the United Provinces as well. At Banaras, H. Bamford reported that the party, excluding Menon and Wilkinson, stayed at the Clarke's Hotel for just twenty-four hours and watched the demonstrations of picketing, flag salutation and burning of cloth which were staged for their benefit. They also paid a visit to the extremely 'volatile' university campus of the city.[254] The magistrate of the district reported that the visiting team interviewed a couple of women involved in the Dashashwamedh police case. The interviews were arranged by Malaviya strictly *in camera*.[255] Once again, it was alleged that the delegates did not approve anything that was conveyed to them against the nationalists. In Allahabad, where Matters and Whately proceeded from Banaras, they decided to stay at the residence of Tej Bahadur Sapru despite his absence from the city. The administration was disposed to discount the impartiality of the proposed report on the basis that several Muslims whom they interviewed were themselves Congressmen and the trip to a village was organized and supervised by one Shyam Lal Nehru with the assistance of an interpreter, the son of Dr Kailash Nath Katju, a leading lawyer of the city and reported to have been the treasurer of the Congress.[256] When Matters and Whately protested against the arrest of a Congress volunteer while 'persuading and pressurizing' villagers to lay their grievances collectively before the deputation, the superintendent of police got the impression that the visitors were prepared to listen to what the Congress told them and were not at all anxious to hear the other side of the story.[257]

The investigation was fairly thorough and Hallett felt obliged to write to the India office that the delegation was entirely controlled by the Congress. As evidence of his position Hallett referred to various local incidents. At Kanpur, they met the local leaders and accepted their hospitality. They declined to meet the secretary of the local Constitutional League. It was also alleged that they refused politely to accept the list of names suggested by the Associated Press representatives for collecting information.[258] It was reported once again that they ventured to visit the *bazar* and spent a good deal of time there to watch the proceedings of an arranged picketing demonstration. They had discussions with the Muzdur Sabha, visited the workers' quarters and inspected the list of members of the trade union. The report of the collector of Kanpur echoed a familiar refrain that the deputation had spent their whole time absorbing Congress propaganda and it depended entirely on their credulity how much they assimilated.[259]

From Kanpur, Matters and Whately moved to Agra where they arrived on 1 October 1932. Their stay, the officials complained, was arranged by prominent Congressmen and they were introduced to a body of twenty to thirty partymen in sheer indifference to the official overtures. At Agra two other delegates, Wilkinson and Menon, joined them and they were taken to visit Baroda village, a stronghold of the no-rent movement at the end of 1930.[260] Following the visit, Matters accosted the officer in charge of the village especially on police atrocities against the villagers. Matters, it was reported by the collector, declined to see the official records, files and entries on Baroda incidents etc. The procession, organized in Agra on 2 October 1932 to celebrate Gandhi's birthday, the officials reported, passed by the streets of Agra without any incident much to the disappointment of the organizers. The following day the authorities sponsored a delegation of *chamars* in order to emphasize the social implications of untouchability despite the Poona Pact and to draw the attention of the delegation to the opposition of the untouchables to a system of joint electorates.[261] Matters and Whately visited Meerut, paid a visit to some villages, addressed a meeting of students at Meerut college, discussed the progress of *khaddar* and heard about the political situation from teachers and Congress leaders. The official report on the visit to Agra and Meerut stressed that the delegation did not visit Lucknow and Aligarh; the implication of such conspicuous omission was the prospect of a different perspective from these areas not complementary to the monotonous Congress propaganda.[262]

Summing up the report, Bamford wrote that it was perfectly clear from the reports of officials from all over India that the delegation put themselves entirely in the hands of their Congress hosts and took no pains at all to learn other than the Congress view. It is reported that the subjects in which they took most interest were the Congress movement, the depressed class problems, female education, police repression, the conditions of tenants, and jails. It was further noted that they tried as far as possible to avoid officials, seldom expressed their views and took copious notes of all that was expressed before them.[263] It was assumed that special items of 'false Congress propaganda' to which they were likely to give publicity, were overcrowding in jails and treatment of political prisoners, ill-treatment of tenants by the zamindars and government's partiality to the latter, police excesses, and the uncontrolled initiative given to the police in India under the ordinances.[264] It was maintained in the course of discussion that before the Gandhi-Irwin settlement Baroda was one of the restive centres of the civil disobedience movement and the tenants of that area refused to pay rents. The zamindars obtained attachment orders from the court, and according to local officials, because of the militant and defiant attitude of the tenants, it became necessary for the police force on the spot to control local opposition during the process of attachment. Even after the pact, the officials maintained, the no-rent movement was not called off and Baroda remained as 'truculent as ever', so much so that the land revenue was either paid by the zamindar without collecting rent, or it was realized from the tenant by the use of the coercive process prescribed by law.[265] The delegation, however, got the impression following a thorough examination of cases that the government punished the tenants on behalf of the zamindars and was not inclined to take any action if excesses were committed by zamindars on tenants. That was the impression they got both in Agra and other districts and similar complaints were made quite frequently in Allahabad district and also in Gujarat and Assam.

The no-tax campaign did not extend over the whole province of Gujarat. It extended over some parts of Kaira district, the *taluk* of Jambusar in Broach district and the *taluk* of Bardoli. In Kaira district, Borsad, Matar and Anand were three *taluks* that carried on the campaign in an organized manner. Borsad was foremost in the fight. Twenty one villages in Borsad, four in Matar and two in Anand carried on the campaign as whole villages. Stray villages and individuals also joined in. Harassments, attachments, sentences, imprisonments, *khalsa* notices and confiscation of land together with police brutality and lawless excesses were some of the elements of normal official retribution. To meet the situation in Kaira alone, the government opened about twenty new police camps in the *taluks* of Borsad, Anand and Matar. No less than seven hundred attachments had been affected in the district. Landlords were taken to the *choras* of the villages and treated to abuses, insults, beating and starvation and often even drinking water was refused. Even women were not spared and all ideas of decency, chivalry or humanity were dropped. The government treated the *satyagrahis* with various seductive methods in order to split the solid block of popular opposition. Bardoli in Surat district was in the forefront in the struggle.

In view of the bold commitment of the peasants to the Gandhian struggle since 1930, the government made special *bandobast* to prevent any organization in the *taluk* from functioning or to take firm roots. The whole *taluk* was besieged and strict vigilance was kept on everyone entering or leaving the *taluk*. A large number of villages were invaded by the police authorities and their legions; villagers were beaten and persecuted indiscriminately and threatened with dire consequences if they showed any inclination not to pay land revenue. Any affiliation with the Congress, or even its programme, meant immediate arrest and sentence of hard labour and a heavy fine. Attachment of property and its auction at a low price were common features. Police *joolum* was at its worst at places of no-tax movement.[266] The delegation was aware that litigation was expensive and poor tenants could not afford to pay for it even where recourse to law was feasible. The official position was fairly inflexible. They maintained that during the preceding three decades, substantial efforts had been made by the government to improve the condition of the peasantry, while the Congress played an opportunistic game of exploiting acute agricultural distress in rural India to its own advantage.[267]

Another area of interaction devolved around the permission sought by the delegation to see the jails and examine the conditions of the prisoners.[268] In spite of Whately's persistent request for permission, the officials declined to give the clearance. It was explained that since the civil disobedience movement there had been much indiscipline in UP jails; one of the causes was that exaggerated and sometimes unfounded stories of jail punishments had been sent out by political prisoners through interviewers and had been circulated by way of propaganda by the Congress press. Thus, the Indian people had been told of jail punishments but not of the violation of rules by political prisoners and this created resentment in the country. It was, therefore, considered necessary to restrict the interviews of political visitors seeking information for the sake of propaganda.[269]

Concluding the report, the Agra officials categorically stated that the delegation was completely in the hands of the Congressmen and they showed little inclination even to consider the official point of view and that the officials were well aware of the damage that 'interested interpreters' could do. Since the projected report was expected merely to echo the run-of-the-mill allegations, the officials thought that a counter-offensive should be launched especially in three areas of suspected allegations: condition of jails, agrarian tension, and police excesses. It appeared from stray references by Matters that the party was much exercised by the fact that proportions of A and B class prisoners were negligible and that jail punishments were too many to be treated casually.[270] It could be maintained, the officials held, that the Congress drew most of their civil disobedience volunteers from the criminal classes and men and women of superior classes or of good social standing were few and far between and they were given superior jail status. Besides, the jails were meant for ordinary criminals and not for the requirements of a mass movement. It was added that a brief report of cases of indiscipline in jails and punishments awarded ought to be prepared where it should also be asserted that every court took into account the social status of the person sentenced and that rules were liberal.[271] It should be added that considerable attention had been paid to the problem of overcrowded jails.

It was recommended that a report on clashes of zamindars and tenants should be prepared with statistics regarding convictions. The administration believed it was quite rational to affirm that 'some figures ought to be manipulated to show that large number of zamindars were punished for ill-treating their tenants'.[272] Besides, a chart on civil disobedience in the districts of UP was to be worked out stating when and the circumstances in which, use of police became necessary to assist the execution of legal processes.[273] Figures of remission and suspension of rent and revenue collection in each district during the preceding three years were to be collated. Lists of legislative and other measures which had been adopted during the last thirty years to improve the lot of the tenants in general were to be prepared. It was believed that with such a statement it would not be difficult to answer effectively all criticisms to be raised by the delegation.[274] The government was somewhat exercised as the delegation was keen to locate the dark and grey areas of its general performance, including excesses and overzealous overtones of the administration, its criminal apathy towards popular well-being and the morbid rule of ordinances carried out by local agencies which had been deliberately ignored or overlooked by superior authorities. It was resolved that open overtures should henceforth be made by officials to befriend the delegation and arrange social functions on a small scale where officials and selected non-officials of moderate views should be invited to meet the delegation in order to elicit information and allay suspicions.[275] The official communication with the delegation henceforth was to become extremely subtle, gentle and restrained and the officials were requested to exhibit a sense of concern over the state of affairs in India owing to the significant loss of trust between the ruler and the ruled.[276]

The district of Midnapur in Bengal had been, since the

non-cooperation movement, one of the prominent centres of the Congress movements under Gandhi's leadership. The two popular leaders of Midnapur during these years were Birendra Nath Sashmal and Mahendra Nath Maity. Tamluk formed a subdivision of the district and, along with Contai, this subdivision suffered and sacrificed enormously, drawing the appreciation of all. Hundreds of villagers were gaoled and fined; thousands were belaboured mercilessly; standing crops and household goods were destroyed; valuables were looted; houses and granaries were pulled down and burnt to ashes; women were insulted; sacred places were desecrated and idols broken; young and old were maimed for life and even killed. The people of Tamluk and Contai bore all these experiences without straying from the path of non-violence. Among the leaders of the non-violent struggle there were a number of women such as Lakshmi Bala Devi, Indu Moti Devi, Pravamayi Maity, Nitya Bala Gole and Subodh Bala Kuity. Here, the police *raj* was vicious and even medical practitioners, ambulance men, the aged and the young and women did not escape gruesome physical assault.[277]

In an address of welcome by the pleaders' association of Tamluk to the League's delegation, the members deplored the existing repression let loose by the government for 'aggravating the distress, distrust and discontent among the people of the country'. It destroyed the spirit of confidence engineered by the Gandhi-Irwin pact. The repressive measures were felt as a challenge to the 'manhood of the nation' and they had been driving even the 'most timid to swell the rank of civil resisters and widening the gulf between the rulers and the ruled'. The delegates were urged to impress upon the British people the urgent necessity of changing policy by releasing Gandhi, 'the greatest living man on earth', and others, withdrawing ordinances and concluding a common understanding with the

Mahatma in framing a constitution of free India. It would be a great service to humanity.[278]

At Tamluk there was a huge meeting attended by about 12,000 people at which addresses were presented on behalf of the villagers, women and pleaders. The enormous crowd was under perfect control. Sashmal made an eloquent plea for unity for saving the Mahatma's life. A roar of approval greeted him when he requested the vast gathering to vow to save Gandhi's life and sustain and support non-violence. To his question if the people would open the temples at once to all classes, the approval was even more stirring. In all their imagination, Matters and Whately vouched, they could never have pictured such impressive scenes. To the suggestion that Congress was a spent force, the visitors felt that if Congress be dead, they had seen `the phantoms of a hundred thousand ghosts of a deathless army'.[279]

The report from Assam was in no way dissimilar. Referring to the sudden flying visit by Menon and Wilkinson, W.L. Scott from Assam complained in his confidential letter that both the delegates had left before the local officials had any information of the visit.[280] The delegates made no attempt to contact the officials and the secrecy of the visit irritated the administration most of all. The objective of the delegates was to visit a group of villages called Bhanubeel, then disturbed by agrarian trouble between the tenants who were mostly Manipuri Hindus and the zamindars who were, by and large, non-resident Muslims. In 1927 when prices were high, the zamindars had decided to enhance rents and they obtained civil court decrees at the higher rate; some of these decrees were contested upto the high court and the zamindars won throughout. In the enforcement of their demand the zamindars obtained decrees of eviction and also police assistance.[281]

Mahal Bhanubeel belonged to the Prithimpasha Estate of South Sylhet. It consisted of nine villages, viz. Uttargaon, Chitlia,

Jhangalia, Niz, Bhanubeel, Majhergaon, Kunagaon, Nayapattan and Tetaigaon. Of its population of about 9,000, about 6,000 were Hindus, mostly Manipuris and the rest Muslims. The tenants had approached the Sylhet Socialist Association which took up their case and initially tried to effect a compromise between the landlords and the tenants. Soon the Congress moved in as the socialist association decided to abandon the tenants to their fate. Apart from the enhancement of rents, the tenants had various grievances such as tenuous communication links, subjection to heavy 'nazar' for the zamindars, insufficient supply of drinking water, illiteracy, absence of medical assistance, etc. But before long the police force, under an English officer and the direction of the subdivisional officer of South Sylhet, and consisting of 50 armed constables, six village chowkidars, four peons, two drummers, two hundred *lathials* and 4 elephants, was pressed into the service of the zamindars. They then organized an officially sponsored episode of vandalism in the whole area with a view to ejecting the tenents, demolishing their tenements and snapping their contact with the Congress.[282]

A government spokesperson maintained that the action thus taken had been interpreted as tyranny of the zamindars aided by the government and exercised on helpless tenants. The fall in prices in the subsequent months in 1932 confirmed that assessment. Scott reported that the local Congress party actively interfered in the dispute and undoubtedly encouraged tenants to active resistance.[283] In fact, even the government fully realized that the time was then inopportune for pressing for enhanced rents and initiated steps towards an agreement. Scott was seriously concerned about the indifference of Wilkinson and Menon to the officials and their views. The delegation, he complained, arrived at Bhanugaon railway station from Chittagong on 13 September 1932, met a leading Congressman of Sylhet who was 'connected with a local Hindu-Congress paper', an editor of a 'Muhammadan nationalist paper at Sylhet', some Congress adherents and a 'crowd of Manipuris holding Congress flags'; they were entertained by the 'Hindus' at a local Indian tea garden, and then they proceeded to Bhanubeel where they visited the site of the houses demolished by order of the court, took photographs and then moved on to Rajshahi and Darjeeling by railway. Scott stressed that they scrupulously avoided the officials 'who could have given them', he presumed, 'an authentic account of the position'.[284]

The report from Delhi echoed similar emotions of suspicion and hostility.[285] It was emphasized that throughout their stay in Delhi from 12 to 14 October 1932, the delegation consisting of Matters and Whately remained under the influence of Congress workers who also dominated the itinerary of the delegation. They received deputations from the Hindu Mahasabha, the depressed classes, the Sikhs, the nationalist Muslims, women's organizations, the Swadeshi League, the Arya Samaj, and the students' union.[286] A deputation of the Muslims failed to turn up and, in a private meeting at the house of one Rashid Ahmed, the members were told that since the India League's deputation consisted of persons handpicked by the Congress, they could only talk to the delegates in their private capacity.

The Hindu Mahasabha deputation led by Ganga Ram stressed the desirability of modifying the communal award to satisfy the demands of the Hindus.[287] The depressed class deputation claimed that separate electorates were detrimental to the interests of the depressed classes and it attributed the intention of government to uphold separate electorates as part of the 'divide and rule' policy. The Sikhs also condemned the communal award and affirmed that direct action would be resorted to if the award was not suitably amended.[288] The women's association denounced separate electorates and narrated some unwholesome experiences of jail life. The Swadeshi League led by Ruchi Ram Sahani, an active member of the Congress with a long-standing connection with the *Hindustan Times*, condemned the system of education and urged the necessity of cottage industry. Sahani also led the Arya Samajists and advocated widow remarriage and abolition of untouchability. Potham Joseph, editor of the *Hindustan Times*, went on to a detailed condemnation of the pending press bill.[289] At a tea party given to the delegation Mangat Rai Kotalwala, a prominent Congress worker, emphasized the non-violent cult of the Congress and chastised the policy of the government as repressive which was designed to obstruct communal settlement and harmony. The students' union led by Chiranji Lal Paliwal, 'a revolutionary suspect', claimed that students had taken no part in the Congress but had been harassed by the police.[290]

The second part of the delegation consisting of Wilkinson and Menon arrived in Delhi on 17 October 1932 and left on 18 October 1932. They interviewed the deputy commissioner and Khan Bahadur Abdul Rahman, vice-chancellor of the University of Delhi. They also saw the deputation of the Indian States' People's Conference of Patiala and those of the Hindu Mahasabha and other bodies 'sponsored' by the Congress.[291] The Jamiat-ul Ulema met the delegation and explained the character of its alliance with the Congress and the Frontier Gandhi. Wilkinson addressed a meeting in the Hindu College hall under the chairmanship of Chiranji Lal Paliwal and she 'lambasted' the ordinances which, she claimed, had drawn a curtain between the British and the Indian people. It was alleged that this part of the delegation also remained under the influence of the Congress and was given special coverage in the *Hindustan Times*.[292]

It was feared in official quarters that the delegation would give publicity to Congress views and counter anti-Congress feelings in England. They were likely to emphasize, C.H. Everett warned from Delhi, the non-violent character of the Congress and make general allegations of government repression and police tyranny.[293] In particular, the ordinances would be denounced. It was also believed that the first public appearance of the delegation in London would probably be at a meeting organized by the India League at the Kingsway Hall on 26 November 1932 at which Bertrand Russell would preside in the presence of George Lansbury, Harold Laski, Rev. A.D. Belden, Tom Williams and Brailsford. Although the delegation would attempt to show that they had made an independent and unbiased investigation, it should be necessary to keep in mind that the various deputations with a variety of names interviewed by the delegation in Delhi and elsewhere were largely under Congress influence. For the first time it was alleged that the expenses of the delegation had been paid by G.D. Birla and hence very little credence should be put on the delegation's much proclaimed neutrality. It was emphasized that the delegation had little or no interaction with the Muslim League or with the RTC representatives. As relevant facts to counter the claims of the Congress of its adherence to non-violence, the officials were to stress that the Congress celebrated Bhagat Singh and Chandrashekhar Azad days, that the Congress workers had been convicted for cutting wires and destroying letters in post boxes and instigating the torching of shops to terrorize cloth dealers. By and large, the officials believed, Congressmen in their individual capacity as well as members of the organization had been morally supporting the terrorists for quite some time.[294]

From Peshawar the local government sent a detailed account of the movements of Wilkinson and Menon with an appraisal of the impressions created by their visit. It expressed the opinion that the governor-in-council was in agreement with the assessment. It was believed that in regard to its general impact, the visit had, on the whole, considerably less harmful repercussions than might have been expected. 'Nonetheless the visit', it argued, 'has not been without its harm', although the immediate and local effects of the Redshirt incidents in the Mardan and Charsadda subdivisions could have been avoided. The basic fear was the use, to which members of the delegation would no doubt put, 'the tainted material' which the delegation had been free to collect in the course of their visit.[295] It was believed that the incident at Mardan would doubtlessly confirm the preconceived idea of the two members about police methods. Efforts were made to keep Menon and Wilkinson in touch with officials, as well as with representatives of moderate views. It was believed that to begin with official efforts seemed somewhat successful. Later on, however, the two members 'managed to slip the official leash' and 'allowed themselves to be taken charge of by the members of the Redshirt-Congress Party'. Officials took note of the fact that John Khan Sahib, son of Dr Khan Sahib, had been commissioned to associate himself with the team throughout its tour. Visits had been arranged, the officials reported with an air of despondency, to places closely associated with Redshirt incidents during the civil disobedience movement in 1930-31 and, on more than one occasion, the 'so-called victims of police excesses' were produced before the members of the delegation. In Utmanzai, the Redshirt office which had been dismantled during the suppression of the civil disobedience movement in 1930 was inspected and no opportunity was lost during that 'conducted tour' of making as much 'anti-government capital' as possible.[296] The report emphasized that this was a strategic province obviously known for police and military *bandobast* and the officials lamented that unfortunately no restriction in the shape of police surveillance was imposed on the party and that there was little opportunity of correcting on the spot the impressions that might have been created in the minds of the delegation by various Congress stories 'embroidered for their benefit'.[297]

The government was uncertain whether in the case of Menon with his 'undisguised Congress bias', it would have been of any use to have attempted to do so. Although it was believed that Wilkinson had a more open mind, it was doutbful if she left the province with any disposition to discount the 'stories of government tyranny and oppression'.[298] On the whole, wrote the chief secretary of the government of North-West Frontier Province, the company that they kept during their visit and towards which they seemed naturally to gravitate was that of the extremist anti-government party and it was perhaps conspicuous that they 'made no attempt to see Sir Abdul Qaiyum'.[299] It was added that Sir Ralph Griffith and Mr Charles Cunningham, who had granted interviews to the members of the delegation, found Wilkinson's conversation perfectly normal. Wilkinson, they reported, hardly asked any question about local conditions and gave the impression 'of being bored with her associate'.[300] The officials were disconcerted by the quick-witted Menon who asked many questions about the future constitution of the province, the possibilities of ministerial responsibility for law and order and the mode of exercise of governor's special power of veto. There ran in Menon a vein of suspicion in the government's *bona fides* and contempt for the British government generally. Menon appeared to the frontier proconsuls to be 'the stuff out of which extremists and communists are made'.[301] They took some comfort from the remark made by the deputy commissioner of Peshawar that to the Pathan eyes the 'exotic appearance of Mr Menon has lent point to the propaganda now making headway in Peshawar district to the effect that the Redshirts are dupes of the Hindu Congress'.[302] It was complained that Menon was instrumental in dragging the team away from the officials and an almost reluctant Wilkinson, though dazed and wide-eyed, moved along with him. Delegates from Charsadda, Utmanzai, Urmar, Mardan, and Takkar made their representations and the party was taken to the Khyber Pass, Kohat Pass, Mohmand Border, Gorkhatri and Peshawar city. They cross-questioned Hindus, Muslims, Sikhs and Pathans and learnt with satisfaction about the presence of complete communal harmony in the area.[303] It was suspected that the statements were manipulated with remarkable ingenuity between a native rascal in Ali Gurkhan, the chief interpreter and a machiavellian bolshie in Menon, the chief questioner.[304]

The local police felt that although Wilkinson was open-minded she was somewhat credulous. She easily showed emotions; as an ex-suffragette she was irrationally sympathetic towards women; in matters of interpreting illiterate Pathan women she was definitely duped.[305] Menon, on the other hand, though elated by his own presence of mind, impressed nobody and probably deceived few except Wilkinson herself.[306] Some of those who saw him, wrote H.J. Vickers with a touch of venom, got the impression that he was an 'objectionable and implacable fanatic'. He made little effort to conceal his feelings and object and he lost no opportunity of switching the limelight on whatever little examples he could find of the high-handed conduct of government officials and exaggerating them out of all proportion to their true value.[307] As a result the atrocities committed by the Redshirts were absolutely forgotten. Vickers thought that Wilkinson was at home in the company of officials and loyalists and wondered if the Congress had gained anything substantial by perambulating 'this little fanatic',[308] who was commonly described by the Pathans of the frontier as a timid Bengali,[309] and by the officials as a prototype of Kipling's 'Girish Chandra De B.A. (Oxon)', the pompous head of a frontier district.

It appeared that the Government of India was somewhat disturbed by the general drift of the Labour Party and its attitudes towards India. It learnt from an intercepted letter from Menon to the *Hindustan Times* that three resolutions on India would be moved by George Lansbury in the forthcoming session of the Labour Party conference in October 1932.[310] The resolutions were to reaffirm the party's faith in the right of the Indian people to choose the form of government which they considered to be in harmony with their national aspirations, to regret the abandonment of the policy of consultations and conferences with the Indian leaders by the Indian government and to condemn the policy of intimidation, internment, imprisonment and recourse to autocratic rule in sharp contrast to the general goodwill that had been attempted during the preceding year. The resolutions would urge the government to adopt a definite policy of conciliation and take steps to reassure Indian opinion that it would return permanently to the avowed policy of establishing a responsible federal order and revive the atmosphere by resorting to the policy of amnesty and cooperation. The conference would also oppose the 'unjust delay' in the Meerut conspiracy case and ask for effective reforms in Indian criminal procedures. Together with the resolutions on labour conditions and promotion of trade unions and the institution of an industrial commission, the proposed political resolutions caused much stir in the Indian administration. The close nexus established by Menon between the Labour Party and advanced public opinion in India and the central place occupied by him in the League's delegation inspired a mixed feeling of uncertainty, tension and animosity in the official mind.[311]

Notes and References

1 Benn to Lansbury, Labour Party research department, 21 February 1932, Stansgate Papers; see also, Benn, 'India Policy: General Lines of Criticism', n.d. 1932 and 'Continuity of Policy', n.d. August 1932, Menon Papers and note by J. Clauson for Wedgwood Benn, n.d. 1932, Lansbury Papers.

2 Text of Samuel Hoare's broadcast on India, 27 January 1932; 'Samuel Hoare in Parliament,' 24 March 1932, Menon Papers.

3 Menon to Lansbury, 4 May 1932, Menon Papers.

4 Menon to Malaviya, 23 April 1932, Menon Papers. Also see, Menon, 'London Letter', for *Hindustan Times*; Menon to Divakar, 12 August 1932; 'Notes on a meeting held at the House of Commons', 28 June 1932; Verrier Elwin, 'Some Really Respectable Information', 11 June 1932, all in Menon Papers.

5 Menon to Malaviya, 28 March, 9 April and 25 April 1932, Menon Papers.

6 Mirabehn to Tom Williams, 7 January, 8 January, 9 January and 29 January 1932, Menon Papers.

7 Menon to Malaviya, 28 March, 9 April and 25 April 1932, Menon Papers.

8 Cf. S. Chakravarty, *V.K. Krishna Menon and the India League,* Vol.II, Delhi 1997, pp. 218-20 and 267-70.

9 Ibid., pp. 268-9; also Menon to G. Malaviya, 18 March 1932 and 28 May 1932, Menon Papers.

10 Menon to Malaviya, 16 June 1932, Menon Papers.

11 Menon to G. Malaviya, 17 June 1932, Menon Papers.

12 Menon to Malaviya, 17 June 1932, Menon Papers.

13 Ibid.

14 Horrabin, 'A Note on the *Indian Review*', 6 May 1932, Menon Papers.

15 Ibid.

16 Horrabin to Menon, 1 August 1932, Menon Papers.

17 Ibid.

18 S. Chakravarty, *The Raj Syndrome, A Study in Imperial Perception*, Delhi 1991, pp.140-2.

19 Ibid.

20 Menon to G. Malaviya, 6 July 1932, Menon Papers.

21 Ibid.

22 Menon to G. Malaviya, 20 July 1932, Menon Papers.

23 Ibid.

24 Ibid.

25 Ibid.

26 G. Malaviya to Menon, 16 June 1932, Menon Papers.

27 Menon to Malaviya, 9 July 1932, Menon Papers.

28 Ibid.

29 Ibid.

30 Menon to G. Malaviya, 14 July 1932, Menon Papers.

31 Ibid.

32 Menon to Malaviya, 16 July 1932, Menon Papers.

33 Ibid.

34 Ibid.

35 Horrabin to Malaviya, 21 July 1932, Menon Papers.

36 Ibid.

37 Menon to Malaviya, 22 July 1932, Menon Papers.

38 Ibid.

39 Menon to Horrabin, 23 July 1932, Menon Papers.

40 Menon to G. Malaviya, 14 July 1932, Menon Papers.

41 Horrabin and Marley to the members of the delegation, 2 August 1932, Menon Papers. See also the same letter in Appendix I. The India League, *Condition of India* (Indian edition), New Delhi 1999, pp.521-2.

42 *The Plebs* was the organ of The National Council of Labour Colleges. See, Horrabin, 'Twenty-one Years After', *The Plebs,* January 1930.

43 Ernest Thurtle, 'India and the Round Table', *The Plebs,* January 1930.

44 Ibid.

45 J.F. Horrabin, 'India', *The Plebs* 1930.

46 Ibid.

47 Fenner Brockway, 'The Labour Government and India', *The Plebs,* December 1930.

48 Ibid.

49 J.F. Horrabin, 'The Bookshelf', *The Plebs,* September 1931.

50 Lester Hutchinson, 'India and the British Working Class', *The Plebs, June* 1931.

51 Ibid.

52 J.F. Horrabin, 'Empire Unity and the Facts of Geography', *The Plebs*, April 1931.

53 Ibid.

54 R. Coppeek, 'Rationalisation and the Worker', *The Plebs,* April 1930. 'What to do with British Empire', *The Plebs,* February 1932.

55 J.P.M. Millar, 'Education as an Empire Builder', *The Plebs,* May 1932.

56 Ibid.

57 Eileen Merrie to Menon, 11 April 1932, Menon Papers.

58 Eileen Merrie to Menon, 19 May 1932, Menon Papers.

59 Ibid.

60 Ibid.

61 Eileen Merrie to Menon, 19 May 1933, Menon Papers.

62 Ibid.

63 Ibid.

64 Eileen Merrie to Menon, 16 April 1932, Menon Papers.

65 Eileen Merrie to Menon, 17 June 1932, Menon Papers.

66 Ibid.

67 Ibid.

68 Menon to Eileen Merrie, 26 June 1932, Menon Papers.

69 Eileen Merrie to Barbara Macnamara, 28 August 1932, Menon Papers.

70 League Against Imperialism, *The Mutiny in Meerut Jail, A Memorial of the Meerut Prisoner,* London 1931, Creek-Jones Papers.

71 D.N. Pritt to Menon, 21 March 1932, Menon Papers.

72 R. Bridgeman, *The Meerut Conspiracy Case, Open Letter to the Labour Party,* London 1931, Creek-Jones Paper.

73 Ibid.

74 Ibid.

75 Ibid.

76 Ibid.

77 Ibid.

78 Menon to Bridgeman, 13 September 1931, Bridgeman Papers; See the following documents on the Meerut Conspiracy Case in Creek Jones Papers:

'Memorandum on the Meerut Case, 25 June 1931'

'The Meerut Conspiracy Case, Open Letter to the Delegates to the Annual Conference of the Labour Party at Scarborough, 5 to 9 October 1931, 29 September 1931.

'The Mutiny in Meerut Jail: Memorial of the Meerut prisoners', League against Imperialism and the National Independence, London, 1932.

79 Ibid. Also, W. P. Kabadi to Menon, 16 August 1931, Menon Papers.

80 Eileen Merrie to Menon, 4 March 1931, Menon Papers.

81 R.P. Dutt, 'The New Phase in Britain and the Communist Party', 1928, R.P. Dutt Papers.

82 R.P. Dutt to Harry Pollitt, 13 February 1928, R.P. Dutt Papers.

83 R.P. Dutt to Harry Pollitt, 26 March 1928, R.P. Dutt Papers.

84 R.P. Dutt, 'The New Phase', etc. op.cit.

85 Ibid.

86 'Anglo-Indian Peace', *Krnasnava-Zvezda* in Remoud Ovoy to

Arthur Henderson, 16 March 1931 (Communication from Moscow), P&J/7/80, India Office.

87 Ibid.

88 Ibid.

89 Ibid.

90 Ibid.

91 Shapurji Saklatvala, 'British Imperialism in India, A World Menace' in *The Colonies and Oppressed Nations in the Struggle for Freedom,* published by The League against Imperialism and for National Independence, Berlin 1931, Bridgeman Papers.

92 Ibid.

93 Ibid.

94 Hallett to Stewart, 4 July 1932, F12/1932/Home Pol.

95 Ibid.

96 Ibid.

97 Hallett to Stewart, 7 July 1932, F12/1932, Home Pol.

98 Hallett to Stewart, 7 July 1932, F12/1932, Home Pol.

99 Ibid.

100 Hallett to J.M. Clay, Secretary, United Provinces, 23 July 1932, F12/1932, Home Pol.

101 R. Peel to Hallett, 15 July 1932, F12/1932/Home Pol.

102 Ibid.

103 Peel to Hallett, 5 August 1932, F12/1932/Home Pol.

104 Ibid.

105 Ibid.

106 Ibid.

107 Confidential note in Ibid.

108 Ibid.

109 Ibid.

110 Ibid.

111 Ibid.

112 Ibid. The following list of persons to whom Lord Lothian wrote introducing the team: Sir Ghulam Hussain Hidayatullah, member of the Governor's Executive Council in Bombay; Sir P.A. Kelly, Commissioner of Police in Bombay city; the acting Home Secretary to the Government of Bombay; Dr B.R. Ambedkar; Rao Bahadur Sir A.P. Patro of Cosmopolitan Club, Madras; Diwan Bahadur Ramaswami Mudaliar, Madras; G.T.H. Bracken, Chief Secretary to the Government of Madras; Sir P.C. Mitter and Sir A.K. Ghaznavi, both members of the Governor's Executive Council of Bengal; B.N. Reid, chief secretary to the Government of Bengal; Sir Ahmed Said Khan, the nawab of Chhattari, member of the Executive Council of United Provinces; Zafarullah Khan and Sir C.P. Ramaswami Aiyer, members of the Viceroy's Executive Council; M.G. Hallett, home Secretary, Government of India; Capt. Sardar Sikander Hyat, Government of the Punjab; and Sir Ralph Griffith, Governor of NWFP. Lothian to Whately, 30 July 1932, Menon Papers.

113 Peel to Hallett, 14 August 1932, F/12/1932 Home Pol.

114 Ibid.

115 Ibid.

116 Confidential covering letter, in Peel to Hallett, 5 August 1932, F/12/1932, Home Pol.

117 Ibid.

118 Ibid.

119 Ibid.

120 Peel Hallett, 14 August 1932, F/12/1932/Home Pol.

121 Ibid.

122 Cf. Chakravarty, *Krishna Menon* etc. op.cit., vols.I and II.

123 Author's interview with Krishna Shelvankar.

124 Author's interviews with Michael Foot, Anna Polak, Julius Silverman, and Mary Shelvankar.

125 Author's interview with Michael Foot.

126 Author's interview with Mary Shelvankar.

127 J.B. Priestley, *English Journey,* London 1933.

128 Arthur Marwick, *Britain in Our Century,* 1968, pp. 91-3.

129 Ibid., pp.93-5.

130 Eric Hobsbawm, *Age of Extremes, The Short Twentieth Century, 1914-1991,* London 1994, pp.21-99.

131 Marvin Jones (ed.), *Kingsley Martin, Portrait and Self-Portrait,* London 1969, pp.14-35.

132 Noveen Branson and Margot Heinemann, *Britain in the Nineteen Thirties,* London 1971, pp.1-8.

133 Hobsbawm, *Age of Extremes,* op.cit., pp.124-31.

134 James Klugmann, 'The Crisis of the Thirties' in Jon Clark, Margot Heinemann, Caril Snee (eds.), *Culture and Crisis in Britain in the 1930s,* London 1979.

135 Branson and Heinemann, *Britain in the Nineteen Thirties,* London 1971, op.cit., p.8.

136 Gary Wersky, *The Visible College,* London 1978, pp.148-52.

137 Ibid., pp.26-7.

138 Isaac Deutscher, *The Prophet Outcast,* London 1963, p.137.

139 Ibid., p.135.

140 Klugmann, 'The Crisis of the Thirties', op.cit.

141 See, for example, the statement of Samuel Hoare in parliament, 24 March 1932, Menon Papers.

142 Author's interview with Michael Foot.

143 Ibid.

144 Ibid.

145 Ibid.

146 Author's interview with Platts-Mills.

147 Ernest Bevin, 'Economic Factors Threatening the Peace of the World', Preliminary Memorandum, Economic Committee,

Trade Union Congress General Council, 5 April 1929, Bevin Papers.

148 Author's interview with Platts-Mills and Michael Foot.

149 Author's interviews with Krishna and Mary Shelvankar.

150 Author's interview with Julius Silverman.

151 Ibid.

152 Author's interview with Mary Shelvankar.

153 Ibid.

154 Author's interview with Julius Silverman.

155 Cf. Menon to Janaki Amma, 25 September 1926, quoted in Janaki Ram, *V.K. Krishna Menon: A Personal Memoir,* Delhi 1997, pp.32-4.

156 Ibid.

157 Based on the author's interviews with Michael Foot and Mary Shelvankar.

158 Menon (Notes on Gandhi), C.I.L, September 1931, Menon Papers.

159 Ibid.

160 See Chakravarty, *Menon and the India League,* op.cit., vol.I, pp.254-6 364-8,393-4; vol.II pp.64-9, 126-30, 257-60.

161 Cf. Janaki Ram, *Personal Memoir,* op.cit., p.22.

162 Author's conversation with Anna Polak and Pam Cullen.

163 Lambah to Menon, 16 April 1932, Menon Papers.

164 Author's conversation with P.N. Haksar.

165 B. Macnamara to Horrabin, 21 August 1932, Menon Papers.

166 B. Macnamara to Menon, 31 August 1932, quoted in J. Ram, 'Personal Memoir', op.cit., p.52.

167 Ibid.

168 Interview with Mary Shelvankar.

169 Ibid.

170 Macnamara to Menon, 6 October 1932, Menon Papers.

171 Author's interview with Mary Shelvankar.

172 India League, 'Circular', 3 September 1932, Menon Papers.

173 Ibid.

174 Horrabin to Malaviya, 25 August 1932, Menon Papers.

175 Ibid.

176 Macnamara to Secretary, ILP, Eastbourne, 28 September 1932, Menon Papers.

177 Horrabin to Malaviya, 25 August 1932, Menon Papers.

178 Ibid.

179 Macnamara to Horrabin, 21 September 1932, Menon Papers.

180 Gangavihari L. Mehta, 'Ordinance and Freedom', 6 March 1932, Menon Papers.

181 Ibid.

182 Ibid.

183 Ibid.

184 Menon to Waughray, 7 August 1932, (from The Mediteranean), Menon Papers.

185 Enclosure in (Confidential), Home Department, Bombay (Poona), 26 August 1932, F12/1932/Home Pol.

186 Notings by Secretary, Bombay, 30 August 1932 in Ibid.

187 Hallett, 'Note on the India League Delegation', 31 October 1932, F12/1932/Home Pol.

188 Ibid.

189 Ibid.

190 Ibid.

191 Ibid.

192 Ibid.

193 Ibid.

194 Ibid.

195 Ibid.

196 Hallett, 'Note on the India League Delegation', 11 October 1932, F12/1932/Home Pol.

197 Ibid.

198 Ibid.

199 Ibid., also, A.K. Sinha, (Railways) Patna to Hirst, 23 September 1932, F12/1932/Home Pol.

200 'Note on The India League Delegation in Madras Presidency', 25 August 1932 to 7 September 1932, F12/1932/Home Pol.

201 Ibid.

202 Ibid.

203 Ibid.

204 Extract, Weekly confidential report, 7 September 1932, district magistrate, Kanara, F12/1932/Home Pol.

205 Ibid.

206 'Note on the activities of India League Delegation', 21 October 1932, F12/1932/Home Pol.

207 Ibid.

208 Note by the home member, 31 October 1932, F12/1932/Home Pol.

209 Ibid.

210 Ibid.

211 Ibid.

212 Ibid.

213 Ibid.

214 Ibid.

215 Ibid.

216 Ibid.

217 Ibid.

218 Ibid.

219 Hallett to Stewart, 14 November 1932, F12/1932/Home Pol.

220 Ibid.

221 Ibid.

222 Hallett, 'A note on the activities of the India League delegation', 19 October 1932, F12/1932/Home Pol.

223 Ibid.

224 Ibid.

225 Ibid.

226 Ibid.

227 Ibid.

228 Ibid.

229 Ibid.

230 Ibid.

231 Ibid.

232 Ibid.

233 Ibid.

234 Hallett, 'A note on the activities of the India League Delegation', 11 October 1932, F12/1932/Home Pol.

235 Ibid.

236 District magistrate, Monghyr to commissioner, Bhagalpur division, 24 September 1932, F12/1932/Home Pol.

237 Hallett, 'A note on the India League Delegation', 11 October 1932, F12/1932/Home Pol.

238 Commissioner, Bhagalpur division to Hallett, 27 September 1932, F12/1932/Home Pol.

239 Memo, 26 September 1932 from Superintendent of Police, Monghyr, F12/1932/Home Pol.

240 Ibid.

241 District magistrate, Monghyr to commissioner, Bhagalpur division, 24 September 1932, F12/1932/Home Pol.

242 Commissioner, Bhagalpur division to Hallett, 27 September 1932,

F12/1932/Home Pol.

243 Ibid.

244 Ibid.

245 District magistrate, Monghyr commissioner, Bhagalpur division, 24 September 1932, F12/1932/Home Pol.

246 Ibid.

247 Extract from the confidential diary (district, Muzaffarpur), 27 September 1932, F12/1932/Home Pol.

248 *The Congress Bulletin,* 13 August 1932, F12/1932/Home Pol.

249 Ibid.

250 Ibid.

251 P.A. Kelly to C.B.S. Clea, 18 August 1932, F12/1932/Home Pol.

252 Ibid.

253 Ibid.

254 H. Bamford to C.M. Trivedi, 26 October 1932, F12/1932/Home Pol.

255 Extract from the report of the district magistrate, Banaras, 11 October 1932, F12/1932/Home Pol.

256 H. Bamford to C.M. Trivedi, 16 October 1932, F12/1932/Home Pol.

257 Ibid.

258 Ibid.

259 Ibid.

260 Khan Bahadur Qazi Azizuddin Ahmed, Agra to Bamford, 5 October 1932, F12/1932/Home Pol.

261 Ibid.

262 Bamford to Trivedi, 26 October 1932, F12/1932/Home Pol.

263 Ibid.

264 Ibid.

265 A.H. Ahmed to Bamford, 5 October 1932, F12/1932/Home Pol.

266 Ibid.

267 Ibid.

268 Ibid.

269 Ibid.

270 Ibid.

271 Ibid.

272 Note on Ibid.

273 Ibid.

274 Ibid.

275 Ibid.

276 Ibid.

277 C.M. Trivedi to Hallett, 5 October 1932, F12/1932/Home Pol.

278 Ibid.

279 Ibid.

280 Confidential report, 6 October 1932, F12/1932/Home Pol.

281 Ibid.

282 Ibid.

283 Ibid.

284 Ibid.

285 Confidential report, 25 October 1932, F/12/1932/Home Pol.

286 Ibid.

287 Ibid.

288 Ibid.

289 Ibid.

290 Ibid.

291 Ibid.

292 Ibid.

293 C.H. Everett, Memo on the visit of Wilkinson and Menon from 9 to 15 October 1932, 18 October 1932, F12/1932/Home Pol.

294 Ibid.

295 Copy of a demi-official (confidential) letter from the chief secretary to the Government of North-West Frontier Province, to the home secretary to the Government of India, 15 November 1932, Mss Eur F165/184.

296 Ibid.

297 Ibid.

298 Ibid.

299 Ibid.

300 Ibid.

301 Ibid.

302 Ibid.

303 Ibid.

304 Ibid.

305 Ibid.

306 Ibid.

307 Ibid.

308 Ibid.

309 Intercepted letter from Menon to the editor, *Hindustan Times,* in C.H. Everett's report, 25 October 1932, F12/1932/Home Pol.

310 Ibid.

311 Ibid.

CHAPTER II

STRAND, ONCE AGAIN

The delegate conferences and public meetings organized by the India League following the return of its mission from India were well-attended and their impact was quite discernible. The deposition of the delegation at different platforms painted a grim and disturbing picture of India. It could not have been glossed over casually. A good deal of introspection took place in public and the ordinance misrule became the talking point if only in liberal and left-wing circles. Although some of the delegates to the League's conferences would have liked to welcome the speedy termination of the ordinances and a renewal of normal life in India within the framework of conciliation, they felt uneasy with Gandhi's movement confronting the administration at the centre of Indian life.[1]

They were not convinced if the civil disobedience movement could be considered as a legitimate instrument to resist even an arbitrary and authoritarian regime. In a leaflet, *Gandhi-Willingdon Correspondence*[2] circulated by the India League, they read all the communications between Gandhi and Willingdon since the return of the Mahatma to India towards the end of 1931. In particular, Gandhi's bold affirmation of moral authority struck them as evidence of his staggering impudence.[3] At one place, Gandhi, while repudiating charges by the viceroy of dishonourable conduct had asserted: 'In my opinion, constitutional issues dwindle into insignificance in the face of Ordinances and Acts' and in the absence of a systematic stubborn resistance by the people, it would lead to 'utter demoralization of the nation'.[4] He hoped that no self-respecting person would run the risk of stifling national spirit 'for the doubtful contingency of securing a constitution'. At another place,

Gandhi stated boldly: 'I believe that Civil Disobedience is not only the natural right of a people, especially when they have no effective voice in their government, but is also a suitable substitute for violence or armed rebellion. I can never therefore deny my creed.'[5] And yet at another place, Gandhi asserted that any government, zealous of the welfare of the masses in its charge, should welcome voluntary cooperation of a big body like the Congress which admittedly exercised 'great influence over the masses and whose one ambition is to serve them faithfully'[6] and that he regarded the withholding of payment of taxes 'as an inalienable ancient and natural right of a people who have exhausted all other means of seeking freedom from an unbearable economic burden'.[7]

To the pacifists and theosophists given to compliant conciliation, Gandhi seemed far too provocative and belligerent. A.L.S. Wilkinson, a delegate from the Theosophical Lodge of Bromley to the November 1932 delegate conference held in London, was one of those many who, having disagreed with the transformation of the CIL and its new orientation, had retained a personal contact with the League, albeit tenuous, for old time's sake. He listened to the speakers attentively, took down copious notes and concluded that unhappily similar atrocities were still being inflicted upon the Indians as had been done years ago when he was in India for nearly 47 years ending 1922. It seemed to him very tragic that those who were prepared to sacrifice their lives for India had been 'instrumental over the years in 'intensifying her sufferings and her crucifixion' by a remarkable lack of wisdom as exemplified by their practice of civil disobedience.

Wilkinson was convinced that civil disobedience was 'worse than crime' and constituted a fundamental 'strategic blunder'.[8] It merely handed over to 'her torturer' a club wherewith India could be 'bludgeoned' without limit. Wilkinson held that the India League should use all its influence and weight on the Labour Party in England and the Congress in India to persuade Gandhi and his associates 'to give up putting this weapon into the hands of India's persecutors'.[9] Instead, they should devise a sincere policy of complete passive resistance and relentless persuasion, which would give no loopholes to the authorities whatever, and render all obedience to the law while unceasingly striving to alter it in every legitimate way.[10] By law, Wilkinson explained, he meant the law that had been in force before the ordinances were promulgated. Wilkinson held that people had every right to resist the ordinances which had been enforced to thwart the civil disobedience movement. But then, he had been given to understand that the Viceroy had assured time and again that the ordinances would be revoked once civil disobedience was withdrawn and it was imperative to enable him to honour his commitment. Wilkinson was uncertain about the objectives of the League. He gave vent to the widely circulated apprehension that the League might be working for a revolution, in which case, he cautioned, any unconstitutional agenda of the League or of the Congress would draw no more than an infinitesimal support in Britain.[11]

Gandhi's message on behalf of India to the British people following RTC II was, ostensibly, a simple and direct statement of India's plight, its causes and the remedy. In this message, circulated by the India League as a pamphlet, entitled *India and the National Congress (1932),* Gandhi explained his creed of non-violence and referred to the pauperization of the country in which Lancashire's interests appeared to have been an important factor. But in the simple formulations of Gandhi, a large number of Wilkinson's associates saw an open threat of secession from the empire and the disintegration of the imperial commonwealth. They noted with concern that the minimum Indian demand after the conclusion of the RTC was complete independence for India. A voluntary partnership and 'safeguards' in 'the interest of India' were acceptable to Gandhi and they were not very exciting propositions for a pacifist, a theosophist or a liberal imperialist.[12]

It was assumed by a sizeable section of liberal public opinion that in criticizing the Government of India as a casual visitor, one would not really know all the facts and considerations and would inevitably tend to be somewhat unfair to the government, especially when one had little experience of handling practical affairs with Indian politicians.[13] Even those who had extensive administrative experience in India and were endowed with sincere liberal disposition and who could 'see the real truths of national feeling behind the disappointing manifestations of individual leaders', came to realize that there were certain wild accusations which one should discount in India.[14] The overworked officials lived in an atmosphere of *ex post facto* criticism on the lines that if only this or that had been done things would have been so different. Harry Haig, an influential member of the Viceroy's executive council, confided to Horace Alexander that although on several occasions the government had sought to meet the demands of the national leaders, there was not, a single occasion when it got any credit for it.[15] Far more often than not, all practical efforts of the government towards conciliation were condemned as a sign of weakness. It was widely believed that an attempt to be responsive in the prevailing Indian atmosphere was beset with extraordinary difficulties.

The function of the administration, Haig felt, was to govern and to establish law and order in the country. True, to be sensitive to strong national demands was axiomatic and in India the national demand for constitutional advance was so strong that government would have liked to assess that demand by a fully representative party.[16] In this context it was believed that the Congress was not a national body reflecting the opinion of diverse elements of the land. It was also generally taken for granted that entire energies and activities of British statesmen at that point of time were concentrated on trying to improvise some plan that would be workable and acceptable on all sides.[17] It was added that there was no viable reason to justify the suspicion that the RTC method did not offer an ideal opportunity for India. It appeared to the government that Gandhi and the Congress were averse to constitutional methods and had been consistent in their attempts to force the hand of the government to adopt repressive measures.[18] It was believed that the desire of the Congress to avoid actual violence made no difference. Their methods were illegal and they were designed to paralyze the government and to compel it to agree to their demands. To yield to these sorts of pressures would be detrimental to the development of a constitutional programme.[19] It was argued that the course of action open to the government would thus be faced, as it were, with a major dilemma. Either the government had to give way and enter into a bargain with an Indian party having sectional representation, or it had to accept a policy of opposition to the Congress. Confrontation with the Congress would inevitably place the government in another set of unfavourable alternatives: either the Congress be given a free course to defy the authority of the government and destroy respect for law, order and authority, or the government be forced, willy-nilly, to adopt a policy of repression.[20]

The success of the Congress campaign and its hold over public imagination depended entirely, it was argued, on its ability to goad the government into this sisyphean dilemma. The Congress was not oblivious to the problems of a government committed to law, order and public security, in dealing with a resolute opposition given to destruction, disorder and paralysis of authority. Responsibility for maintaining law and order could not be exaggerated, for in India life could easily fall into periods of anarchy, brutality and cruelty.[21] There was a major apprehension that revolutionary organizations were getting very active, especially in Bengal, and any apparent weakness on the part of the authorities might create a state of affairs that would soon get out of control.[22] Despite the expressed conviction of the Congress leaders, who might have desired honestly to pursue the policy of non-violence, the officials doubted if they would be able, with a modicum of certainty, to contain the forces of destruction let loose by their non-violent indulgence to brutal criminality.

Although MacDonald continued to maintain a sphinx - like silence on the subject of India, his paper published an article by Sankey which might be regarded as the authoritative exposition of the National Government's policy. Sankey's main thesis was that the Labour Government's policy in regard to reforms remained unchanged and so far as repression was concerned no government could have ignored the Congress attempt to establish a rival revolutionary government, or capitulate to a campaign of sedition, violence and murder. The fashion of clubbing Congress activities with revolutionary violence was a favourite form of bureaucratic propaganda and *The Hindu* felt disappointed that Sankey should have thought it prudent to follow bureaucratic practice in a cavalier manner. *The Hindu* commented that even the few facts that managed to attract the notice of the parliament should have convinced every one that official repression was not distinguished by moderation. Sankey underrated, *The Hindu* stated boldly, the level of alienation and embitterment that repression had been producing throughout the country that made a rapprochement extremely difficult. The paper believed that there had been a sea change in the official policy towards India after the installation of the National Government. It held that the Labour government had been actuated by a spirit of cooperation, despite the brutal supression of the civil-disobedience movement. This was indicated by the attitude of Irwin, the Gandhi-Irwin Pact and the institution of the RTC with Congress participation. In contrast, the National Government did not believe in any settlement by agreement; it had no faith in the legitimacy and credibility of the most powerful political organization in India. Of the Conference method, *The Hindu* concluded, 'while the shell remains, the soul is fled.' Many might still find excuses for the attitude of the government. 'But even they will not, we fancy, endorse Lord Sankey's claim that there has been no change of policy in regard to India.'[23]

Meanwhile, the work of the India League had been severely handicapped by a striking lack of organizational assistance, especially when the official policy of repression towards Indian unrest became very rigid or at best, found itself oscillating between tweedledum and tweedledee.[24] Several areas of the League's programme had been more or less neglected as there were not enough volunteers to do the work required. People were not fully aware that in India civil liberty was supressed on a nation-wide scale and conditions approximated in many respects to those that obtained in medieval times.[25] Imprisonment without trial, police brutality, subversion of the rule of law, etc. were condemned, by and large, by the majority of people in Britain. But, unfortunately, all these had become essential ingredients of normal life in India.[26] In a circular, the India League said that there was a robust working class movement in India and the awakening of the peasantry was a promising feature of the current nationalist upsurge. The determination that appeared to characterize the Indian struggle, Menon presumed, should be greeted by all those who were engaged in the struggle for the expansion of human freedom.[27] Agitation and protest against the repressive regime in India, however, were lukewarm and inadequate and Menon offered all forms of assistance in support of a more vigorous and intensive propaganda in Britain.[28] In particular, Menon thought that it was necessary to renew discussion with trade unions who were keen to grasp something substantial about the existing conditions in India. Although anxious to approach the trade union leaders, Menon was aware that any deliberation with them was going to involve considerable political discussions, especially when presenting the League's views on the subject of India.[29] It was a sensitive matter and it would be unfair if a person not fully conversant with the League's outlook was encouraged to put forth the case. No one with any doubt or reservation should be authorized to represent the League in public and in formal gatherings, conferences and *conversaziones.* At all these meetings, Menon emerged as the principal discussant on the Indian situation, ably supported by Ellen Wilkinson and Monica Whately.

Evidently, there was a growing demand for Menon from near and far pressing heavily on his time, nerves and health. His meal was always unsubstantial: it became irregular. Increasingly, he became impatient with timid mediocrity, unmindful diffidence, teasing prevarication, malicious insinuation and irritating fillibustering.[30] Menon was outraged by the impenitent display by Tory sophists and their intellectual casuistry. They were aroused, he wrote, by the Russian trials, especially by the imprisonments without trial, extraction of confession and forms of jurisprudence. But as the League pointed out, hundreds of Indians had never been tried and allegations of insanity, extortion of apologies from political prisoners and the detention of Meerut prisoners for four years were cases which might be compared with the Russian trials. But then, India, it was added with a touch of frustration, stood on a different platform altogether.[31] The impact of the daily controversies and noisy disturbances at public presentations was to sharpen Menon's repartees and verbal counter-offensives. He had become caustic, even vitriolic, often given to ruthless vivisection of the opponent's arguments *advienna que pourra.* Well-proportioned, dark, attractive and energetic, Menon had kept secret even from his close associates his weak constitution. His swiftly changing moods made him almost enigmatic. He could accomplish a wide range of activities with extraordinary perfection and finesse. Sometimes fretful and restless, sometimes pensive and withdrawn, Menon was given to persistent endeavour, always eager to locate a new and challenging space for his League. Inevitably, he aroused not only loyalty and affection but also bitter animosity. His personal expenses were severely limited and his organization seemed perpetually in a state of impecuniosity. He was a remarkable initiator and a meticulous organizer but, unfortunately, he was somewhat impatient with the problems of consolidation. The efforts required for scintillating popularity did not appeal to him. It was his nature to be stoic. He took things in his stride but nothing really altered his basic objective. He gave the impression that he had brains that could evaluate like lightning the fallout of a proposed initiative, but all the same, he took his decisions carefully, with a good deal of circumspection. He listened patiently and pleasantly but, although not hard-headed, he was rational, consistent and firm, unnerved by flitting emotions. He was strongly attracted to the opposite sex, but aggressive pursuit of any kind of pleasure was not in his bag of tricks. He preferred to attract people instead. He built his empire of affection slowly and surely.

Menon was patient, persistent, stubborn and confident of his objective but, in the steadfast pursuit of his goal he was prone to neglect his health. He often suffered from colds and carried with him a nagging pain from arthritis, but despite increasing addiction to pills, he was partial to prolonged periods of recuperation due to his obstinate refusal to obey the doctor. Very often, the universe seemed to him barren of meaning. He had moved through many dark phases. But he still believed that he would be sustained by his faith in a profound creative purpose. Either he must trust his conviction in the inevitability of freedom of India and the necessity of the relentless struggle for it or he must abandon it. In the course of his involvements, Menon realized that even his small endeavours had been pushing the League into wider networks of publications, world events, media and discussions stimulated by a strong sense of the relevant history. The feeble and unsteady agenda of the League was constantly nursed and fed despite temporary setbacks.[32] From Geneva, Privat had made repeated requests through the India Conciliation Group inviting Menon, Wilkinson and Whately to an international conference. It seemed that Privat was keen to invite the whole team to the European capitals to address informed and influential circles on the condition of India.[33] Despite censorship and blackouts the Indian situation got a good deal of publicity even in the political backwaters in England. People at places were interested to know more about the nature of the ordinance rule in India and there were invitations from various organizations.[34]

The India Conference on 11 February 1933 at 372 Fore Street, Edmonton, under the auspices of the Edmonton Labour Party was a singular event for the League since the return of the delegation.[35] With Fred Messer MP as chairperson, Menon made his presentation. Great Britain and India was the theme. He maintained that the welfare of a population of over 350 million in a country 6,000 miles away from British shores was a responsibility of the British Parliament. Dire poverty and starvation of the people compelled them to demand some rational and tangible social, political and economic changes. An equally fundamental compulsion was the fact that the Indians had, over the years, been a subject people and their government, culture and education had been dominated, directed and restricted by an alien rule. Giving extensive evidence, Menon dwelt at length on the nature of poverty, industrial conditions, taxation and expenditure on defence, security and social overheads. It was evident that all the social and nation-building services were starved and Indian money was being spent for the advantage of the British people and the prestige of the British army. The ordinance rule had been enforced in order to suppress the representative body of the Indian people, although, in spite of the official crackdown, the Congress had emerged as the unofficial parliament of the people. The ordinances sapped the very foundation of civilized rule and alienated the government from the people of all religions, regions and linguistic groups: unless the existing policy was withdrawn forthwith, it would promote and nurture malevolence and racial bitterness that would leave behind tensions of hatred and contentious bickering to vitiate Indo-British relations.[36]

The resolutions moved by Dorothy Woodman and seconded by Ernest Davies were widely disseminated. They supported the right of the Indian people to independence and self-determination, called upon the British government to grant full self-government to India as early as possible and to summon a constituent assembly elected by universal franchise and commissioned to draw up a constitution for India and to decide the country's future relations with Britain. As an earnest gesture of the government's intentions, the conference urged that a responsible ministry enjoying the confidence of the Indian people be immediately appointed by the viceroy to conduct the administration of the country including finance, foreign affairs and defence. Besides, the conference decided to set up a committee to cooperate with the India League in making known India's case for independence in the areas from which delegates to the conference were drawn.[37]

The association of Dorothy Woodman with the resolution was a prominent feature of the conference. The Union of Democratic Control (UDC) had been set up to oppose war and secret diplomacy and to promote peace and democratic participation in major decisions of state and society. Over time it had been pressing for an alternative foreign policy, a total commitment to collective security and the organization of various international paradigms for peace. During the inter-war period the impact of the UDC on the peace and labour movements was disproportionate and abiding.[38] By then the UDC had seen through the lofty hopes and promises of the disarmament conference whose objectives were being severely restricted and hindered by 'unseen powers behind the scenes'.

The UDC paid special attention to the activities of the warmongers and munition -makers. Its careful and detailed research resulted in the publication of *The Secret International* (July 1932) and *Patriotism Ltd.* (February 1933) having extraordinary influence on anti-war propaganda since World War I. Now, for the first time, Dorothy Woodman, its effective secretary, put India on the Union's high-profile agenda. Apparently, the ordinance rule and denial of democratic rights and personal freedom meant for UDC, violation of peace and declaration of war on an inoffensive people. Peace in India, based on equality and goodwill, was considered as an essential pre-condition in the fight against war and against growing fascism in Britain.

On 17 January 1933, Bertrand Russell received a detailed cable from C. Rajagopalachari regarding the Congress reaction on the proposed safeguards, the unchanged official attitude towards Gandhi and the emancipation of the untouchables requiring the government's intervention especially in favour of temple entry, the prominent case being the temple of Guruvayur.[39] Russell, in response, issued a statement reiterating his belief that self-government with a number of severe restrictions would not be acceptable to the Indian people. The Congress had taken note of the formula for safeguards devised at the RTC and found it to be incompatible with its conception of freedom. The British Government had been fighting the Congress for two years in the hope that the new constitution would go far to satisfy Indian aspirations.[40] It was evident that the proposed constitution would do no such thing. It was also affirmed that the government's policy gathered by the India League delegation should be widely spread in Great Britain. There did not seem to be any prospect of better times in India unless British public opinion could exert sufficient pressure on the government to compel it to adapt its policy to the realities of the Indian situation.[41]

It was feared that politically 1933 would be a lean year. Menon reported that nothing would move dramatically in Britain. It was held that the Government of India might advance the claim that the country was no longer ruled by ordinances. This would merely be 'a technical truth'.[42] Even if the official assertion was true in spirit the aftermath of 1932 made any hope of immediate conciliation very dim. The ordinances had been first enacted in January 1932 and they ran out their course of six months. It was the calculation of the government that the extraordinary powers would crush the Indian movement in three months. But by July 1932, the government found India unwilling to accept repression and despotic rule with submission. Since the ordinances could not be renewed lawfully, the government decided to opt for legal justification for the continuance of these drastic powers by what amounted to a subterfuge. It enacted another set of ordinances which were 'the old ones in new garb'.[43] The year passed but the government's remedies of stern rule failed to restore peaceful conditions or reduce the people to submission. The ordinances were therefore re-enacted in another form. They were given the appearance of laws passed by the central and provincial legislatures of India. The world was told, Menon bantered, 'that repression bears the hallmark of popular consent, a ridiculous contradiction in terms'.[44]

Explaining the findings of the delegation, Menon emphasized that Indian villages had asserted their identity and their cosmopolitan viewpoint. It was said at several meetings and assemblies that, contrary to the opinion fostered in Europe that the Indian villagers were push-overs of the urbanized nationalists and the *Raj* was their trustee and safeguard, the Indian villages had responded in a remarkable way to the awakening of India.[45] The empire sat on the masses heavier than on the other classes. The resentment was widespread in India and it was sought to be crushed by force.[46] Liberty in every form was suppressed. Searches of houses, confiscation, destruction and removal of property, restriction of movement of people and deprivation of free speech proved beyond doubt that India was ruled not by law but by force. The wrath of the officials was not confined to grown-ups but also to the young and old irrespective of gender. Torture, humiliation and various atrocities, confiscation of agricultural land, destruction of standing crops, residences and household goods, redistribution of land at cheaper rates to outside parties were essential features of the firm hand policy. Opposition was primarily non-violent, notwithstanding isolated cases of political assassination in Bengal. Menon emphasized that it ought to be recognized that terrorism was the upshot of brutal suppression.[47] Despite tall claims of success of the policy of crushing the Congress and the self-congratulatory appraisals of it in the British press, the fact remained that the Congress committees had continued to work, resistance had been kept up, unlawful bulletins appeared every day and boycott of British goods and firms continued without diminution. Menon held firmly that unless the government reversed its policy, released political prisoners and negotiated with the Congress with a view to making the Government of India Bill embody the minimum demands of the movement, the fight would go on unabated.[48] There was, however, no sign of any change in that direction and the viceroy seemed determined to follow a vindictive and barren policy of firm hand and 'talked in medieval terms of no truck with law breakers'.[49] Menon and the League maintained that there could be no settlement with India without reconciliation with those who represented her and the majority of them had been in prisons.

Calling upon the people of Britain to rise to the occasion and get themselves thoroughly acquainted with the facts relating to the Indian situation, Menon thought that it was futile to claim that the problem was intricate or that there were difficulties nearer home. He asserted that Britain must either abdicate or live up to her responsibilities. Even pacifists could not be indifferent to India's challenge and 'if their conscience does not impel them to action, their instructed judgment should be called into service'.[50] Menon made it clear that behind their indifference to wrong was fear and ignorance: the only way to deal with that was to dispel fear and to become informed. The India League, Menon affirmed, believed that British public opinion, particularly progressive opinion, had a part to play in the struggle of a people against a powerful empire and 'we should be glad to offer our humble services wherever they are requisitioned'.[51] The empire had been built by force and sustained by oppression and 'no more war' was but a vain slogan so long as there was oppression all over.[52]

Theosophical Lodges at Great Yarmouth and Norwich organized two meetings on contemporary India towards the end of 1932 and beginning of 1933 respectively with the assistance of the local Labour parties; the meetings were thrown open to all. The organizers were apprehensive of a hostile audience because of the overwhelming conservative political ambience of the area and added to that was the fact that any meeting arranged under the TS auspices was at once prejudiced. In terms of a sizeable attentive audience who participated in the animated discussion that followed, the meetings were successful.[53] From Hereford came an interesting communication from William A. Barnes who had heard Menon at a meeting on India a few days earlier and was impressed by the presentation and arguments of that 'Indian gentleman'. Barnes knew that whenever one tried to champion a just cause, one suffered from 'press misrepresentation'. Even the 'advanced thinkers of Hereford' ridiculed his suggestion that probably India would 'manage her own affairs better than we can for her'. Thus he told them after a prolonged local debate that so long as there was a suspicion that the British administrators had been doing injustice to the Indian people through lack of other than prejudiced knowledge, 'my conscience at any rate would compel me to retain my unpopular attitude'. He was, therefore, keen to get the same lecturer to the Audit School to speak at a meeting. Barnes was an influential member of the school and was confident of assembling a good audience. He thought that it was better for districts like Hereford to have 'the truth of misrepresented ideas explained to them than that all worthwhile knowledge should be poured into places like Cardiff and other large industrial towns'. Barnes was eager to listen to the lecturer's answer to 'some of the questions put to me with much cynical assurance by some of the biased intellectual ignoramuses who would not admit that the other side might have a case'. The meeting was a challenge for Menon as a consequence of which a branch was enthusiastically formed by purely local initiative.[54] There were Barneses at other places as well.

Speaking at a meeting at Birmingham on 14 February 1933, Menon stressed the nature of prison conditions in India.[55] In 1932 about a hundred thousand people went to prison in India. In several provinces the local governments had to set free criminals to make room for political offenders. About 95 per cent of these were C class prisoners entitled to none of the privileges which were given to political prisoners in other parts of the world. In many cases, they were vindictively treated worse than criminals. The Indian jail system centred round the convict warder and overseer who earned remission of their own prison terms by doing warder duty. They were, by and large, notoriously cruel and overzealous in the harsh treatment of politicals which, they believed, would raise them in the estimation of the jail authorities. The local governments appeared to encourage severe handling of politicals and a copy of a confidential circular issued by the inspector general of prisons in Madras to that effect came into the possession of the League's delegation. Ill -treatment was sanctioned by the jail manuals, the scope of which was arbitrarily extended by warders, supervisors and superintendents. Brutality of jail life, distinguished by hard labour, punishments including flogging, 'chain-gangs' of civil disobedience prisoners, solitary cells, firing and lathi charges, inadequate covers and shelters and vindictive treatment made the medieval character of Indian prisons apparent.[56]

At another meeting held in Bristol on 25 February 1933 Ellen Wilkinson examined before a labour audience the concept and practice of unlawful association as developed by the Government of India. Immediately after the four all-devouring ordinances were promulgated on 4 January 1932, the Bombay government issued notifications in its extraordinary gazette of 5 January 1932 proscribing as many as 132 institutions of the province, known by the names of *mandals, samitis*, leagues, *ashrams, chhavanis* devoted to some organized efforts to develop specific phases of national life, be it political, educational, social, economic or even humanitarian. Soon other provinces were equally affected by the ordinances. The list of the unlawful organizations clearly showed that the government wanted to crush all efforts for the nation's upliftment which were being 'made on the people's initiative and crippled it for years to come'.[57] The intelligence that guided the institutions was incarcerated in prisons and their funds and property were seized by the government. Some of these institutions were doing purely humanitarian work, a few of them were related to the Congress and a few others had nothing to do with any political movement. Some of these organizations were devoted to minority sectional interests and a large number of them were mainly devoted to social service to the backward communities. Wilkinson claimed that the government inflicted heavy fines on political offenders in addition to the terms of imprisonment. Attachment of property was extensively used as a useful method of realization of fines. For poor villages such attachments meant looting of all their belongings including buffaloes, bullocks and agricultural implements. Even doors of houses were unhinged and taken away. The local administration could considerably extend the scope of ordinances and punishments and they saw to it that the victims and families lost their instruments of livelihood.[58]

The delegate conference held on 4 July 1933 at the Friends' Meeting House in London and addressed by the delegation created a good deal of commotion as the speakers spent the whole morning and afternoon sessions dwelling on the special and significant features of the Government of India and its arbitrary and brutal methods.[59] About two hundred delegates from 90 organizations were given a graphic presentation of the police *raj* in action in India, the nature of the ordinance mind, the ascendancy of irrational forces of vindictiveness, assault on women and children, beating of men, women and young boys in lock-ups, the extension of national feelings in rural India, popularity of the Congress, the salient features of social resistance and the remarkable sway of Gandhi. The delegation of the League had witnessed the impact of the Communal Award of MacDonald in India and watched with amazement the 'supreme appeal' by Gandhi to 'the conscience of his countrymen' to preserve the country's social integrity. Tagore cried out in anguish that 'no civilized society can thrive upon victims whose humanity has been permanently mutilated and whose minds have been compelled to dwell in the dark'. Calling upon his countrymen to endeavour in earnest to eradicate untouchability in all its ramifications, Tagore emphasized that 'dismemberment of a large portion of Hindu society is certainly fatal to its wholeness' and the protest of Gandhi was noble, merciful and incredibly extraordinary. Gandhi, the delegation was convinced, reigned over the Indian mind and psyche.[60]

At another conference at Barclay Hall in Layton on 3 October 1933, Fenner Brockway was the principal participant.[61] Attendance was thin due to inclement weather. Nevertheless, more than one hundred persons assembled. R.J. Tallack convened the meeting and Menon also participated in the discussion that followed Brockway's presentation.[62] In a resolution the representatives of political, social and religious organizations of Layton supported the claims of self-government and self-determination of the Indian people and urged the government to seek a solution on those lines and release the political prisoners to ensure an atmosphere of cooperation and goodwill. Fenner Brockway emphasized that the very fact that the English people were intensely absorbed with their own domestic responsibilities and could only give a secondary consideration to India's problems was surely an argument why England should not decide the destinies of India and why India should have self-government. Although the British government had been responsible for the direction of nearly two-thirds of the Indian territory, the mass of the people of India remained in terrible poverty and ignorance. Conditions among the industrial workers in factories, mills and mines were almost equivalent to the conditions of England's industrial workers a hundred years ago. The only section of the Indian people who were resisting self-government in India were the rich landlords and princes.[63]

The speakers at this conference emphasized that despite all the superstitions, misery and poverty, India did not present a picture of a decadent society. India was one of the most renascent countries of the world. It was in the ferment of a reform movement and had been endeavouring with deep enthusiasm to lift India to a higher level of civilization. Referring to Gandhi as a politician by accident, Brockway argued that Gandhi hated violence in all forms and condemned British administration in India, but was keen to extend extraordinary love for the English people. He was appalled to think that such a beautiful personality, a saint and a mystic, should have been put in prison. Methods of repression, Brockway thought, would fail. They would never succeed since they had never succeeded in history. The Simon Commission, the RTCs, the JSC, etc.

were all doomed to failure because they 'did not represent the dynamic and alert force' of Indian nationalism. Therefore, the solution of the problem must be sought in negotiations, peace and democratic equality. The greatest danger, all the speakers emphasized, was that the people of England were beginning to settle down to the Indian situation and were taking it for granted.[64]

For the League, Sapru's statement of 6 February 1933 from Allahabad protesting against high-handedness of the local administration prohibiting a meeting to commemorate the death anniversary of Motilal Nehru proved to be quite convenient. The meeting had been convened by politicians of different schools such as C.Y. Chintamani, Hriday Nath Kunzru, Khwaja Abdul Majid and others. Sapru's letter was circulated by the League widely in order to drive home a point raised by an eminent member of the RTC known for moderation and conciliation.[65] Without going into the legality of the order, Sapru argued that the concerned district magistrate should have been more considerate because it was actions of this character that tended to cause unnecessary and unavoidable irritation and annoyance to public sentiments. Instead of creating a feeling of harmony between the local administration and the citizens, they merely tended to create estrangement and resentment. It was no crime, he averred, to pay a tribute to the memory of a distinguished leader notwithstanding differences on political questions, especially in the case of Motilal Nehru, one of the most outstanding figures in Allahabad and a distinguished Indian. It was time that one realized that there was a limit to the exasperation of public feeling on a question of this character.[66] Menon sought national introspection and a serious second opinion in Britain on the dangerous drift of the Indian situation.

The *India Bulletin,* under an editorial board consisting of Horace Alexander, Will Hayes, Reginald A. Reynolds and Atma S. Kamlani also took up the cause in right earnest and reported in its issue of March 1933 almost an endless catalogue of official trickery, prevarication and cruelty at a distance of 6,000 miles combined with desultory and tendentious news given in the British press, which accounted for the indifference of the average person in England 'to what, after all, he and she is responsible for'. The editors wrote that those whose feelings were in a condition of coma due to official indoctrination should ask themselves whether a steady application of rigorous imprisonment, fines, suppression of speech, beating, insults, tortures and the rest of the 'law and order' programme were likely to be of political and economic benefit to the rulers of British India or to anyone else. The readers were also reminded and made to ruminate over the extraordinary phenomenon that the movement for freedom in India was being carried on under unique conditions of non-violence and love.[67]

One of the principal talking points of the League speakers all over happened to be the nature of Indian poverty, the perpetual hunger of the masses of the people of India, widespread illiteracy and lack of health services. Quoting Linlithgow, the India League's *Information Bulletin* drove the point home: '... those who govern and those who aspire to govern India must never allow themselves to forget that India's wealth in an overwhelming degree is in her agriculture, and that upon the fields of her agriculture is founded the whole structure of India's economy'.[68] The speakers maintained that there was an undeclared famine in India and scarcity of food was the people's daily bread. Poverty stalked naked as the normal state of affairs in the *raiyatwari* villages as much as in the *zamindari* ones. Taxes had to be paid, remissions were rare and belated and agitations were always shut down on political grounds. Rural indebtedness was so heavy that without radical changes in the law, the revenue system and agriculture, no substantial improvement in the condition of the peasant was possible. Debts were owed not merely to professional moneylenders, but to landlords, the government, mortgage holders and town shopkeepers. The state and the landlords were regarded as parasites on the land, the latter more than the former.[69] The *talukdars* of Awadh, who might be taken as typical instances of parasite landlords, lived luxuriously in town homes distinguished by lavish displays of hospitality. The speakers of the League maintained forcefully and with a remarkable array of facts, that agrarian discontent consequent on failure of crops, falling commodity prices, government's revenue policy and the awakening among the villagers had reduced the vision of 'pathetic contentment' of the traditional East to an obsolete and antiquated perception.

In the NWFP and the UP the unrest of the peasantry had resulted in organized protests and in the latter province it caused what the government called a state of 'agrarian revolution'.[70] In Bengal there was far greater mass awakening and discontent in the villages than was usually known. Terrorist murders and arrests eclipsed other items of news about that presidency and it was sometimes believed and circulated that apart from terrorism there was no movement of importance in Bengal. In fact, rural upsurge was a new and an explosive phenomenon in India and in certain areas this formed the effective cushion to absorb violent political processes.[71] It had infused an adequate measure of social realism and the vision of an egalitarian society into the anti-imperialist movement of nationalist India.

The tone of the *Notes for Speakers* became sharper than in previous years. By 1933 the *Notes* encompassed the essential features of British rule under the ordinances. One of them dealt with a comprehensive discussion on the freedom of the press. From the early days of British administration, the press in India had been under rigorous control. Even as early as 1791, the press was subjected to censorship, several editors were deported to Europe and keeping a printing press in India, according to a judge, became a hazardous undertaking. Considering the existing situation, the *Notes* concluded that together with the Press Law

Repeal and Amendment Act of 1922 and the Indian Penal Code, the suppression of the press all over India became a powerful preoccupation of the Government of India under the ordinances. The effect of the operation of the ordinances was draconian in nature. For example, under them news allowed in some provinces was not allowed in others, correct and authentic news might not be published without mutilation; display of certain kinds of news was not allowed; double-column headlines for certain items and certain captions such as the arrest of Muslims and women were prohibited; reports of the proceedings of legislatures and law courts were censored and were not permitted to be published extensively; 'immediate criticism' of the government was prohibited; editors were restrained from all political comments and activities and serious censorship was imposed on the printing of photographs and all other illustrations.[72]

Another *Note* was devoted to the Red Shirt movement of the NWFP and its leader, Abdul Ghaffar Khan, then being vilified by the government (and by such eminent correspondents as Edward Thompson) as a 'dangerous character' leading an aggressive militant movement with strong racial overtones and having long camps which manoeuvred in military formations extending beyond the borders of the province under the patronage of the Congress. The *Note* dispelled the clandestine elements in the official propaganda literature about the Red Shirts, explained that the name of the organization was *Khudai Khidmatgar* or Servants of God, who swore to non-violence and functioned as an affiliated organization of the Congress; their oath of enrolment bound them to be prepared for every suffering and sacrifice and to live chaste, honest and honourable lives. It was explained that the crime of Abdul Ghaffar Khan was his commitment to *purna swaraj* and, despite inducements, his consistent adherence to Indian nationalism as championed by the Congress.[73]

Yet another *Note* made a statistical analysis of the nature and quantum of India's payment for a large number of British wars including World War I.[74] Another set of *Notes for Speakers* examined with facts and figures (culled from official sources) the nature of ordinances giving the total number of political prisoners with provincial breakdown, official crackdown on demonstrations and organizations, atrocities against the rural people including those on the people of the NWFP, analytical exposé of the RTCs, the suppression of the press, boycott and its impact on Lancashire trade, detailed informative account of the policy of firm hand, suppression of postal communications including those of MPs, the nature of income tax in India, the meaning and implications of the home charges and the remarkable and iniquitous distribution of wealth, failure of the government to deal with India's poverty, the inertia of the administration to grapple with social welfare programmes and the practice of *divide et impera* in British India and its impact on social and political development.[75]

In keeping with the League's enthusiastic campaign against the ordinance rule in India, Leonard Matters protested in a strongly worded petition to Samuel Hoare against the arrest and persecution of S. Venkatapathaiya, an advocate and a member of the Bangalore municipality for his association with Matters during his visit to the city. Matters recalled that before undertaking the visit, the India League's delegation obtained the necessary official authority to move freely about the country and pursue their investigations in their own way.[76] It was implicit in that official authority that members of the delegation could use the services of individual Indians as informants, guides, interpreters and so on. That such individuals might be members of the Congress Party and even active cooperators was, in Matters' judgment, equally implicit. Matters was quite aware that understanding could not establish immunity from prosecution of anybody who had broken the law or to conduct illegal activity in the company of the delegation. But no Indian, he maintained, should be penalized because he had assisted the delegation in their investigation. Matters thought it prudent to protest since he read in the charge sheet against Venkatapathaiya 'that he brought to Siddapur ... Mr Leonard Matters, a European, to show him the manner in which the Congress activities were carried on etc.'[77] In his letter Matters considered that the whole case was a 'travesty of justice and fair play'. He was concerned with what was palpably the basis of the specific charges against him — Venkatapathaiya's association with the delegation as guide, interpreter and exponent of the Congress case. In his opinion, the delegation was entitled to avail itself of Venkatapathaiya's services and Matters was entitled, within his broad authority, to make his investigations in his own way using such media for information as he chose, in Karnataka or elsewhere in India. Matters felt that the official reaction was essentially vindictive and he protested in a most emphatic manner against charges against Venkatapathaiya on the assumption that it was a breach of law for him 'to show me the conditions in Karnataka'.[78] Matters was convinced that because he saw with his own eyes what was officially denied and because Venkatapathaiya disputed with authority the accuracy of official statements, the charges were brought against him. Matters protested against breach of understanding that members of the delegation could avail themselves of the services of anybody and those who had assisted them should not be victimized for giving that service and guidance.[79]

Amidst the ascendancy of diehards in Britain and the growing stalemate in India, a white paper was placed on the table of the house on 18 March 1933. Not surprisingly, it met with a cold reception in India from all shades of political opinion. Apart from the views expressed by some Congressmen in a personal capacity which were brushed aside by the government as being 'extremist', what was known as 'politically sober or moderate' opinion had also been overwhelmingly against the proposed scheme.[80] A substantial section of Muslim opinion felt that the government had let them down badly. The white paper did not satisfy that section of Muslim opinion which clamoured for one-third representation in the central legislature and residuary powers in the provinces. They were sore that in provinces where Muslims were in a majority, like the Punjab, it was the governor with his special powers who would rule and not responsible ministers 'who under the communal award should under normal circumstances be Muslims'.[81] Ghaznavi, a member of the RTCs, condemned the white paper wholeheartedly. He claimed that the government had even flouted the opinion of the Bengal legislative council which had passed a resolution not long ago against the establishment of a second chamber in that province. It was also maintained that the proposals did not even conform to the policy enunciated as a result of the three RTCs. RTC I recommended that recruitment and control of all-India services should be in the hands of the Government of India in the future constitution. Hoare's scheme overlooked that recommendation and distinctly laid down that both recruitment and control of these services should remain in the hands of the secretary of state. Again, it was a foregone conclusion that the new constitution would see the end of the India council. This was retained, though in a slightly modified form under the new scheme. Furthermore, conditions were then imposed on the establishment of an all-India Federation with responsibility at the centre. These were that states representing 50 per cent of the total population of the Indian states (as opposed to the British Indian provinces) should express willingness to enter the Federation and that a Reserve Bank should first be established. When these two conditions were to be fulfilled was a matter of grave speculation, but the general opinion was that central responsibility was a distant dream.[82]

The content and goal of central responsibility was also seriously questioned. Only a shadow of authority would be seen in a government, apparently responsible, to the elected legislature but having no control over defence, foreign affairs or finance. Over and above, the money required for these reserved subjects would be non-votable and would rest at the arbitrary discretion of the Viceroy, who would enjoy great power. Apart from being able to pass ordinances, he was going to be given powers to promulgate the Governor-General's acts which would have the full force of law. Besides, the power of veto had been kept intact. Central responsibility would be a farce: this would be confirmed even by a cursory reading of the white paper.[83] Thus, one felt that the whole policy at least promised by the Labour government in 1929 had been thrown overboard and it was feared that the white paper scheme would be even more reactionary than the Simon Report. The latter at least recommended provincial autonomy. Hoare's scheme was surrounded on all sides by safeguards. Powers were given to the governors to override their ministers, pass governor's acts and ordinances and even administer the transferred subjects in case of an emergency. What was more, these measures of the governor would be enforced by the executive officers who would be merely responsible to the secretary of state. They were not liable to be dismissed or dealt with if they refused to obey the orders of the ministers, who would be mere figureheads in the future constitution.[84]

It was widely believed that the whole scheme would have to be revised in toto. If it did not satisfy moderate opinion in India, it could not ever satisfy the Congress. Meetings were held and resolutions had been passed all over condemning the white paper and expressing disappointment that political prisoners had not been released. The most advanced opinion in the country had been prevented from expressing itself. The Congress session in Calcutta had been banned. The reception committee had been declared an unlawful association and its president and secretary were sent to jail. Rigorous imprisonment became the order of the day. Eminent Congressmen with well-known credentials were given punishment with hard labour for running Congress organizations or educational or philanthropic institutions. They included reputed scholars, leading advocates, prominent social activists and seasoned legislators.[85]

These punitive methods of dealing with Congressmen, Menon observed, had not as yet been given up. The paradox of the situation was that while reforms were being considered for India, repression went ahead unabated. It was a matter of speculation if the future constitution would put an end to such arbitrary methods. Evidently, no constitution would be worth its while if it did not safeguard the liberty of the person. About that time, the India League was compelled to publish a long and enlarged letter by Menon to the *New Statesman and Nation* in the form of a pamphlet entitled *Law and Prisons in India (1933)*. The Indian prison system, Menon concluded, was in line with the traditions of the Indian police both in inhumanity and vindictiveness. The results of repression were visible everywhere. 'There is no law in India except the law which translates the will of the executive to suppress and stifle all opposition.' But the ordinances, Menon held, did not dispirit or intimidate the Indians. They could not stop India thinking.[86]

The white paper, Menon wrote in another place, had a chequered career. Six years of inquiry and 20 commissions and conferences preceded it. This was to be the basis of further inquiry. Its proposals might be amended by the joint committee of parliament. In view of the possible composition of that body it was reasonable to anticipate that it would whittle down the government's proposals. In India, Menon wrote, the paper had already been rejected by the Congress, the Moderates, the Muslims, and the Hindu leaders. Gandhi pigeonholed the document. N.M. Joshi, the trade union leader, was exceedingly disappointed. Sapru, a persistent cooperator with the British

Government, reserved full comment but said that the reaction had made its influence felt on the government.[87] Jayakar, Sapru's collaborator, was amazed at the proposals. In contrast, British public opinion, judged by press headlines and comments, unanimously welcomed the white paper and even the more radical journals, who regarded the proposals as conservative, urged India to accept it. There was a complete divergence of view — a gulf which six years of committees and conferences had not bridged. Some of the leading Tory commentators sought to explain away the Indian demur and the British applause: 'The main lines of recent criticism, for instance, are that the Government policy, now crystallized in the White Paper, is a mere inheritance from the Socialist Party, that it is based upon the enfranchisement of millions, that it will end in the domination of Congress and that above all, it will mean the transfer to Indians of responsibility for Law and Order - or in more picturesque language, the handing (sic) over of the police to their hereditary enemies, the politicians ... Nothing, of course, could be more remote from the truth ....' Menon thought that the *Daily Telegraph,* another ministerialist organ, was even more blunt. After enumerating the conservative checks in the plan it concluded with significant cynicism that an 'elementary point', the importance of which was generally overlooked, was the recognition in the white paper that 'the whole enterprise may be held up indefinitely' if financial conditions were unfavourable for a more expensive system of government than what was then available.[88]

The proposals concerned a federal centre, the future relations of the crown and the princes, the functions reserved to the British Government and the Secretary of State for India. In every one of these spheres, Menon noted, the essential feature of the proposed scheme was the insistence that the reality of power and control should not pass effectively to Indian hands. In the centre, the status of the Federal executive, composed of ministers and councillors, was not in a state of mysterious indefiniteness. The truth was that it was not presented as a responsible cabinet. The ministers were nominated and the councillors appointed by the Governor-General, a distinction without a difference as was apparent from the details of the plan. The Governor-General was not bound by ministerial advice in any matter whatever. There were spheres of administration which were reserved for the governor-general, such as army, defence and foreign affairs. In the transferred departments, which were under ministers, the governor had special responsibilities enabling him to override ministers and legislatures. Besides, he possessed powers to reverse ministers' decisions and take over every department and item of administration and legislative action by virtue of his special powers, prerogatives and superior authority. The Governor-General might cut, introduce and reinstate budget items against the decision of the legislature. He could withhold assent to bills passed, stop them at any stage or refuse sanction for their introduction. He could suspend the constitution or rule by ordinance. He could interfere with any finance or legislative proposal on the ground of its being related to his reserved spheres or his special responsibilities. Of all this, of when and how the powers were to be used, the Governor-General alone was the sole judge.[89] The ministers had been spoken of as responsible, and thus, different from the councillors. Although they would be appointed from among the members of the legislatures, it was not specially mentioned that they should be elected members or responsible to the legislature. The white paper definitely referred to occasions when the governor-general and ministers might be ranged in opposition to the legislature and the matter in question be decided by the governor-general.[90]

It was also claimed that the proposals conferred autonomy on the provinces. But popular control of police, responsible government and ministerial responsibilities were not contemplated. The legislatures were not fully elected. The appointed elements together with the European representatives and those of vested interests would be sufficient in most provinces to give the governor a majority for the official view. Further, the governor had overriding powers of the same character and extent as the governor-general. 'He like the superior of Delhi,' Menon commented, 'is the sole judge of when and how to use these Hitlerian powers and for how long,' while the secretary of state became, more than ever, the 'great Mughal' empowered to overwhelm even the actions and proposals of the governor-general.[91] Menon conceded that franchise was extended, but it was still entirely inadequate to the needs of modern India and out of tune with the awakening in the Indian villages. In the provinces, about 30 per cent of the population would vote and less than four per cent were eligible for the federal chamber. Thirty-three per cent in the lower house and about 40 per cent in the upper house were to be the nominees of the princes. Concluding his review of the white paper, Menon claimed that the proposals gave the Governor-General the powers which any Central European dictator would envy. Army, services and finances were placed under the firm control of the viceroy, supplemented by prerogatives and safeguards. Currency was the privilege of the Reserve Bank and through it amenable to the demands of the City of London. It was apparent, Menon claimed, that the white paper was not conceived in terms of a responsible government, partial or complete. The impact of the whole scheme on the political processes of the country would be the development of 'a strained form of responsible government' or a 'government by ordinances', more likely the latter. It was not merely a violation of a series of pledges. The worst features of 'rule based on prestige, race, discrimination and commercial and economic exploitation' were retained in the scheme with 'facades of representative institutions' based on 'a conservative franchise and the enthronement of princes and vested interests'.[92]

The challenge from the die-hards had become somewhat alarming for the government. The die-hards were not disposed to admit that the old *Raj* was vanishing before their eyes as the incomprehensible charisma of Gandhi had moved the whole of India and her millions. True, Churchill had been feeling sequestered within the Conservative high politics over the years as he witnessed the ascendancy of a temporizing 'mediocrity' without a spark. He was vexed at the treatment meted out to him by Baldwin with the 'consummate' dupery of a 'charlatan'. Churchill had been awaiting resentfully the opportunity to oust Baldwin from the party leadership, come what may. Churchill was talented but unreliable. He was energetic, prankish and dissolute and his distinctive feature was his sheer inability to subordinate himself to party loyalty. But, as A.J.P. Taylor observes, Churchill was the remaining giant in British politics after the eclipse of Lloyd George.[93] He had always been animated by the elaborate rituals of the British mission in India, the Heaven's Command. He contributed his bit to make the image of a romantic redolent *Raj* the leitmotif of the conservative British life.[94] It appeared that the opposition under him had become determined. Only one-third of the members of the Conservative Party in parliament voted for the government in the debate on India in early February 1933 when the diehards moved an amendment to obtain the exclusion of the four cabinet ministers on the joint committee.[95] The government's majority was the smallest in any division in parliament and considering the enormous size of its backbenches, this was very significant. The frontbench was somewhat alarmed not because India might be vouchsafed by a measure of independence, but that its own pet scheme of giving India a paper constitution that would throw on the Indians the blame for not working it might be undermined by the overenthusiasm of the die-hards. Menon noted that hitherto the die-hards had been connived at by the Conservative leadership. They had railed and barked but had never been called to book.[96] On the contrary, each time the government made a generous gesture to them they were emboldened to raise their price and a frustrated government felt obliged to yield to their basic point of view. It was, however, feared that the game of appeasement had gone a little too far, especially in view of the growing die-hard opposition to the white paper.[97] It was also not expected to get a large number of witnesses to the JSC who, unless summoned by the government, would have to pay their own fares. Besides, the joint committee had decided to accept the advice of the government with regard to the personnel of the Indian assessors who were to sit on it.[98]

In early March 1933, the India League decided to place before the members of the parliamentary Labour Party the facts relevant to issues of Labour cooperation on the JSC. It was argued that the object of sending the memorandum to the parliamentary party was to provide information which might not be ready in hand. It stressed that the circumstances which had compelled abstention from the RTC still remained unaddressed. The cooperation of Indian parties was not secured; the Congress leadership was still in prison; despite the appeals of the opposition and Indian cooperators, the government had been persistent in its policy of a knock-out blow while the outcome of the third conference was not welcomed even by the moderate Liberals including Sastri and Sapru.[99] 'There is nothing in the circumstances of Indian situation or in the policy and attitude of the Government', the memorandum ran, 'to justify or warrant the Labour Party offering its assistance on the Joint Committee.'[100] The League urged that the party should maintain its independence and pursue its own declared policy of self-determination and continuing cooperation with the Indian people. That strategy would constitute the most effective protest against repression, continued imprisonments of the Congress leadership and refusal to negotiate with the representative Indians. The League carefully appended to its memorandum Sapru's public statement deploring government's remarkable 'lack of imagination' and capacity 'to read the signs of time' and castigating Samuel Hoare's pugnacious political precepts presented in the parliament.[101] 'One cannot understand', Sapru wrote, 'what exactly is meant by saying that there can be no question of Mr. Gandhi or other civil disobedience prisoners being released until the government had convincing reasons to believe that their release would not be followed by a revival of civil disobedience .... If government feels that the Mahatma will now or at any time make a public recantation of his faith and furnish a sort of recognizance for good behaviour, then I think they are applying standards of conduct to Mr Gandhi and his adjutants which no one who understands anything of political psychology can apply to political leaders in the situation of Mr Gandhi and others'.[102]

Apprehensive of the carefully planned parliamentary manoeuvres by the increasingly successful die-hards, Menon had reasons to feel despondent. He was unhappy at the temperate criticism of the Indian papers of the white paper and the absence of any suggestion of the future of nationalist policy in regard to the Indian proposals. These had led to a conviction in the political circles in Britain that the constitution would be accepted and worked under formal protest.[103] The attitude of important Indian journals and the reported conversations with which M.S. Aney was supposed to have set on foot the revival of the *swaraj* party, were frequently cited as reinforcing that view. It was more than evident that the government did not regard the Congress as an important factor in the working of the reformed constitution.[104] Menon discovered that the die-hards proposed to make a special feature of the claims of the Muslims of the Punjab in the constitution. The older claims of reservation of residual powers and statutory majorities were once more to come to the front. The premier's award might also be reopened. It had been amended in view of the Poona pact which was then being challenged by the Hindus of Bengal and regretted by the militant leaders of the depressed classes.[105]

In a sharp and caustic review of the situation, Menon maintained that the internecine feud between rival sections of Tories did not concern itself with the future and aspirations of India and its people. But it was quite apparent to all that the Baldwin-Churchill duel lacked realism so far as India was concerned. In political content, Menon argued, there was little difference between the two points of view however, varying their phraseology. But their 'Kinship lies deeper than the chasm'. It was important, Menon continued, to realize that the Tory party, either in opposition or in power, never committed itself to any policy in India. During the RTC I, Samuel Hoare insisted as the Tory spokesman, that he would express no opinion and commit himself to nothing beyond a willingness to examine the 'picture' when it was completed. In power, the same Hoare had been busy in erasing even such outlines as two years of effort tended to throw into relief. Menon maintained that the white paper did not represent the proposals of the British government for constitutional reform in India. It was an agenda for the joint committee of two houses of Parliament 'at the doorstep of which a few chosen Indians, like Talleyrand at Vienna in 1815, are allowed to sit.' But there was an important distinction: 'Talleyrand knew his mind and had France, vanquished as she was, behind him, our leaders are like balloons sustained by hot air, floating all the time, but aimlessly, in political space and awaiting the crash which contact with political earth renders invariable.' The Federal structure was a matter of promise rather than performance. As contemplated, the centre was to be both 'federal' and 'responsible'. The inverted commas, Menon held, were essential in the interest of political science because Indian national responsibility was conditional on the establishment of the federal structure and the latter was dependent on the adhesion of a large number of princes, the creation of a Reserved Bank, world recovery, a suitable atmosphere in India and the completion of the provincial part of the Act.[106]

Menon argued that the constitution would not work and would reveal at every stage bad craftsmanship. The piston of the engine, he wrote, would either not move or if it was made to move it would snap. Power, Menon asserted, can crush forms of resistance but never resistance itself. It could never transform the spirit of righteous revolt into channels of constructive effort. 'Let Britons', Menon wrote, 'who still believe and care for the destiny of their race, be misled or feel happy about the triumph of Hitlerism in India.'[107]

By March 1933, Menon was clear in his mind that an active interaction with influential individuals, press, organizations and parties in India must be initiated and, if necessary, revived, so as to ensure a creative and uninterrupted two-way communication between the League and India. As a part of the renewed effort to reorganize and stimulate the publicity work of the League, Menon sent a circular to all known personalities and centres in India, intimating the desire of the League to revamp its work. If circumstances made it possible, the League proposed that a printed bulletin of news, summarized from Indian bulletins, press and cable news should be widely circulated. The League thought that it should take out a mimeographed digest, 'Facts and News', useful for teachers and send it to about a thousand lecturers all over the country. Menon was convinced that at least one third of these would make use of the material. The League was also willing to summarize the Indian bulletins and send out a copy each week to selected members on the League's list. The League decided to take suitable steps to make it attractive for the foreign press who might be tempted to opt for some copies. The existing press service bureau of the League would be stimulated to send out to the Labour papers in the provinces an *apercu* of Indian news, which they might use or at any rate, find time to browse through.[108]

Menon wanted to know the extent of support that could be obtained from friends and well-wishers in India. He would be pleased to incorporate suggestions from Indian parties and was anxious to circulate Indian bulletins on their behalf to persons of their choice. Menon was candid that he had no means to do the work all by himself and if a small monthly contribution was made, the League would be able to carry out the scheme as outlined, or any other arrangement could be worked out between them to circulate the Indian bulletins as before.[109] In an earnest appeal to his Indian acquaintances, Menon urged that if the scheme appeared feasible and attractive and if there were interested persons in India, who thought that foreign propaganda was desirable, the League would like to get in touch with them. Menon stressed that it was impossible to finance the work entirely from England. The report of the delegation to India was ready for the press but lack of funds and official opposition had conspired to stall its publication. Menon affirmed that it was an objective document and faithfully reflected 'the investigating character of our visit in India'.[110] Reaction, he added, was then in the saddle and it was feared that the firm hand policy might receive a further shot in the arm. Menon was uncertain if his letters would break through the censor screen and reach their destination. Unfortunately, he was equally unsure of the response of his addressees in view of the state of inertia and doldrums in which political India landed itself with the Mahatma's preoccupation with Harijan welfare, social reform and the *charkha*. The confusion was worse confounded by the misplaced civility of the Indian moderates and their refusal to appreciate the true face of British imperialism beyond the veneer of a liberal constitutional facade.[111]

The renewal of the League's propaganda was based on a wide dissemination of some disconcerting facts of India.[112] But the League was single-minded in its work undaunted by sinking enthusiasm in India for civil disobedience. The handouts of the League declared that in 1932, 100,000 persons in India including women and children were sent to prison under hard labour conditions for their political opinions and a large number of them were subjected to harsh treatment and punishments in jail. Referring to the ordinances, then under the law, the League quoted Lansbury's statement in the House of Commons that it was legal in India to make parents responsible for something their children had done, to tell a person not to leave his village and practically to confine people to their residences and to be circumscribed in areas round their homes.[113] Directing people's attention to the violation of the basic human rights, the India League leaflets declared that there were several thousand people in Indian jails or prison camps who had never been tried or charged with any offence. Some of them suffered several years' imprisonment. The ordinances had been enacted as emergency measures but their main provisions were included on the regular law of the land. Even though the civil disobedience was then suspended, albeit temporarily, the spokesmen of the government had declared that the extraordinary provisions of law must remain. Police raids and arrests were taking place though little was heard of them in papers in Britain. All over India, the forces of the empire were set in motion. Bertrand Russell, chairman of the India League, emphasized that although there was no lack of interest in the misdeeds of the Nazis in Germany, and these were fully reported in the press and commented upon 'with self-righteous indignation', few people in Britain realized that similar misdeeds were being perpetrated by the British in India. He also added that a large number of men and women, including many of the highest idealism, were incarcerated without any hope of being brought to trial.[114] At one of the meetings of the League on 20 April 1933, Lansbury declared: 'I stand here this afternoon in defence of the policy that the only people who have the right to settle how India shall be governed are the Indian people themselves.'[115]

The reponse was mixed. At places, such as the Eastbourne branch of the ILP, the organizers entreated Menon to come and enlighten the audience assuring him a hearty welcome, a good meeting, an enjoyable visit to an unprejudiced and attentive assembly and satisfactory hospitality.[116] Several branches of the League, egged on by the Southampton branch, sent a resolution to Hoare urging the government to terminate the reign of terror and suffering then being experienced in India and arrange, as speedily as possible, a meeting with the leaders of Indian opinion.[117] At places, such as the students' union of the London School of Economics and Political Science, the reception was not very amiable. The council of the LSE union declined to host a meeting of the League politely but firmly. 'While appreciating to a considerable extent the objective of your scheme,' Tarlok Singh, secretary of the union, wrote back in response to Menon's request, 'we now feel that we have no place for your plans for the simple reason that our interest in politics is not acute enough to permit us to make active participation in it. For unless that is what the scheme implies, it is meaningless. We have so many immediate objectives in view that we can ill-afford to spare time for matters extraneous to them.'[118]

Although a good deal of interest was detected by E.M. Tuckett, an India enthusiast at Rochester, he somehow failed in his attempts to inspire either the Chatham Anti-War Committee or the United Church to invite Menon to a discussion on India.[119] Some other organizations were more forthright but apologetic. The general secretary of the National Union of Agricultural Workers confided that owing to the circumstances in which the branch secretaries were placed and their 'liability to be victimised' the executive committee had recently made it a rule not to supply their names and addresses to outside organizations in any circumstances whatever.[120] Menon was assured, however, that the inability to assist the League was not to be taken as an indication that 'we are in any way antagonistic to the object of your League'.[121] Expressing sincere gratefulness to a large number of active sympathizers,

Menon extended his invitation to them to join the League as regular members so that the League could take advantage of their goodwill and commitment more effectively.[122] Menon argued that the League was not set on any particular form of constitution for India and it stood for self-determination for India acknowledging the right of that country to complete independence. The India League, he added, was enjoined by its council to support and promote the cause of a government responsible to the people of India and for complete control by the government of all her affairs and for the ability of that government to decide on the nature of the relations that India would prefer to have with Britain.[123] The League recognized that even among those friendly towards Indian aspirations there could be a difference of opinion with regard to the details of Indian constitutional arrangements and other matters. The essence of the League's object and policy was that the relations of Britain with India should rest on free will and that the domination and coercion of India was wrong, inhuman and impolitic and should be opposed. Menon would be glad, he informed all, to answer any specific points on which any one might have any doubt.[124]

Some activists of the 'No More War movement' needed little persuasion to get involved with the India League.[125] So were many local Labour Party units, notwithstanding the expressed diffidence of their central leadership, who excelled in almost proverbial ambiguity in any controversial political issue.[126] The executive of the Labour Party, for example, carefully considered the view of the League to withdraw the party's participation in the RTC and its committees. But it did not think it wise to withdraw participation in the RTC's committees and decided not to commit a tactical and constitutional blunder for the sake of a dubious self-satisfying gesture. In fact, the imperial committee of the Labour Party, on which its experts on India were Henry Polak and Graham

Pole, bulldozed the issue overriding the parliamentary party under Lansbury, Tom Williams and George Hicks.[127] The ILP units everywhere, the Socialist League and the Communist party offered full and undiluted sympathy and support to the League compensating the lack of it elsewhere. There were many who like Ms Pam Kempster felt unhappy that India, despite a good deal of propaganda, did not stir many English people who remained totally innocent and indifferent about India.[128] Somewhat irritated by the constant reference to Hindu-Muslim tension in the media she held boldly that 'anyone who knows our mean double- dealing ways, would know it was engineered'.[129] She realized that large-scale work was very expensive. Sending a sum of £30 as a donation to the League, she hoped that surely, if thousands of English women were forced to read or hear of the horrors in India, they would rise up and demand that they be stopped.[130] There were some others who saw no point in flogging a dead issue. H.N. Marley enquired from Menon if the united efforts of the ILP and the India League were likely 'to influence the work of the Round Table Conferences in any way'. If not, he declined to indulge helplessly in activity for activity's sake.[131]

Many others underlined the absurdity of the Indian situation and the futility of the India League's endeavour. India seemed to them to be a hotbed of all kinds of troubles, social, political and religious and they felt somewhat inadequate to comprehend the implications of the League's work for India's political emancipation.[132] It was added that whilst requiring the need of widespread knowledge of the condition of India among the English people, a strong feeling persisted in many of her well-wishers that there was no evidence of unity amongst the people of India themselves.[133] It was widely circulated by the India League that it had still been actively engaged in continuing to hold meetings all over the country and addressing those organized for them on India. The League was most anxious to arrange for activities in every area and if any initiative was taken by individuals, groups or organizations in the districts the India League would be very glad to help in organizing study circles, schools, conferences, meetings and other forms of propaganda.[134] 'We do not ask for any fee for the speakers we send out,' Menon made the position clear, only 'travelling expenses and hospitality if that is necessary.' If, however, it was possible to take up a collection at the meeting 'towards the funds of the League we are always glad as we are very hard up'.[135]

The publication of the report of the Indian delegation was being delayed largely owing to official manoeuvres and contrivances and the League was obliged to make the necessary explanations.[136] It claimed that the report of the delegation's travel in India from August to November 1932 together with a historical section, without which background the more immediate issues could not fully be understood, had been consuming a good deal of time. The historical section required intensive research of available literature. The indexing and arrangement of an immense amount of documentary material brought over from India could not well have been accomplished in less time by busy people with only scanty leisure to devote to such an immediate task.[137] But the facts that were being presented, Menon wrote, were not out of date. A delegation that had returned from India only in early April 1933 claimed to have seen practically everything that was described in the manuscript of the volume still in operation there.[138] Menon claimed that despite Gandhi's declining interest in civil disobedience, little had changed. Gandhi's fight continued on a low key but government went on with its policy. Millions of Indians found in Gandhi their most trusted and most charismatic spokesman. The government, however was still reluctant to recognize that obvious fact. But the situation indicated in some measure the extent and intensity of resistance and repression. The organization of law and order, Menon maintained, was done in India in contravention of British ideas of law and justice. And yet, the British administrators in India were somewhat sensitive to public opinion in Britain, and protests and action in England might still alter the course of action in India.[139]

The government was not inclined to let the question of international propaganda on India to be left unattended. Speakers were sent over to USA not as official spokesmen but as well-known government supporters.[140] This was being done even on the continent. The core issue of the official propaganda was that the situation in India had altered for the better, the cooperating moderates and threatened minorities had closed their ranks and surged forward with remarkable unison and determined to provide a democratic social cushion to the instruments of law and order, that in popular perception the Congress and the terrorists had become inseparable, perhaps identical, and that civil disobedience had been sliding downhill unaided.[141] Gandhi, a unique combination of apparently irreconcilable contradictions, stood rejected and relegated to the dustbin of history while the government, despite some setbacks, rediscovered its confidence to drive the engine of progress in India. Lord Lytton, ex-governor of Bengal, captured the trend of the dominant British discourse on Gandhi when he eloquently examined the Mahatma's role: 'Gandhi is an idealist who dreams of a most perfect future, but is without the capacity to remedy an imperfect present. A sincere and determined pacifist, he has accepted the leadership of an organization that believed in violence and war.' He was not himself a hater of the British but the only unity amongst his followers was to be found in their social animosities in the conflict within the Hindu community itself.[142] Gandhi was an ardent reformer, Lytton held, and had he confined himself to the task of social reforms for which he was conspicuously endowed, he might have been the greatest Indian of his generation. 'In politics', Lytton added with a contrived air of satisfaction, 'he is always out of his depth and, though his personal character is deeply revered as ever, India has become tired of his policy and of civil disobedience which has only led to violence which he deprecates.'[143] Menon did not allow Lytton go unchallenged. If one had to accept, Menon quipped, Lytton's estimate of the situation, one would like to ask 'what policy Indian nationalism should adopt instead, especially if it is tired of Gandhi's non-violence'. Menon was quick to respond to the ex-governor's hollow sanctimony. He desired to know if the alternative to the Gandhian method would suit Lytton's book as his experience of Bengal must have reminded him.[144]

By the time the Joint Select Committee (JSC) was summoned in April 1933, it was clear that the moderates had been gloating in their greatness and they had as usual overestimated their importance in Indian politics and in official estimation. It was self-evident to all discerning observers that the JSC would water down the white paper proposals. In the committee, the government would be obliged to accept compromises and in these synthetic agreements the Indians would have no say. Hoare said in Parliament little beyond what he proposed to do to satisfy his friends in India 'by which he means', Menon wrote, 'not Saprus and Jayakars but the Europeans and the Muslims and the anti-Brahmin section that cooperates with the government'.[145] Menon detected that the debate in the House of Commons was a clear 'indication of a complete change in policy' especially when Hoare affirmed that he would not swallow the plans of the Labour government. Evidently, a significant change was in the offing in the programme of the government.

The *Morning Post* had been running a campaign not to rush the princes. It had a correspondent in India who was, Menon thought, 'even more morning post that *Morning Post* itself'.[146] It was generally doled out that the Patiala party was gathering strength and that the princes then realized that they were being coerced into the federation business and they decided to carefully watch Churchill's opposition.[147] It looked as though the die-hards would make common cause with the *Jam-Patiala* faction supported by the extreme sections among the Muslims for whom they were financing a mosque and a club on Carlton Terrace. An Anglo-Muslim-Prince alliance, Menon thought, would be used to create an impression on the waverers on the Tory benches and drive them into the field of the die-hards.[148] It was reported from New Delhi that the Mahasabha, the dominant section of the Muslim League and the officials were neither hostile nor indifferent to Churchill and the die-hard campaign. On the contrary, they were inclined to do what was desirable to terminate the National Government's scheme for federation with central responsibility. Menon was quite convinced that government was in all essentials not opposed to the die-hards. All that the government had been doing was, to 'let them do the barking while they do the biting'.[149]

It appeared that the Tory plan was to use the House of Lords to the full to pare down the bill. The house would be an active agent in the matter and India might dispense with all illusion about there being a bill that would lead to dominion status whatever that phrase meant. All the talk of Sapru about adopting the tactics of de Valera, Menon wrote, 'is sheer nonsense' since the 'new constitution will not permit of this'.[150] It would be interesting, Menon added, to know whether 'the Allahabad Knight' would be willing to 'approve de Valera's sticking to his guns'. Was he really true to him, Menon asked tongue-in-cheek, 'when he said that his opposite number was de Valera and not Mr Cosgrave'?[151] Menon thought that the legality and sanctity of agreement worried Sapru as they did Cosgrave.

Menon noted that it was interesting to observe that imperial policy was given to manipulate every section of Indian opinion in its favour. The participation of the Parsis in the nationalist movement of late came as a surprise to some of their former friends in Britain.[152] The part that the community had been taking in the new life of India instead of confining their activities to such movements as were patronized by officials and Europeans, provoked many questions. In some circles in Manchester the Parsi was attacked. He was described as a complete exploiter whose one object was to 'sweat the Indian masses' with whom he had nothing in common.[153] It was, the local press held with aplomb, necessary in the interest of those masses for whom Britain was trustee, to limit his ambition and exploiting power. The Indian tariffs to keep out British goods and the subsidy given to the firms of Tatas and the cotton magnates of Bombay must be stopped. In contrast, a somewhat less vociferous school of thought had been planning a commercial mission to India to negotiate terms with the Parsis. The assumption was that the best plan would be to rope in some of the Indian leaders who would be willing to play the game. Menon thought that such an ingenious game plan to manipulate the various social forces in India was probably rather too late in the day.[154]

The India League realized that the official responses to Indian aspirations were reflected in the attitude of the government towards Indian students. The National Union of Students (NUS) of Great Britain and Ireland called a special delegate conference in mid-February 1933 at Welwyn Garden City to discuss the problems arising out of the presence of Indian students at British universities.[155] Discrimination with regard to admission to colleges, hostels, officers training corps, and in social life, the presence on the staff and in the capacity of advisers of men who had been ex-Indian officials and men who had spent the best part of their lives in the police or espionage services, had lately attracted the attention of the student body.[156] On the other hand, the conservative section of the NUS and the Tories who financed it, were anxious to be generous to the Indian students so that they felt proud of the empire and did not lapse into extremism. On the council of NUS there were some brilliant English students who were incensed at the treatment meted out to their fellow students who happened to be Indians.[157] The High Commissioner for India and his staff were not too friendly towards the Indians and they often came in for some caustic references at students' conferences. Officials often discussed with Tory politicians various stratagems to work out a plausible scheme of sending a British students' team to India to fraternize with their Indian counterparts. The radical students had been demanding that such a team would be selected by the student bodies and it would have nothing to do with the Indian government and its hospitality, British residents and officials in India. An area of academic resistance to imperial manoeuvres had been growing directly in response to the ongoing India propaganda.[158]

Ellen Wilkinson was an enthusiastic and acerbic orator with a stupendous public image in a world distinguished by a left-wing swing and hunger marches. Her intense loyalty to socialist and democratic principles, integrity, courage, strength of emotions and sheer vitality of personality gave Wilkinson a great influence in left-wing circles. She was one of the League's principal spokespersons. Early in February 1933, she addressed a packed meeting of several hundred at the Dome at Brighton, on India, and did some plain speaking about terrorism practised by the police in India. Her statements about Willingdon were resented by a group of vociferous British blackshirts who were present. But the audience, mostly middle-class and even conservative men and women, were indignant about the alleged state of affairs prevalent in India.[159] Similar meetings addressed by Wilkinson, Krishna Shelvankar, Menon, Whately, Platts Mills, Michael Foot, James Marley and other members of the League were held at various places through political organizations in each locality. They were subjected to a consistent press boycott and little appeared in the newspapers.

The Meerut prisoners' case received a good deal of publicity during the unemployment demonstrations.[160] As against these, there was a mass of anti-Indian and anti-Congress propaganda being carried on all over by the Indian Empire Society, India Defence League and others. Louis Stuart, Hugh Molson MP, Reginald Craddock and Lord Lloyd were some of the Conservative propagandists.

The atmosphere of financial uncertainty and misgivings at the Strand office was to some extent relieved by encouraging communications from sincere friends. D.V. Giri, a medical practitioner from Eastbourn, was, for example, in agreement with the League that the continuation of ordinance rule by other means merely stressed the importance of a vigorous campaign in Britain.[161] His personal view of effective propaganda was that the British should be made to realize that continuance of repression and withholding of full autonomy in India was a boomerang, which would, in the end, do more harm to Britain than to India. It did not require an extraordinary perception to realize that the Indian had every right to be master in his own house. It was the man in the street in England who should be convinced that he was the one that would be hit worst by the policy of the British government in India. Giri was one of the many who had made their home in England. From long years of intimate contact with the people he learnt to love them and esteem their qualities of head and heart and desired ardently to see happy relations established without further delay between the two countries.[162]

By the end of the month a significant event with specific Indian interest attracted Menon's attention. The people of Ireland responded to the call of Éamon de Valera and gave him a majority. In a London Letter, Menon wrote that the victory was all the more significant, because a good deal of intrigue and threat failed and the Irish stood firmly behind their leader in his efforts to rid that country of British domination. English hopes centred in the return of Cosgrave and all the English papers spoke of an inevitable Cosgrave victory. That hope was dashed by the event. Since the Irish model was then talked about in relation to India, Menon sought to identify some of its essential features. De Valera, he wrote, was one of the most honest of living men.[163] As a politician he was comparable to Gandhi in his regard for his followers, in the purity of his personal life and in the straightforwardness of his dealing. Like the Mahatma, he was a lover of peace and compromise, though the imperial world looked on both of them as uncompromising and unreasonable persons. The followers of de Valera, like the membership of the Congress consisted of a mixed group. There were rich and poor, liberals and socialists, the religious and the rationalists. Like the Congressmen they were all self-respecting, patriotic and devoted to the reconstruction of their country. They believed in the destiny of people to rule themselves and refused to be bluffed by the British. De Valera carried his similarity to Gandhi a step further in his dealing with the left wing.[164] The Mahatma made his phrase, *purna swaraj,* cover the aspirations of the independence school and those committed to full dominion status. De Valera, Menon added, had been reluctant to commit himself during the elections to a republic but talked of a free and self-reliant Ireland electing the form of government it desired. Politically de Valera might compromise with the acceptance of some form of allegiance to the British crown if, as a result, he could obtain Irish unity.[165] Unless the Irish could regain the six northern counties and build up a united state of 32 counties they could not look forward to prosperity since the best industrial part of Ireland was in the six counties. De Valera was therefore desirous of reserving for himself some power of bargaining with the British and Menon maintained that he was wise in doing this. Flexibility in non-essentials but firmness in fundamentals constituted, in his view, the essence of statesmanship.[166]

Menon had added to his instinctive Indian sensibilities during his prolonged active public life in Britain a distinct attachment to democratic perceptions. His humanist sentiments did not make any essential difference between freedom and social justice. Over the years, he developed a firm faith in the British ideal of freedom and became a conscious admirer of Britain's stimulating public opinion. He happened to feel instinctively, complete equality with every human being with whom he came into contact. But, even colleagues and acquaintances were not entitled to indulgence when there were conflicts of needs, principles and priorities, and even egos. He could prove that he did not respect rank and could lose his temper as violently with the high and mighty, as with the subordinate and the unfortunate. His tactlessness in dealing with individuals was duly compensated by his unusually alert instinct, his discriminating sense of history, his finely-tuned fund of principles, theories, perceptions, contexts and processes of life, and his endless hunger for knowledge and self-improvement. All these were suitably marinated by a childlike simplicity under his thin, but disturbingly tough exterior.[167] Even to a close acquaintance, Menon would often seem strange indeed, until one penetrated the shell he made to protect his vivid personality and 'one came to know him for an affectionate, devoted creature'.[168]

In Menon's political calculations, strategic and tactical considerations played a crucial role. By then he was convinced that the British government was as determined as ever to carry out its proposals of a constitution for India. All questions of amnesty and cooperation with the Congress had receded into the background. Sankey had been working on the details of the constitution and irrespective of the attitude of the Congress, the Government of India Bill would be passed by the houses and the new Act would be introduced. It was still the conviction of the government that the bulk of the Congress would gradually cooperate and work the reforms, much as the *Swaraj* party had come into being to work the Montagu reforms. Menon seemed convinced that government was inclined to think that it could afford to start the operation of the constitution with the help of the cooperators. He was veering round to accept the construction that the government was too keen to ensure the support of Tej Bahadur Sapru and accommodate his ideas in the formulation of the provincial governments.[169] The federation would be inoperative until at least half the princes came into it. Sankey was keen to establish the federation partly because he took a personal pride in the constitution.[170] Samuel Hoare had also become a convert largely because he did not see any harm in supporting endoring a federal constitution in which all effective powers were reserved in British hands.[171] The policy of the government during the preceding few months had been to encourage the princes to join the federation. The government appeared to be of the opinion that in almost all the provinces the constitution could be worked and that Congress' non-cooperation would certainly be largely ineffective. In any case, the bulk of the spirited and ardent elements of the Congress would remain in prison and the new constitution would be brought into being with the New Public Safety Act 'as its chaperon'. Menon added caustically that this was what 'the great minds of the Whitehall appeared to be thinking'.[172] Rumours were then current in London, that plans for a newspaper from the Punjab had been discussed by a high-profile gentleman of that province, with a few prominent British friends who were disposed to assist. The support of the Muslims, it was believed, was assured and a serious effort was being made to seek the cooperation of the Sikhs and the Hindus. If the attempt succeeded, Menon thought, it was unlikely that similar efforts would not be made in other parts of India. He was convinced that the British tactics during the recent Irish elections lent colour to that belief.[173]

Meanwhile, the correspondent of the *Daily Mail* informed its readers as a part of official counter-propaganda, that the people of India were almost inordinately happy and that the ordinary Indian he saw everywhere in India was well-fed and that he was not in any way touched by the agitations that were reported to be going on.[174] The only work of usefulness undertaken by the Indians, otherwise unworthy of any honourable enterprise, was the Ramakrishna Mission school in Madras which, the correspondent reported, was a marvellous effort since the pupils were as clean, polite and well behaved as those of any English school.[175] Menon felt that Ward Price, the correspondent, would soon be presented in the country as an authority on India and on that authority it would be asserted that the British *Raj* was well loved and fondly desired by the Indians. What Price had to say about the various undesirable qualities of Indians, Menon wrote, was not fit to print. Price had probably read *Mother India*, Menon quipped, 'before he left this country', and 'this is how they educate public opinion over here'.[176]

India kept parliament active. During the second half of February, for example, 48 questions were discussed in the House of Commons. Of the three classes of questions, the first came from the Tory bench who sought to criticize the government for going too fast and not supporting the firm hand. The second set came from the Labour bench about the administration of ordinances and the Meerut case, and some came from all quarters on administrative problems of non-political character. The parliamentary committee of the India League was active and the questions on ordinances and repression constituted their particular area of specialization though putting down of these questions was by no means an easy matter. It was believed that one of the factors that made India important was the world depression. Tory members had been harnessing their political armoury to find out whether they could find ways and means to make India pay for Britain's troubles, but they were faced with the fact that the depression had made things very difficult for the Indian government itself.[177]

On 26 February Menon's London Letter for *Pratap* began with a sensational headline that read: 'The battle has begun.' Menon cautioned that the real significance of the parliamentary debate should not be overlooked. There was not one speech, including that of Hoare, which was very different from that of the die-hard. This was merely the first skirmish in the battle and only a preliminary trial. The forces of reaction had been organizing and government, Menon believed, would yield to their pressure not unwillingly. It seemed the whole die-hard programme had been planned out meticulously. The campaign to obtain a bill, which did not pass very much beyond the Simon report, was to be kept up in the House of Commons. Meanwhile at the annual conference of the Conservative Party, resolutions were being framed. The India Committee was to be gingered up and a formula was to be forged, whereby the government would have to face all the opposition in the JSC and agree to a reactionary bill unless it was prepared to face a defeat on the floor of the house. It was clear that the JSC was to decide the norm and it must agree to a compromise. To facilitate the situation Lord Lloyd would be on it and so would Winterton.[178] If the proposal was not modified sufficiently to suit the substance of the die-hard demands, it would not pass the House of Lords and the government would be forced to fall back on the Indian liberals whose support might be forthcoming in ample measure, although one was uncertain if that would be effective.

Two important facts of the debate of early February were highlighted: forty-two members voted against the party whip, but no action was taken against them, while Hoare did not categorically refuse the demand for a 'free and unfettered vote'. Secondly, the debate was stage-managed while Labour amendments were not allowed. The real battle of the die-hards was being fought in the India Committee, a parliamentary committee of the Conservative Party. Though not an official body but a right-wing committee of the party, it had always supported Churchill, and Samuel Hoare always looked on this committee more or less as the advisory body in the Conservative Party on India. The large volume of feelings on this body of about 150 members was distinctively apprehensive of, if not antagonistic, to all forms of reform.[179] Although the Conservative Party was very different from the conservative parties of the continent, which were often violently reactionary, indifferent and even hostile to democracy and social progress, the British party had its roots in the support of the Crown, the Church and the Constitution. It cannot be denied that between the Wars some Conservatives were deeply distressed by their party's attitude to economic and social affairs and insisted that the party listened to the voice of conscience. But it appeared that the die-hards began to argue that the reformers were the real menace. They had lost all touch with reality which they sought to debunk. Conservative scepticism, with its emphasis on man's imperfections and its useful insight into man's limitations, tended to metamorphose into illiberal reaction and ran the risk of becoming an ideology in its own right.

It was true that the question of staying away from the JSC had been exercising the minds of some of the Labour rank and file. Bertrand Russell had been fighting in the party for non-cooperation with the government. Tom Williams, probably the most sensitive and brilliant man in the small parliamentary party and parliamentary secretary of the India League, called together his colleagues to a meeting to which Menon was invited and asked to speak. The brief narrative of the Indian constitutional struggle was deeply impressive and James Marley, another invitee, was agreeably surprised to find at the end of the meeting that members requested Menon to come over and address them again. The real purpose of the meeting was to assist the party to make up its mind intelligently on the forthcoming issue of participation in the joint committee.[180]

It became increasingly clear that the initiative rested entirely and solely with the British side. Even as early as 11 February 1933, Menon assessed the strength of the revolt in the Conservative Party over the reform proposals and felt that it was more than a storm in the teapot. The final Act that would emerge from parliament, he thought, would fall far short of the expectations of Sapru and his friends and even those of Hoare. The agitation of the backbenches had been gathering momentum. Lord Salisbury's speech in the House of Lords was an indication of the level and intensity of the campaign and mobilization.[181] It appeared that more than a hundred Conservatives in the House of Commons had pledged to oppose any measure that had been designed to go further than the Simon report. The revolt might lead to a bid for leadership at the national level under a combination of Amery, Winterton and Churchill, who were experts in the parliamentary game, backed by Simon and Hailsham within the cabinet, with the moral support of J.H. Thomas and Cunliffe Lister, while Samuel Hoare who was already on the run would save himself.[182] Menon found in Hoare's letters to his constituency an eagerness to emphasize that his policy was an undiluted Conservative endeavour.[183] The *Times,* the *Yorkshire Post* and the *Scotsman* between them covered the whole country and were truly the mouthpieces of the bulk of Conservative opinion. They expressed with remarkable unison, that the Willingdon policy had succeeded and the constitution would be worked by the Indians.[184] It was maintained by the *Times* and the *Yorkshire Post* that Willingdon was a strong man who betrayed no signs of flagging or faintheartedness while facing problems with courage and statesmanship.[185]

The *Scotsman* went a step further. It asserted that civil disobedience had been waning, that Gandhi could no longer obtain funds, that Hindus were split over untouchability and the country was refusing to follow the Mahatma. The *Scotsman* assured its readers that a 'genuine and extensive transfer of power' would not take place and the 'introduction of the new constitution' would 'make a non-cooperative policy suicidal'.[186] Thus, with the Muslims satisfied, the Liberals sobered, the untouchables assured and the Congress dispirited, all seemed safe in India. News about the decision of the Congress to call a conference to discuss the continuance of the movement received wide publicity, while Jam Saheb, who had turned into an important ally of the die-hards, insisted that the interests of the princes should be considered seriously by the government before settling for central responsibility. Menon thought that the Indian participants should count no more in its work than the members of the Indian central committee had done in the forming of the opinions of the Simon commission, or in the discussion on the report afterwards.[187] There was a gradual but steady drift of British public opinion towards Churchill. That group lost the narrow character of a die-hard revolt of disgruntled backbenchers in the parliamentary Tory party, assisted by a few retired reactionary civilians.[188] On the contrary, it became over time, a rank and file Conservative revolt against Baldwinism. Menon anticipated no straight fight between official leadership and the rank and file on the issue. He was convinced that it would not lead to a displacement of the existing leadership.[189] The difference between Hoare and Churchill, he maintained, was, in substance, minute and technical. Menon thought that it was interesting to note that the Conservatives of Bewedly, Baldwin's constituency, had already been demanding a revision of the government's India policy 'a la Churchill'.[190]

Menon knew that it was difficult to make clear to the Indians the relation between the official policy and the Churchill revolt. To suggest that Churchill had been playing the government's game would be untrue, but it would be equally, if not more, untrue to assert that the government regarded him and the forces that he had aroused as 'rank opportunist'.[191] Churchill, Menon held, had hitherto been a convenience of the government. Irwinism, he added, promoted Baldwinism 'to move in phases towards counsels of moderation and progress' and the whole process was solely the 'result of Indian pressure'. Similarly, Irwinism and Baldwinism, so far as India was concerned, would be prepared to 'move equally towards the right if the pressure is strong enough'. This was what Churchill had been contributing.[192] Meanwhile, the whole press of the country had been devoting all its attention in the preparation of the setting.

The principal daily newspapers, with the exception of the *News*, the *Chronicle*, the *Manchester Guardian* (all liberal) and the lurching *Daily Herald,* were all confirmed Tory in interest, outlook and presentation. The press barons, Rothermere *(Daily Mail)* and Beaverbrook *(Daily Express),* were unable to appreciate Baldwin's inclination for the so-called British virtue of compromise, his 'simple moral eloquence' and his affiliation to the best features of 'nineteenth century Anglican Christianity', and were bitterly hostile to the leadership of the Conservative Party. But both of them were high-powered imperialists and opposed vehemently to all socialist proclivities and concessions to Indian nationalism.[193] Menon emphasized that the official side had also an ally in the BBC and in the various 'respectable movements of Christians and other enlightened imperialists'. The government policy was being paraded as the expression of Britain's good faith. Equally disturbing was the fact that even in some of the radical press it was believed that the white paper would ultimately be accepted by responsible opinion in India.[194] The *New Statesman* under Kingsley Martin represented anti-imperialist opinion. However, the journal's views, Menon maintained, had been coloured by experts who were ex-civil servants who had somehow appropriated for themselves the title of being pro-Indian.[195] The *Manchester Guardian* was much in the same category. An ex-civilian and another person, who was arch-imperialist though he occasionally chastised a few English officials, were its experts. C.F. Andrews got a word in, though infrequently, but for the rest of its information it relied on imperialist sources. The *Time and Tide,* Lady Rhonda's paper, claimed to be independent. Its Indian side was advised by an ex-Indian police official who had a great deal to do with the government's information service in India.[196]

As leading exponents of the empirical tradition, the Conservative Party was not frightfully perturbed to proceed with a modest advance in Indian reform. Menon knew fairly well that young men with the right educational background, however unhappy and critical they might be of the party leadership, would still, by and large go into the Conservative Party. This was the party which enjoyed the tradition of ruling and which seemed to them most likely to go on ruling. In a sense, the Conservatives had over the decades, constituted the foundation of the British ruling class, and despite conflicts of authority within the Conservative Party, it was the logic of expediency and compromise that guided it. True, the party had to encounter various vested interests and often there was tension between the old regime and new recruits. But, if there were limits to the resistance of the younger element, there were also the attractions of the established elite. The challenge of the die-hards and the demands of the liberal elements were met either by dignified retreat on the part of parties concerned or by careful adjustments. Distinguished by privileges, wealth and revering birth-rights and prepared to admit commoners, the Conservative Party was imbued with the belief that it had, like the crown, a special role to play in running the empire. By and large, this conviction of the Conservatives remained unimpaired despite the challenge posed by the rise and consolidation of the labour movement. This basic faith sustained the traits, habits and prejudices of British conservatism. In spite of the intense hostility of the die-hards towards Baldwin, he could, in the final analysis, depend on the hierarchical instinct inculcated at the great public schools that ensured loyalty, the secret weapon of the Conservatives.[197] The net result of the British political chemistry was that everywhere the belief that at last a solution to the Indian problem had been found in the white paper proposals gained ground. Sapru, and to a lesser degree, Sastri were largely responsible for the mistaken impression. The participation of Sapru on the joint committee had been a foregone conclusion. It was apparent to Menon even before Sapru left for India in December 1932 that he would come back 'without entering his caveat about government decision'.[198]

The impression left on the British radical mind, Menon observed, might be grasped by quoting the *New Statesman*'s interpretation of Sapru's attitude. 'Men like Sir Tej Bahadur Sapru,' it said, 'have also recognised that the white paper does, in spite of glaring defects, offer a constitutional advance, and have agreed to take their place on the Joint Committee and to see what they can do to make a workable constitution.' It would not be an exaggeration to affirm, Menon commented, that 'the majority of even our friends here think in their innermost minds that even Congress will work the constitution'.[199] They had been led to think that by the attitudes of Sapru, regarded as a liberal, Pheroz Sethna, a fighting representative of Indian commerce, and Rangaswamy Iyengar who, most people think, was coming to the committee at the convenience of the Congress. The official policy, they believed, would triumph at the end and that all the denunciation in the nationalist press could be ignored as sheer bluff. The view, Menon claimed, was strengthened by the policy of the Congress in exploiting the legislatures for untouchability legislation, the collapse of civil resistance, the absence of a fighting lead from anyone and the silence of a constitutionalist Congressman like Malaviya. India was, for the moment, 'comparatively quiescent'.[200]

Menon believed that the confrontation in the JSC would not be between Indians of different persuasions on the one side and the British on the other. On the contrary, it would essentially be between the die-hards and the government. In this friendly contest, neither party would seek to knock the other out.[201] A drawn bout or a compromise would only mean cold storage for the bill. It might also mean that the committee report would dilute the recommendations of the white paper.[202] Menon was convinced that the Labour members on the committee would be encouraged by Sapru and, to a lesser degree, by N.M. Joshi to keep their mouths shut even if they could otherwise be persuaded to speak out'.[203] He felt that the work would be unrelated to the RTC and to a certain extent removed from the white paper and the Indian participants would make no impression at all on the proceedings. Menon implored Sapru to make it abundantly clear that the discussions in the committee were a breach of the statements made in 1931, that they did not represent agreements, that they violated the declaration of 1917 and that their outcome would not satisfy India. Sapru's failure to say this had already created the false impression that the Congress was only biding its time before it fell into line.[204] The government's policy in the eyes of even its opponents represented a significant constitutional advance, the onus of whose rejection would fall on India and no one would believe that India either desired it or dared it. It was, however, held that probably Labour participation on the committee was no longer doubtful.[205] In case the government had released prisoners and sought Congress cooperation, such participation would have been forthcoming. It was hoped that in view of the government's knock-out policy, the Labour Party might still be induced to maintain its relative independence. Constitutionally, Indians should not be able to find places in the committee.[206] Some of them might be invited by the government as assessors. Witnesses would be chosen by the government. The terms of reference of the committee would be pretty rigid and the function of the committee would be to implement the government scheme which would be issued before the appointment of the committee and the debate in parliament.[207]

Menon was certain that British imperialism had been distinguished by its sophisticated internal mechanism and its subtlities. The attempt to coerce India into buying Lancashire goods, which was the function of the newly formed Cotton League, was supported by the Manchester chamber of commerce. Kenneth Lee, one of the leading cotton merchants of Manchester, the India League noted, disagreed with that policy and delivered a scathing indictment of the chamber's inane and pesky attitude in adopting a resolution which called for the use of political power in India to capture markets for Lancashire.[208] Making a general reference to the temper and spirit of Indian nationalism, he pointed out the danger of attempting to build trade on any but a commercial basis. Political weapons, he argued with a good deal of sense, worked like a boomerang and while they appeared serviceable in the immediate run, the reaction in the long run was harmful as it would recoil on its originator.[209]

Menon took special care to look into the nitty-gritty of the liberal dilemma in Britain. With the Labour Party poaching into the traditional Liberal vote and the Conservatives consolidating their hold over the upper class interests, the Liberal party found that its catchment area had been shrinking. There was no significant socio-economic grouping to bank upon. Besides, the war destroyed its leader, Asquith, while Lloyd George was reduced, primarily due to lack of commitment, to the position of the leader of a parliamentary rump. And yet some of the most constructive thinkers came from the Liberals such as J.M. Keynes and H.D. Henderson, both economists; Ramsay Muir and Philip Guedella, both historians; William Beveridge, pioneer of Edwardian social reform; Ted Scott, journalist and E.D. Simon, businessman and politician, who launched the Liberal summer schools as a means towards scientific analysis of social problems.[210] It was observed that Herbert Samuel was being challenged on his liberalism by his own followers. The Liberals in the country seemed totally opposed to the conduct of their parliamentary spokesmen in supporting the government.[211] The parliamentary party, however, had so far taken the view that government policy should be supported on every matter except tariffs. The decision was partly due to the commitments of the Liberals while they were in the government team and to the fact that their place in the Commons was dependent on Tory votes. The radical stance of the local parties would thus make no difference to the Liberal policy on India. Although the *Manchester Guardian* hinted that the government's policy was a denial of liberalism, it was made clear that the parliamentary party would support the Hoare policy and the rank and file would be prevailed upon to fall in line with it.[212]

Meanwhile, the National government had been living from crisis to crisis, each of which it had attempted to solve by a conference, and at each time it acclaimed its efforts as a success. It held out that prosperity was always round the corner. But the truth was then forced into the open.[213] After World War I, British economy and society never regained the relative stability and confidence of pre-war days. It had been optimistically hoped that the turbulence in the industries would gradually die away as production and trade returned to normal peace-time rhythm. Prosperity of the United States was quoted as an example of the success of capitalism when associated with modern mass production technology. But unemployment reached a figure of just under three million, or about 23 per cent, of the insured workers by the beginning of 1933.[214] It was followed by recession and there was a growing feeling that realities did not reflect merely an ephemeral upshot of certain incidental maladjustments in the economy but denoted a fatal disease of capitalism.[215] Poverty in the midst of plenty was an overwhelming fact of life. The overtures of MacDonald and some other leaders to the Conservatives and the emergence of Mond-Turnerism meant Conservatives led or dominated governments for the rest of the decade.[216] Britain, however, was still the centre of the greatest empire the world had seen, though it was an empire in which tensions, stresses and fissures were beginning to manifest. It embraced 500 million people of which 430 million were subject colonial peoples including 360 million in India. And India was in a state of non-violent insurrection and the government was compelled to forgo all references to British liberal traditions.[217]

Menon thought that the government's policy of economy in the salaries of its servants and school teachers tended only to aggravate the depression because the government was no longer afraid of a parliamentary defeat. This was a strange phenomenon as in Britain, parliamentary sovereignty was more than a matter of legal phraseology.[218] The country and parliament, he reported, were no longer *en rapport,* and the government tended of late to deal with parliament with a high hand. It appeared to some concerned intellectuals that democracy was at stake. The struggle for liberty had become once more a vital issue. Political movements not disinclined to use violent methods had been spreading. Liberal intellectuals began to move towards communism. Unemployment, stark realities of British domestic life, old age insecurities and large families depending on meagre incomes created an embittered society with desperate resentments. Menon noticed the impact of a wide popular base of political parties, permanence or continuity of political organizations, the growth of party discipline and the rise of small influential cliques in or about government or at the head of the party machine to guide and direct great masses of electors. Authoritarianism was the order of the day all over. The 'tendency of today,' Menon argued, 'is towards a parliamentary despotism,' which was not 'far different from fascism'.[219] Menon echoed the opinion of a substantial section of the radical left when he emphasized that from that position to a dictatorship was merely a short cut. Democratic form might still be retained, but power had been gradually but definitely passing away from parliament.[220]

Calling for the restoration of calm, goodwill and reconstruction, the India League mobilized about two dozen signatures from public men of liberal persuasion having profound commitment to the methods of conciliation in a statement issued to the people of Britain through the columns of the *Manchester Guardian*.[221] The signatories clarified that a congenial atmosphere could not be obtained so long as Gandhi and thousands of his supporters remained in prison. Their detention, it was maintained, compelled a large part of Indian public opinion to look unfavourably upon any proposal made by the government. It minimized the possibility of cooperation and maximized the difficulty of implementing in practice any proposal embodied in an act of parliament.[222] The existing political impasse compelled great masses of people to concentrate attention upon grievances which needed to be given the highest importance in the proceedings. The signatories also supported the appeal of Sapru, whose moderate opinion was well known, to release Gandhi and his associates as a gesture of goodwill vital to the future of the relationship between the two peoples. It would be a token of 'creative generosity', calculated to help the humane and reasonable spirit triumph in Indo-British affairs. Refusal to be magnanimous in the face of impending events, it was added, would be 'the revelation of a blindness to their significance, pregnant with tragic results'.[223] The signatories included Bertrand Russell, Harold Laski, C.F. Andrews, George Lansbury, Stafford Cripps, James Marley, A.D. Belden, Ellen Wilkinson, G. D. H. Cole and Susan Lawrence.

In another public communication, Bertrand Russell, as chairperson of the League, held that the Government of India continued to remain the ally of social reaction. The viceroy, Russell maintained, sought safety in procrastination.[224] It was the insistence of Gandhi and his followers that had compelled Willingdon to retreat one step on the question of untouchability. The government's antipathy to social reform, however, was evident in the viceroy's statement which permitted the Indian legislatures to discuss a measure to remove the disabilities of the 'untouchable' and, at the same time, insisted on proclaiming that the government would not be bound by the decisions of the legislatures. Meanwhile, Russell pointed out that the bill for enabling the 'untouchable' to enter temples in Madras was disallowed on the ground that the question was an all-India one.[225] But in Madras, the legal power for preventing 'untouchables' from entering temples was derived from the Hindu Religious Endowment Act of the province. That act was not in any way an all-India measure. Thus, Russell maintained, the government's attitude merely confirmed his expressed views that it had been impeding social reform with spurious arguments.[226]

In the face of an almost ceaseless campaign against India and her aspirations, Menon organized a counterblast. Letters to the editors of the leading dailies by Menon and a few activists were meant to supplement the impact of meetings and conferences. In reply to a leader in the *Eastern Daily Press,* Menon drew the attention of the editor to the fort that L.J. Glendenning, one of its India experts, had accused the India League of having given a completely one-sided picture in its presentations on the Indian situation and of having suppressed facts.[227] Contesting the claim of the writer, Menon substantiated the League's position with authentic information based on official statistics, extensive interaction and shrewd observations. As against the comment of Glendenning that the poverty of the Indian peasantry was due to the religion of the Hindus and their conspicuous extravagance on weddings and funerals and because they did not kill off cattle, Menon questioned the reasons for the poverty of the Muslims of the Punjab, Bengal and the NWFP, not to mention the smaller Muslim groups elsewhere, especially when it took no special effort to find that they did not treat the cow as sacred or money on funerals. He doubted the assertion that the Indian administration had spent substantial by contributed towards improving a poor breed of cattle.[228] It was common knowledge, Menon added, that the East India Company brought in a good deal of pasture lands under existing proprietorship, which was supplemented by rigorous forest laws and these measures were directly responsible for inadequate pasture for cattle. Indeed, 'Indians hope that when they have control of government', Menon averred confidently, 'this matter will receive attention and perhaps we shall spend more money on tractors than on armoured cars.'[229]

With regard to Glendenning's contention that taxes were lighter under the British *Raj,* Menon maintained that this was stated in various works of Englishmen and, more often than not, the Indians of a previous generation uncritically accepted that proposition. Menon held that on the contrary the fact was that in the pre-British days taxes were largely realized in kind and they formed a proportion of the net produce. The proportion looked larger than in the British calculation which was on gross produce. The existing system threw the peasants into the hands of moneylenders, the state providing no means for extensive credit to the small peasantry.[230] With regard to the famine code, Menon held that since officials alone were judges of what famine was, it could not be said that the state stepped in to feed the hungry. In any case, famine relief methods were a 'crude, wasteful, uneconomical and undesirable form of state charity', which did not strike at the root of the problem. As against Glendenning's claims that cholera, plague and malaria had been stamped out, Menon pointed out that the official figures of 1930 recorded a million deaths in India from malaria, two million people maimed and 50 million affected by the scourge.[231] Indian plague was a disease of the modern towns. The slums, the products of modern industry unchecked by legislative protection, had created intolerable conditions as in the *chawls* of Bombay and Ahmedabad, the *cheris* of Madras and the *bastis* of Calcutta.[232]

Menon contested the assertion that Indian prosperity was built up by British skill and enterprise. He thought that it was an extravagant surmise and this argument was essentially *non-sequitur,* which even the 'thinking section of imperialists' would 'refrain from using'. He maintained that capital flowed into India because it found an adequate return. India being a subject country, the rulers could follow a policy of exploitation without any compunction. It was not until 1912 or so that the first effort was made by the Indian government to consider the question of Indian industrial reconstruction. No British money, he argued, had ever been invested in India out of motives of charity but 'they were gilt edged securities, often generated on the revenues of India'.[233] If Pax Britannica, Menon wrote, 'secured any advantages for such investments these advantages accrued primarily to the British capitalists and not to the people of India'. The real 'prosperity' of India would become apparent, Menon added, when it was realized that the country with an average income of two and half pence per head of the population carried something like nine million pounds of national debt, all contracted since the British occupation and spent nearly 60 per cent of her revenues in the maintenance of an expensive foreign army while the total expenditure in India on agriculture and industry together was not more than two per cent. Menon presumed that he should be appreciated for trying to remove a few of the misconception and prejudices that existed even in the minds of honest British people resulting from decades of imperialist propaganda.[234]

The situation at the Strand office was almost desperate. Financially, the League was at its lowest ebb. Communications from Menon, Wilkinson and Bertrand Russell to Malaviya had been unacknowledged.[235] It was feared that his replies had probably been waylaid. Menon heard that government had driven in the last nail. The release of Gandhi and others was no longer the prospect that it was thought to be when the Sapru crowd left.[236] Politically, the atmosphere was very dark. Indian witnesses were expected to arrive in London early in May. The Special Powers Act would continue and elections would be held under 'peaceful' conditions.[237] The proposed constitution was the only thing that even progressives cared about. In an interview with Sankey lasting an hour and a half, it was evident to all the members of the League's delegation that in his mind '*his* constitution was the only thing that matters'.[238] There was no room for an attempt at conciliation in any way and even a calamity of national proportion such as the quake in Bihar did not deflect the government from its concentration on the constitution. It was, by and large, expected that the Congress would gradually, but surely, acquiesce. Malaviya's silence under these circumstances appeared fairly conspicuous.[239]

Unsure of the situation, Menon felt that probably there might have been an misunderstanding between the two of them. Menon had sent Malaviya the *India Review* accounts soon after his return as was desired by him. He had become somewhat sceptical about continuing his connection with the India League whose credibility in British politics, he thought, was negligible and whose support for the Indian struggle was perhaps of marginal importance.[240] The paper had been suspended due to a lack of funds and Menon thought that it was very unfortunate especially when there was so much misrepresentation in Britain about the questions concerning unity and the untouchables. According to the British press, the unity effort was a manoeuvre of the Malaviya family to assume leadership. It appeared that the Gandhi side was in alliance with Nehru and wanted independence, while the Malaviyas were satisfied with dominion status. Menon felt that probably the role played by the Malaviya family in the unity effort and their desire for an agreed plan on the dominion status was the basis of press speculations.[241] Indian propaganda was hampered as the League was penniless. Menon was unhappy that his trip to India had resulted in his losing even the few connections he had which had enabled him to carry on.[242] Even the *Hindustan Times* had not been treating him satisfactorily.[243] It had not paid him from the end of May 1932. 'I do not know', he wrote in sheer frustration, 'where my next meal is coming from or how I am to deal with the next demand on account of things here.'[244] Loneliness was reinforced by political isolation; cold penury superimposed an element of melancholic foreboding on Menon's introverted self.

Although it was initially arranged with the *Hindustan Times* that Menon would be paid an honorarium of £12 per month, it was slashed unilaterally from the Indian end to Rs.100 per month, but that was not regular or even forthcoming. The total amount received from the *Hindustan Times* was to the tune of £21.[245] Nothing was paid even for the special article Menon wrote during Gandhi's visit. Menon was 'hopelessly in the stew' and asked Govind Malaviya to help him to 'get some money out of these people'.[246] The suspension of the *India Review* was unfortunate because it was evident from its accounts sent to Malaviya that the paper ran economically, and a first class paper was produced at much less than a third of the expenses which would be incurred by other organizations.[247] It found its way in new circles. Russell had been taking much personal interest in the work of the League. Ellen Wilkinson had been addressing big meetings all over the country and she was keen to bring India into all her speeches. Evidently, public opinion was 'moving to our side' although the government was not amenable to it.[248] Menon confided to friends in India that Sankey mentioned that he was impressed by the change in the public opinion in the country and that the League and its delegation to India were, in a great sense, responsible for it.[249] India became one of the principal talking points in social gatherings and even in polite society, and a good many people had been aroused by the Meerut sentences.[250] Unfortunately, the period of cooperation and cordiality between Menon and Malaviya was at its end. It constituted an element of personal loss that, for a while, engulfed Menon's vision. In one of his last letters to Govind Malaviya, Menon struck a sombre note. 'The accounts will show you how much money I have put into it myself', Menon wrote, 'and how much is owing. Legally I am responsible and I am knowing each day after my return what it means. I do not want to write any more as I feel sure that I took the responsibility with my eyes open. I say this only because I left India with a feeling that I had somehow created a bad impression on Punditji for whom I have a very high degree of respect. It must be my own fault and I am therefore taking my medicine.'[251]

On 20 April 1933 another letter was written to Govind Malaviya. It was a desperate move. Menon informed Govind that he had been dismissed by the *Hindustan Times* who did not pay for four months even at the rate of Rs. 100 per month instead of £12 as fixed. Subsequently, he was given Rs. 10 per month for another four months and finally, without any reason, was summarily dismissed. What Menon wanted to convey to Govind Malaviya was that 'these people do not consider that they owe working men like myself anything'.[252] He claimed that he never pretended to be doing anything more than earning an honest living by writing for that paper. He had done his best to give them news and the *Hindustan Times* never ever gave him a suggestion of what was wanted. He had no reason to think that the readers of the paper were dissatisfied since his pen had written those articles ever since the *Hindustan Times* reappeared three years earlier.[253] Subboo was then their correspondent and Menon had a working arrangement with him. Subboo used to do the cabling for both of them while Menon did the writing. 'So I have written', he wrote, the London Letter 'all along though I was not their correspondent or drawn the money'.[254] But, unfortunately, Subboo never got his remuneration regularly and at last he committed suicide, insolvent and exhausted. The paper owed him a tidy sum which was never paid to anyone. Then Menon stepped in and his services were requisitioned on a paltry sum. But they neither paid nor used his special articles and news cuttings. 'Apparently there was no one competent up there who can use anything.'[255]

Menon thought Joseph, the editor, did not appear very pleased about 'my not appointing Sunder Kabadi as my substitute' during his visit to India. Even the small amount of arrears which came was a cheque on Delhi and one had to wait for another two months. What Menon stressed was that the Delhi 'cheque would not pay my bills, and even poor working people have to live, what is more, they have to and do pay their bills.'[256] More than taken for a ride, Menon was hurt by the way he was treated and in sheer disgust wanted an alienated Malaviya to know that he did the work as had been expected of him. Impatient of mediocrity he made it clear that he believed in professional ethics. Joseph had not told him if he had any complaints and, strangely enough, he had lifted material out of London Letters and 'used them in current topics as though it was their own. Journalists!'[257] 'I do not', he asserted in his characteristic style, 'propose to write sensational stuff for anyone. Nor can I produce currency crank stuff as unfortunately I learnt economics.'[258] The caustic letter ended with a friendly note that eased the tense moment: 'Please be good enough to write me if you have the time and if you are not in jail.'

The political situation in Britain was very gloomy. It was widely believed that Gandhi and a large number of political prisoners would not be released and the government would impose a constitution relying on the Special Powers Act and the cooperation of the Indian liberals and moderates who would, in one way or another, work the constitution. Menon's own reading of the situation was that the constitution would be more conservative than was contemplated by the government or the Indian moderates. It would be full of checks and balances. He had no advice or information from India. Neither Malaviya nor Rangaswami Iyengar had replied to his letters. The League's delegation, having returned to England addressed many small and large meetings and had interviews with several people including Sankey. Although the report was being written and had been coming up well, the League had insurmountable odds as there was little money to be found and, financially, even he personally seemed to be in a hopeless position. He had still been writing for the *Swadesamitran* who paid him £2 a month: Menon wondered if it could be raised a bit and enquired from Iyengar for an opening into the *Hindu*.[259]

As a large number of Indian representatives sailed for London, Menon could not quite comprehend what their exact function would be in their deliberations with the joint select committee. But he was certain that what they said would not make the slightest difference in the framing of the India Bill.[260] It was strange that although the Liberal Federation which recently met at Calcutta passed such strong resolutions condemning the white paper scheme as being far short of Indian demands, the Indian delegation contained a few members of the Liberal Party. The Federation also passed resolutions urging the government to release forthwith all Congress prisoners and protesting against its repressive policy. But they resisted this policy 'by clutching at every straw to cooperate with the government by consenting to go to London!'[261] Menon had no doubt that the proposal would emerge from the joint committee more reactionary than the scheme of the white paper. The press campaign against Gandhi had become rampant and the poet Tagore thought it prudent to issue a statement to the press showing how India was misrepresented abroad and how far his supposed antagonism with Gandhi was a carefully crafted misconstruction.[262] Not long ago Tagore had formally expressed his anguish at the unfortunate disillusionment of his generation with the attractive vision of universal conciliation, goodwill and fraternity held out by the West during his formative years. Operating within the parameters defined by well-synchronized propaganda, British public opinion, including that of its enlightened segments, diffused the real issues of the Indian question and drifted towards an animated discussion on the futility of India's self-determination, the absurdity of the severance of the British link, and the terms of so-called safeguards for the interests of the empire, the princes and the minorities.[263] Meanwhile imperialism got away with its inhuman ordinances, its broken pledges, its autocratic bureaucracy and its facile promise about the prospects and future of the *Raj*.

Notes and References

1 A.L.S. Wilkinson to Menon, 27 November 1932, Menon Papers.

2 India League, *Gandhi-Willingdon Correspondence,* November 1932, Menon Papers.

3 A.L.S. Wilkinson to Menon, 27 November 1932, Menon Papers.

4 India League, *Gandhi-Willingdon Correspondence,* op.cit.

5 Ibid.

6 Ibid.

7 Ibid.

8 A.L.S. Wilkinson to Menon, 27 November 1932, Menon Papers.

9 Ibid.

10 Ibid.

11 Ibid.

12 India League, *India and the National Congress,* London 1932, Menon Papers.

13 Harry Haig to Horace Alexander, 16 May 1932, Horace Alexander Papers (TH).

14 Ibid.

15 Ibid.

16 Ibid.

17 Ibid.

18 Ibid.

19 Ibid.

20 Ibid.

21 Ibid.

22 Ibid. These were some of the recurring ideas in the contemporary political debate. One may refer to the following selected list of pamphlets and articles:

E.P.J. 'The White Paper Proposals with regard to Law and Order', *The Indian Empire Review* (hereafter, IER), October 1933;

Sir Verney Lovett, *The Present Extent of Terrorism in India,* 1933;

Alas the Poor Indians: A Sidelight on the White Papers, 1933;

Sir Evan Cotton, 'The Future of European Services in India', IER, February 1933;

Col. J.H.C. Harrison, *Has Socialism Shaped Our India Policy?* 1933;

K.K. Lalkaka, *Britain's Plain Duty Towards India,* 1934;

Verney Lovett, *The Present Extent of Terrorism II,* 1934;

The British and the 'Scheduled Castes', 1934;

Zeta, *The White Paper* and *The Indian Judicature,* 1934;

British Raj, *The White Paper Plan,* 1933;

Viscount Sumnar, *Looking Forward,* 1931;

Michael O'Dwyer, *Lord Sankey on the Third Round Table Conference,* 1932;

The Provision of Safeguards under the Indian Federal Constitution, 1932;

Lord Sydenham of Combe, *The Tragedy of India: Retrospect and Prospect,* August 1932;

K.K. Lalkaka, *The Parsees in India,* 1932;

J.A. Tassie, *Future Prospects for Britishers in India,* 1935;

Col. J.H.C. Harrison, *What has gone wrong with the British Raj?* 1935;

K.K. Lalkaka, *Some Points A Sympathetic Briton Ought to Know,* 1934;

Duncan McClay, 'Truth and Mr Gandhi', *Nineteenth Century,* January 1934;

John Coatman, 'India and the New Franchise', *Nineteenth Century,* June 1934;

Sir Elliot Colvin, 'India's March to Promised Land', *Nineteenth Century,* October 1933.

Cornelia Sorabji, 'A Bengali Woman Revolutionary', *Nineteenth Century,* November 1933;

23 *The Hindu,* 26 June 1933.

24 India League, 'Circular Letter', 6 February 1933,

25 Ibid.

26 Ibid.

27 Ibid.

28 Ibid.

29 Ibid.

30 Author's interview with John Faithful Fortescue Platts-Mills,

31 Menon, 'Letter to the branches', 3 June 1933, Menon Papers.

32 See the papers relating to the programme of the India League between November 1932 and April 1933, Menon Papers.

33 Dr Privat to Agatha Harrison, 1 January 1993, Menon Papers. also Menon to Dr Privat, 7 January 1933, Menon Papers.

34 See Reports on Kingsway Hall, meeting on 26 November 1932, meeting at ILP, Eastbourne, on 10 August 1933, and meeting at Northumberland, 2 April 1933, all in Menon Papers. It may not be inappropriate to quote from a letter from Hamstead, London: 'It was with the greatest pleasure that I learnt from my cousin ... that you were willing to come and speak at one of our school meetings ... Truly, it will be an event unprecedented in our school history — you know, it is one of those Public schools where the most die-hard British Toryism is hidden under a cloak of seeming broadmindedness. When we had a government official to speak to us not long ago on India, it was thought very tolerant and broadminded! By dint of many promises and pressures I at last squeezed permission from the President of the school branch of the League of Nations Union to have a really anti-British Indian to speak to the Branch on India - if I could find anyone willing .... Now for the subject ... I think what would really be best, is to make *as strong a case as possible* for Indian independence -

with particular reference to India's present day government.' Hilda Kuttner to Menon, 13 May 1933, Menon Papers.

35 'Report on India Conference, Edmonton Labour Party, 11 February 1933', Menon Papers.

36 Ibid; also see the influential tract of the India League, Bertrand Russell, *Know the Facts,* 1932.

37 'Resolutions' moved by Dorothy Woodman in 'Report on India Conference, Edmonton Labour Party', 11 February 1933, Menon Papers.

38 A.J.P. Taylor, *English History, 1914-1945,* London 1977 (ed), pp.51-52, 97, 97, 136, 209. Also see the Collection of Dorothy Woodman papers at the Hull Library. The document, 'Join the Union of Democratic Control' in Dorothy Woodman Collection is very instructive. See also, The Union of Democratic Control, *Annual Report 1932-1933-1934,* Dorothy Woodman Collection.

39 C. Rajagopalachari to Bertrand Russell, 17 January 1933 (cable), Menon Papers.

40 Statement issued by Bertrand Russell, Chairman, India League, 19 January 1933, Menon Papers.

41 Ibid.

42 Menon, 'Note on the political situation in India', 24 March 1933, Menon Papers; also Menon, 'London Letter' (for *Hindu*), 4 February 1933, Menon Papers.

43 Memorandum on 'The Ordinance Rule', February 1933, Menon Papers.

44 Ibid.

45 Menon, 'The Village under Ordinance', February 1933, Menon Papers.

46 Ibid.

47 Ibid.

48 Ibid.

49 Ibid.

50 Menon, *Policy Raj in Action*, February/March 1933, Menon Papers.

51 Ibid.

52 Ibid.

53 'Report on the meetings on India at the Theosophical Lodges at Great Yarmonth and Norwich, 23 December 1932 and 19 January 1933', Menon Papers.

54 A Barnes to Menon, 6 March 1933, and 16 April 1933, Menon Papers.

55 Report on the India League meeting, Birmingham, 14 February 1933, Menon Papers.

56 Ibid.

57 'Meeting at Bristol: Unlawful Association, Ellen Wilkinson, 25 February 1933, Menon Papers.

58 Ibid.

59 Delegate Conference, 4 July 1933, Friends' Meeting House, London, Menon Papers.

60 Ibid.

61 'Delegate Conference, Barclay Hall, Layton, 3 October 1933 - A Report', Menon Papers.

62 Ibid.

63 Ibid.

64 Ibid.

65 'Circular letter: Letter of Tej Bahadur Sapru, 6 February 1933,' Menon Papers.

66 Ibid.

67 *The India Bulletin,* March 1933, Menon Papers.

68 India League, *Information Bulletin,* March 1933, Menon Papers.

69 Ellen Wilkinson at the Friends' Meeting Hall, London, 16 June 1933, Menon Papers.

70 Ibid.

71 Leonard Matters in Ibid.

72 'Press in India', *Notes for Speaker,* March/April 1933, Menon Papers.

73 'Ghaffar Khan and the NWFP', *Notes for Speakers,*' March/April 1933, Menon Papers.

74 'India's payment for British Wars', *Notes for Speakers,* March/April 1933, Menon Papers.

75 'The Ordinance Raj', *Notes for Speakers,* May/June 1933, Menon Papers.

76 Leonard Matters to Samuel Hoare, 12 October 1933, Menon Papers.

77 Ibid.

78 Ibid.

79 Ibid.

80 Menon, 'Note on the White Paper', 24 March 1933, Menon Papers; also Menon to Malaviya, 3 February 1933, Menon Papers.

81 Ibid.

82 Ibid.

83 Ibid.

84 Ibid.

85 Ibid.

86 Menon, *Law and Prisons in India,* India League pamphlet, March 1933, Menon Papers.

87 Menon, *White Paper Examined*, 6 April 1933, Menon Papers; also, see James Marley, 'London Letters', 4 March 1933, Menon Papers.

88 Menon, 'London Letter', 19 March 1933, (for Kaiser-e-Hind), Menon Papers.

89 Menon, 'The Storm: The Political Situation in India', 17 April 1933, Menon Papers.

90 Ibid.

91 Menon, 'London Letter', 1 April 1933, Menon Papers.

92 Menon, 'London Letter', 15 April 1933, Menon Papers.

93 A.J.P. Taylor, *English History 1914-1945,* pp.335-6.

94 S. Chakravarty, *The Raj Syndrome,* op.cit., pp.93, 154, 158, 160, 168, 182; also, see, Patrick French, *Liberty or Death, India's Journey to Independence and Division,* London 1997, pp.92-96, 130-133, 135-138.

95 Menon, 'London Letter', 18 February 1933, Menon Papers.

96 Menon, 'London Letter', 26 February 1933, Menon Papers.

97 Menon, 'London Letter', 18 February 1933, Menon Papers.

98 Ibid.; also Menon, 'London Letter', 26 February 1933, Menon Papers.

99 James Marley to George Lansbury, 6 March 1933, Lansbury Papers.

100 Memorandum in ibid.

101 'Statement issued by Sir Tej Bahadur Sapru', 3 February 1933, Lansbury Papers.

102 Ibid.

103 Menon to Rangaswami Iyengar, 8 February 1933, Menon Papers; also, see, Menon, 'London Letter', 18 February 1933, Menon Papers.

104 Menon, 'London Letter', 19 March 1933, Menon Papers.

105 Menon, 'London Letter', 26 February 1933, Menon Papers.

106 Menon, 'London Letter', 24 March 1933, Menon Papers.

107 Menon, 'London Letter', 20 April 1933, Menon Papers.

108 'Circular Letter to Friends in India', 22 March 1933, Menon Papers.

109 Ibid.

110 Ibid.

111 Menon, 'London Letter', 20 April 1933, Menon Papers.

112 Menon, 'Circular Letter', 24 March 1933, Menon Papers.

113 Ibid.

114 Ibid.

115 Report on the 'Meeting of the India League', 146 Strand, London, 20 April 1933, Menon Papers; also report on *India,* public meeting, 5 October 1933 at Market Hall, Hastings, Menon Papers.

116 E.W. Sterry, Secretary, Eastbourne ILP, to Menon, 10 August 1933 and 11 August 1933, Menon Papers.

117 Report on the Activities of The India League, Southampton branch, 6 February 1933, Menon Papers.

118 Tarlok Singh (Students' Union, LSE) to Menon, 23 November 1933, Menon Papers.

119 E.M. Tuckett to Menon, 16 May 1933, Menon Papers.

120 W. Holmes, Secretary, National Union of Agricultural Workers to Menon, 23 October 1933, Menon Papers.

121 Ibid.

122 Menon, Circular Letter, 12 October 1933, Menon Papers.

123 Ibid.

124 Ibid.

125 F. Wenyon to Menon, 6 April 1933, Menon Papers.

126 Menon to Secretary, Westminister Labour Party, 29 December 1933.

127 Menon to Govind Malaviya, 28 May 1933, Menon Papers.

128 Ms Pam Kampster to Menon, 6 June 1933, Menon Papers.

129 Ibid.

130 Ibid.

131 H.N. Marley to Menon, 10 June 1933, Menon Papers.

132 J.B. Hicks to Menon, 16 July 1933, Menon Papers.

133 Ibid.

134 Menon, Letter to the branches, 24 March 1933, Menon papers; also, Menon to Wenyon, 3 April 1933, Menon Papers.

135 Menon, Letter to the branches, 24 March 1933, Menon Papers.

136 Minutes of the Executive Committee, 2 March 1933, Menon Papers.

137 'Explanation' in Ibid.

138 Proceedings of a public meeting at Hastings on 5 October 1933, Menon Papers.

139 Ibid.

140 Menon, 'London Letter', 25 February 1933, Menon Papers.

141 Ibid.

142 Ibid.

143 Ibid.

144 Ibid.

145 Menon, 'London Letter', 1 April 1933, Menon Papers.

146 Menon, 'London Letter', 26 February 1933, Menon Papers.

147 Menon, 'London Letter', 4 March 1933, Menon Papers.

148 Ibid.

149 Menon, 'London Letter', 12 March 1933, Menon Papers.

150 Menon, 'London Letter', for the *Swadeshamitram,* 19 March 1933, Menon Papers.

151 Ibid.

152 Menon, 'London Letter', 1 April 1933, Menon Papers.

153 Menon, 'London Letter', 19 March 1933, Menon Papers.

154 Ibid.

155 Secretary, National Union of Students to Secretary, Students' Union, LSE, 16 January 1933, Menon Papers.

156 Menon to Saklatvala, 30 January 1933, Menon Papers.

157 Ibid.

158 Ibid.

159 Report on Wilkinson's speech at a meeting in Brighton, 3 February 1933, Menon Papers.

160 V.K. Krishna Menon (Meerut Committee of The India League) to Ernest Winteston, 3 March 1933, Menon Papers.

161 D.V. Giri to Menon, n.d. April 1933, Menon Papers.

162 Ibid.

163 Menon, 'London Letter', 27 January 1933 (for *Swadeshamitram*), Menon Papers.

164 Ibid.

165 Ibid.

166 Ibid.

167 Author's conversation with Michael Foot.

168 Winifred Horrabin, 'Jawaharlal, Indira and Krishna', 1938, Winifred Horrabin Papers.

169 Menon, 'London Letter', 20 May 1933, Menon Papers.

170 Ibid.

171 Ibid.

172 Menon, 'London Letter', 23 May 1933, Menon Papers.

173 Menon, 'London Letter', 3 May 1933, Menon Papers.

174 Menon, 'London Letter', 13 May 1933, Menon Papers.

175 Ibid.

176 Ibid.

177 Menon, 'London Letter', 8 April 1933, Menon Papers.

178 Menon, 'London Letter', 26 February 1933 (for *Pratap*), Menon Papers.

179 Ibid.

180 Menon, 'London Letter', 4 March 1933, Menon Papers; also, Tom Williams, 'Report of Krishna Menon's Speech,' 12 February 1933, Menon Papers.

181 Menon, 'London Letter', 11 February 1933, Menon Papers.

182 Ibid.

183 Ibid.

184 Ibid.

185 Ibid.

186 Ibid.

187 Menon, 'London Letter', 19 March 1933, Menon Papers.

188 Ibid.

189 Ibid.

190 Ibid.

191 Menon, 'London Letter', 1 April 1933, Menon Papers.

192 Ibid.

193 Cf. Arthur Marwick, *Britain in the Century of Total War,* London 1968, pp.198-9.

194 Menon, 'London Letter', 3 June 1933, Menon Papers.

195 Ibid.

196 Ibid.

197 Ralph Miliband, *Capitalist Democracy in Britain,* Oxford 1982, pp.121-30; also, Arthur Marwick, *Britain in the Century of Total War,* London 1968, pp.94-95, 119-20, 169 and 195-200.

198 Menon to Govind Malaviya, 3 February 1933, Menon Papers.

199 Menon, 'London Letter', 19 June 1933, Menon Papers.

200 Ibid.

201 Menon, 'London Letter', 19 March 1933, Menon Papers.

202 Ibid.

203 Menon, 'London Letter', 1 April 1933, Menon Papers.

204 Ibid.

205 Ibid.

206 Menon, 'London Letter', 15 April 1933, Menon Papers.

207 Menon, 'London Letter', 1 April 1933, Menon Papers.

208 Menon, 'London Letter', 4 February 1933, Menon Papers.

209 Ibid.

210 Arthur Marwick, *Britain in the Century of Total War,* op.cit.,

pp.199-200.

211 Ralph Miliband, *Capitalist Democracy in Britain,* op.cit., pp.37 and 127.

212 Menon, 'London Letter', 4 March 1933, Menon Papers.

213 Jon Clark, Margot Heinemann, David Margolies and Carole Snee (ed.), *Culture and Crisis in Britain in the 30s,* London 1979, pp.14-16.

214 Pilgrim Trust, *Men Without Work,* London 1938. See also, A. Marwick, *Britain in the Century of Total War,* op.cit., pp.226-38.

215 Cf. John Strachey, *The Nature of Capitalist Crisis,* London 1935, pp.317-32.

216 Cf. Arthur Marwick, *Britain in the Century of Total War,* op.cit., pp.226-54.

217 Cf. India League, *Condition of India,* London 1934. Also, Menon, 'London Letter', 20 May 1933, Menon Papers.

218 Ibid.

219 Menon, 'London Letter', 26 May 1933, Menon Papers.

220 Ibid.

221 'Release the Prisoners - A Statement', 14 May 1933, Menon Papers.

222 Ibid.

223 Ibid.

224 Bertrand Russell, Chairman, India League: A Statement, 23 May 1933, Menon Papers.

225 Ibid.

226 Ibid.

227 Menon to the Editor, *Eastern Daily Press*, 3 February 1933, Menon Papers.

228 Ibid.

229 Ibid.

230 Ibid.

231 Ibid.

232 Ibid.

233 Ibid.

234 Ibid.

235 'Minutes of the meeting of the executive committee, India League on 2 March 1933,' Menon Papers.

236 Menon to Malaviya, 3 February 1933, Menon Papers.

237 Ibid.

238 Ibid.

239 Ibid.

240 Menon to Govind Malaviya, 20 April 1933, Menon Papers.

241 Menon to Rangaswami Iyengar, 21 April 1933, Menon Papers; also Menon to Malaviya, 3 February 1933, Menon Papers.

242 Menon to Govind Malaviya, 20 April 1933, Menon Papers.

243 Menon to Govind Malaviya, 3 February 1933, Menon Papers.

244 Ibid.

245 Ibid.

246 Ibid.

247 Ibid.

248 Ibid.

249 Menon to C.F. Andrews, 22 March 1933, Menon Papers.

250 Ibid; also see, Menon to E. Winterton, 6 March 1933, Menon Papers.

251 Menon to Govind Malaviya, 2 April 1933, Menon Papers.

252 Menon to Govind Malaviya, 20 April 1933, Menon Papers.

253 Ibid.

254 Ibid.

255 Ibid.

256 Ibid.

257 Ibid.

258 Ibid.

259 Menon to Rangaswami Iyengar, 28 April 1933, Menon Papers.

260 'Notes' February/March 1933, Menon Papers.

261 Ibid.

262 Ibid.

263 Suhash Chakravarty, *The Raj Syndrome,* op.cit., pp.142-3.

CHAPTER III

RIGHT ABOUT TURN

The quiescence of the labour movement immediately following the advent of Hitler to power was extraordinary. Perceptive social scientists, sensitive intellectuals and committed political activists even in Germany had been given over the years to a sort of churlish complacency, smug detachment and self-defeating fantasia. An over-confident Left intelligentsia had cogitated that fascism was perhaps related to backward agricultural economy, lack of organized democratic consciousness and certain obscure Mediterranean particularisms and it was certainly not compatible with the dynamics of advanced Western societies sustained by robust industrialization and distinguished by articulate democratic movements and significant cultural achievements.[1] The standard refrain of the Western intelligentsia, including those of England and Germany right upto the beginning of the 1930s was, 'it can't happen here'.[2] Even after Hitler came to power on 30 January 1933, the orthodox die-hards such as Winston Churchill were reported to have appreciated more than once the efficiency of Mussolini's Italy and the commitments of disciplined nationalism in Nazi Germany. It was generally believed by hard core conservative opinion that Mussolini with his fascist followers, had certainly done Italy immense service by saving it from Bolshevism by wise and energetic administration, by developing the resources of the land and making Italy great.[3] In an atmosphere of suicidal contentment the social democratic political formations, the communist parties and many socially conscious Christians, committed to collective efforts for the weak and the poor, had been too impotent to heed the admonitions and premonitions of many concerned individuals and were unable to rise to the occasion.[4]

It was the struggle against war and for peace that had developed systematically, since World War I, the main path to socialism and Marxism. It was accepted by both the working classes and the intellectuals.[5] Paradoxically, however, by the 1930s there was widespread diffidence in the enlightened Western mind to comprehend the various forms of bourgeois rule and to appreciate their peculiarities and differences from fascism. Examining this enigma, James Klugmann pointed out that after the October revolution of 1917 it had been almost taken for granted, especially in the left-wing circles all over, that the next socialist revolution was to be in Germany where the size of the Communist Party was enormous. The impact of Marxism was extensive beyond the formal communist and social democratic movements and that influence was deeply embedded in German cultural life. It was creative and almost infectious. For a left-wing intellectual, a visit to Berlin offered spiritual and ideological sustenance second only to a journey to Moscow. Berlin was the centre of numberless democratic organizations, as well as of the West European Bureau of Communist International. The influence of the revolutionary rebel culture in Germany was both intensive and extensive. Names of Bertolt Brecht (1898-1956), Georg Kaiser (1878-1945) and Ernst Toller (1879-1939) were the guiding spirits of an invigorating renewal of socialism.[6] Barbara Macnamara, Menon's intense admirer, was an addict of German expressionist theatre and she often dragged Menon to the Gate Theatre, a little playhouse down the Villiers Street by Charing Cross station while Krishna Shelvankar, another close friend, specialized in Brecht and Toller.[7] The India League experienced that German left-wing euphoria; Menon's friend, A.C. Nambiar wrote his regular Berlin letters for friends in England; Menon watched carefully both the effulgence and the fall of the Weimar republic.[8]

Hitler's victory in January 1933 was a bombshell for sensitive souls and progressive spirits. The cumulative impact of what followed constituted a major setback to what hitherto appeared to be an apparently irresistible ascendancy of humanism, economic opportunity, social justice and equality.[9] That struggle against all forms of bondage and deprivation seemed to be thwarted by a single monolithic phenomenon: fascism. A period of tormenting revaluation of revolutionary experience began. Germany under Hitler offered a perspective of desolation and defoliation of life and all that was noble in man. A spectrum of grotesque barbarism appeared every day in the morning newspapers. In that systematic internal destruction, institutions, morality and then humanity perished. Starting with the communists, the Nazi political militia (the *Sturmabteilung*, the *Schutztaffel* and *Geheime Staatspolizei*) proceeded to the socialists, trade unions, Centre party, liberals, pacifists, radicals and the Church, ruthlessly killing, imprisoning, molesting and tormenting millions of Jewish people en route, torching libraries and collections, and ranking as 'cultural bolshevism' most of German culture from the middle ages onwards.[10] Externally, it meant tearing apart the *dictat,* rearmament, *anschluss* and *lebensraum,* threat of war, and war. An agonizing introspection of the social processes and assessment of the situation meant the involvement of democratic people of Britain and elsewhere in the struggle against fascism in its various forms.[11]

The rise of fascism had been spearheaded by the Great Slump, but without the triumph of Hitler in Germany, as Hobsbawm emphasized, fascism would not have become a general movement. The Hungarian Arrow Cross, the Rumanian Iron Guards, the Croatian *Ustashi* terrorists gained ground and were ideologically *fascisized* only with Hitler's support.[12] More significantly, with the advent of Hitler, the idea of fascism as a universal movement, a sort of right-wing parallel of international communism with Berlin as headquarters, was actualized. After 1933, fascism centred around a German hegemony devoted to the irrelevance of conscience, rampant irrationalism and superiority of instinct and will.[13] The infamous Reichstag fire trial held in Berlin and Leipzig (March 1933 - February 1934) not only focussed on the world stature of Georgie Dimitrov as an intrepid hero of the revolution, but added urgency to the fight against fascism. Peace, social stability, economy, liberal institutions and the intellectual values of liberal bourgeois society collapsed before the tide. It was, as Hiren Mukherjee pronounced, 'a diabolic dictatorship aimed chiefly at demolition, not only of communism and socialism, but of all democratic processes and popular forces'. It strengthened the radical Right and saw the retreat of the revolutionary Left perhaps partly due to its own sectarian isolation. Fascism in Germany, the India League was forthright in its condemnation, was the embodiment of intolerance, violence and oppression. It meant the abrogation of the rule of law and justice in the matter of freedom of speech, freedom of writing, freedom of assembly, the right of association and the protection of the property of the working-class organizations and individual anti-fascists from destruction or seizure. It denoted the worship of an abstract entity; a narrow, bigoted, nationalist ideal to which the individual must be sacrificed; a puerile glorification of everything German; a denial of any contribution to German culture of the Jewish race and fierce jealousy of the intellectual achievement of that race expressed in vindictive persecution. It was the subjection of the intellectual and political life of a people to the will of one militarized and barbaric party.[14]

There was a strong undercurrent in British socialism that was inclined to push the labour movement to non-political trade unionism. That trend was stimulated by the General Strike. It meant a growing concern for supporting workers' claims for higher wages and better conditions of work brushing aside all commitments to politics. The Labour leadership feared that the 'wild' political talks against the empire and the British ruling classes and propaganda for socialism would merely alienate the working classes, who, they believed, were primarily interested in bread-and-butter and in little else.[15] In a way, it might be suggested that the Labour leadership entertained, often unknowingly, a very indifferent view of the perception and world-view of the working class and was inclined to overlook the refreshing experience in Russia where workers proved to be the significant politically conscious class when socialist propaganda drove home to them the importance of politics.[16] Menon as an Indian was obliged to look at Britain through alien eyes. He realized more comfortably than many others that propaganda did not mean merely to confront the credulous general public with a striking political advertisement selling an 'idea' as a seductive commodity. For the India League and Menon, propaganda meant just the opposite.

Menon knew that if propaganda for socialism was a difficult proposition especially in Britain, where capitalism had already created its progressive features, its civilizing influence and its attractive democratic atmosphere, it was far more onerous to attempt to mould public opinion against the *Raj* which had become the central theme of British national sensibility.[17] Among his intelligent audience were some sincere socialists with an international outlook, then confronted with a perplexing intellectual problem in comprehending the claims of Indian nationalism in class categories.[18] Some others were bourgeois liberals who often used the Marxian idiom to plead for a progressive capitalism and conjured up the vision of a liberal imperial commonwealth. Some others were willing to promote socialism at home in sheer indifference to the aspirations of the empire and the colonial peoples.[19] Yet, there were some others who were entrenched in the Fabian illusions of gradualness.[20] There were also some to whom the elementary struggle for bread and butter and against unemployment means tests were more than enough to have either the opportunity or the inclination to strive for an imperial salvation.[21] For Menon, propaganda for India meant modest and earnest discussions of realities of India and principles of struggle in small study groups and traffic in ideas, in meetings, delegate conferences and reasoned discourses along with vociferous slogans in large public demonstrations and rallies.[22] It also meant an organized group of persons capable of leading, instructing and coordinating the activities of various local groups and associations.

Menon could only depend on the services of part-time volunteers whose association with the League was tentative depending on the availability of time and leisure, continued interest in and propensity for unrewarded silent service. The problem was that Menon had no party in British parliamentary life working for India's freedom with coherence and a striking power. The strength of Menon and the India League was that they successfully identified themselves with the England of labour, of spiritual power, of the struggle for justice and human freedom and of the great ideals of international solidarity against England with imperial arrogance, an England of the stock exchange, and exclusive area of economic exploitation, the vile and honourless England. The India League's popularity with the liberal democratic public opinion in Britain enhanced as the decade unfolded itself. It was the principal anti-imperialist platform in Britain that swerved overwhelmingly to the Left and converged with the global anti-fascist mobilization. In its turn, the India League found its crucial empathy and support from the international Left, much to the discomfiture and chagrin of the secret service.[23] Under the pressure of events the style of Menon, the principal actor of the League became clear, cutting, concise and precise.. There was no artificiality of manners; the pronounced Malayali accent persisted as he rolled his r's; his language was rich with imagination, rare among contemporary politicians; his metaphors had telling effect. His untrained voice, however, acquired over the years, as Anna Polak confided to the author, an uncanny ventriloquist ring.[24]

Within the Labour Party, a good deal of ideological adjustments had been taking place. The failure of the General Strike had persuaded the labour movement to look towards the parliamentary option to create the legal framework within which trade unions could discharge their individual functions. There were growing consultations between the employers' association and the union leadership.[25] It appeared that the position of the Labour Party, though crucial, was subordinate to the trade unions who were somewhat apprehensive of the expansion of state authority which the compulsions of socialism made almost obligatory.[26] The position of the Labour Parliamentary Party was incoherent as electoral considerations competed with the demands for more radical socialist policies championed by the vocal ILPers.[27] An ILP report, *Socialism in Our Time* (1925), asked for substantial positivist state intervention while Labour Party's *Labour and Nation* (1928) was a limited and tardy response.[28]

By the end of 1931, when the events of the year stunned the socialist movement, it seemed that socialism was being paraded by the Labour Party merely as a form of secular morality. Attempts to revitalize the Labour's ideological frame was undertaken by various initiatives, the most remarkable being the formation of the Socialist League in 1932.[29] It aimed at capturing the Labour Party through socialist policies including immediate nationalization of banks, land, mines, power, transport, iron and steel, cotton and control of foreign trade and restricted compensation.[30] The Socialist League revolved around sound and idealistic leaders such as Stafford Cripps, Aneurin Bevan, Clement Attlee, Harold Laski and many other leading luminaries. Stafford Cripps in *Can Socialism Come by Constitutional Methods?* (1933) placed the urgency of socialist transformation on the agenda of the decade.[31] True, judged by the history of the 1930s and the hindsight of the decade, the Marxist upsurge in the 1930s might have seemed no more than a temperamental ideological overcast. It was also true that the Labour Party was a pattern of inconsistent ideological threads and they were reflected in the emotions and interests of personalities having contradictory interests and sensibilities. Yet, it was equally true that in the early 1930s the formation of the

Socialist League was a bold and positive left-wing affirmation, inspiring ideological ripples all over.[32] The League claimed that it was an organization of convinced socialists pledged to devote themselves 'to one object, and one object only, the achievement of the Socialist Commonwealth in this country within a worldwide system of Socialism'.[33] That Socialist Commonwealth could only be established by an organized working class seeking the cooperation of all socialists to work within the labour, trade union and cooperative movements.[34]

The members were expected to place their energies and devotion at the disposal of the movement for the specific purpose of promoting socialism. Such an immensely charged organization had no option but to operate on a very succinct programme. It ran socialist forums, weekend conferences and summer schools, discussed practical socialist problems, trained its members to play their role in the Labour Party and socialist propaganda, formed study circles and research groups to work out a compatible, intelligible and articulate socialist plan of action, and publish tracts and pamphlets to stimulate discussion.[35] There was an element of urgency and a firm conviction in the whole endeavour not merely for continuity in the British radical tradition, but for complete severance from traditional theories of government with a view to seizing power from the undemocratic ruling class and transfering it to the people as a whole.[36] It was believed that the ruling class might go to any length to defeat parliamentary action if the issue was the continuance of its financial and political hegemony.[37]

Transition to socialism was to be the function of a confirmed socialist party fully prepared to deal with every kind of opposition. What was indispensable was an overwhelming majority in Parliament, whose undivided attention during a full and uninterrupted term should be devoted to the accomplishment of so great a degree of change as to deprive capitalism of its power to stage a comeback. The emergence of a planned and ordered industrial society should be accompanied by a new technique of direction in the industries. The electoral system should be so conditioned as to ensure that the government represented the policy desired by the majority of the electors and the political machinery should be so overhauled as to absorb the tempo of socialism in keeping with the spirit and institutions of democracy. It would mean an extraordinary political support of the whole nation enabling the socialist government to mould political, economic and social life of the people in a fundamental way and remove the capitalist bias of the existing machinery and institutions.[38] Socialist transformation through constitutional means would involve a determined struggle with vigilance, grit and fortitude in an uphill task against the combined forces of opposition of immense strength.[39]

Menon, an active member of this Marxist intellectual wing of the Labour Party, had been pushing the question of India's independence in the forefront of its agenda. As an incisive thinker on international issues, especially on war, peace, fascism, imperialism, progress and development, Menon had acquired a name for himself while he was a member of the old ILP.[40] He was startled to find that some branches of the Socialist League held the view that the League was concerned with internal problems of the British nation to the exclusion of imperialism.[41] In particular, he realized upon a good deal of soul-searching that the Westminster branch of the Socialist League with its introverted world-view was probably no place for him. He argued that the approach to socialism in Britain without a simultaneous and sustained thrust on imperialism was meaningless and hypocritical.[42] Such an approach was fraught with danger and Menon made it unambiguous that what he dreaded most was 'socialist imperialism'.[43] He had declared that he had a deep and inflexible attachment to socialist ideas and could not, therefore, submit to 'this kind of sheltered approach to it'.[44] As a member of the Labour Party, he claimed, he remained in the socialist movement in a general way and he felt that the ILP, as he knew it, was a more active organization when he had joined it. ILP's disaffiliation from the socialist movement was in his view incompatible with socialist achievement and hence he abandoned it.[45] Menon's conviction and its forceful exposition proved effective. In the agenda of the Socialist League conference at Derby a resolution on the empire was included. It was decided that as soon as it was carried, the branches would be expected to get similar resolutions passed by the local Labour parties wherever possible so that something tangible could be done on a satisfactory scale.[46] Soon, a meeting on India was arranged at York with the assistance of a few liberal friends who, though enthusiastic about India, entertained certain inchoate political ideas.[47] But similar speaking engagements were many, for it was widely understood that it was high time that people were enlightened on India and for that Menon, though controversial, seemed indispensable.

The effort of the Socialist League bore fruit and a proposal was adopted to place a resolution on India on the annual Labour Party conference in October 1933.[48] There was by then, a qualitative change in Labour policy towards Indian independence. In the past the party had asserted merely a general principle of self-determination for India. The world situation was such that the party could not still be too explicit in its proposals for implementing such assertion, or even too logical in following the principles it had affirmed.[49] But it was now believed that the party should no longer fight shy of stating boldly that self-determination for India meant and could only mean the right of the Indian people to decide these constitutional questions for themselves. This was what George Lansbury indicated when he declared in the House of Commons that the Indians should be encouraged to draft their own constitution as the Australians had done. The RTC method produced nothing that could be interpreted, even by the biggest stretch of imagination, as self-determination. It was rather an imposed constitution that 'gave excessive power to the Indian princes and other reactionary forces'.[50] Menon was requested to consider, scrutinize and, if necessary, improve the resolution which the local parties were required to adopt and send for inclusion in the agenda of the annual conference. The drafts were to reach Transport House by 18 June 1933. It was believed that the resolution should become the principal item of discussion on Indian policy and it was therefore desirable that a large number of local parties should forward to the conference almost identical texts.[51]

The resolution was Menon's handiwork based on his recent experience in India. It condemned the British government's resort to and persistence in a policy of naked terrorism, wholesale arrests and employment of armed police and troops against unarmed peasants. It protested against the government's repudiation of the pledge repeatedly given by the government that the constitutional settlement of India would be based on agreement with the representatives of the Indian people, and the adoption in its place of an imposed constitutional plan which was not only unacceptable to India but was not based on any democratic principle or calculated to lead to the political and economic emancipation of the Indian people.[52]

The resolution also reaffirmed the policy of self-determination and self-government for India accepted at previous party conferences. In view of the failure of the RTC method to achieve any satisfactory settlement it declared that the Labour Party, even in opposition, should take definite steps to enable India to make its own constitution through a democratically elected assembly with full powers to formulate their constitution. Demanding the withdrawal of the ordinances, release of all political prisoners, remission of fines and other impositions on the peasantry and the abandonment of the existing coercive method of administration, the resolution called for the immediate release of the Meerut prisoners in view of the partisan injustice of these trials and promotion of labour legislation in cooperation with the leaders of the Indian labour movement.[53]

For the India League, India work had now become a fairly complicated affair. Andrews was a receptive contact through whom the 'contents' of the report of the delegation were disseminated to the Congress leadership and others since Malaviya had become silent and incommunicado and Menon's relationship with the *Hindustan Times* sulky and estranged.[54] Menon had to spend a great deal of time in pulling strings to push the Labour Party to the left on the question of cooperation in the joint committee.[55] Many letters passed between Lansbury and others and the League people. Bertrand Russell received a cable from Rajagopalachari rejecting the white paper; Russell took a hand and lectured the party at its private meeting. The India League was also able to plank down the copy of the cable before Cripps, Lansbury and others just before their executive committee meeting.[56] Although the party could not be persuaded to abstain from the joint select committee, the next best result had been attained. The amendment method was an able substitute and they had also explicitly stated that cooperation with the committee was merely a matter of parliamentary courtesy.[57] It was acknowledged and affirmed that the decision of the Churchillites to join the committee was a clear indication that there was no commitment on principle.[58] Menon was able to obtain from the principal Labour men an assurance that speeches in the JSC would make it clear that the party stood for full self-determination, that the white paper scrapped the RTCs and that political prisoners must be released. 'If I am well enough to do so,' Menon confided, 'I hope to be able to coach some of the speakers myself.'[59]

The meeting of the executive committee of the League of 2 March 1933 was attended by nine members with Bertrand Russell in the chair.[60] They were James Francis Horrabin, Tom

Williams, James Marley, Ellen Wilkinson, Winifred Horrabin, Barbara Macnamara, Menon and Fairfax; the leading absentees, who could not attend because of previous engagements, were Horace Alexander, Wilfred Wellock and Anne Wilkinson. It was evident from the proceedings of the meeting that despite the acute financial crunch, League activities had been continuing on a limited scale.[61] Efforts were being made to educate Labour MPs on the question of participation in the joint select committee on India and a satisfactory meeting had been held the previous day at which Menon spoke.[62] A number of meetings were being organized in London and the provinces, for which speakers were being sent by the League. There was a glut of outdated literature; a majority of branches had become non-functioning; the *India Review* had ceased publication; paucity of funds had made large-scale propaganda impossible; there was the increasing liability of the League; the necessity of raising funds was strongly urged. A full summary of the report of the India League delegation and a substantial section of the complete text were put forth for consideration. Russell and Horrabin undertook to read them and express their opinions.[63]

Despite the successful completion of the India mission and in spite of the fact that the report of the delegation was nearly ready for publication with the prospect of a significant strategic fall-out, the situation seemed not very optimistic. Menon's absence from the scene for three months had made it clear that he had been the kingpin of the organization. The opposition of the India Office and the media introduced an element of doubt in the mind of the executive as to the continued support for India work from a vacillating middle class already hard hit by retrenchment and unemployment.[64] The rejuvenation of the League depended entirely on Menon's perception of the League's importance and his own unflagging energy and determination. Ideologically, Menon was, by then, an uncompromising socialist. Backbiters given to petty intrigue were on the increase. Friends were becoming somewhat uneasy and even vexed by the ever increasing demands on them by Menon's fresh endeavours.

One of them clarified the situation by forcing the issue. This was Francis Horrabin, vice-chairman of the League and Menon's long-standing associate. Menon had been a friend *précieux* of the Horrabins. Occasionally, he dropped in for a couple of hours at Horrabin's centrally heated flat at Hampstead on the top floor of a newly built department store gazing from the windows at the wide view of London that included the gold cross on the top of St. Paul's to the east, the tiny twin towers of the west front of Westminster Abbey and to the north the spire of the church on Harrow Hill. In winter, a curtain of mist hid that view and one could only see the ugly sprawl of red brick houses and state roofs. It was a convenient place to stop for a short break as it was situated almost next door to the Finchley Road Underground. Following the executive committee meeting of 2 March 1933, Horrabin decided to write to Bertrand Russell about his own perception of the League and its future. Horrabin concluded that no useful purpose could be served by carrying on the India League in its existing form any longer.[65] Only a few months earlier he had been trying to impress upon Malaviya the importance of the India League in the political life of Britain and the significant role being played by Menon in a planned and synchronized campaign against British imperialism in India.

Years later Winifred Horrabin recalled the creative years of Francis as the vice-chairman of the India League, a small 'subversive' organization 'almost entirely run by Krishna Menon'. 'He often came to talk the business of the League', Winifred Horrabin wrote in amused indulgence, 'and to tire us with discourses on our duty, and, truth to tell, to irritate us a little by his obvious scorn for "middle class English intellectuals", not that he ever flouted it that way. He had a genuine affection for us both, forgiving us for our cold-blooded Anglo-Saxon lack of fanaticism. He felt it was something we could not help! A built-in frigidity.'[66] Now Horrabin of all persons proposed to move at the next council meeting a resolution urging that the League be 'wound up' and that 'we remain then simply a group of Labour people interested in the question of India' and concentrating on such activities as 'a group of that sort can adequately do'.[67] He did not think that there was any use trying to maintain an organization with an office etc. He thought that Menon might be persuaded to remain secretary of such a group and, in case he declined, one has to find a person who could devote rather more time to the work than 'those of us who are busy in a dozen other directions'.[68] The liabilities must be met and the report could just as well be published by that smaller group. He thought that it was unsatisfactory to give friends in India the impression of an organization with a large number of members and varied activities 'when such a picture is so far from the truth and, indeed, far from being possible as things are in Britain just now'.[69] Horrabin concluded that it would be far better to break free and start with a clean slate deciding what they could do then, rather than to go on in an unsatisfactory manner. He was firm that he was not inclined to be associated with the India League in its existing desultory state of being.[70] It meant to reduce the League to a non-functioning body of the Labour Party having a low public profile.

Menon was nonplussed. It was hard to accept the bewildering proposition. As a democrat he desired that the proposal must be discussed at length in the executive. There was now little likelihood of publishing the delegation's report. Funds were wanting and no publisher was available without a large subsidy. Government opposition was intense. The executive committee was at a loss to find adequate funds.[71] The manuscript was all ready. It was widely believed in friendly circles that the white paper was going 'to be worse than even we anticipated'.[72] Menon himself was then engaged in doing all that he could to prevent the Labour Party cooperating heartily on the joint select committee. And the difficulties of the League were rendered complicated on account of the feelings entertained by a genuine left-wing Labour colleague among others that there was no need for a movement outside the Labour Party.

Horrabin's letter had been circulated in the executive.[73] Russell was totally opposed to the idea. Menon himself could not quite see the case as Horrabin put it. Peace movements, Africa, internationalism, movements in favour of democratic consciousness, promotion of the Covenant of the League of Nations, and every kind of reform movement found it necessary to maintain their organizations outside political parties.[74] The principal problem was finance which was in a delicate and difficult state. Pecuniary inadequacy was, however, used as the last straw on the camel's back. It prompted the move and Horrabin's association gave it a touch of credibility.[75] Menon felt the utter helplessness of his situation more keenly than ever before. Over the years he met reality without precipitating a crisis but now he felt as if he could not face it any more.[76] Yet he was convinced that the League had been doing a good deal of useful work and that it should go on, however hopeless the situation appeared to be. The existing adverse situation would certainly pass over.[77]

Menon's enthusiasm was based on a growing appreciation of his work in various organizations and by unattached men and women. There were elements of sympathy and support even at places where the most die-hard British Toryism was hidden under a cloak of seeming broadmindedness.[78] Young persons in the universities grasped the close nexus between anti-imperialism and the struggle for socialism. Gandhi, *ahimsa, satyagraha, swaraj* and soul force had entered the *lingua franca* of sophisticated academia. The basic outlines of the condition of India were becoming clearer to the rebellious generation of the 1930s.[79]

Besides, Russell was in a fighting mood. He had read the manuscript of the delegation's report and had penned a thought-provoking foreword recommending the volume as essential reading material about how the empire was being managed. In a letter to Lansbury, Russell explained that the circumstances which influenced the decision of the Labour Party towards the RTC III still existed as the government refused to release political prisoners and to seek Indian cooperation.[80] The extent of Indian cooperation that was then forthcoming was, if anything, less than it had been some months ago. The government had been persisting in a policy of repression and rule of force with which the Labour Party could never agree. Besides, the refusal to open negotiations with the Congress and the insistence on keeping political opponents in prison while fashioning a new constitution were in keeping only with the best imperialist tradition.[81] Accordingly, the participation of Labour representatives on the joint committee would be fruitless and counterproductive inasmuch as it would alienate the Indians from the Labour Party in any future settlement of the Indian question on the basis of self-determination. 'I recognise', he wrote, 'that the decision is one which rests with the Party, but I have taken the liberty of pointing out some of the relevant facts in view of the importance of the question and my own association with Indian affairs and membership of the Labour Party.'[82] He felt sure that Lansbury's sympathy for the Indian struggle would ensure the continuation of the policy that was adopted by the Labour Party in respect of the RTC III.

In a circular to the Labour parties, Russell declared that British policy had been designed to retain power in the hands of British officials in India and the India Office in London.[83] The Labour protest against imperialist oppression should be 'insistent and emphatic'. The constitutional proposals were opposed to Labour's ideas and declared policies. He emphasized that there was a large body of opinion in the labour movement that was opposed to imperialism and persecution. It was rightly 'incensed about Hitlerism in Germany'. But Hitlerism had been thriving 'within the Empire and we share the responsibility for it'. Labour could not be apathetic to its own interests. The India League called upon every Labour Party and individual for assistance in the fight against imperialism.[84] The League survived. Horrabin was relieved of his responsibility and D.R. Grenfell moved in.

The 'King and Country' debate at Oxford was a significant event in Britain in the early 1930s. It had its reverberations all over the English-knowing world and its resolution was endorsed by almost all British universities. It was the first major political initiative that represented the attitude of modern British youth towards the greatest of all problems of human history: war and the threat of war. It affirmed that the appeals to fight in the name of the king and the country should not be allowed to intervene in the process of individual choice between war and peace on considerations of public morality and expansion of human freedom. This was the first critical assessment of the concept of patriotism and constituted an unalloyed denunciation of war by the young generation of a conservative university.[85] The intellectual impact of the motion was not ephemeral. It signified that the movement for peace as the necessary condition of all-round development of mankind had been growing in the universities. Undergraduates of Oxford had already demonstrated against official remembrance service at the war memorial and against the propaganda of Officers' Training Corps. Students in Australia, New Zealand and South Africa passed similar resolutions; a ballot in the United States confirmed the generation's growing commitment against war and blind patriotism.

The ascendancy of peace enthusiasm in the young generation was, in some measure, due to the spate of literature depicting the horrors of destructive warfare heavily underlining the facts that war had been a recognized institution in history, that it was deliberately prepared for, that by far the largest part of any government's budget was concerned with it, that school boys were conspicuously trained in the art, that it was dinned into their minds by systematic propaganda that was necessary to bring out the best qualities of courage, grit and chivalry in men.[86] In another sense, the resurgence of the peace movement was a reaction against the general worsening of the world situation and the growth of the threat of war since 1931 when the nineteenth century vision of hope, tenuously preserved even after World War I, was brought to an abrupt end by Japan's aggression and the collapse of the whole system of collective security and peace. The new thrust in the peace movement was also a barometer that indicated the remarkable switch of undergraduate interests to left-wing politics. The object of the existing school system, it was argued, had been to promote the values of stability, status quo, loyalty and conformity. It aimed at creating an intellectual climate that sustained adherence to a world order based on force and hatred and not on the principles of conciliation and harmony. Japan's aggression in the Far East, Hitler's accession to power, and the failure of the protracted disarmament conference brought war within the range of possibility.[87]

Menon sought to garner the whole range of ideas and emotions sparked off by the Oxford debate in an intensely argued volume, *Young Oxford and War,* by four Oxford activists.[88] In this attractive publication, Menon claimed in his editorial note, a representative group of the young generation of Britain was called upon to throw into relief some relevant questions opened by the famous Oxford resolution on war. Should the youth of the country respond to appeal to arms? Was the new generation self-centred, cowardly and unpatriotic? Did they have a vision for the future of mankind? All the four contributors to that absorbing symposium belonged to different schools of thought and each of them played an important part in the contemporary history of the university. Frank Hardie was a socialist and a member of the Labour Party. Michael Foot, an ex-president, took a leading part in organizing peace demonstrations and was a liberal by political persuasion although of late he was on his way to the Labour Party, being nursed by Menon in the India League. Keith Steel-Maitland, a Conservative, was an astute debator and had made a positive contribution to a point of view held by many Conservatives in the university, which was philosophically opposed to the position of die-hard Toryism. R.G. Freeman, a Communist, was ex-president of the October Club, an active hunger-marcher and he found himself at ease in the congenial atmosphere created by Menon. In a perceptive preface, Harold Laski maintained that a university ought not to be a mere training ground in technique; it should be a school of citizenship as well.[89]

The virtue of Menon's endeavour was to provide clear evidence of the eagerness of Young Oxford to make its uninhibited contribution to the evolution of national opinion. The idea was to articulate much more substance in defence of international justice than was implied in the acceptance of some vaguely conceived peaceful sentiments. Instead, it meant to bring about a complete break with the past and its mindset and to concentrate on an attempt to undermine the theoretical base of international anarchy and the elimination of force in its various forms for the conduct of national, imperial and international affairs. Henceforth, Menon became a significant left-wing national figure who could no longer be held back.

As has been stated earlier, the die-hard organizations had been carrying on a full-blooded agitation aiming at whittling down the proposals of the government. Their slogan was 'back to the Simon report'.[90] Hoare had been throwing out assurances to his backbenchers that they had nothing to be alarmed about and he, in reality, was making no concession of India. His comparison of India with Ireland and his attempt to show that under the new constitution Britain's authority in India would remain unimpaired was an equivocal explanation of the policy.[91] As for Indian support he had been flouting the Congress Party and had been content to rely on the Muslim League, the depressed classes and other friends who came to the RTC. The general impression in England during the preceding few months, Menon wrote in his London Letters in mid-February 1933, had been that the Congress was completely crushed and its chief was then 'concerned only with the social problem of the untouchables and the privations of his own soul'.[92] In contrast, Hoare's assurances had been assuming an air of reality. It was noted in political circles that the Secretary of State's manifesto was an approval of 'the decision of Simla to crush Gandhi'.[93] There was a report in the *Morning Post* that some followers of the Congress had been planning secret parleys to discuss the question of the abandonment of civil disobedience. A marked decline in the number of political prisoners was self-evident. Delhi had been given almost a free hand to tighten repression. Besides, the reforms sought to alleviate the position of the untouchables, which Gandhi had demanded, and the use of the existing legislative machinery for that purpose was regarded as a surrender and the confession of futility of the Congress method.[94]

Menon felt that at the RTC III Sapru had been encouraged to develop 'a sudden affection' for Hoare. The government also hoped to rally the conservative Hindus against the Congress and at, the same time, exploit the differences that they thought would arise as a result of the untouchability campaign.[95] The backbenchers wanted to go a step further and bring in the orthodox Hindus who, like the orthodox Muslims, would demand the continuance of Britain's power to make India safe for democracy.[96] The next few months, Menon prognosticated, would probably see further legislation or ordinances, which would place the whole of India under the type of administration that had become common on the frontier. The spread of 'revolutionary crime' would be made the ostensible reason for such action. The announcement by the government of India about the extension of revolutionary activities in the provinces of India, other than Bengal, had been widely advertised. Stern remedial steps were demanded and such measures were sought to be placed beyond all forms of so-called namby-pamby sentimentalism.

In common with many of his contemporaries, Menon had sensed feelings of hope during, what might be called, the Locarno period. There was the emergence, superficially at least, of a new spirit of harmony and optimism in Europe. Old-fashioned diplomacy continued to thrive as the principal instrument of foreign affairs and produced in the middle of the decade two somewhat optimistic settlements: the implementing of the Dawes plan in October 1924 and the Locarno agreements of 1925. It had appeared that the payment of reparations had been put on a workable basis creating new confidence in German economy with US investment. The western frontiers of Germany and the permanent demilitarization of the Rhineland had been collectively guaranteed and this cheerful atmosphere was confirmed by the Locarno Pact of autumn 1925.[97] By the end of 1932, however, Europe was on the edge once again as the return to the pre-war methods intensified latent conflicts.

In a series of London Letters, Menon captured the nervous trepidations all around emanating from a developing crisis. The situation was complex. An element of uncertainty engulfed it. There was also a touch of the inevitability of a Greek tragedy. The traffic in arms grew and, as a direct result, suspicion among nations became more acute than it had been for several years. France and Germany were hostile to each other and allegations were made of a secret arms plot between Hungary and Germany. Similarly, Italy was being charged with being responsible for smuggling arms into Austria-Hungary. France, having very large interests in the areas, would not look on silently when other powers were active. Apart from this, the ultra-nationalist movement in Hungary, which sought a revision of the treaty of Trianon (4 June 1920) and wanted to extend her borders to the pre-war size, might any day lead to a tremendous conflagration in which the whole world would be involved.[98]

Complications in the Far East had been driving America and Russia into an alliance against the Anglo-Japanese friendship.[99] Meanwhile, there was trouble brewing on the Polish side in the Polish corridor which Germany wanted to annex.[100] Looking around, Menon saw significant developments in Egypt and Turkey. British-inspired repression in Egypt sent many moderates into the *Wafd.* The government, which had been ruling most tyrannically, had been showing signs of collapse. The *Wafd* were as militant as ever and were determined that they would not surrender.[101] From the experience of Turkey it was clear that the new Turkey was not tied to the opinions of a long past age but was anxious to build up nationhood. Mustafa Kamal Ataturk did not allow Britain to exploit Turkey's religious inclinations and pushed his country to move towards the modern view of national self-esteem.[102]

The overwhelming feature of the contemporary world was, however, the amazing rise of Hitler. He had been once dismissed as a showman whom the suppressed desires of 'a once military nation raised to the level of a hero' and was caricatured as 'measuring himself by the shadow he cast in his own twilight'.[103] He had never been visualized as the leader of a *coup d'état.* But that perception had changed. Leading the vicious Nazi party, Hitler stood prominently on the European stage striving to fulfil the programme of German *Mittleuropa.* Surrounded by Joseph Goebbels as minister of propaganda, Heinrich Himmler as head of S.S. and Gestapo, Ernst Roehm, the chief of SA, and Hermann Goering, in charge of police, Hitler was an image of a diabolical, ruthless and determined dictator having little consideration for human values. Hitler, Menon wrote in his piece for *The Hindu,* 'has cast his shadow over Europe and, may be, the world'.[104]

Menon was almost prophetic: Bismarck plunged the world into the cataclysm of 1914; Hitler, in his turn, threatened to overwhelm the world in another holocaust in less than a fiftieth of the time.[105] The change of government in Germany was still tentative but his appeal to the country on 5 March 1933, Menon wrote, would have only one result because the German election was a farce as Hitler had captured the machinery of government.[106] His men occupied all the important posts. His use of the presidential decree was an essential feature of his shock tactics. He had already outlawed opposition parties, suppressed their newspapers and put opponents in prison. The real opposition, Menon wrote, came from the communists and the rank and file of the working class, who in the face of a Nazi dictatorship, had formed a united front in spite of disagreement amongst the leaders.[107] The proletarians were being suppressed ruthlessly. 'Bolshevism, if unchecked, will change the world', Hitler drew a frightening picture of the growth of communism, 'as completely as Christianity once did .... If this movement continues to develop, three hundred years from now Lenin will be regarded not only as one of the revolutionaries of 1917, but as the founder of a new world doctrine and he will be worshipped as much perhaps as Buddha'.[108] The Nazi party alone was prepared and willing to stem the Red tide. Without that party, there would no longer be a middle class in Germany and only with Hitler could the nation be united and revitalized. Indeed, Hitler launched a crusade against communism.[109] 'Germany will poll under Fascism,' Menon added, 'and under Fascism elections have only one result.'[110] The advent of fascism in Germany had changed the map of Europe almost overnight. Hitler had already set 'the storm centre of Europe', Menon wrote, 'in an anticyclonic circle; and anti-cyclone often precedes a cyclone.'[111] More than new alliances and counter-alliances, Hitler's shadow threw into relief the outlines of the new map of Europe, which carried within it 'the inevitable elements of instability and the utter negation of the only ideas on which stability can be based'. There was no prospect of disarmament. 'It was a dark horizon.' Menon wrote: 'Will it be a cloudburst, a thunderstorm or a cyclone? 1933 will answer.'[112] A recognized political analyst and commentator, Menon switched his attention to examine the prospect of the Indian movement against the new international situation.

Before the farcical German election of 5 March 1933, Menon reported on the persecution of Jews in Germany and its repercussions in Britain. Jews in Britain and elsewhere were alarmed. They feared mass extinction of German Jews. There was an eerie uncertainty that stupefied the community the world over. Jews in Britain were struck by a paralyzing fear that any organized protest might at once lead to reprisals against their co-religionists in Germany.[113] The British newspapers were desperate to emphasize that world opinion would compel Hitler to relent. Then the Reichstag fire (27 February 1933) gave the pretext and within a short span of two days 5,000 socialists and communists, including all left MPs, were in prison and every form of freedom was suppressed. Germany was under ordinances known as martial law. People began to disappear into camps at Dachau, Sachsenhausen and Oranienburg. The only effective check on the suppression of civil liberty, on rule by decree, on the crushing of political opposition and the torture of opponents was organized world opinion. Menon had realized the bitter truth that, generally speaking, such opinion tended to express itself 'when the suppressed people belong to a free country and not to an Empire'.[114]

In response, the politics of the National government took a perceptible right about turn. Soon Menon was to write that while MacDonald had been moving towards the Palace Chamber, his one-time trusted lieutenant Oswald Mosley was touring the country playing Hitler 'to the last T'.[115] By April, Menon reported that Jews in Britain had set aside their class and party distinctions to battle Nazism in Germany. It was striking, Menon wrote, that Lord Reading found himself in agreement with the socialists and communists and even discovered the value of liberty.[116] It was interesting to note, Menon added, that all those respectables had been discovering the virtues of economic boycott as a potent weapon and the government formulated no ordinances against it, although German business was affected by the Jewish protest.[117]

By mid-April 1933, it seemed to Menon that the fascist coup in Germany was complete and had consolidated itself.[118] It appeared that Hitler cared little for engagements and would allow no commitment to bind him. His wicked plans had been made and published, but only a few could read them. Menon was convinced that the man had a programme and he intended to carry it out systematically and even go beyond it. The news of Nazi atrocities from Germany were published in all the newspapers in England, although the right-wing press had largely gone over to Hitler. Menon learnt from private sources that in Germany Hitler was then so fully believed as having stabilized the revolutionary regime that the trade unions and others who opposed him in the past had learnt to submit and, as in Italy, Germany in all probability would have only official and non-political unions.[119]

By May 1933, however, the reaction of British public opinion to Hitler and his method was not in doubt. Part of the press was mildly pro-Hitler but dared not express itself. The persecution of the Jews had queered Hitler's pitch in Britain.[120] If the German chancellor had been merely a political autocrat like Mussolini, Menon wrote, he would have gained the support of the British reactionary press and even some of the prosperous and eminent persons.[121] Hitler's emissary in London had been having a hard time. The House of Commons was more alive to the German issue than it had been to any other and there was considerable liveliness inside the chamber.[122] Great Britain had begun to think along the lines of an economic blockade. France declared that she took British collaboration for granted. She proposed to march her troops before long into the Rhine.[123] Germany had already given some indication of her scheduled actions. The United States had become very curt to the Nazis.[124] It was evident to Menon that while Germany had been drifting away from the English alliance, which the government of the social democrats and the stewardship of Stresemann had promoted and nurtured, the United States and Britain were coming together.[125] Public opinion was definitely anti-Hitler, while the government laid itself open to suspicion that it allowed Nazis greater facilities than political propaganda of other persuasions. In the universities anti-Hitler organizations were formed by students and certain colleges were endeavouring to provide openings for students and staff driven away from Germany by Hitler's persecution.[126]

The German speech at the disarmament conference provoked ripples in Britain but there was no significant attempt to restrain Hitler from becoming another Kaiser Wilhelm. Sympathy for Germany, however, had been steadily waning. German attempts for obtaining relief from the iniquitous provisions of the Treaty of Versailles had been cold-shouldered. Germany might soon find, wrote Menon, that militarily and economically it had raised a hornet's nest.[127] The gender policy of Hitler had opened a new area of fascist perception. German women, who had been enjoying a good deal of democratic freedom for generations, were victims of Hitler's new pogrom. A new spurt was added to the women's movement to resist Nazi policy and in Britain Mrs Pethic-Lawrence, then an ardent India League activist, had been leading the movement.[128]

It was widely realized by then that fascist forces shared in common a commitment to ultra-nationalism, anti-communism, and anti-liberalism. But what Menon underlined was that the most specific area of agreement was the idealization, motivation and enlistment of the masses to the fascist cause. That undemocratic mobilization of the masses was maintained symbolically in the form of public theatre — the Nuremberg, Dresden and Munich rallies, the masses passing under the Brandenburg Gate down the Wilhelmstrasse looking upto Hitler's gestures on the balcony of the Reichstag — even when the Nazis came to power. They were, as Hobsbawm puts it, 'the revolutionaries of counter-revolution';[129] they appealed to all those who imagined to have been victims of society; called for a total transformation of society and adapted the symbols of social revolutionaries; they indulged in the rhetoric of 'return to the traditional past'; denounced liberal gender emancipation; opposed modern cultural forms for their alleged degenerating impact; invented tradition; transformed superficial historical prejudices of the society such as anti-semitism into 'a mechanized mass murder of millions of Jews' based on 'a repulsive ideology of race-hatred'.[130] Words of Marx, Freud, Stefan Zweig, etc. were thrown into the flames of 'spontaneous' book burnings and with them went books of Voltaire, Thomas Mann, Romain Rolland, H.G. Wells. Germans under Hitler were desperately in search of their role as self-styled *Herrenvoek*. Early in November 1932, 39 prominent business houses had come out with a petition to Hindenburg in support of Hitler. Bureaucrats did not find it difficult to serve him. Even a number of intellectuals and literary figures espoused the regeneration of Germany. These included the philosophers Krieck and Bäumler, the poets Buck and Binding and Germany's most distinguished dramatist, Gerhart Hauptmann. In a sense, Menon wrote, fascism was an amalgamation of conservative values, techniques of mass appeal, innovative ideologies of the irrational and the savage, older traditions of intolerance and support of the middle and lower middle strata sandwiched between big business on the one hand, and an organized labour movement on the other.[131]

In another perceptive letter, Menon reported that Europe was inevitably drifting towards war. Internecine strife in Germany was then only a few weeks away. The situation in the Balkans was nearing a dangerous crisis. The internal troubles of Yugoslavia could no longer remain an internal matter. King Alexander was threatened from all sides by his people. Yugoslavia was the object of Italian attention on the Adriatic and the friendship of King Boris of Bulgaria and the Duce was not a happy combination for the well-being of Europe.[132] To add to these, wholesale traffic in arms had been going on. Germany was sending arms to Hungary where a virulent nationalist movement wanted to regain her pre-war boundaries. Italy had been similarly charged with sending arms to Austria where the fascists were gaining strength. France had investments all over the place and watched the situation carefully. She had a finger in the Romanian pie. Oil fields in the ports on the Adriatic, the coal beds in Silesia and the mineral wealth of Transylvania made the situation one of gravity to international peace. The performance of the League of Nations in connection with Manchuria did not warrant a hope that it would be effective in a crisis. Further, while the powers would either discuss the clauses of the covenant or appoint innumerable committees when it was the Chinese that were being slaughtered, it was very unlikely that they would adopt that procedure if it meant any possible thwarting of their own pet national ambitions. 'When there is oil, money and mines mixed up with principles, and a lot of armament manufacturers interested in the whole business,' Menon wrote, 'we have reasons to fear that we are on the edge of a serious trouble.'[133]

By the end of April 1933, Menon warned against the rumblings of war in the Far East. In March 1933, Japan left the League. Russo-Japanese embroilment had then reached the stage of acute crisis and it created a greater confusion in foreign policy than was superficially evident. Menon was firm in his conviction that, although Russia was hated in the British foreign office, Britain could not afford to allow the growth of Japanese hegemony in the Pacific. In any case, Hong Kong had turned out to be a place of first class strategic importance for the British empire.[134] Both France and Britain were not happy about the difficulties in the Malayan empire. The Singapore base was not yet constructed and the complications in India and Burma were not very reassuring either. Japan had been an ally, but she entered the war because it paid her to do so. She captured the German possessions in the Far East and even robbed China, herself a war ally. In Japan, Menon noted with concern, the anti-war movement had been crushed with severity besides which martial law and ordinance rule paled into insignificance. Arrest for entertaining thoughts inimical to the state was increasing. Suicide and growth of radical tendencies went hand in hand. Teachers were being persecuted by the state. Newspapers were afraid to speak the truth and they echoed the thoughts of the warlords who had been precipitating a war with Russia.[135]

The Near East did not make one happy either. The Poles were in a state of ferment. Concentration of troops had taken place in the corridor. Hitler's speeches and demonstrations in eastern Germany about the dismemberment of the Fatherland and the pledges taken by the Nazis to recover the corridor and the free cities, including Danzig set the stage for war. Official organs of Poland asserted that the Third Reich was determined to build up the military power of Germany and that the claws of the old lion had grown. Conservative press in Poland was incapable of restraining the people from denouncing Germany. MacDonald added confusion by his Rome conversation and Poland was thrown into the arms of France.[136] While the disarmament conference failed to produce any real measure of disarmament, the fighting services and their branch departments in Britain and other major countries, scheduled their programmes for an imminent war. The war machine had been speeded up, expenditure on armaments increased; military alliances had been tightened. Added to this was the changed psychology of nations where fascism was the reply to economic crisis as their citizens were drilled to think in terms of patriotism. Under the crumbling facade of international goodwill, the forces of ultra-nationalism and fascism grew.

Menon was quick to see that while political discussions were going on in Westminster, postulates concerning the future of economic relations which were the basis of political policies were being established by the British side. The Indian side in the whole operation was eclipsed by default.[137] At Manchester, Baldwin referred to the voluntary acceptance by India of an idea of preferences and he was followed by other ministers. Side by side with the reforms and the safeguards, a scheme of economic imperialism stronger than before was being planned. It was usual to contrast the policy of the die-hards with that of the Baldwinites, but, as Menon pointed out, the differences were mainly those of manner rather than matter.[138] In this context, Menon alluded to the latest pronouncements of Lord Lloyd which deserved attention. He proposed a tightening of the British grip on the Crown colonies and asserted Britain's tariff rights over India which, he maintained, were legal and constitutional and called for a bargain with India to share in the exploitation of the colonial market in return for obtaining preferences in India.[139] In other words, Menon argued, the mill-owners of Bombay, Calcutta and Ahmedabad were to be told that they could sell the Africans and others some of their jute and cotton on condition that Lancashire and Birmingham held India. What Menon stressed was that the doctrine of imperial preferences was then becoming the closed system of the empire and it was being forced on India. No constitution, Menon was quick to add, even if it gave a little more than the white paper conceded, was 'worth anything in the face of this economic conquest'.[140]

Under the circumstances Menon saw no definite indication that any change in the India policy was in the offing.[141] The Government of India appeared to believe that 'the knock out blow' succeeded and assumed that it could follow up their success by proposing to keep the 'rebels' in prison unless they apologized. 'The Government of India', Menon said in his 'London Letter', 'is not satisfied even with a victory, they want a triumph.' This was the opinion, he added, 'held here by some with regret and by others with approbation'.[142] Gandhi was regarded as being a spent force politically. It was also believed that the government had helped to bring about his political death. Some odd individuals, not commanding any particularly influential political force, were unhappy with such an analysis. They thought that the political eclipse of Gandhi would mean mighty little for the government who would gain nothing. The support of the cooperators could have been taken for granted anyway, Gandhi or no Gandhi. The left-wingers would not have given the government anything more substantial than Gandhi would have done.[143] To all these questions, the answer of the die-hards seemed to be that the King's government was the Government of India and such malcontents as Gandhi or the Congress must be put down till they changed their ways. It was not a question of left-wing or right-wing, Menon wrote, 'every wing that is not under the wing of the government should be clipped'.[144] That seemed to Menon to be the government's case and it proposed to put it into practice. The issue, therefore, appertained to the facts of the Indian situation and the Government of India would decide the trend of official policy as well as the nature of the reform. In Britain, misrepresentation of the Indian situation would continue and the efficacy of the strong-hand policy would constitute the central tenet of official handouts and the preoccupation of the media.[145]

In a passionate appeal to stimulate public opinion to the sordid realities and emphasize the righteousness of India's cause,

Wilkinson continued to express her displeasure against British tyranny in India and the false and mischievous presentation of India's struggle for freedom. At a meeting under the auspices of the Birmingham and District Council for India's Freedom at Digbeth Institute on 11 February 1933, she castigated the self-centred attitude of the middle-class. She claimed that the Indian leadership was composed of men and women of immense courage and high moral and intellectual standards. She described the National Congress as the biggest propaganda machine in the world outside the Soviet Union and as a tremendous cultural effort which had drawn into unity people of different creeds and languages by an ideal of India as a nation. The big difference Congress had made had been to make the Indians realize that they could stand up to the British and if they stood together they could run their country. The official drive against reconstructive work in rural India was even more dreadful than putting into prison Congress volunteers. Gandhi represented to hundreds of millions of poor people in India — someone who understood them and had been fighting for them. There was no other way to peace except through agreement with Gandhi. Opportunities for conciliation were missed. The oppression in India under the Labour Party was phenomenal but owing to the united work of Benn and Lord Irwin, a bridge was built between Gandhi and them on which it was possible for negotiations to take place. It appeared to her that Britain, having opted for a strong hand in India, declared without a touch of remorse that it had not learnt anything from the lessons that Ireland might have taught her.[146]

Recalling the visit of Menon at the Congregational Church, Battersea, to address a meeting, organized by Workers' Fellowship, and his instructive and inspiring presentation, Maurice Hodder, President of the fellowship wrote in February 1933 soliciting Menon to visit them once again. He claimed that the organization was still prospering. Emphasizing that India should find a significant place in the current political movements in Britain, Hodder lamented that the political salvation of India should be closely linked to the problem of rationalization and retrenchment that was the order of the day. The Labour Party, especially its trade union, appreciated the importance of the management of class conflict and the subdual of activism. Hodder claimed that he had been doing everything that he could in the way of educational and instructional nature 'to prevent these men from declining from unemployment to unemployability.[147]

At a crowded meeting organized by the India League, some leading men and women in public life in India and England paid their tribute to Gandhi during his three-week anti-untouchability fast on 23 May 1933. C.F. Andrews was in the chair while Sapru, Aiyangar, N.M. Joshi, Ellen Wilkinson, Lansbury and Morgan Jones spoke to a fairly good gathering at Friends' House.[148] Lansbury's speech breathed sincere admiration for Gandhi. It was an indictment of government policy, an appeal to release political prisoners and a cogent argument against bombing civilian population in India. Upholding Gandhian humanity in contemporary politics, Lansbury emphasized the incompatibility of violence in a democratic polity. Meanwhile, an appeal to the viceroy and the prime minister signed by some 70 outstanding Indians, including Rabindranath Tagore, urged government to respond with sincerity to the gesture of goodwill made by Gandhi and thereby restore an atmosphere favourable to the reception of reforms under consideration.[149] Observers noted with pleasant surprise that Gandhi had been making headway in certain intellectual quarters, in spite of his apparent failure to influence the Government of India.

In fact, Gandhi's moral conviction, steadfastness to truth and his conquest of violence had then been acknowledged, albeit with misgivings, in British political circles. In a signed article in the *India Bulletin,* the organ of the Friends of India, Romain

Rolland had recommended the honest, generous and elegant mood of poet Tagore. Rolland hailed Gandhi as the 'Mahatma of non-violence', 'the Saint of satyagraha' and 'the new St. Thomas, a triumphant example of what Gandhi himself called the sword of self-sacrifice'.[150] Even though one was tempted to pass over the statements of Gandhi's admirers, it was evident to the statesmen and politicals of the *Raj* that Gandhi was not an obdurate and mean politician and that he had given ample evidence of his sincerity to arrive at some respectable settlement with the government in keeping with the honour of his people and the integrity of the Congress. The general impression that had been left in the mind of Herbert Emerson during his long interview with Gandhi on 20 March 1930, was that the Mahatma was keen to implement the settlement with Irwin and come to some genuine long-term understanding.[151] It was feared by Emerson that the opposition from the left and the execution of Bhagat Singh might create complications for him at the Karachi Congress. Gandhi was also not unaware that a resolution in favour of complete independence within a definite time-frame would only add to his difficulties. Emerson was, however, quite convinced that Gandhi had made up his mind to ensure that such a step would not be taken at Karachi and all references to *purna swaraj* would invariably be qualified by speeches 'which would avoid banging the door in the way of peace'.[152] *Purna swaraj*, Emerson believed, might still be adopted by Gandhi before long, since the ideal of dominion status had not as yet found a place in the British agenda for India. Gandhi was, nevertheless, reasonable in his terms and conditions and he gave the impression that he was not frightfully perturbed by open threats held out to him by Emerson on the eve of his departure for England.[153] Gandhi did not fail to comprehend the nature of the threatened official action against Congress attempts to consolidate its position. He had good reason to apprehend that official over-reaction would be followed by a period of reprisals but he showed no sign of uneasy tension. Emerson must have recalled in his pensive moments the statement of Field-Marshal J.C. Smuts that Gandhi had made the Christian motif of the spiritual power of suffering a means of reconciliation and atonement; and the efficacy of prayer and fasting an essential part of his novel technique of reform. The Western man, at least in the preceding 350 years, Smuts elaborated, accepted a creed of progress through material welfare which had no place for the mystical side of Christianity. Gandhi adopted that aspect of Christianity and Indianized it in his quest for truth. In fact, Gandhi strenuously denied that his fast was intended to blackmail his opponent into surrender. He hoped to win by conversion, not by coercion.[154] Gandhi and his credo and conviction were totally alien to imperial perception and Western tradition and sensibilities.

The British press did not attach any political importance to Gandhi's release in May 1933. Both press cables from India and comments in England expressed the view that the government should not revise its policy in any way and he would be put back into prison as an ordinary prisoner if he started organized disobedience again. The *Manchester Guardian* made a cautious suggestion that Gandhi was not an ordinary prisoner after all. But Menon was surprised to find that the rest of the press, including the progressive organs, looked on him as a completely spent force and pointed to the absence in India of public interest in Gandhi and to the nature of his actions as that of a man who once had millions behind him but was no longer a factor in practical politics. Evidently, the idea that impelled such comments was to mobilize the results of Willingdon-Hoare policy and to rally the moderates. Menon thought that the direct result of that strong arm policy was to push India to the place that it used to have before 1927. Even by June 1933 there was no indication at all that the government would change its policy. Gandhi would be allowed to remain free if he devoted himself to untouchability but there was no question of an amnesty or any peaceful gesture of any kind.[155]

Gandhi's peace offer, however, appeared somewhat astounding. Menon thought that for the fast of May 1933 itself there was little sympathy in England and friends of Gandhi thought kindly of him but did not pretend to understand the matter or to explain it. For many, the Indian situation had become more of an enigma than ever. Even Menon and other members of the League, who were then intimately connected with Indian realities, did not quite know how to assess the situation. Menon noted that protest of Vithalbhai Patel and Subhas Bose did not evoke any significant response in India and this was, he thought, an indication that Gandhi even in his retreat, held the Congress in his grip. The government, and the on-line body of the British establishment, viewed Gandhi's declaration as an admission of defeat and was therefore glad that the Government of India had not given away its advantage by offering to retreat while the enemy was on the run. There was no indication that the government's policy would undergo any desirable modifications. Menon felt that political initiative had been fast moving away to the die-hards. Tory reaction on India continued to grow; Tory women's condemnation of Baldwin's 'conciliatory' India policy was a surprise even to the Conservative leaders; the bill was expected to be more die-hard than the white paper making it acceptable to the die-hards except perhaps Churchill, Alfred Knox and Reginald Craddock.[156]

The withdrawal of the movement by Gandhi and the refusal of the government to accept Gandhi's offer of negotiation seemed to endorse the general assessment that it was a confession of the demoralization that had set in the Congress ranks. The campaign against the Congress and the arrest of men like Malaviya confirmed that white paper or no white paper, 'the government proposes to carry on at present'.[157] The constitutional proposals, Marley wrote, would not lead to amnesty; the cooperation that the government sought was not from the Congress. As the white paper conceded less than the

Simon report and since it was presented simply as a tentative proposal which the JSC was empowered to whittle down, it appeared that Churchill 'was banging against an open door'.[158] The die-hards might be tempted to attack the Simon proposals as radical and 'Sir John may thus yet emerge', Menon wrote, ' as the radical reformer'. Menon realized that in the Labour Party there was a tendency for ideas to live in association with each other, so that a revolt on one issue tended to become a revolt on a broad front. In contrast, in the Conservative Party revolts were usually *ad hoc* affairs involving no total attitude and no total rejection of the leadership.[159]

The Mahatma's peace offer was, however, perplexing. Menon felt that opponents were not influenced by it, while friends were confused. If it was a retreat it appeared abrupt and disorderly. It crystallized the die-hard attitude, since it was taken to mean that the Congress was beaten completely. Menon was candid: Willingdon was acclaimed as a saviour and Gandhi's action was cited as testimony of its success.[160] From Irwin, Gandhi obtained terms of peace; to Willingdon he offered surrender. The only redeeming feature was that the volume of opposition to the National government had swelled amazingly in the preceding few months and at the Hitchin by-election, known as a hard core Conservative farmers' Hertfodshire constituency, Labour polled a vote that was better than in the avalanche of 1929.[161]

As Knatchbull was appointed a new governor of Bombay, Menon was not slow to point out that he had been private secretary to Samuel Hoare and was himself a confirmed Baldwinite. The new governor brought with him no record of statesmanship. It was emphasized that he was a reliable and an experienced party man. There would be no change in policies and officials would gain greater power than ever. Looking at the prospect, Menon protested vehemently. The practice of appointing governors from London, Menon held, should have to be given up even under a conservative constitution, as such men would either be in the hands of officials completely or commit egregious blunders that would create crisis after crisis. It was, however, significant, Menon added, that Britain sent to India to command the destiny of millions of people, men 'who aren't considered fit to take a junior ministerial post in this country'.[162]

By the end of June 1933, the situation seemed ominous and events pointed to the inescapable ascendancy of Churchill. The victory of Baldwin in the Conservative meeting on India on 28 June 1933 was illusory. It was hailed as the personal triumph of Baldwin and the party machinery. But it was necessary to realize that the meet was not of parliamentarians mainly, but of chairmen and secretaries of Conservative organizations in the country which meant that it was much more than a mere rebellion in the House of Commons. A poll of 356 for a rebel group against 838 for the party machine and the parliamentary leader in the first round was dreary and the prospect was sombre because it was well known that not all those who disagreed with the issue in question would vote against the officials of the party. All that the decision meant, as had been pointed out by the *Manchester Guardian*, was that the majority had decided to postpone consideration or judgement on the white paper till the joint committee had reported. Baldwin did not make a fighting speech; he was defensive and even apologetic; he took his position on technicalities of procedure, he made no case for the white paper, and merely insisted that the party should await the outcome of the joint committee. Menon commented that once the committee reported, the whole question would be reopened and by then the Churchillites would have gathered momentum. The most significant feature of the Conservative jamboree was Lady Hoare's interjection about the future of communications in India. It was plain, Menon remarked, whatever the nature of constitutional proposals, the military arm of Britain was for ever to be at India's throat and what he heard of the activities of the railway committee made the situation more dismal and gloomy. Worried about the inept handling of the deliberations in the JSC by a set of ambitious but inept Indians, Menon lamented that they had been playing faithfully the game of government and the 'future of India is now a pawn in their game for place and power for themselves'.[163]

There was also a strange phenomenon as the Indian women and the joint committee attracted some reactionary feminist leaders in England. The growing cordiality of the two movements, Menon warned, had dangerous possibilities and had to be carefully watched. Feminism, he wrote, was all very well but it was tragic that feminism should land them in the strange company of those who despised Indians and were antagonistic to their aspirations.[164] The group of women who were then posing as friends of Indian womanhood first came into notice as supporters of Katherine Mayo. They then belonged to groups that were opposed to Indian nationalism and whose outlook was most imperialistic. The Indian women, Menon reiterated, were making a worse mistake of seeking the alliance of India's enemies for particularist claims. Under the wise leadership of Sarojini Naidu and others, the Indian women's movement had been kept away from 'this inane vulgarity and stupidity', Menon wrote in anguish, but that stage of 'women's movement now appears over' and one was confronted with the 'pathetic phenomenon of Indian women in alliance with India's detractors'. It was a tragedy to see the meek representatives of all-India organizations led by Begum Shah Nawaz queuing up to give evidence before the joint committee despite the fact that the Indian delegation was being treated as a mere subsidiary and was not given even free exchange of views with its British colleagues. The joint committee asserted its right to take and hear evidence on its own and in the nature of things it would write its own report.[165] It was widely circulated in the whispering gallery of London that the die-hard attitude towards Indian freedom was hardened partly because of the tenor of Indian politics: persistence of picketing of British goods, general sympathy for revolutionaries, temper of communal feelings, continued agrarian unrest in Bengal, UP and Gujarat and immensity of Lancashire pressure. As a consequence, it seemed to many that Toryism felt justified to demand a strong government in India.[166]

The decision of the Congress conference in Poona (12 to 14 July 1933) not to suspend civil disobedience, which was cabled to London, repudiated the expectation of everyone. The impression that had been given to the officials during the preceding few months was that the retraction of civil disobedience was a certainty. The discussion in the press had all along been only on the point of how it would be done. The 'surrender' of the Congress was accepted as a fact for which only a little more time was required before the actual accomplishment. Indians in Britain, who had the ear of the official side, also genuinely held that opinion and they made no bones about it. The claims that the movement of civil disobedience had been backsliding and gradually fading out for some time, that people were tired and that nothing could revive any extraordinary enthusiasm for it were stated as axiomatic political realities by almost every stray visitor or savant from India both in private conversations and at public presentations. Such views were expressed so often that a somewhat contradictory decision, taken at Poona, came as an incongruous surprise.[167]

In fact, the Poona decision caused much unsettling discomfiture. It was apprehended that the request of Gandhi for an interview would be refused by the viceroy, that the stalemate might continue and the government would reaffirm its proposal to press on with reforms. It had also been expected by his friends in the Conciliation Group that Gandhi would appeal for peace. It was believed with a mélange of glee and relish that he would put untouchablity before everything, that he had mellowed over time and such expressions as 'no surrender' indicating extreme inflexibility, would never appear in his vocabulary again.[168] There was no pressure of any kind from the London end to induce the Government of India to soften its attitude and offer a matching response to Gandhi's malleable gesture. The Indian delegates at the JSC had neither the will nor the ability, Menon wrote, to do anything significant and the government felt sure that they had the situation well under control. Serious observers, however, had been raising two distinct questions: if the Government of India would attenuate its stiff attitude and meet the Congress halfway or if the government would decide to swoop down on the Congress, in that contingency would the Congress be able to stand up to the shock?

Representations had been made to Samuel Hoare by the League but without any effect. Menon reiterated that even in informed circles in England it was believed that the Congress had been suing for peace. There was considerable disillusionment as it was felt widely that suffering had brought nothing. Gandhi was expected to give a lead when he was strong enough to do so. People were inquisitive to know if the Congress would agree to his calling off the movement for good.[169] Gandhi's friends in England were also wondering whether Gandhi would ever agree to a policy which kept Nehru and Ghaffar Khan in prison and left the peasants of Gujarat to their fate.[170] The proceedings of the joint select committee, Menon claimed, had then developed into something like a conference. Samuel Hoare held his own both against die-hards and reformers. He was clear in his mind about what he proposed to do. He had given every one an impression of downright frankness though to those outside the committee and the friendly circles of government, the frankness did not seem very different from the take-it-or-leave-it attitude.

The progressive individuals on the Indian side were unhappy about the situation, but the possibilities of a walk out, which used to be canvassed earlier, were then definitely ruled out. The committee was expected to continue its deliberations till August 1933 and it was very unlikely that all the Indian members would continue to stay on till it reassembled in autumn.[171]

Evidently, as Menon saw, the committee was being directed by the government towards its own desired goal. Those among the Indian delegates who had thrown in their lot with the JSC 'must now be on the bed they have made'. The Indians were not by any means happy and Menon was convinced that men like Sapru and Aiyangar knew full well what the situation was and they were not by any measure satisfied with the work they had been able to do. The choice between them seemed to Menon to be either active civil disobedience or cooperation. Within the limits in which these men had placed themselves, they did their work and put up a case, but they were aware that their role on the committee had been one of subsidiary significance.[172]

Commenting on the situation, Menon continued to warn against complacency, drift, and lack of creative leadership in India and emphasized the need for a bold and united stand in London. In July 1933, it was increasingly felt in political circles in London that the world conference was MacDonald's swansong.[173] With disarmament wrecked partly by British insistence and partly by lack of British initiative, with the world conference ending in a fiasco and with issues fairly joined on India between the die-hards and the nationals, with the domestic situation showing a complete triumph of 'Tory fascism' as seen in the cooperative societies taxation, increasing unemployment, the police report and land tax storm, 'the Premier may find that the time has come for him', Menon wrote cryptically, 'to prefer the air of his Scotch highland to the surf-riding of Westminster'.[174] Baldwin appeared to have realized this and had been preparing to take over. He had, Menon wrote, no intention of going down with the premier and he might, Menon added, easily explain that it was his national duty not to do so.[175] His leadership of the house during the premier's absence at the conference in Geneva was but a step preparatory to it. Meanwhile, Baldwin continued to make significant surrender to the Churchillian wing despite the so-called sensational victory at the Conservative conference on 28 June 1933. 'The White Paper', Menon quipped, 'would have to become whiter still.' It seemed to Menon that time was with Churchill. The Indian issue 'need not reach breaking point' till the middle of next year. Meanwhile government stock would decline further and its national veneer would be thinner.[176]

In that desperate and gloomy atmosphere, Menon called for serious introspection in India. It was time, he wrote in *Andhra Patrika,* that moderate opinion in India asserted itself and called a halt to the performance that was then going on at Westminster, so far as it concerned the Indian side.[177] It was no longer a question of the divergent viewpoints of Congressmen and liberals, of constitutionalists, non-cooperators and gradualists and others.[178] Menon maintained that Indian moderates had been functioning over the years under conditions vastly different from those which obtained then. Since those days India's power to compel or effectively persuade the British side had diminished due to various causes. But none of those justified the presence of Indians 'held in bond by the British government to witness the unseemly spectacle of gratuitous insults and vengeful attacks on the character and antecedents of people whose future was under discussion' without giving a general consideration to the 'ordinary self-respect' of the subject people.[179]

Menon recognized with sympathy the supreme difficulty of the task which had fallen to men like Sapru, isolated as they were, from the moral support of their countrymen. He was even inclined to overlook their many mistakes and shortcomings. But all this was possible only in the hope that ultimately their course of conduct would not for ever scatter to the winds India's title to esteem and self-respect in the eyes of the world. Menon recalled the time when the moderates of India boycotted the Simon Commission; he also recalled the words of a moderate who, when told that a commission was an impartial jury, retorted that 'India was neither in the dock as a criminal nor a corpse in a mortuary to need the service of a jury'.[180] In contrast, at the joint committee witness after witness appeared to malign the Indian people, make *ex parte* statements and indulge in generalization 'which at any conference between two nations would lead to diplomatic rupture'.[181] It was heard for weeks that the Indians did not think that any useful service could be rendered by their continuance on the commission and yet they decided to go on. They talked of sailing but opted to stay put merely to 'mortgage the future of Indian finance by being outmanoeuvred in the committees on the Reserve Bank' and to attend the Secretary of State's 'durbars where he, with commendable frankness and imperial pomp, lectures them all'.[182] Not even personal affront appeared to have had the 'wholesome effect of re-examination of their own position so far as those delegates are concerned'.[183]

Menon concluded that the JSC was primarily engaged in an internal dispute within the Conservative Party and India was projected merely as a pawn. Menon thought that the very presence of John P. Thompson, Edward Villiers and Alfred Watson as representatives of the Union of Britain and India, operating on behalf of Baldwin with their reactionary views on India's progress, was a sufficient indicator of the purpose of the committee. Baldwin's new phrase 'Save India for the Empire' was more explanatory than the earlier phrase 'safeguards demonstrably in the interest of India'. The new slogan should, Menon quipped, have persuaded the moderates and the liberals, with whom friendship and alliance with Britain was an article of faith, cry out: 'Save us from our friends.'[184] The purpose of the JSC, it appeared, was not to make out a case for India's self-government, but to provide justification for the further tightening of safeguards. John Thompson's evidence was in the nature of a homily to Indians not to be anxious to advance in haste without finding the money to run self-government. The general impact of the proceedings of the committee was so humiliating that Menon requested Srinivasa Sastri in India to use his goodwill to recall the delegates. To wait and watch and hang on 'would be to lose self-respect first and everything else after it'.[185]

The world economic and monetary conference was being held between 12 June and 5 July 1933 at the Geological Museum in South Kensington. Menon was convinced that both the conferences had been leading to no hopeful results. The economic conference from the point of view of its avowed objectives failed.[186] It had shown the bankruptcy of statesmanship but in spite of all that, Menon wrote, in comparison with the Indian discussions in Westminster, it might as well claim credit. The small nations were not continually exposed to a humiliating set of lectures.[187] The Kensington conference was not 'an orgy of sadistic revenge and callous heckling of a hapless victim while the relatives helplessly look on'.[188] In response, Menon harped in his various letters that the Indian committee had been turning increasingly into a disgrace from the Indian point of view each week. It was apparent to him that what was being done was to build up a case that handing over of services, Indianization, central responsibility, immediate establishment of a Reserve Bank and so on were matters which were either not possible, or were against the interest of India's progress.[189] The bill, Menon thought, would thus aim at conferring partial responsibiliity in the provinces of India, and place on the statute book a plan for 'a federal structure which would be found to be rather an impediment to development in India than otherwise'.[190]

What was equally disturbing was that even the labour movement was getting more and more nervous at the developing fascist tendencies of the national government.[191] The proposals to militarize the police force and to import into the system men with authoritarian Indian experience, were hotly contested by the opposition. Britain's economic position was not reassuring.[192] In fact, the stable industries of Britain had slumped heavily and there was no hope of real return to prosperity. About 30 per cent of the mining population was out of work. In Wilkinson's constituency on the Tyne, about 85 per cent of the workers were unemployed. The coal areas showed an increase of ten per cent in unemployment. The number of the Blackshirts increased. They were becoming increasingly volatile, and had been enjoying considerable official indulgence.[193]

In another Letter Menon argued that the best way to understand the *mentalite* of the nations then assembled at the World Economic Conference, was to analyze their speeches and discern their core. Without exception, they all claimed that they would agree to this or that policy because it was in their national interests.[194] The conference itself moved in the realm of economic nationalism and its autocratic implications. As a consequence, such discussions 'as were likely to bear fruitful proceeds' had been going on between neighbours and others. The conference provided an opportunity for agreements, but they were not international agreements nor were they based on the desire to reach world settlements.[195] They aimed at self-interest and they sustained the time-honoured ideas of balance of power.[196] The London economic conference, Menon declared, had been laying the foundation of a Europe and an America 'which for the next decade will wage the internecine war born of economic nationalism...'. Out of this anarchy, he added, would emerge dictatorships and the 'worst exaggerations of militarism and capitalism'.[197] In informed circles, Menon thought, it was widely believed that 'the Oxygen treatment' of the world economy could not go on for long and, therefore, before long, so far as England was concerned, it would settle down to a discussion with the United States 'while the rest of the nations will go home', enabling 'Sir John Simon to acquire a relish for the humble pie' and find some legal justification, if not necessity, for calling off the Russian embargo.[198] The two nations were likely to find an agreement on business terms. The National government, Menon wrote, hoped that the transition to higher prices and wages would come about by the 'swing of the pendulum'.[199] But Menon thought that there was little chance of this happening and unless some radical changes were introduced for making use of the plentiful supply of money, the depression, in all probability, would continue.

Menon felt that MacDonald's star had probably set.[200] The Tory parliamentary party was faced with the worst period; to the Indian revolt was added a revolt on tariffs, and opinion had been hardening for an appeal to the country. The size of the party itself had been causing alarm.[201] Discontent was growing at an alarming rate and the failures of government were mounting. The world conference was 'a pricked bubble' already and the younger Tory MPs were unwilling to take on themselves the odium of the National government's failure.[202] Churchill had been trying hard to compel Baldwin to adopt his policies and end the National government. The upshot of such an endeavour would, however, be marginal because the Tory caucus, that had been ruling the government, might adjust its policies.[203] The party machinery was powerful and the Defence of India League was alert but Baldwin was not sure if he would be forced to face a defeat.

Even by the end of May, it seemed that die-hards had become discreet and decided not to fight the official Conservative candidate in the Lancashire by-election as Randolph Churchill hastened to beat a retreat in spite of the cotton magnates' friendly approaches and encouragement.[204] At Hitchin, the Tory candidate had the reputation of a die-hard but he had also been 'cooing gently'.[205] All this, Menon thought, was a clear indication of the authority of the party machine rather than of the popularity of the existing leadership.[206] Although the rift within the Conservative Party had been widening, Menon believed that the government could conveniently rely on the backbenchers who would not allow it to fall.[207] It was known that about 150 members, who would never again see Westminster, did not want a general election. But the volume of discontent had been swelling because of the taxes on cooperative societies, the resolutions of the liberal conferences, the increasing distress in industrial areas combined with the failure of the government's tariff policy.[208] Evidently, the Tory Party machine might think in terms of either a rehabilitation of its position by dropping part of the crew or by sinking the ship altogether. MacDonald was aware of the possibility, but it was widely believed that he might still sail through till autumn.[209]

In any case, by the closing days of June, the Palace Chambers, the headquarters of the Tory Party, started taking serious note of Churchill's revolt and was constrained to treat Churchill's opposition and offensives as constituting the party's principal point of concern.[210] His defiance was no longer dismissed as the antic of a disgruntled cabinet minister and a few hard-boiled colonials and ex-civilians. No one was inclined to believe seriously that Churchill's animosity arose merely out of his opposition to the India policy.[211] India, it was believed, proved to be a convenient rallying point and might yet prove a good weapon to beat the government down.[212] The gossip about Churchill's ambitious plan for an alternative cabinet was given currency by the official Tory leadership in the hope that such a credible rumour would discredit Churchill and proportionately rally the government stock which had been fast falling. But the planted story was but a spoony spoof and it merely underlined the importance of being Churchill in British politics of the day.

The general strike had made it clear that he was 'the British Mussolini' when, as editor of the *Gazette,* and 'as a strong man of British Cabinet, he ruled the country for a few days'.[213] Churchill, Menon commented, had been simply clarifying political issues for the British ruling classes, then locked up in a terrible economic crisis, and the government, unable to detect the nub of the problem, had been preparing the way for him. It was evident that the government had been 'laying the foundations of a British brand of Fascism in their various measures'.[214] Menon believed that Churchill, or whoever succeeded MacDonald, would find the situation ready for them even 'as the Hitlerites found that the German nationalists had done some of their work for them'.[215]

A general apprehension was felt by all, that the government was preparing for a war. Government spokesmen and editorial writers had been protesting against the spread of the idea that what the Tories wanted was another 'jolly old war' and the foreign policy and the attitude towards disarmament were dictated by that desire. Strenous efforts were being made to assure the country that warlike preparations were not being undertaken, that the Conservatives love peace as much as Socialists and that the government was really serious in its efforts towards international disarmament. But it was well-known that the dockyards and arsenals were very busy and the armament manufacturers were quite happy. The die-hard organs found still a number of colonels and ex-officials to write soul-tearing appeals not to leave the masses of India to the mercy of the politicians. The British Medical Associations issued a memorandum criticizing the white paper proposals concerning the civil branch of the India Medical Service.

In a Conservative Party conference on India during Easter, Churchill and his die-hard friends delighted their impressionable audience that they were out to save poor India from being abandoned by her British mother under the monstrous White

Paper scheme. Menon emphasized that it was grossly untrue to pretend, as the diehard claimed, that they had been silenced by the Conservative headquarter's ban on propaganda. On the contrary, neither the 'alleged gad' nor the 'mythical muzzle' prevented the die-hards from sustaining a virulent campaign against the white paper. Indeed, Menon added, the campaign had been very successful. It had been sustained and strident and the change in the attitude of the Conservative Party was made vividly apparent. The opponents of the white paper were steadily gaining strength and they intended to use every method to sabotage and nullify the plans, of which Hoare was the exponent. Indeed, the die-hards were on the warpath and condemned a constitution based on broader democratic basis as a futile chase for a well-o'-the-wisp.[216]

Meanwhile in a paper entitled "The Round Table: An Inside Story", which was circulated by the India League, Menon sought to capture the nature of the Round Table operation in its third round. Menon maintained that the RTC was dead and it only remained for the prime minister to deliver the `funeral oration', `which he always delivers in the form of a valedictory address'.[217] The term crisis, Menon wrote, had lost its urgency and trepidation because MacDonald lived on them and they appeared to be parts of the normal mechanism of political life in Britain. Sapru had been the leading Indian at the RTC. He had been fighting his battle, ditch by ditch, only to be beaten back by the British side before he could 'establish himself in the territory that he conquered'. It appeared that Sapru was particularly inhospitable to pressmen. But 'the burden that he carries is visible on his face'. There was no one of his caliber, or his comprehension, at the conference. Probably, he and Sastri, would have proved a formidable team. The RTC III was not very articulate before the press. A statement which conveyed little and was meant to inform but not to provoke thought was issued each evening after the session. Publicity was thus tightly controlled. At the previous conferences the watchful eyes of Chintamani, who was on the publicity committee, proved an effective check on Whitehall's officials. But the RTC III was unique in the way it treated its proceedings. No record was kept of the speeches except the official summaries. There was no verbatim report of speeches, so that protestors entered no record book. All fine distinctions made and modifications sought were treated by the officials in the way that suited them. Menon happened to know that one of the Indian leaders queried this procedure, only to be told that a summary was made and, basically, that was all that was necessary.[218]

As at the previous conferences the Muslim delegation was a united team. The Aga Khan guided it from behind and Shafa'at Ahmad Khan, the professor from Allahabad, did most of the aside talking. Zafrullah Khan was the leading speaker among the Muslims. On the princes' side, Menon held, Abkar Hydari was suave and clever as ever. He was still devoted to the idea of federation, provided it turned out to be what he liked it to be, and in consequence, Hyderabad and a few others would be running the rest of India. Apart from Gandhi, his was the best-known Indian name in the country. Menon also heard that the Nawab of Pataudi was not likely to be in 'the Indian test team on either side'. He could not 'very well play against India and if he plays for India he may lose his place in the British test team'. Sultan Khan was a protégé of Nawab Sir Umar Hayat Khan and was regarded as a chess marvel. He attracted more attention than all the speeches ever made at the RTCs.[219]

One of the significant documents that created a stir in public opinion on India was the presentation by E.A. Guest, ex-deputy magistrate and deputy collector in Bihar and Orissa, who had just returned from India and sought to catch the eye of Colin Davidson, secretary to the joint committee, to submit his views on Indian constitutional reform and was denied permission.[220] Guest was informed that the joint committee did not consider it necessary for them to invite Guest to tender evidence. Witnesses had already been invited to give all the information that the committee would require on certain questions before reaching conclusions.[221] Guest maintained that India was in a melting pot and at that critical stage, certain serious matters that he would bring forward were the tap-root of half the unrest in India and they should be probed to the core by the joint committee.[222]

In a small note addressed to the committee, Guest held that most people seemed to have the impression that things were settling down in India and the existing trouble and strife were about to terminate. But the fact was that never within living memory had there been so much bitterness as there was then and the gulf between Britain and India was never wider. Guest thought that the unfortunate situation was due to a set of not-very-reliable information that had been supplied by the Government of India to Parliament through the secretary of state. It was the system which was at fault and he thought of demonstrating the defect of that machinery by examining one specific matter. Referring to the example of a *lathi* charge or firing at a given place, followed by loud complaints and a government order for an inquiry, Guest sought to examine the way inquiries were generally conducted in India.[223] In this connection, several facts, he said, had to be kept in mind.

First, the Congress did not complain under the inspiration of Gandhi and took no part in the official inquiry. Very often, witnesses produced on behalf the of government and police were not cross-examined. Witnesses on the official side were at liberty to make statements favourable to themselves. These inquiries were very often conducted by executive officers. In India, there was hardly any separation between executive and judicial functions. Without questioning the bona fides of officials, Guest thought one should not be surprised if the natural leaning of the officials was sometimes towards the official position. The result of such an inquiry was accepted in Britain as the considered opinion of a judge who had arrived at his findings after listening to evidence on both sides, which had been thoroughly checked by cross-examination. These essential anomalies in the Indian situation should be brought to the notice of the secretary of state and the British public in order to enable them to review and revise their estimate of the situation. In this context, Guest made an appeal through the India League that Englishmen should assert their sense of responsibility, do all they could to get acquainted with the facts of India and not allow themselves to be unduly influenced by statements made either in Parliament or in the press.[224]

Guest stated in the memorandum that there was no responsibility in the central government in India, in the Government of Bihar and Orissa or at the India Office. He claimed that the bureaucrats of the Indian civil service, which was the only service that really counted in India and had all the power, would not miss the opportunity that distance from headquarters offered them of usurping powers far greater than those usurped anywhere else.[225] The permanent officials were responsible to nobody, Guest claimed, and 'for that reason, are a law unto themselves'. He thought that, without wishing to be presumptuous, he could claim to know some aspects of the special features of Indian life and character on the basis of his long experience as a student and as a civil servant. He felt that the Indians were 'the most docile, tractable and law-abiding people under the sun and no people more readily respond to any kindness shown to them'.[226] The imprisonment of Gandhi was not fair. Guest's formulation was simple: 'Gandhi, who believed in soul force which has captured the hearts and imagination of the Indians who were essentially a spiritual people' and who would readily respond to 'any gesture of Peace and Goodwill and mutual understanding which I, in my humble way, would urge the National Government to make'.[227] For a permanent partnership, Guest pleaded, there must be freedom and only as a free people would the Indians be able to reach remarkable heights, not otherwise. Dominion status was the indispensable condition. A contented India would be an invaluable asset for world peace.[228] Guest's strong accusation was supplemented by controversy over Malaviya's allegation about police misconduct in Calcutta. The *Manchester Guardian* gave a full report on the statement made by the Government of India endorsing the denial of the Bengal government. In a strongly worded and tightly argued statement, Menon castigated the statements of the government and the *Guardian's* attempt to accuse Malaviya of making false and malicious accusations against the police.[229]

A further stage was reached in September 1933 in the die-hard anti-Indian campaign against government policy. The attack on the government, however, lost its former strength since all concerned knew that the die-hard battle had been won. Henry Page Croft, Conservative member from Bouremouth, was head of the die-hard protectionist group in the House of Commons and he led the attack.[230] It took the form of an amendment to the official resolution demanding the reference of government policy to the electorate. The official tactics were to sidetrack the opposition on the plea that the policy was a matter for decision by Parliament after the joint committee reported and that the whole matter was then something like *sub judice.*[231] In the meanwhile, a war was breeving between the India Defence League and the Tory party machine who had been indulging in mutual recriminations. The Beaverbrook press, which compared to its ally, the Rothermere group, had till recently been rather less anti-Indian and die-hard, was then coming out in full blast. It made the terrorist outrages in Bengal its text and demanded that India should be 'governed' or that Britain must get out. It gave full support to the Page Croft amendment.[232] The attitude of the Beaverbrook papers was indicative of a new Beaverbrook empire campaign against Baldwin and it was the first step in rallying the empire mongers. The defence of the lives of British nationals who had been serving on the outposts of the empire was always a good cry. It might before long even raise the demand for the recall of the Governor of Bengal who was not regarded as a good Tory.[233]

As Sapru decided to leave for India, Menon reported that he was physically in a better condition although lines of care and depression were etched all over his face.[234] It was difficult to deny that all through the JSC session he had stuck to his position in the most disinterested way and endeavoured to make the best of a bad job. He obtained greater goodwill and perhaps 'live and let live attitude', wrote Menon, 'from his Congress opponents in India than his British allies here'.[235] He was let down, Menon added, by his 'co-architects and placed himself a comparative outsider so far as the determination of the future was concerned'.[236]

Misgivings in the liberal mind, outside Parliament, were however accumulating. Apprehensions had arisen, albeit gradually, whether all the paraphernalia of a constitution had any relation to Indian realities.[237] *The Manchester Guardian* talked of the need of a Reserve Bank as a condition precedent. The *Economist* made a very unorthodox suggestion relating to the establishment of a Reserve Bank before everything else. Lloyd George's interesting statement in this context was instructive. Transfer of the portfolio of law and order, according to him, appeared to be very remote. Lloyd George argued in the old 'steel frame' vein that it was dangerous to transfer it.[238] Strangely enough, he was also inclined to refer to those who were competent to speak for India, as against those who were handpicked. Menon was convinced that the future would be decided by extra-Indian considerations. He was certain that the official Liberals were prepared to find a space in the government. Meanwhile, the tradesmen were also busy. Perhaps more interesting than all the committee meetings was the private interview that Sapru had with Lord Derby who apart from being an owner of race horses was one of the larger Lancashire millowners. Britain wanted trade and was beginning to find out that the firm hand was not very helpful in that direction. The economic weapon, on the contrary, was the most potent one.[239]

By autumn 1933 when the JSC reassembled, things crystallized. The process of whittling down the proposals of the white paper continued. Hoare's evidence did great credit to the India office and to the astuteness of Malcolm Hailey. The committee seemed to notice the opinion of the civil services and the Indian government. Annual conferences of the Conservative and the Labour parties in Birmingham and Hastings discussed India policy. Although nothing spectacular happened at either place, Birmingham confirmed Menon's apprehensions.[240] The importance of Birmingham's Indian hubbub had been, Menon reported, that the government put into the field the whole resources of the party machine and the House of Commons patronage to fight the Churchillian opposition. Issues were evaded, attempts were made to fall back on an appeal to fairplay, no attempt was made to meet the Churchillites in battle, and requests were made for postponement of the decision to fight. There was no desire to risk the government's life on its Indian proposals. There was an unprecedented presence of partymen, but 300 delegates opted to remain neutral. Neville Chamberlain re-affirmed in unambiguous language that no Indian proposal which would affect British trade interests would be supported by the party. Menon emphasized once again that this tenacious persistence in imperial sensibility underscored the party's determination to hold India at all cost.[241]

'Those Indians who still consider basking in official sunshine as congenial to them', Menon wrote at the end of his persuasive analysis, 'might do well to ponder over all the past talks of safeguards in the interests of India and of Lord Irwin's dictum that the interests of India and England were not very different one from the other.'[242] Besides, the Conservative opposition felt reassured by their increasing strength among their ranks with a number of active sympathizers sitting on the fence.[243] Some of them felt that the outcome of the JSC would be sufficiently reactionary, the introduction of the bill would be delayed, and the House of Lords would bring greater modifications in the bill.[244] Some of those fence-sitters thought that they would gain their point without joining Churchill. A few astute Conservative politicians such as Lord Derby and Austen Chamberlain had been working to keep the flock together on Indian issues. Derby, representing the Lancashire interests, had been an active advocate of striking through Mody a lasting deal that would enable the Lancashire industrialists to recapture the Indian market and break the Congress boycott.[245] In fact, as the government seemed to relent from its initial position, one witnessed a good deal of sparring with each other among the Conservatives and the retired civil servants, who not long ago were associated with the Defence of India League and advocated official severities in India. They were then found urging in the columns of the *Times* that the white paper should be supported:[246] if it was not done, they argued, the Congress would regain strength as the conservative elements of the princes would be out of the field and the Muslims and other cooperators would be eliminated.[247] Menon, as alert as ever, commented: 'The allies of the White Paper are the best enlightening evidence of its character and if nothing will open the eye of the Indian exponent of it, this fact should do so.'[248] Self-deception, Menon wrote in another place, could hardly go further. Their urge to cooperate with British imperialism was so great that it dimmed their vision.

It may not be amiss here to note that India had moved into the Labour Party's annual conferences with a fair amount

[This D It is requested that special care may be taken to ensure the secrecy of this document. rnment.]

MOST SECRET. Copy No. 3

B.D.G. (31) 9.

CABINET.

[*This paper is circulated on the following conditions:—*

(a) It is not official and in no sense indicates Government conclusions;

(b) It is a statement of matters which must be considered and is purely of the nature of an aid to the British delegates in considering the detailed problems of the Conference;

(c) It is kept absolutely secret, as, should any leakage take place, the consequences might be fatal to continued negotiations.]

INDIAN ROUND-TABLE CONFERENCE.

Cabinet Committee.

Note by Sir Maurice Gwyer on Safeguards.

Since it is upon the question of safeguards that the main controversy in connection with the new Indian Constitution is likely to centre, it may be desirable to consider in greater detail the elements of the problem and the practical difficulties with which it is surrounded.

2. It has been said that every Constitution, that of the United Kingdom included, embodies safeguards of one kind or another. This is no doubt so; but a closer examination discloses little analogy between normal constitutional safeguards and those which would seem to be essential in the case of the Indian Constitution. The former consist for the most part of a series of checks and balances designed at one and the same time to secure the strict accountability of Executive to Legislature and to prevent undue encroachment by the one upon the functions of the other. It is true that the Executive, in more than one modern Constitution, has for the purpose of dealing with sudden and unexpected emergencies been given powers of overriding specified rights guaranteed by the Constitution, but the exercise of these powers is almost invariably limited in point of time and subject to strict control by the Legislature. It is therefore not unfair to say that such safeguards as are embodied in modern Constitutions are intended to secure that the organs of the State do in the long run reflect the public opinion of its citizens. They are not concerned with the quality of the public opinion as such, since *vox populi, vox Dei.* But since it is common ground among all parties in the United Kingdom that in the present composition of Indian society such public opinion as exists in India has neither the quality nor the experience to guarantee by itself a reasonably efficient administration, the just treatment of minorities, or adequate protection of Indian no less than of British financial interests, the safeguards in any Indian Constitution must have other purposes in view, if the obligations assumed by the United Kingdom towards the people of India are to be adequately discharged. Hence the Constitution must be such as to make the Indian Executive accountable not only to the inchoate public opinion of India, but also in some degree to that of the United Kingdom. To make this double accountability effective, the Executive must be twofold in character, and safeguards are necessary to protect one part of it, if the need should arise, against interference or obstruction by the other. Analogies to a situation of this kind will not readily be found in any modern Constitution which purports to confer responsible government upon a people.

3. Although in the United Kingdom and in the Dominions the executive authority is vested in the Crown and is exercised either by the Sovereign in person or by his representative, the essence of responsible government according to British theory is that this executive authority is only exercised on the advice of Ministers, who are

121 50 7.31

Confidential and secret note on safeguards for the aid of British delegates at the Round Table Conference. Wedgwood Benn Papers.

Reception to the Indian delegates to the round Table Conference 1931. Courtesy, Friend's House. M.M. Malaviya, Mahatma Gandhi and Sarojini Naidu on the dias.

A protest meeting in Madras against the arrest of Annie Basant, 1917. Annie Basant Papers.

Gandhi at the Quaker's Centre at Sally Oak. Sally Oak collection.

Mr. and Mrs. Horace Alexander. Courtesy, Friend's House, London

Friend's Home, London, one of the important meeting places of the India League. Courtesy, Friend's House.

Carl Health. Menon Papers.

INDIA & LABOUR

PUBLIC MEETING.

Chairman: **JACK TANNER**

(President: Amalgamated Engineering Union)

SPEAKERS:

S. A. DANGE *(President: All-India T.U.C.)*

WILLIAM DOBBIE, M.P.

MICHAEL FOOT

V. K. KRISHNA MENON

REGINALD SORENSEN, M.P.

ADMISSION FREE.

Doors open 6.30 Res. 2/6 & 1/-

MONDAY, 11th DEC. 7 p.m.

CENTRAL HALL

WESTMINSTER. S.W.1.

THE INDIA LEAGUE, 165 Strand, W.C.2

Telephone: Temple Bar 3689

T. Rankin & Son, Printers (T.U.), [illegible], Upper Street, N.1

Leaflet announcing a meeting of the India League, 1932.
Menon Pepers

EMERGENCY !

FRIENDS AND SYMPATHISERS ARE ALSO INVITED.

CALLING ALL INDIAN MEN AND WOMEN

to

A CONFERENCE

TO RESPOND TO THE CALL OF

INDIA

on SUNDAY the 26th. April at 2-30 P.M.

THE HOLBORN HALL

GRAYS INN ROAD, LONDON, W.C.1

"It is the duty of every Indian who can do so to return to India and face the dangers that threaten us.
"Who lives if India perishes?
"India calls! Every Indian man and woman must listen to that call."

Please return this form at once to:-

THE INDIA LEAGUE, 165, Strand, LONDON, W.C.2.

I desire to attend the conference of Indians at the Holborn Hall on the 26th, April. Enclosed registration fee of 1/-.

Name ....A. Ismail....................

Address ....112 Half Moon....

....Passage E.1 London....

Issued by the India League, 165 Strand, London, W.C.2.
Printed by THE APOLLO PRESS, 53, Theobalds Road, London, W.C.1

India Leaguis poster for a conference against the ordinance Rule, 1932. Menon Papers.

of reservations, uncertainties and confusion. The annual conference at Margate in 1926 was cautious and alive to a possible explosive situation that could be easily sparked off by the left-wing resolution moved by F. Kenyon (Brass and Metal Workers' Union) and seconded by Joseph Southall from Edgbaston. They proposed to send greetings to the coloured people in their freedom struggle against imperialism and to support their demand for self-determination, even to the point of seceding from the empire.[249] J.R. Clynes thought, as did many others, that it was a 'foolish and extravagant' declaration, for in his judgment, it was possible to maintain the British empire without forcible domination and without the exploitation of hundreds of millions of workers. Clynes held that such an 'unnecessary' and 'provocative' resolution would merely fritter away the Labour Party's immense popularity. Freda Utley's resolution, which was finally adopted, declared that the Labour Party should 'do all in its power to help the Native peoples to obtain control of their own land'. It held that in all non-self-governing parts of the empire, the administration should restore the rights of the 'natives' to the land, see that they were educated for self-government and prevent industrial slavery and conscription of labour in any form.[250]

The political atmosphere at Blackpool in 1927 was more congenial and the resolution on India by Lansbury and supported by J. McKendrick (Miners' Federation), C. Roden Buxton (ILP) and A. Fenner Brockway (ILP) was passed with marginal acrimony.[251] The resolution affirmed the right of the Indian people to full self-government and self-determination and the policy of the British government should be one of continuous cooperation with the Indian people, with the object of establishing at the earliest, possible occasion, partnership with other members of the British commonwealth. It also stated that the forthcoming royal statutory commission should be so constituted and its methods of doing work so arranged, that it enjoyed the confidence and cooperation of the Indian people. Lansbury called for a firm resolve against poverty and unemployment and a determined effort to promote industrial development and education. He urged the Simon Commission and the British people to realize that one of the objectives of the commission was to see 'how Britain could give back to Indian peoples the ... right to form their own self-governing Dominion...'. An immediate step towards that goal was spelled out by Brockway, who called for the inauguration of friendly discussion by withdrawing all coercive measures and repressive legislation and by releasing political prisoners.[252]

In 1928, the conference in Birmingham insisted that opposition in India was based on certain misapprehensions, which had been aggravated by the way the government handled the matter. Some form of consultative machinery should have been worked out to ensure the cooperation of the people of India. The absence of Indian members in the commission, the humiliating proposal to examine the fitness of India for self-determination and the absence of the principle of equity caused much consternation. The Indian delegation led by Chaman Lal felt that the Labour Party had been soft-pedalling the issue and, it should work for a round table conference between the representatives of Britain and India in order to forge the best method of applying the principle of self-determination in the Indian situation. C.F. Andrews added his voice and conviction to the demand of Chaman Lal, Fenner Brockway, Wilfred Wellock and Ernest Thurtle took up the Indian position in right earnest.[253] They maintained that the resolution at Blackpool enjoined upon the party to insist with conviction that the commission should be so constituted and its procedures so arranged as to enjoy the confidence of the Indian people and its principal political forum. No attempt was made to ascertain Indian opinion, which was broadly known. It was clear, they asserted, that the Labour Parliamentary Party had deliberately flouted the expressed wish of the conference.[254]

In 1929 at the Brighton conference, Brockway referred to the Meerut trial and following a very critical debate, the relevant paragraph of the parliamentary committee's report was referred back on card vote and was lost. The leadership saved the situation by insisting that the case was *sub judice* and might not be discussed.[255] The session at Llanduduo in 1930 took up the report of the Simon Commission (June 1930), which gave rise to some disappointment but instead of discussing its recommendations the conference welcomed the RTC and hoped that its deliberations would bring conciliation. In the conference, the Indian situation was brought up by Brockway, ably supported by Ms Hilda Oldham, W. Herron (Chorley DLP), Earnest Marklew (SDF) and J.M. Kensworthy (Hull).[256] The essence of their arguments was that the Labour Party, while extending greetings and solidarity of the Indian people in their struggle for political and economic freedom, recognized their right to self-government, self-determination and independence, welcomed the mass movement in India and expressed the hope that the movement would develop into a mass struggle against landlordism and capitalism. The speakers regretted that the Labour government did not, in its early stages, accept full responsible government and release of Indian political prisoners as the basis of a conference with the Indian representatives to ensure an atmosphere of goodwill and strongly condemned the severe repression with which the civil disobedience had been met.[257] They called upon the Labour government to end its self-assigned duty 'as the policemen of imperialism' by withdrawing all repressive measures, liberating all political prisoners and opening negotiations for the transfer of power.

On behalf of the India League, Brockway maintained that the policy of the Labour Party towards India should be unambiguously defined and followed. Brockway affirmed that as expressed in *Labour for the Nation,* that policy should be definitely in favour of self-determination and free partnership in the British

Commonwealth. Echoing the position of the India League, Brockway maintained that if the conference between British and Indian representatives was to be successful, the Indian representatives must speak on behalf of the main body of political opinion in India.[258] The terms on which the conference was to be convened was to include the right to secede from the empire. That right was recognized in the case of dominions and it should not be denied to India. Besides, self-government was a farce and meaningless unless government was able to control the economic life of the country. In order to make the political atmosphere congenial, all political prisoners should be released.[259] All the speakers on the subject asked the conference to carry the resolution and make it clear to government that they wanted a policy which was bold and courageous in its anti-imperialism, which stretched out hands of fellowship to the Indian people without any qualification, accepted their right to govern themselves and to work out their own situation as socialists.[260] Despite Graham Pole's passionate plea to withdraw the resolution, it was carried. The Labour Party conference of 1931 at Scarborough hailed the RTC assembled in London and called for a unique cooperation between the representatives and help establish full self-government and self-determination in India and inaugurate a new era of friendship. Despite the plea of Brockway, Alexander Gossip and John Jagger with regard to Garhwali riflemen, M.N. Roy and Meerut prisoners, the principal resolution did not take note of these issues.[261]

In 1932, the Labour Party was out of power, ordinance rule was clamped down vigorously and, Gandhi and a huge army of prisoners were behind the bar. The Labour Party resolution (Leicester) condemned ordinance rule sought to give the Indians the right to establish a government in consonance with their national aspiration; to ensure peace and cooperation by withdrawing all repressive measures and releasing political prisoners and urged that the Indian penal procedure be immediately reviewed. There was also a remarkable unity of opinion between Lansbury, J. Hallsworth, J.W. Singleton and Wedgwood Benn. 'There is only one thing you can do in India,' Benn asserted, 'you must go back to the methods of peace, go back to the will to peace, and get all the parties in India represented at the Conference together, and if we were willing to give them what they ask and what they ought to have, you might have that bridge between East and West upon which the future peace of the world depends.'[262]

The annual conference of the opposition Labour Party (1933) met at Hastings. JSC was in session; the Labour Party had dropped its non-cooperation and it was evident that civil disobedience in India was petering out.[263] Hastings was preoccupied with German fascism and the struggle about policies within the Labour Party although India came in as a subject of first class importance. Accredited leaders of the Labour opposition having strong India League connection spoke on the subject with a good deal of depth and analysis. They included George Lansbury, Monica Whately, Tom Williams and Ellen Wilkinson.[264] At a meeting arranged by the India League the evening previous to the day on which the India resolution was to be debated by the conference, Lansbury told a crowded gathering that India would no more accept the white paper than the 'working class would accept a Means Test imposed by the Tory government'.[265] He went further to repeat Labour's commitment and condemned terrorism by officials in India. He paid a great tribute to the Congress and Gandhi, who had made conciliation an article of faith in an uncompromising fierce struggle of the Indians against a mighty imperial power.[266]

Tom Williams told his audience how in the House of Commons they never received a satisfactory reply from Hoare about the situation in India and how the secretary of state had to admit that the Indian people lived in conditions of destitution under British rule. He repeated Lansbury's assertion that the party in the House of Commons should insist on India's right to self-determination and oppose tooth and nail the white paper proposals which contained no approach to self-government. The worst feature was that the proposals were not even transitional but they contemplated keeping India under British control in perpetuity.[267] The reservation of what Lansbury called the 'army of occupation' in the hands of a foreign government, Williams continued, did not only indicate that there was to be no self-government, but that the Indians were not to be permitted even conditions which their own self-respect demanded.[268] The two MPs were followed by presentations by members of the India delegation who had a great reception.[269]

The Meerut sentences brought to the surface the travesty of the administration of justice in India. The trial drifted for four years; the sentences passed against the accused were astonishingly severe; the offences that seemed to have been committed by the bulk of the accused were not in any way such as to merit sentences which were far more severe than those normally imposed on people guilty of the most cruel and immoral crimes against society. No overt act involving violence to the person or property of anybody had been proved during the trial. The activities of the accused were mainly confined to actions dealing with the trade union movements and elementary human rights such as the freedom of organization, of speech, of collective bargaining, of demanding equality of status and other similar considerations.[270] It was asserted by the Indian Meerut Committee with J.A.D. Naoroji as the active and energetic secretary that the Meerut prisoners had neither said nor done anything more than what many members of parliament had been saying or doing in England.[271] Relying upon the warm sympathy and support of the democratic segments of public opinion, the Indian Meerut Committee opened a fund to engage counsel and give all other necessary facilities to the accused in their appeal against the inordinately harsh sentences. In response to the Indian Committee's appeal, the India League acted promptly.[272]

There were some difficulties with regard to effective cooperation between all the three committees on the Meerut case. The Meerut Release Committee was a Communist affair, the Meerut Defence Committee was the Labour counterblast including some religious people, and there was the Committee of the Civil Rights people. None of these could be induced to cooperate with the others, especially as the Labour and Communist committees were out to prove each other wrong. Fortunately, the members of the India League were already on all these committees. Bertrand Russell, who was chairman of the League's Jail Committee, decided that his committee should cooperate with the others, act as representative of Naoroji's committee in India and turn over to the Indian Committee whatever assistance was likely to be raised by them in England.[273] The Communists told Menon that they would do that if Bradley did not object to the course and in all probability they would cooperate.[274] The Committee of Civil Rights, led by a feminist, was more difficult, but persuasion worked. The Labour people's committee promised to assist though they were not raising money themselves. Their plan was propaganda, which would enable the League to raise small amounts from Labour people, who were all much concerned about the case.[275] In letters addressed to all the committees, Menon suggested that all funds that were available for defence should be sent to them and pooled for the purpose of legal defence.[276] The India Committee desired to have one senior advocate and several juniors counsels engaged in the case. The League made it clear not to undertake any activity independently which would duplicate work or overstep the work that was being done by one or the other of the existing committees. The League desired to make an appeal to the Labour movement generally under the signatures of Bertrand Russell and other labour and trade union leaders for funds.[277] The League also informed those interested in the movement about the progress of the defence and the work of the Indian Committee.

Before long, Menon felt confident to write to Naoroji about the existing financial condition of the India League, whose indigence was largely responsible for crippling the activities of the organization. Naoroji was informed that the League would, nevertheless, continue its efforts to raise funds, but Menon feared that the result would not be very substantial. The League was in serious difficulties financially, and 'unless we obtain the necessary support immediately we shall very regretfully have to wind up'. It was very difficult to raise money in England then and even the League's supporters of previous years found it impossible 'to help us to carry on'. Those who could well afford substantial donations to organizations were ranged in the ranks of the opponents of Indian independence. In view of the publication of the white paper, the intensive anti-Indian propaganda, the mysterious apathy of the Labour leaders and the continuance of severe repression in India, it would be unfortunate if the League was obliged to close down or stop work for India.[278] Naoroji was aware of its importance and the urgency of the work done for India in England. He realized that such a thankless job would find active support only among the few who were already burdened with other similar responsibilities. The continuance of Indian propaganda therefore required some assured support from Indian friends who were disposed to help such work.[279] The *India Review* had closed down. It was not practicable to run it on such an appreciable style as a fortnightly as before, without a large sum of money which, obviously, could not be raised. Although it was possible to run a successful monthly paper on a small scale for about £120 to £200 a year, the League was not in a position to initiate it without definite support. Even the report of the delegation to India was ready but surreptitious official interventions had made its publication difficult. It would need about £130 for private publication but the League was not only in debt but was also in severe straits.[280] The fact of his being personally on the rocks made the situation even more difficult. The *India Review* etc. left Menon encumbered and penniless. He was convinced that the League had grown in influence and could get some influential people to listen to them but the activities of the League had been impaired.[281] The redeeming feature was that Bertrand Russell was not a figurehead chairman but fully identified with the League and thoroughly involved with it. The League had been busy in its endeavour to persuade the Labour Party not to actively join the joint committee. Hoare put attractive propositions to them in the way of representation in the JSC and there were personal ambitions inside the Labour Party which formed obstacles in the way of the League. The League, however, resolved that even though it did not succeed in preventing them from joining and appointing delegates 'we shall make the position of these delegates uncomfortable in their constituencies'.[282] The *News Bulletin* from India had stopped and in the existing circumstances it was very difficult to know to whom to write. Menon sought to make the best use of the situation.[283] Before long he reported cheerfully that although publicity suffered by the suspension of the *India Review,* the members of the delegation had very good meetings in London and in the provinces and they had done a good deal of lobbying as well. His personal view was to get the Labour Party deeply committed to a radical plan as the existing bill could 'not be improved by anybody'.[284] Menon felt that the worse it was, the better. Meanwhile Menon had been appointed the London representative of the *Bombay Chronicle.* But he was not inclined to do the job without payment. Pushed against the wall, Menon entreated if Naoroji could 'fix this up for me on any terms you can arrange with them' and he promised to give the paper a good return for their money.[285]

In reply to the inquiries from Rev. F.A. Wenyon about the League and the *India Review*, Menon sounded a very depressed, if not a defeated, person. He regretted that the *India Review* had been obliged to suspend publication indefinitely owing to financial difficulties and though efforts were still being made to revive it, Menon thought that there was little hope. He was despondent.[286] The India League was still carrying on, but he found it very difficult to arouse any public enthusiasm or active sympathy. Menon acknowledged that there was a certain amount of goodwill in a limited circle, but there was not the necessary strength that would enable him to meet vicious and hostile propaganda.[287] The League had been making its effort despite the bleak outlook and it would appreciate any assistance in any part of the country that the League was able to garner. In a circular to the friends of India's freedom, Menon declared that it would help him to know the people in the provinces who were willing to do a bit of work for the League. It would also be useful if some people like Rev. Wenyon, would volunteer to write occasionally to the Christian press, which was used as much as any other, as a forum for anti-Indian propaganda.[288]

The impact of the intense anti-Indian propaganda in England had begun to find expression in all the meetings, debates and discussions arranged by various organizations in London and elsewhere. By and large, Germany, fascism, the empire and its future, Indian reforms and some such themes constituted the core of all these public presentations and interactions. London, in particular, was the principal listening post of the empire. The economic crisis, the advent of fascism, political polarization, unique intellectual effulgence, rise of an articulate youth movement, radicalization of the universities, impressive hunger marches, increasing concern for democracy and popular participation, demand for democratic control, collective security, importance of the international body and definition of peace and war had stimulated a debate on the intricate relations between Britain, India and the rest of the world. Associations with different political persuasions sparked off animated public discussions. The right-wing swing of the parliamentary politics gave a fresh spurt to Oswald Mosley, the Blackshirts and anti-communist hooligans. Various fascist groups had been functioning for some time but the inept supervision of the economic crisis gave them a major impetus. They picked up anti-semitism from Hitler, their black uniform from Mussolini and anti-communism from the right-wing politics. The clarion call of the British fascists was sharp and definite: 'To lose the East is to lose all; for a nation which cowered before a *fakir* could never again play any part in the Councils in Europe. Our nation has not yet cowered; the politicians have, but the attitude is so natural to them that the rest of the world has not yet grasped it.'[289] Fascist marches in East London targeting Jewish shops, frequent clashes with communists and left sympathizers and brutal treatment to hecklers which, together with alleged police delinquency in philandering with the fascists, gave sharp edges to issues in current political debates.[290]

Intense spirit of camaraderie and shared feelings of shame and contempt charged the atmosphere of many of these meetings. Following one of the public debates held under the aegis of an organization with conservative orientation, Menon was constrained to protest against uncivil treatment at the hands of the chairman and other speakers. The debate was on Indian self-government and all the speakers gave in their turn a very unambiguous indication of their views.[291] The League had anticipation of Menon's unsavoury reception at the debate and, therefore, had definitely pointed out to the organizers before the arrangements for the meeting were made that the speaker would expect fair treatment and protection of the chair to which he was entitled during the debate. Throughout the debate the audience received Menon warmly and the chairman did not in the least find it necessary to pull him up and it confirmed that

Menon, despite extreme provocation, was well within the bounds of debate. Unfortunately, Menon found himself not in the position of a guest who had been invited to participate in a debate but of someone who had to submit to cross-examination. Menon made it clear that it could not have been 'part of the programme of a debate that I should be insulted by your other guest and that my host, the chairman, should stand aside and say nothing'.[292] Menon felt peeved that Louis Stuart, the other speaker, shouted at him, ordered him to sit down in the most insulting manner and all that the chairman was concerned about was to see that the secretary of the Indian Empire Society was not offended or did not leave the hall in a huff.[293] It was painfully obvious to all, Menon wrote, that the chairman and the organizers were so intensely concerned in paying attention to and cultivating Louis Stuart that they did not seem to mind whether they were being discourteous to someone else. Menon was quite capable of looking after himself if he had to reply the other guest or to treat him 'for the way in which he behaved to me'.[294] He, however, thought it judicious not to create a scene, but he made it quite unambiguous that he had as much right as any one else to expect fair treatment and also that he was as much a guest as Louis Stuart or any one else.[295] The Conservative demonstration against Menon and his League was largely offset by the warm reception from other organized political bodies. The British Universities' League of Nations Society invited Menon to preside over the annual session of the Students' International Assembly.[296] 'Your presence,' the secretary of the society added, would 'give prominence to the International Assembly'. The Society for Socialist Enquiry and Propaganda under Aneurin Bevan, G.D.H. Cole, D.N. Pritt and others promised all possible assistance.

Amidst his hectic schedule all over Britain, Menon observed that parliament had become, since the formation of the National government an institution with a declining political image. An astute parliamentary observer of the Labour Party said that there was an air of ennui and helplessness in the atmosphere. The government had a full legislative programme which had little to do with social justice.[297] There was no freshness in the speeches from the treasury benches. It appeared to many that the prime minister himself looked on the House of Commons as a nuisance and had spoken of the recess as the time for real work. One of his colleagues made a statement in a strange fit of eloquence to the effect that his colleagues in Parliament drew a salary that they did not deserve. The swarm of new MPs had given rise to serious problems. The majority of the new ones never expected to return in the next election and they did not have the equipment to make themselves useful in the place. The House of Commons, except for the opposition protests, was increasingly turning into a place to confirm decisions reached beforehand by the cabinet.[298] The Conservative backbencher, though a confirmed party loyalist, constituted a dead weight. He was essentially an instrument of government and, in the popular image, was a product of 'credulous democracy'.[299]

The Liberal Party appeared to be the pathetic remnant of a historic party. There was Lloyd George and his family still feeling important and claiming to be the chosen few; there was Herbert Samuel, the elected leader and plenipotentiary of the party, 'whose speeches were comic in parts' and who oscillated between the treasury bench and the opposition like a shuttlecock.[300] There was also John Simon 'who made up in pomp what he lacks in other things'.[301] The Liberals were, however, given to fancy that they were the most significant party in the house and in the country because they stood between die-hard reaction and red revolution. Menon wondered if anything without a distinct personality could ever really stand between two opposites without being assimilated by either of them.[302] Meanwhile, Hoare in his constituency had been compelled to assure his electorate that he would not make in India the mistake that had been made in Ireland — surrendering power. The constitutional measure for India would be a firm conservative step and the proposed act would be no departure from Conservative policies. It seemed that Hoare had the comfort that while he could not himself retreat into die-hardism, the pressure of his backbenches, of which he was a willing victim, would help him to do it.[303]

With Baldwin, it was almost a religious faith to preserve the sanctity of his party as also a sacred duty of keeping it together on all issues. He regarded the threatened schism in the party over the Indian question with intense anxiety. He would rather see the National government dissolved and even the beloved empire sundered to pieces than he would see his Tory Party break into fragments over India. That accounted for his flexibility in the Indian policy. The cohesion of the Conservative Party was of more concern that the fate of India. The virulent and consistent die-hard pressure worked. Together with the crusade against Indian reforms, there was also a campaign against Stafford Cripps accused of seeking left dictatorship. Cripps' scheme, emanating from his Socialist League platform for the revitalization of British democracy, was considered by the Labour executive which affirmed its continued adherence of parliamentary democracy and its opposition to all forms of dictatorship.[304]

But the situation for Menon had become dull and tiresome because he could not quite comprehend the complexities of the problem in India. Depressing cables piled up on the desks of the India League during summer and autumn 1933 to indicate that the Congress in India was on the run completely.[305] The figures showed that the boycott and *satyagraha* had slackened and it was anticipated that the Congress would, before long, be compelled to offer an unconditional surrender. Menon thought that it would perhaps be in order that he should write to Malaviya and Gandhi about the state of affairs at the JSC and the League's perception of the nature of the future struggle. He held that things were going unsatisfactorily at the JSC and it had been made plain to the Indians that the central part of the white paper must wait till the Reserve Bank came into function, which incidentally was not a priority item of the agenda.[306] The Indians, Menon thought, were outmanoeuvred and the process of taking evidence could go on long enough to tire every one. After that the Indians would return and the rest of the committee would produce its own report. Menon pointed out that Baldwin's refusal to defend the white paper at the Conservative conference was significant and was commented upon even by the *Guardian*.[307]

On another point, Menon drew the attention of the Congress. It seemed to him that since, after the promulgation of the new act, the Government of India would rest on transitory provisions and constitutionally on the powers of the secretary of state, India might thus be relegated to the status of a Crown Colony and the central government would become a matter for the viceroy and the India Office to look after. Menon's apprehension, he reported, had been confirmed by a few well-known constitutionalists. He claimed that the real aim of the government appeared to be to undo the mistakes of 1917, scotch all talk of dominion status and forestall all future advance.[308] Menon alluded to the readiness of the orthodox Hindus and women to give evidence and cooperate with the committee, indicating that the report of the committee might not give as much as had been contemplated in the Simon report. Besides, the Government and its cohorts were not frightfully anxious that the Congress should cooperate. There was little possibility of the viceroy seeing Gandhi, much less making a settlement. Representations to that effect had been ignored. It was clear that the government would prefer that the new constitution should be operated by their friends in India. Menon was sore that the canard that Indians had been beaten was sedulously circulated and he had heard that, with the exception of K.N. Katju, no Indian would take a different view or, at any rate, express one.[309]

In sharp contrast to the striking consolidation of reactionary opinion on India assembled together various factions and front organizations of the Conservative Party, the Labour Party seemed somewhat baffled by the enormity of the Indian problem. It had become increasingly clear that however much party activists might wish to 'mandate' their MPs on Indian issues, they retained, at least in regard to their activities, an almost total measure of independence. MPs relied on the protection of their party leaders against their constituency parties. Conflict between the natural rebelliousness of the Labour Party and its rigid parliamentary code of conduct remained, by and large, dormant. Party discipline ensured that MPs should remain in line with party policy and not to the left-wing constituency parties. The pronouncements at the annual conferences were prolix but they were distinguished by a definite lack of a sense of direction. Some of the party leaders were persuaded by the India League to articulate sensitive statements on India but, invariably, they looked up for a lead to an overworked Menon and its impoverished League, who had become a source of irritation to a good many right-wingers of the party and the orthodox leaders.[310]

Imperialism had become an essential part of the dominant value system and moral framework that promoted the politics of containment. The Labour MPs were repeatedly required to express an opinion and fight for a policy to which they were strongly opposed and which deeply offended their conviction. Invariably, MPs were able to attenuate the rigours of Labour resolutions and policies. Crucial decisions were diluted in the party's specialized committee on colonial issues and then reversed in the parliamentary committee and awkward matters were prevented from being raised at all. Radical Labour MPs devoted to the cause of the India League had become assailable and their very vulnerability was increased and exploited by the officials and the right-wing leadership in the party in the struggle over policy. The structure of the party had become bureaucratic. A strong hierarchy of centralized administration was built up and power tended to be concentrated in the hands of a few top leaders. Once the position of these leaders had been consolidated, they became established and irremovable, creating a kind of oligarchical rule resembling the Conservative Party. To many of them, the Nazi ascendancy in Germany seemed but a passing phase which rendered the policy of appeasement not so very unattractive after all. The radicalization of the universities appeared transient, sentimental and emotional rather than rational, durable and firm. The socialist/ communist dichotomy was nursed with utmost severity though occasionally relieved by flashes of goodwill and cooperation with optimistic possibilities. The radical MPs might, at times, acquire some influence but not power. They might operate as brakes and accelerator but not the steering wheel.[311]

Amidst the social and political turmoil of the day, rationalization, means tests and growing unemployment, the India League found itself desperately trying to place its programme on the national agenda. The League twaddled along. Even close friends found little time for India work. Assignments from the Indian press had become, over time, very few and most of what Menon wrote was published, but rarely paid for. Many among his former sympathizers saw in the government proposals a promising beginning which could be suitably amended and should not be summarily dropped at any rate. Menon had realized that imperial sensibilities had been fully internalized by the Labour Party. That the British empire was a permanent political structure and that India constituted an organic part of that empire formed the inner core of the imperial consensus. Despite doses of self-government, it was implied in that assertion that India was to remain a British dependency and that the relationship was to be accepted in the natural order of things. Labour and liberal spokesmen of imperialism and its constitutional pedants sought to soften the hard position. India would develop into a self-governing dominion, they tried to persuade an attentive congregation, through a process of constitutional evolution. Both these political positions, however, were dismissed by those who worked incessantly to humanize the much-applauded imperial obligation, which to them, seemed a superficial and shortsighted view based on half-truths. They emphasized the need to dissolve a dominion into a fraternal partnership within the empire. Menon was convinced that these three segments of imperial perception converged and modulated each other as required by the fast moving panorama of the Indian political scene. To many influential Labour activists Menon seemed obdurate and uncompromising, pushing the Labour Party without a modicum of success beyond the rubicon of conciliation. The India Empire Society and India Defence League had targeted him all along in meetings and conferences; sympathetic associations advised caution; calumny and condemnation came from all sides; relationships slackened; friendships got estranged; constant stress and torments of struggle overwhelmed health. Physically and spiritually Menon was emaciated. Overstrained, Menon overstretched himself.

Notes and References

1 James Klugmann, 'The Crisis of the Thirties: A View from the Left', in Jon Clark, Marget Heinemann, David Margolie and Card Snee, *Culture and Crisis in Britain in the Thirties,* op.cit.

2 Ibid.

3 R. Benewick, *Political Violence and Public Order,* London 1972,

pp.110-11; R. Griffiths, *Fellow Travellers of The Right,* London 1980; C. Stuart (ed.) *The Reith Diaries,* London 1975, p.56; F. Donaldson, *Edward VIII,* London 1974, p.192; Ralph Miliband, *Capitalist Democracy in Britain,* London 1984, pp.47-9; also see, Robert Skidelsky, *Oswald Mosley,* London 1975. It may be appropriate to quote here a passage from one of Menon's 'London Letters', 16 April 1933, Menon Papers: 'Reaction, however seems to be on the upward movement. The police bill which the Home Secretary will press for passage is an indication .... Fascism is not far from Albion's shores and its exponents are many. Sir Oswald Mosley may be a comic figure .... But the more formidable blackshirt is Mr Winston Churchill who, having found that India and his gigantic literary occupations do not take up his whole time, is looking with an ambitious glance towards the Nazi movement in Germany. Speaking to the anti-Stalinist union some time ago he said: "The Roman genius expressed by Mussolini, the law-giver among living men, has shown every nation that may be harried by socialism or communism, that there is a way out which democracy is willing to follow provided it is badly led. Mussolini has set up a signpost in the world.

I think of Germany with its splendid, clear-eyed youth marching every one along all the roads of the Reich, singing their ancient songs, demanding to be conscripted into an army, eagerly seeking the weapons of war and to suffer and to die for the fatherland."

Comment is needless'.

4 James Klugmann, 'The Crisis of the Thirties', op.cit.

5 Ibid.

6 Ibid.

7 Author's interview with Krishna Shelvankar.

8 See the file of correspondence between Menon and Nambiar in Menon Papers; also Cf. L. Flower, 'Why Germany went Fascist', *The Plebs.*, May 1934; Maurice Dobb, 'World Capitalism since 1925', *The Plebs,* July 1932; and Edward Conze, 'A Communist looks at Fascism', *The Plebs,* September, 1934.

9 Arthur Marwick, *Britain in the Century of Total War,* London 1968, pp.250-1.

10 See, William Shirer, *The Rise and Fall of the Third Reich,* London 1977; Alan Bullock, *Hitler: A Study in Tyranny*, London 1964; Franz Neumann, *Behemoth: The Structure and Practice of National Socialism,* London 1944; also, George L. Mosse, *Towards the Final Solution, A History of European Racism,* New York, 1978, pp.191-230.

11 Eric Hobsbawm, *Age of Extremes, The Short Twentieth Century, 1914-1991,* London, 1994, esp. Chapter Four, 'The Fall of Liberalism', pp.109-141.

12 Ibid., pp.116-7.

13 Ibid., pp.117-9.

14 Menon, *Circular on Fascism,* The India League, 1933, Menon Papers.

15 Ralph Miliband, *Capitalist Democracy in Britain,* Oxford 1982, pp.131-139. Also see, J.S. Barnes to Jawaharlal Nehru, August 1934, Menon Papers.

16 Ibid., pp.30-38.

17 Menon to Krishna Shelvankar, 16 March 1934, Menon Papers.

18 Cf. Ralph Miliband, *Capitalist Democracy in Britain,* op.cit., esp. pp. 60-93.

19 Ibid.

20 Cf. L. Minkin, *The Labour Party Conference,* London 1973, pp.277-285.

21 Ibid.

22 See, for example, Extracts from New Scotland Yard Report, 25 June 1930, L/PJ/12/356, India Office.

23 See for example, the following:

Extract from New Scotland Yard Report, 25 June 1930, L/PJ/12/356 India Office; Extract from New Scotland Yard Report, 16 August 1933, L/PJ/2/449, India Office; Extract from New Scotland Yard Report, 4 June 1934, L/PJ/12/450, India Office.

24 The author's interview with Anna Polak.

25 Arthur Marwick, *Britain the Century of Total War,* op.cit., pp.163-7. Ralph Miliband, *Capitalist Democracy in Britain,* op.cit., pp.61-65.

26 Ibid.

27 A.J.P. Taylor, *English History 1914-1945,* op.cit., pp. 264-67.

28 Ibid., p.267.

29 Ibid., pp.349 and 354; also Miliband, *Capitalist Democracy, etc.*

30 Arthur Marwick, *Britain in the Century of Total War,* op.cit., p.241.

31 Stafford Cripps, *Can Socialism Come by Constitutional Methods?*, London 1933. A copy of this volume with marginal explanatory notes is available in Menon Papers.

32 Klugmann, 'Crisis in the Thirties', op.cit., p.22.

33 Stafford Cripps, *Can Socialism Come by Constitutional Methods?,* op.cit.

34 Ibid.

35 Menon to Masani, 6 February 1935, Menon Papers.

36 Cripps, *Can Socialism Come by Constitutional Methods?,* op.cit.

37 Ibid.

38 Ibid.

39 Ibid.

40 Fenner Brockway to Bertrand Russell, 28 May 1929, Menon Papers.

41 Menon to Ms M. Miller, Westminster branch, Socialist League, 2 May 1933, Menon Papers.

42 Ibid.

43 Ibid.

44 Ibid.

45 Ibid.

46 Bertha Brewster to Menon, 31 May 1933, Menon Papers.

47 Vera Kemp to Menon, 27 June 1933, Menon Papers.

48 J. Bradfield and others to Menon 20 July 1933, Menon Papers.

49 Ibid.

50 Ibid.

51 Ibid.

52 Resolution in ibid.

53 Ibid.

54 Menon to C.F. Andrews, 22 March 1933, Menon Papers.

55 Ibid.

56 Ibid.

57 Ibid.

58 Ibid.

59 Ibid.

60 Minutes of the meeting of the Executive Committee, India League, 2 March 1933, Menon Papers.

61 Ibid.

62 Ibid.

63 Ibid.

64 Ibid.

65 Horrabin to Bertrand Russell, 3 March 1933, Menon Papers; also Horrabin to Malaviya, 22 August 1932, Menon Papers.

66 Winifred Horrabin, 'Jawaharlal, Indira and Krishna' 1938, Winifred Horrabin Papers.

67 Horrabin to Bertrand Russell, 3 March 1973, Menon Papers.

68 Ibid.

69 Ibid.

70 Ibid.

71 Menon to Bertrand Russell, 7 March 1933, Menon Papers.

72 Ibid.

73 Menon, 'Circular letter', 8 March 1933, Menon Papers.

74 Menon to Horace Alexander 10 March 1933, Menon Papers.

75 Menon to Wilkinson, 8 March 1933, Menon Papers.

76 Ibid.

77 Menon to Wilkinson, 28 March 1933, Menon Papers.

78 Hilda Kuttner to Menon, 13 May 1933, Menon Papers.

79 Bertrand Russell, Chairman, India League, 'Circular letter', 26 March 1933, Menon Papers.

80 Russell to Lansbury, 6 March, 1933, Menon Papers.

81 Ibid.

82 Ibid.

83 Bertrand Russell, Chairman, India League, 'Circular letter' to the Labour Parties, 26 March 1933, Menon Papers.

84 Ibid.

85 The debate was held in February 1933; A.J.P. Taylor, *English History 1914-45,* op.cit., pp.362-3.

86 Cf. Eric Hobsbawm, *Age of Extremes, The Short Twentieth Century, 1914-1945,* London 1994, pp.44-45, 48-49, 124-125; also see, *The Secret International,* London, July 1932; and *Patriotism Ltd,* February 1933 both published by The Union of Democratic Control.

87 Taylor, *English History 1914-15,* op.cit., pp.362-3.

88 Menon (ed.) *Young Oxford and War,* London 1933.

89 Harold Laski, 'Preface' in Ibid.

90 Menon, 'London Letter' (for *Andhra Patrika*), 26 February 1933, Menon Papers.

91 Ibid.

92 Ibid.

165 Ibid.

166 R.J. Moore, *The Crisis of Indian Unity,* Delhi, 1974, pp. 208-18.

167 Menon, 'London Letter', 14 July 1933, Menon Papers.

168 Menon, 'London Letter', 22 July 1933, Menon Papers.

169 Menon, 'London Letter', 29 July 1933, Menon Papers.

170 Ibid.

171 Menon, 'London Letter', 14 July 1933, Menon Papers; also, 'London Letter', 29 July 1933, Menon Papers.

172 Menon, 'London Letter', 3 July 1933, Menon Papers.

173 Menon, 'London Letter', 10 June 1933, Menon Papers.

174 Ibid.

175 Menon, 'London Letter', 8 July 1933, Menon Papers (for *Andhra Patrika*).

176 Ibid.

177 Cf. V.S. Srinivasa Sastri, *The White Paper: A Breach of Faith,* India League, June 1933.

178 Cf. *Demands of the Indian Moderates,* 19 January 1933, India League.

179 Krishna Menon, *Broken Pledges,* May 1933, India League.

180 Ibid.

181 Ibid.

182 Ibid.

183 Ibid.

184 Ibid.

185 Ibid.

186 Menon, 'London Letter', 10 July 1933, Menon Papers.

187 Ibid.

188 Ibid.

189 For example, Menon, 'London Letter', 8 July 1933, Menon Papers.

190 Ibid.

191 Menon, 'London Letter', 8 July 1933, Menon Papers; also, Menon, 'London Letter', 14 July 1933, Menon Papers.

192 Menon, 'London Letter', 8 July 1933, Menon Papers.

193 Ibid.

194 See, Menon, 'The World Economic Conference', 10 June 1933, Menon Papers, also, Menon, 'London Letter', 24 June 1933, Menon Papers.

195 Ibid.

196 Menon, 'The World Economic Conference', 10 June 1933, Menon Papers.

197 Menon, 'London Letter', 24 June 1933, Menon Papers.

198 Ibid.

199 Ibid.

200 Menon, 'London Letter', 10 June 1933, Menon Papers.

201 Ibid.

202 Menon, 'London Letter', 3 June 1933, Menon Papers and Menon, 'London Letter', 24 June 1933, Menon Papers.

203 Menon, 'London Letter', 3 June 1933, Menon Papers and Menon, 'London Letter', 8 July 1933, Menon Papers.

204 Menon, 'London Letter', 26 May 1933, Menon Papers.

205 Ibid.

206 Ibid.

207 Menon, 'London Letter', 1 July 1933, Menon Papers.

208 Menon, 'London Letter', 14 July 1933, Menon Papers.

209 Ibid.

210 Menon, 'London Letter', 21 June 1933, Menon Papers.

211 Ibid.

212 Menon, 'London Letter', 3 June 1933, Menon Papers.

213 Ibid.

214 Ibid.

215 Ibid.

216 Menon, 'London Letter', *The Hindu,* 12 April 1934.

217 Menon, 'The Round Table. An Inside Story', November 1973, Menon Papers.

218 Ibid.

219 Ibid.

220 E.A. Guest to Colin Davidson, 18 May 1933, Menon Papers.

221 Colin Davidson to E.A. Guest, 16 May 1933, Menon Papers; also Colin Davidson to E.A. Guest, 26 May 1933, Menon Papers.

222 E.A. Guest to Colin Davidson, 20 May 1933, Menon Papers.

223 E.A. Guest, 'Memorandum' on Constitutional Reform, 20 May 1933, Menon Papers.

224 Ibid.

225 Ibid.

226 Ibid.

227 Ibid.

228 Ibid.

229 Menon to the editor, *The Manchester Guardian,* 30 August 1933, Menon Papers.

230 Menon, 'London Letter', 30 September 1933, Menon Papers.

231 Ibid.

232 Ibid.

233 Ibid.

234 Menon, 'London Letter', 8 July 1933, Menon Papers.

235 Ibid.

236 Menon, 'London Letter', 20 July 1933, Menon Papers.

237 Menon, 'London Letter', 29 July 1933, Menon Papers.

238 Ibid.

239 Ibid.

240 Menon, 'London Letter', 7 October 1933, Menon Papers.

241 Ibid.

242 Ibid.

243 Ibid.

244 Ibid.

245 Menon, 'London Letter', 30 September 1933, Menon Papers.

246 Ibid.

247 Ibid.

248 Ibid.

249 Proceedings of the Labour Party Conference (hereafter PLPC) (1926) at Morgate, p.252.

250 PLPC (1926) Morgate, pp.252-3.

251 PLPC (1927) Blackpool, pp.255-58.

252 Ibid.

253 PLPC (1928) Birmingham, pp.171-179.

254 Ibid.

255 PLPC (1929) Birmingham, pp.190-94.

256 PLPC (1930) The Pier Pavilion, Llanduduo, pp.216-220.

257 Ibid.

258 Ibid., pp. 216-217.

259 Ibid.

260 Ibid., pp. 216-20.

261 PLPC (1931) Scarborough p. 84, 168-71.

262 PLPC (1932) Leicester, pp. 95-7, 178-181.

263 PLPC (1933), Hastings, pp. 78-9.

264 Ibid., pp. 228-230.

265 Report on the Meeting at Hastings, 1933, Menon Papers.

266 Ibid.

267 Ibid.

268 Ibid.

269 Ibid.

270 Appeal by the Indian Meerut Committee, 3 March 1933, Menon Papers.

271 Ibid.

272 Menon to J.A.D. Naoroji, 5 March 1933, Menon Papers.

273 Bertrand Russell to Naoroji, 18 March 1933, Menon Papers.

274 Menon to J.A.D. Naoroji, 5 March 1933, Menon Papers.

275 Ibid.

276 Menon to Naoroji, 8 March 1933, Menon Papers.

277 Ibid.

278 Menon to Naoroji, 16 March 1933, Menon Papers; also, Russell to Naoroji, 18 March 1933, Menon Papers.

279 Naoroji to Menon, 12 April 1933, Menon Papers; also, Russell to Naoroji, 18 April 1933, Menon Papers.

280 Menon to Naoroji, 19 March 1933, Menon Papers.

281 Ibid.

282 'Minutes of the meeting of the executive committee of the India League on 2 March 1933', Menon Papers; also, Menon to C.F. Andrews, 22 March 1933, Menon Papers.

283 Menon, 'Circular letter', 24 March 1933, Menon Papers.

284 Ibid.

285 Menon to Naoroji, 9 April 1933, Menon Papers.

286 Wenyon to Menon, 1 April 1933, Menon Papers; Menon to Wenyon, 18 April 1933, Menon Papers.

287 Ibid.

288 Ibid.

289 For a comprehensive view of the British Union of Fascists on the Indian empire, see William Joyce, *Fascism and India,* B.U.F. Publications Ltd, London 1933.

290 Arthur Marwick, *Britain in the Century of Total War,* op.cit., p.240; also see for a comprehensive study, C. Cross, *The Fascists in Britain,* London 1961. On the trends of public opinion with regard to fascism, see, Kingsley Martin, 'Fascism and the *Daily Mail', The Political Quarterly,* vol.5, 1934.

291 Menon to Mrs Whitgift, 28 March 1933, Menon Papers.

292 Ibid.

293 Ibid.

294 Ibid.

295 Ibid.

296 Secretary, 'The British Universities' League of Nations Society' to Menon, 18 March 1933, Menon Papers; and Aneurin Bevan (chairman), (the Society for Socialist Enquiry and Propaganda), to Menon, 28 March 1933, Menon Papers.

297 Menon, 'London Letter', 15 April 1933, Menon Papers.

298 Menon, 'London Letter', 23 June 1933, Menon Papers.

299 Ibid.

300 Menon, 'London Letter', 26 June 1933, Menon Papers.

301 Ibid.

302 Menon, 'London Letter', 27 June 1933, Menon Papers.

303 Ibid.

304 Ibid.

305 See, for example, Menon, 'London Letter', 4 May 1933, 13 May 1933, 10 July 1933 and 8 July 1933, all in Menon Papers.

306 Menon, 'London Letter', 13 May 1933, Menon Papers.

307 Menon, 'London Letter', 2 October 1933, Menon Papers.

308 Menon, 'London Letter', 26 September 1933, Menon Papers.

309 Ibid.

310 Cf. the case of Horrabin, Horrabin to Bertrand Russell, 3 March 1933, Menon Papers.

311 Author's Conversation with Mulk Raj Anand and Krishna Shelvankar.

CHAPTER IV

CONDITION OF INDIA

Early in August 1932, the Government of India had begun in earnest to work out the steps which might be taken in order to counteract the propaganda which members of the India League delegation might be expected to put out when they got back to England in the third week of November. Hallett felt that it might be desirable if the India Office, before the delegation themselves started talking, took steps to put out suitable material based on information from India, to show the extent to which members of the delegation from the outset of their tour decided to have themselves 'run' and influenced by the Congress.[1] Hallett made a special reference to the policy of reticence adopted by the delegation.[2] As a result, there was no sure means of anticipating, except in a very general way, what the team was likely to say when they returned home. It was, therefore, not certain what form the official counter-publicity campaign should take. It was also difficult to gauge from the India end political reactions at home and the best possible form that counter-propaganda might ultimately take.[3] Everyone was awaiting the pronouncement of the team on 26 November 1932. From India, a loosely constructed note was prepared by I.M. Stephens, director of public intelligence, as the basis of replies to questions in Parliament.[4] All material in the form of reports from various provinces had already been sent to the India office. The set of reports and the note would supplement each other in giving effective answers to questions raised in the house or outside.[5] Hallett thought that the most effective line for the secretary of state would be to discredit the credentials of the delegation in a 'mildly contemptuous' way and to emphasize that throughout their tour the team allowed themselves to be 'run' by Congress sympathizers. Persistent endeavours were made from one end of the country to the other to stage 'incidents' for their benefit with a view to bringing the police into direct conflict with unruly crowds.[6]

Recommending Stephens' note, Hallett maintained that all facts enumerated in it could be published without reserve.[7] It was suggested that the bold and unambiguous language of the report might be softened at the time of publication and efforts should be made to 'cloak' the 'allegation' in more discreet language.[8] Some of the most effective facts had been culled from intercepted letters.[9] India was used to authoritarian rule and arbitrary methods and such publication would not be questioned in that country. But parliamentary democracy created a delicate situation in England where 'rule of law and legal freedom were fundamental realities'. Therefore, Hallett suggested circumspection and requested the India Office to ensure that these facts of the note were not brought out, at any rate, in so explicit a form. The India Office had requested that the force of argument of the Indian note must indicate the unreliability and bias of the delegation's impressions. Hallett vouched and affirmed that the note effectively performed that task.[10]

The Government of India also claimed that all material concerning the delegation's activities and after-effects had been sent to the secretary of state and the Indian government did not know if the home government would publish any reply to the report.[11] It was anticipated that the report of the delegation would attract attention at home and form the subject of questions in the houses of parliament. A reply to the report would, thus, be more necessary in England than in India where the report would hardly attract attention in the press as it would merely repeat many of the old allegations against the government.[12] But on one point it was very sensitive: the accusation of the delegates that the district officers knew mighty little about India and its conditions and that the complex realities of India were located and grasped by the delegates during their short and casual study trip in rural India. The Government of India thought that such an outrageous accusation was in itself an exposure of their prejudiced point of view.[13] It was enough, wrote Hallett, to say that officers who had spent years of service in their districts and could speak the vernaculars were in a better position to gauge the real feelings of the country than a party of globe trotters who, after a fortnight's hurried tour of half a dozen districts, had the cheek to pronounce judgment on intricate questions which needed years of experience to be fully comprehended.[14]

Hallett thought that Wilkinson was, in particular, a clever person with an able pen and if some effective counter-propaganda were put out before she started publishing herself, it might be useful and also effective except probably amongst a few members of Christian do-gooders, some members of the Conciliation Group and some such persons who, though well-meaning individuals, were capable of confusing public opinion by their very woolly inexactitude both in terms of perception and vocabulary.[15] The India office alerted the press confidentially to its views on the delegation but thought it desirable to await authentic information on the points to be highlighted by the delegation and, if meanwhile a wedge could be driven between Menon and the League on the one hand and Wilkinson and the Labour Party on the other, it would have appreciable fallout in favour of the government and its India policy.[16] Two meetings were held by the India League on 26 November 1932 to initiate a public debate on the condition of India under the ordinances by the delegates then fresh from their hectic sojourn in India.[17] On 1 December, however, the Government of India was informed that the whole affair turned out to be a damp squib and the meetings drew no significant attention in the press. With the exception of a gossip paragraph in the *Daily Herald* having a strong Labour connection, not a line was published in any newspaper.[18] Since there was no special stimulation, thanks to official prompting, this attitude of cold-blooded unconcern was encouraged to continue.

The Government of India was asked to see that as little as possible should come through the press telegrams from India.[19] In some political quarters, however, this perspective was not acceptable and the India Office was obliged to get in touch with certain political organizations such as the Indian Empire Society and some newspapers to arrange a counterblast through them.[20] It was thought indispensable to give some opportunity to the opponents of the India League to discredit the so-called peacemakers and hit the League at its soft underbelly with regard to its professed impartiality as the price of its imprudent impudence. Menon had been especially caustic about Benn and his India policy. It was necessary to exploit that fact to the maximum while the different perspective of Wilkinson, detected by Indian officials, and the intransigence of Whately, Menon and Matters were to be highlighted and exploited with profit and skill.[21] The India Office was careful and while distributing the note prepared by Stephens it saw to it that no evidence was left in the edited version to show that Government of India opened other people's letters.[22] It was certain that when copies of the note were circulated some discerning individuals might think that a few letters had come into the government's hands without interception. On this 'common sense presumption', the note was circulated to some organizations and editors of conservative newspapers and journals who were interested in defending the India policy of the government.[23] Left to itself, the India Office was inclined to ensure that the League continued to be nonchalantly neglected in the press. In any case, the India office thought that for all official purposes the 'precious little delegation' of Menon should be consigned to oblivion.[24]

The counter-propaganda against the League's delegation closely followed the points raised in the confidential letter of the Government of India. Referring to the allegations of a rather disquieting nature about the administration of India made by the delegation, it was resolutely maintained that it would be a matter of grave error of judgement to accept the allegations at their face value.[25] It was politely pointed out that members of the delegation were hardly aware of the situation in India. Ordinary readers and members of parliament were called upon to deduce their own conclusions from the facts that were then placed before them. The India Office claimed that there was irrefutable evidence to prove that the delegation was sponsored and financed by the Congress and its close sympathizers.[26] This evidence established beyond doubt that not only the delegation's travelling expenses were in a large measure provided out of Congress funds or by Congress sympathizers, but also that the Congress, throughout the whole tour in India, was responsible for arranging all the details as to where they went and what they saw and what they heard.[27] It was emphasized that authorities in India and the Congress organization were still engaged in a conflict owing to the continued refusal of the Indian party to terminate the civil disobedience movement.[28] It was, therefore, obvious, it claimed, that the delegation was not concerned about arriving at a correct estimate of the truth. On the contrary, the note claimed, the delegation by putting themselves almost entirely in the hands of one of the two parties to the dispute, did not improve their prospect of reaching impartial or unbiased conclusions or convincing the public that they had attempted to do so.[29]

In the course of the counterblast, it was stressed that the Congress party supported the delegation financially, that shortly before the delegation left for India, Madan Mohan Malaviya contributed a substantial sum to the funds of the League.[30] Menon, a well-known sympathizer of the Congress and secretary of the League, had asked for it and was careful to explain that the money should be treated simply as a donation. It was well-known that Mirabehn, Gandhi's English admirer, had been consulted beforehand, the official handout maintained, as to the places and people the delegation should visit.[31] By the time the delegation reached India, a circular was distributed by the Congress committee, in which detailed instructions were given as to how the various provincial Congress committees should deal with them.[32] These bodies were to prepare the itinerary for the delegation's tour in their jurisdiction and a list of particular things, e.g. confiscated buildings, looted houses and other marks of police atrocities, should be shown to the members.[33] The Karnataka provincial Congress committee issued a more 'illuminating document' which announced that the delegation should carry back striking impressions of civil disobedience in action and it would be effective if Congress activities such as processions, picketing, etc. dispersed by *lathis* could be arranged during their stay and witnessed by them.[34]

In a bid to establish the prejudiced and superficial nature of the mission, the official outburst left no stone unturned. Thus it was maintained that Matters, during his visit to the Kanara district, was presented with fake evidence of so-called police atrocities. Congressmen reported gleefully that Matters was satisfied with his investigation and that he successfully fulfilled commitments assigned to him.[35] It was maintained in the official report that Matters was cognizant of the dubious nature of the evidence but turned a deaf ear to all official correctives.[36]

In Madras, Nageswar Rao, a local Congressman, urged the Congress volunteer in charge of the delegation not to be squeamish about spending money for the comfort of the delegates. The primary intention of Congress assistance was that the projected programme of the delegation should succeed at all costs. Menon reciprocated warmly by thanking Rao for the 'perfect organization and overwhelming hospitality' which enabled the commission to do 'quite useful work'.[37] The officials sought to present the whole operation of work meticulously undertaken, perhaps in some ways, for the personal promotion of Menon himself.[38] With Nageswar Rao's assistance, it was reported that Menon got the assignment from *Andhra Patrika* as its representative in London. With that assignment in hand he proceeded to manage a similar journalistic responsibility from the *Advance* of Calcutta.[39] Authorities held that by the time the deputation reached Calcutta, they were widely recognized throughout the country to be definitely working for the Congress. The success of the role was remarkably demonstrated at a Congress meeting at the Maidan in Calcutta where Whately was seen conspicuously on the topmost step of the Octorlony Monument holding aloft a Congress flag to be cheered by the huge audience.[40] It was small wonder, it appeared to incensed officials, that the mission left Bengal with a firm but fanciful conviction that Gandhi was the only accredited leader of the Hindu population and they were impressed by 'the simple and peaceful ways of the people of India'. Had they been, the officials added cryptically, either in Chittagong or Calcutta a few days later, they might have seen good reasons to revise their opinion.[41]

During the tour in Bihar and Orissa, the official counterblast added, an offer had been made by government officials to provide members of the delegation with an interpreter other than the usual Congressman.[42] It was politely declined and a similar rebuff was administered to the officials when a suggestion was made that it might be worth the members' while to visit some villages in addition to those which had been specially selected by Congress supporters.[43] A typical example of the method the Congress adopted to hoodwink the delegation at Pirbahore and Amhara near Patna, was to show the two houses from which the doors and windows had been unhinged by the police allegedly as part of the general policy of crushing the Congress and its movement. The officials maintained, with a straight face, that the measures were undertaken by the police as part of the attachment orders of the court owing to non-payment of fine.[44] It was pointed out that both at Dhanbad and other places the delegation did not mind accompanying the Congress guides while declining official escorts. It was stressed that the delegation was primarily exposed to those districts, such as Kanara, Sylhet, Midnapur and Monghyr, where the civil disobedience movement had been strongest and they passed by scores of others in which Congress influence was marginal or declining.[45]

The thrust of the official argument was that throughout the country persistent endeavours were made by staging processions, organized picketing and other political demonstrations to bring the police into conflict with disorderly crowds for the benefit and guidance of the delegates. The authorities felt encouraged to complain that at places the delegation's visit was directly responsible for an appreciable revival of civil disobedience activities. All over the United Provinces, especially in Banaras, Allahabad, Kanpur, Agra, Meerut, in various places in the Punjab and the North-West Frontier Province, the Congress volunteers were goaded to rejuvenate the dying movement, to become active again and to lodge complaints against the arbitrary rule of the state machinery to the delegates, including imaginary stories of *lathi* charges, punishment in the prisons, and alleged outrages against women. Amritsar was one of the places which were hotbeds of Congress activities, while the whole of the NWFP was a super-sensitive area and the surprise visit by Menon and Wilkinson to these places was considered an outrageous act of indiscretion by these irresponsible and impetuous personalities. The officials were relieved to report that it was a matter of gratification that no untoward incident took place during this 'guided tour' and they felt that for this they had reasons to congratulate themselves.[46]

It was maintained that since the delegates allowed themselves to be directed by an organization which was in conflict with the government and 'which is renowned for its effectiveness in the arts of publicity and propaganda', the impression that the India League delegation formed was necessarily biased, episodic and one-sided.[47] It was more so since both Congress and the administration had been operating amidst a vast, illiterate and ignorant population which was volatile and lawless.[48] Little did the governors, the home member, the police authorities and district officers realize that their account of an active and popular Congress Party, which was declared illegal, whose front organizations had been pronounced unlawful, whose bulletins and publications had been proscribed, whose entire frontline leadership had been confined to prisons and whose funds had been frozen, constituted adequate and weighty evidence of a virile organization with a distinct and parallel centre of authority, commanding loyalty and obedience of an unarmed people. The whole gamut of facts merely confirmed the instinctive feelings of Menon and the League even before the deputation sailed for India that British rule in India had lost its credibility and that the Congress had presented itself as the nation's acknowledged parliament and that it had been emerging as an irresistible mass movement despite the might of the *Raj*.

The meeting of friends of the India League to welcome back the four delegates to India, held at the flat of J.F. Horrabin on 21 November 1932, was impressive.[49] It was attended by 43 persons including Morgan Jones, Lord Snell, C.F. Andrews, Miss Rathbone MP, Harold Laski, Mr and Mrs S.K. Ratcliffe and Hannah Swaffer. A competent report of the confidential meeting was available in the India office and it drew the appreciation of the secretary of state and the officials. Although the report was comprehensive, the officials of the India Office chuckled as they saw in the proceedings of the meeting no reference to the two points they were interested in, namely, how the delegation was financed and what steps were taken to verify the allegations made through interpreters. The only member, it was added, with knowledge of any Indian tongue was Menon who would himself have been able in all probability to act as interpreter in some parts of India but not in all, much less in the NWFP of which he said as much.[50]

With Laski in the chair, the first speaker was Monica Whately who specialized in police atrocities in India. She alleged that officials in India from the least important right up to the Viceroy were woefully innocent of the real condition of affairs. Indian officers of the provincial services who might be expected to know the situation better were reluctant to report it to their superiors lest this meant a bar to promotion. The delegates found that even Willingdon was curiously uninformed of the situation. There was a 'conspiracy of silence' and wilful ignorance on the part of the officials. Whately alleged that the villages throughout the country were virtually under famine conditions, but that the viceroy dismissed the statements made to him by the delegation on this matter with the remark that there could not be famine conditions since these had not been reported to him. She drew a doleful picture of village conditions and said that the people of the countryside complained bitterly that they were without sanitation, medical attendance, schools or roads, and were permanently in a condition of semi-starvation. Even where the villagers had cows, they were too poor to use milk, which was sent to the market for sale. In spite of that condition of affairs, land revenue was extracted from the cultivators under the lash of a whip.

Whately drew a harrowing picture of the alleged arbitrary power and brutality of the police in rural districts and said that throughout the country there was a system under which punitive police could be imposed upon villages where political crimes had been committed. The authorities could make the punitive police chargeable on the village as a whole or could exempt certain persons or areas from this autocratic exaction. This meant constant exercise of tyranny. Moreover, there was a great deal of extortion by police by hanging the threat of imposition of punitive police on the unfortunate villages. She also spoke of various types of police atrocities of which the delegation had been told. She expressed her surprise that under such conditions the people of India still could retain rational instincts. The people were afraid to speak up. The delegates were told that a couple of youths had been suspended for a few minutes from the roof by their heels and a police inspector confirmed that the allegation was substantially true. Whately claimed that the ordinances had failed to restore the pride of the *Raj,* for the Congress spirit not only existed but had been growing. The police excesses had driven more and more people into sympathy with the Congress ideals. The shopkeepers, even those who were hoping to sell foreign textiles, expressed their dislike and resentment at the rough treatment meted out to pickets. Another point made by Whately was that the women of India were bitterly opposed to the perpetuation of communal divisions in the electorates. They resented the idea of being dragged into a communal tangle. What they demanded was adult franchise and to be placed in exactly the same position as the men.[51]

Leonard Matters, referred to as an ardent supporter of the League against Imperialism, held that almost nothing in India really surprised him. There was no law in India save that of the orders of bureaucracy. The English officials were out of touch with the people and described them by all sorts of epithets ranging from 'nigger' to 'swine'. It was all very well, he argued, for Lord Reading to go to the USA and whitewash the administration of the ordinances, but the fact remained that 'India was under lawless law'. He challenged the British government to answer the charges which the delegation had brought back with them and said that they could not be put off with the soft words of a man like Lord Sankey. The answer to the allegations they brought back should be a readiness to send out to India an independent body of commissioners to see for themselves what was going on. He maintained that Lord Willingdon might believe that there was confidence in India in his government but for the most part there was absolutely none, and where it existed, it had been diminishing. It scarcely breathed even in the minds of some of the individuals who had been brought over to England as members of the RTC. Even Sir Purshottamdas Thakurdas had told the delegation such inhuman stories of brutal police oppression that one wondered if he would get another invitation to attend an official conference in England.[52]

Wilkinson tried to stay close to the political aspects of the tour. She said, probably with a touch of exaggeration that the delegation got to know more of the Indian conditions than the officials, for they went in the villages and lived among the people. They had sympathy for the people and sought to restore their confidence. She admitted that the ordinances had largely succeeded in doing what was intended. They had been carried out with cool persistence and determination that would have done credit to a fascist government. Nowhere was this more marked than in the North-West Frontier Province, where the consideration seemed to be that anything was justifiable because it was the frontier. She admitted that the Congress was on the defensive so far as the big towns were concerned, and very definitely so, apart from Bombay. The pivotal points of the Congress movement had been shifted to the villages. Nationalism was no longer a ferment stirred by the educated classes but had penetrated among the masses of the villages. Everywhere in the countryside, there was determination to resist. Police ruthlessness had permeated rural India and it was not an uncommon thing to find that poor cultivators had been blackmailed.

Wilkinson was convinced that there was greater will to unity in the villages than in the large towns. Muslims and Hindus were united in their efforts to resist authority. The abominable thing about the communal differences of the towns was that the cleavages were distinct and open and they had tended to ruin India's image in the eyes of the world. The rural Indians were magnificent types, physical and mental, and endowed with definite philosophic background. She admitted that she had very serious doubts as to some of the atrocities she had heard of. But such stories were believed and had their effect in the growth of the party favouring violence. That party was growing and was destined to play a significant role in the future. She said that so far as the frontier was concerned, but for Gandhi and his influence upon Ghaffar Khan, there would not have been an Englishman left alive in NWFP amidst 'the flying bullets' and 'the arithmetic of the frontier', especially when the troubles were at their height some months ago.[53]

Menon made his last intervention to add to the strange kaleidoscope of India. The underlying spirit of his remarks was that the efforts of the Indian government to overcome the civil disobedience movement and the armed revolutionaries were a sad commentary on the policy-makers' inability to comprehend and grasp the leading and irresistible forces of history operating in contemporary India. Their commanding heights were actualized in the process of a unique struggle in history by the Indian National Congress, with the active participation of an awakened people, led by a remarkable leader of men given to bold assertion of India's dignity and a compassionate theory of action. Attempting to interpret the mind of Gandhi, Menon referred to his long conversation with C. Rajagopalachari. Menon maintained that Gandhi wished to cooperate, but he would not withdraw the civil disobedience movement save under very definite conditions; one of these was full restoration of property taken from the peasants of Gujarat for non-payment of land revenue. Whether Congress was crushed or not, those who were in sympathy with it would be able to carry out immediate arrangements. The Congress had been watching keenly the proceedings of the three sessions of the RTC. It was not necessary that they were going to boycott the councils.

Gandhi knew that if he withdrew the civil disobedience movement, he would lose his hold on the people of India. The politics of violence was advancing and in Bengal it had 'put the fear of God into the British officials'. The government did not know whether its votaries in Bengal numbered 7,000 or 70,000.[54] The movement had a firm base in the Punjab as well and its impact was so powerful that it could sometimes even issue ultimatums to the Congress as well as to the government. The movement had also been spreading in UP. Menon felt that it was likely that there would be more than one type of resistance to Britain. There was a growing feeling that the people should apply their minds to pressurize the government until it was compelled to grant some method whereby the voice of India could express itself, as for example, in the formation of a constituent assembly. The fact was that Congress workers could not be arrested unless they wished to be arrested.

The general simplicity of life of the people of India greatly helped the movement. Any worker of the Congress could enter any house and be sure of the hospitality of the inmates. The Congress had a wide measure of acceptability to the people. Menon maintained that it was true that there was not much to choose between oppression under Wedgwood Benn and oppression under Samuel Hoare except that the existing regime was entirely vindictive in its action. He was sure that so long as Willingdon remained in India there would be no peace. He had seen to it that everyone who said anything against government should be excluded from the third RTC with one or two exceptions which could not be avoided, such as Sapru. Menon admitted that the financial resources of the Congress were being crippled and that some of the men who had subscribed largely in the past were not ready to do so for fear of sequestration of the amounts they gave. In these circumstances, the centre of gravity of the Congress had shifted to the villages. The Indian villager was a very obstinate being and was not ready to give way when conviction had once formed in his mind. Menon shared the views of other members that they had not seen the worst of the reign of repression in India for the reason that the people were more and more driven to retaliate.[55]

From the report of the meeting, the India office learnt little. They emphasized that the accusations of atrocities had been expressed in vague terms and since there were no specific instances the official reaction should also be couched in vague terms. One thing that was taken serious note of was that Wilkinson seemed to the India office to be more moderate than others and she was also careful and cautious to retain her individuality. The observation that seemed unnerving was that the movement had been reaching the villages and that it had resilience and determination and might soon be taken over by violent outrages especially in Bengal.[56]

The delegate conference of 26 November at Kingsway Hall at 3 p.m. was followed by a public meeting at 7 p.m. The front of the hall was filled with delegates from 255 different organizations and the total number of delegates was about 475. The official report sought to minimize the significance of the assembly. There were the 'usual enthusiastic elderly ladies', a large number of 'nondescript men' from ILP and the various Labour parties, a few Indian youths, very few Indian women and many representatives of women's cooperative guilds. A bookstall outside the hall sold literature of the League and other relevant material. The bulk of the audience, according to the intelligence report, belonged to the working or lower middle class and therefore considered important as voting power. There were a few intellectuals but they did not form a clear, organized driving force as in the case of a communist delegate audience.[57]

John Jagger, in the chair, wasted little time before Matters was handed the floor. He spoke in general terms about the nature of imperial rule of Britain in India. British law, he said, had no application in India where Imperial Britain ruled as a superior power. The Star Chamber was in existence in India. Gandhi was a prisoner on no specific charges. Prisoners were held indefinitely. Willingdon's assertion that the delegates were run by the Congress who spoon-fed them was baseless and betrayed the uneasy conscience of a guilty man. Constantly followed by the CID and police, the delegates found that the government of India and their conservative spokesmen in England thrived on repeatedly asserted untruths and depended on a remarkable lack of perception caused by the web of disinformation indulged in by the media. The truce was not broken by Gandhi but by the Government of India, who had made all the necessary preparation to annul it by the inauguration of a violent regime when Gandhi was still in Britain. The only law that existed in India was the rule of an arbitrary government administered by 'the most illiterate, corrupt and brutalized police in the world'. Torture was being perpetrated on everybody including children and women. He displayed a *lathi* and claimed that this was only a sample *lathi* which was being used without any pretence of law in order to preserve the *Raj.*

Matters added that the ordinances were then being made permanent and if constitutional methods failed what would follow might be a bloody revolution.[58] Whately stressed that the delegation confronted a major spiritual force of the nationalist movement and there was no material force that could crush it. Arrests were common, trials were non-existent, no meetings with prisoners were allowed, the Congress party and its volunteers enabled the delegates to cover a wholly unknown country, the CID gave the delegation extraordinary attention, many of the hosts of the delegates had to pay for their truculence, the officials wanted to monopolize the delegates' time and attention while the police interfered even with the delegates' use of cars and taxis. There was police terrorism which was a scandal to civilized existence. There was little education, none for girls, no doctors, no dispensary. There was grinding poverty, hunger made people look like walking skeletons; there was a perpetual state of undeclared famine, which the viceroy declined to accept; disease was part of the normal process of living; Britons were callous to the condition of India. Police torture was part of everyday diet; boys were beaten into unconsciousness, but the spirit of the people fighting for justice was extraordinary; that spirit was the duty of the British people not to divert into a violent process.[59] Paradoxically, however, the Indian people still believed in the integrity of British public opinion.

Wilkinson concentrated her attention on prison conditions in India. British rule had ruined the prosperous rural civilization of India; racist rule decried the bright men and women of that nation as niggers; agriculture had been neglected wilfully; brutality of the police was inhuman; traditional handicrafts had been virtually wiped out; torture was endemic; racial hatred was intense; unemployment was proverbial; 20,000 leaders were imprisoned; Gandhi was revered everywhere by everybody including the simple villagers and the untouchables; the Indians knew that the RTC was dead before Gandhi reached London; the release of Gandhi was the first condition of peace; India must achieve self-government without interference from England. Life in India was being lived in an eternal background; this gave the people poise and dignity; India had not made a god of Henry Ford but she knew the magnificent possibilities of the human spirit.[60]

Amidst applause and cheers, Menon made a simple formulation that martial law was imposed and brutally executed all over the country; the nickname for the movement in India was war. Imprisonment without trial, beating in lock-ups, constant exhibition of brute force, unemployment, starvation, and economic backwardness together with ferocious ordinance rule had been turning the movement of Gandhi to violence. Gandhi was aware of that; the Congress volunteers were organized and had overwhelming popular support; the delegation was made to realize by the authorities in India that they were afraid of British public opinion; the British people had a responsibility and they could not shirk it.

The delegate conference and the public meeting made a stir. The audience heard, with deep regret of the conditions prevailing in India caused by ordinances and other repressive measures, implemented through a brutal police force and a callous administration. The resolution of the meeting called for the immediate withdrawal of the arbitrary government and restoration of the rule of law and urged the government to initiate negotiations for the transfer of the control of India to her own people.[61] At the public meeting, Bertrand Russell declared that a policy that generated bitterness and hatred was indefensible and that he stood for 'just so much freedom as Indians wished to have'. It was well-nigh impossible to keep 300 million people in subjection, especially when the people were politically stirred. Censorship could not bring the movement of a resurgent people to a standstill. Independence would have to be conceded or it would be won. Such a struggle might not always remain non-violent. Calling for assistance for the dissemination of real news of and views on India, Russell added that 'everyone of us has the responsibility for what is done in India'.[62]

Recalling his experience under the repressive ordinance rule in India, Matters maintained that it was a lawless regime operating through a brutal police force. No responsible Indian had confidence in the government. If the policy was changed, he said, 'we can have the hand of every Indian; if we spurn that hand, God knows what will be the result'. Matters was supported by Whately who maintained that under the ordinances the people had no rights. Imprisonment without trial, brutal physical torture in lock-ups, punitive expeditions, collective fines, confiscation of property, etc. were the order of the day.

'British prestige', she said with remorse, 'has gone beyond all recall' and Britain in India had been trying to break the 'spirit of the people'. Gandhi's teachings have penetrated deep into every home in India. Police had been behaving like 'frenzied madmen'; onlookers and processionists were attacked without any distinction. Official orders denied preferential treatment to civil disobedience prisoners. But the spirit of India showed no sign of humiliating submission.[63] Wilkinson explained that the Congress was the instrument of the people by which the Indians hoped to attain freedom. Although it was an illegal body it had inspired the most wonderful loyalty of the people. India seemed to be endeavouring through an astounding political struggle to regain for herself the spirit of a heroic age.

Gandhi had emerged as the incarnate spirit of India; his word ran through India; his doctrine of non-violence had inspired 300 million people; his work for the untouchables constituted a massive social revolution for fundamental change in human relationships. Wilkinson believed that there was still ample scope for winning back Indian friendship if the Indians were allowed to determine their own form of government.[64] Menon added that the policy in India was one of vindictive terrorism. He believed that the existing policy would push a section of the Congress people away from non-violence. Gandhi had 'made the villager *count*' and he had also 'put the country on the map of the world'. One did not see any feeling in India against the British people but plenty of it against the British government. A war had been forced on the Indian people and the British people might have to witness before long a 'military dictatorship in India'.[65]

The civil disobedience movement, the official policy of repression, the India League's delegation and the publication of various sensational news items in the international press created a good deal of stir in the public mind. It called for a systematic counterblast of propaganda by the India Office, both in India and in England and, if possible, at selected centres in Europe and America. The India Office was concerned about the impact of the clandestine propaganda of the Congress and the League's increasing commitment to an expanding area of public persuasion programme, demands for crucial information by Parliament and the press, the urgency shown by various organizations clamouring for ruthless suppression of all elements of dissidence in India and, in contrast, the quest for conciliation by an influential segment of British public opinion.[66] In a sense, the India office, operating in a media-oriented society, was more sensitized to the demands of persuasion, propaganda and rational explanation than the Government of India, whose daily routine was hardly affected by local public opinion and whose authoritarianism could easily be glossed over as being dictated by considerations of high imperial policy.

In February 1931, the India Office welcomed various suggestions for obtaining greater publicity, at least for the months of the RTC.[67] It was formally acknowledged that to give effect to these suggestions one would require an extended publicity organization which would entail heavy expenditure. The India Office stressed that if the RTC delegates could be persuaded to press for assistance to enable them to organize a counterblast to the nationalist propaganda, government might come forward to help them.[68] In any case, it was found indispensable to prevent the circulation of illegal Congress literature, to organize counter-propaganda and help stimulate various methods by which the government could reach out to the Indian public through meetings, press communiques, the wireless and the cinema.[69] All these measures were thoroughly explored at different times despite a good deal of financial outlay.

Early in June 1931, Wedgwood Benn, then Secretary of State for India, grasped the immediate need for effective propaganda which should be pushed on with, 'if only we can get the right sort'.[70] Benn was keen to give a proper orientation to the nature of the proposed propaganda. It should have a neat blend of subtlety and meaty information.[71] The problem was, as he saw it, that many people in Britain from various organizations had been pressing for propaganda in India but they really meant by it an effort 'to ram down Indian throats policies which they do not wish to swallow'.[72] That sort of propaganda in India, Benn held, would inevitably be counterproductive and would defeat the very ends it had sought to gain. It was not desirable, he declared, to organize a propaganda primarily directed against the Congress. Such an endeavour would render it very obvious that the government had been attempting to carry on a partisan argument.[73] The result would be odious and might even provoke sore criticism rather than cheerful enthusiasm. The Government of India was thus advised to work out a way by which certain facts could be brought home without any frontal attack on the Congress at all.

Benn thought that during the period of truce with the Congress following the Gandhi-Irwin pact, all provincial governments were better off, traders had developed better opportunities in Indian markets and there was a genial and more comfortable spirit abroad despite remnants of bitterness. 'If we could cite facts and figures,' especially about the 'benefits of peace, better opportunities for trade, etc.' and publicize them, it might exhibit by concrete evidence how much the country was better off without civil disobedience and emphasize the government's earnest eagerness to retain the spirit of cooperation.[74] The idea was to avoid the impression that the government had been 'arguing for the status quo' and 'opposing the legitimate nationalist feelings' especially when it had been decided to weaken the case for those Congressmen who talked about a fight to the finish. It was difficult, Benn thought, to prepare a document at the London end to this effect and it was believed that, both at Simla and at provincial headquarters, an effective exercise could be undertaken more conveniently. The 'Indian concoction' could then be exhibited pretty freely in England and the authorities would feel satisfied to have something to say of a positive kind over and above having always to explain that patience was necessary and that things were not as bad as they seemed.[75]

Thus it was believed that propaganda should be flexible enough to assume various forms and should avoid a direct confrontation with the nationalist forces. For example, anything connected with the RTC could be presented as proof that the government was getting on with constitutional reforms. In some provinces, such as the United Provinces, Bombay and Punjab, Benn thought that a good deal could be done in the way of educating the people, particularly in the rural areas with regard to the facts of the agrarian situation and the problems of revenue collection. Some of the methods suggested were the use of the wireless, travelling trucks with silent films using daylight projectors with expounders explaining the contents of the films in local dialects, propaganda in the Indian language press including the hostile ones, speeches of public officials and possibly, explanatory leaflets.[76] An elaborate and complete machinery for propaganda organized centrally and provincially during the preceding years existed and, if necessary, it could be put in motion at short notice. Recommending the whole project and advancing other possibilities and improvisations, Benn held firmly that the key to the whole was the nature and type of propaganda thus advocated.[77] The object, he added, was to persuade and conciliate. If the wrong material was used or a wrong message was indicated, the effort could release results worse than useless.[78] Administrators should be cautious and judicious, but they must not betray indecision and weakness. It was necessary, the home government felt, to transmit to London all published materials and various suggestions for use in England, both inside and outside Parliament.[79]

Willingdon adopted the suggestions. But he was convinced that it was no longer possible to confine official propaganda strictly within the ambit of persuasion and conciliation.[80] The impact of the Congress and Gandhi, he thought, was almost ubiquitous in India. Even a discourse on persuasion would have been incompatible with the proposed policy of Willingdon. 'I cannot quite see at present how Government', he wrote, 'can carry on an active political propaganda in an effort presumably to counteract the Congress influence.'[81] It seemed to Willingdon that there was only one thing that was open then in that direction and he had already examined the theme with Sapru and many others to promote an organized political opposition against the Congress. It was for them, Willingdon stressed, 'when they come back to start a regular organization on a political basis and promote a new party, which will be politically antagonistic to the extreme Congress people'.[82] This party would then start their propaganda system and these politicians would have to be prepared individually to go all over the country and state their case.[83] At that phase of the struggle, Willingdon conceded, the whole thing had been left to the Congress which, over time, acquired an upper hand in Indian politics. They got a perfectly free field without any opposition but for the fact that the government issued periodically somewhat innocuous statements in the press.[84] India office was not entirely satisfied with Willingdon's response. It held that the government case would have to be stated firmly otherwise it would go by default.[85] Besides, it was futile to expect that Sapru would have the conviction or even ability to organize a vigorous campaign against the Congress extremists.[86]

Samuel Hoare, Benn's successor, was keen at the beginning of his tenure at the India office to retain his reputation for moderation. He was aware that probably the temper of the India office was *en rapport* with the Willingdon administration. He sympathized with the harassed and sun-burnt administrators in

India and developed during the RTC, a distinct dislike for what appeared to him a strange political and legal rigmarole couched in dated liberal sentiments and articulated in incomprehensible spiritual verbiage, by a trained Indian barrister, dressed as a naked fakir and wandering all over as the true representative of India with a diverse and variegated demographic map, with conflicting interests and ideas.[87] Emphasizing the position of Benn, his successor saw no reason to softpedal the importance of propaganda in India and Britain. He added to Benn's list the importance of cinema and wireless. Recommending the scheme for a propaganda tour of India through the medium of a talkie-cinema van, he emphasized that the scheme might seem rather nebulous but there was something in the idea and that it would be worth pursuing, especially as he learnt from the fortnightly report from Bengal that there was a government cinema party operating in that province which had met with considerable success in the Dacca district.[88] The experiment, Hoare advised, might profitably be repeated elsewhere and the cinema equipment in the possession of the railway board and the education, agriculture and cooperative departments could be utilized for the purpose and the advantages of successful propaganda in the villages by this method would undoubtedly be great.[89] Broadcasting, he thought, could be turned into an effective means of transmitting 'reliable information' to counter Congress propaganda. He learnt that there was some possibility of the stations at Calcutta and Bombay continuing to operate. He hoped that once broadcasting could be put securely on its feet, it would have a great future in India and when it made sufficient progress and prepared to penetrate into rural areas, it would prove an invaluable medium of propaganda.[90]

Willingdon had, however, other ideas. There was no special place for persuasion, conciliation and sedate propaganda in his 'forward' policy of imperial domination.[91] He made it unambiguous that it was extraordinarily difficult to organize anything resembling a well-ordered and officially sponsored system of propaganda. Anything official had become suspect following Gandhi's arrest and inauguration of the regime of ordinances.[92] On the contrary, he thought, it would be advisable to promote and assist 'all our friends who are constitutionally-minded, the Hindus, the Muslims, the landholders, Europeans, the untouchables and big businessmen, who support us.' They should be goaded to do their own propaganda and start political organizations in every presidency in order to be ready for the general election when the reforms came in.[93]

Hoare had been urging them very strongly whenever he met them to get on to this matter in great earnestness, for, he said, 'I think it is absolutely essential if they are not going to be swamped by the Congress altogether.' He felt that it was always difficult for an imperial government 'to start a political propaganda', and 'if only I could instil courage into some of our leaders and make them get up on public platforms and state our case, then I think we should be able to say that real propaganda had begun'.[94] Willingdon confided to Hoare 'that decimation of the Congress Party' as an effective political organization was his agenda in India, that he had consulted and talked to both Edwin Charles Benthall and Edward Villiers about that plan of action, that they had been moving in the matter, that there were many others who had been persuaded and encouraged to adopt the new official target and that the idea had been going round.[95] Of course, a certain amount of propaganda was being conducted but its importance was marginalized in comparison to the undertaking of starting a new party throughout the country with a credible constitutional programme, 'knocking at the bottom of Congress popularity'.[96] This was a sensational project that Willingdon seemed to be pressing for as hard as he could in sheer indifference to its inherent impracticability.

In April 1932 Hoare forwarded to the Government of India, for its sympathetic consideration, a communication from the director of Visatone Sound System certain well-formulated views on the method of propaganda through films in India.[97] The basic objective of the suggestion was to raise the moral and ethical standards of the Indian people and show them British sympathy.[98] The Indian government declined the offer for financial considerations. In any case, the subject of pro-government propaganda was being seriously considered. It was also universally held that the whole structure of propaganda should be strictly under European supervision and government control.[99] Propaganda work should be thoroughly loyal and trustworthy and should not become the means of seditious propaganda.[100] It was also held that the necessity of spreading correct information in the Indian villages had been proved by the events of recent years and more specifically, by the success of civil disobedience.[101] What was required was an accurate daily bulletin and a moderate expression of opinion on current events in a form suitable for rural comprehension. The Indian Village Welfare Association was formed with Lady Irwin as president and Francis Younghusband as chairman. The association warmly recommended the formation of a system of rural wireless broadcasting in Indian languages which would achieve these objects. To the questions raised in Parliament, Government made it clear that the Indian government had not been entirely idle during the period of truce although the Congress had been openly applying itself to the preparation of a possible renewal of the civil disobedience campaign.[102] It was also indicated that the India office was particularly interested in recruiting retired officials who were intimately acquainted with the minds of the Sikhs and Muslims in Punjab, orthodox Hindus, etc. and some who had special experience in dealing with communist tactics and propaganda.[103]

The tenor of the official propaganda was firm. Its main

object was to disseminate the idea that the repressive actions under the ordinance did not connote any policy of reaction. On the contrary, it was necessary to opt for a strong arm policy in order to clear the field for greater activity in the pursuit of constitutional reform. It was asserted that there was a serious misgiving in the minds of many observers concerning the applicability of democratic principles in India. No solution other than the one suggested by the white paper was feasible in the Indian context. It was argued that even in Europe the institution of democracy had not been found suitable and these institutions could not be suitably planted in the soil and surroundings of India. It was believed that democracy was not understood in India. The hierarchical caste system and the Hindu-Muslim antagonism were the serious impediments for the establishment of democratic spirit. True, it was not desirable to go back. But one could only move forward along an arduous path with circumspection. 'Let us not imagine', it was upheld with firm resolution, 'that we are even yet within easy distance of our destination, and above all let us not encourage the Indians themselves to entertain such an idea'.[104]

The India Office had been more or less convinced that the report of the India League's delegation would find little enthusiasm in London. The strategy of the India Office had been to help fashion an atmosphere of indifference around the activities of the team. H. MacGregor, information officer, India Office, was amused by the unusual concern of a nervy secretary of state about the possible impact of the report of the delegation on sensitive public opinion in Britain. Designating Hoare as the 'big-spectacled pundit, somewhat detached from the world', MacGregor regaled himself by his own ability to swing the trend of public opinion with comfortable ease. He gibed that Hoare seemed to be getting excited over the 'mysterious thing called public opinion for which he has a personal contempt but which professionally gives him jimjams'.[105] MacGregor had been commanding the apparatus of information and propaganda of the India office and over the years had mastered the methods of being heard and listened to. He was happy to vaunt that his department would be able to demolish the attempts of the India League to organize an effective publicity campaign for the delegation.[106] He was convinced that, in all probability, the delegation would give very little trouble in Britain. He found not a single person with marked ability in the League's delegation with the exception of the 'fair Ellen' (Ellen Wilkinson) and perhaps, the 'crafty' Madrasee, who, in any case, had been 'sidelined in the trip'.[107]

MacGregor noted with relish that Wilkinson was then out of a parliamentary job and, having to earn a living, she had been pushing hard with journalism.[108] A free trip to India, he thought, was probably a God-sent opportunity to her. MacGregor found in Wilkinson a fairly reasonable person who could be persuaded to see the brighter side of life without much predicament.[109] He was toying with ideas of 'getting her along to the India Office'. She was, however, reported to be 'intensely political' and a committed 'socialist crusader'.[110] MacGregor was unsure of his project. He was in search of one who could be persuaded 'to bell the cat'.[111] Meanwhile, recommending an article on the activities of the delegation in India in the *Statesman,* he complimented the author for creating a sensation. It appeared to him that Ellians, special correspondent of the *Statesman,* was one who 'could match Winston Churchill as a diehard' and could, if necessary, 'cheerfully put all people of the India League persuasion in *jug,* and so would I - if we could'.[112]

In a trenchant reply to Hoare, who in Parliament accused the India League's delegation of deliberate distortion of the Indian situation and of being biased in favour of Congress propaganda, Wilkinson argued in her article in *The Star* that it was impossible to treat the ostrich-complex that infested the official mind.[113] She was surprised that Government of India had made serious efforts to build 'cardboard villages' in order to create an impression for the delegates during their visit to India and the whole construction toppled down with a touch of reality.[114] Referring to their visit to the NWFP, Wilkinson recounted the special endeavours that were made to make their stay comfortable by arranging a sightseeing tour to the Khyber and some other places away from the experience of the conditions of life of the ordinary people of that province, which was the purpose of the study of the delegation.[115] The party slipped out at dawn one day, right into the interior of the country to the town of Mardan. Recapturing the incident of police outrage, Wilkinson felt sorry that Hoare should not think it necessary to question the authenticity of his own statement.[116] If any charge of staging a fake demonstration was to be made, she wrote, the responsibility of the Mardan incident should be placed squarely on the government. Hoare had also blamed the delegation for having met only the home member at Delhi.[117] Wilkinson stressed that apart from the Big Ones in Delhi, they met and talked to various British officials in every out-of-the-way place they went to. But the 'contrast between the talks on my hosts' verandahs and the informal discussions over the English teacups filled me with despair'.[118] The gulf between India and Britain had widened over the years. The British officials in India might know all about crops, irrigation, land revenue, castes and tribes. But they did not know and had reasons not to learn what the Indians, just beyond their immediate official circles, had been thinking and brooding about.[119] Wilkinson did not think it was necessary to scan the opinion of the civil servants that all those non-cooperating Indians were just an ungrateful lot.[120] What mattered, she thought, was that thousands of them were then in gaol and official contempt would not settle the Indian problem. Hoare might have felt delighted to scoff at the delegates and their report. But this typical imperial attitude had by then percolated down to the district level of English settlements and permeated the sentiments and vocabulary of all official clubs in India. The entire enlightened world, Wilkinson affirmed, had been watching and wondering about the remarkable selective amnesia of British statesmanship in India.[121]

In early 1933, the India Office prepared a note regarding the League's delegation for the guidance of the secretary of state.[122] The opinion they formed, the note claimed, was indicated by Monica Whately in her article in the *New Clarion* of 14 January 1933 and Ellen Wilkinson in *Daily Herald* of 3 January 1933 entitled, "India in Crisis".[123] It was maintained in the note that despite the firm advice of Lothian to the contrary, the delegation allowed itself to be largely guided by their Congress sympathies.[124] They did not avoid official contacts and, in fact, had interviews with the viceroy, the home member as well as with a large number of district officers. The general impression, however, was that they were reluctant to believe information given to them by officials while they were not in the least diffident in absorbing astonishing statements made to them by others. Government had in its possession confirmed evidence, the note said, about the various demonstrations arranged by the Congress for the benefit of the delegation. It was also added that the delegates, on their return, did not show any enthusiasm to meet the secretary of state. On the other hand, they began writing articles for the press and holding meetings all over. It was only towards the end of the year 1932 that Wilkinson thought it appropriate to ask for an interview.[125] But in view of the trying disposition of the delegates, the secretary did not think it judicious to entertain the request for an appointment. The India Office was clear that the delegation had aroused no particular interest in Britain.[126]

Towards the middle of December 1932, for example, a meeting organized at Manchester was attended by no more than 50 people.[127] The authorities, therefore, thought that it was prudent not to stir up controversy or through the maze of public discussions, bring the delegation and its findings from obscurity and neglect into the limelight of time and interest. This state of inconclusive darkness would have been nearly complete but for 'the unnecessary questions' in Parliament sponsored by the India League and 'its naive parliamentary secretariat'.[128] A memorandum, as a result, was prepared by the India Office with the assistance of the reports and notes from India and it was circulated as 'reserve ammunition' to be used only if occasion arose, but till the end of 1932 such an occasion had not presented itself.[129]

The India office found the reports from the Government of India quite informative but also somewhat depressing. They showed, terribly clearly, the frame of mind in which the delegation was likely to come home. It was apparent that they would probably bring an almost 'endless supply of incidents 'as propaganda'.[130] It was also obvious that it was out of the question to expect the Government of India to supply in advance answers to any large proportion of the allegations likely to be made, especially in view of their vagueness. As evidence,the India Office brought out the report on the delegation's visit to Bihar and Orissa. In that report, it was noted with concern that there were only two allegations of Whately with which the Bihar and Orissa police superintendent was able to deal. But in neither case, were the answers given very effective, 'nor indeed could they be in his circumstances'.[131] It seemed, therefore, that in the event of a number of the parliamentary questions being based on the delegation's experiences, it would be necessary to make individual enquiries from the Government of India.[132] It was maintained that though an offer to enquire was a very good answer to parliamentary question from the bureaucratic point of view and might help shelve the question, it was rather ineffective politically. Therefore, while the Government of India had been asked to provide any material they could to rebut possible allegations, it seemed that it would be desirable to tackle the whole matter in a more general kind of way. Since it was unlikely that individual allegations could always or often be met with flat and effective replies, the chief desideratum should be 'to discredit the members of the delegation and their claims of reliability.'[133] The officials were convinced that the whole exercise would be very difficult. It might be hard to persuade the average member of the reading public, that the minister or official in London was a better judge of local incidents or conditions than persons who had visited the place and examined the situation closely. If it was suggested that official sources of information were extremely reliable, it could be retorted that the official's will to believe another official was just as strong or even stronger than a Labour politician's will to believe an anti-government agitator. Moreover, it might be held that both Wilkinson and Whately had no axe to grind and no particular reason for lying about what they had seen, or accepting lies and distortions from others, while on the other hand the official's sense of loyalty could compel him to trust the words of his fellow officials who might have every reason for distorting facts if only to cover a gross irregularity.[134]

That particular process of reasoning,the India office felt, might not sound correct,but surely it must be followed by the ordinary newspaper reader who had 'no preconceptions.' It might, therefore, do little good, if not some harm, to indulge merely in public attacks upon the bona fides and veracity of the delegation. The India office was somewhat perplexed and baffled and it offered two tentative, preliminary suggestions to stimulate further discussion on the subject and, if possible, find a subtle and effective line of approach.[135]

The first line of approach was that the secretary of state might make a point of seeing the members of the delegation in their return and receiving them with sympathy: regret might then be expressed that they did not see more of officials and less of agitators. But since it was no use crying over spilt milk, the members of the delegation might be requested to say, very frankly, what their impressions had been and if they had any complaint or suggestion and to embody them in a written document and convey them personally to the secretary of state. This document could then be sent to the Government of India for observations and it would thus be possible, in reply to any question or allegation based on the delegation's experience, to give the fairly effective reply that all of them were already under close examination. If this line of approach needed supplementing, it would then be possible with some effect to belabour the delegation in a speech.[136]

It seemed to MacGregor, in particular, a rather tepid stand in view of the irresponsible irregularity indulged in by the delegation during their investigation in India and their open and declared hostility towards the administration and the officials. MacGregor took the position that if they were received at the India Office at all, they should be told exactly what was thought of their activities in India.[137] In particular, Whately and Matters ought to be brought to book for their mischievous indiscretions. It was believed that it might not be impossible for *The Times* and perhaps one or two of the 'even more liberal-minded papers' to arrange to receive messages commenting on the visit and impressing the fact that, most unfortunately, the sources of information tapped by the delegation were very untrustworthy.[138] The manner in which evidence was fabricated by the Congress could be shown up with good material in the D.I.B. reports, the failure of the delegation to talk to officials without suspicion of everything they said and their readiness to swallow anything poured into them by 'agitators' would be stressed. Finally, their complete lack of any previous acquaintance with the people of India, with Indian conditions, Indian sentiments, habits, etc. could be suggested to be an inadequate foundation, when combined with a hurried and 'conducted' tour for assessing the true state of affairs and suggesting what steps should be taken to remedy the situation.

Such comment would,no doubt,be greatly strengthened if at the same time it could be stated that, worthless as the allegations were, they had been receiving every possible attention in case they might contain some grains of truth.[139]

Monica Whately's "What we saw in India" published in *The New Clarion* of 14 January 1933 was basically a reply to the criticisms of Hoare and certain sections of the press that the League's reports were biased because the delegates were shown round the country by the Congress and not by government officials. Her principal accusation was that Government of India had decided on a certain course of action which amounted to martial law — arrest without warrant, detention without trial, beating by the police without adequate orders and complete muzzling of the press.[140] As against the viceroy's assertion that the people were 100 per cent happier than they had been 18 months ago, Whately counterquestioned: How could people be happy when they lived in constant fear of arrest? In every family, she claimed, there was a relative or a close friend in gaol. Beating of men and women, boys and girls for picketing shops or taking out processions, the disquieting rumours of prison conditions and nature of punishments, the stagnation of trade, the denial of free speech and the elaborate system of espionage were, in Whately's view, the salient features of the Ordinance rule.[141] Police chased the delegation in an attempt to prevent them to see or hear any other side. They arrested the guides of the delegation and, at places, turned back crowds of people on their way to meet the delegation.[142] Members of the delegation were aware, at an early stage in their investigation, that elaborate precautions had been taken to prevent their witnessing the usual treatment meted out to the pickets or processionists.[143] Whately argued that Hoare must be aware that the government was determined that eye-witness accounts of the manifestation of this policy should not reach the British public. Given an account of the prison conditions in India in general and the treatment given to the political prisoners, Whately claimed that more than official figure of 20,000 political prisoners had been kept in confinement, in spite of the fact that orders had been given to beat rather than to arrest.[144]

Whately's presentation made an impact and the India office was bombarded by a series of agitated reactions from men of eminence. D. Jeffery Williams from St. John's Wood, London, wrote that the account of Whately, who was unknown to him, imbubed him with deep shame not unmixed with horror.[145] 'Is it possible', he asked, 'that those things are possible in India, and done in our name?' He was already worried about appalling poverty in India, rooted in the extreme problem of ignorance and was embarrassed to learn that as trustee in India, the British government had failed so far to tackle the problems.[146] 'The Indians', he argued, could not possibly do worse if they governed themselves, it now seems to me.' He felt ashamed in thinking over what Whately had described.[147]

Graham Pole, whose credentials were beyond reproach, was equally distressed. He was not acquainted with Whately and had not met other members of the delegation since their return from India. His contact with the India League had, over the years become very thin and tenuous. But the things that Whately described in her piece under the headings,barbarism and torture, seemed to Pole to be too revolting to be credible. 'If there is any vestige of truth in such allegations,' Pole wrote, 'I should think it is worthwhile to have a special investigation ordered by the Government of India. If they are untrue, surely the New Clarion could be brought to book'.[148] The initial response of the India Office was evasive. Pole was told categorically that the paragraph he referred to in Whately's article was 'obviously based on an uncritical acceptance of the tales of prisoners' or their friends whose sole object was propaganda.[149] For instance, 'standing handcuffs' was a punishment reserved for repeated and wilful refusal to comply with rules and was regulated in the most careful and detailed manner to avoid anything in the nature of 'torture', such as been decribed in Whately's article.[150] The description, given by the author, was imaginative. Pole was also informed that no good purpose would be served by taking action against the *New Clarion.* Its circulation was small and anything in the nature of public controversy would merely advertise it and stimulate its circulation.[151] It was, however, a serious matter and could not be just glossed over. It led to an earnest official consultation.

The India Office note paper which was approved by the secretary of state on 3 February 1933 clearly stated that there are no reasons to suppose that such facts as were stated by Whately in the paragraph in question were not substantially correct.[152] The political prisoners were unlikely to be given a daily change of clothes or mosquito nets or particularly toothsome food. There were certainly 'forced to associate with criminals' and were locked up at night even if the weather was hot and humid.[153] 'If we are not prepared to say', the official position was candid, 'that Indian prisoners are not comfortable and are not meant to be, then we are bound to be more or less evasive.'[154] Thus Peel, M. Seton and Croft put their heads together and penned a draft that was approved by Hoare.[155] It was at once evasive and assertive, self-righteous and stubborn.

In response to Pole's persistent inquiries, the India Office wrote that it would, of course, be easy to send Whately's article to India for investigation. But after further consultation, Hoare could not honestly see that it would be worthwhile. His experience had been that vague and general allegations were not substantiated in any important particular in such an investigation.[156] This was not to imply, Hoare added, that all allegations were false, but he felt that he was justified in adopting the policy, to which the government endeavoured to adhere, 'of ignoring the general and investigating the particular.'[157] That the government was quite prepared to face the public, in any case, where specific ill-treatment appeared to have taken place was shown for instance by the trial of jail officials at Nasik. But apart from these considerations, he emphasized that the members of the India League delegation were supposed to be writing a report of their investigation which 'presumably will contain chapters and verses in regard to any allegation'.[158] This was likely to furnish suitable material for investigation. In any case, he urged that 'I do not honestly feel we are being really ostrich-like if we ignored loosely-written press articles'.[159]

The India League had by then become, in official perception, a definitely subversive organization requiring very close scrutiny and observation. When in August 1933 it was reported that Leonard Matters, who toured India in the company of Menon and Wilkinson, had been appointed in succession to Frederck Grubb as the London correspondent of the *Hindu* of Madras, Scotland Yard had reasons to feel concerned. It was viewed with apprehensions that Matters had been asked to canvass articles from well-known members of the Labour Party in the country expressing their opinion on the Indian situation. It was feared that Matters' appointment would add substantial influence to the India League, as the *Hindu* had a wide circulation and it would give publicity to the organization as Matters was expected to communicate through his column the proceedings of all its meetings. The officials took note of the displeasure of Atma Santdas Kamlani at Matters' appointment which would be prejudicial to the interests of the rival body, the Friends of India, appreciated in the official circles for its commitment to gradual evolution of home rule within the empire.[160]

By February 1933, it appeared to the India Office that the delegation was a spent force and if there should be any revival of public interest in its work, the officials felt that they had enough ammunition, which could be useful and sufficient.[161] Even in India, it was assumed by the government that propaganda on the subject had died down and nothing might be done to stimulate it.[162] I.M. Stephens had his misgivings, but maintained officially that it was gratifying to note that the activities of the returned members of the delegation continued to be ignored by the press in England, thanks to the efforts of the India Office, which kept the editors in strict discipline.[163] Should it seem necessary to make use of the material to counteract misrepresentation in India, the home department in India would feel free to draw on them.[164] The campaign had done considerable damage to the eminence of the *Raj.* Officials in India, therefore, were vexed for being persuaded by the India Office to keep quiet, especially when they had up their sleeves very effective answers to all the allegations.[165]

The exhaustive report of the delegates in the *Hindustan Times*[166] had not, as of then, been republished in any journal in England, but MacGregor was convinced that it might soon be reproduced in the League's bulletin or 'some other negligible rag of the same kind'.[167] It appeared that even the League was viewed by the India office as an effete organization. A letter was drafted incorporating the basic points of the memorandum of the home department and was sent to the secretary, Newspaper Society.[168] The letter was written in a way as to give the impression of a casual private note from MacGregor to the secretary carefully including a detailed account of the interview the delegates had with the viceroy.[169] The India League, however, continued to hold meetings, duly ignored by the press, and also published a few bulletins giving detailed impressions of the members of the delegation.[170]

In February 1933, MacGregor was obliged to write to H.B. Holmes, secretary, European Association, that with regard to the campaign initiated by the returned members of the India League's delegation from open platforms, it was difficult to see how much could be done to prevent the distribution of the bulletins in the country.[171] In India, the authorities had shown considerable alacrity. Among the recent arrests had been that of Bisheswar Prasad Sinha, a barrister, who had compiled some of the bulletins of the India League on ordinance rule.[172] As reported by the European Association, the League appeared to be in very low ebb.[173] Its offices had not been visited for many days. Unopened letters had accumulated on tables and no one appeared to be there to deal with them. It was expected with a sense of jubilation that 'perhaps they are bust — Let us hope so.'[174] In all probability, lack of funds had forced the League to cease publishing the *India Review*, in place of which bulletins were circulated periodically. But owing to the shortage of funds and the fact that the bulletins were for the most part distributed to the already converted, it was unlikely to prove effective propaganda stuff.[175] The secretary, Newspaper Society, was confidentially advised to ensure that nothing about the delegation's visit to India and their campaign in Britain 'should be particularized too much' in the British newspapers. He was told that the authorities in India had been keeping a close watch to prevent the 'dissemination abroad of lies of this kind and are on the whole successful'.[176] It was added forcefully that it was the moral obligation of the English newspapers to help normalize the disturbed political process in India with an element of self-imposed discretion. 'In this country,' MacGregor, having failed to attract Wilkinson to the India office, wrote, 'it is impossible to stop the mouths of Wilkinson and Co.,'[177] but the redeeming features were that the India League was, by then, financially bankrupt and that it had been preaching over the last few months to the already converted souls with no fresh intake of *advoc-tus di-bolicus* in their ranks.[178]

The situation, as viewed from London, however, did not correspond squarely with the perception of the Government of India. The India Office recognized this divergence of perspectives.[179] It thought it desirable to impress upon the Government of India that the calculations of the India office should not be the conditions determining the initiatives of the

Government in India dealing with local exigencies under specific political and social conventions. MacGregor admitted that a good deal of time and labour had been spent in India in preparing the documents and one would do well to consider that all that labour and effort had not been wasted.[180] On the contrary, officers in India and London deserved to be congratulated for averting an awkward situation that could have been sparked off by an odd turn of events. MacGregor was candid when he claimed that he never expected that the delegation had the capacity for igniting an ugly situation in Britain. He felt that it was ridiculous to think that such a green deputation, composed of some unworthy and unstable elements, under such undesirable auspices as the India League, could ever create a stir in England. 'The English press', MacGregor vouched with a touch of self-righteous pride, 'had not fully lost its perspective and patriotism and the English public has not lost its sanity.'[181]

The Government of India, while conceding the points raised by the India Office, was in no way satisfied by the way the whole scheme of publicity was being given a significant, subtle dimension. To the Indian administration, effective propaganda should have been both flamboyant and extrovert. The officials in India were somewhat out of touch with the parliamentary situation at home to anticipate precisely what line of action members of the delegation would adopt.[182] They were convinced that the India office would be able to take certain definite steps on the basis of the voluminous material supplied by the home department in India.[183] Stephens, Williamson and Hallett were disposed to feel that the India Office was in a better position than the Government of India to prepare the required publicity material for English consumption. They were better equipped to gauge than officials in India the precise political reactions at home which might be expected from 'comments about the delegation's activities, either by themselves or their opponents'.[184]

Stephens, in particular, was not at ease with the decision of the India Office not to take note of the noise made by the returned delegates.[185] But what was most disturbing for him was the disposition of the home department in India, Stephens grumbled, and its 'unwillingness to yield to my clamour for some counter-propaganda at this end irrespective of what you might be doing at yours'.[186] It was a pity, he thought, to let Congress 'get away with it', especially to the degree they did in India and 'to keep so much powerful ammunition as we possessed lying idle'.[187] Unfortunately, to him had fallen the task of plodding through the 'rigmaroles of nonsense about the delegation's activities dished up by the nationalist press'.[188] It was, however, gratifying to him to know that so little importance had been attached to what 'the Labour trio' had said. But he found himself distinctly a 'pelican in the wilderness of this subject'.[189] Strictly from his point of view, it was tiresome to watch helplessly that so little had been done in the way of a counterblast to the delegation's allegations in England. The nationalist press, Stephens wrote in disgust, was 'pretty full of unpleasant articles' while it was increasingly 'difficult for him to counter them' on the basis of notes sent to the India office since he could not tell why actions in London had been apparently so circumscribed or 'what the effect of action on my part would be at your end'.[190] It was intriguing as the second instalment of the notes had not been sent over to the *Times* as suggested earlier and Stephens felt a strange sensation as he had no option but to observe quietly the other side getting away with it so effectively at the India end.[191]

In view of the determined hostility of India office towards the League and its delegation, it was evident that they would do their utmost to prevent the publication of the report and if that was not feasible, to ensure that it received little attention in the press. It was reported that a book prepared by Wilkinson and her delegation on the visit of the India League deputation was being published in London and would be released towards the end of March 1933. It was decided that Home Office should 'secure for the book the kind of review' it deserved.[192] It was decided by MacGregor to take suitable assurances privately from the major newspapers.[193] The India Office was active and it was able to persuade quite a number of printers and publishers to drop the idea of publishing the report.[194] At one stage, Jonathan Cape, publishers, discovered that their printers therw back the manuscript following an informal warning from the India Office against a 'probable libel action'.[195] In fact, E.W. Davies, secretary, Newspaper Society, was able to procure from S. J. King and Hutchins, printers, an unabridged proof copy of the projected volume.[196] It was known that the volume was in the last stage of publication. It was, therefore, urgent that within the next few days, King should come to a final decision whether to proceed or refuse.[197]

Before long, Davies was to receive a letter from MacGregor meant for the members of his association including King.[198] MacGregor maintained in that personal letter that even by a cursory first reading, one could coveniently advise without hesitation that 'this is a publication with which no responsible Englishman should be associated'.[199] MacGregor was harsh and categorical against the publication of the delegation's report: 'Were I your member I should anticipate that at home, the Government would deplore the publication of such a book at any time and especially at a time when conditions in India have greatly improved, and English statesmen are employed in the task of securing the constitutional advance of India on the most reasonable lines.'[200] MacGregor made it pellucid that the Government of India would 'in all probability proscribe the book under the Sea Customs Act'.[201] It was also added that the book would do incalculable harm by suggesting an 'absolutely false picture of British rule'.[202] MacGregor maintained that the object of the book was 'glorification of the Indian National

Congress Party'[203] whose civil disobedience movement was essentially subversive and 'a denunciation of the ordinances or special laws which the Government of India was compelled to enact to cope with that subversive movement'.[204]

The method of the India League, it was maintained, was the translation to England of the Congress use of exaggeration, misrepresentation and suggestion of the exceptional as representing the general.[205] The views, expressed by MacGregor, had an element of urgency and the secretary, Newspaper Society, was prompted to take immediate steps to pursue the matter. MacGregor also added that the book was 'an ignoble production not likely to do us much harm at home' where people could 'value the writers' but it was likely 'to do incalculable harm abroad where absolute and comparative ignorance prevails'.[206] In particular, it was stressed that there was an interview with the viceroy where the secretary of state was virtually called a liar.[207]

The strategy was very subtle. It was argued that MacGregor's letter, communicated to King through Davies, would prompt him not to print off the volume. When the printer declined, Jonathan Cape would also decline or, at least, send the book for examination to an expert who, in their case, would be J. Coatman and he might be restrained from giving a favourable report.[208] If Jonathan Cape then refused, MacGregor believed no reputable publisher would touch the manuscript. Thus, although his letter would by no means prevent publication, it was tolerably certain 'to cause further delay which is all to the good'.[209] There was no better way to frustrate the India League delegation. It was felt unwise for the India office to attempt, by any direct persuasion of printers or publishers, to stop publication.[210] Hurriedly browsing through the volume, R.T. Peel, Secretary, P&J Department, India Office, felt that the book was vicious and the writers had omitted little unfavourable to the government that they had managed to collect. Where the case of the government was mentioned, it was immediately declared to be unacceptable.[211]

In an official circular, it was held by the Government of India that it would certainly provide a dangerous textbook for the circulation of charges against government and the police. It was believed that by then few would consider the reproduction of these charges to their advantage. But it could hardly be expected that anti-government agitation would not be revived by such a publication. On such a revival, the ammunition in the volume would be very valuable especially those many passages in which it was suggested that the government acted illegally, or denied or deprived the people of legal safeguards that were to be found in any civilized country and particularly in Britain. This collection of all the allegations that were made in the course of the civil disobedience movement would certainly form a 'dangerous textbook' capable of doing much mischief in the country.[212]

And yet the book was finally published. By then the India office felt, that much of it was out of date and yet it was likely to be 'a source of trouble to us'.[213] The report was given a push by the *Daily Herald*[214] but the *Times Review* deprecated the document and 'showed up the document in its proper light'.[215] The India office would have felt better if the *Times* had left the document entirely alone. But it appears that the editor did not wish the opportunity of criticising the tactics of the delegation to slip by.[216] Once the volume was proscribed in India, MacGregor made the point clear to Douglas Crawford, editor, *Daily Mail*: 'You are a big innocent! See today's *Daily Mail* reference to the proscription of the book 'Condition of India', i.e., the report of this precious so-called India League delegation, and then look up the '*New Statesman*'. You will then appreciate that you have done what these sentimentalists of the India League want and what they complain they have not received from the British press-given them publicity.'[217] MacGregor emphasized:

'By all means have a go at the politicians over the Indian politics but uphold the administration for all you are worth and in this instance, you should recognize that the India League is a tool used by the Gandhi crowd.'[218] The editor of the *Daily Mail* agreed with the criticism. 'As Marlowe used to say you can deal with foolishness, but you cannot deal with stupidity.'[219] When Reuters' message had been brought to his notice about the proscription, he thought that it was the best thing that 'could have happened to that pestiferous crowd'.[220] The instruction was to give a sarcastic note but, unfortunately, the result of editorial intervention made it look almost like an apology for them. The only redeeming feature was that it appeared in one edition only.[221]

MacGregor, however, maintained that the repercussions at home of this egregious publication had so far been few, in that it was not according to the spirit of the times.[222] But the wheel of events, he wrote, might turn to more favourable circumstances and it was from that point of view of the future rather than the existing situation, that he was inclined to regard the publication with some concern.[223] He enclosed a copy of the letter to Stephens, written in the course of 'our endeavours to keep the book out of the hands of reputable publishers'. He was quite firm in his assertion that in that effort, the India office succeeded, but the 'control of publishers other than the reputable is beyond us'.[224]

The *Times* coverage of the volume was obviously an inspired one.[225] It argued that the volume only emphasized some facts although the situation in India prompted diverse views of the problem. There was no doubt in the mind of the editor that a delegation of the India Defence League would have produced a report exactly contrary to this document. In a country with 352,000,000 people it was comparatively easy to secure material that would support a given view but it did not necessarily follow that the view was that of the people as a whole. The report seemed to the *Times* somewhat partial and lacked objectivity. It was favourable to all such impressions which justified the purpose of the delegation. It was somewhat niggardly in considering opinions contrary to their objective. The ordinances were promulgated to deal with an exceptional situation caused by a concerted effort at severe subversion and lawlessness and a wicked political strategy of the nationalists together with the warped psychology of an Oriental people. The *Times* thought that compared to other eastern administrations, the *Raj* was more tolerant and more liberal. The *Times* also maintained that the dual policy of Willingdon did not preclude the policy of conciliation and cooperation. The delegation ignored that conciliation meant acceptance of the realities, and the Congress and Gandhi had always showed indifference towards that particular pre-condition of peace. The *Times* argued that the writers of the report failed to comprehend that nationalism in India was not the monopoly of the Congress party and that the party was not the sole exponent of the aspirations of the Indian people as a whole. In any case, the government did not view the voice of nationalism in India as an evil thing to be put down forcefully. The fact that the leaders of the Congress found themselves in prison was no proof that the government was bent upon coercing nationalism in India.[226]

In April 1934 Desmond Young, editor of the *Pioneer*, Lucknow, sprang a surprise on the Government of India.[227] A letter from Young of 7 April 1934 and a leading article in the paper on 8 April came as a bolt from the blue.[228] The article, in particular, caused scarcely any jubilation in the home department especially at that juncture when the goodwill of the newspaper was of some importance.[229] There was little scope for discussion, Stephens wrote, because of the very definiteness of the view that has been taken by Young in the article. The subject matter was the proscription of the volume of the India League and Young's very strong criticism of the action.[230] Stephens understood that objection had been taken, in a very general way, to the proscription and on grounds of European liberalism. Stephens, however, contended that the objection was more theoretical than practical and not applicable in Indian conditions, especially when the comments even in the Congress papers regarding the proscription 'have been rather perfunctory'.[231]

Stephens held that an arguable case for proscription might be worked up from an analysis of certain points emanating from the volume. There were strong grounds for believing that the expenses of the delegation were paid from Congress funds. It was, therefore, idle to expect that the report would in any case be unfavourable to those who paid for it.[232] A perusal of the document left no doubt that it was remarkably unfair to the government and it was basically an exhaustive compilation of the anti-government case. In its cumulative impact, the report was, therefore, the ablest piece of Congress propaganda. Under the existing law, no Indian would ever be allowed to publish such a report. Besides the controversies dealt with in the report were then out of date and as a general proposition, re-opening of old sores was undesirable. Owing to a very low standard of literacy and education, it was maintained that public opinion was a different matter in India than there in England and, in consequence, the right to freedom of speech and freedom of publication could be far more dangerously abused in India than in England.[233] These general points might be added to the various inaccuracies, misstatements and distortions in the volume, although Stephens stressed that he and the services, in general, were not totally apathetic about the philosophical questions raised by *Pioneer*. But, honestly, Stephens added, 'both your leader and your letter struck me as somewhat *a priori* and up in the air', — and also 'very ill-timed!'[234]

The volume entitled *Condition of India* was published by the *Essential News* of Portland Place, London in 1934, having passed through a chequered career and amidst an atmosphere of official antipathy and intrigue.[235] It was a volume of 534 pages with twenty-five chapters and seven appendices and with a simple cover designed by Eric Gill. As indicated in the foreword, this report of the India League's delegation contained two types of information and analysis.[236] It was both, an account of the experience in and investigation of India as well as an excellent survey of British rule, focussing on its social and economic impact on the subject people. The historical material formed the background of the contemporary situation investigated by the committee. While the sections dealing with the inquiry were prepared by the team on the basis of the copious notes taken by them during the investigation, the historical part of the document was largely the output of the personal research of Menon himself. In a sense, it presented an analytical study of the life and condition of the people of India under the *Raj,* then groaning under the arbitrary and authoritarian regime fashioned by Wedgwood Benn and re-inforced by the combined initiative of Samuel Hoare and Willingdon. The delegation concluded that the regime unleashed a rule of terror which had been resisted by the Indian people all over, including those of rural India with an unparalleled weapon of non-violence under Gandhi's gentle, civilized and firm leadership. The ordinances continued unabated and, despite opposition of a substantial segment of democratic opinion in Britain, there had been no relaxation in the rigour and tempo of the regime during 10 months. The volume affirmed, with the assistance of a wide variety of evidence, that Gandhi and the Congress were still the trusted leaders of the Indian people while the Indian government had been confined in a claustrophobic atmosphere, refusing to recognize the realities of the situation or to seek a peaceful settlement. The report called upon readers in Britain to grasp the essence of British rule in India which 'would become intolerable to themselves if they lived under it'.[237]

The India League assumed that the Indian administration was extremely sensitive to British public opinion as expressed inside and outside parliament and believed that public protest in England might effectively alter the course of events in India. Recommending the report, Bertrand Russell compared the misdeeds of the British in India with Nazi operations in Germany and hoped that the demand for self-determination should no longer be resisted.[238] He condemned the extensive censorship in India, as well as British apathy towards the real conditions of that unhappy land 'where elementary liberties that make life tolerable' had been taken away from the inhabitants, for the crime of desiring self-government. Russell insisted that widespread oppression, despite its ephemeral success was impolitic and immoral. British attitude towards India was based on force and cruelty against the background of utter ignorance in Britain about India.

Condemning the impact of a euphoric national self-righteousness in Britain, Russell warned that cruelty might provoke counter-atrocities.[239] The situation, as he saw it, would soon become dismal. The sincere idealism of the Congress movement might then be swept aside by young men and women, who had over the years learnt from experience under the British administration that force might possibly be overthrown by superior force. And if the British administration in India was compelled to face the confrontation of an Indian militant agitation, there was every indication that British rule would then be unable to repress that movement and it might in all probability be swept away from the face of the world. Recommending the chapters on prisons and villages, Russell commented that it was unfortunate that the ruling class in British India had lost its former vigour, skill and elan. The impact of the inhuman policy in India would be disastrous. If a new regime was ushered amidst a bloodbath, it might have an adverse impact on the durability and peaceful demeanour of that new administration. He called for serious introspection, reversal of domestic policy and reconciliation with the rising forces of creative nationalism in India. It was imperative to generate feelings of goodwill among the two peoples. It was only on the basis of mutual trust that a sound foundation might be laid for dominion status in India, resting on negotiation and conciliation. Russell was convinced that the continuation of the existing policy would be both immoral and suicidal.[240]

Presenting a brief and succinct account of events and politics leading to the emergence of the ordinance rule, the report of the India League contested the claim of the government that these emergency measures had been necessitated by the threat of passive resistance.[241] It maintained that the so-called dual government of Willingdon was a premeditated policy to destroy the spirit and content of the policy of conciliation initiated by Irwin and to smash the grit and organization of the Congress with a very severe blow. It also contested the claim that the government was fairly successful in its policy and there had been a growing awareness in India as to the righteousness and efficacy of that policy. On the contrary, the Congress had emerged as the basic centre of popular loyalty. Gandhi was revered and followed all over the country as an the embodiment of the invulnerable human spirit.[242] It was true that the Congress might have witnessed periods of introspection, strategic reorientation and even setbacks and in the urban areas the brutality of organized tyranny had succeeded in creating a sort of a peace of the graveyard. But the movement attained new and unprecedented height by moving fast into rural India. The agricultural community had adopted the Congress doctrine with determination and sincerity and hailed the Mahatma as a redeemer.[243] The delegation visited every province of British India, inspected and verified conditions in every important city and town and spent the greater part of their time in rural India. All the four linguistic areas of South India, the North-West Frontier Province, Punjab, Sind, Gujarat, the United Provinces, Bengal, Bihar and Orissa, and Assam and some of the Indian states provided the principal centres of its operation. As directed by the executive committee of the India League, the delegation met every class of social and political opinion and administrators of various ranks and importance.[244] Certainly, it was not a conducted tour and if the Congressmen and other politicals moved forward to assist members of the delegation, the principal obstruction was provided by the officials and their agents. There were many outside the Congress organization who offered their hospitality. Besides, there were innumerable hosts in the villages in their humble environment.[245] Giving the whole account of their finances that made the investigation possible, the delegates made it clear that the fund was raised in Britain and in India and, in no case was the delegation financed by the Congress.[246] The report asserted that the government was in possession of the facts of the situation and the necessary documents to that effect.[247] In fact, the reference to the delegation in the Bombay provincial Congress bulletin to which attention of the delegation was drawn by no less a person than the police commissioner of Bombay, was far from complimentary.[248]

The accusation of the secretary of state in Parliament that all demonstrations were stage-managed by the Congress for the edification of the delegation was also seriously challenged.[249] Processions and picketing were part of the normal activities of the Congress in India and the clashes that were witnessed by the delegation had become the essential features of daily life in India, unleashed by police atrocities on which special chapters were written in the volume.[250] Referring to the allegation made by the secretary of state that the impressions of the delegation had been biased from start to finish was equally unacceptable. The delegation could not have expected an attitude other than one of hostility in view of the nature of obstruction that the administration had put on the way of its commitment. Retributive punishments were given to those who volunteered to disclose the nuances of police *raj* in India.[251] Finally, the delegation made a pertinent point that the secretary of state should not have tried to detract from the importance of their findings by diverting popular attention to some odd and irrelevant issues from the principal problems at stake. 'The facts we have set forth', the report stated firmly, 'in this Report and the analysis we have made of the situation must, in our judgment, be met with more satisfactory answers, than casting doubts on the validity or the *bona fides* of our investigations.'[252] 'Even if we had gone out to India expressly on Congress invitation, and our expenses had been paid by that body', the Report added, 'we do not consider that our enquiry or our conclusions should, for that reason, be invalidated or discounted beforehand.'[253]

The work of the delegation in India had been carried on with as little formality as possible. The members constantly reminded themselves that statistics and memoranda compiled by officials would not give them the picture of the real India that the delegates had been seeking and that an understanding of the feelings and sentiments of the people was of the essence of their work.[254] They, therefore, stayed almost invariably in Indian houses with Indian hosts. The hosts, guides and friends of the delegates were not of one religious or political persuasion. In every province and nearly every district, they took care to see the officials who gave them their points of view.[255]

In towns and cities, however, they came across a variety of diverse opinions. The difference amongst sections appeared largely to centre round the question of the distribution of power among them under *swaraj.* In the desire for self-government and in opposition to repression and the ordinances, there was a remarkable unity. This unanimity had made a deep impression on the members. They also came across a section of Indians who echoed official views and repeated official phrases. Every section, however, had ceased to believe in the credibility and legitimacy of the British and the Indian governments. This absence of confidence in Britain was specially marked in the case of moderate men who had held responsible positions under government. The difference amongst sectional leaders with regard to details did not prevent them from telling the delegation that the Congress was the strongest political party in the country and that, without its cooperation, no constitution could be worked satisfactorily. Even officials shared the view.[256]

In the villages, they saw the India of the masses of her people. The delegation were appalled at the poverty of the Indian villages. The Indian villages were the home of the resilient majority of Indians. It was the same story everywhere of crushing taxation, rack-renting, uneconomic agriculture, indebtedness, illiteracy, and starvation.[257] In some villages they saw a post office and a district board school, which, in normal times, were evidence of the *Raj.* Under the ordinances, police, special and punitive, plain-clothes officers and men became the central features of these villages.[258] They found in the most inaccessible villages armed police, police encampments and altogether excessive display of the coercive power of government.[259]

The Indian villager, in their experience, belied the stories about him that were so common. He was not apathetic nor was he ignorant, though illiterate.[260] He was fully aware of his plight and its economic and political causes. He was no admirer of the British *Raj.* He knew that the fight for *swaraj* had to be carried on till it was won. He looked on the Congressman as his friend. Indeed, in these villages, a Congressman or volunteer was always welcomed. Every house, except that of government loyalists, was open to him and he retained the affection of the people.[261]

The Indian village was a homogeneous unit. It had a voice which covered Hindu and Muslim, farmer and labourer. It was prepared to fight and suffer or make compromise as a whole.[262] The subtle arguments and distinctions which obsessed the town politicians did not agitate the villagers. The womenfolk, old and young, particularly in Hindu areas, were conscious partners in the awakening of the village, and it was this that lent to the resistance put up by the village much of its democratic strength. The village, again, supplied the Congress movement with significant fighting material, and its tenacity of purpose was very great.[263]

It was often stated in England that the masses of the Indian people, who were villagers, were not affected by the ordinances. The experience of the delegates challenged this assertion. Punitive police, for which the villagers had to pay, special police and revenue officers made life in some of these villages unendurable.[264] Property and home were not inviolate. In removing or destroying property the officials transgressed even such laws as obtained under the ordinances. Fines and exactions were a heavy toll on the villagers. Apart from that, the ordinances suppressed even educational and other social service institutions which did not participate in political work.[265] The delegation had come across cases where health resorts and schools run by the Congress had come under the ordinances.[266]

If one was to take the special cases of the no-rent villages in Bengal, Assam, Gujarat and Kanara and other areas, the state of affairs that obtained could hardly be described as consistent with civilized administration. When every allowance had been made for the right of a government to collect its dues or maintain law and order, it would be found that a great deal of what went on would have to be classed as irresponsible policedom. Against that, the villager was becoming increasingly resentful.[267] The district officials were out of touch and out of sympathy with the real village. Some of them pretended that they were appreciated for their disinterested service in the villages and adduced as evidence the collection of people who were present when, on occasion, they had turned up in the village. Others pointed to the figures of land revenue, but the fact that the land revenue was focibly realized, at least in part, was not often stated.[268] In every village in India, Gandhi's name was known and reverenced. In Gujarat, Vallabhbhai Patel and in UP Jawaharlal Nehru were household names. Their imprisonment had only added to the affection in which they were held and increased their prestige.[269]

The die-hards in the House of Commons often agitated for higher pay for the Indian police. They saw in the police the real bulwark of their hold on India and were anxious to ensure the loyalty of the force. The delegation felt that most of the Indians would agree with them in prescribing higher pay and better conditions for the police in its rank and file and would consider it an essential reform.[270] Indeed, it was one of the most disturbing factors of the situation that they were an ill-paid, ill-disciplined and ill-educated body of men holding in their hands very wide powers which placed the liberty, property and self-respect of innocent people at their mercy.[271] In fact, police *raj* became meaningful only when the delegates watched it in operation in India. Petty officials exercised very wide powers which were freely used. The ordinances had destroyed every safeguard against police excesses which obtained all over India and were by no means confined to the ill-paid ranks of the force.[272] It was difficult to assess why force should be used at all in effecting arrest of civil resisters, as it was admitted that they neither resisted nor avoided arrest.[273] The explanation offered to the delegates was that such methods were more effective and cheaper than arrests. The explanation carried with it its condemnation. Another gross abuse that appeared to be widely prevalent was the practice of allowing the police to buy directly or indirectly goods that had been attached or confiscated.[274]

The delegates had great difficulty in obtaining permission to see jails and had to take refusals in several cases. The total number of jails that the delegation saw was eight. They had, however, collected evidence from ex-prisoners in different parts of the country. They had no doubt in their minds that ill-treatment of political prisoners was widely prevalent. Even the jail code was not observed by some officials who imposed several penalties for the same jail offence, though the code allowed only one punishment at a time.[275] The majority of the political prisoners were treated as common criminals and were kept in 'C' class. Their warders were criminals. The quality of food varied from jail to jail. Some of the food they had seen was dirty, deficient and bad.[276]

The officials were willing to listen to the delegation but their attitude was uncritical of excesses.[277] The ordinance mind pervaded the administration. If a bureaucratic form of government was bad, a bureaucracy ruling by ordinances was a serious menace to the most innocent of people. There were district officers who recognized that excesses were going on and some who even regretted them. The delegates felt that the ordinances were responsible for that indifference to wrong-doing which appeared to have affected even the better class of officials.[278]

The delegates placed on record that the officials had everywhere been kind enough to give them interviews and talked to them with comparative informality.[279] They discovered that while a good many of them were well up in figures and statistics, they were entirely out of touch with the sentiments and feelings of the people. They could say without exaggeration that the officials they met, British or Indian, were out of touch and out of sympathy with the masses of the Indian people. Their will was effective not because it echoed the will of the people but on account of the force they were able to command, irrespective of popular feelings.[280]

No statement about India would be complete without a reference to the Hindu-Muslim problem. Briefly, it might be said that the delegates found that in the villages, communal feeling was non-existent. Even in places where one of the communities was in a small minority, it exhibited no fear of the majority. The phrases and fears with which Hindu, Muslim and Sikh leaders made the delegates familiar in the towns, seemed strangely enough unrelated to the life and consciousness of the villages of India. The village, as had been repeated more than once, thought as one and its voice and consciousness covered both the Hindus and the Muslims.[281] In the towns, differences between the two communities were perceptible. At places these differences were acute.[282] It was not, however, true to speak of a homogeneous Hindu opposition to a homogeneous Muslim claim, or *vice versa*, as there were shades of differences in groups in the communities themselves. The younger section of the Muslims were supporters of the Congress and even among the so-called communal section, the feeling of nationalism was very strong, the differences between the Congress and the nationalist Hindus being on points of detail.[283] It is not true that the majority of the Muslims in India were supporters of the British *Raj* or that they were opposed to self-government.[284] During the stay of the delegation they saw the bulk of Hindu and Muslim opinion earnestly endeavouring to come to terms.[285]

Once again in the villages, the delegation saw impressive evidence of the results of Gandhi's stand against untouchability. Gandhi's moral prestige and the democratic awakening that remained unsurpassed even under ordinance rule were breaking down the rigours of caste and custom. The political significance of the Poona agreement was that any settlement of Indian problems that was really worthwhile must be made in India and not at Westminster or Whitehall.[286]

It was admitted even by high officials that repression by itself would not allay discontent. Officialdom claimed that government was making a genuine effort of substantial constitutional advance and dwelt on the immensity of the changes that would take place when power was transferred in the provinces. It was held that when the RTC concluded its work and produced a constitution, there would be peace. The delegates, however, entertained no hope and no illusion in this regard. In the view of the delegation, peace would emerge only when existing policy was abandoned and the Congress and Gandhi were brought into effective cooperation for the purpose of a settlement. All other methods would fail.[287]

The delegation regretted that government persisted in its mistaken view. The way of looking at the nationalist movement as an evil which must be put down was unlikely to win Indian acceptance.[288] It was a tragedy that the Willingdon administration was by its policy blocking every avenue to peace. In the face of such an official perception it was little wonder that no Indian trusted British bona fides or believed in the official declarations of good intentions. The ordinances originally meant for three months, had been in operation for about ten months and they were then being given statutory permanence. No better proof of their failure was required. Ordinances had only produced more nationalists and more discontent.[289]

Examining the situation in 1930-31 and in the period when the truce transformed itself into a period of conflict by the vindictive ingenuity of Willingdon, the report questioned quite effectively, with the assistance of two distinguished Indian members of the legislative assembly, namely, B.L. Mitter and B.R. Puri, the legality of the ordinances.[290] It was held that the ordinances were revolting, sinister, humiliating and liable to dangerous misuse. It was significant that, as Puri put it succinctly, no law 'has been devised nor could it ever be devised, which can force a people to love a government and its agents if they do not choose to do so voluntarily...'.[291] Puri also maintained that a government which 'looks at every combination of men as conspiracy and every patriot as a rebel cannot expect the people to look upon the Government and their agents as people who are here for the benefit of the people'.[292] The report concluded its deliberation on the ordinances by stating that the ordinances endowed the authorities with extraordinary powers of law and order primarily to crush the tenacity of purpose and the force of moral discipline of civil disobedience.

The impact of repression staggered the nationalist force, but it survived, and the spirit of the Congress continued to constitute the strongest moral force of the country.[293] Despite setback it made the desire for freedom and struggle more formidable and it was feared that the current of national resistance might be turned into violent, though not desirable, channels.[294] Examining the strength and organization of the Congress Party, its policies and methods and its constructive programmes and voluntary movements, the delegates, having wide-ranging discussion and in-depth examination of available literature, arrived at certain conclusions as regards its influence and impact in the country. They all agreed that the Congress was the best organized and most powerful movement in the country, that it alone penetrated to the masses whose loyalty it commanded in a large measure, that there were millions of Congressmen at heart who were silent followers of the movement, that if the Congress decided to contest in a general election it would sweep the polls, except perhaps in Punjab and the Tamil part of Madras, and that it was the only nation-wide movement and the only one with a firm base in the countryside.[295] The commitment of the Congress to *purna swaraj*, fundamental rights, democracy, nationalism and equality, self-reliance and *khaddar*, education and national schools, *panchayats*, and rural reconstruction on an egalitarian basis against feudal and caste domination were some of the main parameters of its programme.[296]

The League's delegation asserted quite conspicuously that the civil disobedience movement had animated the younger generation of Congressmen who had been inspired by Jawaharlal Nehru whose commitment to *purna swaraj* was fundamental.[297] *Purna swaraj* in the view of its advocates signified a complete break with the past riddled with a medieval outlook. They wished 'to create a movement which will have a complete new outlook, politically and socially and which would reject the religious and economic ideas which have kept her in national bondage'.[298] Therefore, *purna swaraj*, as distinct from dominion status, the report affirmed, was no longer an idle dream.[299]

Suppression of opposition was thorough. It involved large scale arrest of leaders, excessive physical torture in lock-ups and in various detentions, unabashed use of force on peaceful demonstrators, declaration of a large number of organizations as unlawful, measures to give deterrent punishment and to create an impression on the people of effective power of the state, etc. In fact, the nick name of ordinance rule was police *raj*: police *joolum* was applied without any compunction.[300] It was admitted by officials that the use of force had had a contrary effect. Instead of curbing the movement, it stimulated people's resistance, especially in Bengal, Bihar, Madras, and NWFP. Giving details of the cases in the Bombay presidency, CP, Madras, Bengal and UP of police assaults with *lathis* together with ruthless beating including specific incidents, the report left no doubt as to the authenticity of the cases and of the allegation made by all that the police *raj* was inhuman and diabolical and attempted to 'unman' the whole nation with dehumanized state power.[301] Evidence was given not only by those who suffered but also by those who had respectable positions in the official circles and those who cooperated with the Simon commission and opposed civil disobedience as a matter of principle.[302] Then, there were cases of police firing with the list of dead and wounded victims, evidence of peasants fired upon by the military police, deflated official numbers of victims of police violence, evidence of raids and searches, attacks on women and children, evidence of caning of women, molestation and rape cases, high-handed orders of punishment by magistrates, beating and confinement in lock-ups, cases of prisoners beaten to death, attacks on medical relief, orders to close down hospitals, actions against shopkeepers, gruesome cases of *lathi* charge on girls and children of Chittagong and Sylhet, immolation of a living human being in Madura, cases of inhuman physical torture of young men and well-to-do professionals in Rajshahi jail, police running amok in villages and towns without provocation whatsoever, other cases of a 'lawless law' in operation backed by independent and even by European evidence.[303] Some significant cases against government where despite conviction government thought of turning a deaf ear were the firing at the Hijli detention camp, report of official inquiries into alleged police atrocities at Chittagong, allegations against the jailor of Nasik and the Bezwada memorial against police excesses. In most cases, where complaints were made, government was either silent or their answers were vague, indefinite or flatly denied.[304] In some cases, it was admitted that men on the spot had gone berserk and beyond their instructions and committed errors of judgement. But it was added promptly by officials that in view of the extensive conspiracy of violent lawlessness it was not surprising that a few officers were driven to make some odd mistakes.[305] Even the *Times of India*, an Anglo-Indian newspaper, while exonerating the authorities advised that they should think it prudent to remember that it was essential to keep their activities within the four corners of the measures deemed essential.

Dr Forrester Paton's case created a furore but government of Madras flatly denied the incident.[306] In one of the cases, the *Times of India* felt obliged to write a word of caution: 'Picketing is a public nuisance, but it is not a crime for which offenders should be beaten on sight.'[307] To be pursued by the police was a common sight. The delegates, however, encountered various forms of police action including threats, threatening behaviour, intimidation, surveillance, penalizing those who helped the delegates and sending police agents, as in Agra, Meerut, Lahore, Peshawar and Madras, to represent groups of opinion.[308] The arrest of Jayaprakash Narayan in Madras under a Bombay warrant for having met the team and that of Chaganlal Joshi who was arrested on his way to meet the team at the Ahmedabad railway station were cases in point.[309] During the entire period of their stay in India the delegates were given the impression that they were being followed about. The police also appeared to be on the track of anyone who gave them any assistance. Twice the police was polite enough to suggest gently that the surveillance was for the protection of the honourable delegates.[310]

The extension of the civil disobedience movement in the villages was a new phenomenon in Indian politics and this aspect provoked a powerful and brutal response. In consequence, the administration turned ruthless towards rural life in general. Some of the measures adopted by government to punish agriculturists included collection of landlords' arrears, establishment of police camps, special police camps, attachment machinery with orders to assist tax realization, blockade of villages and prohibition of reaping crops.[311] Among the punitive measures and excesses to which rural India was subject included attachment and illegal seizures, looting and pillage by landlords and government agents, intimidation and humiliation of women and civil resisters, attack on constructive works, punitive police and punitive exactions.[312] In the NWFP a new system of 'undeclared war' was imposed on an already harsh and arbitrary system of *bandobast*.[313] The result was traumatic. Even the most sympathetic of the officials, the report says, appeared to be remote from the main forces of life that stirred India. Their reaction, therefore, appeared strangely unrelated to the environment over which they had full political and administrative control.[314] They all agreed that there was no party in India other than the Congress with such intense devotion to India's progress. Its hold on the popular imagination was unprecedented. Yet, practically none of them would agree that in the interest of peace and progress power should be allowed to pass on to the Congress. They declined to accept the proposition that control of affairs in India had been passing out of their hands despite themselves.[315]

The emergence of the 'Ordinance Mind' was the natural outcome of the system.[316] It made the man on the spot in the villages, districts and provincial headquarters more autocratic than ever. He exercised unchecked and authoritarian power; he was scared of being marked for an alleged weakness; if temperamentally domineering, he tended to become a sadist.[317] His source of information, standard of judgement, concept of prestige and appreciation of contingencies and expediency worked against the better instincts of his nature.[318] Summary methods and autocratic temperament prevented upward movement of information; police officers got a special nudge; a district officer with a strong common sense approach for the settlement of disputes declined in importance and often found himself marginalized and even eclipsed.[319] Contact with India through 'the loyalty leagues' made the administration thrive in a world of ignorance. The result was that the whole system seemed to be hanging in a void supported by misinformation, make-believe and wishful thinking.[320]

The absurdity of the situation was demonstrated by the interview that members of the delegation had with the Viceroy on 13 October 1932. When in the course of the conversation the delegation raised the question of famine in India, the Viceroy felt outraged and reacted sharply.[321] He claimed that there was no famine anywhere in India, that such a situation was required by law to be proclaimed, and that the officials never even casually mentioned to him the existence of such a calamity in India. It was obvious from the viceroy's reaction as if the four members of the team from England were given to some fanciful concoction to malign the administration. On the Poona pact, although the Viceroy expressed his apparent satisfaction, he made it unambiguous that he expected no permanent or substantial improvement in the condition of the untouchables in the near future. On the suggestion that Gandhi might then be released to consolidate the gains of the Poona pact, the viceroy lost his cool. He maintained that Gandhi was no saint and that he was a shrewd politician who repeatedly asserted the legitimacy of civil disobedience, that he was the inspiration behind his lieutenant Jawaharlal Nehru who started the no-tax movement in the United Provinces and his ally Ghaffar Khan who initiated the Redshirt 'rampage' in the NWFP forcing the ablest of officials to plead for the imposition of the ordinances. It was again Gandhi who gave an open threat for the renewal of civil disobedience and therefore was despatched to find his place in prison. 'The little man', the Viceroy thundered, 'can be released tomorrow if he will only agree not to break the law.'[322] The Viceroy felt unhappy that the delegation had decided at the very outset that they should be committed to the Congress and not to listen to the officials; the viceroy was well informed about the predilections of the delegation and its morbid animus against government. He also gave vent to a firm conviction in his mind that the partiality of the delegation was due to the fact that they had visited India on the invitation of the Congress and that their visit was entirely funded by the Congress and its sympathizers and that they had come not to make an impartial investigation of Indian conditions but prepare a charge-sheet against government and to whitewash the Congress and Gandhi. He concluded his indictment with a sonorous claim: 'Eighteen months ago things were in a mess. I will guarantee that conditions are today a 100 per cent better than they were then, and I go further and guarantee that the people are a 100 per cent happier — now that they can be sure of protection and liberty to go about their business as they wish.'[323]

One thing was evident to the delegates that the iceroy was displeased by any attempt to bring about a rapprochement between the leading communities in India. On board *MV Victoria* the delegates had the opportunity of meeting Maulana Shaukat Ali. They had a long conversation with him primarily on the Indian situation touching upon the Viceroy's conversation with the delegates on 13 October 1932.[324] Menon recounted that in the caste Hindu-depressed classes negotiations arising out of Gandhi's fast, the Viceroy remained neutral and said nothing. He did not send any telegram to Ambedkar urging him to remember that there were others whose interests had to be looked into. But in the case of Hindu-Muslim negotiations, he thought it prudent to go out of his way to utter a warning to Shaukat Ali against the negotiations to the effect that Shaukat Ali could not speak for the entire Muslim population of India. Menon claimed that the viceroy could not quite explain, when asked, why in his judgement he thought it judicious to change his priority and stance within a very short period. Shaukat Ali emphasized that it would be impolitic to continue the prolonged tension between the two communities and that in his desire for a permanent peace he had the sympathy of the Hindu leaders such as Madan Mohan Malaviya and a large number of eminent personalities of both the communities. He vouched that he had never entertained with favour civil disobedience and non-cooperation as credible means of political struggle. He was a rebel and desired peace for all including the British. But both he and Malaviya shared a common perception that Gandhi's presence at the peace negotiations would be most fruitful. He was pleased to acknowledge that Gandhi had given his blessings to such an endeavour. Thus, despite the Viceroy's opposition, the peace conference met at Lucknow. As far as the viceroy's doubts about Shaukat Ali's credentials were concerned, the Maulana reminded that he had been a past president of the Muslim Conference and also its vice-president, that 28 of the executive board were present at Lucknow, including four of its executive officers.

The late Maulana Mohamed Ali, his brother, was instrumental in drafting 13 out of its 14 points and that the poet Iqbal had sent his blessings to the conference. Shaukat Ali added that only 'the job-hunters and flatterers' who made the mistake of believing that they could stand out, 'stood by the government'. Following Lucknow, Shaukat Ali met the Viceroy. Government was determined to 'rub the nose of Congress in the dirt', but Shaukat Ali was convinced that there could be quicker and surer peace all round if 'we are free to negotiate it' on a rational basis. If the Viceroy wanted an honourable peace he should release Gandhi forthwith. Shaukat Ali was keen to ensure that civil disobedience should be dropped as a precondition of peace and that the interests of the British must be considered. He was convinced that Gandhi would meet the conference properly and fairly. Everyone including Gandhi, he held, was sick of warring and wanted peace but everyone also knew perfectly well that the only kind of peace 'we can have is one that has justice and honour as its foundations'. If the British did not want that, then they must put up with the consequences.

Shaukat Ali felt that Willingdon was a testy person who wanted to see 'Gandhi going down in the mud'. He was ill-advised by his officials who did not care for creative statesmanship and only wanted people to obey their orders. They wanted 'their own jackals, and their creatures like those they send to the Round Table Conference'. Thus, if they continued to think that they could play the game they had been playing for a century, nothing could 'stop the avalanche and the disaster'. The spirit of the nation could not be smothered. The British must realize the gravity of the situation. They could no longer procrastinate. They must yield. Indians were no longer satisfied with 'a rattle or a bauble to play with'. 'Now we want the real thing,' Shaukat Ali asserted, 'and if Britain will come into the proper peace she can have all our friendship in the future. If not, they can commit suicide and I can't help it.'[325]

Summing up the objections to the points raised by the report, government of India emphasized a few issues which, it thought, had considerable ramifications. The first point to be asserted was that the delegation had placed no reliance on official statistics and memoranda. On the contrary they propounded a number of generalizations based on insufficient and inaccurate data. As a result of a biased investigation, the delegation had committed a series of palpable errors.[326]

One of these was that the claim of the delegation that whatever other differences there might be there was unity of all communities in opposition to the policy of repression and ordinances. They, however, ignored the fact that the government of Madras asserted that in the presidency a majority of the elected members of the legislative council had constantly supported government in the measures taken to combat civil disobedience and refused to accept motions by the opposition designed to censure alleged excesses by the police.[327] Government of Madras also contested the claim that the Congress was the strongest party and would win hands down in a free election. The Justice party, it argued, had been organizing themselves to fight the impending election in opposition to the Congress and had considerable hope of obtaining a majority. In this electoral battle, it was anticipated, the Congress would not fare well in view of the fact that many supporters of the Congress had been alienated by Gandhi's recent political gestures and by his advocacy of temple entry for the depressed classes which had roused the opposition of the orthodox.[328] It was believed that since recommencement of the civil disobedience in January 1932 the Congress and Gandhi had been steadily losing ground. The general public, it was added, had come to realize the barrenness and futility of civil disobedience. Thirdly, it contained false allegations and a strong attack on the police. It was stated that the picture drawn by the delegation of life in the villages made unbearable by the oppression of punitive and special police was fantastic. It was held in opposition to that opinion that at the outbreak of civil disobedience the police force had been strengthened by the re-enlistment of some 300 retired officers but subsequently owing to retrenchment, there was a considerable fall in the sanctioned strength of the force. As for punitive police, it was alleged, a force of 28 men had been quartered in one village in the Madras presidency at the cost of inhabitants for a period of two months; but otherwise no special measures had been necessary.[329] As for the jails, government was categorical: they were allowed to visit eight jails and the delegates were surprised by the cleanliness and good order of the prisons. What government thought a matter of urgency was to refute the assertion of the delegation that in the villages, communal feeling between Hindus and Muslims was non-existent.[330] Even in Madras, where the communal question was not acute, troubles between the two communities had been recurring even in the most out of the way places. There had been outbreaks in districts so far apart as Ramnad, Trichinopoly, North Arcot, Anantapur and Karnool. Even in places where outbreaks had not occurred, special police precaution had been necessary on numerous occasions to prevent clashes between the two communities.[331] Finally, it was stressed that the delegation's 'cheap snear that district officers may be well up in figures and statistics but are entirely out of touch with sentiments and feelings of the people' was vacuous rhetoric indulged in by a set of irresponsible visitors in their motivated political polemics.[332]

The report, however, made it obvious that the delegation had conducted an admirable project in unravelling the mystique of the *Raj* and its grandiloquent assertion. The report claimed that, broadly speaking, the reason for the demand of Indians for freedom to govern themselves was twofold. On the one hand, there was the practical fact that dire poverty and starvation among the masses of the people had made them demand significant changes. On the other hand, there was a different but equally fundamental fact, namely, that the Indian people had been a subject people. Their government, culture and education had been dominated, directed and restricted by an alien rule. To remain subservient willingly to a foreign power would be to submit to their own moral and spiritual degradation as a people. The Indian people, it was maintained, had been awakened to the subtle danger of the continuation of foreign rule and thus the movement of the Indian people had become in reality a struggle for human freedom. The outstanding fact in regard to the masses of the Indian people was poverty. Although official statistics recorded four pence a day as per capita income, recent enquiries in a certain district revealed an average income of one pence per day.

The standard of life in India was very low compared with that of England and people had no vitality to resist diseases and famine. It was again their poverty that could explain the alarming death rates in times of famine. In 1918 when the influenza epidemic swept over the land, three million people died in India. The housing conditions of the workers were appalling, especially in the industrial areas in large cities. In Bombay 97 per cent lived in one-room tenements. In the factory areas of Bombay the death rate for infants had at times exceeded 800 per 1,000. In one district, in a single year, as many as 8 out of 10 babies died before the age of one year. In many of these one-room tenements there were more than one family. They were built with no airspace, shut off from sunlight, and their sanitary conditions were unmentionable. Disease and high death rate were the inevitable consequences of such conditions. The factory conditions, described in the report of the Royal Commission, recorded a low rate of wages which averaged out at £3 a month for a 60-hour week, the appalling starvation rate for women and children and the awful conditions under which they worked. That the Factory Acts in India did not apply to workshops where power was not installed accounted for the existence of abuses banished years ago in Britain. The horrors of child labour existed in factories run by European as well as Indian capital. Little children as young as five years were employed sometimes for two pence per day under threat of corporal punishment. The conditions of work of persons in the tea plantations were equally shocking. Primary education for children of the peasants and industrial workers had been severely neglected. Among men, less than 14 out of every 100 were considered literate and among women, only 3 out of every 100. This fact alone would be sufficient to account for the helplessness of the people when they came to work in factories and workshops managed on similar lines to those in Britain but without all the safeguards of British factories.

These helpless, poverty-stricken and illiterate masses, it was reported, had been subjected always to burdensome taxation which produced a revenue to be spent not on health services or education but for the maintenance of the army. That army had always been necessary for the preservation of internal peace in India, the defence of the frontiers and preparedness to embark at a moment's notice for imperial service in other parts of the world. In these three aspects, India had for long been one of the most important units in the scheme of British imperial defence providing the British government with a striking force with admirable efficiency and assured valour. Curzon had confirmed the position held by the Indian army in the imperial defence system. In that army, 1/3 were British troops and a British soldier cost four times as much as an Indian soldier. Practically all the officers with the exception of a few Indians in junior posts were British. A British officer cost six times as much as an Indian officer. India was in dire poverty and yet she was taxed for active service for the British government. One third of the revenue was spent on the upkeep of the civil services. This meant roughly speaking that £32,000,000 was annually spent on the salaries of British officers. It was not an exaggeration to say that the payment of high officials had always been more than excessive and that the Indian civil services as a whole had provided well-paid careers for educated Englishmen for years past. To the cost of maintaining the army officials and the civil services might be added the long list of pensions paid to retired British officials, the whole of which money was not spent in India but in Great Britain. When all this expenditure was deducted from the revenue, it was evident how little was left for social services. Thus only 1/20 was available for education, 1/12 for health services, and only 1/28 for agriculture, notwithstanding the fact that India was pre-eminently an agricultural country with a large peasant population. The report gave enough facts taken from a solid mass of similar evidence and they suggested a picture of poverty and suffering to prove how impossible it was for one nation to govern another especially when they were so widely separated.

It was small wonder that India had been demanding self-government. The political organization which represented the national movement was the Indian National Congress. This body might almost be described as 'the unofficial parliament' of the people. The policy of the Congress, the report affirmed, was that of non-cooperation with government and resistance to the unjust ordinances, and the method of resistance employed by the Congress volunteers was entirely non-violent. Evidently, the British government was not inclined to grant complete self-determination but was seeking to institute a reformed constitution in which Indians would have a large measure of control but the whole government would still be subject to the British parliament. To this end, the report explained, the RTC had been held in two sessions; the nature of the new constitution was considered but the main issue from the Indian standpoint, that of self-determination, was not discussed. The delegates had been handpicked by government and were not elected by the people and, therefore, could not be said to represent the national point of view.[333]

At the second RTC, Gandhi represented the Congress and two other members were present with him. At its close, committees were formed to continue investigations in India towards the formation of a new constitution. Members of these committees were nominated by government. Reporting on India in the current situation, it was maintained that while the second RTC had been sitting in London, there was a truce in India between the Congress and Government of India. The non-cooperation movement was discontinued by the Congress and government withdrew its repressive measures. Yet, although at the end of the second session of the conference the outlook for a speedy settlement was not bright, Gandhi asked his people not to take any action until after his return. But a few days after his departure for Britain the first of the Bengal ordinaces was issued, followed by others. The official reasons for issuing the ordinances were some isolated cases of violence as for instance the murder committed by two girls in Bengal. All these cases had been repudiated by the Congress whose followers remained by and large non-violent.[334] The issue of ordinances was followed by the arrest of the Congress leaders and others including Gandhi himself. Arrest, censorship and dissemination of misinformation were principal instruments of ordinance rule which was backed by ruthless police terrorism. Attempts had been made to spread a false notion that India was quiet but it was the quiet which remained behind prison doors. The administration indulged in hideous and brutal deeds and obscene methods of torture. The ordinances gave the authorities almost unlimited powers. They could inflict the death penalty without appeal and imprison without trial, impose heavy fines, suppress newspapers and political meetings. The police were encouraged to use brutal methods and terrorize people. Unarmed men, women and children were struck with stout sticks and *lathis*. It was a frequent occurrence for unarmed crowds to be fired upon. English and European people visiting India had actually witnessed such attacks and seen police not only striking down unarmed men but continue to strike them on the ground. A well known missionary Dr F. Paton was himself subjected for no cause to similar treatment. Under the slightest pretext, people's houses were raided and elderly people, invalids and children were turned out of doors. It seemed that the 'worst refinement of cruelty' was committed when government closed down the hospitals run by Congress volunteers. The report emphasized that these ordinances and methods were directed against unarmed and non-violent people irrespective of age or gender.

The Redshirts in the NWFP, the one time proud warriors of the frontier, were then the non-violent patriots with close relations with the Congress. Thousands of them were in prison. Their leader had been deported. They had been mercilessly assailed and, surprisingly enough, they did not retaliate even once. It was in fact legalized state terror and the report wondered how long this reign would continue in the name of the British people. It was going to be a lasting shame in British history and it would certainly sow the seeds of bitterness and resentment among a people otherwise friendly and peace loving. There was optimism that India would win her freedom. The report was, however, despondent about the impact of the rule of the ordinances. It would foster, it claimed, a heritage of ill will and racial hatred for which future generations would condemn the British nation.[335]

The proscription of the *Condition of India* and the suppression of the volume in the British press inaugurated a synchronized assault on the India League as a whole. The upshot was even more galling in view of the publicity given over time to the imperial discourse and a misleading and an almost unending projection of the seamy side of Indian realities. In a series of letters addressed to the editors of the leading newspapers, Menon asked if the press had been paying honest and impartial attention to the evidence which had been offered to the public on the condition of India. The Simon report, Lawrence

Housman held, in the shaping of which Indians were allowed no part, had been given all possible publicity and remained for many minds 'the accepted measure of prudent liberality of action'. The white paper, which was regarded in certain quarters as a dangerous concession to undesirable influences, had received plenty of publicity. The sessions of the JSC constituted, by all standards, a singularly monotonous anti-Indian demonstration. In contrast, no publicity whatever had ever been given to the exhaustively complete report on the Indian situation by the delegation of the India League.[336]

In Bengal, the mere possession of a copy of the book would have entailed imprisonment for the person concerned. The *Condition of India,* Menon argued, was in the main, a record of facts and was fully documented. The authors had drawn liberally on official sources and several chapters of the book contained statements of the points of view of the authorities. Critics like Gwyn, a contributor to the *Manchester Guardian* on Indian topics, pronounced his favourable verdict on the conscientious attempt of the authors to be fair. In any case, if the report was not a true account, the Indian reader, Menon added, would dismiss it as a tissue of lies as he would soon be able to discover its real nature from his own knowledge of the facts. So far as India was concerned, the report made no 'revelation', nor was there any reason to fear that it would 'mislead' the ignorant multitude since it is written in English and, therefore, would be used only by a small section of English educated Indians.[337]

In India, the action of government caused no surprise. The press and public opinion were muzzled and persons daring to express views distasteful to local officials, exposed themselves, their friends and kinsmen and their property to severe penal action. The banning of the report, it was asserted, was in the same category as the ban placed by Hitler on the *Manchester Guardian* and other English journals because they dared to say a few things that were true. Menon argued that though there was nothing extraordinary about that action in the context of administrative policy in India, it gave an opportunity to those who were concerned about India and the policies pursued there by the British authorities to form their opinion as to the ways of the Indian movement.[338] The expression of abhorrence at the curtailment of liberty and ban on the right to dissent in Germany and other places by men and women in Britain led Menon to hope that a similar attitude would be expressed about equally abhorrent actions in India. Menon emphasized that the Indian administration, while it cared nothing for Indian sentiment, was still sensitive to public opinion in Britain. He believed that there was a sizeable volume of opinion in the country which was opposed to Hitlerism and its like wherever it obtained. It was their conviction that in the main induced the League to undertake the publication of the report. Here was a document available to the people of England, Menon concluded, but their agents in India arbitrarily decided to withhold it from the Indian people, including the members of the Indian legislatures, under severe penalties.[339]

In an informative communication to D.N. Pritt, Menon asserted that the conditions described in the volume were not a 'collection of stray stories', nor did they portray any less reprehensible state of affairs than what had obtained in some of the terrorized countries in Europe. As was only to be expected, Menon claimed, the press ignored the book. It was an awkward paradox, Menon added, that while atrocities and illegalities in other parts of the world, Russia and Germany for instance, excited heated comments in the newspapers, the conditions in India, for which England had a direct responsibility, did not appear to attract even marginal attention. Calling upon Pritt as a socialist, a jurist and an advocate of penal reforms, Menon felt that the volume would receive his full consideration.[340] Lawrence Housman, chairman of the Friends of India, was uncertain if his review of the volume would be published in any English journal but he wrote letters to the editors of *Guardian* and *New Statesman* urging them to show an interest in the 'solid and serious' publication of the India League. Housman stressed that during its work of investigation in India, all possible obstacles were thrown in the way by the Indian administration, even to the extent in some cases, of prosecuting, for breach of the ordinances, those who dared to give it information. But what was most tragic and illiberal was that when the report had been published 'an almost complete boycott has been instituted against it in the Press'. Housman argued that much of the material, though well-documented, was no doubt controversial in character and in the main hostile to the case officially put forward for the proposed reforms. 'But is it just or honest,' Housman placed a loaded question, 'in the face of so great a problem, to ignore — because of its controversial character — this weighty pronouncement from the Indian side, and to keep the British public in ignorance of its existence?'[341] From the Indian standpoint, the report, as a forward statement, made the proposals of the white paper 'seem rather over moderate than over-conceding', and for that reason alone and at that precise juncture the volume was of substantial political importance.[342] Menon was persistent. To Stafford Cripps, spokesperson of the Socialist League, Menon wrote for his considered opinion. The last chapter of the report, Menon pointed out, dealt with the impact of the existing policy and the 'way out' of it. He ventured to think, he added, that the plan of a policy based on self-determination which had been outlined there should be adopted by the Labour Party in the near future.[343]

The Friends were keen to assist but were even more eager to seek conciliation and to bridge the gulf of estrangement. It was imperative, they thought, that the tone of the Congress and the India League should be modulated and that the investigative report would merely toughen attitude and harden official perception. In his communication to Menon on 21 March

1934 on the volume, Horace Alexander maintained that although the book looked to be a fine piece of work, he had not had time to go through it. He would see to it that it got noticed in the *Friends* and, if possible, in other Quaker papers and would also find out if C.F. Andrews could be persuaded to undertake a review. The Indian committee of the *Friends* was perhaps philosophically averse to the India League's investigative report and Menon's suggestion for a discussion on the volume met with a very casual and lukewarm response.[344] Following an indepth discussion by the sympathetic India-watchers, it seemed to Alexander not quite practicable to review the volume. But he thought that he would try to do something else. At a small meeting in Birmingham, Wellock spoke of the book and it was reported that he had been trying to organize a fairly well-attended meeting before long.[345]

Meanwhile Grenfell failed to persuade Samuel Hoare to receive a deputation of the League which included Laski on the ground that he had no time. Grenfell suggested that a memorandum could be submitted.[346] The idea of appointing a deputation was to obtain a statement on the League's case on the banning of its report and a discussion which was not possible in letters and memoranda. A question in the House of Commons regarding the proscription of the book drew a sharp answer that the step had been taken because the publication was an offence against the Indian penal laws and therefore was entirely a legal action. No supplementary question could be asked and the meeting was not followed up.[347] Menon also failed to persuade the Transport House even to take interest in the massive strike in Bombay and police atrocities on the processions and demonstrations of the strikers. It seemed that Grenfell could not get his question past the Clerk of the House. In sheer frustration, Menon seemed to throw up his hands: 'Do you think that there is anything more to be done on this at all?'[348]

Menon had realized that the political situation portended continual tension. The optimistic views entertained in England in some quarters had been dampened by a feeling of diffidence. Many members of the exalted civil service in India deplored the gradual but almost inevitable extinction of Indian loyalty. They whined as they helplessly watched its impact on their proverbial confidence. They ascribed the erosion of faith in the *Raj* to the new creed of the administration. Loyalty was no longer considered, they carped, as the spontaneous manifestation of gratitude, to which British rule was legitimately entitled. On the contrary, loyalty was being interpreted, they mumbled, as a sentiment which ought to be won by indulgence, insured by negotiations and retained by compromises and concessions. It was unfortunate, the civil servants complained, that Government of India and public opinion in England had imparted to the Indian nationalists the lessons of mutual adjustments and the notions of political bargaining. As a constructive approach, they proposed, the political scientists should recognize that the British system with all its merits might not necessarily be *comme il faut* in India and would never be gracefully accepted even by a sizeable and politically significant minority. In any case, they insisted that the 'undiluted nationalism' and 'political emotionalism' of the Congress ought to be supplanted by a rational approach with the primacy of viceregal veto as the crucial monitor of the whole system. To surrender at that stage of India's development, they argued, the destinies of India's millions to the hands of a few urban intelligentsia, would be a gross betrayal of trust.[349]

Notes and References

1 Hallett to MacGregor, 13 November 1932, Home Pol.; also in Infn. offr. 803/32/6/1/50, India Office.

2 Ibid.

3 Ibid.

4 Ibid.

5 Ibid.

6 Ibid.

7 Ibid.

8 Hallett to MacGregor, 29 November 1932, Home Pol.

9 Ibid.

10 Ibid.; also, Hallett to Stewart, 18 July 1932, Home Pol.

11 Hallett to M.S. Clauson, 10 October 1932, Home Pol.

12 Hallett to Peel, 14 November 1932, Home Pol.

13 Hallett to MacGregor, 30 November 1932, Home Pol.

14 Ibid.; See also a critical contemporary assessment of the 'Ordinance Rule' in M.M. Malaviya 'Statement on Repression in India' L/I/1/50, India Office.

15 'Note on the India League Delegation', n.d. 1932, L/I/1/50, India Office.

16 Hallett to MacGregor, 26 October, Infn. offr. 732/32, L/I/1/50, India Office.

17 See, 'Private Report, India League Conference', 26 November 1932 at Kingsway Hall and Public meeting at YPM, Infn. offr. L/I/1/50, India Office.

18 MacGregor to Stephens, 1 December 1932, Infn. offr. L/I/1/50, India Office.

19 Ibid.

20 Ibid.

21 Peel to MacGregor, 26 November 1932, Infn. offr. L/I/1/50, India Office.

22 MacGregor to Stephens, 22 November 1932, Infn. offr. L/I/1/50, India Office.

23 Ibid.

24 Ibid.

25 Stephens to MacGregor, 27 October 1932, Infn. offr. L/I/1/50, India Office.

26 Ibid.

27 Ibid.

28 Ibid.

29 Ibid.

30 Memorandum on 'The India League Delegation', home department, government of India in Stephens to MacGregor, 13 November 1932, Infn. offr. L/I/1/50, India Office.

31 Ibid.

32 Ibid.

33 Ibid.

34 Ibid.

35 Ibid.

36 Ibid.

37 Ibid.

38 Ibid.

39 Ibid.

40 Memorandum on 'The India League Delegation', in Stephens to MacGregor, 13 November 1932, Infn. offr. L/I/1/50, India Office.

41 Ibid.

42 Ibid.

43 Ibid.

44 Ibid.

45 Ibid.

46 Ibid.

47 Ibid.

48 Ibid.; see all the reports from the presidencies and provinces in F/12/1932 Home Pol. 1932.

49 'Confidential Report on the meeting of The India League, Welcome to the delegation on 21 November 1932', 24 November 1932, Infn. Infr. L/I/1/50, India Office.

50 Ibid.

51 Ibid.

52 Ibid.

53 Ibid.

54 Ibid.

55 Ibid.

56 MacGregor to Stephens, 24 November 1932, Infn. offr. L/I/1/50, 878/1932, India Office.

57 'Private Report of India League Conference and Public Meeting, 26 November', 27 November 1932, Infn. offr. L/P/J/12/448, India Office.

58 Ibid.

59 Ibid.

60 Ibid.

61 Ibid.

62 Ibid.

63 Ibid.

64 Ibid.

65 Ibid.

66 Polak to MacGregor, 26 April 1932, P&J, India Office, Also, Stewart to Emerson with enclosures, 26 February 1931, P&J, India Office.

67 Ibid.

68 'Specific Instances of Repression and Atrocities quoted by India League Delegation', P&J(S) 1306, 1932 L/P/J/12/448, India Office.

69 Ibid., for official concern about the anti-government propaganda in India; see, confidential draft paper in the office of the secretary of state, 16 December 1935, P&J department, India Office.

70 Wedgwood Benn, 'Note on Propaganda', 26 June 1931, P&J department, India Office; also, Freemantle to Hoare, 'Propaganda in India', 3 June 1931, P&J department, India Office.

71 Ibid.

72 Ibid.

73 Ibid.

74 Ibid.

75 Ibid.

76 Benn to viceroy, 17 August 1931, P&J Collection, India Office; also, 'Note to Secretary of State on Propaganda', ibid.

77 Ibid.

78 Ibid.

79 Ibid.

80 Extract from Willingdon to Wedgwood Benn, 6 July 1931, P&J Collection, India Office.

81 Ibid.

82 Ibid.

83 Ibid.

84 Ibid.

85 Marginal note, 19 July 1931, ibid.

86 Ibid.

87 Samuel Hoare to Willingdon, 17 December 1931, P&J Collection, India Office.

88 Ibid.

89 Ibid.

90 Ibid.; also see, 'Broadcasting in Rural India', Indian Village Welfare Association, 8 June 1932, P&J Collection.

91 Willingdon to Hoare, 8 February 1932, P&J Collection, India Office.

92 Ibid.

93 Ibid.

94 Ibid.

95 Ibid.

96 Ibid.

97 Director of Sales, Visatone Sound System to Samuel Hoare, 7 April 1932, P&J Collection, India Office.

98 Ibid.

99 Ibid.

100 Ibid.

101 Ibid.

102 Ibid., also see papers on broadcasting in rural India, by Indian Village Welfare Association in P&J Collection, India Office.

103 'Note', prepared by under secretary of state, 13 May 1931; Strickland to Peel, 8 June 1931; E. Gilford, 'note' on propaganda, 31 May 1932, all in P&J Collection, India Office.

104 Vicount Sumner, *Looking Forward,* Indian Empire Society, London, 1932. Cf. S. Chakravarty, *The Raj Syndrome,* New Delhi 1991, pp.150-165.

105 MacGregor to Stephens, 4 January 1933, Infn. offr. L/I/1/50 900/192, India Office.

106 Ibid.

107 Ibid.

108 Ibid.

109 Ibid.

110 Ibid.

111 Ibid.

112 Ibid.

113 'Miss Wilkinson's trenchant reply to Sir S. Hoare, '*The Star*', Infn. offr. L/I/1/50, India Office.

114 Ibid.

115 Ibid.

116 Ibid.

117 Ibid.

118 Ibid.

119 Ibid.

120 Ibid.

121 Ibid.

122 'Visit to India of the India League's Delegation', 30 February 1933, Infn. offr. L/I/1/50, India Office.

123 Ibid.

124 Ibid.; office note to MacGregor, 14 January 1933, Infn. offr. L/I/1/50, India Office.

125 Ibid.

126 MacGregor to Stephens, 29 December 1932, Infn. offr. L/I/1/50, 875/32, India Office.

127 Ibid.

128 Ibid.

129 Ibid.

130 MacGregor to Stephens, 25 October, 1932, Infn. offr. L/I/1/50, India Office.

131 Ibid.

132 Ibid.

133 'Note regarding the India League Delegation which visited India during the Summer of 1932'. (prepared on consultation with Lord Irwin) n.d. February 1933, P&J Collection, India Office.

134 Ibid.

135 Ibid.

136 Ibid.

137 Note by MacGregor, dated 11 February 1933 attached with ibid.

138 Ibid.

139 Ibid.

140 Monica Whately, 'What we saw in India', 14 January 1933 enclosed in Jeffrey Williams to Samuel Hoare 12 January 1933, L/PJ/12/449, India Office.

141 Ibid.

142 Ibid.

143 Ibid.

144 Ibid.

145 Jeffrey Williams to Samuel Hoare, 12 January 1933, L/PJ/12/449, India Office.

146 Ibid.

147 Ibid.

148 Graham Pole to Samuel Hoare, 12 January 1933, L/PJ(S)/12/140/1933, India Office.

149 Ibid.

150 Ibid.

151 Ibid.

152 Minute Paper, 3 February 1933, L/PJ(S)/140/1933.

153 Ibid.

154 Ibid.

155 This is Draft Paper, P&J(S)/140/1933 India Office. See also Samuel Hoare to Major D. Graham Pole, 18 January 1933, Pole Papers (India Office).

156 Samuel Hoare to Graham Pole, 6 February 1933, P&J(S)/140/1933, India Office.

157 Ibid.

158 Ibid.

159 Ibid.

160 Extract from New Scotland Yard Report, 16 August 1933, PJ(S)/884/1933, India Office.

161 MacGregor to Hallett, 6 February 1933, Infn. offr. L/I/1/50, India Office.

162 Stephens to MacGregor, 12 January 1933, Infn. ofr. L/I/1/50, India Office.

163 Ibid.

164 Stephens to MacGregor, 25 January 1933, Infn. offr. L/I/1/50, India Office.

165 Stephens to MacGregor, 12 January 1933, Infn. offr. L/I/1/50, India Office.

166 'Peace of present policy is abandoned', *Hindustan Times,* Infn. offr. L/I/1/50, India Office.

167 MacGregor to Stephens, 18 January 1933, Infn. offr. L/I/1/50, India Office.

168 Ibid.

169 Ibid.

170 Peel to MacGregor, 20 February 1933, Infn. offr. L/I/1/50, India Office.

171 The Information Bulletin in India League, 16 December 1932, Infn. offr. L/I/1/50, 138/1933, India Office; and MacGregor to H.B. Holmes, 20 February 1933, Infn. offr. L/I/1/50, India Office.

172 Ibid.

173 H.B. Holmes to MacGregor, 22 February 1933, Infn. offr. L/I/1/50, India Office.

174 Ibid.

175 MacGregor to Holmes, 18 February 1933, Infn. offr. L/I/1/50, India Office.

176 Ibid.

177 Ibid.

178 MacGregor to Stephens, 2 December 1932, Infn. offr. L/I/1/50, 575/32, India Office.

179 Ibid.

180 Ibid.

181 Ibid.

182 Stephens to MacGregor, 12 December 1932, Infn. offr. L/I/1/50, India Office.

183 Ibid.

184 Ibid.

185 Stephens to MacGregor, 27 October 1932, Infn. offr. L/I/1/50, India Office.

186 Ibid.

187 Ibid.

188 Stephens to MacGregor, 19 December 1932, Infn. offr. L/I/1/50, India Office.

189 Ibid.

190 Ibid.

191 Ibid.

192 Stephens to MacGregor, 12 December 1932, Infn. offr. L/I/1/50, India Office.

193 Ibid.; also, MacGregor to Stephens 12 January 1933, Infn. offr. L/I/1/50, India Office.

194 MacGregor to Peel, 22 March 1933, Infn. offr. L/I/1/50, India Office.

195 MacGregor, 'Note' for Peel, 18 October 1933, Infn. offr. L/I/1/50, India Office.

196 Edward N. Davies to MacGregor, 19 October 1933, Infn. offr. L/I/1/50, India Office.

197 MacGregor to Peel, 18 October 1933, Infn. offr. L/I/1/50, India Office.

198 MacGregor to Davies, 18 October 1953, Infn. offr. L/I/1/50, India Office.

199 Ibid.

200 Ibid.

201 Ibid.

202 Ibid.

203 Ibid.

204 Ibid.

205 MacGregor to Peel, 14 October 1933, Infn. offr. L/I/1/50, India Office.

206 Ibid.

207 Ibid.

208 Minute paper on the 'Condition of India Mss', 18 October 1933, Infn. offr. L/I/1/50, India Office.

209 Ibid. Peel wrote on the margin - 'I agree - provided it is understood, as stated in the draft, that so far we have not been consulted officially'.

210 Ibid.

211 Ibid.

212 Ibid.

213 MacGregor to Stephens, 12 March 1934, Infn. offr. L/I/1/50, 840/34, India Office.

214 Ibid.

215 Ibid.

216 Ibid.

217 MacGregor to Douglas Crawford, 31 March 1934, Infn. offr. L/I/1/50 393/34, India Office.

218 Ibid.

219 Douglas Crawford to MacGregor, 2 April 1934, Infn. offr. L/I/1/50 293/34, India Office.

220 Ibid.

221 Ibid.

222 MacGregor to Stephens, 2 May 1934, Infn. offr. L/I/1/50, 400/1934, India Office.

223 Ibid.

224 Ibid.

225 'India League Report', *The Times*, 10 March 1934 in Minute paper, W. Johnston, 26 March 1934, J/PJ/2/449.

226 Ibid.

227 Desmond Young, 7&8 April 1932, *The Pioneer*, in Stephens to Young 11 April 1932, Infn. Offr. L/I/1/50, India Office.

228 Stephens to Young, 11 April 1932, Infn. Offr. L/I/1/50, India Office.

229 Ibid.

230 Ibid.

231 Ibid.

232 Ibid.

233 Ibid.

234 Ibid.

235 *Condition of India, Being the Report of the Delegation Sent to India by the India League in 1932,* London 1934. (hereafter *Report*).

236 Foreword, *Report.*

237 Ibid.

238 Preface, *Report.*

239 Ibid.

240 Ibid.

241 Chapter I, *Report;* also see, Home Pol. files at the National Archives, New Delhi for the months of August to December 1932.

242 Chapter IX, *Report.*

243 Chapter II, ibid.

244 Chapter XII, ibid.

245 Chapter II, ibid., pp.10-11.

246 Chapter II.

247 Ibid.

248 Ibid.

249 Ibid.

250 Ibid.

251 Ibid.

252 See, Ch.XIII and appendices ii and iii, ibid.

253 Ch.II, ibid.

254 Ibid.

255 Chh. II and XXIV, ibid.

256 Ch. II, ibid.

257 Ibid.

258 Ibid.

259 Ibid.

260 Ch. X, esp. pp.112-40, ibid.

261 Ch. XXII(1), ibid.

262 Chh. XVII and XVII esp. pp.350-84, ibid.

263 Ibid.

264 Ibid.

265 Ibid.

266 Ibid.

267 Ibid.

268 Ch. IX, ibid.

269 Ch. XVII, ibid.

270 Ibid.

271 Ibid.

272 Chh. XVII and XVIII, ibid.

273 Ch. XVIII (iii), ibid.

274 Ibid., pp.79-83.

275 Ibid.

276 Ibid.

277 Ch. XVII, ibid.

278 Ibid.

279 Ch. XIII, ibid.

280 Ch. XII, ibid.

281 Ibid.

282 Ibid.

283 Ch. XIV, ibid.

284 Ibid.

285 Ch. XXII (i), ibid.

286 Ibid.

287 Ibid.

288 Ibid.

289 Ibid.

290 Ibid.

291 Ch. XXII (i), ibid.

292 Ibid.

293 Ch. X, esp. pp.120-2, ibid.

294 Ch. X.

295 Ibid.

296 Ibid.

297 Ibid.

298 Ch. XXIII (i) ibid.

299 Ch. XXV, ibid.

300 Ibid.

301 Chh. XXII and XXV, ibid.

302 Chh. V, VII and XI, ibid.

303 Ibid.

304 Ibid.

305 Ibid.

306 Ibid.

307 Ibid.

308 Ch. XIII.

309 Ibid.

310 Ibid.

311 Ch. XXII, pp.454-60, ibid.

312 Ch. I, pp.5-6, ibid.

313 Chh. XVIII (ii), XIV, pp.401-3, ibid.

314 Ch. XIII, pp.441-2, ibid.

315 Ibid., pp.239-41.

316 Ibid., pp.24-44.

317 Ch. XVIII, ibid.

318 Ibid.

319 Ch. XX, ibid.

320 Ch. XXII, p.456, ibid.

321 Ibid., pp.463-67.

322 Ibid.

323 Ibid.

324 'Conversation with Maulana Shaukat Ali on board, *MV* Victoria, 8 November 1932', Menon Papers.

325 Ibid.

326 Bracken to Hallett, 3 November 1932, F 12/1932 Home Pol.

327 Ibid.

328 Ibid.

329 Ibid.

330 Ibid.

331 Ibid.

332 Ibid.

333 See *Report*, pp.489-91, 509-11.

334 See the following chapters of the *Report*:

Civil Disobedience Movement, pp.72-87; The Congress, pp. 88-111; Suppression of the Nationalist Movement, pp.141-158; The Police Raj in Action, pp.177-244; Political Prisoners and Jails, pp. 245-281; The Village under Ordinance, pp.352-384; The Boycott and Picketing, pp.384-403; and Some Important Political Issues and Events, pp.485-492.

335 See Ch. XX, The North-Western Frontier, pp.404-430, *Report.*

336 Lawrence Housman to Menon, 11 December 1934, Menon Papers; Arthur Wenyon to Menon 15 June 1934, Menon Papers.

337 Menon to Arthur Wenyon, 3 August 1934, Menon Papers; also, see, Menon to editor, *The Manchester Guardian,* 21 August 1934, Menon Papers.

338 Menon, 'Circular letter', India League, 24 September 1934, Menon Papers.

339 Ibid.; See for an analysis of the events around and impact of the publication of the *Condition of India* in an undated note by Menon on the volume in Menon Papers.

340 Menon to D.N. Pritt, 16 September 1934, Menon Papers.

341 Lawrence Housman to the Editor, *Guardian/New Statesman*, 10 August 1934, copies in Lawrence Housman to Menon, 12 August 1934, Menon Papers.

342 Ibid.

343 Menon to Stafford Cripps, 16 September 1934, Menon Papers.

344 Horace Alexander to Menon, 21 March 1934, Menon Papers.

345 Horace Alexander to Menon, 29 March 1934, Menon Papers.

346 Grenfell to Menon, 16 May 1934, Menon Papers.

347 Ibid.

348 Grenfell to Menon, 21 May 1934, Menon Papers.

349 Cf. Suhash Chakravarty, *The Raj Syndrome,* op.cit., pp.148-53.

CHAPTER V

STIRRINGS

In August 1933, Victor Gollancz, teacher, publisher, author and public campaigner, brought out *The Brown Book of the Hitler Terror.*[1] The volume was compiled by the World Committee for the Relief of the Victims of German Fascism. It offered irrefutable evidence that the Nazis had been fabricating data for implicating the communists for the Reichstag fire of 27 February 1933, in a desperate bid to find an excuse for suspending civil liberties. What happened during the summer of that year was best described by the term, *Gleichltung,* or coordination, under which every aspect of German life was brought under Nazi control. The purge of 30 June 1933 completed the 'national socialist revolution.' The *Brown Book* examined scrupulously the content and contours of the Nazi rule, its implications and significance. Thanks to the publication, it was all very clear as early as autumn 1933, that Hitler was definitely and inescapably committed to war. However, even in the left circle in England there was an element of diffidence arising out of the fear of inflaming an irrational anti-German commotion. There was also a touch of uneasy pragmatism probably emanating from a feeling of unpreparedness. Nevertheless, the publication made it difficult to condone and accept the atmosphere of intense hatred, gross degeneration and unconcealed violence, engineered by the Nazis, as matters to be taken for granted.[2]

Initially run down by the events in Germany and Europe, some of the leaders of the labour movement in England paused for a while, took stock of the situation, pulled themselves together and a few of them decided to go for in serious introspection.[3] In fact, the leftward deviation of the rebellious generation of the 1930s had already become a milestone of the age. A host of writers, poets, critics and university undergraduates found themselves overwhelmed in what appeared to the Establishment to be a disturbing seditious inclination. The vital prominence enjoyed by that group of intellectuals was primarily due to the crucial position commanded by them in Britain's dominant culture.[4] Thus, it was but natural that when a bunch of young poets published a semi-political manifesto or the Oxford Union took an extraordinary pledge not to support King and Country in the future war or a combination of Cambridge undergraduates staged a conspicuous pacifist demonstration and joined enthusiastically impressive hunger marches, both the press and the authorities felt alarmed and often overreacted.[5] The social animation of the period encouraged the Left leadership to expect enthusiastically that the stirrings in the two ancient universities might explore a novel area for exciting intellectual articulation. Indeed, the decade was inseminated by profound and provocative ideas.[6]

Fenner Brockway, undisputed leader of ILP, was one of those concerned politicals who decided to examine seriously the tactics of the social democrats and communists in the continent and in England, with a view to assessing the situation and reviewing the rise of fascism in Germany and the right-wing swing in British politics, paradoxically, in sharp contrast to the increasing social and intellectual ascendancy of the Left ideology. Brockway thought that it could probably be illustrated by concrete historical evidence that the failure of the moderate social democratic policy and the perplexing communist tactics enabled the Nazis to make their decisive advances in politics. Over the years, India had been Brockway's special area of interest. His political career had been dominated by anti-imperialism and racial equality ever since Saklatvala, the Communist MP for Battersea, entreated him to become one of the organizers of the India League under Krishna Menon.

Brockway placed conviction before career, accepting for a time loneliness and unpopularity among his old associates because he was certain that he was right. He gave an impression of a dogmatic and pugilistic person but rarely did he show publicly his other side; tolerance, fellowship and compassion, charm and friendliness.[7] A member of the India League's executive council, Brockway warmly welcomed Nehru's advent 'to freedom' following his release on 30 August 1933. But like many others on the left, he could not quite comprehend Gandhi's withdrawal from politics to social reform, temple entry and the general emancipation of the untouchables, thus allowing the civil disobedience to fizzle out.[8] He had doubts about Gandhi's methods. Early in 1921 he had thought that non-cooperation, though a powerful and perfectly justifiable weapon, 'solves no racial or economic problem whatever'. Gandhi's new 'tactics' mystified Brockway and his colleagues. They watched with dismay the decline in the enthusiasm for civil disobedience in India, Gandhi's preoccupation with the *harijans,* the continuance of a firm hand by the government towards the Congress, especially its radical elements, the pusillanimous cooperation of the liberals and constitutionalists such as Sapru, Jayakar and Sastri. The spineless collaboration of these pussyfooters with Willingdon and Hoare, the short-sighted trade union policy of the communists and their anti-Congress activists and the general dementia in the Labour perception of India under a weak and compromising leadership were viewed by the National government as definite symptoms of the end of the Congress resistance and the inauguration of a period of rejuvenated *Raj.*[9]

And yet there were signs of a new breakthrough in Indian politics. Since the days of Gandhi's fast preceding the Poona Pact in 1932, Jawaharlal Nehru, then incarcerated in Dehra Dun jail, had been at a loss to comprehend Gandhi's mind and to grasp the intricacies of his moves.[10] Nehru was alive to the demands of the anti-imperialist struggle. He was also conscious of the limitations of Congress as a conglomeration of various shades of opinion and its innate inclination in favour of compromise and consensus.[11] But, over time, as a result of a good deal of internal debate, soul searching and extensive public discussion the objective of *purna swaraj* outlined in Lahore and the programme sketched in the Fundamental Rights in Karachi had been internalized by the political culture of the Congress, notwithstanding strong reservations jealously guarded by its fairly compact body of right-wing.[12] Peasant movements were rife all over, especially in the United Provinces, Bihar and Bengal,[13] restlessness of the working class was noticeable[14] and the long and languid trial of the Meerut poisoners ended in severe judicial indictments.[15] The interests of the native princes had been successfully projected by the *Raj* to redress the balance of the imperial system then being upset by the disturbing aspirations of democratic forces.[16] Communal disharmony between the Hindus and the Muslims had been sharpened since the RTC days: the Mahasabha placed its Hindu card unambiguously on the constitutional table and in India's political vocabulary, Vinayak Damodar Savarkar's *Hindutva: Who is a Hindu?* (1923) was being read by some enthusiastically,[17] the *suddhi* and *sangathan* and the *tabligh* and *tanzim* movements had been stimulating communal consciousness leading to recurring riots,[18] B.S. Moonje and militant Hindu leaders sought salvation of a Hindu *swarajya* in the ideology and organization of Mussolini's fascism.[19] A vibrant section of untouchables/*dalits* under Ambedkar got a glimpse of its separate destiny outside the Congress; the Muslim League, had been assessing the importance of mass following and communal consolidation.[20] In short, political life in India had become complex, polyphagous and, at places, quite murky. Some issues got clearly focussed, some others became somewhat fuzzy, while a sizeable section of the Congress found itself crying aloud for a definite social orientation.[21] Even Gandhi concentrated increasingly on social affairs, identifying himself with India's landless peasantry and preaching and writing on rural sanitation, nutrition and health.[22] Within the Congress, Marxism and class analysis became a point of departure for a substantial section of young political activists. Socialism coloured their vision. To them the charisma of Gandhi and his hold over the masses remained attractive, though his social philosophy appeared archaic and his economic propositions conservative and retrogressive. His natural proclivity towards compromise and adjustments tended to present him in their eyes as a credible prop to social reaction. However, on the basis of some marked demonstrations it was judged by quite a few reasonably sound political observers that Gandhi's popularity and his immense hold over the masses continued to be very nearly the same as before. Though there might be perhaps an apathy on the part of the people to make sacrifices for the cause of political emancipation, but for many the effort for the removal of untouchability was equally great. It appeared to many others that in the course of his campaign against untouchability, the mission of the Mahatma's life was going to be fulfilled. He had been carrying on with his work despite great stress. It was so despite a superficial assessment assiduously circulated by the intelligence department that Gandhi was surrounded by sycophants and oddballs and had been persuing an eccentric agenda.[23] It was amazing to watch that even Sapru and Jayakar joined in the chorus of praise for Gandhi exhibiting, as Menon put it, an 'unparalleled' shamefacedness.[24]

Evidently, no one could dismiss Gandhi. He was honest, unambiguous and close to the helpless downtrodden and social underclass. He practised what he preached. He was a shrewd tactician and a simple, but articulate, communicator. He was intensely patriotic and was firm in his convictions. In June 1934, Gandhi rebuffed Moonje for his invitation to join the Hindu Sabha. 'As to my joining the Hindu Sabha,' Gandhi wrote curtly, 'I am sure you are joking.'[25] There were many others in the Sabha such as Bhai Paramanand who thought the Congress was composed of persons who were 'enemies of the Hindus and much more dangerous than others for the reason that they are Hindus.'[26] Gandhi, 'the soul of the Congress', and his followers did not care, Paramanand declared, 'a bit whether Hindus live or die'[27] and the Mahasabha could not afford to function 'as a hand maid of Gandhi and the Congress.'[28] The Poona Pact was condemned as 'the very negation of nationalism' and it was apprehended that Gandhi's *swarajya* could rise only on the ashes of Hindu community.[29] The socialists on the other end of the Congress spectrum sought to scan, scrutinize and impugn the Mahatma and his-ism but with the exception of a few they did not consider it wise to disown him.[30] These angry young men and women found in Jawaharlal a reluctant leader, one who inspired them but one who inexplicably declined to lead them. In his splendid isolation, Jawaharlal's restless spirit conceptualized a socialist vision for India as an integrated and vibrant member of the world community in sympathy with the toiling millions of the colonial world and the underdogs of the advanced economies struggling for human dignity, social justice and democratic participation in political and economic processes and upholding social relations based on modern scientific perceptions and sensibilities.[31]

Dinkar Mehta, young Congress activist of Surat, had met Nehru at the Gujarat Vidyapith at Ahmedabad and listened carefully to Nehru's illuminating talk on the conditions of socialism in India along with some young activists.[32] For them socialism had become a compulsive ideological attraction. Economic clarity had been rapidly drawing upon their perception and they began to understand the basic class character of the social structure. They realized that the feudal and the capitalist elements of the society were conscious of their class integrity and were better equipped than others to comprehend the need for coherent and collective action. Evidently, the question of all questions before the rebellious generation was whether the Congress, then standing expectantly at the crossroad, should be led by the masses or by the classes. They were aware that in many western countries, reformist politics following misguided paths had led to dictatorships of various forms. Even the prospects of British democracy were darkened by the shadow of fascism.[33] The new generation of nationalists read and heard Ben Bradley, Jawaharlal Nehru and Henry Noel Brailsford. They had been reading the *Modern Review,* the *Hindu,* the *Living Age,* the *New Statesman,* the *New Leader* and the like. They had been following closely the Soviet developments and the informative 'London Letters' of Krishna Menon, James Marley, Krishna Shelvankar and Konni Zilliacus. They were intellectually drawn to new ideas. They became conscious of the significance of revolutionary social transformation and the urgency of liberal sensitivity and were committed to pluralist social and political perceptions amidst the mind-boggling Indian diversities. They were convinced that all countries were not similarly placed while life, perceptions and sensibilities were somewhat historically conditioned. They made it loud and clear that the future trend of the Congress and the nationalist movement was to be socialistic and nothing else. Under the existing circumstances caution might be necessary and yet clarity and speed should not be sacrificed for circumspection. The vastness and diversity of the country were extraordinary and it was clear that perception of reality would vary from place to place in an uneven social canvas as what was applicable to UP might not be suitable to Gujarat.[34] Pluralism was essential for the growth of unity and socialism in India but it must be allowed to develop and should not be impeded by dubious sentiments and a regressive historical backlog. Socialist propaganda should aim at the dissemination of its ideology and, along with it, it must help foster a definite line of action.

Menon learnt that Nehru was alive to the problems and questions of this *generation curieux*. 'I quite agree with you', Nehru wrote in response to the young Dinkar Mehta's probing literary reconnaissance, 'that the future trend of the Congress must be socialistic. Not only the trend but the actions also.' Apart from ideology, the spread of which was essential, 'right action, if it is of a revolutionary nature, inevitably releases mass forces.'[35] In a bid to clarify the objective conditions for India's struggle for socialism, he brought up the case of Soviet revolution. Unlike pre-revolutionary Russia, he wrote, power in India was not concentrated in the hands of an effete aristocratic group in a few headquarters having a strong and organized working class capable of influencing events effectively and even subvert and upturn the system of governance. There were no concentrated centres of power and industry such as Moscow and Petrograd had been.

Power in India, Nehru argued, was not focussed in a few centres but was effectively diffused all over the country, so that in India one was to contend with a significantly mighty imperial opponent with strong military and administrative command, having its source of strength in various advanced international outposts and armed with an enormous striking power.[36] Besides, in 1917 Russia had witnessed a set of unusual circumstances which overwhelmed the Romanovs and these contingencies could not ever be repeated.[37] In a letter to Charles Mascarenas, Nehru maintained that he was conscious of the growing social awareness of the Indian intelligentsia, its grasp and competence and he wrote primarily for their observation a series of articles expressing his views on the international situation and conditions of socialism which were republished in a volume entitled *Whither India*? (October 1933).[38] Basically he was keen to see Congress activists concern themselves with the peasantry and the working class and evolve a distinct Indian path to socialism. In Indian conditions, he thought, it required patience, sincerity and a rational scientific outlook.[39] The Karachi resolution might have been inadequate in its formulations, but it was not, as had been dubbed by some, an exercise in deception. On the contrary, it recognized the urgency of an economic policy for the Congress and prepared a background for the evolution of a sensitive policy with socialistic bearings and elan.[40]

It seemed to many that there was a steady decline in Gandhi's ideological leadership. Even as early as 1931 Vijayalakshmi Pundit had been constrained to write: 'I must confess the Gandhi-Irwin agreement came as a shock to me. I have no faith in it. I mean to say this does not seem to be the road to India's freedom. After the tremendous effort the country put forward last year it seems to me in the nature of a betrayal of the Indian masses, but it is not for me to criticise the Mahatma. As a humble soldier of the Congress I must abide by whatever that great body decides.'[41] Gandhi's concern for social stability, compromise, inner soul and support for 'reactionary' social forces were being questioned. In contrast, a firm commitment to democracy, scientific outlook and significant changes in India's social system constituted the salient features of Nehru's attractive vision. Nehru argued convincingly that the basic outlook and ideology and the scientific interpretation of history in Marxism must be adjusted to the requirements of Indian conditions.[42] Evidently, both in terms of ideology and short-term strategy, the Congress should have nothing to do with communal consolidation. The majority community had a democratic responsibility, Nehru seemed to suggest, to assuage the apprehensions of the minority, especially in that remarkable world of a composite culture. Anti-imperialist struggle must be dovetailed to a stout opposition to feudal forces and exploitation of the peasants and workers so as to buttress the democratic movement and its thrust towards socialism. In Nehru's perception the Indian National Congress was a vibrant movement of diverse elements and his idea was to strengthen the Congress for socialist action and not to weaken it with various parallel organizations.[43]

In a letter to Dinkar Mehta, by then one of Menon's regular correspondents from India, Nehru affirmed that he had already given the publication rights of the volume to a concern in Allahabad for its Hindi and Urdu versions and, a little later, probably in Bengali and Marathi editions and if Mehta cared to bring it out in Gujarati, he might as well find himself free to do so.[44] Nehru also confided that it was his desire to write a few more articles partly in answer to some of the criticisms and also to continue the argument.[45] Nehru was not enthused by the tenor of the criticisms. He thought that they were basically trivial and casual. On the one side, the purely nationalist criticism failed to appreciate the pith of the argument, while from the vantage point of the left, Nehru was reprimanded for not going to the logical conclusion of the socialist perspective and for having sidetracked the implication of his own conviction and line of analysis. Nehru was somewhat baffled for he felt that he was being reproached for the contradictions in Indian life.[46] As a pragmatic politician he thought it necessary to emphasize that his target audience was not very mature and almost totally unaware of socialist analysis and ideas. He had to carry that audience with him and not merely to make a brave show.[47] Nehru held that much of his so-called inconsistencies and diffidence emanated from the fact that he had to function as the general secretary of the Congress Party and in that capacity he could have, at most, expressed opinions which were in consonance with Congress resolutions.

Nehru was convinced that the future of the Congress party, its organization and hegemony constituted his principal social and political concern and it was imperative to go along with it. It might be assumed, he argued, that in due course the accumulation and maturity of socialist ideas and propaganda might initiate a schism in the Congress movement and the situation might then be tackled accordingly. But, because of that hypothetical eventuality, Nehru saw no reason why he should insulate himself from the Congress and 'leave the organization which has so much influence over people's minds in India to other people with reactionary outlook.'[48] Nehru had already attracted the attention of the Mahasabha for his radical pronouncements. He was castigated for being carried away 'by impulses aroused by the study of dogmas and doctrines derived from books written under circumstances which are very little in common with the conditions that obtain in this country.'[49] Nehru was upbraided for his 'juvenile exuberance in communism', and his irresponsible 'command performance' against the Mahasabha. Characterized as the 'spoilt child of Mahatma Gandhi',[50] Jawaharlal was admonished for living 'in a world of dreams' and believing that the Hindu masses would care to take his advice in preference to that of the Mahasabha.[51]

Nehru's uncompromising views on the Congress's role, his engagement with *purna swaraj* and his affiliation to socialism together with the general perception of Nehru as the inevitable successor of the Mahatma caused a good deal of flutter in the official and unofficial European circles, both in India and England. It was considered essential to ascertain Nehru's attitude with regard to the British interests in India and his perception of the destiny of the Congress and finally, to garner his support, if possible, for a dialogue over some of the issues around the question of the possible secession of British connection. H. K. Hales MP for Hanley and British manufacturers' representative in India, Ceylon and Burma, Federated Malay states and Dutch East Indies was encouraged to make an effort to initiate the discussion.[52] Hales, as many others, was apprehensive of the policy that might be pursued by the Congress in the near future under Nehru's leadership. In particular, Nehru's avowed programme of snapping the British connection and of economic freedom gave Hales a sufficient cause for alarm. This design, he maintained, stood in sharp contrast to the salient features of the arguments of those leading luminaries of India whom he had been meeting over the past two years or so in London in the context of the prolonged conferences and enquiries on India.[53]

A successful policy of the Congress, Hales wrote to Nehru, must be based on love and conciliation and not hatred. A policy, which had for his object the severance of India from the British empire, would bring in its trains complete disaster upon England, the empire and India. It would mean a mortal blow to all the partners of the empire. It was, he counselled, a moment of creative statesmanship and certainly not for mercurial sentimentality and vindictive destruction.[54] Mutual understanding and fellow feeling should be the maxim in place of contempt and enmity. In response to Nehru's firm resolution against all adjustments and short-term compromises and his fierce opposition to the prospect of an uneven patron-client relationship, Hales argued that the programme as regards the severance of India from Britain would under no circumstances be 'eventual in your lifetime' and by following Nehru's line of reasoning, India would be placed in a position of dangerous insecurity.[55] Hales was convinced that the white paper was evidently unwelcome to every community in India and the select committee had been unable to acquaint itself with the opinion of India as a whole. Hales was, therefore, toying with the idea of an informal round table discussion with Sastri, Gandhi, Malaviya, Shaukat Ali, Nehru and some others at a suitable place in India so that on his return to England he would be able to place before the House of Commons durable and constructive points of view of some eminent Indian leaders of 'conflicting communities and interest.'[56]

In another letter Hales confessed his inability to appreciate Nehru's vehemence against the British connection which seemed to him materially different and diametrically opposed to the opinion of the majority of Indian leaders. He urged Nehru to appreciate that, in fullness of time, the mantle of Gandhi with all its grave responsibilities would fall on his shoulder as a leader of the Congress. But he felt unhappy as he was compelled to prognosticate that by pursuing an acrimonious policy Nehru would merely split the organization and as a hopeless minority his group would in the end gradually disperse from sheer inanition.[57] H.S.L. Polak in common with many others in the Labour Party was inclined to view that Jawaharlal's advent in politics would have a positive advantage. Polak felt that it would remove the 'veil of Gandhi's humbug' that had 'hitherto helped to conceal wide and fundamental differences among divergent parties and groups within the Congress itself.' Polak was keen to emphasize that one ought to realize 'in recognising both Jawaharlal's sincerity and ruthlessness' that he was partly a 'creature of circumstances' and partly a 'theorist' who for years had been withdrawn from the trials of public life and thus forced to brood upon all kinds of injustices and injuries. 'Egocentricity', Polak added, 'is an almost a natural result of long confinement and withdrawal from affairs.'[58] Official uneasiness was heightened by intelligence reports on Nehru's confabulations with Indian revolutionaries operating from various centres in Europe and his almost uninterrupted link with the international Communist movement.[59] Hales hailed Nehru for his rare, urbane sensibilities and recommended that 'in the interests of every community of India'[60] Nehru should take care to modulate his extreme views and learn the urgency of moderation, lenity and cooperation with other political opinions and, of course, with the British parliament.[61] Nehru would not have it. But, more intriguing than his 'reckless audacity', was the staggering fact that the restive generation of younger nationalists affirmed more than once its unflinching confidence in Jawaharlal.[62]

In 1933, Premchand's *Godan* was yet to be published. Saratchandra's *Pather Dabi* (1926) had already made a splash in the world of letters. S. V. Ketkar's *Brahmo Kanya* (1930) had challenged orthodoxy, caste, status and *shastras* in defence of humanity. Bibhutibhushan Bandopadhyaya's *Pather Panchali* (1929) mingled both playful innocence and earthy emanation with scarcity and hunger of rural Bengal and juxtaposed them besides the creeping commercialization that almost stood stupefied in the face of the tenderness of nature. Tarashankar and Manik Bandyopadhyaya were to bring before long their sensitivity to poverty, hunger and fear of the underdog in a sprawling Bengali society. In Assam with Dinanath Kalita's *Sadhana* (1929) and Daivachandra Talukdar's *Apurna* (1931), the stoic Gandhian hero of contemporary life entered the field. The intense realism of Premchand had merged in Nanak Singh's *Fauladi Phul* (1935) and *Kagtan Di Beri* (1936) amidst the lively sensation of a resurgent Punjabi poetry steeped in self-awareness and humanism; psychological overtones entered in the world of the Gujarati writers such as Suresh Joshi and then Manubhai Panchali who were conscious of the crisis in convictions amidst the cross-currents of changing social values. Kalindi Charan Panigrahi was prepared to treat intimately the land and people of Orissa in *Matira Manisa* (1934), Hare Krushna Mahtab made the resurgent village the epicentre of his social movement in *Pratibha* (1922), while Ramprasad captured the determination of a struggling people during the salt *Satyagraha* in *Pujara Bali* (1930). By then, in Tamil Nadu, Ramatirtha Thammal had created a stir in the conservative society with her *Mohana Rajani* (1931) projecting a sharp tract on social experience, while K. S. Venkataramani's *Deshbhakta Kundan* (1932) offered political struggle as an exclusive theme of creative writing.[63] Premchand carried the day with his realism depicting the men, manners and ethos of colonial India and dissecting the declining rural social structure like a literary surgeon endowed with profound sympathy for the dead, the living and the resurgent. Jainendra and Ilachandra Joshi were not left far behind. The interest of the Indian intelligentsia was focussed on a new and satisfying space for exploration and analysis. The value system of regulated stability was compelled to share the literary platform with the fresh and challenging norms of relativity, changing perspectives, comparative societal modules and the stern and naked realities of existence. Conciliation and the inevitability of gradualness took, for a while, a back seat in the *avant-garde* creative writing.[64]

Purna swaraj and the statement on Fundamental Rights appeared to them remarkably bold steps towards the right direction. Violation of the salt law at an obscure sea-shore in Western India was a momentous decision: Dandi released a dynamic historical force that overwhelmed Irwin and his administration.[65] Already Iqbal, Aziz Lakhnavi, Hasrat Mohani, Kazi Nazrul Islam, Ramakrishna Pillai, Veerappa, Ghulam Hussain, Premchand and Tarashankar had been drawn to social realism however romantic that attraction might have been.[66] The Communist Party had been formed; socialism was being talked about and it inspired a good deal of inspiring debate[67]; the Meerut Conspiracy case had become a national point of reference.[68] Official terrorism went ahead unconcerned with popular opposition.[69] Sajjad Zaheer and Sophia Wadia had taken the preliminary steps towards the formation of the Progressive Writers' Association; Zaheer's *Angare* (1932) encapsulated the spirit of social resistance to empty values and their concrete authoritarian institutions; Nazrul Islam's concern for a plural society, a set of rational values, the end of imperialism and his vision for a sustained endeavour for social justice found explicit articulation in the publication of the journal, *Langol* (1925) and then in its invigorated incarnation, *Ganabani* (1926).[70] Social scientists such as Hiren Mukherji and Shushobhan Sarkar sought to place the Russian revolution and World War I in perspective and indicated the emergence of masses as the triumphant hero in modern Indian history under the direction of a half-naked frail man leading them on to a promised land of the future.[71] There was the slow, but confident, genesis of a *dalit* literature and the formation of the Congress Socialist Party in early 1934 gave a formal political shape to the new intellectual awareness and emotional resurgence for freedom and equality.[72] India seemed to have actualized in its stimulating literary output the aspiration to find a place in the modern world. Gandhi continued to remain the dominant personage, but popular attention was also focussed on Ramprasad Bismil, Bhagat Singh,

Chandrashekhar Azad, Surya Sen, Bagha Jatin and many others.[73] Congress was the national platform: but one could not pass over the Congress Socialist Party, the Communist Party and the Hindustan Socialist Republican Association. Anti-imperialism was the motivator of political and social action but the ideal of socialist transformation turned out to be, in the perception of many, the condition precedent of *purna swaraj*. Organization of the expropriated mute peasantry had become the principal occupation of a fairly sizeable body of thinking intelligentsia, not as a generous gesture but as a social obligation fashioned by a committed outlook.[74]

Parichaya, a Bengali monthly, appeared in 1933. Almost instantaneously it began to articulate the new awareness and soon developed into the *Left Review* of Bengal. And then on, it engaged itself endlessly in debates and discussions on left literary theory: if scholarship and literature were instruments of propaganda, if all art was class art, if bourgeois education promoted the ideology of the ruling class, if literature could be appreciated only in terms of social reality, if realism was closely related to class struggle, if literature was invariably to become a school teacher, if the social commitment of the writer was actualized in his prose, if the relationship between fine arts and social formation, poetry, emotions and class struggle should be integrated, if the dialectical unity between form and content should be closely examined, if the distinction between literary sentimentalism and poetry of commitment, the urgency of historical perspective, the need to grapple with and assimilate reality and so and so forth should necessarily constitute the concern of the literary theory. Despite incompleteness, weakness, incongruities and even juvenile eccentricities, there was an overpowering excitement in projecting all human endeavours in a single vision.[75] Rabindranath Tagore stood apart as an indulgent patron and, at times, even participated in the discussion. Some of its leading luminaries drifted away before long, but *Parichaya* created an *environs vivant.*[76] There developed a remarkable interaction between various creative writers of Indian literature and a lively reception of the literary theories of the West. Readership grew. Many of the protagonists of that literary restlessness had been in England for higher education and nearly all of them had been the League's part-time unpaid volunteers. Menon, in London, had been a perspicuous observer of men, events and processes of Indian life.[77]

By then, the underlying assumption of the National government appeared to Menon and the League very dangerous and disturbing. To many discreet observers, the continuation of the coalition had become 'a sort of conspiracy against representative government.'[78] It meant, to all intents and purposes, a collection of men who avoided both the exploration of their own differences and the effective consultation of the electorate 'lest the result be their loss of power.' The so-called 'national' unity, Laski was categorical, was built upon the acceptance of phrases rather than their critical evaluation.[79] It appeared that the principal intention of the National government had been to adopt measures to keep itself in power since it could not adopt measures on coherent principles. The National government had been consistently following an opportunistic policy. It was for the League of Nations, so long as it was not expected to stand by the principles of the Covenant. It was for disarmament, so long as it was understood that it was not necessary to be emphatic at Geneva. Although it asserted the absurdity of economic nationalism, it did not hesitate to adopt a policy of protection. It drastically reduced wages, avoided all significant advances in education, public health and housing and followed an insensitive strong arm policy towards India. In fact, in the entire tenor of the outlook of the National government one could merely see the typical indica of a normal Tory policy.[80] It appeared that the fusion of the Conservative Party with its partners was complete.

MacDonald had been using his majority to consolidate 'the citadel of old order' and to consider the opposition with utter contempt because of its small numerical parliamentary strength. The left-wing of the Labour Party felt free to go for a systematic scrutiny of the National government. By then, Harold Laski, Stafford Cripps, Aneurin Bevan and Kingsley Martin had become the ideologues of an uncompromising opposition to MacDonald who, they maintained, borrowed Baldwin's majority to carry on the government of the country to ensure that 'no shadow of his former conviction shall appear in the legislation for which he is responsible.'[81] His success in that endeavour meant his willingness to overlook the fallout of Japan's victory in Manchuria, the failure of the World Economic Conference, the breakdown of the process of disarmament, the withdrawal from social reform, continued operation of the means tests, the growing hostility to free speech and the policy of unalloyed repression in India. It was, the Left Labour felt, an organized hypocrisy and a denial of democratic foundation of the political fabric that echoed the suppression of basic human rights in Hitler's Germany.

In fact, so far as India was concerned, the National government had, by then, virtually closed its ranks. George Lansbury, gentle Labour leader, confided to Bhulabhai Desai, a distinguished jurist, that the government had convinced itself that its policy towards India was rational and just and that it had overcome Indian resistance completely. To all suggestions for conciliation, friendliness and corporation, the government's answer was straightforward: they knew their business and all these suggestions constituted a concerted but futile interference by infantile sentimentalists in high politics. Lansbury felt that the Indian perception of the situation was not being properly focussed and, as a result, it had become difficult for some of the Labour MPs to project a line of action forcefully for they believed in the Indian people managing their affairs in their own way.[82] They were at a loss to know what line to take since some of the Indians themselves had passed on to the government the impression that either they were satisfied with the RTC proposals or that the constitution would be acceptable if framed on the proposed lines. It appeared to Lansbury that the government would laugh at his suggestions for a meaningful self-determination for India saying that he was being more royalist than the King and more Indian than the Indians themselves. An authoritative expression of opinion in India was, therefore, indispensable. Otherwise, it would be officially asserted that the country was satisfied with the white paper proposals 'which all of us who know India realize is not the case.'[83] Bhulabhai Desai had made it clear that even the right-wing Congressmen would not accept the white paper constitution and many liberals such as C.Y. Chintamini and Chimanlal Setalvad, who had opposed civil disobedience, were equally critical of government proposals.[84]

The *Manchester Guardian* developed grave doubts whether the white paper scheme retained any interest for India. The *Guardian* made it plain enough that India had won nothing of substance under the scheme and her future was largely a gamble. Most of the Indian contingent, Menon wrote, endorsed the opinion that there was no desire either to minimize the difficulty or to exaggerate the progress. Over the preceding many months, the contingent was tired of being told, day in and day out, that the well-guarded secrets of government, the mystique of British rule and a well-ordered administration would be vitiated by the advent of the Indian ministers. That process of Indianization was an evil phenomenon - far-reaching in character and reprehensible in its nature.

Lansbury was keen that the Congress, in its full session, should put forward the demands to make it known that the country was far from reconciled to the government's policy and its assent had still to be obtained. Lansbury asserted that

India should make her own constitution. 'If it were possible, for the Congress', Lansbury added, 'to draw up an agreed formula in which some connection with Britain, as under the Statute of Westminster, were incorporated, it may prove a useful alternative to the Government's constitution.'[85] Lansbury was apprehensive if it was feasible. He knew that the younger generation of Indians would not agree. But, as a socialist, he would have welcomed any settlement in which more nations could cooperate as free partners and he wanted to see it extended to the whole world. But it was India who must decide its own future. Lansbury felt that since civil disobedience was no longer practised, the government would not venture to suppress a Congress meeting. He also maintained that there was not even the remotest indication that Gandhi might be re-arrested as he was not any longer officially perceived as harmful. Lansbury was dismayed to observe that there was hardly any statesman on the British side who could be persuaded to brush aside the die-hards altogether, in order to strike a permanent or lasting solution out of the existing embittered situation.[86] He had heard that very strong pressure from Friends had been brought to bear on Gandhi to give up political work and to concentrate on untouchability. But Lansbury was firm in his conviction that Gandhi was a great name and a unifying political and moral power and the political withdrawal of the Mahatma, would be unfortunate for India. He earnestly hoped that probably it was just a change of tactics or a strategic retreat on the part of Gandhi primarily to enable the Congress to proceed from a different position for a time.[87]

In keeping with his firm conviction Lansbury prepared a rough draft of a statement on behalf of the Labour Party in March 1933. Evidently, the draft was formulated in consultation with Menon. It stressed that full responsible self-government for India had been declared by every political party as its goal. There were differences of opinion as to the rate at which progress towards that end could be made. Lansbury felt that the Labour Party should believe that nothing should be left undone to make that progress as rapid as possible in close cooperation with Indians. This, he added, had been promised to India by Great Britain over the years. The reform proposals, by no stretch of imagination, Lansbury argued, offered a responsible self-government. It was hedged about on every side with safeguards and emergency powers 'which undoubtedly do prejudice the advance of India through the new Constitution to full responsibility for her own government.' Unfortunately, the proposed authoritarian constitution did not contain even the necessary provision of its own development. It is difficult to overlook that the draft internalized, in a large measure, the position of the India League.[88]

The advisory committee on imperial questions of the Labour Party, however, had other ideas. Its perspective was at variance with Lansbury's liberal disposition. That specialized committee of the party decided in its wisdom to overlook Lansbury's liberal prescription and, instead, sought to examine the *modus operandi* of Gandhi's non-violent revolutionary technique and its implications for the stability of the Indian empire.

In a closely argued memorandum prepared by John Maynard, the committee sought to assess the intricacies of Gandhi's movements.[89] Maynard thought that Gandhi's plan was to put the government in such a position that it was compelled to defend law and order by repression: the abuse and excesses which would be committed in the process would inevitably alienate the potential cooperator. The counter-plan of the government was the achievement of a *modus vivendi* such as the Gandhi-Irwin Pact. That, Maynard wrote, 'spoilt the game.' During Gandhi's absence, the memorandum continued, his more irreconcilable lieutenants got to work on restoring the lost advantage and found their chance mainly in the agrarian situation. The Hoare-Willingdon combination ran straight into that trap. The advisory committee did not think that the government could altogether have escaped the necessity of exceptional actions in meeting Gandhi's challenge. Terrorist outrages in Bengal were the necessary fallout of non-violent revolutionary technique and they called for harsh official response. It was believed that even the no-rent campaign in the United Provinces would not have been dealt with by the ordinary law. It was affirmed that the Labour Party in opposition should not, at any rate, condemn all legislations by ordinance.[90] The committee avowed that the ordinance rule was several degrees better than any martial law administration and the refusal to apply extraordinary legal powers in difficult and exacting times might have led to something worse. In support of this contention, it was held that even Hari Singh Gaur's vote of censure in the legislative assembly on 1 February 1932 did not demand the repeal of the ordinances, although it complained of the harshness of their administration. It was recalled that the Labour government itself found it necessary to resort to ordinances when 'Gandhi self-making campaign set Civil Disobedience going in 1930.' It was certain, the memorandum asserted, that even a Labour government could not possibly withdraw all exceptional laws. It would be undesirable, the committee cautioned, to convey the impression that it believed that the acceptance of Congress demands would solve the Indian problem. This was as complete a fallacy as was Samuel Hoare's conception of the Congress as 'dogs who bark while the caravan passes along.'[91] The Labour committee conceded that the Congress was the largest and the best organized body in India and that it enjoyed enormous advantages of its association with Gandhi's name. Besides, the party had been fortified in public regard by the hammer- and-tongs working of the ordinances. It was, however, added that the princes, the large landholders, five-sixth of the Muslim population, a large proportion of those 'who have a low place in the Hindu hierarchy of castes' and the bulk of the rural population regarded the Congress with feelings that ranged 'from hostility to indifference.'[92] Against the background of such a inflexible perception of Indian situation and Gandhi's *satyagraha,* the Labour Party's specialized committee on India concluded that no solution of the constitutional problem was feasible without efficacious application of experience and judgement. A solution of the tangled problem could be arrived at only after a patient examination and analysis of the antagonistic social forces of a vast continent having diverse historical contradictions. Its intention must be to arrive at the greatest common measure of agreement between the conflicting network of interest. The Labour Party was persuaded to take the position that a sincere attempt to strike an agreement had begun in the sessions of the RTCI, supplemented by a provisional settlement by the government, for the purpose of working out the new constitutional statute and franchise rules of the communal difference. It was also maintained that after Gandhi had landed in Bombay from his visit to the RTC, the extremist elements of the Congress avowed that Gandhi's attitude in the RTC was hardly consistent with the spirit of the Congress mandate and the RTC's decision completely ignored Congress demands. The Labour Party concluded that the extremist section of the Congress had been pressing for the impossibles and its obduracy threatened to terminate the credibility of Gandhi as a 'potential mediator and co-operator.'[93] The Committee, however, realized that despite his diminished political capacity and credibility, Gandhi's word was still 'law with the Indian masses.' The Labour Party thus thought it prudent to reproach Willingdon for throwing away 'that potential instrument of peace' and for alienating the 'political cooperators, the great Moderates'. The very large and ill-defined powers conferred by the ordinances stimulated the administration to opt for harsh and reckless interpretations in the use of exceptional powers. The Labour Party was urged to assert that firm administration created an eerie atmosphere of consternation and despair in the face of an indefinite renewal of ordinances. Even people committed to the ordinances began 'to ask themselves uneasily where they are really leading?'[94] The Labour Party was encouraged to affirm that while it was necessary to take action in certain cases, it was clear that excessive powers had been used to imprison many Indian critics, many of whom alone could cooperate with the government in the formation of a federal constitution. The ordinances should be extended to certain areas where the ordinary machinery of administration had broken down and even in those areas it might have been possible to forego a number of emergency powers which had proved to be unnecessary and even provocative. In any case, the Labour Party was prodded to state boldly that if the viceroy could not descend to negotiate with Gandhi, he could perhaps negotiate with Sapru by way of a stepping stone to something new.[95]

Evidently, the Labour Party's response to the Indian situation was tardy and hesitant. The party was more than uncertain of itself. Its left wing felt that a rational response to India's demand for self-determination would release a gusty wind of change. The political map of Asia and Africa, as a consequence, would witness an unprecedented whirlpool. This extrovert, but numerically and politically insignificant left wing, looked forward to associate itself with the growing national movement in India for the expansion of human freedom. But, although the appeal of Indian nationalism was compelling, the right wing of the party could carry with it an overwhelmingly large body of rank and file to its own perception that it was necessary for the good of humanity to restrain the forces of nationalism in India with a powerful garrison to keep it down.[96]

Thus in March 1933, Graham Pole examined, in a comprehensive memorandum on the white paper, the areas where the Labour Party could find a space for itself in the ongoing debate in the parliament.[97] It was observed that the white paper did not envisage a responsible self-government. Pole felt that the object of Ramsay MacDonald's white paper of 1 December 1931 had been a 'responsible government, qualified during a period of transition, by limitations in certain directions.' Pole added that during the RTC II, MacDonald repeated that the reservations and safeguards were meant for a transitional period. In the document under review, Pole stated that there was no period of transition and there was also no mention of a statutory period. Since there was no provision for the responsibility automatically passing gradually into the hands of Indians, the white paper proposals would be bound to produce the maximum agitation from the very start. It was believed that by refusing Indians real responsibility, the proposals would provoke irresponsible talk and violent action. Besides, in view of the undefined status of India, the extensive reserved powers of the governor-general and his 'special responsibilities' together with his authority to make sweeping ordinances, the British hold on India would be absolutely 'iron and rigid.' By May 1934, in the context of the discussions in the JSC, the advisory committee on imperial questions desired to call the attention of the Labour executive committee to the grave situation in India. It felt that two things were especially regrettable. The first feature was that the great position of the Labour Party in the eyes of political India during the RTC I was in danger of being altogether lost. The second feature of the then political situation was that there was no powerful political body in England which stood for a position significantly advanced than of the white paper. Besides, since there was a sizeable element in the Labour Party which was committed to leave the question alone until the report of the JSC was issued, a large body of public opinion was being persuaded to commit itself to the die-hard view which was 'entirely hostile to Indian aspirations.'[98] The Labour advisory committee believed that as a result of the concerted political compulsions, it appeared that there was only one cleavage of opinion between those who supported the white paper with its very modest instalment of self-government and those who supported 'the die-hard view', which was entirely hostile to Indian aspirations'. It was, therefore, felt necessary that since the party held neither of the two views, the Labour Party should emphasize that it was pledged by its general policy to demand 'something far more advance than the White Paper'. This policy, the committee held, must be articulated in a clear and an ambiguous way. The idea should be to neutralize all misapprehensions in India. A condition of frustration and despair, it was added, would make the successful operation of any scheme impossible. It was therefore emphasized that it might be judicious and prudent to examine the documents by the Indians to the JSC. It was a memorandum by Tej Bahadur Sapru on behalf of himself and three colleagues.[99] The main points of the memorandum were entirely in accord with the Labour Party's ostensible policy. It was maintained that the Labour policy should stress that the reserve powers must not prejudice the advance of India to full responsibility, that the act should contain a definite statement that the natural issue of India's constitutional progress was the attainment of dominion status, that a definite date should be fixed for the inauguration of Federation, that the army should be Indianized within a definite limit, that the financial safeguards were excessive and must be toned down, that fears and apprehensions of the nationalist designs were exaggerated and might make the scheme inoperative, that the system of direct election should be retained for the lower federal chamber and that the department of law and order should be completely transferred to the provincial governments. Besides, it was to be stressed that the Indian legislatures should have the power to initiate proposals for constitutional changes. The advisory committee concluded that these proposals constituted the 'very minimum' that would suffice to garner the cooperation of the moderate sections of Indian political opinion. Without this minimum, the Labour committee tended to agree with Sapru that it would be impossible to find a sufficient body of men to work the scheme at all.[100] Labour policy, it was held with aplomb, should go further than the memorandum of Sapru and his associates. The Labour Party should insist on the whole question of franchise as vital to the new scheme. It maintained that the proposals gave an electorate unfairly weighted in favour of the rich as against the poor, men as against women, townsmen as against countrymen, landlords as against tenants, moneylenders as against ryots and factory-owners as against their workmen. It was decided that without holding out for complete adult suffrage, property and educational qualifications should be considered as temporary expedients only and the act should contain machinery for the extension of the franchise.[101] The Attlee draft was a diluted version of Pole's recommendations. The Labour Parliamentary Party moved at the third reading of the bill for the establishment of the constitution for India a resolution that declined to assent the bill because it did not 'contain the means for the realization of Dominion status, imposes undue restrictions on the exercise of self-government, fails to make adequate provision for the franchisement and representation of the workers, both men and women, and entrenches in the legislatures the forces of wealth, privilege and reaction.'[102] There was no reference to the principle of self-determination to which the party was officially committed.

Before very long, Menon had worked out the details of his asseveration on the much discussed dominion status for India. He emphasized that the dominion status as a practical solution to the problem of Indo-British relations depended essentially on three distinct determinants. He argued that India should be willing to accept such a solution, that the transition should be speedy and administratively workable and British statesmen must have the grit and courage to carry through such a policy and sufficiently large volume of instructed opinion should be mobilized by them and their parties to that end.[103] Menon felt that the first of these considerations entered little into the calculations of British politicians. But it was integral to any practical plan of a solution of the Indian problem. Evidently, dominion status evoked much less enthusiasm in India then than it had done ten years or even five years earlier. Menon argued that if the dominion status carried with it full implications of the Statute of Westminster, if the acceptance of such a solution and framing of the new constitution were left to self-determination by India through a constituent assembly elected on the basis of adult franchise and if India could be impressed by the bona fides of the offer, a new atmosphere might, in all probability, be created and India would respond prudently.[104]

Menon maintained that the process of transition to dominion status would present the minimum of difficulty if Indian civil servants were convinced beyond doubt that the home government meant business and would tolerate no obstruction or sabotage and the responsibility of meeting the difficulties — such as the problem of minorities — would then be faced by the Indians with firmness, conviction and realism. The preparation of British opinion for such a change was the function of the labour movement. Menon held firmly that imperialism and socialism were incompatible and urged the Labour Party to recognize that reality without any reservation. Such a perception should form, he added, a clearly distinguishable part of the Labour policy. This meant, that Labour's imperial policy must be so adjusted as to signify a clear break with the past and with that of other parties and not be just some benevolent modifications of the existing position. The principle of 'self-determination' was already the accepted basis of Labour's India policy. What was required was a strict adherence to that principle and taking of steps to implement it, when the party would move in power, by calling a constituent assembly in India which British authority in India alone had the competence to undertake. In opposition, the party should similarly insist on the adherence to the principle of self-determination and not willy-nilly be jockeyed into the acceptance of an alternative plan like that contained in the Attlee draft, which denied the very principle of self-determination and was entirely unacceptable to the Indian opinion.[105]

Menon was present at Hastings when in the winter of 1933-34 the Labour conference endorsed a comprehensive resolution on India moved by Rev. R.W. Sorensen (Leyton West D.L.P.). It condemned the policy of internments and imprisonments and protested against the government's repudiation of pledges that the new constitution would be negotiated and settled in consultation with the representatives of the Indian people. It reaffirmed the policy of self-determination and self-government for India and enjoined the party both in office and in opposition to work for a constitution for India based on the principles of equality, consultation, conference and agreement and in harmony with the national aspirations of the Indians. Among other things, it demanded the release of all prisoners including the Meerut detainees and implementation of the recommendations of the Whitley commission. Sorensen, Fred Hughes (National Union of Clerks) and Lansbury piloted the resolution through. Sorensen was warmly applauded when he asserted that imperialism in India was, in essence, no different from the operation of fascism in Germany and if democracy was on trial, the real test would come not so much in the Western world as in the Eastern world. 'It is in India', he claimed, 'that we who claim to be protectors of democracy will prove our sincerity.' There was, however, confusion as to the party's attitude towards the white paper and the JSC, its report and to the bill which would arise out of the report.[106] In view of the participation of the Labour Party in the JSP, as Wilfred Wellock (Stourbridge) pointed out at the annual conference (Southport 1934), Labour policy had been noticed for the absence of a definitive clarity as to whether the Labour Party would be committed to the findings of the JSC.[107]

As Attlee's assurance to abide by the previous year's resolution did not remove the doubt, Menon (Westminster Abbey) sought to get the party committed to the idea of a constituent assembly for India. By all reckonings, Menon's resolution was much better than the one proposed by Sorensen, but the executive of the party felt that his resolution should be withdrawn in view of the resolution of Sorensen and the positive assurances of Attlee, deputy leader of the parliamentary party.[108] Arthur Henderson, (secretary-treasurer) emphasized that the position held by the party and expounded by Attlee should satisfy everybody and the party leadership was not in a position to give any further undertaking.[109]

The simmering discontent developed into a skirmish at the Labour conference at Brighton in 1935.[110] The India bill had been placed on the table of the house and the issue at the Labour conference was the role of the Labour member in the deliberations of the JSC and it was occasioned by the presentation of a note by the Labour executive on the Indian constitutional reform. Moving a resolution to stand by the policy of self-determination and self-government and the establishment of a representative constituent assembly, Mrs Berry Fraser (London University Labour Party) affirmed that since 1933, events in the House of Commons did not inspire confidence in the sincerity of the parliamentary Labour Party which, it appeared, had not been faithfully following the proceedings of the annual conference.[111] Fraser maintained that the minority report produced by the four Labour members, known as the Attlee draft, was a very considerable improvement upon the government's own recommendation. The draft, however, fell far short of the party line. The Attlee draft, she maintained, advocated the same Conservative principle of veto and the only real improvement it sought to make upon the majority report was to try to set up provisions for adult suffrage in India.

The draft did not endeavour to work for self-determination. She argued that in the light of the Labour policy, the party was committed to the policy of self-determination which simply meant the setting up in India of a constitutional assembly to formulate its own administrative machinery.[112] The Attlee draft, the India League argued, was inconsistent with the Labour policy. Tony Greenwood (Westminster Labour Party) added that the resolution was indispensable because the Labour Parliamentary Party was indifferent to the fact that 'as Socialists we are convinced that the principles which are embodied in it are the principles for which we have got to stand.' He reminded the officials of the party that the Labour government would, in all probability, pursue an oppressive imperialist policy in India as it had over time internalized the *pukka sahib* tradition. He also reiterated that it was not the parliamentary Labour Party but the annual conference that should decide the Labour policy.[113] In India, he added, there was a growing and determined socialist movement, one third of the Congress Party were convinced socialists and it was the duty of the socialist movement in Britain to do everything 'we can to foster the growth of Socialism in India.'[114] There were others who warned that there was a serious danger of Labour leadership joining hands with those who were the enemies of the Indian people and that it was imperative to emphasize the urgency of a constituent assembly.

The official version of the Labour Party conference offered a diametrically different perspective. The left-wing movement within the party, according to Polak, was heavily defeated as had been expected. Polak reported that unexpecedly the whole affair was by and large a tame affair, especially in view of the long and detailed amendments put forward by the Socialist League. In a large measure, he reported gleefully, the League 'capitulated to the Party.' The Conference refused to reopen the Indian constitutional question upon the advice of Henderson in spite of Krishna Menon's appeal for the endorsement of an idea of a constitution devised by a constituent assembly in India. The only visible sign of success for the Socialist League was discipline, democratic principles and national interests.'[115]

Polak's assessment of the Conservative meet was equally interesting. In the Conservative conference, a good deal of discussion had taken place on Henry Page Croft's resolution. There had previously been a considerable exchange of correspondence between Page Croft and Baldwin on the question as to whether that was the last possible occasion for a representative Conservative body to consider the proposal before the Bill was introduced. Despite Baldwin's assurance, the resolution was put forward. A large number of people, Polak reported, voted for the resolution out of 'sheer muddle-headedness.' Polak felt that Page Croft's assumption that the majority of the Tory party were with him was very wide off the mark. On the contrary, his activities caused a great deal of resentment in the party. 'It is true', Polak wrote, 'that Baldwin is not going to have an easy time, but on the whole I think that he will win through.'[116]

Bhulabhai Desai was then one of the close associates of Menon in India in projecting the idea of the constituent assembly. Correspondence between Menon and Desai had been kept alive despite interception of letters by authorities, causing a good deal of irritation. On 4 May 1934, Menon had assured Desai that so far as the London end was concerned, he had been pursuing the basic policy agreed upon by the two of them during Desai's visit to England in the preceding winter. In a fairly informative letter, Menon sketched the steps engaged in by him in order to advocate the cause of a constituent assembly. The task of obtaining currency for the constituent assembly was necessarily slow having no spectacular effort, especially in the early stages of the campaign.[117] But that somewhat colourless proceeding was an essential prologue to the League's elaborate programme. Menon maintained that the League had gained the first ground. A resolution drafted in the League's office was scheduled to be on the agenda of the Socialist League conference in Whitsun. If Menon could rake in some money by then, he proposed to go to the conference himself and speak on the resolution and amplify its nuances. He was confident that the resolution would no doubt, be adopted in that conference.[118] All that had to be done through the proper channels within the movement. The second stage was also well advanced. A memorandum of the constituent assembly was then under preparation and it would closely correspond to the last section of the last chapter of the League's report on India. The delegates had made these suggestions while in India, both to Dr. Syed Mahamud and Malaviya. Menon confided that the memorandum would be signed by prominent Labour leaders and intellectuals and Laski would help sponsor it. Menon believed that it would be adopted by the League's executive very soon. He would, before long, send to Desai copies of the memorandum along with the proscribed report of the League, surreptitiously. The third step was to wait in deputation on the Labour executive and other useful organizations in order to press the idea. 'Our task now here is to make', Menon stressed, 'constituent assembly an accepted cliche.'[119] The total rejection of the white paper in India, Menon reiterated, was an immense help as it would enable the League to go all out on the attack and it had not come out a moment too early. Now that the movement had been taking an aggressive line from all fronts, Menon hoped that 'you will give us all possible assistance from your side.'[120] Ostensibly it might appear that things were hopeless with a terrific reactionary wave all over, but with the rejection of the white paper, the futility of the existing policy would assert itself and any party in power or in opposition would be obliged to take note of it. Menon was happy to see that all sections of the Congress appeared to be agreed on the idea of constituent assembly[121] — an idea which enjoyed the approval of Nehru whose consent had been secured before he was sent to jail.[122]

On 18 May 1934, Menon informed Laski that the memorandum had been adopted by the executive of the League and Grenfell signed it. In the absence of Laski, the executive was told that Laski had gone through the basis of the draft and agreed to sign it. A few verbal alterations were made partly as improvement in language and partly to clarify a few ambiguities. But no modifications in substance were made.[123] In his letters to Lansbury, Stafford Cripps, Brailsford, D.N. Pritt and others, Menon explained that the draft had been carefully considered by Laski. He took all precautions to avoid misunderstandings because most of the people whose signatures 'we want are not familiar with the problems and would probably want to have some assurances that the substance of it is all right.'[124] An element of urgency in the formation of the constituent assembly was carefully fused in the text so that the plan should not be procrastinated and, instead, be immediately taken over.[125]

Recommending the memorandum to Brailsford, for his signature, Menon emphasized that it had the approval and signature of Laski, Russell and Grenfell while the Swaraj party, 'the parliamentary wing of the Congress', adopted the demand for a constituent assembly as one of three main planks of its platform.[126] Brailsford was also informed that Jawaharlal Nehru, before his imprisonment, had approved the concept and in a letter to Menon, put the idea forward as the only solution of the Indian problem.[127] The Socialist group, formed inside the Congress, included the constituent assembly as one of the items of its programme. The League would endeavour to obtain its acceptance by the Labour Party as its policy in relation to India. Menon reiterated that a constituent assembly was the obvious method of implementing self-determination which was the accepted Labour policy.[128] In view of the comparative lack of knowledge of the Indian problem on the part of those whose signatures had to be obtained, the memorandum was made slightly longer than what was probably desirable but Menon could not quite help it.[129]

Contact with India, so consistently tampered by official agencies, was gradually being revived. Sachidananda Sinha from Patna was one of the few from eastern India whose letters managed to reach Menon. Copies of the *Condition of India* had been sent to him but, in all probability they had found their way into the custom department of the Indian government. Menon arranged to send a few more copies.[130] He was in dire need of money and offered to write for the *Hindustan Review* in case Sinha so desired.[131] Menon had, by then, completed his law terms and passed his examinations for the Bar. He could not be called the previous term as he had no money to pay for it, but he had by then adequate money maturing at the publishers, for whom he had been working, to enable him to be called the next term in autumn.[132]

Reviewing the whole political situation, Menon, though not jubilant, had by mid 1935, reasons to feel that things had been shaping well. He claimed that he had always believed that the best thing that could happen to India was that the white paper proposals 'should move to the right and kill itself by its reactionary character.'[133] He was, he wrote, not a prophet, but he thought, not without reason, that by the time the government announced its policy in the form of a bill the die-hards and the Baldwinites would come together. Churchill might either be clever enough to come back or Baldwin might be cleverer and be able to unite the party with Churchill outside. However, Menon thought that was a purely internal matter.[134] Besides, Menon argued, if the Congress along with other parties like the advanced liberals secured the rejection of the government proposals, the government in Britain would either slow down further the pace of reform or shelve the measure.[135] The economic and political situation, the condition of Bengal and the rise of the socialist movement in the Congress would induce them to do so.[136] The only factor that operated against the probable course of events was the personal position of Hoare.

He was to stand and fall by the reforms. He had been tipped by some for the future leadership of the party but in Britain, Menon wrote, 'they do not make leaders from failures, however magnificent the failure be.'[137] Menon did not think that Hoare would be able to resist the outcry for doing nothing in view of the changing conditions. On the basis of his experience, Menon concluded that in all probability the League would gradually be able to commit the Labour opposition to the idea of a constituent assembly. The next step forward constitutionally in India would not materialize till there was a Labour government in the country. Menon had already obtained some good support on his proposal. The vital feature of the campaign was that Laski was with the League on constituent assembly and that he signed the memorandum along with Grenfell, who was the member of the parliamentary executive of the party. The memorandum made a modest, though significant, impact as Lansbury publicly stated that it was the only way out.[138]

The memorandum on a constitutional assembly was drafted in clear logical terms and it adopted as its base certain definite liberal principles acceptable to the informed public opinion in Britain. It placed the nationalist demands in the context of a historical process having phases of qualitative transformation.[139] Even a casual perusal of the document indicated that it was the brainchild of an exceptionally sharp mind, trained in the theory and practice of political science. Menon's basic idea was to affirm that time and method constituted the essence of policies and they tended to change and modify the character and content of political doctrines and measures. He maintained that the demands of Indian nationalism including those of the moderate school and the trends of British policy and its intentions in respect of constitutional advance in India, point in different directions and between them there was a wide gulf. In this context Menon contested the frequently stated proposition that the British government and Indian nationalism had the same objectives and the differences between them, sharp as they might appear, appertained only to the methods and the pace of advance. Menon argued that vague and facile generalization, 'which, like the rest of its kind in politics, accommodates all pairs of opposites.'[140] Politically, that aberrant postulate served the purpose of mobilizing on the side of reaction a large body of public opinion of men and women of undoubted sincerity and goodwill, but who might easily be satisfied by certain eclectic formulations. The memorandum argued that, broadly speaking, the Indians were concerned with a government amenable to Indian opinion and responsive to Indian needs which would place the interests of the Indian people above the imperial and national requirements of Great Britain or the interests of her British or Indian allies in India. They looked forward to a government which would enable their country to take its place of equality and self-respect among the nations of the world. They also thought of the transition to the full functions of self-government within a definite, determined period not longer than required for the necessary administrative adjustments. In other words, Indians would decline to entertain or accept the idea of probation and examination or even an intermediate period of transition. No amount of elaboration of the difficulties in the way of establishing such a government or arguments about the unfitness of the Indian people to govern themselves would any longer serve to alter that view. The memorandum went ahead to argue that within the limits of the implications of these ideas, even the extremists would agree to compromise and that in disregard of them, no effective section of Indian opinion would accept any term.[141]

In sharp contrast to the essentials of Indian demands, the memorandum stated boldly, British policy had been directed to ensure the security and perpetuation of British interests in India and the demands of British imperialism had been the keystone of any scheme of constitutional advance. Besides, the official position considered Indian constitutional advance and, indeed, the destiny of India as matters on which Great Britain was the arbiter. The content, method and pace of any advance, the memorandum asserted, were, as a consequence, determined by Great Britain. British imperial policy viewed Indian constitutional reform as that degree of concession which, in imperial interests, it was prudent to make and which could not be withheld without immediate danger. Menon thus went ahead to argue that if the future held nothing more than or different from what the existing policies contemplated, one could look forward with little hope to any agreeable prospect in India.[142] It was true that the RTC represented, as a method, an advance on the older idea of examining committees and commissions but all of them failed because they embodied out of date ideas and assumptions. The principle of free discussion and negotiation which was the essence of the RTC method had been abandoned and even that method then stood discredited and should thus be removed from the perception of all who could entertain any hope for the future. The most important function before those who continued to work for a way out was the recognition of the task that the forces of the Indian awakening had to be harnessed for a settlement. The making of the new constitution must 'largely depend on the initiative, the sense of responsibility and the pride of effort of an awakened India.' In other words,the way out was in the recognition and fulfilment of the principle of self-determination.[143] The memorandum admitted that it might be easy to dismiss that view with such arguments as there was no 'self' capable of determination, and even if there were, it was the prerogative of the British parliament to determine. Menon argued that the emergence of a 'self' in this context in definable form was itself a process in some ways parallel to the 'determination'. Granted the will to allow and assist India in that task, 'the time is opportune and the difficulties are not insurmountable.' The memorandum affirmed that the principle of self-determination could only be implemented through a constituent assembly. An *ad hoc* conference tended to offer false values on representatives and such a body would not meet the full needs of the situation. A constituent assembly, on the other hand, would consist of representatives having the mandate of their constituents and would be amenable to a democratic procedure.

It was essential, the memorandum maintained, that the representatives should be elected on an adult franchise or as near adult franchise as possible. The signatories felt that for the purpose of convening a constituent assembly, the existing state of communal distribution in franchise and electoral arrangements should be accepted. In view of the well defined tasks, the signatories suggested the acceptance of the Lothian franchise so as to avoid delays and disagreements subject to the condition that the disabilities imposed on women under the franchise should be removed. Constituent assemblies on this basis should be convened in each province. These provincial assemblies should elect, by proportional representation, a central assembly which should deal with important matters of an all India nature and adequately mirror the divergences of opinion in the country. The provincial assemblies should also deliberate upon and decide on all such matters as were decided by the central assembly as being of provincial concern exclusively and also act as a body whose views should influence the opinion of the members in the central assembly elected by it.[144] It might yet be argued that the relative functions of the centre and the provinces were the outstanding controversies in the Indian constitutional discussion. The signatories pointed out that the significant feature was that this was one of the points on which the unity conference at Allahabad in 1932 was able to come to a satisfactory agreement that reflected a remarkable degree of ingenuity and commonsense. The signatories took note of the problems of the Indian states that had been thrown into relief by the discussions of recent years and the plan of federation on which the white paper proposals were based. It was entirely practical, the memorandum thought, to frame and work a constitution for a self-governing India which, at the same time, would contain provisions for the entry of new units into a state that it created. The plan was in keeping with British policy in India from the time of Warren Hastings.[145] It was suggested that the constituent assembly, after formulating its proposals, should appoint a delegation to negotiate with the British government on all points on which such negotiations were necessary and agreement reached should then be embodied into an act of parliament. This procedure did in no way conflict with the sovereignty of the parliament and had the sanction of precedents such as the New South Wales Constitution Act of 1855, the Victorian Constitution Act of 1855, the Tasmanian Act of 1856, and the Western Australian Act of 1896.[146]

The signatories believed that the memorandum was a serious contribution to the solution of the Indian problem and that it would meet with a response in India which no RTC or commission of enquiry had been able to evoke. Under the proposed scheme the onus of reaching agreements, of negotiating compromises and the reconciliation of combating interests were all to be thrown on the very people who had to work and live under the constitution. Their actions would be discussed in the Indian press and would receive the benefit of public criticism, which the RTC procedure did not. At the same time, the memorandum noted, it did not demand 'a change over till the tracks and engines are ready.'[147] The constituent assembly would have no responsibility for the government of the country which would be carried on under the existing constitution. The maintenance of a comparatively calm political atmosphere, while the task of constitution-making was in progress, was an essential condition and both direct action and repression must be abandoned during the period. The proposed procedure, it was suggested, would cut away much dead wood while, at the same time, it did not rule out the use of past experience or material which the RTC or the royal commission had accumulated. The position would be much the same as contemplated by Lord Irwin in his speech on 29 June 1930.[148] It shifted the responsibility for producing a workable constitution on those on whom it should rest, the representatives of the Indian people. If the process of internal agreement in India protracted the proceedings of the constituent assembly, the delay would not, in itself, breed suspicion and resentment. Besides, a constituent assembly was open to none of the objections usually advanced against plans of self-government for India. In fact, it was argued, it would test the validity of most of them in a definite and practical manner. It would harness the Indian opposition to constructive work and paved the way to the birth and development of political parties within the constitution, instead of the main opposition being outside it. It was affirmed that there was nothing utopian and little that was novel in the suggestions. They appeared to the signatories 'eminently practicable' having behind them the sanction of constitutional experience and the weight of precedents. The memorandum was concluded with a firm statement: 'It is only those who fear agreement amongst Indians and who desire to avoid their presenting this country with a definite set of proposals, which will undoubtedly mean the surrender of power in India, that will find this plan unworthy of consideration.'[149]

Elucidating the various nuances of the proposed Constituent Assembly, Menon wrote to a young volunteer of the League that he could give no answer that could satisfy those who could think or act only in terms of an impotent constitutionalism. 'Constitutionalism is dead', he wrote, 'and the worms have already been at it, and there is going to be no resurrection. Not even the National Congress can revive it by resolution for we have passed that historical stage of growth.' Every national movement, he added, every social movement, when it was strong enough to endanger the existing order, passed that stage and could not go back though individuals or groups might collapse or retire. Menon claimed that 'an impasse' had been created and this would continue till the existing order broke down. To suggest that the 'impasse' should be resolved 'by an attempt to revive the corpse of constitutionalism' was to ignore the historical precedents and existing facts. The conditions, he wrote, that had created the 'impasse' would continue and function more intensely and thus would bring about a worse 'impasse'. Therefore, Menon advised that the only alternative was to carry on the struggle for freedom without compromise. Menon was quite explicit about the proposal. No person who understood the implication of a constituent assembly, he explained, could ever imagine that it could meet under the distinguished patronage of the British government. Its patron could only be the people of India. Because the Indian people, then, had been held down by the imperialist machine in the most abject conditions, there could be no constituent assembly. It would come in good time when the Indian people gained the upper hand. Meanwhile all talk of 'All-Parties' conference and conventions was much shadow talk, not even resulting in shadow action.[150]

It was now that Menon emphasized that the Indian movement could no longer be comprehended in isolation without any reference to the specific form in which world issues confronted it. Propaganda would be ineffective if it was not informative and if the dissemination of information was not constantly reviewed. The contents of propaganda, Menon recognized, should not be dull and repetitious. They must be given a new orientation. They must always cover a fresh space and indicate a specific direction. In the preparation of a syllabus on India for the youth movement, Menon contributed a background paper for the comprehension of the members. This became the central theme of the League's programme of propaganda. Apart from its poverty, Menon stressed, the outstanding fact about India had been its unity. Despite diversities of various forms, culturally, institutionally and ideologically, the Indian people showed a common heritage and had been playing collectively a progressive role in the modern world.[151] From time immemorial, the history of India had been an integral part of the history of Asia which was synonymous with at least two-third of the history of civilization. The remains of the urban civilization in the Indus valley displayed remarkable affinities with the civilization of Sumer, Elam and Mesopotamia. Throughout history, India never ceased to exercise an important influence on world culture.[152] Within India, the course of events was decisively shaped by the advent of the Aryans. The subsequent development of their religious and political institutions and ideas — both greatly modified by contact with the cultures of the earlier inhabitants of India, the Dravidians and others — led to the formation of the Mauryan empire which, for the first time, knit together almost the whole of the sub-continent. The economic, religious and cultural developments of the people rose to unprecedented heights under the Guptas which was sustained with vigour and brilliance in the Chola and Vijayanagar empires. A new element in the complex amalgam of Indian culture was introduced, Menon wrote, by the Arabs, Turks, Afghans and other Islamic peoples who began to penetrate India as early as the eighth century. By the twelfth century they succeeded in building up a stable kingdom and in the Mughal empire (1525 AD-1767 AD) India once again achieved political unity.[153]

The Mughal period, Menon wrote, with a refreshing insight into the India historical process, was notable for two things: it saw the culmination of a long process by which the Hindu cultural traditions were impregnated with those of West and Central Asia, resulting in a remarkable efflorescence of creative power in the arts, architecture and literature. Ceasing to be 'foreigners', the Muslims took a leading part in the growth of a civilization 'that was distinctly Indian — neither Hindu nor Muslim — in every phase.'[154] Secondly, it was during the Mughal period that India's foreign trade came to be monopolized by European chartered companies and ultimately by the East India Company. Capitalist Europe thus reached out to India.

The break-up of the Mughal empire was followed by a hundred years of disorder, not a little of which was due to the intrigues of such ambitious and unscrupulous agents of the English East India Company as Clive, Hastings and Dalhousie. The stubborn and prolonged resistance of the Indian people, particularly of the Marathas and Sikhs, was finally scotched and after the suppression of the great rebellion, the piecemeal conquest of India came to an end and the rule of the East India Company was dissolved. The political and administrative system that had been functioning since that date was marked by the sovereignty of British Parliament and the division of India into states and provinces. The sovereignty of Parliament meant in practice a government by a bureaucracy in which most of the key positions, whether political, financial or military, were held by the hand-picked members of the foreign ruling race. It also meant that regardless of the wishes of the Indian people, the revenues and manpower of India might be used by the British for their own imperialist and war-like ends. The native states were ruled by feudatory princes whose power rested on British bayonets. The states and the provinces were both ultimately controlled by the viceroy and governor-general who was appointed by and responsible to the British cabinet.[155]

In this outstanding survey of Indian history, Menon focussed his attention on its principal dynamics and the various facets of Indian life. The economic exploitation, he wrote, which was the purpose of the political system to defend, had resulted in complete disruption of the base of the historic culture of India. It subordinated India to the industrial requirements of

British capitalism, extinguished the arts and crafts which had given India her former pre-eminence and compelled scores of additional millions into agriculture for their livelihood. That pressure on land was reflected in the size of the peasant holdings which were invariably, and in many cases, absurdly small. The majority of them were uneconomic while, as a result, the rural economy was ill-organized and inefficient and had been steadily deteriorating so that the number of landless peasants increased by 33 per cent between the years 1921 and 1931. The number of employed in large-scale or organized industries never rose above one per cent or so of the population. The industrial backwardness of India was due, among other things, to the actually hostile policy pursued by the alien government until recent years and to the widespread poverty of the masses.[156]

The organization of production in India, though fundamentally unsound, benefited certain classes. Above all it served the landowners whose ability to rack-rent their tenants increased with the pressure on land and profited the industrial and financial interest, mainly British, which dominated the economic life of the country. Rural indebtedness was rampant, which swelled the ranks of the rural proletariat. In the towns, by 1935, the lower middle classes were being crushed by unemployment and workers with meagre income lived in the worst slums of the world. The significant fact of India's growing poverty was that with the exception of kerosene and sugar, the per capita consumption of every necessity of life including salt, had gone down since the pre-war years. Sickness and malnutrition were extraordinary; life expectancy was 24 years; the average number of deaths resulting every year from preventable disease was about six million. Of the total population of 350 million, the overwhelming majority could neither read nor write. Schools, colleges, hospitals and dispensaries were scarce. Public finance in India was characterized by a complete absence of expenditure on such social service as unemployment relief, old age pensions, sickness insurance, etc. Giving the significant indicators of the economy, Menon concluded, that 75 per cent of the revenues of India were devoted to the upkeep of a state machine which had been 'relentlessly killing, starving and maiming the masses of Indian people.'[157]

Menon wrote that the political ferment in India must be re-examined against the light of these harsh realities. That national effervescence, Menon argued, was deeply coloured by the conviction that the existing all-round regression could be halted and standard of life improved only by a concerted effort at social and economic reconstruction, which would not be possible until the deadly impact of British imperialism had been rooted out.[158] This conviction had been asserted, most uncompromisingly, by the National Congress having an unrivalled place in the esteem of the common people and in many parts of the country had greater authority than the established government.[159] Indisputedly, it represented the voice of a resurgent India. Its aim was complete independence and the mode of opposition was organized mass disobedience, non-violent but unyielding to the imperialist state. The Congress, however, represented one phase of a multiparous awakening during the preceding half-a-century.[160] The disintegration of the old order sparked off a reappraisal of accepted values and despite misery and degradation India was pulsating with a new ardent energy. In response, imperialism armed the authorities with powers of coercion such 'as one associates with a Fascist regime.'[161] Bureaucracy had been brutalized; political activities penalized and labour organizations obstructed; civil liberties lay at the mercy of magistrates or police officers; censorship had become ubiquitous. The official policy was designed to isolate India from progressive movements abroad and prevent the dissemination within the country of what the Japanese authorities called the 'dangerous thoughts.'[162] Simultaneously, imperialism had been seeking to divide the ranks of the Indian people by the offer of an allegedly democratic constitution with a spurious federal structure which made no concession to the Indian demand for freedom. It invested the governor-general with virtually dictatorial powers and provided for a federal legislature packed with princes and Indo-British financial and commercial interests — a body that would have no control over foreign affairs, the army, railways, credit and currency nor over 80 per cent of the Indian budgets. Rejecting that 'mockery of a free constitution' designed as a device for strengthening British grip on India, the Congress resolved to work for the convocation of a constituent assembly elected on the basis of adult suffrage.[163]

Of late, Menon thought, the national liberation movement in India had been strengthened and driven forward by the growth of class organizations with specific objectives. Of these, the most significant were the Peasant Leagues *(Kisan Sabhas)* aiming at a radical transformation of the land systems of India. Handicapped by various difficulties the Labour movement, Menon maintained, had been growing its way towards socialism. In those organizations as well as in the Congress, a small but increasing number of socialists had been active. Jawaharlal Nehru, one of the most trusted leaders in India, was a socialist with a strong universalist outlook.[164] Under his inspiration, the Congress had been following with the closest attention the course of events beyond their frontiers. Appreciation of international affairs taught the Congress a singularly instructive lesson — that British imperialism was not only the enemy of the colonial peoples, but by reasons of its treacherous, dishonourable and pro-fascist policy, the enemy of all who desired peace and freedom. This had led to the realization that by striving to shake off British domination, India had been helping to weaken the anti-people forces and lay the foundations of a better world order. The aims of the Indian people were essentially the goals of those of the other lands including China, Abyssinia and Spain, who were engaged in fighting fascist and imperialist aggression. Out of this realization came a strong sense of solidarity with the popular and progressive forces everywhere.[165]

Shadowed by Scotland Yard, targeted by the Conservative front organizations and deserted by fair-weather friends, the League was ever eager to welcome a word of encouragement or grasp a friendly hand. The tense atmosphere in the League, heightened by Menon's constant endeavour to forge his way through a maze of misinformation, was relieved by evocative communications from some enthusiastic friends. One of these from Revd. D. Chellappa of Hatfield College, Durham came towards the end of January 1935 in response to the invitation of the League to attend one of its conferences on India.[166] Chellappa was convinced that it was perhaps futile to think of influencing the British public to the Indian point of view by means of persuasive writings and meetings. Faced against 'the titanic imperial force commanding a host of mass media', these attempts might only mean a cry in the wilderness. Chellappa called for action in place of words, service in place of oratory, sacrifice in place of emotionalism. The scene of action, he maintained, was India and not England and one must prepare oneself, tenaciously and carefully and get ready for the grim struggle that awaited the expatriate Indians. What was termed and respected in the British empire as patriotism for Englishmen was condemned as sedition for Indians. A struggle for national emancipation for India was not just an opportunity to let off steam: it was a test of manhood and an assertion of the genuineness of conviction.[167]

Revd. Chellappa was convinced that the first essential condition for a united struggle for freedom was to rise above the petty parochial and provincial affiliations in language, society and religion. Some of the dissensions had been engineered by powerful agencies over which one had no control but, once one recognized their character, one ought to be on one's guard and refuse to succumb to their alluring seductions. Finally, Chellappa sent, in his message, best wishes for a consuming sincerity of purpose, a burning conviction in the righteousness of the cause and a self-effacing love for the masses of Indians. He thought that there was no reason for despair for the paucity of committed nationalist crusaders for so vast a country as India. Christianity started, he argued, as the religion of despised subject race whose Apostles were men of little culture or prestige. But so great was their faith and fortitude that they 'turned the world upside down.'[168]

Despite short spates of melancholia, Menon had enough verve and spirit not to overlook the fact that the situation was not without hope. Menon realized that his life in London had become meaningful only against the backdrop of his role in the India League, even if it meant that he consciously overlooked much of his own personal side. Since his arrival in the city as a student under the patronage of Annie Besant, his life and endeavours were inextricably bound up with the CIL, subsequently renamed as the India League, and its struggle for independence. Despite tactical adjustments in the professed objectives and priorities of the League, Menon did not adopt a public image different from his private character. A man of exceptional integrity and varied interests, Menon could view, even in the midst of a hectic campaign, India as a distinct, but not an isolated, social, political and cultural phenomenon and also as a significant part of an international movement devoted to the expansion of human freedom. He was subject to moods and emotional outbursts, but his personal feelings and inclinations were never allowed to interfere with the collective decisions taken in the interest of the movement. At each stage he worked in consultation with close associates, accepting justified criticisms and delegating responsibility when it seemed best.[169]

By then, he had forged a line of contact with a reliable source of information about the condition in Germany and the movement against fascism in Comrade Evelyn Lend.[170] Friends of India, under Lawrence Housman and Reginald Reynolds were cooperative and saw to it that their representatives attend all the rallies and meetings of the League.[171] Menon became a special guest speaker in almost all the branches of the Labour Party's League of Youth and was inspired to speak on the India League and aspects of the Indian situation, dwelling extensively on imperial mindset, the carefully crafted reform proposals that merely stimulated opposition and the urgency of a constituent assembly in India as the only way out of the complicated political impasse. The fervent appeal of the Hornsey League captured Menon's magic spell on his audience: 'We are looking forward to this meeting very much and we appreciate your willingness to oblige us.... We usually allow speakers about an hour and then follow with discussion, but this procedure may be varied to suit you. We want to learn from you.'[172]

Gandhi's perception of the Indian political scenario as outlined in his letter to Carl Heath had, by then, become a subject of considerable public discussion. In a comprehensive communication in response to Heath's persuasive epistle of 21 December 1934 urging the Mahatma to reconsider favourably the constitutional proposals, Gandhi stoutly maintained that he had nothing to suggest in the way of alterations to his earlier position.[173] Gandhi was aware that Heath was cognizant of the existing repressive laws in India. But he was not convinced that Heath could have comprehended the impact of those laws on the life and condition of the people of India. Gandhi thought that probably both Dr. Maud Rayden and Andrews would be able to give first-hand testimony of what they saw and learnt in Bengal. It was amazing, he added, how little was known in England of the intolerable situation of India. While Heath had maintained that the withdrawal of the bill would be 'a calamity', Gandhi resolutely held that such a withdrawal would constitute 'a blessing both for England and India' in the face of 'an almost unanimous Indian opposition to it.'[174] Gandhi was aghast by the persistent, obdurate attitude of Parliament and its bitter contempt for Indian public opinion. In support of his position, Gandhi referred to the opposition to the proposed reforms by moderate men like Sastri and Chintamani who had been, over the years, recognized and recommended by the India Office for their consistent abhorrence to 'Congress attitude in unmeasured language.' Gandhi had read the white paper and the report as one single document. They left an indelible impression upon his mind that 'bad as the existing constitution is, the threatened new one will be infinitely worse' and if it was passed, it would be most difficult to undo the mischief.[175] Having enumerated the objections that he entertained about the proposed reforms, Gandhi held forcefully that to clinch the whole of the objections it is well to remember that the constitution was sought to be imposed upon the people who were already groaning under repression. Such a policy of suppression had not been equalled in British Indian history. 'I have a vivid memory', he wrote in anguish, 'of Jallianwala Bagh. I have read Kaye and Malleson's volumes on the Sepoy Revolt, as it has been called, of 1857. Both make gruesome reading. Then, it was naked sword. The repression represents the gloved fist, but deadlier on that account.'[176]

Since the withdrawal of Eileen Merrie and the dissolution of the branch, the presence of the India League in Bristol was in a dormant state. Now in January 1935, Menon located, with the assistance of Reginald Reynolds, a silent but creative political activitist in Chris Lewis.[177] The principal task assigned to Lewis was to revive and reorganize the Bristol branch in the course of participating in the current public controversy centred around the proposed India reforms. Little was known, Menon wrote, in Britain as to what the Indians had been thinking of the proposals and how they would affect the masses of the Indian people or how far they were calculated to repudiate the interests of the Indian people. It seemed that to start with an ad hoc committee in Bristol would be a satisfactory arrangement. Besides, it would be adequate to have a one day or a weekend school plus a public meeting in the evening and if that was not practicable one should be satisfied with a good delegate conference.[178] In any case, the upshot of the endeavour was that the Bristol branch was revived once again.

Gandhi's modest but inflexible presentation, together with Menon's unceasing persuation was able to underline one point—that Indian opposition to the constitutional bill was unanimous. Although that opposition was not based on hatred, it was firm in its refusal to accept a constitution imposed upon them by alien conquerors. George Lansbury, a gentle Christian socialist then leading the parliamentary Labour Party, was convinced that the Indian leaders, themselves trained in British liberal traditions and educational system, desire nothing better than to be partners with the British people to work for a new India, free from foreign domination and of equal status with the rest of the world. In this context, Lansbury's broadcast speech of 1 February 1935 was a resounding success for the India League, as it declared without any diplomatic ambiguity that the bill was a cumbersome, costly and undemocratic document and had completely failed to offer India a 'government by the people.' 'Autocracy', he added, 'veiled by a facade of make-believe democracy' was the best description of the scheme. Calling for the immediate withdrawal of the bill, Lansbury strongly advocated the idea of giving the Indian people the responsibility to draft proposals of constitutional arrangements so as to 'enable us to reach as full agreement as possible.' This, he thought, would be a brotherhood of action' and would demonstrate 'our faith in the religion we profess.' Emphasizing the importance of a constitutional assembly in India, Lansbury added: 'Our interests cannot be served by domination, force or make-believe. The old teaching of the Gospels are true: "what shall it profit a man if he gains the whole world and lose his own soul.'"[179]

The Midland's Churches' Committee of No More War Movement, who was committed to work for total disarmament and the establishment of a new social and international order based on pacifist principles, came out with a definite offer of goodwill and active support. Assuring Menon of the committee's sincere interest in the welfare of India, the organizers announced their decision to reprint and circulate an article by Wilfred Wellock, the noted ethical socialist, forcefully advocating justice for India for the general approval of a wide and receptive readership.[180] This would be done to arouse interest and might be followed by a series of conferences, meetings, poster parades, etc. as would seem most suitable. The organizers sought Menon's suggestions and cooperation for chalking out the programme.[181] Albert Purcell, writing on behalf of the Manchester and Salford Trades Council, invited Menon to a delegate meeting of the Council on 20 January 1935 giving him full freedom to 'say just what you think is of the greatest value.'[182] Although it was difficult to whip up enthusiasm for a big public meeting, Manchester continued to stimulate India work. In particular the Manchester branch of the League was engaged in combating the anti-Indian propaganda launched by officially sponsored agencies.

P. Waughray, organizing secretary, strongly protested against a public display of fireworks widely advertised as Cawnpore Massacre.[183] Waughray, in his sharp note, held that one could guess it would mean either of the two incidents in the modern history of Indo-British relationship: the first possibility was a highly inflammable story of 'Cawnpore massacre' of 1857 as over the years 'Cawnpore' symbolized, in British propaganda, the triumph of British justice over Asiatic barbarism. The second possibility was that the firework referred to the communal riots of 1934. But these incidents could certainly not be classified as items of entertainment 'particularly when so much fondness is displayed today in many quarters over the Empire and the equality of its citizens!' The project of entertainment, the League maintained, should be judiciously pruned and altered, especially 'in view of the current vicious propaganda as has been going on in such a subtle and disgusting manner.'[184]

From Hull came a letter from Harold Bing on behalf of the No War Movement, inviting Menon to participate in a one day school. All local organizations such as trade unions, Labour Party branches and cooperative guilds would be circularized and urged to send delegates. A book stall with all the League's books and pamphlets could be organized.[185] Harold Bing was an old associate of Menon since the days of the British Federation of Youth. Over the years Hull had been nursed for India work by the Friends of India. Now, Menon and the League found a sympathetic hearing from an already sensitized audience.[186] One of the areas where the India League had lost out its influence was Wales. The League had quite an active organization at Cardiff and other places, which broke down with the depression and its workers leaving the place. A new centre was then being organized at Swansea with the assistance of Dorothy Stevens with the prospect of a good deal of extension. A public meeting was held at Swansea in February 1935 when those interested were grouped together.[187] Similar initiatives were also taken in Edinburgh and Dundee and these exercises proved fruitful and synergistic.[188] In fact, the problem of India had become so acute that some specialized initiative was called for. The meeting of the Middlesborough branch of Women's Freedom Movement found stubborn opposition from district authorities, but it was able to pass a resolution demanding the release of political prisoners not guilty of acts of violence.[189]

Menon noted with satisfaction that the demand of League's pamphlets, especially from the universities had been increasing.

Pamphlets such as *India and the National Congress, Terrorism by Ordinance, Indian View on the White Paper, Report of Investigations into the Conditions of Indian Textile Workers, Chittagong, Hijli, Indian Labour and Self-Government* (1933-34) were popular.[190] Requests from various centres came for assistance in order to neutralize the impact of the meetings of the India Defence League and the Indian Empire Society addressed by retired colonels and civil servants 'who put over the usual tosh about the divisions in India.'[191] Menon, Shelvankar, Platts-Mills and Ellen Wilkinson were invited by various organizations to let people know something of India, its desires and aspirations which 'should do some good.'[192] In Manchester University, a little over 60 delegates attended a meeting; at Durham, over 400 delegates were present.[193] About the same time, Reginald Bridgeman, the ebullient left-wing publicist and Harry Pollitt, the enthusiastic general secretary of CPGB, extended their support to the India League, without reservation, in its struggle for *swaraj* for India. Bridgeman affirmed that he would be pleased to do anything to advance the work of the India League by becoming a member. He made it clear that despite his strong CPGB connection he was not inclined to do anything which could, in any way, even unconsciously, embarrass the efforts of the League.[194]

Bridgeman, honorary international secretary, British Anti-War Movement (AWM), was on the same wave length as John Strachey, chairman of the movement. Despite some odd theoretical misgivings, they were keen to push the anti-war movement to obtain the services of Menon as an important speaker of their demonstrations. In other words, they had intellectually internalized the agenda of the Indian crusader. In a communication to Menon, N.B. Hunter, Secretary, AWM, emphasized the menacing events that had taken place in Austria and the anti-war demonstration proposed by the Movement should be representative of all sections and societies that were opposed to war. The platform would include people of all shades of opinion. 'We believe', Hunter pleaded, 'it would be extremely valuable if you yourself could speak on the occasion.' In case, Menon found it absolutely impossible because of pressure of work, 'we would greatly appreciate from you a letter of greetings that could be read out.'[195]

It was, however, evident that despite a good deal of public sympathy, a sharp and meaningful headway was somewhat unattainable because of the ambivalence of the Labour Party's India policy. Jim Saunders from Sunderland, reported that despite the awareness of the members of the ILP and No War Movement of the urgency for the dissemination of reliable information about India, there was serious opposition from the Labour Party towards the ILP to which Saunders and his organization were affiliated. The cooperative movement was largely controlled by the Labour Party which, together with trades union council, were hostile towards ILP and they would invariably boycott anything initiated by it.[196] Sunderland was a very depressed area with about 30,000 unemployed hands and the region was by and large under the Labour Party's influence. In that political backwater the only source of information was the unreliable press. Saunders stressed that if Menon could contact D.N. Pritt, the Labour's prospective candidate, it was certain he would be able to mobilize the local Labour Party agents.[197] From Sheffield, Frank Dawtry, chairman of the body of the Friends of India, though not a wet-blanket, was not frightfully optimistic either. The local branch of Friends of India was loosely held and inordinately ill-informed but it was nevertheless hoped that the No War Movement might still be exhorted to undertake a bit of India work and drag the sloppy Friends of India along a little later in the year.[198] Alexander Keeble from Birmingham was more forthright and a meeting under Horace Alexander was organized. But the resolution proposed by Alexander was not sharp enough and it called for a compromise formula to end the stalemate.[199] Meanwhile,

Menon found the interactions in the Discussion Group at the Memorial Club on 13 January 1935, organized by Dorothy Woodman, stimulating though the conclusions were couched in tangling indefiniteness.[200]

'The present situation in India' by K.S. Shelvankar, by then Menon's very close associate, had appeared on 26 April 1934, in a paper in Stockholm and the India office carefully scanned the piece. Shelvankar had come into contact with Menon in London in 1931 and the following year deputised for Menon as editor of the *India Review,* Menon being then in India. He again deputised for him when he was ill for several months in 1935. Since 1932, the two had been closely associated. Menon relied upon him to a very considerable extent as a speaker at India League meetings and an authority on facts and statistics, although they did not always agree on the nuances in the handling of Indian political questions. It was evident that Shelvankar was not a member of the CPGB. But his association with R.P. Dutt, the communist theoretician was sufficient ground to condemn him as a suspect requiring constant surveillance on the part of Scotland Yard. His views were, it was reported, 'distinctly inclined towards Communism' and in his public pronouncements, he gave the impression of being 'a staunch supporter of the Indian National Congress.'[201] The India Office did not overlook the Stockholm paper especially because it presented in a nutshell the standpoint of the India League.[202] After a review of the development of nationalist opposition to British rule in India and a sketch of the proposal contained in the white paper of March 1933, Shelvankar observed that there were two major reasons why nationalist India was still dissatisfied. One of the reasons was that the policy of the white paper did not correspond to India's expectations. The right to responsible government was granted only in a limited form; it was hedged by innumerable restrictions; it was not extended to any important sphere and its exercise was liable to be impeded by the British supreme authorities. And the federation, though sound in principle, would merely tend to prolong the petty autocracy of the princes and give them a position which would retard democratic progress. Even the Indian liberals and moderates, Shelvankar remarked, had withdrawn themselves from the role of collaboration, somewhat defeated and disappointed.

The second reason was the general state of contemporary India. Shelvankar summarised the basic findings of the *Condition of India* and concluded that the country had received a stunning blow from an authoritarian government from which it scarcely recovered. He maintained that when the activities of the Congress movement became annoying, a policy of inhuman repression was released which had since been maintained unabated. Exceedingly harsh and cruel measures were issued and subsequently incorporated in the ordinary legislation of Government of India by a submissive legislative assembly. In Bengal, in particular, any criticism of the government, however mild, was regarded as seditious and was dealt in a summary and ruthless manner. Only a small number of Indians had not joined in the demand for radical changes despite the continued repressive policy. Only these few had not been reached by the heavy, oppressive and persecuting hand of the authorities.[203]

The bitterness to which these unfair and offensive methods had given rise, the author continued, had been aggravated by the economic depression. These factors, Shelvankar added, plunged the country into a state of profound depression. The essence or central tenet of the argument was that Indian nationalism was a tremendous material force and its demand for self-government was legitimate and irresistible. Until that demand was satisfied, it was futile to hope for peace. India might consent to cooperate with Great Britain but only as an equal partner in a true federation. But the short-sighted statesmen who were then in power were pursuing a myopic policy which rendered it difficult, even impossible, to attain that aim.

Amidst the queer political stalemate, Shiva Rao informed Menon that Polak was frantically working to get the Indian liberals to bless the white paper. 'I always knew', Shiva Rao added, 'he was at heart a Tory, but I did not know he was such an ass.'[204] Sastri's speeches castigating the thrust of the official proposals seemed to have disturbed a number of people in England. Shiva Rao was uncertain if the constituent assembly idea would catch public imagination easily in India. Nehru was then in prison and Shiva Rao found it difficult to see anyone else in India who could carry on his work in the same way. Menon felt somewhat diffident in that politically claustrophobic atmosphere. He was not in a position to offer a cheerful perspective. To all his friends he made it clear that the India business needed the assistance of all those 'who are with us politically.' With such legislation as would enable the police to get people hanged and suppress all press criticism, 'we are much worse in India than the Communists in Germany!'[205]

In the course of the public debate since the release of the white paper, Menon's ideas had crystallized. He was convinced that so far as Congressmen were concerned or those who cared to think along Congress lines, there was no room for compromise on vital issues. He reiterated that the Congress stood for independence and the fullest self-determination by the people of India, without any interference by an alien authority.[206] It was obvious, he argued, that any attempt to consider the white paper and to try to improve it was incompatible with what was termed as dominion status or even a small measure of political or economic freedom. In reference to the proposed all-parties conference at Bombay, Menon felt that only those who were prepared to give up their objectives, forget their pledges and accept even for a distant future the 'steel chains of British imperialism' and its political, financial and military control might find it judicious to discuss the white paper and its offshoots. Menon thought that for the Congress and others who would have liked to work for a fundamental change in India, there should be no compromise on the issue, whatever happened. He maintained that for the Congressmen to associate themselves with any step to adopt the white paper would be a betrayal of all they stood for. It would stimulate the reactionary elements in the country and promote the interest of British imperialism. Any attempt at modification of the white paper would be an exercise in deception.[207]

Misgivings about Menon's credence on the Labour Party were heard in India. Even some of his close acquaintances were eager to know what Menon's attitude was to the Labour Party, the official policy of which was clearly not calculated to satisfy the Indian demands. It was asserted by C.B. Kumar, representative of *Matrubhumi* in London, that Attlee was desirous of only a compromise formula of the white paper proposals and Indian aspirations. Kumar and many others felt uneasy as they thought that Menon seemed to rely too much on the possibility of a 'Labour' support for Indian independence.[208] Paradoxically, however, Menon's pronouncements on the white paper was rated highly by none other than Kumar himself and he publicized Menon's views through his weekly report to his journal in India.[209] Menon's views had become the points of discussion in political circles and the Publicity Club of London invited him to share the platform with many other eminent speakers on the white paper. Menon was considered a creative interpreter of events and movements — one whose range of interests seemed never confined by the frothy outpourings at the party's annual conferences.[210] Reginald Bridgeman requested Menon to come over for a detailed discussion on the constitutional reform proposals in the light of the recommendations of the joint committee to develop some kind of a wide, organized action.[211] He regretted that the only agitation then of a vigorous character against the proposals was being conducted by die-hard Conservatives, giving the impression that the rest of the country with the solitary exception of the India League regarded the project, (which was 'extremely reactionary in its every details'), with complacency. Soon, on 19 December 1934, Menon, Lansbury and Brailsford addressed a meeting at Conway Hall, Holbern on India and the reform proposals. Menon's lucid analysis on the urgency of a constituent assembly was widely appreciated.[212]

One of his public presentations on India was a talk at the Panther's, a writer's club, which caused a great sensation. Menon was called upon by a book club to participate in a discussion of Edward Thompson's novel called *An Indian Day (1932),*[213] which, apart from being a well known piece of creative writing was, at the same time, a perspicacious exposition of the Indian problem. It was believed that the book was a genuine attempt to state the case with fairness to the Indian as well as the English side and was likely to have a considerable impact on cultured and intellectual opinion in England.[214] In view of Menon's speech at the Panthers', it was presumed that Menon would be able state the case from the other side with poise and felicity. In particular, it had been noted with satisfaction that Menon had been stating and elaborating his case with the help of statistics and facts on the economic and historical sides of British rule which were scarcely touched upon by Thompson. Examining at length the nature of poverty and misery of the peasants due to British rule, Menon, in the course of the book discussion, sought to pick holes in the oft-repeated assertion that English rule meant peace, order and as near as approximation to justice as was possible 'among the vast hordes of native races who would be much worse off if left to the tender mercies of their own countrymen.'[215] In view of the importance of the Indian question not only in the parliamentary session and but for years to come, Menon was naturally anxious that the labour movement should be as well informed on it as possible. Calling upon the agents of the Labour Party, he requested them to call delegate conferences on India, promising assistance by supplying effective speakers.[216]

A positive and cheerful response came from the Universal Publishing Co. from New York. Congratulating Menon for the splendid report on the existing conditions in India, Haridas T. Mazumdar emphasized in his open-hearted communication that the report would go a long way towards dispelling 'the clouds of misrepresentation and ignorance' in America, so ingeniously promoted by British propaganda. It appeared to the American publishing house that the report should not be confined to the British public. In Mazumdar's judgement the report could be distributed to great advantage in America, accuring enormous international significance. Mazumdar offered his cooperation for the distribution of 500 volumes and even more copies in the near future. Even that, he thought, was a very conservative estimate as he spoke with considerable experience in the field of publication. Soon the American edition was out in the market.[217]

One of the principal engagements of the League following the release of its report was to supply specific informations about ordinance rule and police *raj*. On 3 August 1934, for example, Menon sent through a courier of ILP school at Swansea to Mirabehn in India, many solid instances of oppression. He informed that Khan Abdul Ghaffar Khan was detained under Regulation III of 1818 and for more information one could refer to pages 19 and 407 to 411 of *Condition of India*. It was added that the regulation was the Bengal counterpart of Regulation 25 1827 of Bombay under which Gandhi was arrested on 4 January 1932 at 3:15 am which might be verified from p.24 of the same volume. Nehru was then jailed for two years beginning in February 1934 under a sentence for sedition. He was tried by an Indian magistrate and the speech for which he was arrested and convicted was one which demanded independence for India and contained no incitement to violence although Nehru agreed with the magistrate that under the existing penal system the speech could be considered seditious. In reality, that speech was an impassioned appeal against violence and Nehru was at that time engaged in relief work for the victims of the earthquake. His arrest prevented him for making a report of the investigation he had made. Menon added that if Nehru was guilty of sedition, then all Congressmen were, as Congress was committed to *purna swaraj*. In reply to other queries, Menon instructed that chapter III of *Condition of India* would give all the information of the facts leading to the arrest of Khan Abdul Ghaffar Khan and Gandhi's correspondence with the Viceroy. Besides, chapter XX offered a fairly elaborate outline of the Khudai Khidmadgars and the Khan's work and the resistance in the NWFP.[218]

Hemmed in on all sides, Menon, however, was becoming restless while his intensity grew. He became far more persuasive. One was struck by his eloquence, his remarkable sense of reference and his integrated mind. On an average he had been addressing four meetings a day. He did not enjoy robust health but was endowed with indomitable energy and clear perception. His pungent analysis of men and events had become overpowering and despite a cordial demeanour, he began to inspire vengeful responses from persons with limited interests. 'I enjoyed my talk with you', Allan Young, editor, MacMillan & Co. Ltd. wrote to Menon following an intriguing encounter with this vivacious India League enthusiast, 'although, on reflection, I am more than ever convinced that moderation is a virtue — even in politics.'[219] But there were some remarkable personalities, distinguished by sharp intellectual qualities and idealistic commitments, who rallied round him and were prepared to address his meetings and conferences. A.A. Purcell, Gordon MacDonald, George Hicks, Michael Foot, John Jagger, Harold Laski, Harry Pollitt, Ellen Wilkinson, Monica Whately, Krishna Shelvankar, Platts-Mills, to mention a few, were to be found frequenting the Strand office with an extraordinary sense of purpose. There was a conscious collective decision to stand by Menon in his hour of crisis to help him tide over the difficult situation. Mary Shelvankar recalled that Menon's clothes required mending, his shoes were shabby, he looked emaciated and lived on poached eggs and cups of tea. He was financially hardup; gout and ill health bogged him. Menon was in and out of hospital; opposition closed its ranks; loneliness haunted from all sides; the Labour Party had been asking for unprincipled pragmatic adjustments with imperialism. In September 1935, Barbara MacNamara finally decided to walk out of Menon's life. The relationship between them rested on an understanding that each must allow the other the space to reach one's goal in a divergent manner. But that loving and trustful relationship did not last. For MacNamara, Menon's life was a bitter struggle chasing a dream that eluded him. She failed to teach Menon how to unwind and how to turn his talents into reality. Both shared strong discipline, morals, and goal-oriented hard work which they admired in each other.[220]

In September 1935 Menon received the final communication from MacNamara from Buxham: 'I should naturally have been ready to come if necessary and if I felt any good could be done to either of us. But however much it hurts to hear it I feel I should say honestly that I do not think it is any use going on as we are now. I am afraid it is only prolonging the agony for both; I feel that is hopeless and I want to end an unhappy and unsatisfactory position. There is no use writing at length or saying much of what one feels, or what a step like this costs me, but I am afraid I should not be happy with you, and consequently could not make you happy. There is a chance of my being happy elsewhere; I am going to take that chance. I have thought and worried over the situation ever since it first arose and particularly since I have had a chance to think while down here. The only possible way I think is to cut off and both try to start afresh. I know what you will say as far as you are concerned but I can only ask you to remember the past and give me a chance to be happy without making it too difficult. I do not think, in these circumstances, you will want to see me again; I do not think it would be any good and would only cause more misery.... Please forgive me for not having made a success of what I wanted more than any thing else to make a success of, and for all the pain I have [caused] and am causing you.'[221] They parted company leaving behind deep scars. Years later Anna Polak, a close associate of Menon since the late 1930s, wrote to me about Krishna and his admirers:

> I have been thinking over my inadequate, meandering talk into your machine and remember now that something diverted me when you mentioned Barbara MacNamara. She was just a name to me when I first met Krishna but I gathered he had had a special relationship with her but was pipped at the post of a rival. He did, I think, in those days find certain young English women attractive and probably longed for a share of distraction and warmth but I also think his temperament (inhibition?), obsessive pilgrimage and arduous workload would never have allowed him to be tied down in a conventional way. Though he never said so, he must above all have felt vulnerable to any gossip, innocent or malicious, among his associates; so many, especially Indians, on the look out for 'human weakness' and ready to pounce.
>
> I believe my long and rewarding friendship with him persisted because I was not feminine enough to make trivial demands and, in any case, had my own career to build and living to earn! You see, Krishna was totally dependent on so-called voluntary workers. He couldn't afford paid staff and he no doubt sensed at once whom he could or could not trust. We were a mixed bunch of idealistic young women, ready to type, file (K called it "pickling".), clean and run errands; all had other paid jobs and interests but *all* were of course fascinated by Krishna's

fervour, dynamism and *selfless* compulsion despite the long hours and many discomforts (cold, heat, interruptions for tea, tea, tea; journeys home with bomb fallings, etc. etc.). Finally, when independence came and what can only be called revolutionary work ended, Krishna expressed vividly in articles and speeches his appreciation of and affection for 'the India League Workers'.[222]

The striking ambivalence in the Labour Party's attitude towards India and the of Attlee's constitutional recipe had an extensive fall out. They dampened many enthusiastic spirits and caused widespread diffidence. Miss M. Dormer Harris was a typical example of the sinking spirit of the rank and file of the party who began to doubt India's capability for independence and democracy.[223] Harris had been a sympathetic observer of the Indian situation and often sent a few shillings towards the League's fund. But now she was not convinced of the authenticity of India's demand for freedom because of the prevailing poverty and social evil in the country. Menon made it clear time and again to various observers that he was unable to accept the view held by some people that the facts connected with 'child marriage and maternal morality' should alienate sympathy of liberal opinion from the cause of Indian freedom. Menon held that it was legitimate to assume that Indians were as concerned as others to rid their country of social evils. The history of events would show that such efforts had been made and to a certain extent, carried out by Indian people in the teeth of official opposition, the child marriage legislation being a glaring example.[224]

It was unfortunate, Menon argued, for those English people who were genuinely interested in India and her social generation, that facts about it should be misrepresented.[225] It was only too true that the British people had no ill will towards the Indians, but those of them who were articulate should be able to discern that facts had been so consistently distorted and

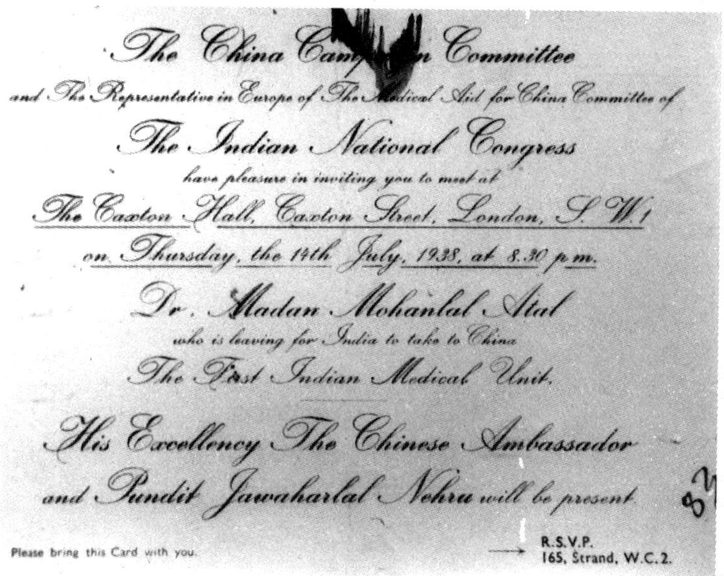

The China Cam[illegible]n Committee

and The Representative in Europe of The [illegible]edical Aid for China Committee of

The Indian National Congress

have pleasure in inviting you to meet at

The Caxton Hall, Caxton Street, London, S.W.1

on Thursday, the 14th July, 1938, at 8.30 p.m.

Dr. Madan Mohanlal Atal

who is leaving for India to take to China

The First Indian Medical Unit.

His Excellency The Chinese Ambassador

and Pundit Jawaharlal Nehru will be present

Please bring this Card with you.

R.S.V.P.
165, Strand, W.C.2.

Invitation card of the India League's the China campaign Committee to meet Dr. Madan Mohan Lal Atal July 1938. Menon Papers.

INDIA

speaks

with a foreword
by Professor
Harold J. Laski

2D

PUBLISHED BY THE INDIA LEAGUE, 165, STRAND, W.C.2

Frontispiece of an inflnential publication of the India League entitled, *India Speaks*, 1935. Menon Papers.

26th April 1934.

Dear Bevan,

Mr. Grenfell, I understand, is not in the House today, nor is Tom Williams as you know, and I am therefore obliged to trouble you.

As you have probably noticed from the papers, 65,000 textile workers have come out on strike in Bombay as a protest against a cut in wages of about 12½%, and the authorities have prohibited processions and demonstrations, and lathi charges have been made by the police on the crowds and demonstrations broken up. It is also stated that the leaders have been arrested and that armed police are being drafted to the area. It looks as though all labour activity is going to be suppressed under Ordinance provisions just as Congress activity was treated.

I do hope that you will feel interested in this matter and raise it by a private notice question today. Surely whatever might be the view of the Labour Party with regard to their support of "Nationalists agitation, it would be agreed that the beating up and dispersal of labour demonstrations and imprisonment of leaders is a matter that concerns us at least as much as similar matters in Germany or elsewhere.

Perhaps you are also aware that the textile workers at Sholapur were similarly treated a few weeks ago. Some of the mill workers came out on strike protesting against wages cuts of 12½% and the employers locked the others out. 14,000 operatives were implicated, and the district magistrate at once issued orders, under the special powers that he possesses according to the new laws which incorporate Ordinance powers, and prohibited all meetings of strikers, and served orders on labour leaders also prohibiting them from attending or taking part in any activities.

The Indian Trade Disputes Act, wicked as it is, provides for the appointment of Boards of Arbitration and Conciliation appointed by the Government when there are industrial disputes. The district magistrate could at least have availed himself of this instead of using political and punitive powers against the workers.

Menon to Anaurin Bevan, 26 April 1934. Menon papers

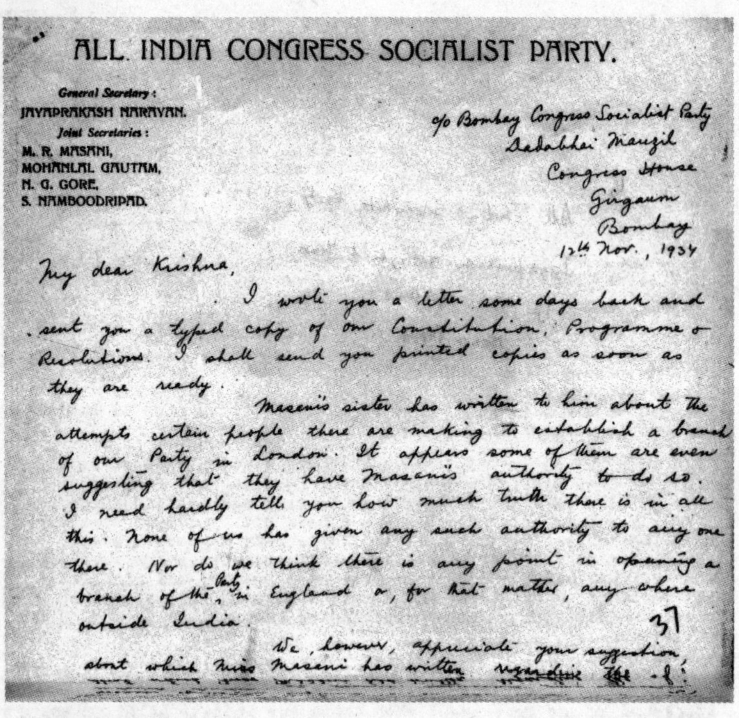

ALL INDIA CONGRESS SOCIALIST PARTY.

General Secretary:
JAYAPRAKASH NARAYAN.
Joint Secretaries:
M. R. MASANI,
MOHANLAL GAUTAM,
N. G. GORE,
S. NAMBOODRIPAD.

c/o Bombay Congress Socialist Party
Dadabhai Manzil
Congress House
Girgaum
Bombay
12th Nov., 1934

My dear Krishna,

I wrote you a letter some days back and sent you a typed copy of our Constitution, Programme & Resolutions. I shall send you printed copies as soon as they are ready.

Masani's sister has written to him about the attempts certain people there are making to establish a branch of our Party in London. It appears some of them are even suggesting that they have Masani's authority to do so. I need hardly tell you how much truth there is in all this. None of us has given any such authority to any one there. Nor do we think there is any point in opening a branch of the Party in England or, for that matter, any where outside India.

37

We, however, appreciate your suggestion, about which Miss Masani has written regarding the [illegible]

Jayaprakash Narayan to Menon, 12 November, 1934.
Menon Papers.

British Anti-War Movement

(British Section of the World Movement Against War and Fascism)

National Council:

Telephone: HOLborn 5364

Telegrams: Council, Holborn 5364 London

Chairman (acting) and Treasurer: JOHN STRACHEY

Vice-Chairmen: PERCY COLLICK, Mrs. WADDINGTON, J. GASTER, J. MARVILL

Honorary International Secretary: R. BRIDGEMAN

Hon. Secretary: N. B. HUNTER

53, GRAY'S INN ROAD
LONDON, W.C.1.

28th July 1934.

Krishna Menon,
165 Strand
W.C.2.

Dear Comrade,

The special Committee which is organising the 20th anniversary Anti-War Demonstration in Hyde Park on August 5th at 6 p.m. has decided that we should endeavour to obtain your services as a speaker at that Demonstration.

Our Demonstration this year is of paramount importance not only because it is the Twentieth Anniversary of the last Imperialist war, but because of the very menacing events that have taken place in Austria during the last few days. We intend that our August 5th Demonstration shall be representative of all sections and societies that are opposed to war and we anticipate a most impressive rally. The platforms will include people of all shades of opinion who are opposed to war and we believe it would be extremely valuable if you yourself could speak on this occasion. If you find it absolutely impossible because of pressure of work or prior engagements we would greatly appreciate from you a letter of greetings that could be read out.

Hoping for a favourable reply at your convenience.

Yours faithfully,

N. B. Hunter

Hon. Sec: Anti-War Movement.

18

N. B. Hunter (Secretary, British Anti-war Movement), 28 July 1934. Menon Pepers.

SOCIALIST YOUTH DEMONSTRATION

ON SATURDAY, 19th OCTOBER, 1935,
IN THE MINERS' HALL, Red Hill, DURHAM CITY

Convened by the Durham University Labour Club and the Durham County Federation of Divisional Labour Parties.

Recognising the precarious position of the National and International political situation, this CONFERENCE desires to give expression to the principles of Socialism, in the continual struggle of the WORKING CLASS AGAINST FASCISM, IMPERIALISM, AND CAPITALISM.

The position of the Working Class in Europe clearly illustrates it is imperative that we must create such a Socialist outlook in the country, that Labour will march to full power at the next General Election, culminating in the abolition of the anomalies and injustices of Capitalism, by the creation of a Socialist Society.

Working Class Youth must realise, that in order to protect their liberties and institutions, they must march straight forward with a policy of Socialism, and in this struggle, the apathy of the older and younger generations must be destroyed. All sections of opinion must be aroused by constant propaganda and Socialist Education as the result of Conferences and Meetings, and in this respect this Conference will serve such a purpose, preparing the way for the building of the new Socialist Order.

SPEAKERS—

PRESIDENTIAL ADDRESS BY:

Mr. FRED PEART, B.Sc.
(President Durham University Labour Club);

Mr. M. R. MASANI
(Secretary of the All-India Congress Socialist Party and Ex-Chairman London School of Economics Labour Party).

Conference will begin at 2-30 p.m.

NOTE.—Masani is an authority on Indian problems, and is the first Representative the Indian Socialist Party have sent to this country. In January, 1933, he was arrested and imprisoned for one year for having participated in the Civil Disobedience Movement.

It is desirable that every Trade Union and Political Organisation should send as many young delegates as possible. (No delegation fees will be charged).

VISITORS ARE WELCOME.

Yours faithfully,

FRED PEART, } JOINT
J. W. FOSTER. } SECRETARIES.

47

Socialist Youth Demonstration against fascism, imperialism and capitalism with M.R. Masani as one of leading speakers in October 1935 in Durham city. Menon Papers.

misrepresented that Indians were not very grateful to them for it. Referring to one simple fact, Menon asked why was it that Katherine Mayo's yellow book received so much support and 'the child marriage reformers' were her first supporters; why was it that the people so interested in Indian child marriage reform refused to castigate their government for blocking the reforms; why was it that the good Christians in Britain did not record their protest against the attitudes of their own co-religionists and representatives in the assembly?[226] Menon was candid. 'Is it any use diverting attention', he asked, 'from the factors of hunger, poverty, pestilence and disease for which the administration has the responsibility to end?'[227] Indeed, Menon became very invective. The same government, he added, that put 1,00,000 men and women into prison and treated a majority of them as ordinary felons and criminals in jail 'the condition of which defied description', had been neglecting its duty and abetting social reactionaries to break the law against child marriage. Menon emphasized that Indian women would take to reform their social system and their liberation and that awakening had come largely through the efforts of Indian people and through the movement of human liberty.[228] Indians, as a people were, very appreciative of sympathy and help. They were also forgetful of past troubles and wrongs. But they were in those dismal days 'a bit sensitive' about 'all this talk of the social iniquities of people' by those who were not inclined to end the greatest inquity of all, namely the subjection of their country by others. By then Menon had decided to cast aside all covers. He was incensed by the sanctimony and pretence of the counterpropagandists. 'Please forgive me', he wrote in anguish, 'if I have been in any way disagreeable. My own experience is that it is best to tell people who seek information the facts without reservations' and he hoped that his observations would be taken in the spirit in which they had been made.[229] Menon affirmed that all rational observers would agree with him that the case against the Indians would be much more legitimate if they were in a position to put their house in order. A government, he added forcefully, which was politically reactionary, invariably sought alliances with all other reactionary groups. It is not, therefore, surprising that the allies of the government in the legislatures and in the press were reactionaries among the Hindus and the Muslims in regard to social affairs.[230]

In keeping with the left-wing trend of the British public opinion, however, the League of Youth, South-West St. Pancras Labour Party decided to form an Educational and Study Group and start an educational programme on socialist theory as per the 'outline' prepared by the headquarters. Each course contained lists of suitable books and questions for discussion. It was decided that a leader be appointed who would supervise the activities of the group throughout the course. Wherever possible the parliamentary candidate or some experienced adult person should take sole charge.[231] The offer of that responsibility to Menon by the St. Pancras League of Youth was in harmony with Menon's political interests and intellectual inclinations. It gave Menon the opportunity to integrate a course on imperialism and on the importance of self-determination for India in the quest for a socialist salvation for Britain.[232] In no time the St. Pancras syllabus on socialism became the most popular and sought-after course in Labour Party's educational programme.[233]

About the same time, Menon became an active associate of the Socialist Press Service which was founded with the aim of making and keeping contacts with the socialist journals in all parts of the country, which had been running entirely by trade unions or local labour parties.[234] There was no central body to coordinate their endeavours. It was generally felt that these local initiatives did not wish to lose their local form but they found it difficult to get authors of national importance to write for them on topics of current and vital interests. Nor could they be certain of well-informed and authoritative discussions on the main lines along which the policy of the Labour Party was going.

Through this press service, it was believed, the writers could be assured that what they wrote could have a much wider circulation and readers would be given a wide variety of articles on various items of the reinvigorated socialist discourse. One of the series sponsored by the Socialist Press Service was on socialist policies and Menon's article on 'Socialism and the White Paper' encapsulated his views expressed in conference and lectures.[235]

Since mid-1933, Saklatvala, Menon and J. Vakil had been working in unison for organizing a vigorous India propaganda.[236] Mass meetings were on the agenda. Vakil and Saklatvala agreed with Menon that the cause was such that all of them should do their best in unison to rouse the British public and get as much publicity as possible and the proposed meetings should not be fiascos. Even if the Indian students had paid their contributions, Vakil felt, it was their duty to turn up in numbers. Vakil maintained that the unenthusiastic response and meagre participation of the Indian students betrayed a remarkable lack of urgency on the part of the organizers and one should pull one's socks to see that attendance of the Indians could be maximized. One could not expect Britain to take an interest in India, if more interest was not shown by the Indians themselves.[237]

It was natural, therefore, that by 1934 the thrust of the League's literature had also become pithy. The League followed up Menon's discourses on the condition in India at various branches at the Labour League of Youth by writing to these organizations if some of the members were interested in imperialism as a historical phenomenon and, as socialists, in fighting imperialism in a systematic way, apart from the conventional but flaccid official opposition of the Labour Party.[238] The central branch of the League was a new formation and it was composed of young socialists with strong Marxist orientation and there was lot of work for them to do. Its principal function was to push the League's propaganda to an advanced stage and sharpen its punch. 'Is there anyone in your branch,' Audrey Hus of the Central branch asked, 'who could spare two or three hours a week in working with us ...?'[239] It was informed that the India League had undertaken an intensive propaganda against imperialism generally and imperialism in India particularly. The urgency of the programme was underlined by a determination to carry out the campaign against imperialism as an outstanding accomplishment. The need to score a resounding success was imperative because unless it was possible to obtain the services of men and women genuinely devoted to the emancipation of India, the League feared that public opinion in Britain would remain innocent of Indian realities.[240] It would not realize how inadequate the government proposals seemed to the Indians and a defective public opinion was the ground work of future tragedy. It was, therefore, indispensable to get help from every one, who was sufficiently civic minded, to realize the importance of averting such a development.[241]

J. Rubenstein, secretary of the Central branch, had announced in a circular that no problem was more difficult, or more urgent, than that of India. The proposals of the National government tended further to exasperate Indian opinion and to accentuate the miseries of the masses of India.[242] He also held that little was known of the great mass-awakening of the people of India and of its political and economic causes. The entire problem and its solution were of the utmost importance to every concerned individual. It was, therefore, decided to convene a conference for placing before the branches first-hand information and to consider what effective steps might be taken to rouse public opinion and to mobilize support for that common cause.[243]

A good deal of preparation went in to the organization of a delegate conference on 16 March 1935 at the Memorial Hall, Farringdon Street, London, in order to focus public opinion on a problem which was of permanent importance to the English public. It was asserted by L.E. Goodrich of the Central branch that India and the whole question of imperialism concerned 'us the young people very gravely.'[244] The inheritance left by the National government with regard to India was one which would make 'us the agents of coercion in India, and also the victims of imperialism ourselves.' Goodrich reminded that should Labour came to power at the next election it would have the unpleasant task of imposing 'this wretched piece of legislation' upon the exploited workers of India. This was to be the first public protest against the India bill that was being organized in London. Discussion in the conference and the deliberations in the public meeting concentrated on the constitutional proposals. They took into account the League's comprehensive analysis of what had been happening in India and took a close look at the proposed devolution of authority under the new bill. Menon gave a critical resume of the various strands of Indian response to the white paper and the bill. In this context, speakers recalled the various pledges given by the British government to India demanding *purna swaraj*. Speaker after speaker explained the true meaning of self-determination and the dynamics of constituent assembly based on popular support.[245]

It was asserted by the central branch that in Menon and Shelvankar the League had the two most competent authorities in Britain on contemporary India and their expertise had been requisitioned for the enlightenment of the delegates who had been invited to participate in the conference. In September, October and November 1934, the same scholars were called upon to give a set of lectures on imperialism and British rule in India. In view of the significance of imperialism in world affairs and the impending legislation by the National government, it was believed that all thinking people would be interested in informing themselves of the problem.[246] The syllabus of the lectures included a short assessment of the British empire in

India between 1600 to 1900, an analysis of the agrarian problems and an investigation into industry, trade and finance in the context of the crisis in imperialism, an examination of Indian parties and their programmes, a scrutiny of the proposed constitutional project as the advanced imperialist machination and a careful and logical projection of the future including a possible way out of the situation.[247] The whole idea was to give wide currency to the demand of a constituent assembly in the public opinion as an essential step in the process of Indian political development.

The essence of the argument spelled out, both at the conference as well as at the set of lectures, was the inevitability of India's freedom. It sought to question and analyse the imperial stereotypes and propositions which, with minor modifications, had over the years been talked about and accepted as axiomatic by a substantial section of labour and liberal opinion and had been basically culled from the inflexible conservative pride and prejudices.[248] In all the meetings, conferences and lectures organized by the Central branch, the speakers made it amply clear that the demands of Indian nationalism of every school stood in sharp contrast to the very gradual and marginal constitutional advance inherent in British ideas and intentions. The Indians, it was argued, were concerned with a government amenable to Indian opinion and responsive to Indian needs which would place the interests of the Indian people above the imperial requirements of Britain.[249] It was unfortunate that the content, method and pace of India's constitutional advance were sought to be determined by the British government. *Manchester Guardian* elucidated the point succinctly: 'We can neither govern nor get out, and so it is necessary to devise a constitution that seems like self-government in India and at Westminster like British *Raj*.'[250] The only way out of the situation, Menon held, was the actualization for the principles of self-determination through a constituent assembly and not any ad hoc body with picked up members endowed with a set of false values.[251] Evidently, since 1934 there was a good deal of interaction between the Communist Party and the India League. The League's demonstrations and meetings drew a substantial number of communists and fellow travellers. Intelligence reports did not overlook the significance of this trend and the drift of the League's policy.

By the end of January 1934, Menon had established contact with Nehru and saw to it that an article from Jawaharlal was published in the *Daily Herald.* A second article from Nehru created some problems for the editor.[252] It was very similar to the first article. It was also far too intricate to be effective. The editor felt that Nehru seemed to assume considerable knowledge of the Indian situation on the part of his readers and without it the comments might become ineffective and the article might lose much of its punch. The editor desired to know if Menon had in his possession the text of the various orders and ordinances because, in case these were available, the editor could make something out of the Nehru article. He wanted some definite, conclusive and unchallengable facts such as an order about welcoming troops or saluting the flag under penalty, or explicitly forbidding the expression of undue concern for detainees or regulations proscribing a whole range of literature.[253] The situation was ripe for a wholesale exposition of arbitrary executive actions, especially as the Nazis had performed a service in making such things unpopular. Since these hard facts were not known to the readers, the editor managed to draw out from Menon concrete evidence so that Nehru's article might not go unnoticed. Menon saw to it that G. Parthasarathi, a student of Wadham College, Oxford, took care to give facts to substantiate all his conclusions in the report of a conference on India quoting extensively from the *Condition of India.* In particular, Parthasarathi sought to popularize the idea of the constituent assembly and lifted a whole paragraph from the League's report. This was necessary, Parthasarathi thought, as although the whole lot of people had been talking about the constituent assembly, no one thought it prudent to sketch an outline of it.[254]

Pressure on the university Labour clubs about the need for a India conference evinced a good deal of response everywhere. The International Student Service (ISS) in Oxford, somewhat disturbed by the condition of India as portrayed by the League's report, organized a conference on 16 and 17 February 1935, on the main issues involved in the relationship between Britain and India and to let students confront the main points of view on the question and discuss the whole problem in a rational and objective way.[255] The idea was to create better understanding between the protagonists of very diverse points of view. It was in keeping with the ideals of the ISS to forge a meeting-ground for various shades of opinion. It also resolved to do something to lessen, by means of rational discussion, the antagonisms that existed between different national, racial and ideological opinions in Oxford. Among the speakers were Atul Chatterjee, Geoffrey Corbett, Horace Alexander, Rvd. Jack Winslow and Menon.[256]

Evidently, G. Parthasarathi was unable to cope with the manoeuvres of the local Labour leadership. 'You understand', Parthasarathi wrote in anguish to Menon, 'how difficult it is for us, Indians, to talk to these Labour people who claim to have very definite views on all these things.'[257] Parthasarathi felt very strongly that the organizers should not have thought of getting a Tory to share the platform with Menon to discuss British imperialism and India, but he felt that all the same it was too late to withdraw from it.[258] In fact, Parthasarathi was unable to grasp the full significance of the seemingly innocuous decision to initiate a discussion in which all points of view would take part on the problem of the existing relationship between India and Britain, using the proposals for reform as a focal point for the discussion. The ISS ventured to put Menon down to lead the discussion in the second session on the political reforms, the first session having been devoted to a general review of the Indian problem by Geoffrey Corbet and Sir Atul Chatterjee. All that was required of Menon at the beginning of the second session was to give a short account of the Indian nationalist views of the proposed reforms which would be followed by another statement by a British die-hard. This would lead, it was hoped, to a general discussion on the part of the conference, as a whole, on the reform proposals and on the wider issues involved in the question. It was also decided that Menon should feel free to take part in the general discussion. This, in all essentials, corresponded to the position held by a substantial section of the Labour Party led by Attlee, who desired the Indian nationalists to accept and work a modified version of the proposals.[259] Menon felt outwitted primarily because of the ineptitude of his close associates in Oxford. Having accepted the invitation, Menon agreed with Parthasarathi that it would be inopportune to withdraw altogether, although he made it clear that he did not see much point in taking part with a die-hard in an Indian debate. The net result of it would be to make many people believe that the policy of the government was balanced, legitmate and judicious.

To the India League and those who were seriously concerned in the Indian problem, the real opposition to Indian freedom came from the supporters of the National government who, Menon thought, misled a number of well-meaning people by covering up their reactionary proposals with a lot of wordy eloquence. It would have been much more rewarding, Menon wrote frankly, if he had not been put down 'for the unrealistic and fruitless debate' as there would be 'two of us attacking the government policy and thereby making it look the right thing which it is not.'[260] He understood that it would be a serious effort to understand the Indian problem but in that case it was unfortunate that the die-hard view, which was already well-known and was very simple, should have been pitted against the Indian case presented by Menon.[261] Menon's clear and firm stand was fruitful. The die-hard spokesman withdrew. Horace Alexander and Jack Winslow joined the conference upholding liberal positions. Menon participated in all the sessions of the conference and an inquisitive audience heard and debated the questions on India with a good deal of sympathy for Indian aspirations.[262]

Not long after, Menon found himself contesting an 'unfortunate' misrepresentation in the official journal of the Labour Party. Menon was sorry to bring to the notice of Hubert Tracey, editor, *Labour,* that in a much advertised symposium on dominion status for India the publishers thought it necessary to put Menon's contribution under the caption, 'The Hindu standpoint.'[263] 'You may remember,' Menon recalled, 'I was not asked for a Hindu standpoint nor did I give one.'[264] Several people drew his attention to that gross distortion and Menon thought that the least he could have done was to tell the editor about it. Of course, Menon felt sure that he had been labelled in such a way unintentionally. But it was unjustified and unfair and it was a pity that the official organ of the Labour Party should, even unconsciously, have thought it judicious to present the issue in such a manner and project the viewpoint of the national organization of India as a sectional demand.[265]

By then Menon felt obliged to examine the the reform proposals in the context of the over all imperial policy towards India.[266] He claimed that in the existing political discussion, the Indian people did not appear to figure in the imperial calculations at all. Two sections of die-hard imperialists, he jibed, had been wondering how best to fight the Indian people. One section maintained, Menon explained at a receptive symposium at Liverpool, 'we are not going to give India to the Indians', and the other section from opposition declared with great aplomb, 'we are going to give India to the Indians — but we are going to keep it all the same.'[267] Menon contested the idea that India was in the empire for its own good had long evanesced even from the imperial propaganda. The existing formulation maintained that India was in the empire for the good of the empire. India was Britain's by conquest.[268] It did not belong to the Indians; the Indians were merely born there. Menon maintained that the Indian problem could not possibly be solved by a policy of bribing and flattering Indian princes. Under the India bill, finance, defence, foreign affairs and internal government were all left in the hands of the governor-general.[269] The viceroy, endowed with special powers, could suspend the whole of the constitution, take over any department, stop the discussion of any measure of legislation and veto anything that had been passed by the Indian legislature. Menon emphasized that the existing unemployment in Lancashire owed its origin not to the trouble in India caused by Gandhi but to a conflict of worldwide imperialism. The economically backward countries had not the necessary purchasing power to obtain British products and the Lancashire mill owners had been taking their capital to utilize the sweated labour of India against the labour in their own country.[270] Politically, Menon then found himself at the left spectrum of Indian politics. As a socialist, he had become somewhat sceptical of Gandhi's political and social stances. A few of his London Letters had been thinly disguised criticisms of the decline of civil disobedience and of Gandhi's unaccountable withdrawal from political struggle to a course of social reform under what appeared to be the undesirable influence of Agatha Harrison and Horace Alexander.[271]

There was little enthusiasm in India about the report. Most of its departure from the white Paper had been anticipated by the press by a process of conjecture. All the important public men and newspapers condemned the report. It appeared even to Sapru that people seemed to have lost all faith in any substantial proceedings from England. It was, Sapru commented, a very unfortunate feeling, but he felt that there was considerable justification for it. Sapru acknowledged, that Attlee's alternative report incorporated some of the suggestions of the memorandum Sapru-Jayakar of December 1933, but they were flouted by the majority of the Conservative members in utter indifference to moderate Indian sentiments.[272]

Polak had been in constant touch with Sapru and Jayakar. All through 1934, Polak thought it prudent to impress upon the moderates that the Attlee draft was substantially to the left of the white paper proposals and more along the lines suggested by Sapru and Jayakar. But he was not certain if the Labour Party would vote against the bill in Parliament. Polak was convinced that the party would be obliged to act according to the established convention of the British constitution. He held that faced with the new constitution, even the Congress 'will have to work it.'[273] All talk about destroying the constitution by deliberately working for deadlocks appeared to Polak to be the most reckless piece of advice. It would create the worst kind of opinion abroad and unleash mischief in the country. Polak asserted that even a universal condemnation would play into the hands of dieh-ards in Britain. Besides, there was not the slightest chance of anything better emerging out of the existing Parliament. There was also very little, if any chance at all, of the Labour Party being able, even if willing, to do anything in the way of introducing a new and advance scheme of constitutional reform for India, 'except in the remote furture.'[274] Polak, himself a member of the Labour Party's specialized committee on India, was confident that the party would have neither the mandate nor the will to deal with the Indian question exclusively as a party matter. Unless there was a 'terrific landslide in Britain politically', of which there was no indication anywhere, no substantial reforms could be expected, without the consent of the Conservatives. It was evident, Polak sought to convince Jayakar, that whilst the Labour Party would seek to amend whatever possible in the Indian constitutional bill, they had no intention of 'playing the die-hard game of obstruction', nor would they prevent, however small a measure, the Indian constitutional reform. It was apparent from the pronouncement of the leaders that though the party had voted against the report, it was not going 'to help the diehards to wreck the Bill.'[275]

By August 1934, Polak had already thought it judicious to discuss the significant features of the Labour perception of the Indian constitutional proposals. Polak was certain that the new constitution would be 'something less, though not in principle, than the White Paper scheme.'[276] In the assessment of the Labour Party, Polak added, there was no coherence of purpose or unity of action in Indian responses. The Labour leaders were convinced that despite universal dissatisfaction with the government's final proposals, there was so much weakness, disorganization and factional hostility throughout the country that no effective opposition to the reform could be offered. Polak advised Jayakar to give a lead to public opinion in favour of the acceptance of the reforms. He thought that the projected constitutional scheme had a few significant features which might conveniently be advertised to attract the nationalist forces in India. He stressed that the mere fact that it would bring all India together, for the first time, within one political organism should justify its acceptance. Recommending the scheme, Polak held that the Indian people would gain invaluable experience from the collaboration between the States and British India operating in tandem in the interests of the country as a whole.[277] With the inevitable increase in national consciousness, the political process would help the formulation of national objectives. The process would be assisted by the inexorable development of world events. Polak believed that dominion status 'cannot ultimately be denied her' and it would come sooner than she was prepared for it. But the situation was as yet not favourable.[278]

In fact, the authorities in Britain were eagerly awaiting the split in the Congress in more than one direction. They relished the developments that drove Malaviya into the arms of the Mahasabha. They anticipated that Malaviya was bound to take the line of opposition to the legislature in socio-religious matters. Whatever the merit of the issue in principles, Polak was convinced that to support Malaviya on these issues would be to stand in the way of progressive ideas and Sapru and Jayakar could not be expected to line up with Malaviya. Besides, Polak felt that the ideological positions in the Congress itself were disturbing. He argued that it was difficult for the Congress to carry at the same time the landholders and commercial men on the one hand, and the socialist group on the other. They were poles apart both in interest and in method and Polak did not think that the 'latent instability can remain without outward consequences.'[279] Polak represented the position of the Labour leadership when he wrote that he did not contemplate the political prospect in India, with all 'the confusion of parties and policies and lack of policies, with any equanimity.' On these grounds, Polak sought to persuade Sapru, Jayakar and Sastri to accept and work the reforms. They were repeatedly assured that their work exercised a profound influence on the minds of the members of the JSC. Evidently, in those days of racial feelings, violent nationalisms, dictatorships and terrorism all over the world, it was impossible to expect enthusiasm or smooth passage for the proposals either in India or in England. But a moderate constitutional line had been adopted in keeping with the liberal way of life. It was believed that if India produced political parties and leaders capable of maintaining stable legislatures and strong ministries, power would pass to them 'by the quiet road of constitutional evolution exactly as it has in Canada, Australia and elsewhere.'[280] Polak had persuaded the Labour leadership to appreciate that Indian public opinion naturally concerned itself with the 'multitudinous legal limitations' 'implicit in safeguards.' He was, however, equally convinced that English public opinion 'was rightly inclined to multiply safeguards', partly because powers might very rapidly pass from its hands to an Indian 'dominion' once the principle of responsible government was recognised.[281] British public opinion was also apprehensive of the danger of the breakdown of unity and government in India in view of the rapid transfer of power to the hands of inexperienced politicians distinguished by the absence of strong party foundations and certain liberal ideas of governance. Polak emphasized that the more the JSC proposals were attacked in India, the more the Conservatives were likely to listen to the die-hards. The only alternative, Polak advised was to set the constitution in motion and so to give a field of useful political responsibility to young India. The alternative, according to Polak, was the repetition of the history of Ireland — a prolonged bloody and bitter struggle between Indian revolutionaries and British diehards, eventual break-up of India, the triumph of the spirit of violence 'corresponding to the partition and the struggle of the gunmen in Ireland since 1922.'[282] Polak commended the courage and focussed ability displayed by Hoare, secretary of state, throughout the course of the JSC and urged the responsible Indian opinion to accept and launch a moderate form of constitution which 'would lead to full responsibility in proportion to the political ability displayed by Indian political parties.'[283]

Lord Lothian, with whom the Indian constitution had become a supreme preoccupation over the years, was keen to emphasize in his correspondence with Sapru that much had been salvaged for the Indian development and progress. The report of the JSC, he stressed, preserved quite intact the three fundamentals of what 'may perhaps be called the Round Table agreement.' They were federation, provincial autonomy and central responsibility with safeguards. It was true, he acknowledged, that the JSC had stiffened up the safeguards. But the principle of responsibility was not infringed in any case.

The position of Lothian closely corresponded to that of Polak. Both of them agreed that all the changes had been made in order to make the white paper 'more palatable to the Conservative Party' but these alterations did not undermine its basic principles. At first sight the JSC proposals might look like 'a very restricted affair.'[284] It was assumed that in due course of time, by conventions and by the process of practice, the constitution would assume the character of a responsible parliamentary democracy. The basic problem was to get the act on the statute book. The authorities had before them a choice between conciliating Indian opinion and winning moderate Conservative support. They opted for the second alternative. The future of India, Lothian was assertive, 'depended fundamentally on whether the Indian electorate would return competent legislatures capable of maintaining stable Ministers or not.' If they did, power would inevitably and inexorably pass into their hands. If, on the other, they failed to return constructive political leadership, the safeguards should preserve the political and constitutional unity of India. Lothian made it abundantly clear that the utmost which the Labour Party could expect at the next election was a position of equality and not an overwhelming majority to put through a more liberal constitutional experiment in the teeth of the opposition of a really formidable Conservative Party.[285] Polak endorsed Lothian's persuasive appeal. He made it clear to Jayakar that those who entertained the idea that the Labour Party would introduce a large measure of more liberal constitutional reforms in India would be doomed to disappointment. They would be so involved in domestic affairs that they would have no leisure to deal with India. Besides, they would be prevented to think of a more liberal constitutional measure by the powerful adverse public opinion. Morgan Jones virtually confirmed that view in conservation with Polak and Andrews.[286]

Carefully examining the Indian opposition, Agatha Harrison presented a note to her group on the Congress opposition. Harrison believed that two of the objections seemed to be fundamental in the Congress standpoint.[287] It appeared to the Congress that the constitution was being thrust on India as it was not drawn up by the representatives of India. Besides, there was no popular control over army, finance and foreign affairs constituting what Gandhi termed as the 'substance of freedom.' Other objections included British guilt of breach of faith and the carefully drafted phrase as the goal for India avoiding dominion status and tending more to emphasize and perpetuate sectional interests detrimental to national interest. The Congress also opposed the unlimited dictatorial power to the Viceroy, safeguards designed to protect British interests and not Indian interests, indirect responsibility to federal assembly, representations of the states by the nominees of the rulers, no representation of state subject, 80 per cent non-votable revenue, dictatorial powers extended to provincial governors, services not under popular ministers, reactionary nature of second chambers, ministers in provinces with non-votable salaries and without joint responsibility, non-transfer of law and order portfolios, and dyarchy in federation. The whole measure was designed, the Congress asserted, to facilitate, perpetuate and consolidate domination of India by Britain.[288]

Agatha Harrison's note emphasized that if it could be shown that the framers of the constitution had been making efforts to meet the second set of objects which the Congress held in common with the other groups, it would then be open for Congressmen to consider if they could not possibly modify, for the time being, some of their fundamental objections. In the absence of any such assurance it would be useless on the part of the Congress to sacrifice principles or ignore the pledges.[289] The Conciliation Group was not a propagandist body and unlike the India League, Carl Heath maintained, it did not commit itself to the advocacy of a particular body of opinion. Over the years, the Group had nursed close and friendly relations with prominent members of governments at home and in India, various men and institutions engaged in social service in India and a large number of leaders of modern India having diverse points of view. It could, Heath averred, not start any initiative in India with a bias in favour of any significant opinion.[290] The Group was eager to know and carefully weigh facts as they had always done before. This detached involvement helped the Group to pursue with some measure of success, a great deal of 'private reconciliatory work' in interviews, correspondence and discussions.[291]

The efforts of the Conciliation Group had been helpful in some sense. But the result invariably got enmeshed in a confusing web of sentimental personal relationships. The main purpose of the Group, as Heath informed the members in a circular letter, was the building of a real understanding and cooperating sympathy between Indians and the British. Heath was apprehensive that in the matter of the constitution bill, the Group might be in some danger of losing sight of the wood because of the trees. He felt that in 'a guerrilla warfare' by the Churchillians and a mass of amendments from the regular Labour and Liberal opposition, the main problem had failed to stand out in the public mind.[292] It was, therefore, felt necessary for the sake of conciliation to concentrate on these main issues. It was accordingly decided to organize a few kindred working groups in the country — in Manchester, Oxford, Birmingham, London and one in India — to consider some such issues of an agreed list and to work out a reasoned statement from the point of view of 'free, cooperative reconciliatory relationships.'[293] That statement could then be presented to 'reasonable' members of the House of Lords, the purpose being not that of 'propagandist' but 'an intelligent understanding.' To make the initiative effective it was thought prudent to induce 'our friends in India' to establish something like a watching and working committee in London, sending over to England one or two prominent men and women.

By March 1935, the Conciliation Group was ready with its note on the constitution proposals.[294] It stressed that in the discussion then proceeding upon the Indian constitutional problem, efforts should be made to concentrate public opinion upon certain key questions. Accordingly, it sought to draw the attention of the members of Parliament to certain points of importance such as: (a) status of India to be announced in a clear and unequivocal statement defining dominion status as the ultimate goal of Indian constitutional development, (b) growth of the constitution through Indian initiative by including a clause in the bill that any time after the passing of the Act, a resolution calling for constitutional change by a three-fourths majority of an Indian legislature should be brought before Parliament for due consideration, (c) measures to be adopted for increasing Indian control of finance, defence, foreign affairs, currency policies and the public services, (d) direct election; and (e) representation of labour, depressed classes and women in all upper houses of all legislatures.[295]

This perspective was totally at variance with the India League's approach. The Conciliation Group worked for a compromise and a marginal adjustment in government proposals. The League desired a complete rejection of the proposals and asked for a constituent assembly. It may be added that there developed, despite difference in objective and perception, a good deal of cooperation and give and take between the India League and the Concilation Group. Often they supplemented each other but there was also a fair amount of rivalry and jealousy, and sharp divergence of objectives and perceptions. There was, as Shelvankar conceptualized in his conversation with the author, an undercurrent of tension for jurisdiction and influence and the 'cold war' between the two continued till India's independence despite Alexander's periodical sensitive overtures, Menon's critical responses and Harrison's sincere concern for Menon's health and welfare.[296]

In autumn 1934, it looked as though that the Nationalist split in the Congress was going to paralyze Congress in the elections. The Nationalist Party under Malaviya was based partly on Hindu communal feeling and partly on what appeared to many as Malaviya's private jealousy of Gandhi. By April 1935, the events showed that the communal Hindus were not so strong as they imagined and the Congress was all the more healthy for having shed them. However, they just prevented Congress from getting a clear majority of elected members and left the independents under Jinnah once more with the balance of power. It seemed to the British power elite in general that the result on the whole justified Willingdon's idea of holding an election. Yet it was clear to all who were committed to the continuation of British rule that the situation was not very hopeful. The Congress' return to the assembly was not due to any real change of convictions but because they felt Gandhi's extraordinary policy of private civil disobedience had been leading them nowhere and that they realized that they were not strong enough to revive real civil disobedience. They were cooperating pro-tem, Percival Spear confided to Horace Alexander, in order to see what the reforms would bring forth, and were ready at the next favourable moment to leave the legislature once more and try their hand at a new campaign. The intransigent attitude of the Congress, Spear thought, dated from the rough suppression of civil disobedience movement in the very first month of 1932. That attitude was far more resolute then than it had been under Lord Irwin. Cooperation under Willingdon was a matter of tactics only while the permanent attitude was non-cooperation. In contrast, the civil disobedience had been a matter of tactics, the permanent attitude being really a cooperating one. The Congress, therefore, presented to government a 'grave political danger' which would become real whenever there was a new economic crisis in India or political embarrassment in Europe. This was to be the permanent feature of the existing regime in India. Spear added that it was generally felt by educated Indians that government was inclined to settle the Indian question without the Congress. 'The difference between Irwin and Willingdon', Spear explained, 'is that the one wanted to include Congress within the framework of the Indian settlement, while the other thinks that he can have them out.' As to future Spear's prognostications were reflective of the official mindset. The 'safeguards,' the 'communal settlement' and the concessions to the princes and vested interests would ensure that every government would be 'a coalition of communal blocks.' These coalitions would be 'permanent just because the blocks are permanent.' They would be formed on 'the basis of allotment of public office and appointments.' It was hoped that there was no reason why they should not last for ever. It was believed that the government would revolve round the loaves and fishes and the principle would be to keep things as they were. As a consequence, it would be a paradise for vested interests while 'the inherent weakness of Indian life — overpowering traditionalism and excessive conservatism - will have full scope.'[297]

The Labour Party did not fail to take note of the tremendous urge for revitalization of the party which had got a fresh spurt after the formation of the Socialist League. Menon was invariably considered as an experienced and erudite socialist educator and a stimulating communicator. His mastery of national and international issues was unquestioned; his associations with the labour movement in responsible positions was long-standing; his record in the official memory of the party as an ardent activist was significant and honourable; his contribution in Labour's adult educational movement had been exemplary.[298] He was then in search of a parliamentary constituency. Monica Whately, herself in search of one, was keen to get one for Menon. But there were various constraints. It seemed that headquarters were not really interested in any but big people or those who had money. Some constituencies would not consider Jews, some would not have anyone who was not English, some would not provide for a candidate known to be a strong feminist, some would not touch one who had been fighting for colonial freedom and some others would not deal with a suspected fellow-traveller.[299] The Labour Party was in doldrums and the Labour men, somewhat stupefied, were in a state of pleasant idleness. It was evident to all perceptive observers that there were three roads open to the Labour Party: it could abandon reformism and shift to the right as MacDonald had done, or it might abandon reformism and shift to the left and adopt a revolutionary outlook though retaining significant identity for itself and the third alternative was to hold on to reformism in its decaying, unstable form. It seemed to Menon and many others that the Labour leadership might be inclined to conclude that the third alternative constituted perhaps the most convenient course of action.[300]

Notes and References

1 The World Committee for the Relief of the Victims of German Fascism, *The Brown Book of the Hitler Terror.* Victor Gollancz, August 1933. Also see, Menon on the release of the book, 22 August 1933, Menon Papers.

2 Ruth Dudley Edwards, *Victor Gollancz, A Biography,* London 1987, pp. 218-20.

3 John Strachey, *The Menace of Fascism,* London 1933, pp.11-18; S. Samuels, 'English Intellectuals and Politics in the 1930s', in P. Rieff (ed.), *On Intellectuals; Theoretical Studies, Case Studies,* Garden City, 1969, pp.196-247. Gary Wrskey, *The Visible College,* op.cit., pp.160, 216-219, 249-57, 328-35.

4 Arthur Marwick, *Britain in the Century of Total War,* op. cit., pp.217, 226, 239-9.

5 A.J.P. Taylor, *English History 1914-1945,* op.cit., pp.362 and 364.

6 See, Jon Clark, Margot Heinemann, David Margolies, and Carole Snee, *Culture and Crisis in Britain in the 30s,* op.cit.

7 D.A.N. Jones, 'The 20th Century Remembered', 10-2 July 1981, BBC, in Brockway Papers 25a/5; also, Brockway on Manny Shinmell, 3 April 1981, Brockway papers, 55a(3).

8 Fenner Brockway to Jawaharlal Nehru, 8 September 1933, Menon Papers; also see, Brockway to Henry Mayers Hyndman, 18 July 1921, Brockway Papers.

9 Brockway to Jawaharlal Nehru, 8 September 1933, Menon Papers.

10 Sarvepalli Gopal, *Jawaharlal Nehru, A Biography,* Vol.I (1889-1947), Delhi 1975, pp.176-78.

11 Ibid., p.177.

12 Ibid., p.178.

13 Ibid., pp.178-9; also see, K. Gopalan Kutty, 'The integration of Anti-Landlord Movement in the Movement Against Imperialism', in Bipan Chandra (ed.), *The Indian Left,* A.R. Desai (ed.) *Peasant Struggles in India.*

14 Sukomal Sen, *Working Class of India, History of Emergence and Movement,* 1830-1970, Calcutta 1977.

15 Cf. The appeal of the Indian Meerut Committee, March 1933, Menon Papers.

16 See, Urmila Phadnis, *Towards the Integration of Indian States, 1919-47,* Bombay 1968.

17 Vinayak Damodar Savarkar, *Hindutva: Who is a Hindu?,* Bombay 1923.

18 Bipan Chandra, *Communalism in Modern India,* New Delhi

1987; D.R. Goyal, *Rashtriya Swayamsewak Sangh,* New Delhi 1979.

19 There are extensive references to this aspect of 'Hindu' communal organization in Moonje Papers.

20 Balabushevich and Dyakov (ed), *A Contemporary History of India,* New Delhi, 1964, pp.150, 240-2.

21 Acharya Narendra Dev, *Socialism and the National Revolution,* Bombay 1946 p.4; Girja Shankar, *Socialist Trends in Indian National Movement,* Meerut, 1987 and S. Gopal, *Nehru,* vol.I, op.cit., pp.570-4.

22 Judith Brown, *Gandhi: Prisoner of Hope,* New Haven 1989, pp.301-2.

23 Patrick French, *Liberty or Death,* London 1997 pp.104-5.

24 Menon to Rangswami Aiyengar, 18 April 1933, Menon Papers.

25 Gandhi to Moonje, 15 June 1934, B.S. Moonje Papers.

26 Bhai Paramanand to Moonje, 26 June 1934, Moonje Papers.

27 Ibid.

28 Ibid.

29 Central Hindu Yuvak Sabha, Lahore, 'An Open Letter to Mahatma Gandhi', July 1934, Moonje Papers.

30 Cf. 'A Statement by Bengal Socialists on Gandhi's decision to retire', *The Congress Socialist,* 29 September 1934.

31 Dinkar Mehta to Jawaharlal Nehru, 4 December 1933, Menon Papers.

32 Ibid.

33 Ibid.

34 Ibid.

35 Jawaharlal Nehru to Dinkar Mehta, 9 December 1933, Menon Papers.

36 Ibid.

37 Jawaharlal Nehru to Dinkar Mehta, 18 December 1933, Menon Papers.

38 Jawaharlal Nehru to Charles Mascarenas, 10 November 1933, Menon Papers.

39 Ibid.

40 Ibid.

41 Vijayalakshmi Pundit to Graham Pole, 21 June 1931, Graham Pole Papers. (India Office).

42 Jawaharlal Nehru to Dinkar Mehta, 9 December 1933, Menon Papers.

43 Jawaharlal Nehru to Mascarenas, 10 November 1933, Menon Papers.

44 Jawaharlal Nehru to Dinkar Mehta, 9 December 1933, Menon Papers.

45 Ibid.

46 Ibid.

47 Ibid.

48 Jawaharlal Nehru to Charles Mascarenas, 10 November 1933, Menon Papers. Also see, Gopal, *Jawaharlal Nehru, A Biography,* vol.I, op.cit., p.181.

49 'B.S. Moonje's rejoinder to the statement of Jawaharlal Nehru', *Hindustan Times,* 24 November 1933, B.S. Moonje Papers.

50 Ibid.

51 Ibid.

52 H.K. Hales to Jawaharlal Nehru, 6 October 1933, Menon Papers.

53 Ibid.

54 H.K. Hales to Jawaharlal Nehru, 25 October 1933, Menon Papers.

55 Ibid.

56 Ibid.

57 H.K. Hales to Jawaharlal Nehru, 7 November 1933, Menon Papers.

58 Polak to Jayakar, 12 June 1936, Jayakar Papers.

59 See Scotland Yard papers in P&J(S) series in India Office Library; also, Gopal, *Nehru,* vol.I, op.cit., p.154.

60 H.K. Hales to Jawaharlal Nehru, 7 November 1933, Menon Papers.

61 Ibid.

62 Ibid.

63 Culled from a significant work of Sisir Kumar Das, *A History of Indian Literature, 1911-1956, Struggle for Freedom: Triumph and Tragedy,* New Delhi 1995.

64 Ibid.

65 See, Suhash Chakravarty, *Menon*, vol.II, pp.78-109; also cf. *Sisir Kumar Das, Indian Literature,* op.cit., pp.64-90, for Gandhi's impact on Indian creative imagination.

66 Sisir Kumar Das, *Indian Literature,* ibid., esp. pp.195-214.

67 Cf. Jawaharlal Nehru, *Whither India?* Allahabad 1933.

68 Cf. Sisir Kumar Das, *Indian Literature,* op.cit., pp. 223-227.

69 India League, *Condition of India,* London 1934.

70 Sisir Kumar Das, *Indian Literature,* op.cit., esp. pp.13-14, 81-83, 195-96, 224-5, 271, 318, 321.

71 Hiren Kumar Sanyal, *Parichaer Kuri Bachar O Anyanya Smritichitra* (in Bengali), Calcutta 1978; also see, Sisir Kumar Das, *Indian Literature etc.,* op.cit., p.83.

72 Sisir Das, *Indian Literature,* op.cit., p.22.

73 See, Ibid., pp.83-84, for the popular impact.

74 Ibid.

75 Hirendra Kumar Sanyal, *Parichaer Kuri Bachar,* etc., op.cit.

76 Ibid.

77 Cf. files on the Indian volunteers and speakers of the India League, Menon Papers.

78 Harold Laski, 'The Underlying Assumptions of the National Government', *Political Quarterly,* Vol.5, 1935.

79 Ibid.

80 Ibid.

81 Ibid.

82 Lansbury to Bhulabhai Desai, 28 January 1933, Menon Papers, also, Menon to Rangaswami Aiyengar, 18 February 1933, Menon Papers.

83 Lansbury to Bhulabhai Desai, 28 January 1933, Menon Papers.

84 Bhulabhai Desai to Menon, 31 January 1933, Menon Papers.

85 Lansbury to Bhulabhai Desai, 28 January 1933, Menon Papers.

86 Ibid.

87 Ibid.

88 Lansbury, 'India: Suggested Rough Draft: Statement on behalf of the Labour Party', March 1933, Lansbury Papers.

89 No. 100, 'Indian Policy', Advisory Committee on Imperial Questions, May 1932, Labour Archives.

90 Ibid.

91 Ibid.

92 'The Situation in India and Party Policy', May 1932

Advisory Committee on Imperial Questions, May 1932, Labour Archives.

93 No. 134 C.R. Buxton, 'Memorandum on the Present Situation', Advisory Committee on Imperial Question, April 1934, Labour Archives.

94 No. 100, John Maynard, 'India Policy', Advisory Committee on Imperial Questions, op.cit.

95 Ibid.

96 No. 134, 'Memorandum on the Present Situation', Advisory Committee on Imperial Questions, May 1934, Labour Archives.

97 Suhash Chakravarty, *The Raj Syndrome,* op.cit., pp.153-165.

98 D. Graham Pole, No. 113, 'Memorandum on the Indian White Paper', Advisory Committee on Imperial Questions, March 1933, Labour Archives.

99 Ibid.

100 No. 134, 'Memorandum on the Present Situation', Advisory Committee on Imperial Questions, May 1934, Labour Archives.

101 No.113, D. Graham Pole, 'Memorandum on the White Paper',

102 Ibid.

103 Menon, 'Dominion Status for India, a note', 9 March 1934, Menon Papers.

104 Ibid.

105 Ibid.; also see, Sidney Spencer to Menon, 28 November 1934; also, Menon at Social Problem Circle, Hope Street Church; Liverpool, 1 December 1934, Menon Papers.

106 See the Statement of Monica Whately at Hastings, PLPC (1933) Hastings, p.229.

107 PLPC (1934) Southport, p.179.

108 Ibid., Arthur Hinderson, p.179.

109 Ibid.

110 PLPC (1935) Brighton, Ms Betty Fraser, (London University L.P.), p.240.

111 Ibid.

112 PLPC (1935) Brighton, p.85.

113 Tonny Greenwood, in the conference, ibid., pp.240-41.

114 Ibid.

115 H.S.L. Polak to Jayakar, 5 October 1934, Jayakar Papers.

116 Ibid.

117 Menon to Bhulabhai Desai, 4 May 1934, Menon Papers.

118 Ibid.

119 Ibid.

120 Ibid.

121 Ibid.

122 Ibid.

123 Menon to Laski, 18 May 1934, Menon Papers.

124 Menon to Lansbury, 21 May 1934, Menon Papers.

125 Ibid.

126 Menon to Brailsford, 30 May 1934, Menon Papers.

127 Ibid.

128 Menon to Stafford Cripps, 29 May 1934, Menon Papers.

129 Ibid.

130 Menon to Sachidananda Sinha, 11 May 1935, Menon Papers.

131 Ibid.

132 Ibid.

133 Ibid.

134 Ibid. Also note the following official observation:

'Churchill is less anti-Reform than anti-National Government, and there is reason to believe that his contact with the Indian Delegates in the Joint Select Committee brought to him some realization of the Imperial dangers of his attitude towards the Reforms. At any rate you may have noticed that since then his particular part in the Campaign has lost much of its former avidity and that in its choice of controversial points is much more cautious from the Imperial point of view than formerly.'

H. MacGregor to S.L. Polak, 27 March 1934, Polak Papers.

135 Menon to Shiva Rao, 21 May 1934, Menon Papers.

136 Ibid.

137 Ibid.

138 Menon to Bhulabhai Desai, 27 May 1934, Menon Papers.

139 David Grenfell, Harold J. Laski and Horace G. Alexander, 'A Constituent Assembly for India: A Memorandum', enclosed in New Scotland Yard Report, 4 June 1934, L/PJ/12/450.

140 'A Memorandum' in ibid.

141 Ibid.

142 Ibid.

143 Ibid.

144 Ibid.

145 Ibid.

146 Ibid.

147 Ibid.

148 Ibid.

149 Ibid.

150 Menon to G. Parthasarathi, 11 May 1934, Menon Papers; also Cf. Menon to Harry Pollitt, 23 May 1934, Menon Papers.

151 'Memorandum on India', 1935, n.d. Menon Papers.

152 Ibid.

153 Ibid.

154 Ibid.

155 Ibid.

156 Ibid.

157 Ibid.

158 Ibid.

159 Ibid.

160 Ibid.

161 Ibid.

162 Ibid.

163 Menon, 'Circular letter' to the branches, 16 July 1935, Menon Papers.

164 Ibid.

165 Ibid.

166 Revd. D. Chellappa to Menon, 23 January 1935, Menon Papers.

167 Ibid.

168 Ibid.

169 Author's interviews with Michael Foot, Anna Polak, Julius Silverman and Pam Cullen.

170 Evelyn Lend to Menon, 20 January 1935, Menon Papers.

171 Reginald Reynolds to Menon, 26 January 1935, Menon Papers.

172 Secretary, Hornsey League to Menon, 3 February 1935, Menon Papers.

173 M.K. Gandhi to Carl Heath, 3 January 1935, Lansbury Papers.

174 Ibid.

175 Ibid.

176 Ibid.

177 Reginald Reynolds to Menon, 28 January 1935, Menon Papers.

178 Menon to Chris Lewis, 16 February 1935, Menon Papers.

179 Lansbury, 'Broadcast', 1 February 1935, Lansbury, Papers; See also, 'The White Paper: A Breech of Faith by Srinivasa Sastri; 'The Demands of Indian Moderates', Setalvad, Setna, Mody, Chagla etc.; 'The Indian View of the White Paper', From *The Statesman* and *Nation*; 'Broken Pledges' by V.K. Krishna Menon, all May 1933 in Menon Papers.

180 Secretary, 'No War Movement', Midland's Churches' Committee, 3 March 1935, Menon Papers.

181 Ibid.

182 Purcell to Menon, 10 January 1935, Menon Papers.

183 P. Waughray, (Organizing Secretary, India League, Manchester branch) to Secretary, Manchester Diamament Council, 31 May 1935, Manchester City Council: Manchester Central Library.

184 Ibid.

185 Harold Bing to Menon, 14 April 1934, Menon Papers.

186 Menon to Bing, 2 January 1935, Menon Papers.

187 'Report of the public meeting at Swansea, 16 February 1935, Menon Papers.

188 Report from Dundee, 1 March 1935, Menon Papers.

189 Report on the meeting held by Women's Freedom Movement, 28 March 1935, Menon Papers.

190 Menon to Horrabin, 3 March 1935, Menon Papers; also see, Albert E. Rye (Suffolk) to Menon, 28 February 1935, Menon Papers and Fred Peart to Menon, 6 October 1935, Menon Papers.

191 Albert, E. Rye to Menon, 28 February 1935, Menon Papers.

192 Ibid.

193 Ibid.

194 Harry Pollitt to Menon, 6 March 1935, Menon Papers and Bridgeman to Menon, 10 March 1935, Menon Papers.

195 N.B. Hunter to Menon, 21 March 1935, Menon Papers.

196 Jum Saunders to Menon, 21 December 1934, Menon Papers.

197 Ibid.

198 Menon to Frank Dawtry, 6 April 1935, Menon Papers.

199 Alexander Keeble to Menon, 10 April 1935, Menon Papers.

200 Menon to Horrabin, 14 January 1935, Menon Papers.

201 Shelvankar File, Dr. Krishna Rao Shiva Rao Shelvankar, L/I/1912, 21 July 1943), India Office.

202 K.S. Shelvankar, 'The Present Situation in India', 26 April 1934, Infr. off. 475 (1934), India Office.

203 Ibid.

204 Shiva Rao to Menon, 16 September 1934, Menon Papers.

205 Menon to Shiva Rao, 1 November 1934, Menon Papers.

206 See, Menon to Sahni (ed.) *Hindustan Times,* 23 September 1934, Menon Papers along with the drafts of three articles for publication, namely (1) At the Cross Roads?, (2) Who is choosing the Blind Alley? and (3) Where does India stand? - all in Menon Papers.

207 Menon, 'India at the Cross Roads', 23 September 1934, Menon Papers.

208 See, for example, C.B. Kumar to Menon, 5 December 1934, Menon Papers.

209 Ibid.

210 Charles W. Cropper, The Publicity Club, London to Menon, 7 December 1934, Menon Papers.

211 Reginald Bridgeman to Menon, 8 December 1934, Menon Papers.

212 Report on the Meeting at Conway Hall, Holbern, on 19 December 1934, 21 December 1934, Menon Papers.

213 Secretary, St. Pancras Book Club to Menon, 15 December 1934, Menon Papers.

214 Ibid.

215 Menon on 'An Indian Day', 27 December 1934, Menon Papers.

216 Menon to R. Lewis, 21 December 1934, Menon Papers.

217 Haridas Mazumdar to Krishna Menon, 18 September 1934, Menon Papers.

218 Menon to Mirabehn, 3 August 1934, Menon Papers.

219 Allan Young to Krishna Menon, 16 September 1934, Menon Papers.

220 Author's interview with Mary Shelvankar.

221 Barbara MacNamara to Menon, 16 September 1935, Menon Papers.

222 Anna Polak to the author, 7 May 1992 (in personal possession of the author).

223 M. Dormer Harris to Menon, 31 March 1934, Menon Papers.

224 Menon to M. Dormer Harris, 2 April 1934, Menon Papers.

225 Ibid.

226 Ibid.

227 Ibid.

228 Ibid.

229 Ibid.

230 Ibid.

231 Secretary, St. Pancras Labour Party to Menon, 18 August 1934, Menon Papers.

232 Draft, 'Syllabus', no date 1934, St. Pancras Labour Party, Menon Papers.

233 Secretary, St. Pancras Labour Party to Menon, 29 October, 1934, Menon Papers.

234 Menon to K. Shelvankar, 9 September 1934, Menon Papers.

235 G. Thomson, (editor), Socialist Press Service, London to Menon, 1 August 1934.

236 See, J. Vakil to Menon, 10 May 1933, Menon Papers.

237 J. Vakil to Menon, 1 March 1934, Menon Papers.

238 Andrey Hus, 'Open Letter', 11 October 1934, Menon Papers.

239 Ibid.

240 L.E. Goodrich, 'Open Letter', 10 March 1934, Menon Papers.

241 Ibid.

242 J. Robenstein, 'Circular Letter', August 1934, Menon Papers.

243 Ibid.

244 L.E. Goodrich, 'India and Imperialism', 8 March 1934, Menon Papers.

245 Report on the delegated Conference, 16 March 1934, Menon Papers.

246 J. Rubenstein, 'Circular Letter', 3 August 1934, Menon Papers.

247 India League, 'Outline Syllabus of Study Lectures on Imperialism with Special Reference to India', September to November 1934, Menon Papers.

248 Ibid.; also see, Menon to Wilkinson, 18 September 1934, Menon Papers.

249 Secretary, Central Branch to Arthur Peacock, Editor, *New Nation,* 21 August 1934, Menon Papers.

250 Ibid.

251 Menon to Pollitt, 6 October 1934, Menon Papers.

252 Editor, *Daily Herald,* 29 January 1934, Menon Papers.

253 Ibid.

254 G. Parthasarathi to Menon, 8 February 1934, Menon Papers.

255 J.W.F. Morton to Menon, 4 February 1935, Menon Papers.

256 Morton to Menon, 10 February 1935, Menon Papers.

257 G. Parthasarathi to Menon, 11 February 1935, Menon Papers.

258 Ibid.

259 Menon to Morton, 11 February 1935, Menon Papers.

260 Ibid.

261 Ibid.

262 Parthasarathi to Menon, 20 February 1935, Menon Papers.

263 Menon to Hubert Tracey, 23 February 1935, Menon Papers.

264 Ibid.

265 Ibid.

266 'Note on the reform proposals', n.d. 1935, Menon Papers.

267 Report on Menon's views of the India Bill, Social Problem Circle, Hope Street Church, Liverpool, 13 February 1934, Menon Papers.

268 Ibid.

269 Ibid.

270 Ibid.

271 Tej Bahadur Sapru to H.S.L. Polak, 22 July 1934, Jayakar Papers. The joint select committee had reported in November 1934. It was not unanimous with two minority reports but the majority report was adopted by Parliament as the basis of the bill which became a law on 2 August 1935.

272 Sapru to Edward Thompson, 22 August 1934, Jayakar Papers.

273 H.S.L. Polak to Jayakar, 19 October 1934, Jayakar Papers.

274 H.S.L. Polak to Sapru, 10 November 1934, Jayakar Papers.

275 Polak to Jayakar, 4 October 1934, Jayakar Papers.

276 Polak to Jayakar, 2 August 1934, Jayakar Papers.

277 Ibid.

278 Ibid.

279 Polak to Jayakar, 14 August 1934, Jayakar Papers.

280 Polak to Jayakar, 14 September 1934, Jayakar Papers.

281 Ibid.

282 Ibid.

283 Ibid.

284 Lothian to Sapru, 16 November 1934, Jayakar Papers.

285 Ibid.

286 Polak to Jayakar, 20 November 1974, Jayakar Papers.

287 'Note for discussion on the Constitution', 7 November 1934, India Conciliation Group Papers.

288 Ibid.

289 Ibid.

290 Agatha Harrison to Horace Alexander, 9 February 1934, Horace Alexander Papers and Carl Heath to Irwin, 9 November 1934, India Conciliation Group Papers.

291 Ibid.

292 Carl Heath, 'Circular Letter', February 1935, India Conciliation Group Papers.

293 Ibid.

294 'Note on the Constitutional Proposals', 6 March 1935, India Conciliation Group Papers.

295 Ibid.

296 Author's conversation with Krishna Shelvankar.

297 T.G.P. Spear to Horace Alexander, 17, April 1935, Horace Alexander Papers (T.M.).

298 Author's conversation with Michael Foot.

299 Barbara Castle to Menon, 16 July 1934, Menon Papers.

300 Menon to Harry Pollitt, 16 August 1935, Menon Papers.

CHAPTER VI

PROPAGANDA: CONTEXTS AND PERSPECTIVES

For Menon it was not surprising that Baldwin all along maintained in his public pronouncements that his policy towards India had been distinguished by consistency and continuity. Baldwin held that the Montagu declaration of 1917 and the Act of 1919 had promised the progressive realization of responsible government in India 'as an integral part of the British Empire' and the Simon commission was set up in 1927 to review the situation as envisaged by the Act.[1] Although the Simon commission reported to the Labour government, the government took a position in consonance with a national consensus. The prime minister at that time was anxious to keep the Indian question out of British politics and for that reason when RTC I was set up, MacDonald invited representatives of the Liberal and the Conservative Parties to meet with his Labour Party and see how far a common path could be trodden. Baldwin affirmed that the path had been traversed amiably until before RTC III 'when we were deserted by the Socialists.' Baldwin recapitulated the sincerity and meticulous care with which the Conservative statesmen, who attended the conference in all its sessions, examined the problem of India, discussed the issues at stake and analysed the situation intensely. The collaboration between members of the different parties in Britain, Baldwin argued, had been of inestimable value, not for any reason of compromise, but in view of the danger of allowing the Indian question to become a matter of contention in British political life as the Irish question had become a domestic issue causing a good deal of political instability. Samuel Hoare, Lord Peel, Oliver Stanley and Lord Zetland made their presence felt along with others at the conference. Before RTC III, three committees were sent to India to study certain aspects of the projected policy in keeping with the ground realities and a number of qualified and distinguished members of the Conservative Party in company with others, Baldwin added, went all over the country to complete their assignment.[2]

In fact, in the case of India, Baldwin claimed that he had taken up the threads where the Lloyd George coalition had left off. In close association with Irwin and Hoare, he shared an assumption that the western-educated Indians should not be precluded indefinitely from the government because their active collaboration was indispensable for the continued maintenance of British rule in India. He was keen to initiate and develop a centrist, conciliatory and liberal brand of Conservative policy that alienated Churchill and his die-hards from Baldwin since the controversial declaration by Irwin on dominion status in 1929.[3] Baldwin sought to push his line under the aegis of the National government and presented it as Britain's long-term bulwark against the dictatorships of the right and the left. It seemed to many that he was eager to project his perception as a credible Conservative perspective for England, especially as the European states had been passing under totalitarian regimes. Even when the economic crisis was nearly over, Baldwin continued to promote the centrist policy as a reliable *modus operandi,* preserving the country's stability under the direction of the Conservative Party against a possible resurgent left.[4] Yet, as Menon noticed, Baldwin lacked both confidence and faith in his own policy which was jerky and suffered from an amazing absence of decisive consistency. At each stage, therefore, it quivered and, then, surrendered to an increasing pressure of a well-synchronized assault organized by Churchill.[5]

The proposed constitutional reform in India involved two significant features which were the principal bone of contention within the Conservative Party: the questions of federation and safeguards.[6] The joint select committee, which had been set up, would not have the final word on these issues. Baldwin insisted that the ultimate say would rest with Parliament as to whether it would accept the bill or accept it with modifications. Baldwin maintained that the Conservative Party believed that in all colonial and dominion matters one must trust the judgement of the man on the spot. He assured that with regard to the proposed reforms various important officials in India were behind the government. Successive post-war viceroys — Reading, Irwin, and then, Willingdon — with their extensive Indian experience, had been wholeheartedly in favour of the step forward embodied in the white paper presented to parliament. Similarly, all the provincial governors stood firmly and resolutely by the government. Baldwin agreed that the policy was constructive and extensively reviewed by the Simon commission and in the successive RTCs and subsequently by the three committees that toured India.[7] In the European Association right through India there were thousands of men who were all *en rapport* with the government, who also enjoyed the support of the overwhelming balance of opinion in the civil service. It was strongly favoured by the younger men who did not remember the pre-war India which unfortunately 'looms large in the minds of the older men who are now at home.'[8] Baldwin held that it would not be judicious to turn down the views of all those men who were responsible for the tremendous task of governing India in adverse circumstances. With due respect to the concerns of the older generation, he felt that it was the duty of government and the parliament to listen to the men who had been facing Indian intransigence. Inviting the Conservative opposition to participate in the committee and thrash out the questions, he repeatedly appealed that they should not split up the Conservative Party on India. He stressed that England was probably the only country in the world which had been steering 'the ship of popular government in safety through stormy waters,' and if in a strange fit of insanity, rational public opinion was rent asunder in the country, then some form of Bolshevism or Fascism might eventually overwhelm it. He made his stand clear that 'if we do not advance to India the right hand of generous fellowship', before long 'we shall lose that great Empire and lose it for ever.'[9]

In this context, Baldwin, himself distinguished by a modicum of democratic consciousness and a concern for orderly development of society, emphasized the dangers inherent in the explosive situation in India. The country was passing through, Baldwin stressed a period of unrest and political agitation. But unlike what the die-hards would have liked people to believe, Baldwin insisted that India did not signify only the extremist agitators although they had been conspicuous during the preceding few years. On the contrary, Baldwin underlined that there were millions of Indians of goodwill who wished 'to live in peace and amity with us.' He called for a statesmanlike policy to 'use every legitimate effort to cooperate with our Indian friends' and together with them build for India a system of government that would be appropriate to 'the future requirements of a great continent as big and as diverse as Europe.'[10]

Baldwin argued that the Simon report had emphasized the need for the abolition of dyarchy in the provinces and the RTCs stressed the possibility of the idea of an all-India federation as the princes and politicians from India arrived in England and interacted 'in an unexpected spirit of cooperation with one another.'[11] They gave a new and hopeful turn to the discussions. From that time onward, the concept of a federal government at the centre held the field. The RTC did not fill the details and it was left for a cooperative endeavour on the part of the different segments of Parliament to determine how far it was feasible to achieve the federal idea without surrendering any of the essential safeguards that had been clearly and definitely stated and what 'we consider fundamental in any future settlement.' In the meantime, it was essential to give full support to the Government of India in sustaining law and order 'as the first requisite of every civilized community.'[12] Concerned about the impact of the boycott on British trade in India, Baldwin was convinced that the government would employ all its influence in support of British traders and would insist that, in any future settlement of the Indian constitution, there should be a crucial provision prohibiting unwholesome discrimination against British trade. He emphasized that it was the first time that the forces of moderation in India itself had triumphed over the forces of extremism. Applauding the constructive cooperation, goodwill and honesty of purpose of such men as Sapru, Sastri and Jayakar, Baldwin called for a true appreciation of the noble imperial task of the Conservative Party in harmonizing the 'ideals of the East and West' and 'ensuring the closest and most permanent friendship between India and Britain.' Far from being a source of division among Conservatives, he added, it should rejuvenate the 'bond of union that keeps us together.'[13] Baldwin's reference to the British mission in India was expressed in terms of pluralism and incrementalism. He was inciteful to the general conservative opinion; he helped amplify the heartbeats of a sedate conservative generation when he said:

> Remember: what have we taught India for a century? We have preached English institutions and democracy and all the rest of it. We have taught her the lesson and she wants us to pay the bill. There is a wind of nationalism and freedom blowing round the world and blowing as strongly in Asia as anywhere in the world. And are we less true Conservatives because we say: 'the time has now come?' Are those who say 'the time may come -some day', are they the truer Conservatives?"[14]

As a sequel to Baldwin's subtle exposition, Hoare explained the position of the government in an article in the *Morning Post,* in early February 1933, in unequivocal terms. Hoare might not have been effective and popular and probably was 'too prim — too old-maidish.' But, in an attempt to win over the Conservative opponents led by Churchill and Lord Lloyd, Hoare gave a pathfinder prospectus.[15] He acknowledged that there was good cause for anxiety in India. He alluded to the obvious feeling of uneasiness in the minds of many Conservatives arising from the apprehension that grave issues had been dangerously drifting for quite some time, that law and order were being undermined and that the efficiency of British administration in India, built up by generations of devoted toil, was being endangered.[16] Hoare, however, emphasized the two preliminary conditions which the Indian participants in the RTC acknowledged as the basis of any constitutional reform in India. These imperatives were that the imperial safeguards must be full and effective and that any new constitution must on the face of it be workable.[17] Hoare underlined these points adding that there was hardly an Indian who did not understand the British attitude and not any influential British newspaper that failed to appreciate the official standpoint. It was a pity, Hoare thought, that Baldwin and Churchill did not share the same or even a similar perspective with regard to India. While Churchill believed that the Indian future was one of unrelieved gloom and that there was little chance of cooperation between the English and any substantial body of Indian opinion, Baldwin was less of a pessimist and was enthusiastic in inaugurating a more optimistic phase in the India policy.

In support of Baldwin, Hoare maintained that in the atmosphere of goodwill created by the RTC, the government could enlist the latent forces of loyal Indian opinion on its side.[18] He did not imply that all the hundreds of unsettled propositions would be overcome or resolved overnight. Nor did he give the impression that even a single of 'our great imperial obligations' would be surrendered. Hoare was eager to convey that the government would do its best to ensure Indian cooperation in order to fashion an agreeable all-India federation. It was an attempt to consolidate peace but not peace at any extraordinary price. The government would do its utmost to make it once again possible for British trade with India to prosper by doing away with the harm that 'Gandhi and Co.' had been inflicting 'on the work of generations of British traders.'[19] Hoare avowed that the constitution of an all-India federation would not jeopardize 'the obligations that we have already undertaken.' Among other things, it would include complete and undisputed British command of the army and foreign relations and the existing framework of association with the princes. Besides, internal security and financial stability must be effectively safeguarded. Minorities must be protected. There must be no unfair economic and commercial discrimination against the British traders. The rights of the services recruited by the secretary of state must be preserved. The federal constitution must be workable, stable and permanent. All these constituted the fundamental interests of England in India which the government or the Conservative Party had not the least intention of whittling down.[20]

Observers were reminded, time and again, that India was then faced with a very difficult chapter in its history. The political imbroglio in India was being aggravated by the increasing weight of the economic crisis. Prices had crashed, poverty had increased, and it was repeatedly asserted that in that odd and onerous background, the agitators had been trying to impose their malignant influence.[21] In the face of grave troubles, therefore, the Conservative statesmen were urged to maintain steady judgement and sturdy courage. If disturbances continued, Hoare declared, 'we must throw the whole weight of our party into the scale of law and order.' At the same time, 'we must make it quite clear that we are prepared to work with the forces of goodwill and to try our hand at bringing about an All-India Federation' in which the so-called stabilizing forces of the Indian states would be brought into the consitutional balance. Evidently, the Baldwinites had been trying desperately to appease and, if necessary, allay the anxiety and tension caused by the white paper policy in the Churchill camp. Zetland and Oliver Stanley were in communication with Lord Lloyd and Lord Rankeillour with regard to financial safeguards for the benefit of civil servants in service and in retirement while Hoare addressed a series of memorials to his constituency, stressing that the gap between the perceptions of the die-hards and the Baldwinites was marginal and one of minor tactical requirement.[22]

While men like Zetland and Stanley entirely endorsed the government's India policy and noted with satisfaction Hoare's attempt to correct the misrepresentation of Baldwin's speech in the House of Commons and outside, O'Dwyer, Sydenham, Craddock and many other die-hards drifted towards Churchill and Lloyd and decided to stand by them. O'Dwyer, though somewhat reassured by Hoare's pronouncements, feared that with the Government of India responsible to an all-India assembly and with full provincial autonomy, the fulfilment of imperial obligations would be impossible. In any case, political conflicts and contradictions would be sharpened as it was axiomatic that the responsibility of the Government of India to Parliament should be jealously guarded and it could never be brushed aside.[23] Sydenham added that Baldwin's resolution to bring about a federal constitution in India was regarded in political circles as going beyond the commitment of the party and the prime minister. He reiterated that the Conservative parliamentary leadership would never overlook the interests of some 310 million helpless people 'who know no politics, and for whose security and progress — now arrested — we are responsible.'[24] Craddock agreed with him. The die-hard of ex-civilians maintained that far too much stress was being laid by the official party on safeguards, while the real difficulty was to determine the contents of these safeguards and the most pertinent of all questions was to know if the safeguards would work after all.[25]

Indeed, Churchill's policy was remarkably unambivalent. He maintained, without mincing words, that the onus for splitting the Conservative Party rested upon a leader who forced on his party a policy on which it had never been consulted and 'which runs directly counter to its deepest instincts and traditions.'[26] History, he added, always assigned the responsibility for splitting a party to the leader who proposed the departure. Baldwin and his associates had been pressing forward a policy which would not be accepted by the great mass of their party and, hence, they were the real splitters. The lips of the civil servants, Churchill maintained, were sealed by the very nature of their administrative responsibility. They could neither speak nor answer. Churchill held that a very large proportion of the officials, civil and military, in India who had been carrying forward the government's policy had been doing so with serious misgivings. The British mercantile community had been left with no other option than to make the best terms it could in the situation. Applauding the policy of Willingdon, Churchill emphasized that by firm administration of law wholly out of keeping with the policies of Irwin, RTC and the Socialist and National governments and by 'drastic repressive ordinances completely contrary to the policy of responsible self-government,' Willingdon produced an almost instant improvement in the situation. This achievement was then actually used by Hoare and Baldwin 'in justification of a policy which would make its repetition impossible'. Churchill accused Baldwin and his men of resolving to force the 'India abdication policy' through at all costs and by every party machinery at their disposal. Churchill hailed the resolve of all those who decided to defend the empire and to oppose the attempt 'to strike the death-knell of the greatness of the British empire and inflict vital injury upon the economic life of the English working classes.'[27] Empire, Churchill underscored, was a grand human symphony beyond the comprehension of puny men preoccupied in a set of constitutional punctilios.[28]

Differences and discords, even within the ranks of the die-hards became so intense that it led to the emergence of the India Defence League in 1933, under the chairmanship of Viscount Fitzalan, with Lord Lloyd of Dolobran having considerable Indian experience as one of the vice-presidents, taking a leading position in its council.[29] Others in the executive included such eminent persons as Churchill, Earl Howe, Lord Carson, the Duke of Westminster, Sir Claud Jacob, Henry Page Croft, Rudyard Kipling, the Marquess of Harlington, P.W. Doner, Viscount Wolmer, Michael O'Dwyer, Alfred Knox and many others.

In fact, the India Defence League was formed with the object of bringing before the British public the salient facts with regard to the Indian white paper and to the 'dangers' that would attend the enactment of the proposals of that document. In a circular of the League of 21 September 1933, the white paper and its uncertain possibilities were sought to be exposed.[30] The circular stated that the white paper had been designed to appease a small caucus of mischievous politicians in India and, if implemented, would unleash a series of movements and countermovements that would undo the creative endeavours of over a century. The circular examined a few of the significant proposals of the document. It was particularly disturbed by four distinct propositions: the transfer of central authority to a federal government of a nature previously unknown in world history, the transfer of finance, railways and general administration to the over-riding powers of the governor-general who might be an Indian, the divorce of the control of the army from that of the police and the transport services and the transfer of the Court and of the police to the control of political parties in the provinces with the consequent introduction of politics into the administration of civil and criminal law. The circular prognosticated serious threats to the life and security of the *Raj* from these proposals. They would cause grave disorder and risk of internal chaos, stimulate agitation for complete severance from the empire, encourage repudiation of British loans, lead to a good deal of loss of British trade and shipping business, risk the confiscation of pensions earned by British subjects, discard British standards of justice and all 'our pledges' to protect the safety and defence of all ranks, classes, castes and religious communities in India. It was asserted that no enactment of Federation should be contemplated until provincial autonomy was proved a success. In their conception, provincial ministers should not administer law and order which must be reserved. Besides, some sort of control by the centre over the provinces should be incorporated in order to take corrective measures over the provincial authorities.[31] The League insisted that the blunder of dyarchy should not be repeated and it was inadvisable to embark upon expensive constitutional experiments until the necessary finance was available. The India Defence League argued that Indians should prove their capacity to govern successfully the great Indian provinces under provincial autonomy before any attempt was made to consider establishment of responsible government at the centre. A federation of units at that stage would amount to an abrogation of British authority at the centre of the Government of India. They appealed to the government only to proceed with that part of the Report on which they could unite all their supporters. 'Nothing in the new Constitution,' Fitzalan and Wolmer avowed, 'will work successfully unless we have faith in our moral right and duty to guide India's diverse peoples sympathetically along the path of progress by the route and at the pace our judgement and experience dictate. Surrender of duty to the clamour of inexperience will justify its Nemesis.'[32]

In another leaflet, the India Defence League declared that safeguards of any certain efficiency could never be put into an act of Parliament. It also said that in Ireland safeguards had proved worthless and there was no reason to expect that in India safeguards would be more reliable and abiding. It appealed to all, who realized the grave dangers inherent in the official policy, to give the League their support and subscribe liberally to its funds. The India Defence League did not direct its energy against the Indian Empire Society nor did it cross swords with the European Society of Bengal. But they differed and, at times, the League examined the futility of the tepid gestures of these societies and their inability to formulate firm lines of action and to persistently adhere to their convictions.[33]

Lord Lloyd held that great efforts were being made by Baldwin and Hoare to obscure harsh realities to the public and to the rank and file of the party by what seemed to many of them 'an ambiguous and misleading terminology'.[34] At certain points of time the public had been invited to subscribe to dominion status; at others, to a federal constitution and at yet others, to the policy of responsibility at the centre with safeguards. The official leadership of the party, the die-hards argued, was given to perfidious tergiversation. To Lloyd, the main issue was simple. Opinion divided itself into two princial groups. One advocated, in effect, surrender to the Congress demand for the early grant of full responsibility at the centre; the other stood firmly by the Act of 1919 and its steady fulfilment and pressed for the due consideration of the report furnished by the statutory commission.[35] The former group demanded, Lloyd explained, responsibility at the centre with safeguards. But he maintained that there could be no such thing for the proposition was not only a contradiction in terms, but utterly unworkable in practice. It must, on the other hand, be clear that if such safeguards were devisable and effective, responsibility given to the Indians would, *pro tanto,* become a sham while the British position would be weakened, and the pretext for opposition would in no way be diminished. 'I say without hesitation that no man can devise safeguards.'[36] These safeguards, Lloyd declared, would not in practice invest the Viceroy with effective and exercisable powers adequate to discharge his duties to the Indian states, the great minorities, and last, but by no means the least, the British commercial and strategic interests in India. It was a profound conviction of the India Defence League that the Conservative Party should be firm in refusing 'surrender' to the Congress demand for the early grant of full responsibility at the centre. They would also not abandon to the Congress, responsibility for the guardianship of the masses of India's people until the Indians were sufficiently advanced to undertake it for themselves. It was indispensable that the truth of the matter should be placed before the electorate with conviction, courage and clarity. The country's sensitive feelings on India, the die-hards claimed, had been touched and developed spontaneously and not as a result of, but in spite of, the views put forward by some of the most powerful organs of publicity in Britain. When the future of India was at stake, they argued, one must subordinate the consideration of party harmony to the fate of the empire.[37]

In a letter to the *Times,* the India Defence League thought it proper to correct the main contention of the weighty arguments of Sir Hubert Carr in defence of the government's policy. Carr's argument, reduced to its bare outline, appeared to the League somewhat mischievous and misleading. Carr maintained, according to the League, that in 1919 the British Government had taken 'the wrong path' and having chosen it, 'we must continue to tread in it.'[38] Even if it was argued that a serious error of judgement was made in 1919, Lloyd wrote, Carr would have to be reminded that he was quite misinformed in imagining that the government had still been pursuing it and that the new proposals were the logical and inevitable outcome of the 1919 reforms. Lloyd maintained that the coherent upshot of 1919 was indisputably the report of the Simon commission which in the clearest terms, condemned the principles upon which the existing government proposals were founded.[39] The Simon report, he held firmly, was categorical on these issues. It laid down without hesitation, the proposition that dyarchy at the Centre, or any system of divided responsibility resembling dyarchy, was quite impossible. Unity in the Central executive must be preserved at all costs. As against Carr's argument that the refusal to endorse the white paper proposals was to decline the Indian aspirations which had been openly and persistently encouraged since 1919, Lloyd reminded Carr that the Simon commission contained proposals which constituted a sweeping and unparalleled advance towards self-government of the 350 million people. It appeared to the die-hards that the official policy merely confirmed a dangerous thesis that 'the path we are now upon in India is so surrounded with horrors that for our own comfort we had better shut our eyes and run along it as fast as our legs can carry us.'[40]

The India Defence League believed that even the European Association of India and the Royalists had taken up purely an opportunistic line and such a line of action could never succeed in the conduct of great affairs. Contradicting the tactical inadequacies of the India policy advocated by the European Association, Lloyd explained the various nuances of the League's stand. He maintained that the idea of creative cooperation with moderate Indian opinion had been conceived within the limbo of a remarkable mental inertia and such an attempt was destined to end in a void of uncertainty that obscured unpleasant hard realities. He affirmed that all factions and front organizations of the Conservatives knew perfectly well that no fundamental difference separated the moderates and the extremists in India. They had both, in the main, pledged to the same goal and in this context to attempt to tie 'our programme to the Moderates must lead to disaster.' The moderates, it was believed, had no fixed position. They were always exactly 'the same distance behind the extremists' position that was, in its turn, not static but 'moved forward every time we make concessions.'[41]

The die-hards believed that while the extremists advocated and carried out a frontal attack — boycott, passive resistance and even publicly applauded the political assassin, the moderates held a carefully prepared and steadily pursued policy of sapping and sabotage. The victory that the moderates had been seeking, Michael O'Dwyer wrote, would be achieved slowly but surely. It was believed that the moderate 'hoodwinked' Montagu and Chelmsford and some of their successors, such as Benn and Irwin, into believing that they would honestly and effectively cooperate in gradually establishing self-government in India as *an integral part of the British empire.* The intellectual distinction and dialectical ability of such persons as Sapru, Sastri and Jayakar had given the impression that they represented 'a well-organized body of reasonable public opinion' in India. But, O'Dwyer alleged, these 'distinguished personalities' did not openly oppose Gandhi and his civil disobedience and its disastrous consequences. O'Dwyer thought that the moderate leaders who played a prominent role in the RTCs were clever and ambitious urban Hindu Brahmins who, despite their remarkable intellectual subtlety, had neither the courage nor the influence to assist the administration in times of crisis. O'Dwyer thought that the aims of the moderates was not the gradual development of self-governing institutions but to acquire control of the central government by a small, ambitious and not influential clique of urban Hindus.[42]

The Europeans in India had been asked to consider carefully the measure of concession that the government could safely make to Indian politicians. They were urged to take into account both direct British interests and the welfare of the masses of the Indian people and then stand steadfastly on that and not waver from the position. The die-hards noted with concern that the European Association had been unable to make up its mind and, as a result, it was compelled by circumstances to adopt a line of action which might engage it in a series of rearguard actions from which it might not emerge with success or even a modicum of credit.[43]

The India Defence League viewed the whole operation of the Conservative high command as a game of planned deception. It claimed that it had been led on, stage by stage, with disastrous dexterity by the secretary of state. At each stage the die-hards had been invited not to oppose, 'because our assent at that stage would commit us to nothing.'[44] Arrived at the next stage, the same arguments were used. When the white paper was issued, the diehards were assured that by assenting to it they were not committing themselves to approval of the government's policy, but to a further exploration and examination of the problem. Finally, they were told that when the joint parliamentary committee would be set up, the whole policy could be impartially reviewed. But when the JSC was finally installed, it was found to be packed with an unprecedented and overwhelming government majority, 'irrevocably pledged to the principles to which we have all along taken exception.'[45] Besides, it was apprehended that the government had resolved that the inquiry should be rushed through with the minimum delay. Finally, there was a serious difference of opinion with regard to the native states, their willingness to participate and necessarily to exercise a moderating influence. Some might be expected to do so but others might decide to opt for a different way.

The European Association of Calcutta, however, remained unconvinced by the view of the India Defence League that 'we are either for the White Paper or we are against it.'[46] The Calcutta association was in favour of the broad outlines of the official scheme. But although the association agreed that the reservations went very deep to the root of the scheme, it did not consider that these conditions had upset its fundamental principles. 'I think', F.C. Brasher wrote, 'it would be fair to say that where you and we differ is that whereas you have no confidence in Federation, we believe that Federation is the best scheme under the circumstances.'[47] On the question of the participation of the princes, it was asserted that with minor exceptions, the majority of them were in favour of it. The European Association believed that only two courses were open: to take a substantial step forward or to go right back and start afresh with the knowledge of the mistakes of the preceding 30 years and with the intention of avoiding them.[48] The Association favoured the former course because it was far from certain that merely to give a small measure of advance to the Indians would aggravate the trouble. On the contrary, it would certainly not make the situation worse. In Bengal, it asserted, the situation was already very dangerous and the need was felt for the bare minimum of safety. It was held firmly that their position was not based on a peculiarly Bengal situation inasmuch as they believed that unless the trouble was dealt with firmly, it would spread all over India within the next few years.[49] In fact, the Calcutta Europeans were quite categorical in declining to accept any halfway compromise couched in ambiguous terms. If there was, they asserted, a party in England strong enough to carry out an inflexible policy of impliability and prepared to say firmly and openly that not only did it believe that further advance in India was wrong but that it would retrogress and make a fresh start, the association would warmly support its stand.[50]

In June 1933, the position of a substantial section of the viceroy's executive council was known to Lord Lloyd. It was clear that a sizeable fraction of it did not aspire to consider any significant devolution of authority to nationalist politicians. The commander-in-chief of the Indian army could not afford to criticize constitutionally the actions of his colleagues. But, by then, matters had been moving rapidly towards a dangerous state of affairs. It threatened the stability of the empire and the c-in-c was constrained to set down his opinion on a few issues in strict privacy in order to stress the need for resisting the official move for a new constitution. He emphasized that even the Indians did not entertain a passion for a rapid progress towards self-government. The new trend in the official policy of going forward intensified the campaign by all religions, castes, minorities and special interests to secure for their 'own particular *jat* or interests as many loaves and fishes of office in the future Government as they could possibly secure.'[51] Intense rivalry and competition was inevitable in India having irreconcilable factions and interests. It was held that there was practically no public opinion working for India as a nation and a country. It was contended that once the *hukm* of His Majesty's government was promulgated through the medium of a bill, people would accept the decision and work loyally for the general good. But the c-in-c was not inclined to accept such a construct. He had, at his command, most extensive and reliable information about Indian conditions and he was not frightfully optimistic of the situation.[52] He believed that far from a grand reconciliation, the differences between various factions in India would tend to become more acute than they had been. He held that the attempt to force on India a western form of government would prove to be a futile gesture. Neither by temperament nor by tradition were Indians competent for such institutions. Besides, such a form of government could not function without parties divided by political ideals and objectives. There was not even a remote possibility of such a development in India. It was true that India was sharply disunited but not on political issues. On the contrary, it was religious, racial and caste questions that stimulated Indian political life and aspirations.[53] Other than the Congress, he held, there was no party organization in India at all. The Congress should either follow the 'vague futilities of Gandhi' or emerge surely and steadily as an 'increasingly Left-Wing, and indeed a Bolshevik formation, under the leadership of Jawaharlal Nehru and his fellow Left Wingers'.

Chetwode reported that the Viceroy, over the last few years, had done his best to inspire moderate Indians to form a centre party or at least a moderate constitutional party, but he failed. Chetwode argued that the Lothian committee, in its recommendations, supported to a great extent by Government of India, did their best to perpetuate and exacerbate the communal and other divisions 'by advocating a distribution of seats devised on a population basis of the two main religious factions.'[54] In addition, the committee definitely prevented a rapprochement between the Hindus and depressed classes by allotting separate seats for the latter. Such a classification would thus permanently 'create the sharpest possible cleavage between the two groups.' The Hindus, Muslims and depressed classes would, therefore, he wrote, 'be permanently held apart' and stand face to face as antagonized social identities politically as well as on religious grounds.[55]

In the case of the native states, Chetwode thought only a few of the unimportant ones such as Bikaner, Alwar, Bhopal, etc., had given top priority to the federal principle. But the big princes, such as the Nizam, Mysore, Baroda, Indore, Gwalior, etc., had never even taken part in the work of the Chamber of Princes and they were the ones who really counted in India. The c-in-c believed that they would not venture to come in unless they were sure of getting a great deal more out of the arrangement than British India would ever be willing to give them. Meanwhile, it had been repeatedly emphasized by the prime minister that the essential condition of the grant of Federation was that it must be of all India and include the princes, 'thereby putting the Joker into the hands of the Princes, and allowing them to dictate zero hour.'[56] The whole trend tended to show that there were great big forces to get over before one arrived at a workable constitution but these were some of the minor fences by comparison with the really big hurdles of finance, defence and safeguards generally at the centre.[57]

Chetwode also felt that it was the worst possible moment to introduce provincial responsibility and extended powers at the centre especially when, in common with the rest of the world, India was faced with difficulties in making both ends meet even though her credit was still high and the financial world had confidence in her government.[58] None of the provinces was in a sound financial condition. The province of NWFP had been inaugurated with no prospect of financial self-sufficiency. Now, separate provinces of Orissa and Sind, both in deficit, and the separation of Burma, involving considerable loss to Indian revenues, were being proposed. To this might be added the 'very expensive luxuries' such as extension of franchise and increased number of provincial legislatures. And finally, as *terminus ad quem* of the discourse, Chetwode claimed that what disturbed him the most was that it was then being seriously proposed to reduce the strength of the army, already seriously weakened over the years by reduced recruitment, shoddy maintenance, weak supply line, lack of effective striking power and general inefficiency caused by all-round economies, primarily to bolster up 'a political experiment the success of which is more than doubtful.' In India, the exasperated c-in-c maintained, emergency might arise at a moment's notice, and, if not met at once, the consequences might be disastrous and 'all your reforms go by the board like so many houses of cards.'[59] 'Who sits on the throne at Delhi sits there by leave of the Army [on the] loyalty and efficiency of which the whole present and future of India depends.' Chetwode was frantic and he pleaded with Lord Lloyd to be alert and vigilant against the sentimental approaches of some irresponsible politicians. 'I count on you, and people like you, who know the facts, to put the whole weight of your influence in the scales against such a mad policy, if it is seriously pressed, as I fear it will be.'[60]

The debate over the feasibility of federalism, as proposed by the white paper, was carried out by the British press for

INDIA

A PETITION TO PARLIAMENT
for the conferring of
"DOMINION STATUS" FOR INDIA

To the Honourable the House of Commons of the United Kingdom of Great Britain and Northern Ireland in Parliament assembled:

THE HUMBLE PETITION OF THE UNDERMENTIONED BRITISH SUBJECTS SHEWETH:

That your Petitioners believe that the people of India are justly entitled to Self-Government within the British Commonwealth of Nations,

WHEREFORE

Your Petitioners pray that a measure be introduced into Parliament at the earliest possible moment, for the conferring of the Status of a Self-Governing Dominion on India in accordance with the declared goal of British Policy,

AND

Your Petitioners, as in duty bound, will ever pray, etc.

	NAME.	ADDRESS.
1	Hodgson Smith	10, East Parade, Harrogate
2	Bertha Hodgson Smith	" " "
3	A. Burtt Woodhead	13 Lancaster Park "
4	Elizabeth Young	67, East Parade, Harrogate
5	E. E. Jagger	" " "
6	Agnes H. Brook	67 East Parade, Harrogate
7	Gertrude E. Rocliffe	5 Glebe Flats, Glebe Rd, Harrogate
8	T. L. J. [illegible]	Trevil Croft Harrogate
9	[illegible]	Glen Rd. Eldwick. Bingley
10	Mary M. Hall.	18 Dragon Avenue, Harrogate.
11	L. Eugenie Crook	Charlwood, Wetherby Lane Harrogate
12	H. Crook	121 Fairfield Gardens, London
13	Jean Bishop	Lake House Pittville Lawn Cheltenham
14	[illegible]	Indore Central India
15	Clara Hooper	Omar, Old Bath Road, Cheltenham
16	Mabel Hooper	" " "
17	Lillie Chandler	The Parsonage Cheltenham
18	Mrs E. Dodd	12 St. [illegible] St
19	H. Greening	[illegible] Hewlett Rd Cheltenham
20	M. Fison	Cheltenham

1. Only British Subjects over sixteen may sign this Petition.
2. Each signature must be in ink and accompanied by the Petitioner's full address.

A Petition to Parliament for Dominion states for India, Commonwealth of India League 1927. Menon Papers.

Published Monthly.

INDIA BULLETIN

Vol. I. No. 3. APRIL, 1932. One Penny.

To Our Readers.

This month we are giving our readers news from India. It would be easy to fill a good-sized book with details of what has happened there since the Civil Disobedience Movement began in January last, an endless catalogue of official trickery, prevarication and cruelty. We have but taken a few typical instances from the mass of information at our disposal. Heaven knows, they are disgraceful enough! These things are happening daily, but at a distance of 6,000 miles, and that fact, combined with the desultory and tendencious "news" given in the British Press, may account for the indifference of the average person in this country to what, after all, he and she is responsible for.

We are determined to get people to feel that "something must be done about it." Those whose feelings are in a condition of coma, as the result of an expensive education or a series of tough experiences, can at least apply their commonsense to the question and ask themselves whether a steady application of rigorous imprisonments, fines, suppression of speech, beatings, insults, tortures and the rest of the "law and order" programme, are likely to be of political or economical benefit to the present rulers of British India, or to anyone else.

Our readers must be reminded of what is only too hasily realised, viz.: that this movement for freedom is being carried on under conditions that are unique. Resistance to the unjust exactions of authority is no new thing in the world's history, and clubs, pitchforks, battle-axes, bows and arrows, spears and guns have all played their parts in the business. But the miracle performed by Mahatma Gandhi of convincing millions of men and women that a bully of a policeman with a club in his hand is a human being, who must not be hit back, but treated like a brother, is something new indeed. Yet it is happening all over India.

A LETTER FROM BENGAL.

[We have received a long letter from Bengal, giving a consecutive account of the Civil Disobedience Movement from January 4th. As authentic news from Bengal has been very scarce, we give the most important passages from this letter.—Ed. *India Bulletin.*]

Report of Civil Disobedience Movement in Bengal for January and February, 1932.

On January 5th the Government promulgated the ordinances almost in all the districts of Bengal. Several associations, numbering forty-five, including the B.P.C.C., were declared unlawful on the same date. From January 6th the local authorities served notices under the Emergency Powers Ordinance in Calcutta as well as in the mofussil towns and more than 100 prominent Congressmen were arrested and detained under the E.P. Ordinance. In January and February 230 notices have been served in Calcutta only. Orders [illegible]

Bengal welcomed this challenge and took up the fight by defying the humiliating ordinances and the notices. The salient feature of the movement being that ladies—in very large numbers—have come forward to court arrest and imprisonments.

Many papers have suspended publication and several editors have courted imprisonment under the Sedition Act. Some six or seven Press proprietors have been asked to pay huge sums as securities, and in cases of their non-payment the presses have been locked up. The newspapers are strictly forbidden to publish any news concerning the movement, excepting arrests and convictions.

Unlawful Associations.

In January and February as many as 515 associations have been declared unlawful. Besides the provincial and local Congress committees, the Abhoy Ashram with all its branches, the Banripara National School in Barisal and the Kanya Sikshalaya of Comilla, the only National Girls' High School in Bengal, have been declared unlawful. The houses, buildings, movable properties with cash are now in police possession, Khadi stocks of the All-India Spinners' Association at Comilla and Bankura worth about Rs. 15,000/- have been seized by the police.

Repressions, Lathi Charges and Assaults.

Lathi charges and assaults were confined to Sylhet, Tippera and Jalpaiguri districts at the commencement of the movement. But now it has been the general feature throughout the province.

In Sylhet repression was inaugurated in the brutal assaults and dispersal of the processionists on January 26th, in which the Assistant District Magistrate himself took a leading part. The leader of the Sylhet Congress, Sjt. Brajendra Narayan Choudhury was assaulted, throttled and dragged by a wrapper round his neck. Sjt. Dhirendra Nath Das Gupta, the President of the Vidyashram was beaten unconscious and arrested. The ladies participating in the procession were assaulted and pushed into a drain. In connection with the no-rent campaign in Bhunabil in Sylhet, many houses have been demolished by elephants with the help of the police.

In Tippera, the Mussalmans, who form about 70 per cent. of the population and are freely participating in the movement, have not been exempted from their share of police repression. In Kasba and Elliotgunge, houses have been demolished by police with the help of elephants, men are yoked and made to parade in the villages and vilely abused. A building in the town of Comilla, where twelve assaulted persons were being treated for their injuries, have been taken possession of by the police and the injured persons have been arrested. Two hundred Gurkhas (armed) divided into four batches are visiting different parts of the district and are carrying on indiscriminate assaults and loot. Even ladies are not escaping from their indecent assaults and vile abuses.

India Bulletin, Friends of India, April 1932. Menon Papers

Box No. 11
f. No. 6

In a few weeks His Majesty's government will be announcing their proposals about the future government of India for submission to the Joint Committee of both Houses of Parliament. It is common ground between all parties that they need to be discussed, both here and in India itself, in an atmosphere of calm and of goodwill.

We do not believe such an atmosphere can be attained as long as Mr Gandhi and thousands of his supporters remain in prison. Their detention compels a large part of Indian public opinion to look unfavourably upon any proposals made by the government of this country. It minimises the possibility of co-operation both immediately and in the future. It maximises the difficulty of implementing in practice any proposals embodied in an Act of Parliament. It persuades great masses of people to concentrate upon grievances attention which needs, in a mood of high seriousness, to be given to proceedings of the highest importance to the future of the British Commonwealth of Nations.

The recent session of the Round Table Conference concluded with a strong appeal from Sir Tej Sapru, the moderation of whose opinions is well known, for the release of Mr Gandhi and his associates. We desire to support

2)

that appeal with all the emphasis at our command. We believe that no other way is available by which Indian opinion can be persuaded to approach the government's proposals in a spirit of reasoned criticism. We are convinced that a gesture of goodwill such as this may well be vital to the future of our relationship with the Indian people. We recognise the many difficulties which stand in the way. But we are certain that a policy of creative generosity is at this time the one method of securing the triumph of a reasonable spirit in Anglo-Indian affairs. A failure to show now a temper of magnanimity will only increase in every direction the difficulties before those who will be responsible in the future for the conduct of Indian government. A refusal to be magnanimous in the face of impending events would be the revelation of a blindness to their significance pregnant, we think, with tragic results.

Statement by Harold Laski
Feb. 1933
Menon Papers

Statement issued by Prof. Harold Laski, February1933. Menon Papers.

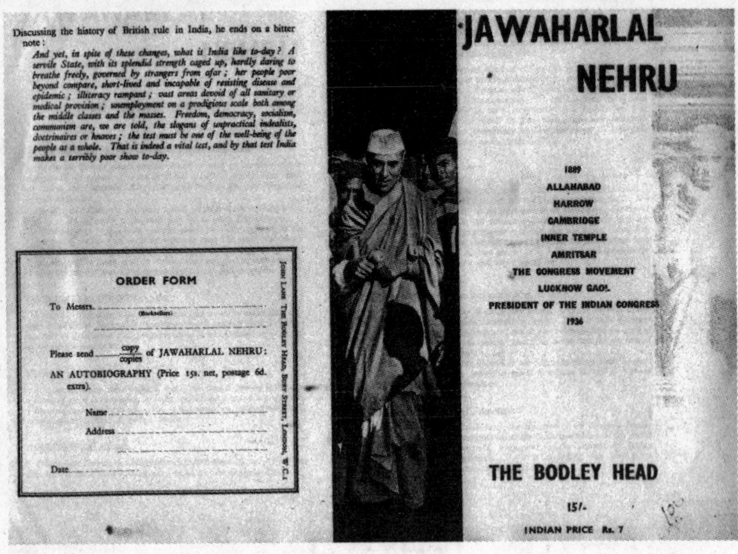

Publicity campaign for Jawaharlal Nehru's *An Autobiography*. Menon Papers.

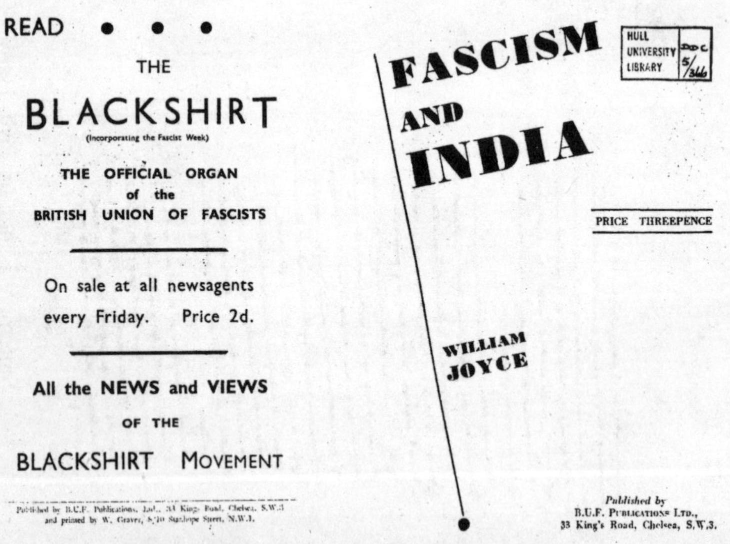

A significant publication of the British Union of Fascists, Dorothy Woodman Papers.

RELEASE NEHRU

Well-known Anti-Fascist and Democrat. Leader of Indian Independence.

PROMINENT SPEAKERS

TO BE ANNOUNCED

PUBLIC MEETING

HOLBORN HALL

GRAY'S INN RD W.C

SAT 23rd NOV

2.15 p.m.

ADMISSION FREE. Reserved Seats 2 6 and 1 -

A notice for a meeting organised by the India league for the release of Jawaharlal Nehru. November 1942, Menon Papers

By JAWAHARLAL NEHRU

GLIMPSES OF WORLD HISTORY

FROM EARLIEST TIMES TO THE PRESENT DAY

A NEW AND REVISED EDITION IN 1 VOLUME

With 50 maps by J. F. Horrabin

English Edition 10/6. Indian Edition Rs 5

DETAILED PROSPECTUS FREE ON APPLICATION

The Publishers will be pleased to send a copy of their complete list which contains books on politics, sociology, natural history, biography, history, etc.,

free on application to

LINDSAY DRUMMOND LTD.

6-7 Buckingham Street, London, W.C.2

By V. K. Krishna Menon

Why must India fight ?

price one penny

Frontispiece of an important pamphlet of the India League, 1940. Menon Papers.

BOMBAY PRESIDENCY CONGRESS SOCIALIST GROUP.

240/42, Walkeshwar Road,
Malabar Hill,

Bombay, 4th June '34.

My dear Krishna Menon,

I found your telegram waiting for me when I returned to Bombay this morning. You will therefore understand what must have seemed to you my long silence. I was away on this time first at Patna where I had gone to attend the All-India Congress Socialist Conference and also watch the All India Congress Committee meeting and then, in Orissa where I accompanied Mahatmaji on his walking tour having accepted his invitation to discuss our Socialist Programme with him. Except that he is definitely not a Socialist but on the other hand he feels well inclined towards us, there is ~~ix~~ nothing of any importance to be mentioned to you arising out of my conversations with him. He agrees that we have a place within the Congress as an organised left attempting to convert the Congress to our point of view.

Now as regards your telegramme I must admit that I do not quite understand what "situation"it is on which you want facts for the House of Commons debate. There are three possible topics, one is the Textile strike, second the general political situation in this country and the third is as regards the Congress Socialist movement. Having regard to our previous correspondence which you mentioned in your telegram, I take it that the information that you want is with regard to our Group. ~~and~~ I am enclosing herewith cuttings of the Ranchi Conference, the Bombay Congressmen's Conference, Patna All-India Socialist Conference and the A.I.C.C. and also an interview of mine to the press as well as the statement issued by the Bombay Group. These will give you as many information as it is within my power to give you in the course of this letter. You will appreciate that I returned after a long journey this morning and have been working all day till within an hour of posting of this letter. I shall however mention what I feel to be the position as regards our Group and the Congress. I think the Ranchi and Patna votes show that we have about a third of the Congress with us already. It may be that faced with this new menace those in power of the Congress organisation may rally their forces and with their superior money power will ~~gat~~ keep us from making any demonstrable progress in voting strength in the near future. But I feel that we have the future with us and are bound to make the Congress accept more and more of our power.

Immediately after the A.I.C.C. the Draft Committee

Masani to Menon, 14 July 1934, Menon Papers.

nearly a whole year and a half. J.H. Morgan, a leading constitutional expert, made the most significant contribution in the debate by a series of six articles in the *Morning Post.* Federalism, he held, even under the most favourable conditions, was notorious as being a complex and disconcerting and probably, the weakest of all forms of government.[61] It was believed that under a federal constitution there was a grave possibility of a temptation to discriminate between the state laws and the federal laws, disturbing the stability of all federal institutions. Divided authority was always weak and the more divided it was, the weaker it would be. The Indian fellow subjects under it would pay obedience to six or seven different and often conflicting legislative authorities. The prospects would be both supefying and dangerous. In India, the opportunities of 'political mischief' would thus be multiplied enormously, especially as disobedience in the country had become a creed and litigation almost a disease. The only door of escape open to the governor-general would be to proclaim a 'breakdown' and an 'emergency' encouraging the politicians to fight the executive both inside and outside the courts.[62] The exercise of its 'reserved' powers and 'special responsibilities' would merely stimulate the Congress leaders to repudiate them, egged on by the clamour for dominion status. The active opposition, thus encouraged and prompted, would compromise the governor-general so ostentatiously as to paralyze his legislative authority.[63]

Morgan affirmed that one of the disturbing things in the proposal was that there was no contract or agreement binding on the constituent states or provinces to bear and forbear at all. To try to build a federal constitution upon such foundations was to build it upon sand. It was also added that the catchword of the proposal was 'safeguards'. To Morgan, the startling thing was that for the first time in its history, Parliament was invited to bestow self-government on a 'gigantic collection of communities' on the expressed assumption that it would not be abused and also a set of safeguards against such abuse.[64] It was argued that all these safeguards would prove utterly worthless because any legislative assembly with the 'popular' will behind it would get the better of all checks and balances. Discrimination would be enforced without impunity and communal strife would be intensified and accentuated.[65] A boycott, it was added, would be beyond the reach of the most ingenious safeguard ever devised by the wit of man. If a provincial government decided to boycott members of any particular community or any English firm, no court would be able to interfere. If a municipal corporation in India determined to discriminate against English firms and the ministers of the province supported them, the governor would be powerless. There was no way to compel a government, Morgan asserted, to govern justly.[66]

Morgan argued that the very provision in the event of a breakdown was a glowing testimony that the situation was extraordinary and institutions were based on shifting sands. Constitutions had always been granted on the assumption that government would be carried on constitutionally. If that assumption could not be made, Morgan wrote, there was only one course open to statesmen and that was not to grant that constitution at all. Morgan asserted that Lord Sankey failed where no man, living or dead, could have succeeded. There would be a danger of chronic martial law.[67] It was a niggardly sort of gift, Morgan argued, to offer India as a solution of the existing discontents, a constitution the only effect of which would be to reduce the country to 'a state of chronic litigation tempered by martial law.'[68] There was an element of fantasy, he added, in the official expectations which consisted of 'smooth assumptions of normal conditions qualified by intermittent apprehensions of grave emergencies.' Morgan found that the whole exercise was so bizarre as to suggest 'a jig-saw puzzle of which most of the pieces had gone astray' and 'texture is so criss-crossed with brittle threads that it was impossible to discover any trace of design in it.'[69]

It was argued that the whole scheme would mean that an imperial sovereignty distinguished by long conscientious service based on justice, progress, unity, stability and peace being forced to yield to the agitation of a few thousand Europeanized Indians and to the 'meddling and peddling theorising of the Lionel Curtis school of political doctrinaires.'[70] It would place formidable power in the hands of the craftiest castes and the most illiberal social system known in human record and plunge vast masses of the population into a sanguinary struggle between the Muslims and the Hindus. India would thus 'fall back into the dark ages of barbarism, from which she has been slowly rescued by British arms and administration.'[71] Shorn of the great dependency of India, which had been the chief source of her imperial development and her international personality, Britain would sink to the position of a third rate power, quite incapable of sustaining its existing predominance in the world. No British home would be unaffected by such a shameful surrender of British rights and privileges in India by politicians without a mandate and without any moral authority. All patriotic Britons were called upon to pull up their socks and defeat the purpose of MacDonald, Baldwin, Hoare and their supporters with regard to India.[72]

A more popular and political tract of significance was Lord Sydenham's *The Federation of India: A Dangerous Illusion,* published by the India Empire Society[73] and circulated by the League. Sydenham maintained that since the RTC in November 1930, the orderly course of procedure of constitutional programme was widely disturbed and the question of the future of India assumed a new and peculiarly dangerous aspect as the federal idea was allowed to dominate the 'promiscuous' talks that followed. Thus, Sydenham quipped, the government joined the Congress Party 'in boycotting the results of two years' hard and conscientious work by the Simon commission, and the official Conservative Party internalized that confounding constitutional prescription armed with safeguards. But the specific problems of India of eight provinces arose from the fact that they differed widely in political and material progress and their legislatures were 'oligarchical bodies', whose responsibility in the democratic sense to their population was farcical. The 'backward areas' with 13 million people, were manifestly unqualified and inept for representative institutions. They could not, by any reckoning be incorporated in any federal system. The provinces were dependent for their economic and other advancement and for the maintenance of order on the British central government, the governors and the British or British-trained Indian elements in the public services. In fact, Sydenham echoed the words of the ultra-die-hards when he held that it was just to say that all the measures which had benefited the masses had been initiated and administered by British elements often in the face of the hostility of Indian politicians. He added that the experience of purely Indian administration on democratic lines in municipal and local governments was, in most cases, appalling and that it should be obvious that at least a full trial of provincial autonomy was essential before the federation of British India could come within the scope of practical policies. Sydenham emphasized that the whole responsibility for the peaceful progress of India towards nationhood and for the guardianship of her territory against invasion and internal disorder 'rest solely upon us'.[74] The attempt by the government to transfer authority 'to a small urban faction, mainly consisting of high caste privileged Hindus' riven by internal divisions was a blatant betrayal of a national obligation. 'We cannot', Sydenham wrote, 'hand over our trust deeds, sealed with the blood and the life-work of tens of thousands of our best manhood to the little faction, mainly Hindu, which calls itself a *National* party.'[75] Anybody, he added, who 'pictures to himself the anarchy and the bloody chaos' which would follow from any ‘such deplorable steps might shrink from that sinister decision’.

The Indian Empire Society was conceived at the time when the Simon Commission had been conducting enquiries in 1928 by Lord Sydenham, Sir Michael O’Dwyer and Sir Reginald Craddock, all of whom had outstanding Indian experience. The object of the endeavour was to work out the best methods of directing the changes in India which were then imminent.[76] The group was joined by another distinguished India hand in Mark Hunter, as treasurer, and then Lord Sumner, a prominent English judge, as the president. The aims of the Society were to secure and discharge the responsibilities incurred by Britain towards the peoples of India. The Society believed that the introduction of the Act of 1919 had not proved a success, that the administration had deteriorated in the intervening years and that India was not ripe for any significant extension of self-government. The presence of the Labour government instilled in the Society the feeling that the authorities would concede to the Congress and, in sheer desperation, the group turned towards the Conservatives and Liberals. The publication of the Simon report, successive RTCs and the policy of Baldwin intensified its uneasiness and the Society was pushed towards the die-hards. The Society opposed the white paper which was released in March 1933 and escalated its campaign against any concession to Indian nationalism. Despite a setback due the death of some of its leading lights, the Society carried its message to many tens of thousands. The contributions by its members to the Press had gone very far. Its pamphlets were many and had been widely circulated.[77] The *Indian Empire Review* supplemented the propaganda. Then there were speeches on its own platforms as well as from a large variety of organizations. Parliamentary contacts increased and the formation of the India Defence League augmented the die-hard pressure on what they thought to be the wishy-washy ‘sentimentalism’ of the Baldwinites.

While the Indian Empire Society was composed of retired Indian administrators, the founders of the India Defence League were men inside the two houses.[78] Together, they represented 'a non-party' conservative public opinion reflecting the acute apprehension excited within Parliament. Both the groups functioned with a good deal of cooperation, although they decided to retain their respective identity. They were housed in the same building, remained side by side and decided to act in cooperation. Lord Sumner, president of the Society, accepted the post of president of the League as well, as a symbolic gesture of close association. While the propaganda side was taken over almost entirely by the League, the Society assisted in its preparation and provided many of the speakers at the numerous League meetings. The League, owing to its for greater resources, conducted the campaign on a scale that had never been contemplated by the Society.[79] Once the Act was passed, nothing more could be done in that direction. The collection of information and its dissemination with comments was left to the Society, while the League came to an end in 1936, leaving behind with the Society 'pleasant memory of harmonious association and generous assistance.'[80]

The official response to the Conservative opposition to the reform proposals was gradual but it went ahead to fashion an organized body of opinion. The Union of Britain and India (UBI) sought to clarify the situation and place the white paper in perspective. Active in 1934 and 1935, the Union of Britain and India was an officially blessed organization to counter the excesses of the propaganda sponsored by the India Defence League and the Indian Empire Society and it functioned under the direction of Sir John Perronet Thompson.[81] Thompson claimed that the reform proposals had been developed from the original conception of devolution of authority in India. Under the existing system, he maintained, many of the subjects concerning the welfare of the people had been under responsible ministers such as agriculture, health, medicine, roads, etc. The verdict of the Simon commission was, by no means, unfavourable. Partial transfer of responsibilities in the provinces had served its term and its continuance produced unsatisfactory results. It was almost an universal agreement that the transfer of responsibilities should be extended.[82] As regards the criticism that the white paper proposal was the negation of the principle that a strong centre alone could check a tendency of deterioration in the provinces, Thompson held that the formulation was based on a dated situation by about 15 years.

In the course of the campaign for the white paper, the UBI worked out a comprehensive paper on the effects of the civil disobedience and boycott movements on the economic environment of the country. It was maintained that industrial depression was primarily due to the panic caused by the movements. There was also direct loss to hundreds of Indian dealers in foreign goods and indirect loss to many more by the worsening of general trade conditions. Many working people had been thrown out of employment reducing the purchasing power of consumers. The nationalist agitation had also produced a general feeling of insecurity which operated against the movement of goods and paralyzed the will to launch business undertakings. Hundreds of *hartal* and demonstrations grossly hampered production and exchange of commodities. Besides, political prejudices, boycott and coercion worked against the freedom of trade. Added to these, various items of local trade were adversely affected and tied-up capital created problems of shrinking of liquid currency. The upshot of the movement in economic terms was disastrous and the total responsibility for all of those was the strategy and tactics of a 'diabolical' Gandhi.[83] A practical adjustment of policy, the UBI maintained, was dictated by the creative statesmanship of Baldwin. It believed that the proposed scheme would serve the imperial mission better for its inherent strength and flexibility. It offered a genuine measure of autonomy in the provinces, inviting the cooperation of the constructive and stable elements in Indian politics. It was also an interesting feature that the franchise would be broadened and political power would then cease to rest upon a narrow basis. The relations between the centre and the provinces would be defined and rationalized. The central legislature would benefit from the sobering impact of responsibility and its radical impulses would be tempered by the representatives of the Indian states. The whole scheme, the UBI argued, would go a long way to satisfy Indian political aspirations and remove much of the bitterness. The real power of Parliament to discharge its ultimate responsibility for good government in India would be strengthened by reservations and safeguards. It would assure defence and financial stability and would protect the actions of the executive on occasions of real emergency from the blighting influence of irresponsible criticisms.[84]

Thompson emphasized, time and again, that the necessity of strong administration as had been organized by Michael O'Dwyer during the time of the Punjab disturbances of 1919 was compatible with the desirability of modest political advance as proposed. It was imperative, he thought, to organize the campaign to impress upon public opinion that the white paper had been on the right lines. The basis of its conviction was the overriding support and assistance the UBI enjoyed in the India Office.[85] As a result, in a very short time the UBI prepared a comprehensive list of eminent men and women with interest in and commitment to the *Raj* producing literature and leaflets, organizing a mechanism of distribution, marshalling impressive speakers for meetings and conferences, contradicting misstatements and misrepresentations of official points of view in newspaper and journals, securing financial and other material assistance and finally, rebutting and demoralizing India League's 'scandalous propaganda.'[86] Before long, the organized official propaganda bore fruit, Hailey found it useful and effective. Butler congratulated Thompson for the 'birth of the great venture' and also 'for the psychological moment for launching it.'[87] Meston shared the views of many retired civil servants and army generals when he extended his entire sympathy and support to Thompson.[88]

In the course of the campaign for and against the reform proposals the combined force of Conservative propaganda argued that any democratic devalution constituted a danger to the empire, that the introduction of provincial autonomy, however regulated, might hand over the control of the greater part of India to the avowed enemies of Great Britain, that increased safeguards should be added to make the proposals inoperative, that Indian nationalism was a transitory phenomenon and an ephemeral gesture and that Gandhi was the most powerful personality in India and a ruthless autocrat who, with all his cunning stunts — non-violence, civil disobedience, *khadi, charkha,* loin-cloth, anti-untouchability, — had been masquerading as a saint and was committed to the dismemberment of the empire.[89] The extension of franchise, it was added, would mean Hindu Congress rule led by a Brahmin oligarchy and would stimulate Hindu-Muslim tension and also inspire Congress to clamour for more independence seeking severance from Britain.[90] It was affirmed that 'our duty' to India as distinct from 'gestures and promises' were three-fold: The first was to protect and to help govern wisely the inchoate many-headed millions of Indians; the second duty was to protect those who gave their lives and sacrificed their families in helping to govern India and the third was to protect those at home and in India who did honest productive trade for the mutual benefit of each country. The first duty, the die-hards claimed, the white paper and the proposed bill could not perform, the second duty it would betray and the third it could not justify.[91]

Michael O'Dwyer put the case of die-hards forcefully when he asserted that the scheme would neither work nor last. It would not give the masses of India more food, more peace in their streets, greater justice in the courts, higher protection and security against the oppression of caste and race, nor would it give what the Indian politicians themselves asked for. Besides the proposals would merely whet the appetite of the Indian politicians without any hope of tranquillity even for a breathing space. 'One wonders', O'Dwyer wrote, 'why the Government persists in a scheme which no one in India wants, which no one in this country has ever yet tried to defend on the merits and ... which will inevitably break up the main bulwark in the country against predatory Socialism.'[92] The only explanation that O'Dwyer could offer was fear. The IDL thought that the whole constitutional experiment was based on a false premise and an absurd assessment of Indian realities. The contention that India 'whose 300 millions are wholly devoted to their fields, their cows and their religious worship' would rise in revolt unless federalism and ballot-box were introduced forthwith 'might only provoke a smile of derision to all those civil servants who knew India'.[93] These presentiments, the IDL dismissed, as 'the foolish dreams of town-bred westerners.'

These ideas found adequate expression in the private correspondence of some well-known English businessmen having long experience in India. One of them concluded his observations by saying that the white paper was an almost purely sentimental document and the authors did more credit to the hearts than the heads of its supporters.[94] If implemented, the scheme would destroy the unifying power and leave the country a prey to disorder and anarchy. No true friend of India 'would have us shirk the heavy and responsible task which still awaits us'. It was just a mockery to talk of introducing democratic institutions on the western model in a country where 90 per cent of the people were 'illiterate hardly knowing their right hand from the left' and to hand them over to the unchecked control of a mere handful of their countrymen 'who are avowedly hostile to the British connection in any form'.[95] Supporters of the white paper were urged not to be one-eyed, not to overlook and not to exaggerate. What was required in 'the great India debate' was 'more of vision and less of party feelings.' Common prudence and honesty should have suggested to government the propriety of consulting the British electorate before seeking to commit the country to a policy that might as well result in disrupting the empire.[96]

Face the Facts in India was based on an article in the *Sunday Pictorial* and issued by the Indian Empire Society and created a good deal of commotion in the vast conservative circles in the country.[97] Representing the conservative backlash against the reform proposals for India, this tract from Ward Price maintained that 'sentimentality' had always been a British weakness but her statesmen had always been kept in restraint by adequate knowledge of facts. It appeared that, of late, rational coordination relaxed its hold over the minds of the power-elite and, as a consequence, a people wholly unfitted for self-administration was being offered political and democratic self-assertion. 'If we go', Price wrote, 'barbarism will recover more ground than it has regained anywhere in the world since history began.'[98] Those were not 'nightmare dreams'. Price exhorted that real statesmanship should speedily displace the feeble mushiness of the socialist and semi-socialist leaders. The critical hour had come at last for the withdrawal of trust from the faint-hearted politicians who had been persuaded to yield to the bitter enemies of the British empire.

There were, however, a large number of backbenchers who were being persuaded to see the trend of events and the desperate need for unity. In a way, they saw the strength of the opposition's arguments. They were, however, handicapped by the paucity of Indian experience and needed guidance as to the best policy or procedure to be followed there. In India, they felt almost instinctively, the stability of administration was indispensable. It must be based on needs of the special time and the specificities of circumstances. Democracy, they thought, was peculiarly unsuitable for India. They were, however, endowed with a remarkable pragmatic approach to parliamentary life. They were, as a consequence, inclined to take the lead from the government and agreed to support it.[99] The Conservative backbenchers saw Great Britain as being still the most stable unit in a world torn asunder by violent upheavals, unsuccessful changes and futile and fatal aspirations against the background of a prolonged economic crisis. Great Britain, they believed, had the best chance of leading western civilization towards a better ethical, economical and political future. They held that the British Government was in need of a solid, united and decisive majority to give the maximum effect to the country's deliberations and actions in the world. Like many others they would counsel themselves to subordinate their personal views on any individual issue to the main theme and to work for the elimination of sectarianism within the ranks of the Conservative Party. Any other step would elucidate no new fact or theory but would almost certainly confuse the main issues, objects and endeavours of the National government.[100]

The situation of India during the high noon of civil disobedience was viewed from the official vantage point in an atmosphere of cool and callous detachment by Harry Haig, home member of the executive council. He assured the secretary of state that the campaign against civil disobedience had been going on satisfactorily and reports from local governments had been on the whole encouraging.[101] He referred to a 'strong propaganda offensive' against official policy, both in India and in England, aimed at spreading an impression that despite apparent success on the surface, the official offensive had been in fact 'creating feelings of sullen resentment and laying up for ourselves much troubles in the future.'[102] Haig was uncertain if the impression was totally untrue but he thought that the function of his government was to deal with such demoralizing allegations with some authority. He maintained that those who had been 'so assiduously advising us of the futility of repression are precisely those who are anxious that we should not succeed'.[103] There were many, he thought, outside the professed ranks of the Congress who had considerable sympathy with it.

Haig was quite contemptuous of the Indian moderates and liberals whom he dismissed as typical 'trimmers.' He argued that these liberals did not want the Congress movement of civil disobedience to succeed because they realized the disastrous effects that would ensue; but, at the same time, they did not want the Congress to be beaten, for, 'after all the Congress was the spearhead of the nationalist attack', and if it was weakened too much, then they were apprehensive that the government might find itself in a position to take a stiffer line on reforms. Haig concluded that it was natural, therefore, that 'the Liberals should have given us some verbal support at the beginning of the movement', and that as the policy of repression appeared to be succeeding, 'they should become more and more critical', continually insisting on the need for moderation. Haig thought what the liberals would have liked to see was 'a draw in favour of Congress.' Another argument that primarily emanated from England, Haig wrote, was 'now that we have asserted our strength we can afford to be conciliatory.' He thought that this was wholly unacceptable. He argued that there was no worse policy than one that advocated 'first to assert our strength and then assert our weakness.' The movement was checked at that moment but by no means beaten. Haig was convinced that it would take time to wear down a movement of that kind and hence the policy should not be slackened. Gandhi, according to him was an 'inveterate bargainer' and one should not concede to his 'various childish antics.'[104] The object was to see that the movement should gradually die down as its supporters became more and more disheartened. It would then be possible, he wrote, to let the prisoners out in ever increasing numbers, though gradually and not dramatically. By then, the constructive policy should practically be ready. In this context, Haig thought both provincial autonomy and the federal part should come together. Although Federation might offer difficulties and from the point of keeping the Muslims quiet it was important that they should be given a communal decision as early as possible and Sind should go out as a separate province.[105]

By March 1932, the government felt that there had been an emphatic change in the atmosphere in India, that the country was settling down and the worst of the crisis was past. Yet, the possibility of a renewal of the no-rent movement especially in the UP offered an ominous prospect. It was evident that the strong official policy would be carried on even at the risk of irritating Sapru and Jayakar. But this did not exclude tactical adjustments. Hoare confided to MacDonald that there was a good deal of substance in what Dr Paton said about Madras. It seemed that the Madras government had been acting 'rather on its own line'. There had been isolated instances of provocative incidents initiated by the local officials and orders were issued insisting upon restraint and caution in dealing with emergency powers. The Government of India was instructed to stick to a position that without breaking the morale of the police 'we must show willingness to admit mistakes if mistakes are really made.'[106]

Alexander Inglis, the seasoned journalist with an intimate acquaintance of the political temper of India, had been commissioned by the government to assess the impact of the report of the JSC on Indian constitutional reform. Inglis stressed that the omission of any reference to dominion status in the report and the seeming reluctance of the committee to define the constitutional goal of the country as being dominion status had serious implications. The avoidance of the term together with the extensive powers which would vest in the governors and the governor-general, Inglis thought, had a characteristic psychological reaction upon a people whose political feelings were primarily emotional and who were largely influenced by questions of prestige.[107] In Inglis' perception, nationalist opinion frankly contended that British pledges had been violated; moderates maintained that the omission would place an undesirable impediment in the way of constructive work by perpetuating a sense of distrust and struggle; the Liberals complained that one of their principal grievances was the failure of the report to state explicitly that the goal was dominion status. British newspapers in India deplored the absence of the phrase in the report.

Inglis made it clear that if statesmanship called for a calculated policy to touch the imagination of the various strands of liberal and moderate opinion, this flaw in the document should be rectified. Otherwise, the general sentiment running through all India was that the committee's lapse on that score implied that British intentions had been re-oriented. The resultant animosity, he reiterated, would assume dangerous proportions.[108] It was true that in view of the avowed policy of the Congress in favour of complete independence and the definition of dominion status in the Statute of Westminster as conceding the right of secession on the part of units of the British Commonwealth of Nations, the reference to dominion status would not have satisfied the nationalist school which would, in all probability, have argued that the safeguards constitute a firm denial of the objective. Inglis, however, held that some cooperative moderates felt that conceding the legitimacy of emergency powers, reservations and safeguards, it would have been far better and even more conciliatory to mention dominion status as the goal in order to ensure sympathetic cooperation of the moderates who could be energized by the prospect of reaching the ultimate objective before long.[109] Dominion status, Inglis emphasized, had become the symbol of equal partnership, a part of the political process that was directed at removing the stigma of inferiority, a signal of British commitment to fair play and justice and a constitutional fixation of India's nationalist psyche. The Indians conceded that their final constitution was bound to differ from that of Canada, Australia and South Africa; nor did they hold that it must inevitably take the form of any other dominion constitution. But, allowing for the different circumstances prevailing in India, Inglis argued, they desired equality of status with the other dominions. Even Aga Khan, with all his unflinching loyalty, sensed the need for allaying that distrust.[110]

The India Office thought otherwise. In a note on Inglis, it was maintained firmly that the Indians craved for the status of a dominion for the same reason that the Irish wanted the principle of equal nationality admitted for themselves, i.e. 'because they feel like many other victims of historical disaster that Providence owes them some satisfaction.' Neither nationhood nor dominion status were applicable to India. But they seemed adamant and had been pressing for dominion status. 'If, as Inglis says, the Viceroy and Aga Khan and most of the thoughtful British in India', the official note explained, 'sympathize with the Indian desire for the use of the phrase and if these magic words are likely to be of temporary value in pacifying the timid elephant on which the British *Raj* is riding, why not use them? They may mean little; there will be British garrisons in India; Native State India will remain under the paramountcy of the Kaiser-i-Hind, etc. But does this really matter at all?'[111] A little imagination in the case of India might save a great deal of trouble in the future. However, in consultation with the viceroy, it was decided by the cabinet committee, that it would be highly undesirable to use the vague and misleading expression 'dominion status'. Any substitute for this phrase would be misunderstood and criticized in India. It was agreed that the aim of British policy was the attainment by India of the position of a self-governing community within the British empire and it should be unambiguously phrased and understood as such.[112]

All through 1933, the fluid situation in India and trends in British politics were carefully monitored by Willingdon, the Viceroy and Malcolm Hailey, then in the India Office. Both were keen to see that the white paper was deftly chaperoned through the Parliament with the minimum of political wear and tear. It was evident that although Winston Churchill had not been able to command the House of Commons, he and his friends succeeded in filling the minds of people at large with a sense that there was something inappropriate and hazardous in making fresh concessions to India.[113] But the real problem of the secretary of state, Hailey noted, did not lie in the general air of mistrust of the white paper proposals but in the attitude of the JSC. Hoare was doubtful of the responses of men like Salisbury and Simon who seemed to entertain an underlying suspicion of the changes as a whole. It seemed that Hoare himself had dropped a very cautious and conservative attitude that had distinguished him in 1930, having attracted, due to his 'pro-reform' policy, to his own head the brickbats which a short time earlier used to be directed at Irwin.[114] Only a small band of Conservatives stood by him with conviction upholding his India policy endowed with 'all the fervour of discretionary statesmanship'.[115] By May 1933, it appeared that the white paper and the bill were likely to have a very rough passage through Parliament. There was a concerted attempt to remove Baldwin, and Willingdon had occasions to foreglimpse 'gloomy' future prospects in matters of finances.[116] Willingdon was keen to emphasize the key role that should be played by the administration in India and the need to push the secretary of state in the background. 'The time has come', he wrote anxiously, 'for the Cabinet and the India Office to realise that we should run this country from here and not from Whitehall, and that the Secretary of State should as far as possible be removed from the picture in the future.'[117] He was distressed to think what the position of a viceroy would be with an autonomous province, an irremoval executive and an irresponsible majority. Hailey was eager to rescue the perspective from all hazy and misleading prejudices and sentiments. He thought many of the die-hards such as Churchill, Lloyd, O'Dwyer and Craddock would have liked to sweep away everything that had been done since the days of Lord Morley. Hailey was convinced that the dislike of the die-hards of the ministerial system and Indianization goaded them to affirm that 'we must swing back to the pre-Morley rule.'[118] They were irritated by the modern tendencies which might have justified these new concepts and political perspective. But, as Hailey added, they declined to be honest and say so openly.

Despite Willingdon's almost pathological dislike of Gandhi, he did not fail to appreciate the destructive policy of the die-hards. 'At this distance', Willingdon wrote with anxiety, 'it is extremely difficult to gauge the situation, but I cannot believe that the Conservative Party will turn down Baldwin and split literally into two parts.'[119] It would mean, he added, general election and if Labour came, 'it seems perfectly clear that I and a good many others would come home.'[120] The position, he thought, was full of anxiety for British imperialism and 'most satisfying to the Congress'. Willingdon prayed for the victory of Baldwin with a big majority on 28 June 1933 at the Conservative conference, which would 'reduce Winston, George Lloyd & Co., very soon to pulp.'[121]

Willingdon was contemptuous of Gandhi and his politics. On 29 May 1933, as Gandhi was about to finish his fast, Willingdon confided to Hailey that he never expected Gandhi 'to be removed from this planet, however satisfactory it might have been to me from an administrative point of view.'[122] Willingdon was determined and refused negotiation with Gandhi even if he so desired. Orthodox people, he wrote, had been active on the matter of temple entry and if Gandhi made it his focal point, he would 'have a very troublesome time.'[123] Willingdon enjoyed Gandhi's predicament. 'Most wealthy Congressmen,' he wrote, 'are strongly orthodox in their views.' By the end of June 1933, Willingdon was candid: 'I am brutal enough to say to Gandhi that I don't feel much inclined to start negotiating with the commander of a rather defeated force.'[124] By 22 July 1933, it appeared to Willingdon that Gandhi was veering round to suspending the civil disobedience. But he, all the same, 'put himself into a terrible hole', and Willingdon could not 'really see how he is going to get out of it or that anything that he does is going to restore his prestige.'[125] But then he could not be too sanguine, for Gandhi was 'a machiavellian little devil', and might 'twist matters round to give him an advantage once more.'[126]

Gandhi was behind the bar once again in early August 1933 and Willingdon reported gleefully that the curious result had been that every Congress paper or nearly everyone had then been fulminating vociferously against 'the want of political *nous* of their one-time leader, in whom apparently they had faith.'[127] He was excited to note the rebellious old Congress Party was being renewed as a constitutional body. Willingdon was jubilant as he reported that Gandhi had been receiving nothing but the most adverse comments from all the nationalist newspapers. When he was arrested on 1 August 1933 and sentenced, there was, Willingdon observed, no outcry of any sort. Willingdon was convinced that 'as a political factor, Gandhi for the moment at all events, has practically disappeared.'[128] He supposed that Gandhi might try fasting again, but he did not think that in the existing temper of the country he would receive much sympathy. 'The little man' he wrote, 'has overshot the mark, and the response of his lead had been very small.'[129]

Official arrogance was stupendous. Correspondence between Hailey and Willingdon during the summer of 1933 was extraordinary. Willingdon complained that it appeared to him by the proceedings of the RTC that the Indian delegates had been endeavouring to drive the representatives of the provinces into an embarrassing position. He deplored the lack of a spirit of cooperation. He detected a sense of despair as each group had been trying to help its own interests. The Muslims, Willingdon wrote, 'really seem to be the only people who have got any political sense at all and who largely combine for their own political advantage.' Willingdon agreed with Hailey that under those circumstances, it would be preposterous to suggest that the princes' representatives should not use their influence if they were members of the Assembly on all matters connected with federal affairs.[130] The overriding consideration in official mind had been that the princes should be 'a steadying influence on general legislation at the Centre.'[131] Willingdon was not inclined even to consider Sapru as a reliable person. Politically he did not trust Sapru 'a yard' and considered his position towards Gandhi all through 'quite deplorable'.[132] Hari Singh Gaur, Abdur Rahim and Sapru, Hailey wrote, 'have been making a perfect nuisance of themselves'. Sapru, in particular, 'pours forth the floods of oratory at inordinate length' and had been 'driving the Committee to despair'.[133] Increasingly, Hailey lost his cool. 'They really are an extraordinary stupid lot, who seem to have no imagination at all, and I honestly confess that if I were the Joint Select Committee, I would make up my mind to finish by the end of July and let them all go home.'[134]

The Indian delegates, Hailey thought, had been trying to exploit the 'weak attitude' of the government although they were aware of the fact that in any case they could get from the JSC nothing in advance of the white papers and that they might even get less.[135] From their point of view, their position was embarrassing and it would prejudice them in India subsequently.

By the end of July 1933 Hailey could conveniently report that there had been no scope for effective contributions by the Indians. The official idea was to create an atmosphere in which concessions and safeguards could be so arranged as 'to convince the bulk of the Conservatives that the position had been rendered materially safer.'[136] It was believed that the opposition to the main lines of the scheme would be marginal and it could be overcome if the moderate thinkers in Parliament could announce concessions. Hailey felt that the Indian delegates had settled down to a realization that they would be lucky if they could get the content of the white paper scheme and that they could not hope for more. They were 'not fully satisfied' but they were 'not seriously dissatisfied' either.[137] It was believed that England must grasp the psychological needs of the situation as even an imperfect decision would be better than great delay. A feeling that the white paper policy had been greatly improved in the JSC was being consciously promoted and press joined in the general hullabaloo enthusiastically. It was generally disseminated that people were prepared to accept the general position of the Government of India, subject to anything that the JSC might say and the select committee must decide on merit and 'not under Cabinet pressure.'[138]

Thompson's organization had begun to issue opinions of men recently in India who were in favour of the white paper and whose names were 'quite impressive.' Lord Meston and many others, though not favourable, would not oppose the white paper as a whole. Butler refused to take an active part in things but he was committed to the white paper as a fair line of improvement as the existing 'hybrid constitution' could not carry on.[139] The essence of Willingdon's demand was to keep the white paper scheme untampered. The Government of India, he maintained, wanted to be sure that the JSC and Parliament did not whittle away the proposals in any material way. It was well-known, he added, that if they did, this would give the Congress people a good chance of recovering their position and would 'reduce the friendly feelings of the Muhammadans for the Government in the future; and this is particularly important just now, because I really and honestly feel we have got that little devil Gandhi practically on his back.'[140]

Cornelia Sorabji was a restless publicist for the Raj. Over the years she had established a warm connection with I.M. Stephens, director, public information, Government of India, and was *l'amiable* with MacGregor of the India Office, who found her an apt and useful instrument to debunk Gandhi and deprecate the importance of nationalist agitation.[141] She was encouraged by Stephens to claim in her counterpropaganda that the dacoities, terrorist crimes and incidents connected with civil disobedience were all parts of one coherent political agenda. Stephens confided to her that it would be dangerous to risk making the same remarks officially as he was not in a position to substantiate these claims.[142] But it would be politically correct and even helpful if a determined public noise could be made by persons with acknowledged commitment to orderly public life. She was also encouraged to reveal the implications of the terrorist movement from its inner side.[143] Thus, on the basis of official briefings she asserted periodically that for the preceding 15 years or so, officers of the central and provincial governments in India had done their best to convince nationalists of the reality and gravity of the situation but they, with a few exceptions, met with no response beyond incredulity of unpleasant insinuations.[144] It was but natural, she argued, that no further attempt at renewed persuasion was likely to succeed and would even be 'misunderstood and exploited politically in an undesirable way'.[145] To make the terrorist story appear more authentic, colourful and alarming, it might be asserted, Stephens advised with a touch of optimism, that a substantial number of Indian students in Moscow, about 75 in 1928, had been trained in Soviet methods of revolution and some of them had been working in India for subversive activities. Sorabji was also informed that nearly 9,700 women were convicted up till the end of May 1933 and about 65 women of considerable educational attainments were said to have engaged in various subversive activities in India.[146]

In fact, terrorism in India was one of the recurring items in official counterpropaganda. The points were highlighted by Sir Charles Tegart, who had served in the Indian Police Service for years. In his speech, in 1932, at a meeting organized by the Royal Empire Society which was subsequently published in 1933, Tegart laid bare the intricacies and nuances of Indian terrorism.[147] Based on a good deal of solid information, unflinching commitment and the single-minded persuasiveness of a trained officer dealing with terrorism in Bengal for three decades, Tegart's pamphlet was effective ammunition for the ebullient publicist. The first point that was asserted was that although the genesis and development of terrorist crime in India formed more or less a continuous chain, the civil disobedience movement gave it a second wind.[148] From the point of view of an impartial administrator committed to the preservation of the essentials of civilized existence, one was tempted to say that, for all intents and proposes, the terrorist resurgence and the civil disobedience movement supplemented each other. Though fundamentally different, both the movements aimed at paralyzing the overnment. Terrorism penetrated the Congress machine in Bengal. The rank and file were generally students.[149] Its network, though not spread all over India, was ever expanding; it relied for its efficacy on secrecy; it burrowed underground; there was no outward sign of it. It emerged and struck its victims suddenly and then disappeared from view.[150] It was essentially a Hindu movement and drew its recruits by persistent and malignant representation of the policy and actions of the government. Although it had branches all over India,

Tegart reported that 'it has taken firm root in Bengal'.[151] Both the Calcutta university and the Calcutta corporation under the influence of the Congress had been impregnated with terrorists, their sympathizers and fellow-travellers.[152] In fact there was scarcely an educational institution in Bengal where there was not a terrorist group. The leaders evaded arrest and their energies were spent in inciting murder. The Chittagong raid of 18 April 1930 was the *annuntiator* of the third phase of the movement, and the most recent development in that new outburst of outrages and murders was the advent of female terrorists.[153]

Cornelia Sorabji was closely attached to the Royal Empire Society and also with the Indian Empire Society and the India Defence League. Her principal patron had been, for quite some time, Lady Maud Warrander, chairfperson, Royal Empire Society and for years moved around comfortably amidst Tory high society.[154] She belonged to an affluent Parsee family. She believed in the righteousness of British rule in India as the greatest gift of providence and worked and prayed for its continuance. She was appalled by the seamy side of Indian life and welcomed Katherine Mayo's *Mother India* as the most liberating exposé of debased Indian institutions, the flimflam of Indian nationalism and its hypocritical primate, Gandhi. She was considered by the Tory leadership and conservative socialites as a valued friend of the *Raj* having rendered inestimable service, both in England and America, as an extrovert publicist of its cause by out-mayoing Mayo.[155]

With firm official patronage, Sorabji had a field day. In a large number of lectures, signed and unsigned pieces, reviews, commentaries, essays, articles and position papers and frequent emotional interventions in meetings and conferences, Sorabji castigated the nature and perspective of the Congress and debunked Gandhi, much of which became the talking points of the Conservative circles.[156] If Menon was to be taken at his face value, she repeated *ad nauseam,* his statements would have an unfavourable impact on the credibility of the *Raj* in England and on British prestige in the United States and she was commissioned to counter him. Her presentations were closely monitored by Louis Stuart, Alfred Knox and Angus Fletcher. Describing Gandhi's prayer meetings as amazing and hypnotic, she compared them with the magic of high service in a continental cathedral. She proceeded to affirm that it was to these daily rituals that 'we must look for the maintenance of Gandhi's hold on his disciples'.[157] It was a clever claptrap, she chuckled disdainfully, to project the atmosphere of the prayer meeting and along with the myth of the legendary 'Mahatma' with all his 'benedictions' and 'maledictions' silhouetted against the background of a country's turmoils to the innocent crowd of dazed followers incapable of grasping the ambivalent gospel of Gandhi, the political and moral reformer.[158] Gandhi was surrounded, she claimed, 'by the most pretentious propaganda' whereby 'our opinions are moulded like wax'.[159] In a review in 1932, she gave vent to her morbid anti-Indian frenzy when she wrote that although Gandhi had been fighting for democracy and the British politicians had promised India democracy, the two 'put different meanings to the word'. Whether, she added, 'it is our politicians' democracy or Gandhi's, the common platform will be removed' and each community would fight only for itself 'without any thought to the good of country'. Surely Gandhi must realize this. Sorabji wondered if Gandhi was really a sincere man or he was laughing up his sleeves at his dupes, who raised him to a position of a demigod as the arbiter of the country.[160]

India on the Brink, a compendium of ideas on Indian nationalism, written by a British Indian merchant, corresponded very closely to the writings and discourses of Sorabji. Its principal preoccupation was to unmask the hollowness of Gandhi's *satyagraha* movement revealing that in its very inception it had been inspired by an implacable hatred of the *Raj*. This political tract was acclaimed by William Birdwood, Earl of Inchcape, Lord Sydenham, Leslie Wilson, Reginald Craddock, Henry Adamson, Michael O'Dwyer, Thomas Holland, Arthur Knapp, James Mackenna, Geoffrey Clarke, Charles McLeod, Clark Jacob, R.W.K. Dunlop and Viscount Burnham.[161] The volume was issued by the Indian Empire Society and found a proud place in Sorabji's papers at the India office.[162] Sorabji toiled hard over the years to prove the ugliness and deceitfulness of a pompous and pretentious Gandhi, much to Gandhi's total indifference. An unpublished article, "Mr Gandhi at the Crossroads", written in January 1933, gave a critical evaluation of Gandhi's *swaraj* which, along with a large number of other tracts by Sorabji, might be examined in her papers to illustrate and evaluate the point.[163]

Symmetrical projection of government policy, careful selection of the views and opinions of the Indian opposition and a systematic blackout of all unsavoury Indian facts and views had become an imperative official obligation since World War I. But it was found during the civil disobedience movement that the government had been increasingly unable to rely on any particular newspaper for the development and justification of its views and policies.[164] The India Study Circle was one of the organizations which, under the chairmanship of Professor L.F. Rushbrook-Williams, sought to clarify views and prepare a 'just' public opinion on various Indian issues. Yet the problem persisted and it became a matter of vital importance when the organization of government was given statutory sanction: the permanent executive was to be confronted with an elected opposition in the legislatures.[165] The solution of the paradoxical problem appeared to be in the enunciation of the principle that if the administration of the country was worth maintaining in the interests of the majority of the people of India, it was emphatically the duty of those who were anxious to maintain the existing order of things to 'provide adequate journalistic reinforcement of the Government's actions'.[166] In this context, it was decided to contact Reuters and the directors of the department of public information, at Delhi and Simla. They were invited to coordinate with the *Telegraph* and the *Times,* who were to have their representatives in Simla along with the Associated Press.[167] The idea was to make a combination of European edited newspapers in order to fight extremist views, meaning the opinion of the nationalist forces. 'The trouble has been that in the past and probably in the present, jealousies as between individual newspapers', the official note maintained, 'has prevented cooperation and combination on points of management which are really vital to the maintenance of a strong European tone in the papers as a whole.'[168] To support and sustain the efforts of government the media should be controlled by 'men with a real stake in the country'.[169] The superior technique of the European edited newspapers and their probable command of greater financial resources should give them powerful influence over editors of newspapers of Indian opinion.[170]

Press propaganda was persistent and ubiquitous. More than once some proponents of 'pious and conciliatory' imperial commonwealth brought to the notice of the India Office evidence of 'disgusting exhibition of ignorance and vulgarity' calculated 'to damage British prestige in India where one does expect of a representative of the English press some degree of decency and self-restraint in writing'.[171] The India Office was urged to find a way to deal with that 'almost unending flow of vulgar sentimentalism'.[172] Refuting the calumnious representation of Gandhi's Italian visit, Graham Pole, on the basis of reliable information, explained to the India office that Gandhi had not said anything with regard to his intention to revive civil disobedience on his return to India and that the interpretation put upon that interview in England was wholly wrong and mischievous and should be publicly repudiated.[173]

'With all my differences with Mr Gandhi', Baldwin added, 'I am not prepared to attribute to him any falsehood. I think he is incapable of that.'[174] The India office, whose inspiration behind the concerted propaganda was transparent and real, adopted a policy of benevolent neutrality in the face of a 'sentimental' opposition: 'On the whole, the best course', the India Office ventured to suggest, 'is to ignore the articles' which 'by their very thrust fully advertised their true nature'.[175] Pole and others were advised to show restraint and tolerance of diverse strands of public opinion of contradictory perceptions which were largely evoked, it was held, by the 'liberal ambience' of British public life.[176]

The impact of this active media policy was effective. Agatha Harrison was persuaded to consider Haig's proposition that abstract principles were not applicable in the case of India. All objections to the proscription of India League's *Condition of India* could not be judged merely on theoretical grounds. Assessments of political situations should be made only in view of certain practical objections operating under Indian conditions.[177] The delegation's expenses were borne by the Congress and the report was not unfavourable to the host. Harrison was persuaded to take cognizance of the view that the report of the League's delegation had become a cleverly compiled presentation of the anti-government case. It was stressed that no Indian would ever be permitted to publish such a one-sided report based on inaccuracies, misstatements and distortions merely to whip up dead issues and to vitiate all initiatives of constructive statesmanship.[178]

Official propaganda became incisive and all the more effecive when a deputation of the Indian Empire Society(IES) led by Louis Stuart called at the India office in early May 1935.[179] It was organized in the context of a letter by Alfred Knox to the secretary of state, offering all possible assistance to work for the India policy.[180] The India Office took note of the fact that, in principle, the IES was opposed to the very concept of federation and to further advance on democratic lines in India, however illusory it might be. On both these issues, the India office was apprehensive that the IES might find itself in opposition once again in the future.[181] The India Office, however, did not overlook that the Society could be a very valuable ally and should be welcomed, although a certain amount of caution was imperative. The necessary pre-condition for cooperation insisted upon by the India office was that IES activities should be conducted with 'open and unqualified acceptance of recent statements of government policy'.[182] The delegation was briefed on the activities of the India League, the London Committee of Congressmen, and the Communist party and 'our difficulties as an official organization in adequately coping with these activities'.[183]

The India Office was particularly interested in combating the letters of Communist press agents in the small local papers and the statements issued by the India League in noisy meetings and conferences, in correcting ill-informed ideas put forward by small local editors and also by correspondents in the greater press, both under the inspiration of the India League and the Communist party, in having debaters 'present and ready to heckle the opposition at public meetings, however small, in holding counter meetings when circumstances required and when such meetings were held, in producing pamphlets in reply to Congress and Communist charges 'against us in relation to India' and in having literature distributed among those attending Communist and India League meetings, in ensuring a small body of MPs watchful over parliamentary questions inspired by the India League and ready by 'supplementaries' to aid in dealing effectively with the questions, etc.[184] On the 'positive' side, the deputation was made to appreciate the need to get 'the right sort of articles and letters to the editors' in the press and meetings supporting the government. The India Office, in its own turn, offered to the delegation a steady supply of all official matters and 'such help as may be wanted from time to time in securing information and guidance'.[185] The Office also offered to examine the possibilities of extending the circulation of the official News Sheet in the UK and USA. Besides, it was decided that UBI (Union of Britain and India) should be encouraged to adopt common course of actions with 'our new ally'. The officially organized body under John Perronet Thompson was prodded to drop its vehemence against its die-hard incarnation.[186]

Between the extrovert publicists of the *Raj* and the so-called lunatic fringe of the British left, there were many who found it difficult to make up their minds. In a sense, they were caught up between the reality of an arrogant empire and the much publicized British liberal inheritance. As has been explained earlier, the Fellowship of Conciliation and its specialized India group rose out of an army of self-assured liberal idealists as a definite group of humanists seeking reconciliation between estranged peoples, antagonistic emotions and contradictory political positions separated by closed doors and unfortunate misunderstandings. Agatha Harrison became the indefatigable secretary of the ICG with Carl Heath as its chairman and Alexander Wilson as treasurer. Henry Polak and some concerned individuals, such as William Paton, Dr Harold Mann, Grace Lankester and several ex-missionaries became active members, while C.F. Andrews was the sympathetic conduit and confidant of the Group. The basis of the endeavours of the India Conciliation Group was their belief in the unity of mankind and their faith in the efficacy of negotiations and peaceful settlement through the process of unhindered dialogue. They sought to strengthen the moderates of all faiths in India, make them sit together, deny all possibilities of giving offence to one another, soften the blows of unsympathetic official actions and make both sides appreciate the problems and difficulties of each other.[187] A quiet, steady and determined progress in India towards a greater measure of political freedom, Horace Alexander thought, had been the significant feature of the post-World War I situation. This trend was vital in view of the ominous attitudes of the ultra-conservatives in Britain, the irrational behaviour of the harassed administrators in an alien country and the impetuosities of the angry young men in India.[188] The Group sought to humanize imperialism and temper its harsh realities; they were often intrigued by Gandhi's uncompromising adherence to truth and were appalled by the enigmatic embrace of an imperial psychology sapping the vitality of the free and adventurous British people.[189] Evidently, it was not easy to close any door before Agatha Harrison and her associates. They always assumed that the man inside the door was one with a warm heart and decent human feelings even when they were struggling to get him to change his policy. India and Gandhi were central to Harrison's conception for two decades.

The Group tried to draw empathy from as many areas as possible and welcomed all those who acknowledged the merit of conciliation in a strife-torn world. They had Conservatives, Liberals and Labourites, administrators, clergymen and missionaries in their extensive network in Britain. At the India end, there were Gandhi, Malaviya, Sapru, Sastri, Amrit Kaur, Jamnalal Bajaj, Birla, Maulana Azad, Rajagopalachari, Tagore, Ambedkar, Pyarelal and many others. Live contacts with Menon, Masani and Nehru were nursed to feel the pulse of the radical young men.[190] The uneasy conscience of the British nation provided imperialism, Menon concluded, with a suitable instrument to manipulate divergent emotions and keep a channel of communication unbarred between advanced Indian opinion and British ruling impulses.

There was a good deal of consternation in the Friends' House about the lack of communication in 1931 between

MacDonald and Gandhi. Maud Royden, like many others, did not quite understand Gandhi although she admired him profoundly. Strangely enough, Royden did not wholly understand MacDonald either. Both the leaders seemed to some of the Friends very shy and remote souls and the Friends constantly prayed that they might understand each other better than 'we fear'.[191] This was a reason good enough for disquietude and they hoped that at that stage of the conference, substantial tasks must be achieved and if any significant conclusions on the fundamental issues were not reached, the conference should be adjourned and not scrapped altogether.[192]

Polak, who knew Gandhi well enough and had been watching the changing panorama of India over the years as a trusted observer of the Labour Party, was called upon to educate the Friends on the various nuances of Indian politics and Gandhi's movements.[193] He claimed authoritatively that the 1917-20 period was one in which if not 'moderates', at least 'moderating influences' were still active within the Congress. Polak did not think that it was right to regard the *Swadeshi* movement as a particular form of direct action. It was, at any rate, an active agitation. Polak thought that it was something different from ordinary constitutional agitation, though it was not 'unconstitutional'. So far as the Congress was concerned, whilst it undoubtedly gave moral sustenance to the 'support Indian industries cry', it never, upto 1920, formally adopted the slogan 'Boycott British goods' and that Gandhi 'allowed him, as I think, wrongly', Polak emphasized, to be overwhelmed 'thereon by the majority of his colleagues'.[194] Boycott of the legislatures by the Congress in 1920 harmed the political processes in two ways.[195] It deprived the administration of the services of some of the most distinguished liberals who had begun to try out the new constitution and by practical experience would have been able to locate effectively its inherent weaknesses. Secondly, it deprived the Congress leaders of invaluable administrative experience and delayed the inevitable realization that substantial and fundamental alterations in the constitution were necessary. Non-constitutional methods, Polak stated firmly, destroyed the possibility of political unity, delayed the accomplishment of a common end, built up barriers against early introduction of the new constitution and raised dangerous apprehensions which, in their turn, prompted the cry for crippling safeguards.[196]

Polak was convinced that had the various nationalist groups, from the right to the left, combined to act with a single purpose on well-organized constitutional methods, they would have 'secured today a far nearer approach to full responsible government' than was possible under the existing political atmosphere. Polak emphasized that the unconstitutional demeanour of the Congress under Gandhi prevented for certain a real rapprochement between Hindus and Muslims largely as a result of the refusal of Muslims to follow the Congress lead after the 1920 session.[197] Polak entirely agreed with the formulation that the Mahatma's personality had helped enormously to create 'a political and social self-consciousness in India' such as had never been known earlier and would invariably, in due course, produce its full consequences. But, he also maintained that Gandhi had 'retarded the realization of national aspirations', and his political leadership on the whole 'injured the National cause'.[198] One of the worst features of Gandhi's impact had been the subordination of all other political personalities to his, especially since the death of C. R. Das (1925) and Motilal Nehru (1931) and the subjection of those who were increasingly inclined to disagree with him but had neither the courage nor the character or even the desire to take a firm line with Gandhi that the circumstances increasingly required. Polak held that those views about the Mahatma and his impact were held by an increasing number of thoughtful people in India, many of whom had begun to regret that 'they allowed themselves' under 'the Mahatma's magic influence' to depart from more useful and fruitful methods.[199]

During the civil disobedience movement, visiting Friends went to India with the support of the 'Meetings of Sufferings' and they tried to build a bridge over the chasm of distrust. The Friends were not pleased to listen to Hoare's proud and uncompromising defence of the Government of India in Parliament and they, along with Christian forces, were afflicted by a sense of frustration with the reversal of the policy of conciliation.[200] Letters from missionaries about the deadlock in India and the urgency of a breakthrough had been pouring in.[201] Communications were sent to a few 'strategic persons' to say that Gandhi had asked Harrison to work for a mutual understanding between the two countries and that the group would be working between all political and social formations and that it would be in touch with all those close to Gandhi in India.[202] Harrison was, in particular, assured by Gandhi that the doors of all these persons would always be ajar for her to see them and pass on to them strategic information that she should have and what they would not be otherwise getting.[203]

As Harrison made her way to the political circuits of British society, she discovered for herself that the catchment area of the Group in Britain was far too limited to make any significant impact on public opinion.[204] The ordinary men and women on the street, Harrison thought, were primarily involved in the questions of disarmament, unemployment, means test and so on, if they were interested in any thing at all.[205] They were prone to forget that, under these circumstances, a state of war was prevalent in India. Even those who had been supporting missionary work did not quite comprehend that 'negation of Christianity' had been taking place in that unfortunate country. There was, perhaps, an element of self-righteous assertion in the Group's conviction. It did not take its line from anyone but prepared material for people who believed that what 'we are doing in India is justified' and for all 'those who had been working quite honestly for peace'.[206] It was also reported that the India League and the Friends of India were anxiously seeking assistance from the Group in some official capacity. But the Group could not afford to acquiesce in such requests for it was neither feasible nor desirable to be identified with the propagandist organizations as the Group would like to retain its freedom to move between all of them.[207]

Polak gave a cogent explanation of the network of personal relationships proposed by the India Conciliation Group over the years. In a reasoned article, he argued that no right-minded person could honestly deny the many admirable services rendered to India by a splendidly organized and highly efficient bureaucratic machine, whose technique had been perfected over a long series of years. The significant feature of that apparatus, Polak identified, was that 'it has worked from above'. It had been, as a consequence, irresponsible, privileged, largely unresponsive to criticism and jealous of the challenge to its authority. At its best, it adopted a patriarchal attitude and 'never recognized the ruled as the equals of the rulers'. The non-official British population had been too absorbed in its preoccupation with trade and commerce to ponder over and share the emotions and ideals of the people of the land. The formulation as a general proposition, Polak argued, was 'substantially accurate' even in 1934 despite the fact that the relations between some of the British officials and non-officials and some Indians, particularly those in the legislatures, had become more cordial and mutually responsive since the Montagu-Chelmsford reforms. There were many individual officials who were friendly, frank, sympathetic and approachable. Polak was convinced that the so-called change of heart had not gone very deep. Racial superiority, Polak added, was so ingrained in the British community that, over the years, it became very complex and the bitter reaction of Indians towards its constant demonstration was not even understood.

The most disquieting feature of the situation was a 'grave spiritual estrangement between Britain and India'. Polak agreed with most of the members of the Conciliation Group that many opportunities of 'justifying British control of Indian affairs' had been lost by lack of imagination, hypocrisy, false prestige, patronage, religiosity, pride of race, suspicion of the Indian peoples and contempt for their culture. Polak called for an entirely different attitude on the part of the British in India, based on better inter-racial relationships that would resolve half the problems of India.[208]

Conciliation between warring factions, it was claimed, was an act of self-denial and abstinence.[209] Horace Alexander made it abundantly clear that it was an emotionally colourless undertaking, based on supreme self-effacement and self-control and was dedicated to international amity.[210] Harrison noted that the India League had a powerful committee in Parliament, where the Labour MPs were briefed for questions in the house. The Conciliation Group, she claimed, undertook to concentrate on people, whom the India League could never reach, the Liberals and the honest Conservatives, with an interest in Indian developments who would be enriched by the presentation of Indian news in a detached way judging issues on merit.[211]

The attitudes of the Conciliation Group towards India under the ordinance rule was distinguished by contradictory pulls and complex sensibilities. In reponse to Horrabin's invitation to join a protest meeting against Gandhi's arrest, Carl Heath of Friends' Service Council and a leading member of the Group complained of being overworked within a limited time-frame in a busy world.[212] Personally, he was rather more concerned for private action than press conferences and protest meetings. Heath assured Horrabin that he had a great deal of sympathy for the India League's agenda, but then he was far too involved in his attempt towards a meaningful permanent conciliation to spare any time for any gesture that would only stiffen attitudes rather than soften people's hearts.[213]

Two meetings of the Group on 5 and 13 April 1932, dwelling on the condition of India, clearly illustrated the perception of the Group. On 5 April 1932, Carl Heath presided over the meeting to discuss with Friends how best to bring the 'serious situation' in India to the public's notice.[214] Information reaching the Group showed a growing estrangement and bitterness on the part of 'reasonable' opinion in India on account of the harshness of the ordinance administration. The moderates in India urged that the prime minister should speak out and take the situation more directly under his control. The feeling expressed in India was that the real difficulty was the attitude of the secretary of state. His perception had been hardening and it was viewed with distrust even by the liberals such as Sapru who had been writing regularly to Polak, an active member of the Group.[215] It was believed that nothing would restore confidence in the intentions of the government so much as a clear lead from the prime minister. There must be some sort of 'time table order' for conciliation and ending the ordinances if belief in the intentions of the government to promote reform was to be effectively reinstated.[216]

Eleanor Rathbone MP, who had just returned from India, found great bitterness of feelings in Bombay owing to the stringency of the ordinances, the 'cat and mouse' provisions effectively used by the police and the absence of any natural vent for nationalistic emotions for the young men and women. Strangely enough in Bengal, Rathbone claimed, the bitter feeling was less pronounced because owing to the revolutionary menace people were less critical of government measures for the preservation of order.[217] Amidst a good deal of animated discussion the position of the Group became clear, especially by the efforts of Lord Allen, who recapitulated the principles of conciliation as applied in the Indian situation. In a pointed reference to the role of the India League, Allen asserted that the accumulation of alleged atrocities and the asking of questions in Parliament thereon would not carry them much further. Conciliation should attempt 'to conciliate on both sides'. It should seek 'to heal and not to widen the breach'.[218] Indian friends, Heath added, 'should be urged to give up their systematic undermining of authority'.[219] If an attempt was made to seek the intervention of the prime minister, its success 'would depend on the tone of the voice'. If the tone was aggressive and partisan it would not impress the prime minister nor would a flood of questions and allegations of oppression. There should be 'a spirit of anxiety to help, not to hinder' and 'with a recognition that the peace move could not be on one side alone and the tone of the voice should be conciliatory'.[220] Conciliation should be a continuous effort. Rathbone clarified that the prime minister's intervention should be more 'on account of his superior office than on grounds of differentiating him from Samuel Hoare'.[221]

A meeting of the Group was arranged on 13 April 1932 to give interested individuals and associations an opportunity of considering together the existing situation in India.[222] On the basis of available information the Group concluded that there was nothing like an intellectual tension in provinces other than Bombay. It was pointed out that in the East if drastic powers were given to the police, cases of brutality were certain to occur. The difficulty was that in most cases allegations could neither be proved nor disproved for usually it was a case of one man's word against that of another. But the point of importance was that such allegations of excesses were believed by the public. In such odd circumstances, nothing could be done by bringing allegations to the knowledge of the authorities, denouncing the ordinances and demanding their revocation.[223] It was unlikely that the government would admit that the ordinances were uncalled for and ineffective.

Rathbone affirmed confidently that the ordinances had

been efficacious in bringing order in the country. She was also keen to add that they had been producing a good deal of resentment and hostile feelings. It was clear that there was hardly any chance of goodwill for the new constitution with a large majority of prominent people of the largest party in jail and amidst an atmosphere of acute tension.[224] The way out of the impasse was to incorporate in the new constitution a rational set of policies with regard to ordinances which might open a new departure.[225] Meanwhile, the Conciliation Group thought it prudent to advise caution. They urged that people should show restraint. Even in face of evidence of brutal punishments and inhuman methods they should bear in mind that 'the move for conciliation must come from both sides'.[226] Rathbone had found, she claimed, among the Congress people and supporters, a strange inability to explain satisfactorily the reasons for recommencing civil disobedience in the winter of 1931-32. The replies invariably resolved themselves into blunt suspicion of the government and refusal to believe British pledges.[227] The Group, however, maintained that it was a mistake and a great pity that the government thought it prudent to opt for a policy of large-scale arrests and political oppression. But it did not entertain all cases of alleged interception of letters, rigour of prison rules and bombing of villages due to lack of any firsthand knowledge or experience. They were, however, quite clear that there was a good deal of controversy in India as to whether the ordinances were the cause of civil disobedience or the inevitable result of its recommencement.[228] It was believed by the Group that one could not 'suddenly throw into the melting pot all the sovereignty we exercised for two centuries'.[229] But since repression was the obstacle to conciliation, the Group underscored the assertion that 'the bridge must be built on both sides so that there could be a meeting in the middle of it'. But they seemed to look over yet another proposition that the proposed bridge could not be built save only on the basis of absolute equality.

When the communal award was announced, the Group considered the situation seriously. The award was 'as bad as it could be', but 'we must not reject it' as it would be a mistake to allow 'want of a communal decision to stand in the way of constitutional progress'.[230] Any 'bad electoral system' could be changed if one secured a constitution which was acceptable in other respects. During Gandhi's fast in opposition to the award, Harrison urged N. M. Joshi to exhaust himself talking to Ambedkar and bringing him to settle the issue because Gandhi's life was precious. The Mahatma was adamant and there was no use talking to him: 'We work from both ends — with powers that be and public opinion.'[231]

One of the organizations that drew sympathetic consideration of the Conciliation Group was the Union of Britain and India under the chairmanship of Sir John Thompson, assisted by Sir Alfred Watson and Edward Villiers. The organization was endowed with a good deal of official support and patronage.[232] Its avowed policy was to further the government's programme of constitutional advance as outlined in the white paper while insisting on the maintenance of adequate safeguards. In support of UBI and in opposition to O'Dwyer and his pamphlet, the *Indian White Paper,* the internal discussion of the Conciliation Group maintained that the essential fact of India since 1914 had been that it became politically self-conscious, assisted by the promotion of western education, the Japanese victory over Russia, the Chinese revolution and the participation of Indian troops in combat operations during World War I. These experiences of the twentieth century helped to produce among the educated Indians a demand for equality and a greater share in the administration of their country, although dominion status and *purna swaraj* were premature formulations and out of the question at that stage of India's political maturity and development.[233]

Round the corner in London's Whitehall, Agatha Harrison was happy that the Group, during its long conversation with Sankey, was able 'to disturb him'. She reported that Sankey 'showed very plainly that he was very troubled' by affairs in India but he would like to wait until further discussion in Parliament.[234] It was pointed out to him that the Congress, the 'chief group in India', had no part in the findings and that 'Gandhi and his group' would have to be treated well to achieve any chance of success.[235] Agatha Harrison, optimistic as ever, thought that they had made a powerful dent in the heart of the establishment and Andrews was left to pick up the threads.[236] Among the intellectuals it was suggested that Laski was the person 'that we should tie very tightly' for he touched 'circles that some of the rest of us do not'.[237] Whenever Sapru wrote to Polak about the position of moderate opinion, Polak passed it on to Harrison who went over to the India office and Sydney Welton for an expert opinion. Within hours it was at the offices of all the London papers with a special plea to some of the editors for publicity.[238] Then there was Nagen Ganguli getting into places like the Empire Society and needing a pep talk because he had spoken indiscreetly against self-government for India.[239] When Cornelia Sorabji was 'given to tongue again' Agatha Harrison saw to it that she was to be covered by someone else who would put forth a counterpoint of view.[240] Irwin, not happy with the treatment at the hands of the India office, had to be nursed;[241] Malcolm MacDonald, a useful contact at the prime minister's breakfast table, might be kept in good humour;[242] Atma Kamlani, Menon's rival, should be maintained on friendly relations;[243] and Menon had to be restrained.[244] It was also decided that Polak ought to meet Menon on a friendly footing and, if necessary, pat him on the back.[245] If required, Polak should also be seen in the front row in the India League's meetings, even if he did not share the platform.[246] Further, the press was to be carefully treated and press lunches should be organized as occasional interludes where Walter Layton, Lord Allen, J.A. Spender, Kingsley Martin, H.M. Smith, Evelyn

Wrench and the editors of the *Christian World* and the *Star* should invariably be invited.[247]

Both the secretary of state and the prime minister were cheery, chatty and nice to the Group's delegation. Agatha Harrison began to appreciate that there was a real problem in that if the government gave way to one group they would have the others clamouring.[248] All this while, Birla and Polak were in active communication. Lothian and Irwin were pressurized to work for the release of Gandhi which would, it was insisted, enable the achievement of a satisfactory solution for the problem of the depressed classes.[249] Accordingly, at a meeting at Chatham House, Heath and Alexander strongly supported the demand for Gandhi's release. Irwin, unable to take a prominent part, agreed to be present at the meeting, adding 'great strategic importance' to the gathering.[250] P. Hartog put the case before the audience on behalf of the Group. 'By case,' Agatha Harrison explained in no uncertain terms, 'I mean to present the expressed feelings of moderate men in India' and 'about the estrangement of these men towards the present policy'.[251] This would be covered, if necessary, by quoting the debate in the legislative assembly, the Madras council, the Bombay council, the Welfare of India League and the National Liberal Federation. The position would be strengthened, Agatha Harrison added, if Hoare's statements in the parliamentary debate or to his constituency were cited. Andrews was chided for describing Gandhi in close circles as 'pathological', which could mean 'unbalanced', while Polak was despatched to Geneva to meet Privat and Rolland to tell them of the existence and purpose of the Group and ensure their willingness to cooperate.[252] Irwin and Sankey were brought closer to the Group as they were found more sympathetic and sensitive to the spiritual significance of Gandhi than anybody else.[253]

When, in the summer of 1933, the Indian leaders of moderate vintage arrived in London, the Group kept up its close contact with 'Sapru, Joshi and Co.'[254] When accosted with a hostile 'savage' state of mind in the Indian hotel, the Group activated itself in order to diffuse the critical situation.[255] To the Group, it was a problem of crisis management and the crisis was diagnosed mainly as one of subjective perception. Few seemed to understand, Agatha Harrison wrote to Alexander, the psychology of these men, who had been busy and important people, and had been listening, day after day, to the most humiliating things about their fitness to govern themselves.[256] There was an alarming ascendancy of the die-hards, Agatha reported, in the India office despite her effort to counter that evil and the Indians, she felt, were once again mismanaged.[257] The papers had been vituperative against India in general and the Indian delegation in particular; there had been an excessive concentration of interest on an alleged split amongst them and a considerable fuss about the economic conference.[258] The knowledge that the white paper might be whittled down and the fact that people who 'should be talking with them have no time to sit down quietly with them' had resulted in a curious temper of frustration and anger.[259] It was a pity, Agatha Harrison thought, that Lothian, Irwin, Hoare and others had been ignorant of the feelings of the delegates, that they did not have time to come together with 'Sapru and Co.' and talk to them 'as man to man'.[260] The atmosphere in the hotel, as a result, was full of 'depression, suspicion and poison'.[261] Someone had to watch the situation behind the scenes, sense the feelings and bring the people together, for that was the missing link.[262] In order to salvage the situation, Polak was made to dispatch letters to Lothian, Irwin and Reading urging them to take proper steps in view of the grave situation.[263] John Coatman from the London School of Economics, himself adept in the art of 'sensing', was pushed to meet Hoare. Arrangements were made to make Sapru, Jayakar and others feel at home and to explore their very sensitive inclinations.[264] As Gandhi busied himself with his Harijan work, the Conciliation Group grew eager in anticipation. It was concluded that the most practical thing was to get the *Harijan* paper as widely circulated as possible for people to see what was being done by the reformers themselves. It was believed that with the knowledge of this social evil and the efforts of Gandhi to eradicate it, people would be able to defend the Mahatma's actions and, if they were impeded, the Group would raise its voice.[265]

It was, however, becoming somewhat difficult to sustain interest in India unless an agreed basis of work was chalked out.[266] Polak had prepared, with the consent of the Group, a short draft on the leading points of the white paper that ought to be modified in order to satisfy moderate opinion.[267] This was largely 'the Sapru-Jayakar-Sastri and Co.' and it was quite likely, Agatha Harrison thought, that this could be a good basis for an agreement that could be put before Muslims with the views of the Congress enclosed in the preamble.[268] It appeared to some others that that was an opportunity to act and a few important delegates could be encouraged to issue a joint statement urging the government to take advantage of the truce. This was considered important because the white paper could pale into insignificance before long as the political situation in India could also alter overnight 'either by the death of Gandhi or by the fact that he survives, and at the end of his fast [in May 1933] realises that no move has taken place as a result of his gesture. He will, I imagine, call on C.D. again and go to prison ...'[269] Thus, as hours would go by, the situation would harden, wrote Agatha Harrison, and much discussion would go on in the official circles whether Gandhi had been playing a game in precipitating a crisis. Harrison was convinced that there was an opening and the Group ought to take advantage of it immediately, which could help to break through the stalemate.[270]

By mid-1934, the Group began to waver and felt uneasy at the prospect of being dubbed as 'Gandhi, Gandhi and

Gandhi'[271] although it was also keen to ensure that the 'untouchable' attitude towards Gandhi and the Congress should not be continued any longer and that some means must be discovered of bridging the gulf.[272] Polak was not happy with the new stance of the Group and had been gradually drifting away,[273] while unlike Andrews, Agatha Harrison and Alexander had concluded that they should broaden the base of the work and were desirous of opening the door wide for anyone who would like to come.[274] The secretary of state, ex-viceroys, governors of provinces, the Servants of India Society, and a host of others were to be roped in effectively. While Sapru and Co. would be the favoured group in India, Gandhi, still the revered one, would be subjected to the objective scrutiny of Harrison and Alexander. In 1934, both Harrison and Alexander had been intrigued by Nehru's letters to his daughter. Both had watched with surprise the strange ways in which the children of modern India were expected to learn history. The Friends were intrigued by Nehru's concept and theory of history and his social and cultural values. Nehru's history, they thought, was fairly different from their own concepts for it did not include any idea 'of the world beyond' — beyond the struggles, tensions and conflicts — and of 'all its wonders'.[275]

Irwin had a soft corner for the Conciliation Group and he appreciated the frank assessment of the Indian situation by the Group. He acknowledged the feeling existing in many quarters in India about the proposals of JSC and, those, the government had made to Parliament. But Irwin was convinced that for a multitude of reasons Alexander's suggestion that someone like Linlithgow or Peel should visit India and got in touch with those, who stood in opposition to the bill, was not really practical politics. It would be likely to place the secretary of state and the Viceroy in an almost hopeless position vis-a-vis the critics in Britain and would generally appear in India as going behind the Viceroy.[276]

In February 1934, Agatha Harrison decided to sail for India with the expressed approval of Gandhi, primarily to gain some first hand knowledge of the situation and to visit some of the places where Gandhi had been conducting his Harijan campaign in order to assess Gandhi's accomplishments.[277] She had informed Gandhi and Andrews that she wished to maintain complete freedom with regard to her plans in India and wanted to obtain views from other quarters and also to discuss the situation with officials.[278] Informing I. M. Stephens about the visit, A. H. Joyce of the India office, whom Harrison called on 16 February 1934, requested Stephens to make himself available for Harrison to meet while in Delhi and also arrange some other official meetings if necessary.[279] Introducing Harrison, Joyce mentioned that her efforts in England 'are inspired mainly by members of the Society of Friends towards spreading the Gospel preached by Gandhi'.[280] She had been well described, Joyce wrote tongue-in-cheek, as a sentimental, well-intentioned and harmless person, who 'distresses herself quite unnecessarily about the state of affairs in India'.[281] Soon Stephens, who had hitherto been sceptical about Harrison, her financial contacts with Birla and her professed 'Congressism', learnt the real importance of being Agatha Harrison, the Quaker friend and admirer of Gandhi. The note dictated by James David Sifton, governor of Bihar and Orissa, following a conversation with Harrison was promptly despatched by Stephens to Joyce who might, it was suggested, find in the note some strategic information.[282] Agatha found during her tour all over the quake-affected north Bihar in Gandhi's entourage, that the Mahatma's magnetism in drawing a crowd everywhere was astounding.[283] It seemed to the governor that her main purpose of seeing him was to suggest that as Gandhi had at the Patna meeting insisted on 'tendering respectful cooperation to Government', the governor should reciprocate and take the opportunity of renewing contact between him and the government.[284] The governor took a difficult stance. Gandhi had taken twice in Patna a position affirming his adherence to civil disobedience and while he persisted in this creed the governor was not prepared to open communication although he was satisfied that both, Gandhi and the district Congress leaders had, for the time being, abandoned politics and had been working actively on quake relief.[285] Agatha Harrison, however, was emphatic that the move was entirely her own and had not been suggested by anybody in the Congress camp etc.[286]

The governor was much impressed by Harrison who seemed to him not of the class of some of Gandhi's admirers who could see no good in the British administratiion and was ready to believe everything bad of it. Her theme was the possibility of reconciliation and getting back to idealistic conditions which, she thought, might have resulted from a generous observance by both parties of the Irwin-Gandhi pact.[287] I. M. Stephens was a prisoner of the constraints and prejudices of Indian administration which had very little to do with the liberal-democratic culture in which imperialism was nurtured in Britain and which made it very subtle and penetrating. Suspicion of any note of dissent or even any honest desire to probe and comprehend political realities was endemic in Indian officialdom.[288] It was hostile to all quests beyond official explanations. Stephens found Harrison somewhat defensive. Despite her parade of being entirely detached and impartial in her approach to the Indian problem, she appeared initially to be 'almost completely Congressy' and struck Stephens as a typical 'theoretical radical' who assumed that her compatriots who 'run an Empire' necessarily tended to disregard and repress subject peoples.[289] But, for a change, Stephens felt that there was a perceptible modulation in her disposition. He thought that it was possible to 'convince her that there really was another way of looking at things, and that those who do so are not necessarily brutal and unimaginative bureaucrats'.[290] She was not frightfully unhappy with all the bureaucrats she met and was particularly impressed by the perceptions and concerns of men like Maxwell in Bombay and Reid in Bengal.[291] Incidentally, both the officials were supremely stretched in suppressing civil disobedience in Bombay and terrorism in Bengal. In short, Stephens, with all his angularities, which his long stint in India in trying times bred in him, was satisfied that the lady, if tactfully and courteously handled, would carry back to England a better 'understanding of the official point of view' and a 'heightened personal respect for several of the big men out here' and, as a result, would, in all probability, not be very bothersome. She might as well be encouraged to serve as a sympathetic internal critic of the *Raj*.[292] Stephens was convinced that there was a good deal of cheerful prospect for such a rewarding outcome.

One of the 'unfortunate' impressions that Harrison had been carrying over to Britain was on the point of government propaganda. She felt that the general impression conveyed by the news that had been appearing in the British press during the preceding two years was most misleading. It had suppressed the Congress or Indian point of view almost entirely and suggested, instead, that the country was contented and at peace and had been awaiting with cautious optimism the inauguration of the reforms.[293] Evidently, it was clear to all perceptive observers that, in arranging for the presentation of that picture to the British public, Stephens was the chief performer and the operation was primarily based on a combination of press censorship and 'inspired' messages, together with a judicious management of the media by the India Office.[294]

In fact, the explanation of the non-appearance of Congress/Indian views in the British press generally was a factor which could not be glossed over *ad infinitum*. Stephens was given by MacGregor a simple formulation as an effective antidote. To all such enquiries, Stephens was advised to say with a straight face, that the silence had nothing to do with censorship or official 'inspiration', but was due wholly to the fact that the British press considered these views so puerile and futile that it refused to find room for them. No doubt, MacGregor maintained, this attitude was too rigidly maintained and except the *Manchester Guardian*, Congress did not get the hearing it deserved on occasions. But, for all this, the Congress had itself to blame because of the 'general silliness of its views and charges discounting and prejudicing the point which now and then matters and is deserving of attention'.[295] It was also argued that British editors had been fed up with half-truths and *ex parte* statements and became permanently alienated from the sources from which these had emanated. Agatha Harrison was mellowed on the question but was not fully satisfied.[296]

Another point of interest that intrigued Harrison was the attitude of the government towards the Congress arguing that the right policy was to make a 'magnanimous gesture' towards Gandhi such as suggested by the *Manchester Guardian*.[297] She realized that the Government of India did not think that it was an opportune moment for such a gesture. On the proscription of the India League report she was told by Harry Haig that it was a mischievous document, full of apocryphal stories, motivated and false interpretations, magnified versions of an over-charged law and order situation, disproportionate enlargement of the so-called 'ordinance mind' and 'prison conditions', etc.[298] It was not an objective study of the situation but a command performance on behalf of its financiers and promoters, the Congress Party, calculated to do a lot of harm in India and to her sensitive law-abiding citizens. In Bengal, Harrison was certain to find 'some other way out' because the existing repressive policy was only a palliative but not a cure and unless the root cause of terrorism had been examined and removed, the problem would remain.[299] Thus there was scope 'for the work by people of goodwill' in investigating the psychological and economic motives from which terrorism sprang.[300] Her general approach to the Indian situation including terrorism, Stephens reported with some satisfaction, seemed to him and other officials more 'realistic and less *a priori*' than other fact-finders.[301]

MacGregor had assured Stephens forcefully that despite the connection with Gandhi and his apostles and financial obligations to Birla, the India office did not 'regard Miss Agatha Harrison with any great concern'.[302] She was 'merely a female Polak, likely to be influenced by common sense in spite of ultra-Liberal sentiments' and far less dangerous than 'our fair Ellen (Wilkinson) on the other'.[303] Doubtless the India Office would make it convenient to see her very soon after her return and would report to relevant authorities its reactions.[304] Stephens reciprocated the sentiments. In his subsequent communication Stephens was more congenial about Harrison than ever before. He informed that the general impression in his earlier letter seemed not very incorrect as he met her with Muriel Lester, both of whom, he added, seemed to be 'obsessed by Gandhi'.[305] But they were friendly and intelligent people and in many ways level-headed. They were 'interesting creatures' and stimulating conversationalists. Stephens discovered several interests in common including similar tastes in music, concern for the evolution of stability in India and personal veneration for Lowes Dickinson.[306]

Cornelia Sorabji, the inflamed *Raj* enthusiast, raised doubts with regard to the reliability of the India Conciliation Group. She questioned the sincerity of the Group as to their effort in bringing about goodwill and cooperation between the British Government and the Indian leaders and princes.[307] The India Office, however, maintained that this small body of well-meaning people associated with the Society of Friends, had been trying, over time, to contribute to the evolution, however ineffectually, of a rational India policy. One thing was certain that the India Office always maintained that harmless groups of do-gooders could always be manipulated to work for ending a deadlock with the Congress, if ever such a measure became necessary.[308] Agatha Harrison, the moving spirit of the group, was assessed as 'a thoroughly well-meaning but woolly-minded sentimentalist.'[309] In their utter innocence of the nuances and compulsions of imperial responsibilities, Sorabji contended, these simplistic and spirited admirers of Gandhi might, at times, find themselves engulfed in the Congress miasma.[310] Considering realistically the feasibility of such an occurrence, A.H. Joyce concluded if these people willy-nilly inspired and encouraged the kind of propaganda put out by the India League, they should not expect others to sit back and allow the misrepresentations of actual situations to go unanswered.[311] Thus, while some established and concerned academics and publicists were encouraged to contest publicly the positions of the India League and the 'implied reverberations' of those ideas in the presentations of the Conciliation Group, the India Office thought it judicious to come to a definite understanding with the Group as to the specific use of the official papers which, from time to time, might be passed on to them as a friendly group interested in India and India policy.[312] In fact, on behalf of the India Office, A.H. Joyce carried on a discussion at length with Harrison and Carl Heath on the question of providing selected members of the group authentic and reliable information on India. In return, both Harrison and Heath felt obliged to offer positive assurance to consider them as classified documents not to be divulged to anybody. It enjoined the group to regard all material from the India office as confidential and not to use it for propaganda or publicity purposes.[313] Harrison recognized that much of this material might provide an effective ammunition for people like Krishna Menon or any one else who was 'likely to use it in a way that would embarrass us.'[314]

The attempts at reconciliation continued unabated. Both the Governments of India and Britain could afford to depend on the Conciliation Group as an effective channel of communication with nationalist India, especially when a particular move was contemplated. Throughout, Menon found that this group of soppy sentimentalists was being used by the India office surreptitiously for 'sensing' the nationalist camp and to promote an optimistic outlook in public. It represented areas in British politics where the enlightened conservative opinion, restrained and reserved labour views, tepid liberal opinion, and vague humanitarian and ethical attitudes of organized Church and of the right wing sections of the Christian socialists could comfortably coexist. This was the plane where imperialism in distress could always retreat for support from every segment of British public opinion. Some would welcome it as a necessary and tactical withdrawal, some, as the *sine qua non* of Indian cooperation, some others with the fanciful thought of the emergence of a happy commonwealth, and others as a deterrent, albeit temporary, on unbridled aggression of imperialism.[315] By 1935, the Friends had established extensive contacts which cut across party lines; they could move around with ease between diverse organized opinions, sense the pulse of men and groups and could always depend on their own immense experience and their 'feelings in the bones'. In terms of Indian sympathy they were at home with Gandhi and his gentle ways and enthusiastic about the moderates and liberals like Sapru, Sastri, Kunzru, Birla, and subsequently, Vijayalakshmi Pandit, Rajagopalachari and Amrit Kaur. They were sceptical of Nehru's radical opinions, his concept of history, his reluctance to meet men in authority, his firm faith in Menon with his outspoken views on international situations.[316]

Polak's perception of India during and following the RTC was largely based on his continual correspondence with Sapru and Jayakar. Together with Graham Pole, he occupied an influential position. They were members of the Labour Party's specialized committee on imperial issues and on India they were the party's established authorities. Polak was a revered member of the India Conciliation Group. Both had a cordial personal relationship with Gandhi. They were also inclined to listen carefully to the opinions and ideas of the moderates and the liberals in Indian politics, Sapru being their favoured political *amie.* They were in constant touch with that eminent Indian jurist. In England, Pole was keen to have him in his country bungalow during weekends to enjoy the peaceful and picturesque surroundings amidst an informal middle class environment.[317]

Forwarding one of Polak's letters to Andrews to the India office through F.H. Brown of the *Times,*[318] Agatha Harrison recommended in early 1933, Polak's estimate of the situation in India. She thought that the letter contained significant material which should be considered seriously as it was widely believed that Polak, a sedate political observer, was not used to offer 'hasty generalizations'.[319] It appeared to Polak that towards the end of February 1933, Hoare and his administration were apprehensive that if Gandhi and his colleagues were released they might start civil disobedience once again. Polak thought that there was a real likelihood of such a recurrence. Willingdon and his colleagues, on the other hand, really wanted 'to bring the Congress to subjection and compel a recantation'.[320] The result was, Polak wrote, 'not the thinning of the partition walls, but a thickening of them'.[321] It would be a complete deadlock. Polak was convinced that Gandhi deserved to be treated as a gentleman who might be talked to with the help of a trusted intermediary having the confidence of both sides. Otherwise, he might be kept in jail *ad infinitum* and the government might as well be content to face cheerfully its awesome consequences.[322] Polak was absolutely certain that the Government of India, together with all the provincial governors and bureaucracy, were bent upon 'driving out of public life all the progressive elements and not the Congress alone'.[323] In this they would depend on the active cooperation of the communalists, zamindars, placemen and other conservatives and reactionaries. If they could not succeed in doing this they would do their best to see that the constitution was so weighted that these elements might stand the best chance of being returned to the legislatures.[324]

It was also evident to Polak that the Indian bureacuracy was intent on wrecking the proposed federation.[325] The British cabinet, Polak maintained, had made the mistake of supposing that they could rely upon the loyalty of the public services to carry out the federal proposal. The political officers in the native states were being promoted for their success in inducing the princes to hold aloof or maintain an attitude of lukewarmness.[326] They were determined to see that, as far as possible, nothing but a sort of provincial autonomy resulted after all and that central responsibility under a federal system would never come into being except with such restrictions — political, economic, financial, administrative — as would 'strangle it at birth or make it a mockery and just a byword'. If they succeeded, all MacDonald's hopes and aspirations would be blown up, Polak held, and along with it, whatever success he might appear to achieve in Parliament. This was a close approximation to the official position in India, however emphatic and voluble the denial might be.[327] Polak was equally convinced that there was 'an active conspiracy in high quarters' to keep out of the JSC the 'progressive' Indians who had already contributed quite so much.[328] Yet it was certain that there was a clear indication in Sapru's pronouncements that he was willing to cooperate at the JSC stage.[329]

As early as August 1932, Sapru had made it quite plain that the British press did not appreciate the fact that the moderates and liberals in India had been working against the high tide of Indian politics.[330] The press was incapable of taking an independent line of its own, differing from the government on any Indian question and was more actuated by compulsions of party politics than anything else. Sapru was troubled that Simla was 'very angry with Jayakar and myself' primarily because they believed that even if the bill was judicious and progressive, good intentions would be frustrated by clumsy methods, controversies, doubts and a suspicious frame of mind.[331] Sapru was seriously apprehensive that the conference was being throttled by the Conservatives as a whole. Sympathetic to the cause of Sapru, Pole was somewhat discomposed that the British Government and the Labour Party had been ungrateful and very discouraging to the moderates and their aspirations. Pole reported that Sapru and the liberals were getting increasingly chary about Sankey and his growing opposition to the federation idea, the unimaginative composition of the Indian delegation out to wreck the whole idea and the nature of the safeguards which would swallow up the principle of responsibility.[332] Unfortunately, unlike 1930-31, both Sapru and Jayakar could no longer count upon Irwin's support.[333] By the time they set out on their voyage to England for the third round, they were convinced that both Whitehall and the Government of India were 'dead opposed' to any idea of advance in the centre and, in any case, finance would be frankly reserved.[334]

Sapru and Jayakar thought it was their duty to tell 'our English friends to their face what we think of the present situation and what gloomy view we take of the future'. There was 'a sense of struggle oppressing the mind of every one of us'.[335] To Pole, Sapru gave a 'warning as a personal friend' that the country was in no mood to put up with half-hearted measures, that the self-flattering assessment of the success of the dual policy was apocryphal and mischievous and the depth and dimension of bitterness had been growing every month.[336] He was not a believer in the philosophy and efficacy of civil disobedience. But he could not reconcile himself to the ostrich-like wisdom of the government which meant 'piling up trouble for them and for us'.[337] 'When you put 60,000 men in jail, he added, 'you cannot have disturbances in public street — but 60,000 men leave behind millions of sympathizers who are thus drawn into the vortex of politics.'[338] In January 1933, Sapru again reiterated that if political prisoners were released there would be a great change in the internal situation and would enable Sapru and Jayakar to interact fruitfully with the Congress leaders on constitutional issues.[339]

It was clear to both the leading liberals that the government did not want the Congress people and would, by all means, encourage the Indian conservatives and reactionaries to seize the new constitution.[340] Some Congressmen had been appreciative of the task undertaken by them in London and Sapru was convinced that they might be able to influence the course of events if a policy of conciliation even at that juncture was initiated by the government. The condition would further deteriorate if the government proceeded in a leisurely fashion.[341] Jayakar goaded Moonje to appreciate the extreme necessity of making the comments of the Hindu Mahasabha on the white paper as helpful as possible to those who would be in charge of the Indian case during the deliberations of the JSC. 'By all means criticize the scheme of the white paper,' Jayakar wrote passionately, 'make distinct proposals as to in what directions it could be made better to suit our national demand, but while doing this please convey no idea of any boycott or non-cooperation or anything savouring of such notions. You can be as strong as you like in your criticism, but convey the impression that you are doing your best to see that the scheme is radically altered, improved and modified to suit Indian aspirations'.[342]

Jayakar made it clear that it would be a blunder if Indian comments took a form 'which our enemies in England' would find very convenient in their agitation against the white paper.

'You know it is more true in politics', Jayakar cautioned Moonje, 'than in any other departments of human activity that extremes meet and that is what we have to guard against.'[343] The white paper and continued detention of political prisoners, however, made the task of the liberals not too easy in India. Pole felt alarmed at the way the government continued to hug 'our blindness to that issue'.[344] Government's decision to prevent the Congress session at Calcutta in December 1933, Sapru maintained, and Congress's insistence to hold it nevertheless was 'to a very large extent' a question of 'pride and prestige on the side of the Congress as it is on the side of the government'.[345] In one of his letters Sapru commented that 'there is no longer the same zest or the spirit of hopefulness in my case as there was until some time ago. Government here and in England have not, by any means, been a source of strength to some of us who have wholeheartedly worked for peace'.[346] Pole noted with concern that the government and significant political forces did not listen to Sapru and his seasoned advice. In any consideration of that transitional period in India's history, Pole added, 'regret must be deep that the British — here and in India — did not listen to Sapru'.[347]

Sapru had always been, Pole thought, on the side of moderation and always ready to make the best of a given situation. But the government with its own conceit, preferred its old confusions, i.e. imprisoning Congress leaders for civil disobedience, harping on safeguards, and so on.[348] It could have been drawn out of the impasse by Sapru. But it decided to cherish its 'problems' and made repression seem necessary. Pole agreed with Sapru that government's declaration of no peace with the Congress until it definitely gave up the cry of *purna swaraj* was calculated to put 'the Congress and other extremists' on their mettle.[349] Both Congress and the government shared 'a weakness for face-saving formulae and prestige'.[350] Pole and Sapru concluded in unison that if British statesmen could talk to the

Congress leaders in a conciliatory spirit, 'the whole situation might easily change'. But there was no chance of a change so long one left the situation to be handled by some unresponsive administrators who, however good, 'have no knowledge of human psychology'.[351]

There was an element of fatuity in Pole's exhortations. By the end of December 1933, Pole seemed keen to convince Sapru that Churchill had, in a way, distinctly helped the situation because his attitude of purblind extremism might push Winterton, Peel and company into the position held by Baldwinites.[352] It was, however, then evident that, in all probability, the white paper scheme would go through but it would not be much 'improved' upon. If the bill was ultimately introduced it would have an easy passage. It would be opposed by Labour for not having gone far enough and by the Churchill group for going too far. It would be carried through by the docile Tory members who could not vote against the bill and by the carefully cultivated acquiescence of all.[353]

By February 1934 Polak decided to be more forceful than he had hitherto been. In a pithy letter he gave out to M. MacGregor of the India Office the other side of the story of India. He reported that he had learnt from all quarters that there was no interest left in the white paper in India. On the Congress side, not even the right-wing attributed any good motive to Britain.[354] He believed that whatever was done, these Congressmen would interpret it as having been done under the compulsion of circumstances and not from goodwill. Besides, it would be looked upon as being far less than India was entitled to.[355] The Gandhi core group would be indifferent to politics and constitutional advance and would, for the time being, continue to strive after social reform and, if necessary, would reserve energy for renewed *satyagraha*.[356] The left-wing was hopeless. It would look for economic revolution and a section of it would aim at separation by violence.[357] Polak wrote that

Gandhi had lost leadership of the Congress although, quite paradoxically, he retained unimpaired command over the masses.[358]

But the most ominous phenomenon was, Polak emphasized, that 'we have definitely lost the moral support of the Liberals'.[359] They represented 'the intellectual leadership and constructive political experience of the country'.[360] Unfortunately, Polak remarked, they were then just in querulous opposition, and their left-wing was almost indistinguishable from the Congress right-wing.[361] Whether that attitude was final and irrevocable, Polak wrote, depended entirely upon how far government and parliament were responsive to Sapru, Jayakar and Co. He felt that it was a fatal blunder to have ignored the Liberal Party as such. Sapru resigned from it in 1930 and Jayakar was never a formal member of it. There was, Polak confided, deep resentment within the party against both and they were regarded as 'having misled or been misled'.[362] To have omitted any representative of the Liberal Party in 1933 from the Indian delegation to the joint select committee was 'sheer political folly and ineptitude'.[363] Either Sastri, Sivaswami Iyer, Chimanlal Setalvad or C. Y. Chintamini would have sufficed. The government had been forewarned, Polak wrote, but it took its own line obstinately, only to suffer accordingly.[364]

The situation in the so-called liberal camp then, as Polak was able to comprehend it, was fairly complex vis-a-vis the reform proposals. Instead of a homogeneous liberal-responsivist group committed to critical support, the liberals, as a body, had turned out unanimously hostile to the white paper and had been demanding 'very substantial modifications of its proposals before they could be made acceptable to the most conservative section of political India'.[365] The liberals were divided among themselves as to whether it should be rejected out of hand or it should be taken for what it was worth. It was largely believed in India that it should soon be scrapped and replaced by 'something nearer to the heart's desire'.[366] Sapru had retired from active public life and had given a strong lead in his memorandum. Jayakar was of the opinion that if the constitution was found to be workable it should be worked.[367] Examining the Indian situation, Polak concluded that the constitution might result in entrenching the conservative, immobile and unconstructive elements, in securing the 'haves' against the 'have-nots', in dividing the country communally and sectionally even more deeply than before. These were not ungrounded fears and might result in immobilizing the liberals.[368] The common acceptable feeling in India, Pole wrote in sheer political inanition, was that 'we are not, in politics, a generous people unless and until our fears are aroused',[369] that the British were compelled to act only in panic, and to accept the white paper would be merely an invitation to Parliament not to proceed beyond it.

Polak was aghast to note the inevitable social ascendancy of die-hard conservatism in Britain. 'A country struggling', wrote Polak, 'for its freedom will feel that it cannot afford to attribute magnanimity to the country that it accuses of holding it down.'[370] Every activity, every speech of Churchill-Lloyd-Page Croft was magnified out of proportion in India.[371] But, what was worse, the most moderate friends read Hoare's evidence with the utmost dismay.[372] They regarded him as having put up a facade of responsible government to hide carefully reaction, reservations, safeguards, special powers and every other sort of obstacle to true reform so that they would prevent any vital development in India or any real exercise of responsibility on the part of the people.[373] Hoare was regarded as having capitulated entirely to the pressure of his own party. He feared that the position of the official party differed from the Churchill group only in being more hypocritical in its pretence and less forthright and outspoken in its concept and distrust.[374] Polak was convinced that the bulk of the liberal-responsivist group was about to settle down to the prospect of an India doomed to frustration and struggle for a couple of decades, at the end of which the country would be physically and morally emaciated and would not have advanced a hands breadth towards emancipation from her own intrinsic evils. It was a gloomy outlook and Polak underlined the urgency of considering the requirements of the signatories of the two memoranda and meeting them to the maximum extent and with the minimum of hesitation.[375]

By the end of August 1935, it seemed to many that when the bill became an act and came into operation, the reactionary interest would be so 'safely entrenched' that it would be impossible to change over to anything like a democratic constitution without overthrowing the whole federation. There was a talk of an election in the autumn and there were possibilities of the advent of a Labour government. Pole hoped that Lansbury would continue to be the leader of the party. 'One thing is certain: he would not send Attlee to the India Office'. There was considerable pressure about dominion status so that there was quite a possibility of its being introduced into the act. Pole thought that the possibility would be transformed into a probability if only there were some united demand from India instead of the Congress independence talk. The question of secession had been troubling many people. But so far as India was concerned it was purely academic. 'If the Princes', Pole comforted, 'who are bound by their treaties with the Crown come into the federation then no question can ever rise'. It was believed that Lansbury had been working on Attlee whose attitude towards Indian matters was being constantly modulated.[376] But significantly, both Pole and Polak before long, found themselves willy-nilly sliding with Lothian and Baldwin.

The suspension of the publication of the *India Review* soon after the delegation's return from India in November 1932 caused some concern among sympathetic readers who followed Indian events closely. Rev. F. Arthur Wenyon was one of those who learnt from the observations in the *India Review* that the outlook was dark. The situation appeared darker as the government looked like conceding nothing. Wenyon was anguished to learn that the government and most of the English people were convinced that the firm hand, even if brutality and injustice were included in it, was the policy that India needed and believed that India had been 'suppressed satisfactorily'.[377] Wenyon was a sensitive humanist and believed in the efficacy of persuasion. He was convinced that a great deal of propaganda was necessary before an appreciable number of English people would believe the truth about India.[378] He thought that missionaries were ill-informed as a rule. Most of them never had even a single, private, frank, personal heart to heart talk on the political situation with an educated non-Christian Indian, who was for self-determination. Because of this unfortunate lack of interaction they had been doing the cause of Indian freedom a lamentable amount of harm by their speeches, conversations and writings. It was equally unfortunate that many people naturally thought that they must know and their words could be absolutely trusted. Wenyon believed that pressure might be brought to bear on them to see to it that they were better informed concerning the 'other side' or refrain from writing or speaking, in public or in private, irresponsibly against the Mahatma and the Congress.[379]

Wenyon was convinced that most India hands in Britain swallowed official statements and never tried, independently, to find out the truth for themselves. The majority of missionaries seemed to be unduly ignorant of the Indian situation, and being speakers and often writers, they did the cause of India's claim to real self-determination more malfeasance than almost all the rest put together. Many letters and articles by missionaries enraged Revd. Wenyon periodically. Their silence, he thought, had been harmful and betrayed lack of character and moral weakness. The religious papers and journals were generally weak and misleading on the subject of India. Wenyon thought the reason for the suppliant attitude was directly due to the fact that the missionary societies had been receiving thousands of pounds to support aid India work and that fund was taxed out of the desperately poor millions of India.[380]

In sharp contrast to Wenyon's perception, the liberal paternalism of Edward Thompson, the celebrated historian of India and a sensitive creative writer with his long intimate association with Bengal and a close *associé* of poet Tagore, drifted away towards the ruling impulses of the white governing race amidst a prostrated brown people. Menon witnessed the tragic metamorphosis of Thompson closely.[381] By 1930 Thompson was unsure of himself, placed as he was on an unsteady equilibrium of conflicting emotions. But he helped mould educated British opinion and supplement the die-hard orthodoxy of the day.

Edward Thompson, having acclaimed the fulfilment of the British goal in India, gazed remorsefully at the decline of the *Raj*. He had sought to recapitulate the thoughts of his countrymen at Fort William and so many points of isolation in an unknown and hostile land. He had witnessed the pageantry and splendour of an arrogant empire. It was as certain as Rome had been. He had foreseen the last days of British rule as he helplessly watched a rising tide of opposition around the issue of the partition of Bengal. In 1931 he was preparing himself to bid farewell to India. By then, the 'childish' nationalism of 1905, Thompson sighed, had grown into a powerful political contender. 'Education was on sufferance, an imperious and reckless Nationalism ruled the stage', Thompson lamented, 'jerking his students back and forth like puppets.' British presence had become a waste of time in the 'flat monotony of the Indian existence'.[382] Indian nationalism, Thompson thought, had been turned into an uncompromising dogma based on some obstinate abstractions deduced from Western experience and political thought. The new India was beyond Thompson's comprehension though he could detect some of its conspicuous features. It was not, for example, overtly Hindu. It viewed non-violence as a private 'fad' of Gandhi and treated him with scant respect. The unchanging India had become a 'Vesuvius' and even more mysterious.[383] He was convinced that so long as a 'non-violent humbug' confronted the 'look-what-we-have-done-for-India humbug', there could be no room for agreement.[384] As had been the case with many others, Thompson could not quite figure out the impulses of the new India. 'Past is king', and it was sitting pretty, waiting for 'us to go', and wondering 'how much longer we shall take or how many hints we need'.[385] Gandhi, a disturbed Thompson cogitated, was no longer guided by reason. Under pressure, the Mahatma, Thompson lamented, had been living almost invariably impelled by an unstable soul force. To Thompson, it meant spontaneous instincts, irrational passions and the promptings of an uncanny past.[386]

In a sense, Thompson reflected what is somewhat indulgently styled as the liberal dilemma. In the early 1930s, Thompson had been closely watching the Indian political realities on behalf of the Rhodes Trustees with a view to locating possible areas of cooperation between Indian and British writers while operating as a special correspondent for the *Manchester Guardian*. The outcome of his experience was *A Letter from India*.[387] This was a characteristic liberal tract centred around the problems emanating from the Irwin-Gandhi pact. Viewed superficially, Thompson seemed remarkably objective. To him the arrest of Gandhi in January 1932 was both premature and a blunder, while the Gandhi-Irwin pact was vitiated by undesirable circumstances. A sense of self-righteousness saturated all his observations. Negotiations between the ruler and the ruled, he argued, were inevitable and had been delayed far too long. The economic and social outlook in India was worse than disquieting and might even render a 'revolution' and its 'attendant sufferings' almost inevitable.[388] A disturbed Thompson hastened to add that the need of the hour was for a more decided and a more reckless government. The backdrop of the prescription was his firm conviction that no democracy or colourful imitation of democracy could ever handle the affairs of India.[389] Authority, when exercised repressively, he expatiated, might postpone a crisis while aggravating the final explosion. Authority, when exercised constructively, had a chance of winning through. If one did not pretend to negotiate one might as well be prepared for a system of police and military rule sitting over an alleged self-government which was, in its turn, destined to be a sure failure.[390]

By then Thompson did not think it necessary even to adopt a liberal posture. The Indian government, Thompson wrote gleefully, was not 'very wicked' as many supposed, 'but there is a good deal of evidence that they are sometimes half-witted' and often subjected to 'an unfair press'.[391] Commenting on the political upheaval of the North-West Frontier Province, Thompson defended stern official measures. It was a 'storm centre' and 'an exceptional area of violence' demanding harsh treatment but requiring honest explanations as well. Shooting in the Hijli detention camp, he thundered, was justified, and reprisals in Chittagong were understandable. He recommended the reports of the Congress on both the incidents as honest and accurate even though they had been drawn up unwillingly. In both the episodes, Thompson argued, government had a case. He was for a frank assessment of the situation because suppression of facts merely led to exaggeration. Rumours might, he warned, push even 'moderate men' into opposition. He believed that it was fair to assert that the 'poor English community' of Calcutta had been 'so threatened and so murderously used' that it had been goaded into a policy of force; that the Congress was in constant communication with the terrorists; that the Bengal Congress was no exception to the general rule and that it had been playing a deceptive role; that Gandhi's diabolical spiritual references were designed to offer 'one meaning to a dull listener and another to an intelligent one' and that Hollywood's contribution to the low estimation in which Europe was held in India was immense.[392] About India's independent future, Thompson had been harping on the familiar stereotype. The temporary unification of India under British rule had been consolidated. But it was breaking up, by political agitation and activity since World War I, he prognosticated, as the Roman empire had been broken up into the nations of Europe. Bengal, Bombay, Madras and the Punjab, Thompson was convinced, were different countries, 'yearly growing into a wider disparateness'. In the face of the precarious political situation and episodic violence and brutality, Thompson commended the remarkable perseverance and tenacity of purpose of the government and expressed, in no uncertain terms, three cheers for the British mission in India. He was conscious of the fact that the educated Indians resented the argument that Britain had a trust in India.[393] He condescended to acknowledge that it was impolitic to use the term and Englishmen should be careful not to prattle it. But he was not oblivious of the fact that an abrupt departure of the British from India would cause very great suffering, 'though we should be the gainers in everything but self-respect'.[394] If India 'secures a peaceful passage to freedom', Thompson stressed the unprecedented British experiment, 'garlands will be due to us, no less than to India'.[395]

Charlie Andrews, Thompson added, agreed with him that a deep deterioration of the *satyagraha* movement in India had set in. It was no longer as pure as it had been in South Africa. Non-violence, Thompson claimed, had been reduced to 'undiluted nonsense'.[396] He scoffed at the 'infinite duplicity' of Gandhi. Both he and Andrews, Thompson claimed, were convinced that the Mahatma had been, at one stage, capable of 'the highest form of truth'. But over the years, he reluctantly concluded, Gandhi had become elusive, evasive and even untruthful. This transformation was so acute and so complete, Thompson complained, that the official view of a Gandhi juggling and quibbling, having no intention to cooperate, acquired credibility and extensive acceptance.[397] Thompson's liberal consciousness had long been submerged in the irresistible flood of an autocratic backlash of a self-righteous imperialism.

In August 1932, Edward Thompson extended to Tej Bahadur Sapru the sincere sympathy of Lord Lothian and the National government for the Indian moderates whose efforts helped mature 'a sense of comradeship in a common cause' in England.[398] Edward Thompson urged Sapru, Jayakar and Sastri to continue their endeavour notwithstanding the stiff opposition at home and in Britain. Thompson shared their distrust of the 'Conservatives'. But he stressed that it was mistake 'to let our memory of "Conservatism" be ruled by memory of the Carson/Birkenhead/Churchill sequence, with the infinite harm it wrought.'[399] The creative political leadership in Britain, Thompson cogitated, was 'in a hole today' with 'Liberalism snowed under' led by Lloyd George and 'Labour out after a record of really shocking folly and levity'.[400] Edward Thompson was then in intimate touch with the residuum of constructive British politics and men whom he respected. He was convinced that the 'young Conservatives', such as Duff Cooper, George Ormsby-Gore, Robert Boothby, Harold Macmillan, Walter Elliot, were 'the best folk we have in politics'.[401] They were the successors of Baldwin's generation and the conservative opponents of die-hardism. They have, Thompson assured a diffident Sapru, profound respect and admiration for the Indian moderates.[402] Thompson felt that Sapru and Jayakar had met 'the wrong people' when they were in London. He entreated that the moderate spokesperson of India should respond to the positive gestures of the young Conservatives. Together, they should, in mutual respect, work to build up India and England 'when the whole world seems to be going to quag'. In a desperate attempt to work out a stable moderate triumvirate (Sapru, Jayakar and Sastri), he questioned the wisdom of Jayakar's futile attempt to tag along with Moonje, 'the high priest of shameless communalism.'[403] The three Indian moderates, along with the younger Conservatives, Thompson emphasized, would have to do the effective fighting in England. They had before them 'as fierce a battle as any in the Mahabharath.'[404] Unless the Moderates cooperated, Thompson added, one could not escape India either disrupting 'with a Muslim State on its Northwest fringes', or else splitting up into 'civil war and revolutions'.[405] The Muslim case, he argued, had been absurdly overstated. Moonje, he argued, had been the greatest possible assistance to the Muslims as were also Gandhi and Malaviya.[406] Sapru was reminded, time and again, that there was an advantage in working with the Conservatives. 'If you can keep them reasonable they can deliver the goods. The Labour people cannot'.[407] Thompson thought that the Labour Party had always suffered from ignorance of everything outside England and its insularity was supplemented by a slavish subservience to the official world with the exception of Wedgewood Benn who was 'a bigwig of little significance' and might be dismissed as 'an interesting amateur of Indian politics'.[408] Ramsay MacDonald was of no use whatever 'except to make burring Scots speeches that say nothing but make a fine noise'.[409] On the other hand, the Conservatives were keen to work and play with the Indian Moderates as they 'have their own Winston Churchill to fight'.[410] By then, Thompson had become the enthusiastic spokesman of the young Conservative wing: 'I want to see you, Jayakar and Sastri confront Winston Churchill across a table, which is what you would do if you stayed for the Committee stage. He is shockingly ignorant on India that you could eat him alive'.[411] Thompson was convinced that all the three of them could exercise a compelling influence over the whole course of passing the Bill. He was also certain that the Conservatives and the Indian Moderates were 'the soldiers in a common cause'.[412] They should bring over Gandhi and Nehru 'to a real reconciliation'. But if 'G and N are bent on stupidity', Sapru should publish a frank statement to the effect that 'they had proved to be really impossible' and deserved to be dropped unceremoniously.[413] Thompson was persuasive and insistent on this line of thought. In case, the Parliament, in its wisdom, decided to abandon the vital principles of British liberalism, Sapru was advised 'to protest as plainly as you can, and if necessary, wash your hands of the whole business'. But until that happened, 'give your friends a chance'.[414] Thompson was eloquent in his appeal and the projected prospect of a joint Conservative-Moderate political initiative. 'Please believe', Thompson entreated, 'that you have, all three, our warm affection here, as well as respect, and that as regards you and some of us the common "Empire Citizenship" has been at last achieved; we do not think of you as Indian, just as we hope you do not think of us as "Englishmen". You have served India well, by teaching the world to respect her'.[415]

By 1933, Thompson's assessment of Indian developments had become mono-dimensional. In a sense, Indian nationalism exhibited, Thompson argued, the shifty mentality of an impulsive, spoilt child. Thompson condescended to assign some responsibility to the stern aloofness, chill efficiency and morbid arrogance of the officialdom for the estrangement of the Congress.[416] But such an alienation, it was resolutely upheld, was inevitable as the Congress refused to accept the reality of life: the Indians were not yet proficient in self-government.[417] Increasingly, this prophet of human understanding had become an arrogant spokesman of ultra-Tory imperialism.

In that hour of intense self-introspection Menon sought to underscore that imperial sensitivity was fairly seductive and infectious and eroded all desultory tenderness of Thompson for

India. He was left to churn certain simulated sentiments for the consumption of a host of simpletons and a fairly large number of diabolical publicists cutting across party affiliations. For many, Menon felt, it was difficult to comprehend that the author of *Atonement: A Play of Modern India* (London, 1924) and *The Other Side of the Medal* (London, 1925) was also the author of *Farewell to India* (London, 1931), *The Reconstruction of India* (London, 1930) and *A Letter from India* (London, 1932) and the communications to the *Spectator* and the *Times.* It was a different personality and a different mind. The former Thompson, Menon wrote in anguish, had been seen by the sick bed of Indians of a remote district town in Bengal, the latter was now being seen at official dinners and parties in East End hotels. 'The fact is that Mr Edward Thompson (perhaps unwittingly) is now playing', Menon wrote, 'the role of a disguised imperialist.'[418]

Menon dissected Thompson's views as expressed in scores of articles in the *Spectator* carefully: Thompson summarily dismissed Sunderlands' *India in Bondage* as an unreliable book without stopping for a moment to point out the author's inaccuracies; he fell foul of Menon because of his suggestion that the Hindu-Muslim ill-feeling was due to sinister official influence; he also made a significant contribution to the imperialist cant by his thesis that England did not exploit India simply because India was not rich in natural resources.[419] Gandhi's views on cow and caste might not be quite modern, Menon wrote in reply, but he did not confuse between greed and trusteeship. Nor did he make the mistake of forcing opium and liquor down the throat of a helpless nation for the sake of individual liberty. In reference to Thompson's facile platitudes, Menon raised the realities of the cruel and inhuman police *raj* perpetrated by the official ordinance mind in India in sheer indifference to the considerations of gender and age.[420] 'As a matter of fact,' Menon wrote, 'we are passing through a period of Black and Tans in India'. Hoping optimistically that brute force was not the last thing in human affairs, Menon added that when the whole truth about Peshawar, Dacca and Sholapur would be known, the world would have seen 'more instances of Dyerism'.[421]

Menon thought that Thompson often overplayed his hands. Menon challenged him to prove his accusation that Gandhi wanted to ban foreign cloth out of spite against Lancashire. Menon maintained that what Gandhi said, on the contrary, was that India could and ought to produce her own cloth and if she did so, she would also improve the lot of the masses. In this context, Menon felt provoked and became caustic: 'Mr Thompson's soft heart bleeds at the injustice Gandhi does to Indian women by asking them to spin. Such cant may very well prejudice those who know nothing of the conditions of life in India, where the majority of women hardly enjoy any social or intellectual amenities.'[422] To the 70 million of the poor and hungry population, Menon asserted, the spinning wheel, as ancillary to their ordinary profession, would supplement their scanty income and probably enable them to earn a modest livelihood.[423] In fact, Menon pointed out, Thompson and his friends could never comprehend that the strength of the Congress organization could not be measured by the pronouncements of some odd set of individuals consisting of 'a bunch of illustrious obscures and sheer nitwits' but by the forces of the larger masses. In that test, the Congress organization was far greater than it had ever been.[424] It was amazing, Menon thought, that the problems of poverty and unemployment and the issues around authoritarianism and ordinances and even the demand for democracy in India did not excite Thompson's imagination. Even the profession of socialism by the Congress Left was dismissed by him as a bad tactic, pregnant with a terrible and damaging reaction.[425] Menon was, however, quite convinced that both in triumphs and defeats, Indian politics was increasingly being shaped by mass urges and that it was not possible for the British empire ever to shed its imperialism without liquidating its old structure and building afresh on a new basis.[426]

The perspective of Thompson might also be garnered from the Lindsay report of a learned commission on Christian higher education in India (1931) that emphasized the futility of scientific education and secular thought and the insolent defiance of all rational ideas by superstitious Hinduism.[427] The ascendancy of a superficial secularism, typified in Motilal Nehru's plan for an Indian constitution and in the personality of Jawaharlal Nehru, the Lindsay commission declared, breathed new life into the spirit of easy accommodation of a pantheistic attitude blurring distinctions between truth and untruth and between right and wrong. This had sapped the moral strength of India through the ages, wrote the Lindsay commission, and it continued to exercise its enervating influence.[428] It quenched the spirit of free enquiry and 'lulled people into a slothful contentment with things as they were'. With regard to the various efforts by eminent Indians to recondition Hinduism, two superficial motives were discerned. The first was the desire to give Hinduism a place in the modern world of activity and competition and the other was to render it respectable before a Western audience.[429] An apathetical demeanour in the face of a much-trumpeted unreal world, the commission noted, reflected the indifference to the problems of life which were projected as illusion and the desire to fly from reality rather than to come to terms with it. That attitude formed the background of Indian initiatives. The general flow of life and its orderings, the commission noted, were still believed to be determined by forces with which one could have no relationship save that of submission.[430] Western civilization, the Lindsay commission lamented, found Hinduism so firmly entrenched in the Indian ethos that they could only touch it marginally. The future seemed uncertain and this uncertainty released a feeling of melancholic frustration which, in turn, reinforced the claims of righteousness and dressed imperialism with a touch-me-not aloofness.[431]

Katherine Mayo had summed up some of the imperial stereotypes in her *Mother India*; a number of civil servants recommended them in their memoirs written in retirement; official reports such as that of the Simon commission put an authoritative stamp on them; the Round Table Conferences turned them into the talking points of British public opinion; administrators and Viceroys explained their uncomfortable hard line on these terms of reference; the British press picked up the threads of these arguments and wove their own warped and macabre patterns; delegate conferences were held in Britain to popularize the imperialist image of India and even a genuine liberal opinion was obliged to appreciate the so-called tragic dilemma of an over-worked and misunderstood civil service operating in an ungrateful and turbulent land. Menon was convinced that the *Raj* had become an essential part of British social history. It helped stimulate the median artery of the imperial culture and fashioned the dominant ideology of the British nation cutting across party affiliations. That the *Raj* was the fulcrum of the empire and was to be preserved at all events was the imperial consensus despite acute tactical differences conditioned by the dialectics of British parliamentary politics. In its larger sense, liberalism was viewed as a deep-seated moral attitude which sought to analyze and integrate various intellectual, social, religious, political, moral and economic relationships. Its principal postulate, the spiritual freedom of mankind, upheld a free individual consciousness of his capacity for unfettered development and self-expression. Menon was aware that political liberalism in Britain had been in touch with the past as well as future: it had been able to strike an equilibrium between conservatism and radicalism by recognizing the credibility of traditional institutions and the validity of reforms. During the inter-war period, liberalism had been under sustained pressures from the left and the forces of plutocracy from the right. So far as the brown and black colonies of the British empire were concerned, liberalism was reduced to a thin cheese paste spread unevenly. But by the mid-1930s the liberal discourse of the British colonial establishment on India had become an unsure slogan, not very convincing to the ears of the liberal spokesmen themselves.[432] It could take no other form than one of evasion of fundamental issues and addition of high moral postures. It dwelt with fragmented minds, projected India as a mystifying muddle and and raised uncanny questions about its survival without British caliber. In its refusal to identify itself with the struggling realities of imperial India, the Conciliation Group, the most significant liberal initiative towards India, merely blotted out its own social and individual face in a mystical fog of personal relationships and walked unsteadily between nothingness and nothingness. The *Raj,* Menon had learnt over the years, was a romantic sentiment, an enormously profitable material concern, an amoral attitude, a particularly provocative perception, a weighty counterpoise in international politics, an applause-seeking vanity, a diabolical policy and a terse reality.

Notes and References

1 Mr Baldwin on India: 'White Paper Policy Defended', *The Times,* 1 May 1933, Lord Llyod Papers.

2 Ibid.

3 Ibid.

4 Ibid; also, cf., Arthur Marwick, *Britain in the Century of Total War,* op.cit., pp.194, 196, 205 and 341.

5 Menon, 'London Letter', 10 June 1934, Menon Papers.

6 'Baldwin on India', *The Times,* 1 May 1933.

7 Ibid.

8 'Mr Baldwin Speaks to Lancashire', *Manchester Guardian,* 30 June 1933, Lord Lloyd Papers.

9 Ibid.

10 'Baldwin and his Critics', *The Times,* 6 March 1931, Lord Lloyd Papers.

11 Ibid.

12 Baldwin, 'Future of India', Lord Lloyd Papers.

13 'Baldwin on India', op.cit.

14 Quoted in H. Macmillan, *Winds of Change,* London 1966.

15 Sir Samuel Hoare, 'Future of India: Anxieties and Realities', *Morning Post,* 5 February 1931, Lord Lloyd Papers.

16 Ibid.

17 Ibid.

18 Ibid.

19 Ibid.

20 Ibid.; also see, 'India - The Longer View', *The Nineteenth Century,* May 1933.

21 Ibid.

22 'Support for Sir Samuel Hoare', 6 February 1931, Lord Lloyd Papers; also see, Zetland to Lord Lloyd, 16 July 1935, Lloyd Papers.

23 'Support for Samuel Hoare', Lord Lloyd Papers, op.cit.

24 Ibid.

25 Ibid.

26 'Mr Baldwin on India and Mr Churchill's Reply', 2 May 1933, Lloyd Papers.

27 Ibid.

28 Ibid., A.J.P. Taylor in his *English History, 1914-1945* was convinced that India was one of the leading subjects that attracted men's minds between the Wars. He held, however, that 'measured by the columns that it took up in Hansard' one got an erroneous impression that the entire nation was haunted and perplexed by the 'intricacies of India's constitutional future'. Taylor categorically declared: it was not so. He overlooked with an element of inexplicable indifference the Indian issue that rocked parliament and sharply divided the Baldwinites from the rebellious diehards. On the contrary, Taylor was keen to affirm that the English people had lost interest in India. Arthur Marwick did not think that Gandhi, civil disobedience and ordinance rule should find even for once a significant appearance in his monumental works on Britain in the twentieth century. Reference to ordinance rule in India and the public debate in England and the nature of popular resistance in India found no place in Hobsbawm's distinguished history of the short twentieth century.

29 Louis Stuart, 'The Story of the Indian Empire Society', *The Indian Empire Review,* June 1939.

30 India Defence League, 'Circular', 21 September 1933, Lord Lloyd Papers.

31 Ibid.

32 Fitzalan and Wolmer, 'The Indian Crisis', 1933, Lord Lloyd Papers. See also, Mark Hunter, 'Circular', N.D. 1931; Mark Hunter to Louis Stuart, 22 February 1931; C.J. Smith to Mark Hunter, 4 May 1931; secretary, Indian Empire Society to Mr. Tillotson, 9 May 1971; H.B. Holme

to Lord Greenway, 4 August 1931; G.B. Sanford to Louis Stuart, September 1932; K.K. Lalkaka to Louis Stuart, 23 December 1933; and J.P. Hewett to Clifton Brown, 30 January 1933; all in Louis Stuart Papers.

33 India Defence League, The Prime Minister on Safeguards, Lord Lloyd Papers.

34 'Lord Lloyd's answer to Mr Baldwin', *Morning Post,* 2 May 1933, Lord Lloyd Papers.

35 Ibid.

36 Ibid.

37 Ibid.

38 Lord Lloyd to the editors, *The Times,* 4 May 1973, Lord Lloyd Papers.

39 Ibid.

40 Ibid.

41 'Statement to the Press by Lord Lloyd, on Mr Baldwin's Monchester Speech', 2 May 1933, Lord Lloyd Papers.

42 Sir Michael O'Dwyer, 'Non-Cooperation by Sir T.B. Sapru and the Moderates', *The Indian Empire Review,* July 1933.

43 Viscount Lymington, 'Our Duty to India', *The Indian Empire Review,* December 1934; also, Lord Lloyd to F.C. Brasher, 27 April 1933, Lloyd Papers.

44 F. Victor Fisher, *The Threatened Indian Crisis,* Indian Empire Society, London 1934.

45 Ibid.

46 F.C. Basher to Lord Lloyd, 6 June 1934, Lord Lloyd Papers.

47 Ibid.

48 Ibid.

49 Ibid.

50 It may not be amiss to quote here what Edward C. Benthall wrote in his diary on 25 December 1928:

'But I am not afraid of the future of India, in which country all my problems will be worked out, at any rate for years to come. We have for the moment apparently lost our grip of Government: the old regime which from our own point of view worked so well for so long is dead, and we have embarked upon a course, the end of whereof no man can pretend to see, and if the truth be known, no man can tell where we are now or why we ever sail upon that course! I believe therefore that we shall come safely through, principally because I have the sublimest faith in England's ability to solve such strange and difficult problems, by methods which in such cases are probably worth a good deal of well thought out theory, and secondly because if we fail to set a happy self-governing country (even in 50 or 100 years), we have sufficient wit to look after our own interests, by force of arms if the worst comes to the worst. We may have a gigantic Hindu bloc against us but we have the potential in the Mussalmans and Sikhs, and even a Labour Government and with a further swing of opinion against Imperialism and towards Nationalism, I am confident that India will remain within the Empire, the greatest of Great Britain's customers and the cornerstone of our Empire. Granted a period of peace and granted the solidity of India, nothing can prevent the country going steadily ahead as a field for merchant adventurers and, in this progress Bird & Co. should lead the race. 'Benthall Papers', Box VII Diaries.

51 PL. Chetwode to Lord Lloyd, 17 June 1933, Lord Lloyd Papers.

52 Ibid.

53 Ibid.

54 Ibid.

55 Ibid.

56 Ibid.

57 Ibid.

58 Ibid.

59 Ibid.

60 Ibid.

61 J. H. Morgan, *The Dangers of Federation,* June 1933, India Defence League, Lord Lloyd Papers.

62 Ibid.

63 Ibid.

64 Ibid.

65 Ibid.

66 Ibid.

67 Ibid.

68 Ibid.

69 Ibid.

70 Sir Michael O'Dwyer, *The Indian States and Federation,* 1934, Lord Lloyd Papers.

71 Morgan, *The Dangers of Federalism,* op.cit.

72 Ibid.

73 Lord Sydenham, *The Federation of India: A Dangerous Illusion,* London 1930, Louis Stuart Papers.

74 Ibid.

75 Ibid.; see, 'Statement of Policy', issued by the president, chairman of the executive committee and the secretary. The Indian Empire Society, 4 July 1930, Louis' Stuart

Papers; also, Viscount Lymington, 'Our Duty to India', *Indian Empire Review,* December 1934.

76 Sir Louis Stuart, 'Activities of the Indian Empire Society: A Review', *The Indian Empire Review,* May 1939; also, Sir Louis Stuart, 'A note on the present situation in India with some suggestions', November 1931. Louis Stuart Papers.

77 Ibid.; also, 'Policy Recommended by the Indian Empire Society, March 1933, Louis Stuart Papers.

78 Sir Louis Stuart, 'Activities of the Indian Empire Society', *The Indian Empire Review',* op.cit.

79 Ibid.

80 Ibid.

81 See, the papers of the Union of Britain and India (UBI) in the collection of Sir John Perronet Thompson in the India Office Library and Records (hereafter, Thompson Collection).

82 'Draft letter to Michael O'Dwyer', 17 May 1933, Thompson Collection.

83 UBI, *Effects of Civil Disobedience and Boycott Movement in India,* London 1934, Thompson Collection.

84 John Thompson, *The Reform Proposals and their Reasons,* London 1933, Thompson Collection.

85 M. Hailey, *6 Crucial Aspects of Reform,* London, 1933; also see, Draft letter to Michael O'Dwyer, 17 May 1933, Thompson Collection.

86 UBI, 'Announcement of 20 May 1933', Thompson Collection.

87 Butler to Thompson, 22 May 1933, Thompson Collection.

88 Meston to Thompson, 31 May 1933, Thompson Collection.

89 Cf. Viscount Lymington, 'Our Duty to India', op.cit.; Michael O'Dwyer, 'Non-Co-operation by Sir T.B. Sapru and the Moderates', op.cit.; 'Lord Sumner's Notes,' Lloyd Papers; 'The Prime Minister on Safeguards', India Defence League, Lloyd Papers; Lord Lloyd to Lord Salisbury, 16 November 1934, Lloyd Papers; F. Victor Fisher, 'The Threatened Indian Chaos', op.cit.; Michael O'Dwyer, 'The Indian States and Federation', Lloyd Papers.

90 See the following pamphlets in Thompson Collection for a balanced perspective of the internal debate of the Conservative Party on the Indian reform:

Facts - The Indian Empire Society, 1933;

The Pledges We Gave to India, India Defence League, 1934;

Report of Joint Select Committee, India Defence League, 1934;

The Threatened Indian Chaos, by F. Victor Fisher, Indian Empire Society, 1933;

The White Paper: What India Thinks, An MPs Impressions, Union of Britain and India, 1934;

India: The White Paper, John Perronet Thompson, 1933, Union of British and India;

The Great Surrender by Lady Houston 1933, India Defence League;

The White Paper with the Black Border, India Defence League, 1934.

91 Viscount Lymington, 'Our Duty to India', op.cit.

92 Michael O'Dwyer, *The Indian States and Federation,* London 1934, Lloyd Papers and Michael O'Dwyer, *The Indian Report: A Minority View,* 1934.

93 Hamish Blair, *India - The Eleventh Hour,* Defence of India League, Thompson Collection, 1934. For a fairly comprehensive compendium on the debate between the

various factions of the Conservative Party on the proposed Indian reforms, the RTC, the White Paper, the JSC etc. see, 11/-4, 17/15-32 and 23/5, Lord Lloyd Papers, Churchill College Cambridge.

94 A Resident of Calcutta: 'Indian Reforms', enclosed in C.R.C. Nixon to Lord Lloyd, 12 February 1935, Lord Lloyd Papers.

95 Ibid.

96 Ibid.

97 Ward Price, *Face to Face in India,* the Indian Empire Society, London 1934, Louis Stuart Papers.

98 Ibid.

99 Some Conservative members of parliament to Lloyd, 11 May 1933, Lloyd Papers.

100 Ibid.

101 Harry Haig to Samuel Hoare, 11 February 1932, Hoare Papers, Templewood Papers.

102 Ibid.

103 Ibid.

104 Ibid.

105 Ibid.

106 Samuel Hoare to Ramsay MacDonald, 20 March 1932, Templewood Papers.

107 Alexander Inglis, 'Future Status of India', n.d. December 1934, Templewood Papers VII:5.

108 Ibid.

109 Ibid.

110 Ibid.

111 *Note on Inglis,* Dominion status discussion (India) 1934-35,

Templewood Papers.

112 'Note for Cabinet Committee', Dominion Status discussion, (India) 1934-35, Templewood Papers, VII:5.

113 Hailey to Willingdon, 26 April 1933, Hailey Papers.

114 Ibid.

115 Ibid.

116 Hailey to Willngdon, 18 May 1933, Hailey Papers.

117 Willingdon to Hailey, 29 May 1933, Hailey Papers.

118 Hailey to Willingdon, 9 June 1933, Hailey Papers.

119 Willingdon to Hailey, 12 June 1933, Hailey Papers.

120 Ibid.

121 Willingdon to Hailey, 23 June 1933, Hailey Papers.

122 Willingdon to Hailey, 29 May 1933, Hailey Papers.

123 Ibid.

124 Willingdon to Hailey, 9 June 1933, Hailey Papers.

125 Willingdon to Hailey, 22 July 1933, Hailey Papers.

126 Ibid.

127 Willingdon to Hailey, 6 August 1933, Hailey Papers.

128 Ibid.

129 Willingdon to Hailey, 12 August 1933, Hailey Papers.

130 Willingdon to Hailey, 5 June 1933, Hailey Papers.

131 Hailey to Willingdon, 16 June 1933, Hailey Papers.

132 Willingdon to Hailey, 5 June 1933, Hailey Papers.

133 Willingdon to Hailey, 12 June 1933, Hailey Papers.

134 Hailey to Willingdon, 9 June 1933, Hailey Papers.

135 Hailey to Willingdon, 24 June 1933, Hailey Papers.

136 Hailey to Willingdon, 28 July 1933, Hailey Papers.

137 Ibid.

138 For a sophisticated official explanation of the relations of the Indian executive and legislature in the proposed constitutional arrangement, see Hailey to Lothian, 10 December 1930, Hailey papers.

139 Butler to John Perronet Thompson, 11 May 1933, Thompson Papers.

140 Willingdon to Hailey, 12 August 1933, Hailey Papers.

141 I.M. Stephens to Cornelia Sorabji, 6 September 1931, Cornelia Sorabji Papers.

142 I.M. Stephens to Cornelia Sorabji, 13 August 1932, Cornelia Sorabji Papers.

143 Ibid.

144 Cornelia Sorabji to Stephens, 16 July 1932, Cornelia Sorabji Papers.

145 Ibid.

146 I.M. Stephens to Cornelia Sorabji, 29 May 1933, Cornelia Sorabji Papers.

147 Charles Tegart, *Terrorism in India,* London 1933, Cornelia Sorabji Papers.

148 Ibid.

149 Ibid.

150 Ibid.

151 Ibid.

152 Ibid.

153 Ibid.

154 See for details the compact body of collection of the private papers of Cornelia Sorabji in the India Office Library.

155 See, 'True Blue' (Cornelia Sorabji), 'The Power of Gandhi',

The Indian Empire Review, December 1934; See the copy of this article under Cornelia Sorabji's signature in her Papers.

156 See Sorabji's engagements all over England and the United States in her papers.

157 'True Blue', 'The Power of Gandhi', *The Indian Empire Review,* December 1934.

158 Ibid.

159 Ibid.

160 Cornelia Sorabji, 'Mr Gandhi at the Crossroads', (unpublished paper) January 1933, Cornelia Sorabji Papers.

161 A British Indian merchant, *India on the Brink,* London 1934.

162 See the volume in Cornelia Sorabji Papers along with the comments of large number of eminent personalities on the content of the volume.

163 Cornelia Sorabji, 'Mr Gandhi at the Crossroads', unpublished typescript, January 1933, Cornelia Sorabji Papers.

164 File 'The India Study Circle', Infn. offr. L/I/1/50, India Office.

165 Rushbrook Williams, Note on Indian Press, 16 June 1933, Ibid.

166 Ibid.

167 Ibid.

168 Ibid.

169 Ibid.

170 Ibid.

171 Graham Pole to Samuel Hoare, 12 January 1933 L/PJ(S)/12/140/1933 India, Office.

172 Ibid.

173 Graham Pole to Samuel Hoare, 9 February 1932, L/PJ(S)/12/153/1932, India Office.

174 Baldwin to Samuel Hoare, 16 February 1932, Hailey Papers.

175 Samuel Hoare to G. Pole, 18 January 1933, Pole Papers (India Office).

176 Ibid.

177 Stephens to MacGregor, 20 April 1934, Infn. No. offr. 408, 1934, India Office.

178 Ibid.

179 Report on the meeting with the delegates of the India Empire Society, 2 May 1935 Infr. offr. No. L/I/1/50, India Office.

180 Alfred Knox to Secretary of State, 22 April 1935, Infr. offr. L/I/1/50 India Office.

181 Report on the meeting with the delegation of the Indian Empire Society, 2 May 1935, Infr. offr. L/I/1/50, India Office.

182 Ibid.

183 Ibid.

184 Ibid.

185 Ibid.

186 Ibid.

187 S. Chakravarty, *The Raj Syndrome, A Study in Imperial Perceptions,* op.cit., pp.165-182.

188 Horace Alexander, 'Friends and India', 2 January 1942, Alexander Papers (Teen Murti).

189 Alexander, 'India', *New Statesman and Nation,* 14 April 1934, Alexander Papers (Teen Murti).

190 H. Alexander, 'Friends and India', op.cit.

191 Maud Royden to Agatha Harrison, 18 September 1931, Agatha Harrison Papers.

192 Ibid.

193 Polak on 'the Indian unrest', 3 September 1931, Agatha Harrison Papers.

194 Ibid.

195 Ibid.

196 Ibid.

197 Ibid.

198 Ibid.

199 Ibid.

200 Horace Alexander, 'Friends and India', 2 January 1942, issued by *The Friends Committee,* Alexander Papers (T.M.).

201 Ibid.

202 Horace Alexander, 'India', *New Statesman and Nation,* 14 April 1934, Alexander Papers (T.M.).

203 Agatha Harrison to Horace Alexander, 3 September 1932, Alexander Papers (T.M.).

204 Agatha Harrison to Horace Alexander, 3 September 1932, Alexander Papers (T.M.).

205 Ibid.

206 Horace Alexander to Andrews, 26 June 1931, Alexander Papers, T.M.).

207 Ibid.

208 Cf. S.L. Polak, 'Wasted Opportunities in India', *The Contemporary Review,* 1934.

209 Carl Heath, 'Circular letter', February 1933, Agatha Harrison Papers.

210 Horace Alexander, 'Note for circulation', 7 March 1933, Agatha Harrison Papers.

211 Harrison to Alexander, 18 April 1933; Alexander Papers, (T.M.).

212 Carl Heath to Horrabin, 16 January 1932, Menon Papers.

213 Ibid.

214 Report of the meeting of the India Conciliation Group on 5 April 1932, Infn. offr. No. 1932, India Office.

215 Ibid.

216 Ibid.

217 Ibid.

218 Ibid.

219 Ibid.

220 Ibid.

221 Ibid.

222 Report on the meeting of the India Conciliation Group on 13 April 1932. Infn. offr. No. 1932, India Office.

223 Ibid.

224 Ibid.

225 Ibid.

226 Ibid.

227 Ibid.

228 Ibid.

229 Ibid.

230 Harrison to Alexander, September 1932, Alexander Papers.

231 Ibid.; also 'Circular Letter', 29 September 1932, Agatha Harrison Papers.

232 Resume of a discussion on 'The Union of Britain and

India', 26 October 1934, Agatha Harrison Papers; also see, John Perronet Thompson Papers, India Office Library and Records.

233 Harrison, 'Report on the discussion on: O'Dwyer, *The Indian White Paper,'* 18 November 1934, Agatha Harrison Papers.

234 Agatha Harrison to Horace Alexander, 26 March 1932, Alexander Papers (T.M.).

235 Ibid.

236 Ibid.

237 Ibid.

238 Harrison to Alexander, April 1933, Alexander Papers (T.M.).

239 Ibid.

240 Harrison to Alexander, April 1932, Alexander Papers (T.M.).

241 Ibid.

242 Harrison to Alexander, April 1933, Alexander Papers.

243 Ibid.

244 Ibid.

245 Harrison to Alexander, April 1933, Alexander Papers.

246 Ibid.

247 Harrison to Alexander, 13-14 September 1932, Alexander Papers.

248 Ibid.

249 Harrison to Alexander, 17 September 1932, Alexander Papers.

250 Harrison to Alexander 24 September 1932, Alexander Papers.

251 Ibid.

252 Ibid.

253 Ibid.

254 Harrison to Alexander, April/May 1933, Alexander Papers (T.M.).

255 Ibid.

256 Harrison to Alexander, April 1933, Alexander Papers (T.M.).

257 Ibid.

258 Ibid.

259 Ibid.

260 Ibid.

261 Ibid.

262 Ibid.

263 Ibid.

264 Harrison to Andrews and Alexander, May 1933, Alexander Papers (T.M.).

265 Ibid.

266 Harrison to Alexander, 11 May 1933, Alexander Papers (T.M.).

267 Ibid.

268 Ibid.

269 Ibid.

270 Ibid.

271 Harrison to Alexander, 9 June 1934, Alexander Papers (T.M.).

272 Ibid.

273 Ibid.

274 Ibid.

275 Harrison to Alexander, 1 February 1934, Alexander Papers (T.M.).

276 Irwin to Alexander, 17 March 1934, Alexander Papers.

277 A.H. Joyce to I.M. Stephens, 16 February 1934, Infn. offr. No. 145, 1934, India Office.

278 Ibid.

279 Ibid.

280 Ibid.

281 Ibid.

282 Note by James David Sifton, 9 April 1934, Infn offr. No. 500, 1934, India Office.

283 Ibid.

284 Ibid.

285 Ibid.

286 Ibid.

287 Ibid.

288 Stephens to MacGregor, 20 April 1934, Infn. No. offr. 408, 1934, India Office.

289 Ibid.

290 Ibid.

291 Ibid.

292 Ibid.; also see, Joyce to Harrison, 8 February 1938, Infn. offr. 99/38, India Office and office note: Infn. offr. 99/38, 4 February 1938.

293 Ibid.

294 Ibid.

295 MacGregor to Stephens, 4 May 1934, Infn. offr. No.408, 1934, India Office.

296 Ibid.

297 Stephens to MacGregor, 20 April 1934, Infn. offr., No.408, 1934, India Office.

298 Ibid.

299 Ibid.

300 Ibid.

301 Ibid.

302 MacGregor to Stephens, 1 April 1934, Infn. offr. No. 439, 1934, India Office.

303 Ibid.

304 Ibid.

305 Stephens to MacGregor, 15 May 1934, Infn. offr. No. 499, 1934, India Office.

306 Ibid.

307 Cornelia Sorabji to MacGregor, 19 May 1934, Infn. offr. No.515, 1934, India Office.

308 MacGregor to Sorabji, 21 May 1934, Infr. offr. No.617, 1934, India Office.

309 Ibid.

310 Sorabji to MacGregor, 1 June 1934, Infr. offr., No.619, 1934 India Office.

311 A.H. Joyce marginal note in ibid.

312 Ibid.

313 Harrison to MacGregor, 23 June 1934, Infr. offr. No.715, 1934, India Office.

314 Ibid.

315 Suhash Chakravarty, *The Raj Syndrome,* op.cit., pp.181-2.

316 Cf. 'Private Discussion Meeting, held on 9 March 1944' speaker: Horace Alexander, Alexander Papers (T.M.).

317 Pole to Sapru, 16 August 1932, Pole Papers (India Office).

318 S.L. Polak to C.F. Andrews, 25 February 1933 Infn. offr. No.407 1933, India Office.

319 Harrison to F.H. Brown, 6 March 1933, Infn offr. No.407 1933, India Office.

320 Polak to Andrews, 25 February 1933, Infn. offr. No.407, 1933, India Office.

321 Ibid.

322 Ibid.

323 Ibid.

324 Ibid.

325 Ibid.

326 Ibid.

327 Ibid.

328 Ibid.

329 MacGregor to Brown, 7 March 1933, Infn. offr. No. 239, 1933, India Office.

330 Tej Bahadur Sapru to Pole, 27 August 1932, Jayakar Papers.

331 Ibid.

332 Pole to Jayakar, 12 September 1932, Jayakar Papers.

333 Jayakar to Pole, 29 August 1932, Jayakar Papers.

334 Ibid.

335 Jayakar to Pole, 3 September 1932, Jayakar Papers.

336 Sapru to Pole, 6 September 1932, Pole Papers (India Office).

337 Ibid.

338 Ibid.

339 Sapru to Pole, 13 January 1933, Pole Papers (India Office).

340 Ibid.

341 Sapru to Pole, 27 August 1933, Pole Papers (India Office).

342 Jayakar to Moonje, 27 March 1933, B.S. Moonje Papers.

343 Ibid.

344 Pole to Jayakar, 23 April 1933, Jayakar Papers.

345 Sapru to Pole, 2 January 1934, Pole Papers (India Office).

346 Sapru to Pole, 16 February 1934, Pole Papers (India Office).

347 Pole to Sapru, 27 September 1933, Pole Papers (India Office).

348 Ibid.

349 Ibid.

350 Ibid.

351 Ibid.

352 Pole to Sapru, 28 December 1933, Pole Papers (India Office).

353 Ibid.

354 Polak to MacGregor, 25 February 1934, Infn. offr. No. 1934, India Office.

355 Ibid.

356 Ibid.

357 Ibid.

358 Ibid.

359 Ibid.

360 Ibid.

361 Ibid.

362 Ibid.

363 Ibid.

364 Ibid.

365 Ibid.

366 Ibid.

367 Ibid.

368 Polak to Jayakar, 3 February 1934, Jayakar Papers.

369 Ibid.

370 Polak to MacGregor, 7 February 1933, Infr. offr. 320, 1934, India Office.

371 Ibid.

372 Ibid.

373 Ibid.

374 Ibid.

375 Ibid.

376 Pole to Lansbury, 15 August 1935, Pole Papers (Hull).

377 Arthur Wenyon to Menon, 15 June 1933, Menon Papers.

378 Ibid.; also see, L. Housman to editor, *The Times,* 24 March 1934, Menon Papers.

379 Arthur Wenyon to Menon, 11 December 1933, Menon Papers.

380 Ibid.

381 S. Chakravarty, *The Raj Syndrome,* op.cit., pp.108-110.

382 Edward Thompson, *A Farewell to India,* London 1931, pp.40-42.

383 Ibid., p.85.

384 Ibid., p.93.

385 Ibid., p.120.

386 Ibid., p.141.

387 Edward Thompson, *A Letter from India,* London 1932.

388 Ibid., p.14.

389 Ibid., p.15.

390 Ibid.

391 Ibid., p.18.

392 Ibid., pp. 20-22, 26-27, and 30.

393 Ibid., p.114.

394 Ibid., p.40.

395 Ibid., pp.30-31.

396 Ibid., p.48.

397 Ibid.

398 Edward Thompson to Tej Bahadur Sapru, 4 August 1932, Jayakar Papers.

399 Ibid.

400 Ibid.

401 Ibid.

402 Ibid.

403 Ibid.

404 Ibid.

405 Ibid.

406 Ibid.

407 Ibid.

408 Ibid.

409 Ibid.

410 Ibid.

411 Ibid.

412 Ibid.

413 Ibid.

414 Ibid.

415 It may be instructive to quote from Sapru's reply to Thompson: 'Your main point in your letter is that we must make Conservatives work with us. I should be glad if that was possible. But the Conservatives avoided us as a hateful thing at both the Sessions of the Round Table Conference. I wonder whether you remember... that they were dead opposed to any genuine advance towards self-government.... Their policy and actions had nothing in them calculated to inspire confidence in us. ... The Conservatives live in a world of their own. Either they do not believe or do not like to believe that India has changed. They think that we stand where we did in the eighties or the ninetees of the last century. The talk of our difference in languages, dress, food, religion and culture, but they overlook the points of contact or the changes that have come about in our social system or are likely to come about soon. I have heard so much of the young Conservatives and know some of them, but they have not yet openly asserted themselves against the die-hards. All this will explain to you why there was so little touch between the Conservatives and ourselves. Nothing will give greater pleasure than to know that the Conservatives are coming out of the trenches of their old-time prejudices against Indian self-government. (Sapru to Thompson, 22 August 1932, Jayakar Papers).

416 Edward Thompson, *The Reconstruction of India,* London 1933 (edn).

417 Ibid.

418 'Thompson on Sunderland' - a note, 1930, Menon Papers.

419 Ibid.

420 Ibid.

421 Cf. S. Chakravarty, *The Raj Syndrome,* op.cit., pp.108-117.

422 Menon, 'Thompson on Sunderland - a note', 1930, Menon Papers.

423 Ibid.

424 Ibid.

425 Ibid.

426 Ibid.

427 Lindsay Commission, *Report of the Commission on Christian Education in India,* London 1931, esp. see, pp.43-45 and pp.45-50.

428 Ibid., p.48.

429 Ibid., pp.49-50.

430 Ibid., pp.54-55.

431 Chakravarty, *The Raj Syndrome,* op.cit., pp.188-203.

432 Cf. Nicholas Owen, 'Critics of Empire in Britain', in J.M. Brown (ed.), *Oxford History of British Empire* iv, Oxford 1999; G.R. Searle, *Eugenics and Politics in Britain 1900-1914,* Leiden 1976; Catherine Hall, *Culture of Empire, Colonisers in Britain and the Empire of the Nineteenth and Twentieth Centuries, A Reader,* Manchester 2000; John MacKenzie, (ed.), *Propaganda and Empire: The Manipulation of British Public Opinion, 1880-1960,* Manchester 1984.

CHAPTER VII

ENTER NEHRU

By the end of March 1934, the first newsletter arrived from the Congress Socialist Group from India. In a covering letter, Minoo Masani, an old friend from the LSE days, wrote enthusiastically about the group which some of them had formed in the Bombay presidency. The large number of enclosures included half-a-dozen copies of the programme of the Congress Socialist group, its opening manifesto and the copy of a letter that Jawaharlal Nehru had given him for publication on the formation of the group in the event of his prior arrest.[1] The group had restricted membership only to Congressmen who were prepared to cooperate actively. Masani was confident that with the prospect of a large number of new recruits 'we shall meet with growing response and support'.[2] The group had participated in the 'Unemployment Workers' Day' demonstration on 4 March which was organized under the auspices of the All India Trade Union Congress and also arranged a public meeting in support of the Sholapur strikers and appealed for funds for their relief.[3] The Bombay group wanted to make and maintain contacts with the British labour movement and Masani was convinced that Menon could help the group in England in a very substantial way.[4] Masani had also written to Fenner Brockway requesting him to send, as the chairman of the ILP, a message of welcome and the group was keen to get considerable political mileage out of it. Menon was requested to meet the IIP people and to see to it that the suggestion was given due attention. He was also urged to come up with concrete proposals regarding communication and contact between the socialist group and the India League and between the group and the British labour organizations and individuals interested in India.[5]

Towards the end of April 1934, the labour situation in Bombay took an ominous turn as 65,000 textile workers in Bombay came out on strike. *Lathi* charge had been made by the police on the crowds and demonstrations were broken up. Leaders were arrested, armed police were being drafted to the area. The matter was considered serious following a similar situation at Sholapur where the district officer, under his special powers, prohibited all meetings of strikers, served orders on labour leaders prohibiting them from attending or taking part in protest marches and activities. The textile workers in the presidency were restive against a cut in the wages of about 12 per cent. The district magistrate of Sholapur did not even appoint the board of arbitration and conciliation as provided by the Indian Trade Disputes Act.[6] It appeared to Menon as though the labour agitation was going to be suppressed under ordinances just as the Congress activity had been treated. Since Tom Williams and Grenfell were away from the House, Aneurin Bevan was requested by Menon to raise the issue by a private notice question.[7] Irrespective of the misgivings in the Labour Party with regard to the tenor of the Congress stir and the party's qualified support to the 'nationalist agitation', Menon argued that violent dispersal of labour demonstrations and imprisonment of leaders were matters of concern for all progressive citizens at least as much as similar matters in Germany or elsewhere.[8] Anticipating the official arguments, Menon stated firmly that it was irrational to argue that the Bombay and Sholapur troubles were engineered by communists, as the communists in India were not strong enough to bring 65,000 workers out on strike and face *lathi* charges. The situation was rather different from what it was stated to be. A socialist group, he confided to Bevan, had been formed within the Congress who had been devoting themselves to the interest of the working classes and providing them with organization and leadership.[9]

In a sense, the Congress Socialist Party was born in prison among the large number of young men interned between 1932-33 in various jails as they all realised the urgency of an effective socialist propaganda. Following the release of these socialist dreamers, provincial groups were formed.[10] The Bombay group was the first to be convened on 25 February 1934. On 17 May 1934, an All India Socialist conference met at Patna under Acharya Narendra Dev and on 21 October 1934 on the eve of the Congress session, the All India Congress Socialist Party was established with Jayaprakash Narayan as the first general secretary.[11] The new party within the Congress stressed the need for change in the policies of the Congress and the trade union movement, emphasized the need to end exploitation and to radicalize its methods hoping to amplify the objectives in the near future.[12] The socialist formation upheld that the isolation and ultra-leftist tactics of the AITUC and Red TUC needed to be rectified, a rapprochement with the Congress should be put into effect, Indian workers were to be guided to take a proper place in the national movement and to bring their due influence on the party's policy. Even in the field of trade unions, the factional infighting must be brought to an end and serious efforts should be made to bring about a united front if not a merger.[13] The specific objectives included the achievement of *purna swaraj* or complete independence and the establishment of a socialist society, transfer of all powers to the producing masses, development of the economic life of the country to be planned and controlled by the state, socialization of the key industries, state monopoly of foreign trade, organization of cooperatives in socialist sectors, elimination of the property of the princes, landlords and 'other exploiters' without compensation, redistribution of land to peasants, promotion of cooperative and collective farming, legalization of debts of peasants and workers. Besides the socialist state should work to implement the principle: to everyone according to his needs and from everyone to his capacity. Adult franchise should be on a functional basis; no discrimination between religions, caste, community or sexes should be accepted and repudiation of public debt of India should be complete and final. It was decided to work within the Indian National Congress to help develop it into the principal anti-imperialist organization complete with peasants' and workers' bodies devoted to the intensification of class struggle.[14] It should have active youth organization and militant women's association, it must offer active opposition to imperialistic wars and support intensification of the national struggles all the world over. It should refuse to enter into any negotiations on constitutional issues with the British Government and should be firm in its commitment to convene after the capture of power of a constituent assembly representing all exploited classes for framing a constitution.[15] It was believed that, tactically, it was sound to form a party within the Congress. Jayaprakash Narayan explained that far from contradicting each other, the socialist and the Congress perspectives were 'interdependent in the peculiar colonial situation in India.'[16] Socialism without the overthrow of imperialism was a senseless undertaking. Narayan emphasized that the National Congress was the only political organization which had led major struggles against imperialism in India and there was no reason to expect that it would abandon its anti-imperialist agenda at that stage. He clarified that he did not imply that the Congress, as it was then, was competent to overthrow imperialism. The exact task of the CSP was to so develop the Congress that it became such a militant body. The formation of an alternative organization outside the Congress would mean wanton and irrational waste of energy. Evidently, it was assumed that those who entertained any doubt in the efficacy of the CSP to change the Congress into an authentic and militant anti-imperialist body should have no place in that political formation. Narendra Dev was circumspect. He cautioned against an optimistic euphoria. Socialism, he maintained, was a weak force in India and there was not much scope for latitude.[17] There was, however, a general conviction that only socialist perception and practice could lead India to freedom and that it was the immediate task of the CSP to wean away the petite bourgeoisie and revolutionary masses from the bourgeois leadership by remaining within the Congress.[18] Masani wrote to Menon in 1935 that without any contradiction it might be asserted that the party within the span of a year of its existence placed socialism on the political map of India. What had hitherto been only an intellectual interest, became a real issue in Indian politics with a message of hope to the countless peasants, workers and lower middle classses.[19] The party organ, *Congress Socialist,* was regularly published under Ram Manohar Lohia and Ashok Mehta; several books were published in leading languages in India, the most outstanding being Jayaprakash Narayan's *Why Socialism?*, M.R. Masani's *Soviet Sidelights,* Babu Sampurnanda's *Samyavad,* Yusuf Meherally's *What to Read?* and Ashok Mehta's *Gandhism and Socialism.* Besides, there were various tracts and pamphlets.[20]

Following the Patna and the Bombay sessions, a broad assessment of the political situation was attempted by Masani. Having discussed the socialist programme with Gandhi, Masani concluded that although Gandhi was certainly not a socialist, he was nonetheless sympathetically 'inclined towards us'. The Mahatma definitely agreed with the proposition that the socialist group had a place within the Congress as an organized left attempting to convert the Congress to its views.[21] The group, in its turn, was confident that about a third of the Congress were with them already. It was, however, apprehended that faced with a militant socialist challenge, those in power in the Congress might rally their forces and with their superior 'money power' would seek to keep the socialists away from having any demonstrable advance in voting strength in the near future.[22] The socialists, nevertheless, felt strongly that the future was with them and the Congress would increasingly be constrained to accept 'more of our policy'.[23] A constitutional programme for the All India Congress Socialist Party had been chalked out. The work of the CSP would naturally be organizational and propagandist within the Congress and that it would attempt to win as many seats as possible on local and provincial committees and be strongly represented at the Congress session.[24] At the same time, labour and peasant work had to be done on certain definitive lines which the socialists wanted the Congress to adopt.[25] They had no contact with N.M. Joshi and Shiva Rao and they felt no need to antagonize them either.[26] They had informed the ILP of their political presence in India but had not received fraternal greetings or even a cordial reply from them.[27] There was then no question of exclusive cooperation with any one organization. As far as the Third International was concerned the socialist group had nothing whatever to do and it was, in fact, denounced by the communists as an agent of imperialism.[28] Menon was asked to get the socialist movement in India familiarized in the Labour Party circles. In fact, he was informed that the group would be glad to have him as an associate member. He was told that Pulin Seal had been doing the group's work in England but whenever a change was considered they would bear Menon's name in mind.[29]

Menon was definitely drawn towards the Congress socialists. Offering himself for enrolment as a member of the socialist group either in Bombay or its national body, he hoped that Indian socialism was not going to make the mistake of the Congress in allowing the foreign side to be neglected or in failing to establish the necessary contacts.[30] He was quite happy that it had been decided that at the initial stage the movement should not seek any foreign affiliation. But he desired the socialist colleagues of Masani to consider if they would arrange for a representation of the organization in London as a bureau rather than a branch having no responsibility for policy making and, in case the decision was in the affirmative, he should be glad to undertake the job and do the best he could.[31] There was a supplementary query: if this should be done by the India League or as a separate committee. Menon confided that difficulty with the India League was that it had often taken a somewhat artificial pose of being non-party and often decided to put forward the majority view in India even though it was not fully approved by the socialist group. The League stood by self-determination and *swaraj* though 'most of our support is socialist'.[32]

By mid-November 1934, the typed copy of the constitution, programme and resolution of the All India Congress Socialist party (CSP) arrived from Bombay. With Jayaprakash Narayan as general secretary and four joint-secretaries in M.R. Masani, Mohanlal Gautam, H.G. Gore and E.M.S. Namboodripad, the new formation represented youth, dynamism and commitment.[33] Masani's sister had informed Jayaprakash Narayan about the attempts that certain persons had been making in London to establish a branch of the CSP. They had even been claiming that they had Masani's authority to do so. No such authority had been given by any one.[34] In fact, the party did not think there was any point in opening a branch in England or, for that matter, anywhere outside India. Narayan, however, appreciated Menon's suggestion regarding the advisability of setting up a propaganda committee. In a separate official letter, Narayan appointed Menon and Miss Masani as provisional secretaries of such a committee so that one could go ahead with the work equipped with the necessary authority, and this information was sent over to *the Daily Herald* for publication to forestall any move from undesirable quarters.[35] Narayan did not want to exclude the communists *per se* from fraternal associations as a matter of policy. Menon was given a free hand to include some of the communists with strong common sense and perceptive judgement which would be welcomed by the party's high command.[36]

Menon was sensitive to the new consciousness for social justice in India and he gave extraordinary encomium to the newly formed socialist group within the Congress. 'As you know', Menon wrote persuasively to Masani, 'and I have never hidden the fact, I am not a member of the C.P. [Communist party] and I do not find it possible or consider it useful at this end to get mixed up with them organizationally. I am very critical of the Labour Party's policy, who would not be, but the position is the same as in your case rightly emphasizing that you and the party are *Congress Socialists*'.[37] Menon did not see any difficulty in obtaining for the socialist formation in India, the official support of the Socialist League and various other movements which were not ancilliary to the Communist Party. All the same, Menon did not see any reason at all why the CSP should not contact the communists and liberals. But it would be, however, the wisest course, Menon counselled, to follow to remain independent.[38]

Responding to the suggestions of Masani, Menon thought that it was an excellent idea to have a deputation of the CSP visiting England.[39] But the ground should be well prepared. It was unfortunate that most of the trade union delegates who visited England, did not get the opportunity of going round to the rank and file.[40] It could not be done without an organized effort. Shiva Rao and N.M. Joshi had been fraternal delegates to the TUC. But the better approach, Menon thought, would be the political side of the Labour Party and that had to be well prepared and the preparation time should be about three months.[41] Menon desired to know if such a deputation was feasible both in terms of time and funds. He was also keen to be advised on the duration of its stay, its exepectations and perspective.[42] Menon counselled that it would be desirable for the CSP to gain the adherence of the masses of India. Its voice could then be heard with greater respect. The whole business of deputation should be considered as a serious affair and Menon suggested that a team of two or three should be appointed at the annual session with all the prestige and publicity that went along with it.[43] The proper time for such a deputation dependend on many things. If there was a general election in the autumn it would have to be done after that. The new year, he added, was a good time as it would be either after an election or well before that.[44] Menon did not attach much importance to Masani being asked as a fraternal delegate to the Labour Party conference, as in 1935, it would primarily be an election conference and because fraternal delegates would have only ten minutes to speak. Besides, as Menon put it cynically, 'you and the Labour Party, both, may have your own doubts about fraternisation!'[45] Menon thought that if the deputation idea was seriously taken up, the ideal combination would be Jayaprakash, Masani and a woman, preferably a Muslim, and they should be empowered to coopt 'any one of us' as might be necessary to join the deputation in London.[46] If the deputation came off, Menon should look round and get a reception committee with some of the left-wing elements within the Labour Party and obtain some rank and file support.[47] Menon thought that the passport difficulty was not a very serious one. The authorities in India could cancel Masani's passport at any moment if they wanted to do so. But, on the other hand, Menon did not think they would refuse to give Masani a passport as a deputation, if properly planned, would lead to a loud and emphatic protest in Britain and Menon was certain that he might be relied upon to ensure that.[48]

Within a few days of his arrival in England, Masani was informed by the Foreign Office that his passport had been impounded at the request of the Government of India and when he desired to return to India he would be given a special permit for the journey back to that country. In his note of protest, Menon held that it was absurd to claim that His Majesty's Government had begun 'to take orders from the subordinate Government of India.'[49] The granting and withholding of a British passport was a matter for the exercise of his discretion by the foreign secretary for which he was responsible to

Parliament. It was surprising that the foreign secretary seemed to have surrendered that discretion on that occasion in favour of the Indian government.[50] In a firm representation, the League reminded that the arbitrary action of the Foreign Office had been taken against an official of a political party which had been functioning legally and openly in India. The Congress Socialist Party was composed exclusively of Congressmen who subscribed to the creed of complete independence by peaceful and legitimate means and no one had so far suggested that it was associated, however remotely, with any terrorist movement.[51]

On the basis of the League's representation, the matter was raised in the House of Commons in the form of a question. The League argued that the duty of the Labour opposition was to resort to every possible form of protest against the attempt to prevent a more intimate contact between the rising socialist movement in India and the working-class movement in Britain and abroad.[52] That step of the Government of India was not an isolated act, but a part of a systematic policy of prosecution and persecution of socialists by that government, along with the suppression of even so-called legitimate trade unions affiliated to the AITUC.[53]

Following Grenfell's intervention, the foreign secretary replied that owing to Masani's communist activities, he was deprived of the passport facility for travelling abroad.[54] In a letter addressed to the leading editors of the British press under the signature of Bertrand Russell, Harold J. Laski and H.N. Brailsford, the League questioned the propriety of the whole episode and the official defense. It sought to direct the attention of public opinion to an unusual step by the Indian government to penalize advanced opinion in India.[55] The signatories maintained that the implications of the official position in the house was extraordinary. A passport was apparently regarded by the Government of India as a reward for meritorious opinions -- a doctrine as dangerous as it was novel. It was a very sinister proposition to claim that one's belief in communism should be considered by a liberal democratic state as an adequate ground for refusing the right to travel. In any case, the signatories held firmly that Masani was not a communist.[56] During his stay in England, he had been a member of the Labour Party. He was then a councillor of the Bombay municipality and a member of the executive committee of the Bombay provincial Congress committee and also one of the secretaries of the Socialist Party within the Indian National Congress. This group, like the larger organization to which it belonged, was a lawful association pledged to non-violence. Besides, Masani came to England with an invitation from the Socialist League of the Labour Party to address meetings under its auspices.[57] The authors affirmed that the Government of India could hardly obscure the fact that Masani's party, far from having any affiliation with the Third International, was the target of continual communist attacks.[58] To call every liberal, a radical and every socialist, a communist was a crafty machination of the party-hack that rarely fails to do much harm. It was, however, a grave matter when the government resorted to it.[59] The Indian government had recoursed to a dubious trial at Meerut for over three years of a number of socialists and trade unionists for activities and expression of opinion that the whole labour movement 'in this country would endorse'.[60] The case was, in itself, a sordid violation of civil rights. The same confused thinking had prompted the step against Masani.[61] The League affirmed that the bureaucracy in India named anyone whom it disliked a communist. It was strange, the League claimed, that opinions that were no bar to the highest office in Britain should condemn Indians to segregation within their own borders.[62]

It was more than evident that Menon, from his sickbed, had been keeping only a technical distance between the India

League and Congress Socialist Party. Masani's visit had been so arranged by Menon as to propagate and popularize the cause of socialism in India as the dynamic force operating within the Congress for a radical transformation of its ideological thrust.[63] In his letter to T. Eaton, secretary, Sheffield Trades and Labour Council, Menon explained that the India League arranged for Masani to address a series of public meetings in the big industrial towns during the latter half of October 1935.[64] The approximate date at which he would be in each town had already been fixed. Masani's itinerary included a series of lectures to the various University Labour and Socialist clubs, the arrangement for these having already been made by the University Labour Federation.[65] Menon's prolonged illness was a nettling problem as his active participation in the organization was missing and in the absence of the principal motivator the League seemed somewhat rudderless. Eaton and many others were urged to come forward to extend their time in organizing the meetings and ensuring the cooperation of the No More War Movement and the Socialist League. Menon was keen to stress that the India League was particularly anxious that the scope of Masani's meetings should be as wide as possible and that the audience should be predominantly composed of the working class. He added that the India League should do everything possible in the way of supplying literature for sale and urged its local leaders to assist in any direction they could. But the League must insist that the actual organization of the meetings should be undertaken by the respective local Labour Parties.[66]

Towards the concluding phase of Masani's visit the India League decided to hold an afternoon conference and evening public meeting on 2 November 1935, at the Memorial Hall in London.[67] The conference was to be in the nature of a farewell meeting to Masani after he had toured the industrial areas where local meetings had been arranged. Requesting Brailsford to speak at the evening public meeting failing which, to help the League at the conference in the afternoon, Menon entreated him to accept the invitation. The Indian movement, he thought, should be tied up with the international situation.[68] Brailsford was requested to consider the suggestion that it was advisable to make a wider appeal for the conference than the subject of India alone. Together with the international implications and ramifications, the question of imperialism must be taken up as well with the repercussions of imperialism in India as the main theme and, finally, the whole issue might be related to the Italian-Abyssinian dispute.[69]

Meanwhile, some cheerful information inspirited Menon into action: *Kaise-i-Hind* decided Menon on as their correspondent; the *United Press* had been urged to consider Menon favourably for the London office whenever it was opened; Amritlal Shah had been requested to drop Pulin Seal and appoint Menon as the representative of the *Janmabhoomi*.[70] It was decided that the weekly of the CSP would resume publication from December 1935, and Ashok Mehta urged that it being the only socialist journal in India, a weekly 'London Letter' by Menon and similar political letters from some continental centres were quite imperative for its reputation.[71] Menon was also entreated to get contributions from radical writers and leaders in the West. If it was not possible to get these contributions as fraternal gestures, the *Congress Socialist* would be willing to pay a reasonable amount for an article of average length.[72] By then, Menon, as an accredited representative of the *Congress Socialist*, had been urging and prodding men of eminence such as Konni Zilliacus and Harold Laski to write for the *Congress Socialist*. Menon, however, had been still out of action due to illness.[73] By 22 August 1935, Madame Morins in France was informed by Joan Bourne that Menon seemed somewhat better, though he was still very weak. He had a very bad time and worried a great deal about not being able to attend to all his India League and other works.[74] There were quite a few of his admirers who made it a point to come to the Strand regularly and try to carry on his work with the hope that he would not have quite so much to do when he was better.[75]

In his communication to Wedgwood Benn, Menon had expressed his desire that Benn should meet Masani basically to know and assess all the latest developments in India. The Congress Socialist movement, Menon wrote enthusiastically, was then the most vital force in India and represented at least one-third of the strength of the Congress.[76] That force, he added, would play an influential part for many years to come. He would have accompanied Masani to Benn, but for the fact that he was ill for the preceding four months and for 10 weeks he had been confined to a hospital bed.[77] To Attlee he recommended Masani, emphasizing that very little was known in England of the socialist advance in India which had been challenging the old leadership of the Congress, and demanding that the overthrow of imperialism should be simultaneous with the victory of the masses.[78] Menon clarified that although Menon and the Congress Socialist Party profoundly disagreed with many of the views on India represented by Attlee, he thought that face to face interaction with a number of representative Labour leaders, including Attlee, would help them appreciate and understand each other's viewpoints on a rational plane and this was one of the reasons why Masani attended the Labour Party conference as a visitor.[79] To Arthur Greenwood, MP, Menon was more forthright. He was keen to impress upon Greenwood that Masani represented the most lively force in India and that he should not go by the stereotyped information supplied by the International Department of Transport House.[80] The CSP whose real leader was Nehru, he confided, contained 'all the younger men who are not wedded to the spinning wheel philosophy'.[81] Menon felt that it was most important that someone like Greenwood, in official circles of the Labour Party, should have an intimate knowledge of the movement which was at least as near to the British Labour movement as the Austrian one. It was with much difficulty that the initial misgivings of the No More War Movement under the chairmanship of a sympathetic Wilfred Wellock were overcome. It was persuaded to organize a meeting on India and Menon goaded that pacifist Gandhian outfit to welcome Masani warmly.[82]

On his return home, Masani gracefully reciprocated Menon's ungrudging assistance in Britain.[83] Assessing the currents of opinion in India, he sought to communicate to Menon the substance of his perception of the Indian situation.[84] It seemed to him that Nehru was certain to become president of the Congress as Gandhi himself had been supporting Nehru and there was no other candidate in the field.[85] There were two conflicting points of view on Nehru's candidature for the position. While the socialists were, by and large, of the opinion that Nehru's accession might be in favour of the progressives and the radical young men, the right-wing of the Congress Party was equally confident that by putting him in the president's chair they 'will be gagging Nehru and make him carry out the Mahatma's policies.'[86] The socialists, however, were not prepared to accept that Nehru with all his progressive pronouncements, enlightened worldview and commitments to socialism would allow himself to be used as an artifice for counterrevolution.[87] Masani also reported that an all-out effort was known to be in the offing to oust all Congress socialists from the Congress organization, which prompted the CSP to issue an unambiguous manifesto refuting some of the insinuations. The strength of the socialists was that Nehru was far too well-read and far too sincere an intellectual to fall for any form of irrational dogmatism.[88]

In conformity with this cordial state of cooperation Menon felt that it would be worth his while to persuade Jayaprakash

Narayan to keep in touch with him in a meaningful way.[89] Menon complained that even the AICC circulars were not received any longer by the India League, although the League was expected to do a good deal of India work in England.[90] Menon wondered if the CSP friends could raise the matter at relevant places. Making an oblique reference to the perception and policies of the Conciliation Group, Menon felt uneasy at the misplaced confidence entertained by that group from the leading nationalist platform in India.[91] 'It seems to me', he wrote, 'a pity why the reliance of Congress leaders should be entirely placed on those whose politics are least like that of Congress'.[92] Menon wondered cryptically if, 'the Congress was a completely one man cult now'.[93] He entreated Masani to take up the question in earnest and in view of 'our work on the deputation, and what we have done here and so on, see to it that at least we are not boycotted'.[94] Menon was excited at the overall success of the CSP and strongly felt that if the party could obtain some mass support, the future would certainly belong to it.[95]

It was small wonder that a stray acquaintance of the LSE days would blossom into an assured and confident political fellowship. Menon wrote long and explanatory letters often enough and Masani replied with sincere warmth of a rekindled camaraderie.[96] At one stage Menon overheard that there was some talk of an appeal by the Government of India to the Privy Council urging Masani's suspension from the Bar.[97] In case it was so, Menon desired to know who had been handling 'your side of it.'[98] He was himself then practising at the Bar and offered his service: 'I shall do my own best but if government takes the course, I fear it would cost you money.'[99] Pritt might be interested in the matter but there was the major question of solicitors. Menon was enthusiastic to help, if required.[100] Seeking Masani's assistance for securing a London assignment of any Indian newspaper, Menon sounded quite spirited: 'Being a mere Indian and not particularly good at being all things to all men I am afraid I am not good enough for the Nationalist press. But one lives until one finds it impossible even to live.'[101] He gave Masani the permission to use his personal letters as much of them as he liked for official purposes 'within your own discretion.'[102] Living on a few weekend schools, Menon nevertheless volunteered to do what he could to interest returning Indians in the work of the CSP. 'Please do not hesitate', Menon concluded his newsy letter to Masani, 'to write to me at any time if there is anything you would like me to do personally or otherwise.'[103]

Gandhi's strategy and direction of India's struggle had been facing an uncompromising opposition from the international communist movement. In an open letter to the Indian communists, the Central Committee of the Communist Party of China revealed and discussed the communist perspective of the Indian 'revolution'. It asserted that the chief causes of the defeat of the Paris Commune was the absence of a party of revolutionary proletariat. The revolutionary experience in Germany, Austria and Italy in the period, 1918-20 showed that without a strong communist party, the proletariat was unable to defeat the bourgeoisie and suffered a defeat. In contrast, the working class of Russia was able to overthrow the 'hated monarchy', to put a complete end to the oppression of the landlords, to destroy the capitalist exploitation, to establish the dictatorship of the proletariat and fashion a radical improvement of the conditions of the working class. This remarkable transformation was possible due to the leadership of an 'iron, monolithic Communist Party' created in the course of a bitter struggle. The consistent ideological and organizational growth of the Chinese Communist Party, the letter asserted, was owing to the fighting powers, correct understanding and the dedicated loyalty of the Chinese party to the interests of the people. The success of the revolutionary struggle of the Chinese Soviet movement and the Red Army was primarily due to the party's comprehension of the ground realities, its singlemindedness in spearheading the movement and its disciplined loyalty to the defined objective. In contrast, in India the 'tremendous movement of strikes' and 'a big movement of the peasant masses' did not find an effective militant leadership of a communist party and the massive upsurge of the national independence petered out as the National Congress capitulated before imperialism. The Chinese Communist Party claimed that the Congress, led by Gandhi, called off the mass civil disobedience movement and did its best to transfer the struggle against the constitution into the 'channels of peaceful reformist activities' for improving the caste system and for an agreement 'with the Mussalman priesthood and the landed gentry.' The Chinese party stated categorically, with a touch of self-righteousness, that the experience had proved that the path of non-violence and passive resistance and conciliatory negotiations pursued by the leaders of the National Congress was 'totally bankrupt.' It was destined to play into the hands of imperialism and invariably led to the further enslavement of India. The experience, the Chinese party affirmed, confirmed once more the prophetic teaching of Lenin that, in that epoch of imperialism there was no salvation for the colonial peoples, except through the path of the people's revolution under the leadership of the proletariat, headed by the Communist Party. The task of the revolutionary party in India, it was suggested, should be to expose the true character of the National Congress, to paralyze its attempt to exert influence on the masses and to sharpen the struggle against the Congress and its machiavellian 'left' reformist leadership. In that hour of crisis in world history, the CPI was called upon to organize and prepare the masses for a 'decisive' struggle against imperialism and its henchmen.[104]

Ben Bradley and R. Palme Dutt sought to scan the programme of the new socialist formation within the Congress in order to 'unmask' the rhetoric of the party and uphold its real intentions. Bradley argued that the disappointment of masses of India was intense as they watched helplessly the withdrawal of the civil disobedience movement by the Congress leadership whose concern for negotiations was an overwhelming consideration leading to periodical betrayal of peoples' democratic upsurge. The working class, the peasantry and the broad strata of the urban petty bourgeoisie were no longer inclined to have faith in Gandhi and his followers. It was precisely at that hour of crisis, Bradley wrote, that Congress leaders organized the All-India Congress Socialist Party with an extensive programme full of good intentions and promises. But behind the platitudes, engagements and espousals there was a sinister design to utilize socialist slogans for keeping the masses from going over to the side of the revolution. The CSP, therefore, had been conspicuously silent about the revolutionary seizure of power, about the establishment of a rerevolutionary dictatorship and about the Soviets. The CSP, unlike the CPI, did not desire to fight, did not indicate the path of the mass revolutionary struggle; and they were compelled to fight against the communists. In that context, Bradley expatiated that *Purna Swaraj,* based on non-violent action, was merely a false label for misleading and doping the masses. It was asserted that every honest adherent to the cause of Indian independence would understand that the CSP was at the service of Indian conciliatory bourgeoisie. The party did not seriously consider the question of class struggle and it had no intention of fighting imperialism. Bradley thought that Gandhi, Nehru and others had long since been bargaining for getting concessions from the British rulers. Nehru and his adherents had moved one step away from Gandhi, only to make it easier to mislead the masses by promising to introduce socialism in India by peaceful and lawful means. Bradley argued that the Congress Socialists would not find even one example from the history of humanity where radical change in the whole social order occurred without a violent struggle, without a bitter resistance by the classes that were being overthrown and without an armed struggle between the oppressor and the oppressed. Socialism through *purna swaraj,* Bradley harangued, merely represented 'charlatan jugglery' serving the interests of Indian capital, parasite landowners and rural usury. It was a clumsy endeavour, he wrote, to help Gandhi and his followers out of the difficulty of explanations with the workers. The Indian bourgeoisie and its agents, he added, were afraid of a real national revolution. In the process of self-awakening and self-organization of the Indian proletariat, the Indian bourgeoisie saw the danger of an agrarian peasant revolution and an urban uprising. That is why the bourgeois had been so anxious to welcome the Congress Socialist Party as a new weapon for deceiving the masses. It would serve as an instrument to enfeeble the working class, to divide the ranks of the workers and peasants and to put obstacle in the way of spreading proletarian revolutionary influence in the rural and urban sectors. British 'jailors' would not find 'any better assistants' than 'these falsifiers, masquerading under the cloak of socialism.'[105]

Palme Dutt's critique of the Congress Socialism was more pointed. Referring to the programme of the Socialist Group of Bombay released in February 1934 under the signature of Krishna Menon, M. Setty, M.R. Masani and others with an approving letter from Jawaharlal Nehru, Dutt could not quite appreciate the objective of the new formation. Palme Dutt maintained that the significance of the development must be sought only in the context of the ignonimous capitulation of the Congress movement and the widespread confusion in the ranks of the national movement. He felt that the national bourgeoisie, which led the Congress campaign had been alarmed by the overwhelming forces of the mass movement that might menace its own interests. As a consequence, it hastened to call off the whole campaign and took moves for closer cooperation with the British Government. In the face of the disillusionment of the mass movement with the temporising leadership of the Congress, increasing numbers of the Congress supporters began to turn to the attractive revolutionary programme of Communism. It is at this point that the Congress Socialist group was brought to the front under the direct sponsorship of the official Congress leadership responsible for the capitulation represented by Jawaharlald Nehru and even with the blessings of Gandhi. Dutt's considered opinion was that the CSP was not a genuine new political outfit but 'a manoeuvre of the bankrupt Congress leadership to conceal its bankruptcy and adapt it forcibly under a new "socialist" coat of paint (the Nazis also call themselves "socialist") to the new currents among the masses.' Despite the presence of some sincere elements in the formation, it was clear to Dutt that the whole exercise was 'being politically exploited for the benefit of the bourgeoisie.' Palme Dutt emphasized that the CSP ignored the basic fundamentals of socialism and its programme confirmed that analysis. Socialism was the movement, Dutt expatiated, for the emancipation of the working class and the overthrow of bourgeois rule and the establishment of a new society of collective production. The heart of socialism, Dutt wrote, was the class struggle, the organization of an independent working class political party, a socialist programme and the dictatorship of the proletariat. The omission of the 'ABC of socialism' in the CSP programme amply illustrated that the real essence of the CSP was the subordination of the working class and peasantry to the political leadership of the bourgeoisie represented by the Congress. The combination of Gandhi and Nehru represented the cunning duplicity of the new strategy. In the final analysis, the new formation the of CSP echoed the familiar line of class cooperation. Calling for building the independent political organization of the working class, Palme Dutt declared that the task of socialists in India was 'to strive to establish the hegemony of the working class in the mass struggle in opposition to the leadership of the national bourgeoisie represented by the Congress.'[106]

No perceptive observer, and Menon was one of them, could have doubted that the ideology of the CSP was a curious blend of Marxist elements, British socialism of the Labour Party vintage, a strong social democracy strand mixed with Gandhian concepts of *satyagraha* and civil disobedience techniques, and *vedanta* socialism which stressed the values of ancient India's heritage. Indeed, the leaders of the CSP formed an inharmonious conglomerate. Jayaprakash Narayan and Narendra Dev represented the first element; Minoo R. Masani and Ashok Mehta, the second; Achchyuta Patwardhan and R.M. Lohia, the third strand while Sampurnanand stood for the fourth component. In fact, it was the specific peculiarities of the unique historical situation of India's struggle than any conformity in ideology, which brought the leaders together on one platform. Even in the Nasik jail, where the formation of the party was being discussed, sharp differences between the protagonists of scientific socialism and those of social democracy were focussed. The contradiction remained unresolved and this ideological confusion plagued the party's existence even in the year of its foundation.[107]

Menon had developed a firm conviction that the National Congress was not a political party but a movement. The principal attribute of that movement was its increasingly vibrant mass affiliation. Its essential thrust was anti-imperialism. A secular united identity of that mass-movement was its essence. The goal was a disciplined struggle against the mighty empire which was the foundation of the basic problem—the problem of poverty and backwardness. But, the political revolution was indispensable for a complete social revolution. A united front of socially conscious political forces under the Congress umbrella was imperative.

In view of the consolidation of the fascist forces in the continent and the increasing membership of the volatile British Union of Fascists (which in 1934 and 1935 ranged from 1,700 and 35,000), there was a sincere review and introspection in the Left which called, at various levels, for the unity of progressive socialist forces aiming at a new order of society. The fascist forces depended heavily on economic crises and unemployment. Its ideological position was rooted in anti-semitism, anti-communism, an obsession with international financiers, belief in the efficacy of social credit, sympathy for Nazi Germany, safeguard and guarantee against foreign competition, a firm hand in India, protection of the Lancashire cotton industry and latent authoritarianism masquerading as parliamentary reform.[108] R. Benewick noted that many people in the leadership of the British Union of Fascists had a public-school background and it included a significant number of ex-officers. Besides, Mussolini and Hitler drew a good of deal approval from many members of the Establishment throughout the 1930s because of the anti-communist thrust of fascist politics. It meant a marked indulgence of conservative forces towards authoritarianism.[109]

The annual conference of the University Labour Federation, in the first week of January 1935, encapsulated the growing urge of the British student societies, the youth leagues, and young workers associations for industrial democracy, socialist unity and an economic system based not on profit, but human needs. Calling upon the younger generation to come forward with creative suggestions for the foundation of a Socialist Commonwealth and solving once and for all the problems of war, Arthur Greenwood MP, one of the active members of the India League, emphasized in his presidential address that war and socialism were incompatible, that the empire was perpetual aggression based on naked force and that the new order of society could only be fashioned by socialists. James Klugmann, the incisive Marxist theoretician, added to this, the importance of anti-war and anti-fascist programme of the new awareness and he applauded the firm determination of widely differing schools of opinion represented in the Federation to work for a peaceful constructive world order. There should be, it was agreed, a broad understanding between Student's Christian Movement, League of Nations Union, orthodox socialists, communists and the India League and together they should be able to work out a common line of action.[110]

In March 1935 came the news of the massacre at Karachi on 19 March, when a platoon of the Sussex Regiment was ordered to open fire on an excited crowd of Muslims with the result that 35 were killed and 100 wounded. The large number of casualties was due to close range of firing. Equally disturbing was the announcement that the demand for an enquiry had been refused. The League Against Imperialism and the India League came together and their joint statement deplored the incident as an evidence of state terrorism in India. It was also felt that the British Government never lost an opportunity of provoking communal sentiments in India and it was difficult to overlook that the same mindset had been operating in the Karachi incident.[111] This was the first serious attempt to make a united demonstration of protest. The deputation of this new combination included, apart from Bridgeman and Menon, representatives of the National Council for Civil Liberties, the Indian Conciliation Group and Friends of India and many other organized groups. The deputation which waited on the Secretary of State was representative not only of the Muslims, Hindus and Parsis but also of persons of British and other nationalities. Its character was not national but international.[112] It recorded strong feelings which were widely held about the uncalled-for shooting by British troops on an unarmed Muslim crowd demonstrating peacefully. No warning had been given and the firing was indiscriminate and excessive. The refusal of an enquiry merely confirmed an impression that there was something to conceal. The Karachi incident was placed in the context of the consolidation of authoritarian and repressive forces as an international phenomenon: employment of British troops in Egypt and Sikh troops in Shanghai, Spanish government deploying troops from Morocco to suppress movement in the province of Austrians, and Algerian, Senegalese and Annamite regiments being stationed within easy reach of Paris and big industrial cities.[113] The deputation urged the appointemnt of a commission of enquiry to investigate the Karachi incident, and to recommend a scheme by which the use of armed forces in civil administration could be avoided. The India Office declined to receive the deputation and both Brailsford and Bridgeman agreed that it was imperative to encourage the India League to organize a broad front with all the persons and institutions who were anti-imperialist in inspiration to resist the constitutional scheme of the British Government for the future of India.[114] By then, the celebration of Indian independence on 26 January had become an annual affair with a firm united demonstration against the British government and its India policy.[115]

But Bridgeman's suggestion for the formation of an India Freedom Committee to campaign against the Government of India bill evoked mixed feelings. The executive of the India League felt that the League would not be able to embark on an active campaign of big meetings, rallies and conferences. The League, Menon reported, did not have at its disposal the resources for undertaking or forming an inclusive organization. The India League, had on its hands, a large number of meetings. It had also to provide speakers and look after the output of a substantial amount quantity of literature so that it was quite unable to undertake any more responsibility. Menon felt that with the existing composition of the League's executive committee and the 'nature of support we obtain' it would be of little consequence to our common cause 'if we proceed on the lines you suggest.'[116] Evidently, Menon had been jealously guarding the India League's position as the dominant spokesman for India's *purna swaraj.* That claim was appreciated by a substantial section of informed public opinion. Menon believed that the League's credibility would be braced up by the participation of various organizations under its banner. Its hegemony in India's struggle in Britain should nevertheless be maintained unimpaired and Menon was eager to ensure that commanding position. It should not be diluted, he thought, by joint and equal partnerships by political units and organizations of uneven strength, fading tenacity and marginal importance under the veneer of unity, goodwill and camaraderie.

The socialist thrust of the League since 1934 found its comprehensive expression in the pamphlet entitled, *India Speaks.*[117] It is a compilation of a few excerpts with a stimulating foreword by Laski. In his sharply worded introductory remarks, Laski detected in India a shadow of the repressive dictatorships of Italy and Germany. The suppression of freedom of speech, imprisonments without trial, the use, as the recent Nehru case showed, of an enormous system of informers, and the reliance upon a rule of ordinance were so savage and inhuman that the system should not be tolerated by the British people.[118] The repressive press legislation had become commonplace in Indian political life. There was no cure for them as they were the inevitable consequences of the existing regime which rested on coercion and not on consent, having lost all credibility and respect. Laski maintained that it was a classic example of imperialism subjecting a nation to itself because force was on its side. It intensified arrogance in those who ruled, deepened servility in those who accepted arbitrary restraint, violence and indignity and stimulated annoyance and resentment in those who believed in liberal values and political decency. Repression of India's right to self-expression and self-determination would invariably 'breed a habit of suppression among ourselves'. Laski reminded that those who had been fighting for India's democratic rights were the true guardians of 'our own liberties'.

India Speaks consisted of a few political discourses that encapsulated the spirit and urge of India's struggle. The first was India's declaration of independence, the proclamation by Jawaharlal Nehru in Christmas week at the Lahore session of the Congress in 1929, where he declared that it was 'the inalienable right' of the Indian people 'to have freedom and to enjoy the fruits of their toil and have the necessities of life so that they may have full opportunities of growth', and resolved to establish *purna swaraj* in order to engage in the glorious pursuits of life. The second piece by Nehru, 'The Indian Struggle' was an extract from his *Recent Essay and Writings* in which Nehru expounded the proposition that the Indian struggle was a part of the international struggle for the emancipation of the oppressed. It was basically 'an economic struggle, with hunger and want as its driving forces, although it puts on a nationalist dress'. Politically, it meant independence and severance of the British connection, and economically and socially it meant the termination of all special class privileges and vested interests. Freedom, Nehru maintained, could not be divorced from life and the vital economic issues. The welfare of the masses could no longer be the concern of 'palace intrigues', 'parlour politics' or the 'manners of the drawing room'. The masses had entered politics. 'Their school is the school of events and suffering is their teacher.' They learnt their politics 'from great movements which bring out the true nature of individuals and classes' and the civil disobedience movement had taught the Indian masses many lessons which they would never pass over. Isolation in a world which was becoming more of a unit through cooperation and interdependence was neither desirable nor a feasible ideal. Indian national resurgence could not go against this irresistible historical tendency. But world cooperation was feasible only after the attainment of freedom from all imperialist countries. If imperialism, Nehru asserted, was wiped out of Britain 'we shall gladly cooperate with her in the wider international field not otherwise.'

There was also in the League's pamphlet an excerpt from Gandhi's statement, *India and the National Congress,* published by the League in early 1932. In *What India Demands,* Gandhi reiterated that India was essentially an agricultural country where cultivation largely depended on the rainfall, that the average income of an Indian, including the millionaires, was 2d per day in contrast with the British average of 4S. per day, that the result of British rule was abject pauperization and the emasculation of an entire nation, that the whole population was disarmed and the government was not responsible in the real sense. Of the various organizations whose object was to free India, the most popular and effective body was the Indian National Congress which had been daily growing in influence and popularity. The Congress demand for complete independence necessarily included full control in the hands of the responsible government over the defence forces, external affairs and finance with such safeguards as might be necessary in the interests of India and complete independence did not exclude partnership but only on absolutely equal terms.

In another informative piece, Menon gave *Some Facts and Figures* that presented the contours of an average Indian life in a most blatant and startling way. There were at least 70 million people in India who were hungry each and every day in their lives, the masses of the Indian people subsisted on less nourishment than the amount laid down for convicts in the jail manual; Dr A.C. Bentley, director of health services, Bengal, in his report for 1927-8 stated that the peasantry of Bengal were, in a very large proportion, accustomed to a diet on which even rats could not live more than five weeks; the average annual income in India was stated by Indian economists to be about £3 per head although the Simon commission placed it much higher;

in the towns and villages the people were heavily debt-laden; only 9 per cent of the population could read or write; the sanitary conditions defied description; in cities there were thousands of tenaments where six families lived in one room, where all the cooking was done, the babies were born and the parents died; 75 per cent of the babies of working-class mothers in some areas were drugged with opium; it was estimated that a million people died, million were maimed and 50 million suffered from malaria each year; in 1930 the infant death-rate was 180-83 per 1000 as against 173-77 in 1929, etc. etc.

Nehru's article on 'The States of the Indian Princes' set the context and perspective of the proposed federation and official singsong about it. Nehru stressed that in India all the reactionary elements -- British and Indian -- had been combining together to delay and, if possible, prevent the freedom of the Indian people and the white paper was an attempt to consolidate the hold of all these vested interests. Nothing was more significant than the utterly reactionary attitude of the Indian princes and the backing it received from the government. Nehru argued that it was quite probable that free India would be a federation but the proposed federation in the white paper was meant to prevent India's growth and to enchain her still further to feudal and out-of-date systems. It was quite impossible, Nehru wrote, 'to progress from this federation to freedom without breaking the federation to pieces'. Nehru was clear that one must stick to *purna swaraj* which meant, complete absence of foreign control as well as the establishment of a fully democratic form of government. The existing state system must go, root and branch.

The central piece of the pamphlet was *Labour and the Congress* by Jawaharlal Nehru. It recalled the significant role of Labour in the Indian struggle then caught up in the grip of the social and economic crisis of the world. He stressed that the burden of ideological leadership must remain with Labour. In India, Nehru argued, it was but natural that the national struggle covered and hid social stratifications and tensions. But the pace of world events had been working for a meaningful socialistic orientation of national movement. It was becoming more social and economic. The struggle between the forces of Labour and those of vested interest had become the crucial and inexorable phenomenon. In India, the social struggle and national struggle had been entwined intimately, and it was not feasible or even desirable to compromise with petty social and political demands any longer. In view of the world situation, it was indispensable that one was to prepare oneself for a complete change of regime. 'Nothing else', Nehru reminded, 'should satisfy us, nothing else can solve our problems.'

Nehru maintained that India was then in a confused state of mind. The old nationalist ideology did not harmonize with the changing circumstances of the world. The adaptation of the old nationalism to the impulses of socialism, given rise to by the contemporary economic forces, might be laboured and painful but it was inevitable. It was only by fusing progressive ideology of social revolution with nationalism that India would be able to participate effectively in the freedom struggle as well as in the world struggle and in that struggle Labour had to be in a dominant position. The national struggle and the economic struggle must join hands and close their ranks for the emancipation of the people of India. Nehru asserted that economically and historically, Labour was the most important class of the future endowed with a clear perception and a purposeful ideology. But this revolutionary group must appreciate the nuances of imperial domination. It must recognize that national problems in India overshadowed social problems and made nationalism 'more revolutionary than the social struggle.' The Congress, Nehru concluded, was a national organization striving for political freedom and included many classes and groups with conflicting social interests. But the common national programme kept them together. Though inclined to favour a socialist programme, it was far from socialist. Elements in the Congress movement were backward and often very reactionary, reflecting the uneven nature of the country's social and ideological growth and the presence of conflicting interests under one umbrella. Nevertheless, it was a militant organization. Evidently, judged by its social base, the Congress programme did not offer an advanced socialist perspective. Yet, it was possible to have its cooperation in the course of militant activities while trying to push the Congress on to an economic orientation in consonance with the labour programme. In fact, *India Speaks* was presented as an overall estimate of the national movement in India from the viewpoint of a new and young generation of socialist activists under the guidance of a charismatic personality. Menon was then the accredited representative of the Congress Socialist Party in charge of the party's propaganda in Europe and one of its principal interpreters. He had assessed the main currents of India's political life carefully.

In a world overrun by fascism and militarism, even an ordinary observer could not overlook the sure and steady decline of the League of Nations as a reliable international body, and the gradual decay of the spirit of collective security. Harry Pollitt's assessment of the National government between 1931 and 1935 offered a depressing prospect: at home -- cuts in wages and benefits; continued unemployment; reduced expenditure on housing; education and all social services; high food prices; the Sedition Act; blackshirts, their frequent rallies and bitter clashes with communists; considerable police indulgence and a modicum of social recognition for Oswald Mosley. Abroad -- a tariff war on Ireland, a repressive regime and an oppressive constitution for India; no representative government for Egypt; connivance of Japan's seizure of Manchuria and Hitler's increased armament; tolerance of Mussolini's preparation for war on Abyssinia and a hostile, belligerent stance against the Soviet Union.[119]

The Nazi revolution had a deep impression throughout. The dominant feeling was one of moral indignation at Nazi excesses. But there was also a sense of anxiety at the blatant opposition to peace settlement. It was evident that Germany's initial advance should be southward, threatening Austria. The revival of Germany made French concern for security somewhat unsettled. The summer of 1933 witnessed a rapid *rapprochement,* based on a common fear of Germany, between the Soviet Union and France. M. Litvinov's visit to Washington in November 1933 and the American recognition of the Soviet government were aimed at neutralizing the threat from Germany and Japan.[120] In July 1934, France, Great Britain and Italy began canvassing for the admission in the League of the Soviet Union. Soon there was also a move to work out the Eastern Pact between France and the Soviet Union approved by Britain and in 1935 the pre-war France-Russian alliance was reconstituted.[121] By March 1933, broadcasts attacking the Austrian government had become a constant feature of the Munich programme. The general indignation against Hitler's excesses was intensified by the German campaign against Austria. In January 1935, the fate of Saar was decided by a plebiscite; on 16 March 1935 Hitler announced that Germany no longer considered herself bound by the military clauses of the Versailles treaty; in June 1935, an Anglo-German naval agreement explicitly recognized the German right to ignore naval restrictions imposed by the treaty.[122] The vacillation of British policy was conspicuous. During the first two years of Nazi rule, the British government had encouraged the French, the Italians and the Soviet governments to build a system of defensive alliance. But by January 1935, when that system was virtually completed, there was a growing body of opinion in British political life which

£ 1,000 APPEAL

We need £1,000 for THE INDIA WEEK inaugurating the 1944 National Campaign for a settlement with India.

We appeal to you for as generous a donation as it is possible for you to make.

REGINALD SORENSEN.
V K. KRISHNA MENON.

December, 1943.

DONATION FORM

To THE INDIA LEAGUE,
165 Strand, London, W C 2.

Enclosed please find cheque/postal order for £ 1 s. / d. which is our/my donation to your funds in response to your £1,000 Appeal for India Week.

N.B.—Cheques should be made payable to The India League, and crossed.

Signature [signature]

NAME Dr Eustace Chesser

ADDRESS 43 Upper Brook Str
W.1

Printed by The Apollo Press, 53 Theobalds Road, London, W.C.1.

Appeal by the India league for a fighting fund of £1000, December, 1943. Menon Papers

With the Indian students in Manchester in 1941. Courtesy Mr and Mrs. Bolt.

With Julius Silverman and Yusuf Dandoo, 1952. Menon Pepers

THE NATIONAL COUNCIL FOR CIVIL LIBERTIES

3 DANSEY PLACE, WARDOUR STREET
LONDON, W.1

TELEPHONE: GERRARD 2337
TELEGRAMS: GERRARD 2337 LONDON

Secretary: RONALD KIDD
Joint Honorary Treasurers: HUGH FRANKLIN AND SYLVIA CROWTHER-SMITH, B.A.

RK/VW. 11th March, 1935.

Krishna Menon Esq.,
The India League,
165, Strand,
W.C.2.

Dear Krishna Menon,

I must apologise for not having sent you a postal order for 1/11d a long time ago for a copy of the Condition of India. I now enclose a postal order herewith. Unfortunately, the matter was overlooked when I disposed of my bookshop in Villiers Street.

My Committee instructed me to ask you whether you have had any information about the banning in India of "The Indian Struggle 1920 to 1934" by Subhas C. Bose published recently by Wishart.

We have in our possession a certain amount of information about the extraordinary methods of repression carried out in India and we have been intending for some time to publish some kind of leaflet or pamphlet protesting against the denial of civil rights to Indians. We feel that our Council ought to make some pronouncement on the grosser features of repression in India and I am wondering whether you and Monica Whately might be able to spare me a little time in which you could suggest the best way to handle this matter. You and she would have first hand knowledge of the subject and could give us some very useful advice if you could spare the time.

With kind regards,

Yours sincerely,

Ronald Kidd

520 Secretary.

Encl. P.O.

Ronald kidd (the National Concil for Civil Liberaties) to Menon, 11 March 1935. Menon Papers

165 Strand,
London W.C.2.

Dear Sub-Warden

I regret the delay in writing to you as promised when I met you last. I should be gladto come to Toynbee Hall and do a few lectures voluntarily as you suggested.

With regard to my qualifications on which you wanted a memorandum, ther are:

B.A. in History and Economics Madras University, India
B.Sc. (Econ) with First Class Honours (Political Science as special subject)
M.A. by research in psychology (University College London)
Teachers' Diploma (London University)
Intermediate in Laws) Completing Law studies for LL.B.
Part I Bar exams) and Barrister at Law degrees this summer.

In addition to this I have done all the subjectsand taken the B.A. Honours examination of London in Psychology with philosophy as subsidiary subject, without a degree, prior to my M.A.
I have also been engaged in research on pyschology and politics for the last so manyyears.

My experience of speaking and discussion with working class audiences extends to about six years and I have spoken on political and economic subjects to hundreds of labour parties, Trade Unions Adult schools &c. I have also taken W.E.A. classes occasionally and am hoping to do regular tutorial work in the coming winter.

I hope the above particulars is what you want. I am grateful to you for giving me your time the other day.

Yours sincerely
V.K.Krishna Menon

Meno to the Warden, Toynbee Hall, 20 Febuary 1934, Menon Papers

Photograph of the ambulance contributed by the League's Spain - India Aid Committee in the name of the people of India to the Spanish democrats. Menon Papers.

INDIAN CONCILIATION GROUP.

Chairman:—CARL HEATH.
Hon. Secretary:—AGATHA HARRISON.

Please reply to:—
at—
2, CRANBOURNE COURT,
ALBERT BRIDGE ROAD, S.W.11
BATTERSEA 2400.

Oct.23rd 1935

Dear Horace,

About Nehru. Mrs Dutt has just rung up to tell me that they are forming a cttee to receive J.N. when he arrives on Tuesday-and plan a gathering for tea on the Thursday. They may have already asked you to serve on this cttee-she asked me to send names as they are anxious to get it as representative as possible. I have sent yours and C.H's names-and I do hope that both of you will serve. Polak,C.F.A. and I have all said yes. I take it you will be down next week-in that case you may be able to be at the station-it comes at a time of that Christian College thing. But if he does not get here till 4 or so-we could go to both.

About his coming to you. It will have to be left until he comes. I agree with you that he and C.H. must talk alone- and this I shall manage somehow.

About Krishna. Oh the hours of trying to disentangle his affairs. It looks as though Mrs Travis may be able to have him a little later on-and Mrs Haeglers daughter is taking him in as soon as he gets out of the Hospital. She talked for ages to me on the money question. She says that any money he gets she feels is poured into the League-she feels that his friends could collect some for the next three or six months-but is strongly of the opinion that this ought to be given him each week for living. She thought that Polak would be a good person to have this in hand. C.F.A. feels that Krishna would not like this. I told her you had been active-and what I would suggest is that the whole thing is left over till you come and can talk with him and some of us. Else wires will be crossed. He has the extraordinary faculty of getting many of his friends all working alone on his situation. Please let me know when I can see you as soon as you come-for I believe we could clear this.

Hastily.

Agatha

Agatha Harrison (India Conciliation Group) to Harace Alexender, 23 October 1935. Horace Alexander Papers (Teen Murti) began to appreciate the view that the system of defensive alliance had merely aggravated German danger and it was imperative that Germany should be assuaged.[123] The Anglo-German naval agreement (16 March 1935), concessions to the Abyssinian design of Mussolini leading to the Hoare-Laval plan (December 1935); the repudiation of the Locarno treaty and the system of collective security, the occupation of the Rhineland (7 March 1936), the formal inauguration of the civil war in Spain (July 1936), following a precarious balance between democratic and socialist forces on the one hand, and the royalist and reactionary forces on the other, by the military rebellion of General Franco and finally, the agreement between Germany, Japan and Italy as a counterpart of the Franco-Soviet Pact followed in quick succession. The policy of 'cautious neutrality' of Britain merely stimulated the situation and aggravated Germany's bellicosity.[124]

Notwithstanding the gathering storm, there was a tremendous Marxist ideological ascension in Britain. Ideology, as Geoffrey Barraclough puts it succintly, did not operate in a void and Marxism could never have exercised so wide and so powerful an influence if it had been nothing more than an ideological support system of Russian national interests.[125] As a theory, Marxism gave to the intelligentsia an impression of systematic coherence, self-sufficiency and comprehensiveness; it had a universal applicability and a significant 'appropriateness as a response to the newly arising conditions of mass civilization.'[126] The moderate leadership of the Labour Party and the Trades Union Congress were largely responsible for diverting the new socialist stirrings into communist channels. The Labour Party, as stated earlier, was in a state of continued entropy: in foreign policy it opted for empty gestures, unwillingness to enforce action in defence of peace and justice and ineffective pressure on the government to strive for collective security. The official mind of the party was doused in a deep-seated confusion with regard to the condition of Europe, leading to a remarkable inertia that immobilized all democratic perceptions and inclinations.[127] In national affairs its steadfast refusal to put forward radical policy and adherence to Mond-Turnerism and industrial peace were fashioned in order to retain its distance from the Communist Party.[128] Menon reported with dismay the inability of the Labour leadership to take note of the urgency of a united left force even after the three by-elections in 1933 of Rhondda East, Clay Cross and East Fulham.[129] The success of the Peace Pledge Union (founded in 1934-1935) which drew support from the Christian and Labour pacifists and the Peace ballot, an offshoot of the League of Nations Union, which managed to collect eleven and a half million signatures in 1934-1935, did not energize the self-centred Labour leadership.[130] As the Nazi terror was unleashed, the Communist International appealed for a working class united front in Germany. Anti-fascist committees in Britain sprang up everywhere; the CP continued to expose the complicity of the National government in Hitler's advances; the National Hunger March and the United Congress in February 1934 almost caused a national upheaval.[131] The growing visibility of a vigorous unity campaign enthusiastically entered into by the Socialist League and other left-wing Labour intellectuals and activists and even the high-profile Hyde Park anti-fascist demonstrations on 9 and 10 September 1934, failed to stir the complacent Labour leadership.[132] Herbert Morrison, clarified in no uncertain terms that the difference between the Labour and the Communist Parties were irreconcilable and association with the Communists 'would lose us hundreds of thousands of voters.'[133]

In contrast, there was a good deal of introspection in the Communist Party which had begun to moderate, unofficially, its self-isolation since the *class against class* thesis.[134] Following the advent of Hitler, the process of re-examination and renewal of communist positions was accelerated both in terms of the class position of its adherents and its tactics. Radicalized students, teachers, academics, artists and professionals were openly recruited. The agonising reappraisal was gradual and consistent and the whole process found a momentous expression at the 7th Congress of the Communist International in July/August 1935.[135] It acknowledged that by promoting sharp conflict between the workers and the capitalists and between communists and social democrats, the tactics of *class against class* had prevented an effective united effort to thwart the triumph of National Socialism.[136] The Congress declared emphatically that fascism was qualitatively different from and dangerous than the normal bourgeois rule and it called for a United Peoples' Front against fascism.[137] It was an affirmation of the strategy of united front already initiated in Spain and France[138], and no appreciation of the development of the India League in the mid-1930s would be complete without an assessment of the 7th Congress and the theory of United Front that was put forward by an integrated and creative Marxist thinker and activist, Georgie Dimitrov.[139] It was more so because Menon, by virtue of his relentless advocacy for India's independence, his association with the socialist movement in India, his crucial position as the chief exponent of India's freedom struggle in England, as one of the experienced theoreticians of the Labour Party and of its Socialist League, his comprehension of the international situation, his perception of progressive movements all over the world and his editorial contact with numerous socialist and creative authors had, over the years, fashioned for himself a wide space for consistent intellectual intervention in British life and politics.

Menon and his generation had been watching the formidable advance in all spheres by the Soviet Union which attracted millions of people throughout the world, especially against the background of the ever deepening crisis of the entire capitalist system. The Bolshevik baby had grown in sturdy manhood that prodded the most reactionary sections of the ruling cass in the imperialist countries to undertake a vicious programme against the Soviet Union and communism. They also noticed that the rise and consolidation of fascism was rendered possible because of the failure of the socialist revolution in Germany, Italy, Hungary and Bulgaria. As early as July 1923, Kara Zetkin cried out: 'Historically fascism is the punishment of the proletariat in Western and Central Europe for failing to carry out the revolution begun in Russia.'[140] The triumph of counterrevolution was possible as the feeble socialist leadership capitulated everywhere to the savage and repressive apparatus of the fascists. The advancement of fascism became irresistible since the socialists and the communists failed to forge a united struggle against fascism.[141]

Dimitrov's presentation began with an analysis of the levels of consciousness of the working class and of the broader mass of working people. Since the economic crisis, Dimitrov argued, the common working people had been confronted with unprecedented hardship and were compelled by circumstances to fight the effects of capitalism-in-crisis, before they came to fight and comprehend capitalism itself. It was natural that the communists must find for themselves a rational place at the centre of the daily struggles against all injustices people had been receiving from the capitalist society. These struggles for bread and butter, if properly conducted, would create a sense of solidarity and a spirit of fraternity among the struggling people despite apparent class differentiations. This meant the creation of a united front of the working class and the popular unity of the whole working people and middle class at all levels and on all issues.[142] The basic commitment was that the platforms of the united front should never be appropriated by communists for their exclusive ends. The experiment of united front was to be open, public, sincere, transparent and never a political manoeuvre. In the communist movement, sectarianism was no longer an infantile disorder, but a 'deeply rooted vice' which had to be shaken off. This was a novel and unprecedented experiment in the history of the working class.[143] One important by-product of the new strategy was to put the struggle for democracy back into the centre of the fight for socialism after the lapse of about 8 years or so. Democracy had so far been a debating point in the socialist and communist movement but it was now a concept of enormous importance for the British communist movement, who had aready begun working for a qualitative expansion of the struggle for democracy under capitalism. Every liberty that dealt with human freedom would, henceforth, become the concern of a Marxist.[144] Freedom was indispensable and indivisible and no theoretical casuistry could make, once again, the struggle for India's freedom against imperialism a matter of secondary importance.[145] And, in close proximity to the renewal of socialist democracy was the 're-establishment' of the Marxist concept of patriotism and nationalism. It was now realized that one of the major errors of the communist movement in Germany since the 1930s had been to hand over to the Nazis the wounded national feelings on a platter.[146] It seemed that the communists had virtually equated internationalism with anti-nationalism. One found now that genuine, progressive national feelings and patriotism on the side of popular and proletarian internationalism.[147] Marxist revolutionaries learnt how to internalize the cultural heritage of the past. The French communists put the red flag side by side with the tricolour: British communists in their turn went beyond assessing the insufficiencies of Wat Tyler and the inadequacies of the Jacobins and endeavoured to discover the legacy of the Peasants' revolt, of the left of the English revolution, of the Chartist movement and of the women's suffrage movement since 1790.[148] Marxism linked the past, the present and the future and India League's line of propaganda became relevant to the reinvigorated Marxian probings.[149] The result of the new strategy was extraordinary. The rallying-cry of the communists: 'Fascism means war' had been convincing to all committed socialists. The new slogan, 'If Hitler is a menace to Europe, it was because of Baldwin' was approved even by the liberals and a whole range of politically uncommitted open minds.[150] The defence of bourgeois democracy from fascist onslaught became one of the planks in the struggle for democratic rights and liberties. It constituted an important element in the new tactical and strategic orientation of the international communist movement. It meant to all intents and purposes a struggle to defend the democratic institutions that would broaden itself into a struggle for power. The right-wing of the ILP was for an immediate return to the Labour Party; some left-wingers sought a revolutionary salvation away from the communists; the bulk of the ILP around Maxton and Brockway dithered for a while but then opted for a united front.[151] The Labour leadership, in contrast, maintained in no uncertain terms that differences with the CPGB were irreconcilable and any form of communist affiliation was not the path to power but the sure road to ruin.[152] Despite the obduracy and self-centred opposition of the Labour leadership, the unity movement surged forward, acquired ample space and forged a support base at the very heart of the Labour Party focussed on an exhilarating body of men and women of the highest intellectual attainments and political commitment.[153] The leading lights of the campaign included Stafford Cripps, a prominent Labour MP and a recent and enthusiastic Marxist convert; Harold Laski, the formidable academic theoretician; John Strachey, the gifted popularizer of socialism and imperial issues; Victor Gollancz, whose genius for synthesizing and publicizing the 'ideas of the other' found its notable expression in the Left Book Club; Ivor Montagu, a leading expert on the Soviet Union; R.P. Dutt, the outstanding Marxist analyst, theoretician and communist leader; G.D.H. Cole, author and university professor specializing in social and political theory and an ardent Fabian socialist, Harry Pollitt, general secretary of the CPGB who never failed to strengthen the socialist purpose of his audience and inspire them to further efforts, D.N. Pritt, a member of the executive of parliamentary Labour Party and a leading legal luminary of the empire and many others. With its new networks of factory militants and the Marxist intellectuals, here was a Left which no one who pretended to be a socialist could afford to ignore.[154] One way or another they had to relate their politics to it. The 'United Front' was dedicated to the immediate defeat of fascism and the ultimate triumph of socialism. When the Second World War commenced, the British left was effectively led by the communists. Its membership increased from 2,500 in January 1930 to about 11,500 in 1936 and 17,000 in 1939 reaching 56,000 in 1943. In the process, the professional people, culture workers, people in all types of creative activity and of different class origins became conscious of the class nature of Britain and shared a commitment for socialist transformation.[155]

Most of these leading personalities shared in common the urgency of a united front exacerbated by the reunification of Saarland on 13 January 1935, German conscription on 16 March 1935 and also their contempt for pacifism and the simplistic Christian ethics in the face of fascism. They were stunned by the efficacy of Goebbel's propaganda machine. In sheer desperation they decided to trim some of their ideological idiosyncracies to come together.[156] They feared that fascist bellicosity would result in a European catastrophe. They were convinced that the National government under Stanley Baldwin was impervious to the need of the time and the Communist Party was the only major party to show enthusiasm. Spain was quickly adopted by the United Front as its rallying cry. It absorbed the anti-war movement. The anti-fascist cause continued to dominate the political scene. The necessity of armed defence of Republican Spain against General Franco helped emerge a consistent line of militant anti-fascism for permanent peace by curbing the aggressive tendencies of the fascist powers. Without coming out explicitly in favour of rearmament, the peace movement and the unity propaganda were conveniently used to propagate the virtues of an alliance with France and the Soviet Union.[157]

The strength of anti-fascism was that it mobilized all those who feared war. If fascism meant war, the convincing reaction to that threat was preparedness for war. For the communist and more so for the non-communist left, a commitment against war and militarism was fundamental.[158] It found its eloquent expression in their refusal to support even the necessary military measures to make resistance to fascism effective such as rearmament and conscription. The memory of the First World War was sharp as the impact of that war was both unprecedented and universal. It seemed that the Western world was caught between a reluctance to go to war and a refusal to fight. Yet, unqualified pacifism, though quite popular in Britain in the 1930s, was never a mass movement. 'Conscientious objectors', as Hobsbawm puts it, enjoyed extensive tolerance but the numbers who claimed the right to refuse to fight were small.[159] For Britain it was no longer feasible to hold a global empire with insufficient military might and inadequate navy operating in the three great oceans and in the Mediterranean. It was, therefore, attractive to many in authority to conduct a prolonged negotiation with revived Germany and establish a more durable European peace settlement. But the tragedy was that the revived Germany meant Hitler's Germany. A second world war, the power-elite foreboded, would have certainly meant the ruin of the British economy, the disbandment of large parts of the empire, the victory of colonial movements for freedom, championed by Gandhi and all the rest and the emergence of a third world. It is small wonder, therefore, that for a section of the British elite, even though the German fascism was the barbarous outgrowth of a systematic development of intolerance, it was an infinitely better choice than the destructive social revolution and Bolshevism. But perhaps even appeasement had its limits. Determined efforts were made to detach Italy from Germany or to wean away Mussolini from Hitler and even Chamberlain's Britain was not cheerfully inclined to endorse a Hitler-dominated Europe. It may be conveniently surmised that amidst the various expositions and explanations of the policy of appeasement, the left nationalists such as Nehru and Menon did not overlook the significance of a crucial historical premonition: Hitler's defeat would mean the collapse of authoritarian systems, including the *Raj*.

By November 1935, it was evident that Nehru was the rising star in Indian politics and the successor of a retiring Gandhi.[160] He was to make a short visit to England from the sick-bed of his wife in Lausanne[161] and Agatha Harrison cudgelled her brains as to ascertain the importance of Nehru in Indian politics and mulled over the urgency of ingratiating the sophisticated Indian nationalist to the British left-wing *haute monde* away from the palsied, uncertain and ineffectual combination of a few 'neurotic demagogues' assembled by Menon, who was dismissed by the Quakers in their private correspondence as a 'theoretical babbler'.[162] Accordingly, Lothian was encouraged to invite Nehru to come down to his Norfolk residence for a couple of nights, possibly with Agatha Harrison out of the rush of London, Lord Halifax having expressed his desire to come down from Yorkshire to Blickling Hall, Norfolk to fall in with the refreshing assembly and its *joie de vivre.*[163] Lothian had no doubt that his own views on the Indian situation differed widely from those held by Nehru. But he was all the same convinced that the destinies of India and England were still very closely interlinked. Interactions between a few British statesmen who had been concerned about Indian welfare and some of the younger leaders of India was considered both useful and necessary.[164] That personal relationship was valued by all those who cared for amity and goodwill and their anxiety was shared and nurtured by the India Conciliation Group.[165] Mankind,

Lothian felt, had been passing through certain momentous changes as the old international order and old economic system were breaking up. People were not necessarily myopic in their visions but only a few could comprehend the totality of the transformation of life. This was why one was confronted with a situation when agreements were difficult to make, progress was slow and life was full of agonizing tensions and conflicts.[166] In this context, Lothian and Halifax were keen to establish personal contacts, which, though might lead to no immediate agreement or rapport, might yet pave the way for a lasting understanding later on.[167] Nehru agreed with Lothian that much of the tensions of the world were due to limited perceptions and narrowness of approach and differences between perspectives and comprehensions of statesmen in a conflict-ridden world.[168] Lothian, Nehru wrote, had always had a stimulating impact on his mind. Nehru, however, was quick to affirm that individuals played only a marginal role, especially when 'vast elemental forces were at play against each other.' Thus it was impossible 'to charm away the conflicts merely by friendly contacts between well-intentioned persons.'[169] The conflicts were largely based on ingrained prejudices, varying mindsets, contradictory outlooks and antagonistic convictions. Personal contacts, however, Nehru added, could help to open minds, widen an individual's horizon and lessen bitterness and prejudices. The proposed meeting between the two perceptive observers, endowed with cosmopolitan outlook, could not take place due to prior engagements of both Lothian and Nehru.[170] Lothian, all the same, passed on to Nehru some of his ideas about India and Britain.

Lothian reminded Nehru that they were in the midst of 'one of the most creative epochs of human history' resplendent with the ideals represented by the word socialism.[171] Lothian insisted that Britain had been shedding the old imperialism and was then actively engaged in exploring a way to prevent anarchy, arising out of the universal quest for national self-determination. Lothian was apprehensive that the historical process might end in a fresh war or in a deluge of imperialism.[172] He held forth optimistically that Britain would also shortly embark on the practical problem of reconciling socialism with the liberal traditions of individual liberty and initiative.[173] In this context, he maintained that as power passed into the hands of the political classes in India and as education and the press enhanced and deepened their influence, religion, race and language would assume increasing political importance and authority and they would become viviparous in effect. He, like many of his compatriots, asserted that religion was still the most powerful influence with the masses in India as it had been in Europe.[174] If the constitutional road was rejected, he was certain that India would inevitably follow the example of Europe. To start with, Lothian argued, religious wars would become endemic, especially when they were stimulated for political purposes and India would not emerge out of the chaos in a united body, but divided into a number of dictatorial states separated by race, religion and language and armed to the teeth against one another. Both militarily and economically, India would, with these internal developments, either be completely paralyzed or she would once more fall under the control of some external imperialist power as had been happening in China.[175] To Lothian, therefore, the greatest disaster which menaced India was the risk of a breakdown in its governmental or constitutional unity. That danger would assert itself, he thought, unless India proved able to maintain her own internal unity as a self-governing community. The supreme question for India, he wrote, was whether India was going to work out its salvation as a fundamentally democratic and constitutional federation. If by way of a catastrophe, India managed to lose its constitutional identity, everything would be lost.[176] Nehru grasped the essence of Lothian's gentle solicitation. A wide gulf stood between them.

Nehru had experienced mass movements and witnessed a democratic upsurge for freedom. He was a part of that process. He had been watching the social and economic reconstructions in the Soviet Union, albeit with some misgivings. He was convinced that a meaningful application of socialism keeping in mind the historical specificities of India was feasible although it would demand supreme dedication and intense commitment.[177] He was aware of the historic significance assumed by the Congress in the Indian subcontinent. He was also cognizant of the inability of imperialism to transform itself into a fraternal partnership.[178] *Purna Swaraj* had become for him a vision for a new India. Menon had grasped Nehru's conception in all its essentials. They were *en rapport* with each other. Together, they were destined to form a unique ensemble of inspirited passions engaged in a quest for freedom and social justice.

Even as early as 1926, Jawaharlal Nehru had been marked by Scotland Yard as an energetic and a capable leader whose influence among 'subversive' elements in India had been rapdily increasing.[179] The intelligence department could not quite comprehend the behavioural pattern of this Harrow and Cambridge-educated Indian who took to politics in India and indentified himself with *Satyagraha* and non-cooperation movements, was convicted and imprisoned many times for political offences and had been a 'devoted follower' of Gandhi.[180] It was noted frequently that Nehru was a much respected person and he carried great influence with in his party. He had been the chairman of the Allahabad municipal board for several years.[181] Scotland Yard noted with misgivings that Nehru was given a passport despite his advanced views primarily in consideration of his wife's illness. It took exception to that piece of 'misplaced clemency' on the part of the government, complaining that it should not have overlooked the staggering fact that Nehru had been, over the years, in constant communication with professional agitators in Europe.[182] His association with the persistent propaganda conducted by the League Against Imperialism rendered him potentially very dangerous.[183] The 'charge-sheet' of Scotland Yard was thorough and well founded. By the end of 1926, Nehru was well-acquainted with the leading members of the ILP such as Fenner Brockway, Reginald Bridgeman, James Maxton and George Lansbury. At Brussels, in February 1927, he had been a significant attraction. He established firm contact with the Kuomintang representatives in Europe and was a signatory of a 'joint declaration' by the Indian and Chinese delegates.[184] He had been in touch with Saklatvala, Chatto (Birendranath Chattopadhyaya), M.N. Roy, Henry Barbusse, Willy Munzenburg and Roger Baldwin. It was also noted that under the influence of some extreme elements of ILP and CPGB, Nehru insisted that the Congress should declare itself unequivocally in favour of complete independence of India.[185] At Bombay, in May 1927, the AICC recommended the Congress to recognize the League Against Imperialism as an associated organization.[186] Though he posed as a non-communist, Nehru was presented by Scotland Yard as a shrewd tactician and a confirmed communist who visited the Soviet Union in November 1927 and was full of admiration for the achievements of the Soviet state.[187] At the Madras session of the Congress in December 1927, he took a prominent role in pushing a resolution on complete independence.[188] He had been seeking the support of the youth movement for the reconstruction of the country after independence and in the formulation of that strategy, the impact of M.N. Roy and Chatto (Birendranath Chattopadhyaya) was clearly perceptible.[189] Though still a young man, Scotland Yard stressed, Nehru had already 'an unenviable record' in Indian nationalist affairs and there was no reason to believe that Nehru's future conduct 'will be less disreputable.'[190] From the point of view of Scotland Yard, four significant points were deduced from the 'history sheet' of Jawaharlal Nehru. His education, cultural excellence together with his undoubted ability as a writer and orator and unflincting commitment to *purna swaraj* added to the aura of this attractive personality. Scotland Yard emphasized that since his connection with the Indian National Congress, Nehru had been consistently deprecating the isolation of the Congress from international political affairs and it was he, more than any other leader, who might be considered responsible for the comparatively close liaison between Congress and the political groups abroad. The third point of interest was his success in establishing active contacts with a large number of revolutionaries and communist organizations and personalities all over the world. Finally, Nehru's commitment to complete national independence and his avowal of socialism had become, increasingly, very intense.[191] Nehru's choice of Menon as his spokesman in 1935, Scotland Yard cogitated, would prove perilous for the empire.

Way back in 1927, Scotland Yard had taken note of Menon. He was viewed as an Indian extremist with firm anti-British views and conviction having steady connections with the London Indian *Majlis*.[192] In fact, Menon had already taken a few firm steps towards the left since the General Strike. What impelled him was the growing brutalization of state apparatus that exposed the class character of the state, then given to a systematic suppression of the working class militancy.[193] In June 1930, when Robert Spurrier, C. Jinarajadasa and H.S.L. Polak were still at the helm of affairs in the League, Scotland Yard did not overlook the significant shift in the spirit and tempo of its propaganda for India.[194] Both Spurrier and Jinarajadasa detected that the officials and the media had been effectively coordinating their efforts to shield British imperial interests in India and the growing unrest in the country. They noticed that India had been rapidly becoming an enlightened and a literate country. The most striking phenomenon was that even the peasants had been taking an active interest in political affairs.[195] Both Spurrier and Jinarajadasa expressed their sympathy for the Indian cause and blamed the government for its apathetic attitude towards

India's aspirations. Jinarajadasa felt somewhat troubled by the situation and argued that in the absence of urgent palliatives, 'a widespread revolution would eventuate' as the freedom movement, hitherto guided by a responsible middle class, would pass on to the masses and the ancient culture of India might be swept away by a militant upsurge from below.[196] Polak, known for his sense of moderation and circumspection, was disposed to agree with Spurrier and Jinarajadasa.[197] In contrast, Scotland Yard found that Menon, a teetotaller with an austere disposition, was more forceful and belligerent. It was reported that he had claimed, more than once, in private conversations and public engagements that he was a confirmed believer in India for Indians.[198] As a pacifist, he deplored the use of arms but 'if weapons had to be used, he would prefer that they be wielded by him.' In such a contingency, he had resolved to be 'at the butt-end of the gun' as he was endowed with all the pacifists' instincts for self-preservation.[199]

Scotland Yard noted with concern that Menon had opted to follow, surreptitiously, the banner of liberation which was being raised in India. His commitment to dominion status was not viewed without mistrust.[200] He stresssed repeatedly that he was not disinclined to see India breaking away from the empire. Such a historical process could be conducted without remorse or compunction, although he maintained that it was still possible for India to remain on friendly terms with Britain.[201] Scotland Yard saw in the whole scheme a diabolical game, for it was certain that Menon entertained serious doubts as to the longevity of the proposed Indo-British friendship.[202] Menon maintained, more often than not, in public pronouncements that there was not a nation that had not at one time or another come under 'the exploitative schemes for British capital'. British rule in India, Menon maintained, had been utterly repressive and 'the British lion had an insatiable appetite for wealth.'[203] With regard to the forebodings that if the British evacuated India, the Indians would 'cut one another's throats', Menon quipped casually that 'it was no worse to have one's throat cut than to be shot down for a demonstration for one's political convictions'.[204] It was evident to Scotland Yard that despite the presence of forces of moderation and conciliation within the League, Menon had been relentless in his malevolent efforts to push the League towards the object of *purna swaraj*. Scotland Yard claimed that none of the League's distinguished speakers in those early days including Marion Phillips, Srinivasa Sastri, Lady Tata, Mrs Gillett-Gatti, Mrs Freda Laski, Annie Besant and Miss Chesley could quite comprehend the true import of Menon's machiavellian resolutions couched in conciliatory verbiage entirely suggestive of a close and amiable cooperation between the peoples of Britain and India.[205]

During the first session of the RTC, the headquarters of the metropolitan police of London was struck by the energetic steps taken by Menon, who deftly coordinated the diverse and often disparate opinions voiced by the delegates from India and guided them through the various strands of public opinion in Britain.[206] During the second session of the conference, Menon attracted the attention of Gandhi and Malaviya, altered the objective of the League and wrapped it up in mystifying terminology which meant dominion status to one set of members and *purna swaraj* to another.[207] Despite an exodus of prominent members including a number of theosophists from the CIL, the League established itself before long as the principal organization committed to India's freedom.[208] It drew a good deal of sympathy from various sections of enlightened British opinion as Menon roped in several intellectuals, authors, playwrights, journalists and leading political personalities at different levels of affiliation with the League.[209] Scotland Yard was taken aback by the sudden spurt of meetings, conventions, delegate conferences and Sunday schools conducted by experienced speakers and experts all over the London area and in the provinces under the general direction of this peripatetic nationalist advocate committed to India's political, social and economic resurgence. Some of the League's public meetings were attended by more than 700 attentive sympathizers.[210] In particular, Scotland Yard was impatient to locate the ideological specificities of Menon's renovated League.

During the Mahatma's visit, the situation was rendered complicated as the Labour Party was in the midst of a devastating internal crisis. The National government was formed while the numerical strength of the party in Parliament became marginal.[211] Scotland Yard watched how Menon, with consummate skill, fashioned extensive contacts. It was also noted that despite the formation of an alternate, if not a rival, body in the India Conciliation Group with Gandhi's support and sympathy, Menon managed to monopolize Gandhi's political image and projected Gandhi's firm commitment to freedom and self-determination together with his conviction in non-violence, compromise and conciliation.[212] Throughout 1932, the League's campaign against a 'ruthless and lawless' Government of India gained in momentum and tempo. Scotland Yard thought that the propaganda was primarily marked for its viciousness and untruth.[213] The *Indian News,* the *India Review,* the *Bulletins* and the *Speakers' Note* were widely circulated and the 'restless' propaganda culminated in the despatch of a team of high-profile Labour members, having significant political clout, to India and the operation was accompanied by an extensive publicity campaign.[214] The Scotland Yard decided to publicize widely that the delegation was entirely sponsored and financed by the National Congress. The investigation conducted by the delegation and its published report passed through a chequered career amidst an atmosphere of official antipathy, hostility and intrigue. Reputed concerns were persuaded not to undertake its publication; printers were goaded to throw the manuscript back; editors were inspired to ignore the report and instructions were issued to newspapers to overlook the meetings and seminars to celebrate the publication and discuss its findings. In India, the volume was promptly proscribed.[215] But the impact of the volume, Scotland Yard acknowledged, was impeded but not thwarted. A number of questions and supplementary questions were asked in the Parliament to chivvy ministers. Officials were encouraged to put on a bold face but they could not quite cover up their embarrassment and discomfiture.[216] Scotland Yard was sore to note that the cumulative emanation of the publication was both substantial and significant. The report gave an authoritative imprint against the credibility of the widely publicized notion of a humane imperial rule in India.[217] As an antidote, die-hard organizations were officially encouraged to sponsor a counterpropaganda and a fund was released to assist their endeavours.[218] The League's publications were closely scrutinized, even the meetings of its executive council were covered by 'moles' and the reports of these agents were scanned by expert committees of the police headquarters and the information department of the India Office.[219]

Increasingly, the shadow of the intelligence covered every aspect of the League's activities. Letters and cables of the League were intercepted; opposition forces against Menon were located and encouraged and his relations with the CPGB and some of the leading members of that party were periodically scrutinized.[220] Menon's personal track-record was closely followed: He was elected Labour candidate in the St. Pancras municipal elections in November 1934, appointed secretary of the propaganda committee set up in England by the CSP, distinguished himself as a keen partisan of the Socialist group of the Westminster Labour Party, attended the Labour Party Congress at Southport in 1934, campaigned for a constituent assembly for India, concentrated on making journalistic connections for himself and was in frequent demand as a speaker in London and elsewhere. His Hyde Park meetings invariably attracted a wide cross section of attentive audience. He manipulated to arrange that all Congress publications should regularly be despatched to the League from India and inaugurated an information bureau in London.[221] As Menon sidelined all other bodies, including the Conciliation Group and a few liberal organizations, and adopted an independent line of analysis of the principal trends of the contemporary world and its problems, Scotland Yard began to appreciate the position of the Conservative Party that Menon fell far short of being the ideal contact for Nehru.[222] As he went ahead to add Abyssinia, Spain, China and the unity movement within the scope of the League's propaganda, Scotland Yard resorted to an orchestrated campaign that Menon was pretentious and jealous of his own prestige and exceedingly contemptuous of other Indians associated with pro-Indian propaganda.[223] It was observed with uneasiness that Menon's outstanding intellectual qualities, attractive personality and his ready wit, repartee and aphorisms placed him in an intriguingly conspicuous position in the communist perception.[224] He was in regular touch with the leaders of the CPGB but retained his individuality and freedom of action. His position was accepted by the party, though not without a touch of uneasy uncertainty.[225] It was noted with concern that Menon enjoyed the confidence of men like Reginald Bridgeman, H.N. Brailsford, Ben Bradley, Harry Pollitt and James Klugmann with whose concurrence the League issued various statements consolidating his position as the leading figure in Indian political circles in London.[226]

The ambit of the secret service was wide. By 1923, the issue of India's stability had become a 'home' matter and the Indian intelligence was linked to the MI5. Under Philip Vickery, the department extended its transactions enormously, so much so that the Indian regime and its policy formulations both in India and in London, depended largely on the vast amount of secret intelligence gathered and sifted by the department of

Indian political intelligence. A number of Indians were periodically recruited in the network of surveillance and infiltration. It was a highly secretive organization and its financial resources were primarily garnered from the secret service funds of the Indian budgets. The scope of its proceedings rose in direct proportion to the political ascendancy of the Congress movement.[227] It is but natural that the file on Krishna Menon was substantial and exhaustive. From the innocuous beginning as a school teacher in 1924, ascending to the position of the prominent Indian activist and finally, to the status of the unofficial spokesman of Nehru operating as a roving ambassador for the Congress in Europe, the whole gamut of Menon's London career was closely monitored by the intelligence department.[228] Although only a part of Scotland Yard papers have been released for public scrutiny, one is amazed by the rich wealth of details in them.[229] Menon's daily activities, his engagements, conversations, public postures and speeches, the proceedings of the India League's executive council, Menon's intercepted correspondence with British and Indian politicians, his meetings with the Soviet emissary in London, papers connected with constant official insinuations about his being a communist, confidential medical reports on the condition of his health, his bank balance and all the entries in his account, his love life, emotional weaknesses and frailties and his editorial assignments, international contacts and association with African nationalists had been exhaustively covered, giving the impression that probably he had become specifically the most marked man in London.[230] There was a serious attempt to present Menon all through these documents as a controversial personality despised even by the Congress bigwigs and the leaders of the CPGB and condemned by an increasing number of the Indian associates for his alleged self-centredness and insatiable urge for fame and recognition.[231] The fact is that Scotland Yard found it disturbing that Menon's ascendancy became, despite its vicious propaganda, almost irresistible.[232] Menon's firm convictions, his comprehension of the world situation, extensive intellectual attainments and acumen, rich texture of mind, his political finesse, tenacity and judgement made him a shrewd and mercurial adversary.[233] Menon was particularly popular with the mining and railway workers and 'service' people. The intelligence department sought to manipulate the jealousy and hostility of rival Indian activists and a few parallel organizations with a view to immobilizing him. But Menon moved undeterred. Often he walked on the verge of the precipice. But seldom did he overreach himself. Scotland Yard tried hard but invariably recognized that it was not easy to make a move against this extraordinary man who had fashioned over the years an extensive field of contacts in the literary and publishing world and with the various political forces of his time. He corresponded regularly with Nehru. He was popular in the vibrant left-wing circles and was widely known for his scintillating presentations at all meetings at which Indian affairs were discussed.[234]

Menon's academic accomplishments were staggering. To a B.A. degree in history and economics from Madras University, he added a B.Sc. (Econ) with first class honours with Political Science as a special subject from L.S.E., a M.A. by research in Psychology from University College, London, a Teacher's Diploma from London University and a Law degree. Soon he qualified for the English Bar. In addition, he had done all the subjects and taken the B.A. Honours examination of London in Psychology with Philosophy as subsidiary subject without a degree prior to his M.A. and had been engaged in research in Psychology and Politics for many years. His special area of academics interests had been political thought, the process of reasoning and psychology of theatre. He had edited the Twentieth Century Library and had been the first editor of the Pelican series - an unusual distinction for an Indian in 1935. As a Labour councillor in the borough of St. Pancras since 1934 he established his reputation as a creative activist given to the promotion of education, culture and decent life to his electorate. His experience of speaking, writing and discussion extended to about six years and he had so far spoken on political and economic subjects to hundreds of labour and trade union meetings, adult schools and academic seminars.[235]

Despite considerable backbiting and intrigues indulged in by a few fleeting rival bodies, the dingy little office at the Strand, one of London's great arteries connecting the West End with the city, became by 1935, the principal institution where the points of view of the Indian National Congress could be discussed, debated and analysed.[236] This cramped room was frequented by distinguished men and women of the capital of the empire as volunteers, lecturers and discussants. From here, the nationalist perceptions of Indian struggles and its various episodes were disseminated, all imperialist distortions were challenged and official misrepresentations were seriously interrogated.[237] The audience at that not-so-comfortable ambience of the Strand listened attentively to the series of discourses on imperial sensibilities and perceptions that had become almost a national obsession from the exclusive Mayfair drawing rooms to the modest homes of the millions of British working people. Menon also lectured on the prospects of a socialist British Commonwealth, on the concern of the League for the protection of the freedom not only of British peoples but of other peoples as well, on the proposition that the government was 'common sense coupled with human dignity', on the British sense of justice and equity, on the lofty idealism of the Labour Party modulated by the pressure of the powerful right-wing and its concept of narrow economic interests, on the nature of British rule in India, on the metamorphosis of the principle of self-determination in the Transport House, on the suggestion of a mutually beneficial imperial partnership between Britain and India, on Nehru's vision, embodying the radical, socialist and democratic aspirations of new India, on India's freedom struggle as an integral part of the international struggle for self-determination, on the fundamentals and nuances of fascism and imperialism and the concept of social justice or on the communal tangle in India and its manipulation by officials in imperial interests.[238] To Menon, his was a historic mission. His target audience was the growing intelligentsia that was becoming increasingly conscious of its own potentialities despite the domination of 'Tory Socialists' and the harassed industrial workers who formed, despite the weaknesses of the Trade Union Congress, a strong phalanx of public opinion as they were clearly fascinated by the pulls of 'Labour democracy'.[239] Menon gave most of his audience the feeling that he was completely preoccupied with India. Michael Foot and Anna Polak confided to the author that it seemed Krishna Menon was 'reading, writing, thinking, dreaming India'.[240] Menon's sincerity was transparent. His intensity was proverbial. His broad-mindedness was above board. His tongue was acerbic. His manners were simple. His vision and perceptions were international. Behind his inharmonious and strident postures, there was a cultivated mind with enormous intellectual power and intense human sympathy.[241]

Menon was an extremely imaginative and influential speaker. Michael Foot, Platts-Mills and Julius Silverman, Krishna Shelvankar, V.R. Krishna Iyer, Mulk Raj Anand and Anna Polak made no bones about the impact of Menon's intellectual presentations on his audience. They were enthralled both by his philosophical discourses and his performances at public debates on problems facing humanity. 'You could almost hear the pounding of his heart', Anna Polak noted.[242] Anand thought that Menon could be classed with Saklatvala, Harry Pollitt and Winston Churchill as one of the significant and influential orators of the period. The young Labour Party members who were commissioned to attend the classes and lectures of the India

League returned with a sense of fulfilment as Menon helped expand their intellectual horizons. Some listened to Menon's criticial assessment of British rule with mixed feelings. And yet, for some others, it was a novel experience of sharing an amazing intellectual camaraderie.[243] Menon's eloquent eyes, his expressive words, the twists of his heavy lips, his rapturous glances together with his intensity of purpose had an intoxicating impact on his sympathizers. Every public presentation of his was an open defiance of British imperialism. It was not an exhibition of empty rhetoric of a capricious demagogue.[244] Menon displayed an intuitive grasp of the situation and a sensitive tactfulness. He avoided distortion and was a master of felicitous phrases. He was not averse to the art of compromise without abandoning principles or national interests. He was not pedantic but convincing. He was persuasive but not dogmatic.[245] Menon's annoyance with mediocrity and the insinuations of mischievous interlocutors had been intensified overtime. His frustration was intensified by his inability to break through the rigid right wing of the Labour leadership. But he was conscious of his inadequacy and tried, not very successfully, to command his own untrammelled temper. The very fact that, over the years, the grimy office at the Strand became a corporate body was a tribute to Menon who had developed into an institution all by himself.[246] The impress of his presentation was resounding. It accommodated the analytical power of an involved social scientist, the total commitment of a socialist idealist, the profound fervour of an anti-imperialist crusader, the integrity and intelligence of a trained modern mind and the relentlessness of a Marxist campaigner.

With the possible exception of the scenes in London when Gandhi arrived for the RTC, no demonstration of Indians and friends of India had excelled in enthusiasm more than which was witnessed at Victoria Station on 29 October 1935 when Nehru, accompanied by his daughter, Indira, was welcomed.

They looked worn out and strained. It seemed that there was no evidence of discrimination between the various Indian groups assembled there. It was a huge crowd of Indians -- including turbaned *lascars* from the East India docks, Hindus, Sikhs, Muslims, doctors, teachers, students, Indian and English -- all eager to greet the visitors with admiration and sympathy. The name of the members of the organizing committee consisted of people of all shades of political thought and activity. They included ardent supporters of the Congress Party, intense critics of that organization, Liberals, Labourites, Communists and just ordinary people. Among others, the welcome party included Agatha Harrison, Bertrand Russell, Horace Alexander, Ellen Wilkinson and Krishna Menon, (straight from St. Pancras Hospital where he was being treated during his prolonged illness).[247]

A visit to Somerville College, Oxford, to make the necessary arrangements for Indira's admission, a few informal meetings with some eminent persons and representatives of political and cultural organizations and with a few publishers, summed up the visible itinerary of Nehru during his short sojourn. Nehru was in search of a publisher for his autobiography and as an erudite and competent editor, Menon was by then a name to be reckoned with in the publishing circles. He readily agreed to act as Nehru's literary agent and also as his daughter's guardian in Britain.[248] It may be noted that they had exchanged nothing more than pleasantries in 1927, when the Nehrus visited London. They met again in Allahabad in 1932, during the League's India delegation. Subsequently, they exchanged a few letters on the idea of the constituent assembly, on the content of the reform proposals and on the ascendancy of the right reaction in Europe. But this was the first occasion when they had a long, almost uninterrupted, one-to-one interaction. Nehru affirmed his commitment to socialism and *purna swaraj* and his unequivocal opposition to imperialism and fascism. Menon opened his heart on Abyssinia, Spain, Austria, Germany, Italy, the Japanese aggression on China and the duplicity of British policy in India. Both were urbane intellectuals and were, by then, fairly well-known to the leaders of radical opinion in the West.[249] For them, socialism was a way of life. Both of them were committed to integrate India's struggle for freedom with the international historical forces engaged in a desperate effort to extend the frontiers of freedom. Their universalism was not obfuscated by irrational parochial considerations. A remarkable intellectual fellowship was fashioned between them almost overnight. The fraternity between Nehru, an enthusiastic, optimistic and popular hero in his stately loneliness and Menon, a somewhat sceptical, caustic and withdrawn crusader in self-exile in London with his ascetic habits, matured. That relàtionship was based on complete confidence in each other's judgements. Often they had free and frank discussions on the objectives and priorities. Invariably, they evolved a consensus representing a common outlook and an attitude on national and international aspects of contemporary struggles.

By the time Nehru returned to his wife's sickbed, Menon was almost ecstatic about Nehru. He thought that Nehru had made an impression in Britain which even the optimistic observer had not dared hope.[250] Nehru, Menon wrote, acted like some sort of a new prophet. Although a quiet and arresting personality, Nehru had a remarkable ability not to circumlocate and to go straight for the anti-imperialist issues. Besides, with comfortable ease he could reach out to the problems of scarcity, poverty, hunger and illiteracy that made some of the distinguished men in London 'sit up and think.'[251] For the conventional Labour leaders it was a new experience, Menon wrote, as they felt that a fresh chapter had been opened in the relations of the labour to Indian affairs.[252] Menon was confident that the socialist movement in India would successfully endeavour under Nehru's leadership to link up Indian socialism with the rest of the world. The magnitude of problems that had been facing the movement in India was overwhelming. But Menon appreciated that the beginning had been made under the charismatic personality, with care and not with hesitation and manoeuvring.[253]

Giving Menon full authority to publish all his statements and articles at the London end, Nehru had informed Menon, as early as 1934, that the various measures that the government had been taking in Bengal seemed to him to be worse even than the martial law regime in the Punjab in 1919. He thought that the Bengal measures were 'cold-blooded'.[254] In agreement with Menon, Nehru had written in one of his letters that he had been laying stress on the calling in India of a constituent assembly elected under adult or near-adult franchise. He strongly felt that it was the only feasible solution of the political and the communal problems in India'.[255] Nehru thought that it was the strategy to which no one could possibly object in theory at least. Even Gandhi, to some extent, accepted the proposal as evidenced by his answer to Muhammad Iqbal.[256] He was happy that the proposal had been initiated and put forward in England by Menon, who carried with him some of the responsible persons and parties.[257]

As Nehru was preparing himself to make a second visit to London, he turned to Menon as his confidant. He made it clear that he was not particularly inclined to meet 'people of importance' whom he would not like to convert. On the contrary, he would like to see 'interesting people', such as the *New Statesman* group as suggested by Amiya Chakravarti from Oxford.[258] He was unhappy at the request of Horace Alexander to meet George Schuster to discuss Indian finances with him. He wonderd, if Horace Alexander could be persuaded to drop the idea. There was no affinity between the two and if Alexander was keen, or if an appointment was fixed already, Nehru would have no excuse to get out of it.[259] The persons Nehru was keen to meet, were Cedric Dover, an Anglo-Indian left-winger and through him Paul Robeson, celebrated singer, and George Padmore, secretary of the Trade Union Committee of the Negro workers and author of a sensational book, *Britannica Rules the Black* and R. Palme Dutta, communist activist and theoretician.[260] To Nehru's request to keep the reception committee a broadbased and a cooperative affair, Menon responded with his unambiguous opposition. 'I am glad', Nehru replied with a touch of amusement, 'you are occasionally non-modest. I would welcome even immodesty at times for I suffer from it myself.'[261] Menon was assured that Nehru had full confidence in his ability to make excellent and efficient arrangements. But Nehru was not inclined to appear in England under the auspices of one particular organization, 'however worthy it might be'.[262] Nehru, therefore, requested Menon to act in his personal capacity. Nehru made it clear that he was on the whole a fairly efficient person but he disliked 'useless fuss and waste of time' and meeting people who were of no consequence for him and his mission. He confessed that he had to force himself to submit to waste of time and energy in India and very often he could not suppress his indignation. But it was difficult to escape from all that unless 'I want to function in an intellectual vacuum.'[263]

Examining his own role in Indian public life, Nehru was quite candid. 'If I am popular or effective in India', Nehru wrote, 'it is not chiefly because of my intellectual attainments, such as they are, but because, *inter alia,* of a certain human element that I possess. I am not looked upon as a machine but a human being who is easily accessible to the most ignorant peasant.'[264] Nehru's outlook was supported by his intuitive knowledge of his countrymen. He knew them pretty well and knew 'what interests them and moves them in India.'[265] Nehru claimed that he was an individualist and to a 'certain extent a bit of a highbrow', but close contacts with large masses of people 'has invariably made me think of the reactions on the masses of anything I do.'[266] The long letter ended with a modest request made sincerely to one who enjoyed Nehru's confidence and excelled in his sense of judgement. 'But the main thing is that I want you to take charge of me during my visit to London, but to manage things in such a way that no one feels that I am a conducted show or a high and mighty person sitting in a higher plane apart from the common run of humanity.'[267]

On 31 December 1935, Nehru informed Menon that he could make his London visit not later than the last week of January 1936. His wife, Nehru reported, was carrying on pretty well and was on the whole better than expected, and by about 12 January he could be expected to be in London.[268] It was absolutely necessary to avoid the visits to Manchester and Oxford. Among the moots he should like to meet were the India Conciliation Group, the Friends of India and the Saklatvala group. He also referred to a mischievous assembly of imposters calling themselves the Indian National Congress of Great Britain who had been firmly forbidden to do so. In case, the group desired to meet Nehru, he would not deny them the opportunity.[269] Of the individuals, he was keen to meet were Aldous Huxley, Ellen Wilkinson and Reginald Reynolds on personal grounds and Reginald Bridgeman as a friend and an active sympathizer of India's freedom.[270] The short and snappy letter ended with an endearing note: 'I am grateful to you for having dropped the 'Pundit'. Why not allow 'Mr' to go the same way. The ceremony in personal relations bores me.'[271]

Menon was overwhelmed. Nehru had, over the preceding few months, spelled out the situation in India against the background of the imposed constitution. He underlined that the nationalist urge to political freedom would remain a dominant factor till all imperialist control was removed. What gave that demand substance was the economic problems of grinding poverty, immense unemployment, arrested industrialization, overwhelming presence of foreign capital under British direction, uneconomic land holdings, continual depression and the feeble and pathetic attempts to meet the situation. 'For a socialist', Nehru emphasized, 'the solution can only be on socialist lines'.[272] In Nehru's vision that socialist salvation was possible through a planning process that would affect agriculture, industry, education, health, sanitation, irrigation, housing, roads, transportation -- all 'tackled at something approaching the Russian pace.'[273] Nehru was categorical that the proposed transformation of India could not be undertaken so long as imperialism dominated India. It protected all vested, reactionary and feudal interests. In a sense, it was the negation of civil liberties. Evidently, both Nehru and Menon realized that the one of the basic problems of Indian unity was the Hindu-Muslim question. It was politically a middle-class affair which would be sorted out in the course of the political and social revolutions. Yet, perhaps at that point, they underestimated the dangers of the issue for the future development.

Menon was amazed by the felicity with which Nehru, a participant and a spectator of the vast and dramatic changes in the world scene, attained a rational admixture of intense activity with lofty vision and clinical detachment. As the editor of Nehru's *Autobiography,* Menon read through the manuscript with rapt attention. The proposed title of the volume, *In and Out of Prison,* was dropped on Menon's suggestion and Nehru unhesitatingly agreed to opt for the new title offered by Menon as the alternative.[274] Nehru's grasp of history, direct, forceful yet simplicity of articulation and his foresight and imagination were remarkable qualities. Menon was simply swayed by them and developed complete confidence in Nehru's qualities as author, his historical perspective, consistency of thought and sense of reality. Nehru was aware of the uniqueness of the

Gandhian method of struggle and efficacy of the mobilization and organization of the masses as an effective material force of history. He admired Gandhi's mass appeal and insistence on the moral content of the national struggle. But Nehru thought that a new India had to be envisaged where all the benefits of science and technology would be harnessed for the common weal. Menon found in Nehru's presentation a penetrating analysis of India's conditions and a programme of comprehensive reform of Indian social system and its economic stagnation. Nehru endowed his manuscript with a sense of living reality. It was clear that Nehru examined the process through which India moved ahead in its attempt to merge with world history as an active participant, and how the whole world itself was involved in the great process of change.

In particular, Menon was attracted by the fact that although Nehru was one of Gandhi's chosen disciples and there was a deep attachment between them, yet they were men of sharply contrasting sensibilities. If Gandhi, the ascetic and a sort of a pluralist mystic, represented the India of the ages, modern India was represented in Nehru. His mind bore the impress of a Western scientific education. He appreciated the significance of economic realities and hoped to make economic growth the basis of India's regeneration. His extensive interaction with various representatives of European intelligentsia served to develop and confirm his socialist ideas. Since 1923, he participated in mass organizations and trade unions, communicated with the young people throughout the country and mobilized them in an organized way to combat imperial authority, social obscurantism and religious prejudices. The rulers were apprehensive of his growing influence and left him little leisure to work for Indian emancipation. In fact, since the 1930 civil disobedience movement, he had hardly spent more than a few months out of prison. Should he be released, a meeting, an article or a conversation served for a pretext and he was once more behind the bar. He would be still completing a sentence but for the serious illness of his wife who was being treated in Europe.[275] In England, the importance of his future role was heavily underlined. He became the object of signal and complimentary attentions. He was discussed in the newspapers and favourably compared with Gandhi who was far too eccentric to appeal to British innate conservatism. Nehru's manner and development were approved. It was noted with satisfaction by the organized Left that he had nothing of the Hindu ascetic, that he preferred Lenin to Tolstoy and the Marxian economics to the Sermon on the Mount. It appeared to some political commentators that Nehru would be a more redoubtable adversary than Gandhi. Menon found Nehru quite resolute in his conviction that the new constitution would not be approved, either by the Congress or by moderate Indian opinion. Sooner or later, India would achieve independence and Nehru stressed that it was far too late to offer India dominion status.

Notes and References

1 Minoo Masani to Menon, 16 March 1935, Menon Papers.

2 Ibid.

3 Ibid.

4 Ibid.

5 Ibid.

6 Masani to Menon, 27 April 1934, Menon Papers

7 Menon to Aneurin Bevan, 10 May 1934, Menon Papers.

8 Ibid.

9 Ibid.

10 Masani to Menon, 6 May 1934, Menon Papers.

11 Masani to Menon, 9 November 1934, Menon Papers.

12 M.R. Masani, 'No Deviation - Right or Left', *Congress Socialist,* 10 March 1935, Menon Papers.

13 Gonavardhan, 'The Objective Stated', *Congress Socialist,* 25 November 1934, Menon Papers.

14 Ibid.

15 Ibid.

16 Masani to Menon, 21 December 1934, Menon Papers; also see 'Why within the Congress', *Congress Socialist,* 29 September 1934.

17 Narendradev, 'Task before us', *Congress Socialist,* 29 September 1934, Menon Papers.

18 'Why Within the Congress', *Congress Socialist,* 29 September 1934, Menon Papers.

19 Masani to Menon, 16 May 1935, Menon Papers; also see: 'Congress Socialist Party'; 'Trade Union and Labour Movement'; 'Peasant Movement' and 'Attack on Socialism - British and Indian' in Masani to Menon, 6 May 1937, Menon Papers.

20 See a good collection of these and other tracts, pamphlets and other publications of the Congress Socialist party in Menon Papers.

21 Masani to Menon, 9 November 1934, Menon Papers.

22 Ibid.

23 Ibid.

24 Masani to Menon, 6 May 1935, Menon Papers.

25 Ibid.

26 Ibid.

27 Ibid.

28 See, Ben Bradley, 'What the Congress Socialists Want', 15 December 1934; and R. Palme Dutt, 'Congress Socialism, — A Contradiction in Terms', October ? in P.C. Joshi Collection.

29 Masani to Menon, 16 April 1935, Menon Papers.

30 Menon to Masani, 9 April 1935, Menon Papers.

31 Ibid.

32 Ibid.

33 Masani to Menon, 20 November 1934, with enclosures, Menon Papers.

34 Jayaprakash Narayan to Menon, 23 December 1934, Menon Papers.

35 Ibid.

36 Ibid.

37 Menon to M.R. Masani, 26 April 1935, Menon Papers.

38 Ibid.

39 Ibid.

40 Ibid.

41 Ibid.

42 Ibid.

43 Ibid.

44 Ibid.

45 Ibid.

46 Ibid.

47 Ibid.

48 Ibid.

49 'A Note on the Impoundment of Mr M.R. Masani's Passport', n.d. 1935, Menon Papers.

50 Ibid.

51 Representation of the India League on Masani's passport, 8 July 1935, Menon Papers.

52 'A Note on the Impoundment of M.R. Masani's Passport', n.d. 1935, Menon Papers.

53 Ibid.

54 Menon to Wedgewood Benn, 19 September 1935, Menon Papers. Government of India held: 'We have no definite evidence that Masani is a communist, but we feel strongly that his general record and associations with communists made it desirable that he should not be allowed to travel freely in Europe. We, therefore, recommend total refusal of passport having regard to the principle laid down in secretary of state's telegram ...' Government of India, Home Department to secretary of state for India, 28 July 1935, Infn. offr. L/I/1/1453, P.J. 1935, India Office.

55 Bertrand Russell, Harold Laski and H.N. Brailsford to the editors, *New Statesman and Nation, The Spectator, Time and Tide, The New Leader, Manchester Guardian, The Times,* etc. 24 July 1935, Menon Papers.

56 Ibid.

57 Ibid.

58 Ibid.

59 Ibid.

60 Ibid.

61 Ibid.

62 Ibid.

63 Menon to J.C. Jagger, National Union of Distributive and Allied Workers, Manchester, 22 August 1935, Menon Papers.

64 Menon to T. Eaton, 15 September 1935, Menon Papers.

65 Ibid; also Menon to Jagger, 22 August 1935; Menon to Joan Bourne, 26 August 1935; Menon to Madam Morin, 22 August 1935; Menon to Kistenmacher, 12 July 1935;

G.C. Whitehouse (Manchester) to Menon, 2 August 1935; Robert M'Intyre (Edinburgh) to Menon, 19 October 1935; Fred Peart (Durham) to Menon, 14 October 1935; Henry Solomon to secretary, Croydon Labour Party, Surrey, 26 July 1935, all in Menon Papers.

66 Menon to T. Eaton, 15 September 1935, Menon Papers; also see, papers connected with the Socialist Youth Demonstration on 19 October 1935 in the Miners' Hall, Durham city, Menon Papers.

67 Menon to Brailsford, 20 October 1935, Menon Papers.

68 Ibid.

69 Ibid.

70 Menon to Masani, 17 November 1935, Menon Papers.

71 Masani to Menon, 13 December 1935, Menon Papers.

72 Ibid.

73 Stafford Cripps to Menon, 23 October 1935, Menon Papers; also see, K.P. Keshava Menon to Krishna Menon, 10 October 1935, Menon Papers; Monica Whately to Menon, 19 August 1935, Menon Papers; Shelvankar to Menon, 16 December 1935, Menon Papers.

74 Joan Bourne to Madam Morins, 22 August 1935, Menon papers; also see, L. Morins to Menon, 28 August 1935, Menon Papers.

75 Ibid.

76 Menon to Wedgwood Benn, 19 September 1935, Menon Papers.

77 Ibid.

78 Menon to Clement Attlee, 19 September 1935, Menon Papers.

79 Ibid.

80 Menon to Arthur Greenwood, 19 September 1935, Menon Papers.

81 Ibid.

82 Joan Bourne to Horace G. Alexander, 7 October 1935, Menon Papers.

83 'Mr Masani on his Tour Impressions', *Hindustan Times*, 18 November 1935, Menon Papers.

84 Masani to Menon, 29 November 1935, Menon Papers.

85 Ibid.

86 Ibid.

87 Ibid.

88 Ibid.

89 Menon to Masani, 21 December 1935, Menon Papers.

90 Menon to Masani, 26 April 1935, Menon Papers.

91 Ibid.

92 Ibid.

93 Ibid.

94 Ibid.

95 Ibid.

96 Masani to Menon, 29 November 1935, Menon Papers.

97 Menon to Masani, 26 April 1935, Menon Papers.

98 Ibid.

99 Ibid.

100 Ibid.

101 Menon to Masani, 29 November, 1935, Menon Papers.

102 Ibid.

103 Ibid.

104 Open Letter to the Indian Communists from the C.C. of the C.P. of China, 24 November 1933, P.C. Joshi Collection, Berlin.

105 Ben Bradley, 'What the Congress Socialists Want', 15 December 1934, P.C. Joshi Collection, Berlin.

106 R. Palme Dutt, 'Congress Socialism: A Contradiction in Terms'. October 1934, P.C. Joshi Collection.

107 Erhard Schaller, 'Jawaharlal Nehru and the Formation of the Congress Socialist Party', in N.L. Gupta and Vinod Bhatia, *Jawaharlal Nehru, Statesman, National Leader and Thinker,* Delhi, 1989.

108 Ralph Miliband, *Capitalist Democracy in Britain,* op.cit., pp.48-49.

109 R. Benewick, *Political Violence and Public Order,* London 1972, p.110.

110 Report of Annual Conference, University Labour Federation, 4 to 7 January 1935, Heathmount Hall, Ilkley, Yorkshire, Menon Papers.

111 R. Bridgeman to Menon, 5 April 1935, Menon Papers; also, Krishna Menon to George Lansbury, 9 April 1935, Menon Papers.

112 R. Bridgeman to Menon, 26 April 1935, Menon Papers.

113 'Draft statement to be communicated to the secretary of state for India on the Karachi shootings', 26 April 1935, Menon Papers.

114 Bridgeman to Menon, 26 April 1935, Menon Papers; also, see Bridgeman to Menon, 15 February 1935, Menon Papers.

115 Extract from New Scotland Yard Report, 30 January 1936, P&J(S) 194(1935), India Office.

116 Menon to the Mrs Green/Bridgeman, 18 July 1935, Menon Papers.

117 India League, *India Speaks,* London, August 1935.

118 This section is based on Ibid.

119 John Mahon, *Harry Pollitt, A Biography,* London 1976, pp.180-81.

120 E.H. Carr, *International Relations since the Peace Treaties,* London 1945 (edn.) pp.200-205.

121 Ibid., pp.202-24.

122 Ibid., pp.217-221.

123 Ibid., pp.220-21.

124 A.J.P. Taylor, *English History, 1914-1945 op. cit.* London 1965, pp.405-21; see for the reaction of the left opinion, Ruth Dudley Edwards, *Victor Gollancz, A Biography,* London 1987, esp. pp.401-23; also, Betty D. Vernon, *Ellen Wilkinson,* London 1982, esp. pp.134-37.

125 Geoffrey Barraclough, *An Introduction to Contemporary History,* London, 1967 (ed.), pp.199-232.

126 Ibid., p.208.

127 Arthur Marwick, *Britain in the Century of Total War, War, Peace and Social Change 1900-1967,* op. cit., pp.242-3.

128 Arthur Marwick, *Britain in our Century,* London 1984, pp.93-94; also see, John Mahon, *Harry Pollitt,* op.cit., pp.136-61.

129 Menon, 'London Letter', 18 September 1933, *Hindu.*

130 Arthur Marwick, *Britain in the Century of Total War,* op.cit., p.253.

131 John Mahon, *Harry Pollitt,* op.cit., pp.181-89.

132 Ibid., pp.192-4.

133 Official discussion between Herbert Morrison and Harry Pollitt, in quoted in Ibid., p.199.

134 James Klugmann, 'The Crisis of the Thirties: A View from

the Left', in Jon Clark, Margot Heinemann, David Margolies and Carole Snee (ed.), *Culture and Crisis in Britain in the Thirties* op. cit.

135 Ibid.; also see, Gary Werskey, *The Visible College,* A Collective *Biography of British Scientists and Socialists of the 1930s,* op. cit., pp.150-153, 216-9 and 249-57.

136 Ibid.

137 John Mahon, *Harry Pollitt,* op.cit., p.195-6.

138 Ibid.

139 Georgi Dimitrov, *United Front of The Working Class Against Fascism,* (Reply to the Seventh World Congress of the Communist International 1935 with Reply and Resolution), Calcutta 1969.

140 Quoted in Gary Wersky, *The Visible College,* op.cit., p. 29.

141 Ibid.

142 Dimitrov, *United Front etc.* op.cit.

143 Ibid.

144 Ibid.

145 Klugmann, 'The Crisis of the Thirties', in Jon Clark etc. (ed), *Culture and Crisis in Britain etc.,* op.cit.

146 Ibid.

147 Ibid.

148 Ibid.

149 India League, *India Speaks,* 1935, Menon Papers.

150 John Mahon, *Harry Pollitt,* op.cit., pp.200-203.

151 Ibid., pp.202-205.

152 Ibid., pp.199; also see, Ralph Miliband, *Capitalist Democracy in Britain,* Oxford 1984, pp.74-6.

153 Marwick, *Britain in the Century of Total War,* op.cit., pp.240-

1; also, Gary Werskey, *The Visible College,* op.cit., pp.224-5, 251-4, 268-9, 290-92, 294-300.

154 Klugmann in Jon Clark etc. (ed.), *Culture and Crisis* etc. op.cit.; Gary Werskey, *The Visible College,* op.cit., pp.212-256.

155 Marwick, *Britain in the Century of Total War,* etc., op.cit., p.241; also, Klugmann, in Jon Clark, etc. (ed.), *Culture and Crisis,* etc. op.cit., p.27.

156 Cf. Eric Hobsbawm, *Age of Extremes, The Short History of the Twentieth Century, 1914-1991,* op.cit., pp.146-52.

157 Marwick, *Britain in The Century of Total War, etc.,* op.cit., pp.240, 253-5; also Klugmann in Jon Clark etc. (ed.), *Culture and Crisis* etc. op.cit., pp.17-20; Hobsbawm, *Age of Extremes* etc., op.cit., pp.152-163.

158 Hobsbawm, ibid., pp.152-53.

159 Ibid., p.152.

160 Agatha Harrison to Menon, 1 November 1935, Menon Papers.

161 Ibid.

162 Agatha Harrison to Horace Alexander, 13 August 1934, Agatha Harrison Papers.

163 Lord Lothian to Nehru, 8 November 1935 and 6 December 1935, Menon papers. Also see the letters in Jawaharlal Nehru, *A Bunch of Old Letters,* Bombay 1958, pp.128-130.

164 Lothian to Nehru, 6 December 1935, ibid. Lord Lothian was anxious that the Congress accept and work the 1935 Constitution.

165 Ibid.

166 Ibid.

167 Ibid.

168 Nehru to Lothian, 9 December 1935, Menon Papers. See the letter in Nehru, *A Bunch of Old Letters,* op.cit., pp.130-132.

169 Ibid.

170 Ibid.

171 Lothian to Nehru, 31 December 1935, Menon Papers. See the letter in Nehru, *A Bunch of Old Letters,* op.cit., pp.133-140.

172 Ibid.

173 Ibid.

174 Ibid.

175 Ibid.

176 Ibid.

177 Nehru to Lothian, 17 January 1936, Nehru, *A Bunch of Old Letters.* op.cit., pp.140-154.

178 Ibid.

179 Extract from New Scotland Yard, Report, 28 December 1927, L/PJ/12/313, India Office.

180 'Jawaharlal Nehru', Secret File Copy, Scotland Yard Report, 12 February 1936, L/PJ/12/293, India Office.

181 'Two Indian Leaders', Scotland Yard Report, 24 February 1936, L/PJ/12/293, India Office.

182 'Jawaharlal Nehru', Secret File Copy, Scotland Yard Report, 12 February 1936, L/PJ/12/293, India Office.

183 Extract from New Scotland Yard Report, 28 December 1927, L/PJ/12/313, India Office.

184 Jawaharlal Nehru', Secret File Copy, Scotland Yard Report, 12 February 1936, L/PJ/12/293, India Office.

185 Ibid.

186 Ibid.

187 Ibid.

188 Ibid.

189 'Jawaharlal Nehru', Secret File Copy, Scotland Yard Report, 12 February 1936, L/PJ/12/293, India Office.

190 Ibid.

191 'Two Great Indian Leaders', New Scotland Yard Report, 24 February 1936, L/PJ/12/293, India Office.

192 Ibid.

193 Conversation with Mulk Raj Anand.

194 'Commonwealth of India League, Extract from New Scotland Yard Report', 25 June 1930, L/PJ/12/356, India Office.

195 Ibid.

196 Ibid.

197 Ibid.

198 Ibid.

199 Ibid.

200 Report on India League, 30 October 1931, L/PJ/12/323, India Office.

201 Ibid.

202 Ibid.

203 Ibid.

204 Ibid.

205 Report on India League, New Scotland Yard, 3 December 1931, L/PJ/12/323, India Office.

206 'India League (Formerly called the Commonwealth of India League), Scotland Yard Report, P&J(S) 721/1932 L/PJ/12/451, India Office.

207 Ibid.

208 Ibid.

209 Ibid.

210 'Note on Vengalil Krishnan Krishna Menon', 30 October 1939, Scotland Yard Report. L/PJ/12/323, India Office.

211 Ibid.

212 Ibid.

213 Ibid.

214 Ibid.

215 Cf. Ch.IV above.

216 Note on Vengalil Krishnan Krishna Menon, 30 October 1939, Now Scotland Yard Report, L/PJ/12/323, India Office.

217 Ibid.

218 See Ch. VI above.

219 See Ch. IV above.

220 Extract from New Scotland Yard Report No. 54, 1 January 1936, L/PJ/12/365, India Office.

221 Note on Vengalil Krishnan Krishna Menon, 30 October 1939, New Scotland Yard Report, L/PJ/12/323, India Office.

222 'Jawaharlal Nehru', 12 February 1936, New Scotland Yard Report, L/PJ/12/293, India Office.

223 'India League', 721/1932-1938, New Scotland Yard Report, L/P&J/12/451, India Office.

224 Extract from Scotland Yard Report No. 63, 6 May 1936, L/PJ/12/450, India Office.

225 'India League and Communist Party of Great Britain', Extract from Scotland Yard Report No. 87, 7 April 1937, L/PJ/12/450.

226 'India League', 1938, Scotland Yard Report, L/PJ/12/ 451, India Office.

227 Cf. Patrick French, *Liberty or Death,* London 1997, pp.98-101.

228 For example, see, 'Note on Vengalil Krishnan Krishna Menon', 30 October 1939, New Scotland Yard Report, L/PJ/12/323, India Office.

229 Ibid.

230 Ibid.

231 Ibid; also see, 'India League and Communist Party', Extracts from Scotland Yard Report No.87, 7 April 1937, L/PJ/12/450.

232 Ibid.

233 'Note on Vengalil Krishnan Krishna Menon', 30 October 1939, New Scotland Yard Report, L/PJ/12/323, India Office.

234 See, for example, 'India, Kingsway Hall Conference', 26 November 1932, Scotland Yard Report, L/PJ/12/448, India Office.

235 Menon to Sub-Warden, Toynbee Hall, London, 26 March 1935, Menon Papers.

236 See, for example, 'Extracts from New Scotland Yard Report', 30 January 1935, L/PJ/12/450, India Office; 'Report on India League', 28 February 1935, L/PJ/12/450, India Office; 'Extracts from Scotland Yard Report' no.34, 27 March 1935, L/PJ/12/450, India Office.

237 Author's conversation with Michael Foot, Krishna Shelvankar and Mulk Raj Anand.

238 Interview with Michael Foot.

239 Ibid.

240 Interview with Anna Polak.

241 Interviews with Mulk Raj Anand and Mary Shelvankar.

242 Interview with Anna Polak.

243 Interview with Michael Foot.

244 Interviews with Julius Silverman and P.N. Haksar.

245 Interviews with Michael Foot and P.N. Haksar.

246 'Extract from Scotland Yard Report No.34, 27 March 1935, L/PJ/12/450, India Office.

247 'Our London Letter', *The Hindu,* 18 November 1935.

248 Nehru's visits to England in November 1935 and January 1936 are covered in Ch. 14 in Sarvepalli Gopal, *Jawaharlal Nehru, A Biography*, op.cit.

249 Reporting his experience in London to Rajendra Prasad, Nehru wrote about Menon: 'He is very able and energetic and is highly thought of in intellectual, journalistic and left wing circles. He has the virtues and failings of the intellectual.' Nehru to Rajendra Prasad, 22 November 1935, Home Pol. File 1/2/36.

250 For the public appreciation of Nehru in Britain see *The Tribune,* 16 November 1935.

251 Menon, 'Our London Letter', *The Hindu*, 18 November 1935.

252 Ibid.

253 Ibid.

254 Nehru to Menon, 1 February 1934, Menon Papers.

255 Nehru to Menon, 16 March 1934, Menon Papers.

256 Ibid.

257 Ibid.

258 Nehru to Menon, 16 October 1935, Menon Papers and 23 October 1935, Menon Papers.

259 Nehru to Menon, 18 January 1936, Menon Papers.

260 Nehru to Menon, 19 January 1936, Menon Papers.

261 Nehru to Menon, 23 December 1935, Menon Papers.

262 Ibid.

263 Ibid.

264 Ibid.

265 Ibid.

266 Ibid.

267 Ibid.

268 Jawaharlal Nehru to Menon, 31 December 1935, Menon Papers.

269 Ibid.

270 Ibid.

271 Ibid.

272 Nehru to Menon, 9 December 1935, Menon Papers.

273 Ibid.

274 Agatha Harrison, Sunday and Thursday, October 1935, Menon Papers; Menon to Nehru, 26 December 1935, Menon Papers; Menon to Menon, 31 December 1935, Menon Papers.

275 Menon to Reginald Bridgeman, 25 January 1936, Menon Papers.

Biographical Index

Aga Khan (1875-1957). Spiritual head of the Ismaili Muslims; active in Indian politics till 1947; supporter of British rule.

Aiyer, Sir C.P. Ramaswami (1879-1966). Madras lawyer and politician; left Congress during non-cooperation; law member, viceroy's executive council, 1931; acting commerce and industry member, viceroy's executive council, 1932.

Aiyer, P.S. Sivaswami (1864-1946). Lawyer, administrator, statesman; liberal in politics; member of the governor's executive council, 1912-17; opposed Annie Besant's internment; served as vice-chancellor of Banaras and Madras universities; elected to Madras legislative council, 1904 and Indian legislative assembly, 1920; presided over annual sessions of National Liberal Federation, 1919, 1926.

Ajmal Khan, Hakim (1865-1927). Well-known physician of Delhi; president of Congress, 1921.

Alexander, Horace (1889-1989). Quaker; secretary, Friends Peace Committee 1915-16; 1919, lecturer in International Relations at Woodbrooke; 1943, leader of the Friends Ambulance Unit team in Calcutta; 1947, accompanied Gandhi on foot through Noakhali; India, Gandhi, Tagore and Congress were some of his varied interests; member, India Conciliation Group.

Allen, Reginald Clifford (Lord Allen of Hurtwood) (1889-1939). Pacifist and socialist; a complex, attractive and fascinating personality; totally involved in public life that was largely enriched by controversies and arguments, one of the forerunners of the League of Nations Association, the Nationl Peace Council.

Ambedkar, Bhimrao Ramji (1891-1956). Indian statesman, led the depressed classes; attended the Round Table Conferences,

1930-2; signatory to the Poona agreement of 1932 which rejected separate electorates for Harijans; member of viceroy's executive council, 1942-6; member of Nehru's cabinet, 1947-51; one of the architects of India's republican constitution.

Amery, Leopold Charles Maurice Stennett (1873-1955). Conservative M.P. (1911-45); first lord of admiralty, 1922-23; colonial secretary, 1924-29; secretary of state for India, 1940-45.

Amrit Kaur, Rajkumari (1889-1964). Leading nationalist; foundation member, All India Women's Conference; secretary to Mahatma Gandhi for 16 years; member, Lok Sabha and minister of health, 1947-57, etc.

Andrews, C.F. (1871-1940). Educationist, author, publicist of India's cause; came to India in 1904 as member of the Cambridge brotherhood; friend of Gandhi and Tagore; one of the architects of India Conciliation group; became a Quaker.

Angell, Norman (1872-1967). Author, internationalist, free-lance peace activist; Labour MP, 1929-31; Nobel peace prize, 1933; wrote about 40 books; famous for his much acclaimed *The Great Illusion* (1910).

Anand, Mulk Raj (1905-2004). Man of letters; art critic; novelist; author of much celebrated and acclaimed works; professor of art and literature, Punjab University 1962-65; chairman, Lalit Kala Academy; awarded international Peace Prize by the World Peace Council, 1952; Padma Bhushan 1967; more than 40 publications including untouchables (1935) and Coolie (1936).

Ansari, Mukhtar Ahmed (1880-1936). Nationalist leader; led the Indian medical mission to Turkey, 1912-13; founded the Home Rule League in 1917 in Delhi; chairman, reception committee of the Muslim League, 1918 etc.

Arundale, George Sydney (1878-1945). Theosophist and English academician; adopted India as his home; professor in Central Hindu College, Banaras; attracted by Annie Besant and her Home Rule movement; organizing secretary of the League; rector, National University, Adyar; president, Madras Labour Union, 1944; president, Theosophical Society, 1933-45.

Attlee, Clement Richard, first earl (1883-1967). Labour MP, 1922-55; under-secretary for war, 1924; member of the Indian Statutory Commission, 1927-30; deputy leader of the opposition, 1931-5, and leader, 1935-40; lord privy seal 1940-2; deputy prime minister, 1942-5; prime minister, 1945- 51.

Azad, Chandra Shekhar (1906-1931). Nationalist and revolutionary; participated in the non-cooperation movement and imprisonment; joined the revolutionary group, 1922; formed the Hindustan Socialist Republican army; active role in Kakori mail dacoity; responsible for the bomb explosion in the Central Legislative Assembly, 8 April 1929; fought at Alfred Park at Allahabad with the police and died, 17 February 1931.

Bailey, Vernon Gerald (1903-72). Quaker, peace activist; ran the National Peace Council for 19 years; played a leading role in the creation of the World Union of Peace Organizations at Geneva in 1948.

Bajaj, Ramakrishna Jamnalal (1889-1942). Indian industrialist; participated in the freedom movement; courted imprisonment thrice between 1940-45; managing director, Bajaj Electronics Ltd; cotton merchant and banker.

Baldwin, Stanley (1867-1947). British statesman; prime minister, 1923, 1924-9, 1936-7; member of MacDonald's National government, 1931-5; supported Government of India Bill 1935; target of Rothermere, Beaverbrook and Churchill for being inadequate in the Empire free-trade movement and for supporting dominion status for India.

Baldwin, Roger (1884-1981). Founder of the American Civil Liberties Union (ACLU) and political reformer; executive director, ACLU, 1920-50; regarded as leftist because of his defence of radical labour unions and other left groups in the 1920s and 1930s.

Balfour, Arthur James (1848-1941). British Conservative statesman; prime minister, 1902-5; lord privy seal, 1902-3; first lord of the admiralty 1915-16; secretary of state for foreign affairs, 1916-19; etc.

Barlett, Percy Walter (1888-1980). Member of the Society of Friends; conscientious objector; secretary, International Fellowship of Reconciliation, 1936-56.

Barry, Gerald Reid (1898-1968). Journalist and administrator; editor, *Saturday Review,* 1925-30; *Weekened Review,* 1930-34; managing editor, *News Chronicle,* 1936-47, etc.

Beaverbrook, Atkin Maxwell, Lord (1897-1964). Proprietor of Express newspapers; Conservative politician and senior minister; exercised full editorial control over *Daily Express, Sunday Express* and *London Evening Standard;* his conservatism was firmly rooted in the empire; invariably at odds with his party leaders with the exception of Bonar Law and Churchill; along with Northcliffe and Rothermere, Beaverbrook was founding father of modern, mass-circulation popular journalism; his Empire Crusade (1929-31) challenged Baldwin's party leadership.

Beckett, John Warburten (1894-1964). Labour politician; MP, 1924-31; joined ILP, 1931; co-founder with the Duke of Bedford of the British People's Party, 1938.

Benn, William Wedgwood, first viscount Stansgate (1877-1960). Joined Labour Party, 1927; secretary of state for India, 1929-31; secretary of state for air, 1945-6.

Benthall, Edwin Charles (1893-1961). Senior partner of Bird and Co.; close adviser to the Government of India; participated in the RTCs; member, viceroy's executive council, 1942-45.

Bernal, John Desmond (1901-71). Physicist; member of Communist Party; wrote *The Social Function of Science* (1936), *Science in History* (1954), etc.; contributed to scientific planning of invasion of Europe; leading Marxist scientist; emphasized revolutionary potentialities of science and its social base.

Besant, Annie (1847-1933). British Theosophist, educationist and Indian patriot; from 1895 active in India; president, Theosophical Society, 1907-33; initiated Home Rule for India League, 1916; president of Congress, 1918; one of the founders of Banaras Hindu University; lived at the Theosophical Society headquarters; editor, *New India* and *Commonweal.*

Bevan, Aneurin (1897-1960). Labour politician; Labour MP, 1929-60; founder, contributor and editor (1942-5) of the *Tribune;* elected to national executive of the Labour Party, 1944; minister of health and housing, 1945-51; obtained passage of National Health Service Act, 1946, etc.; deputy leader, parliamentary party, 1959; had vitalizing influence in labour politics.

Bevin, Ernest (1881-1951). Labour politician; leader of Docker's Union, 1920-1; creator and general secretary of Transport and General Workers Union, 1921-40; one of the architects of Mond-Turnerism; minister of labour and national service and member of war cabinet, 1940-5; foreign secretary, 1945-51.

Bhagat Singh, (1907-31). Indian nationalist; revolutionary; founded Nav Jawan Bharat Sabha with a broad programme to establish a non-exploitative egalitarian society; also founded the Hindustan Socialist Republican Army; arrested and tried for a whole series of charges including throwing of bombs in the Legislative Assembly on 8 April 1929 and was executed on 2 March 1931.

Bikaner, Ganga Singh Bahadur, Maharaja of (1880-1940), Indian prince; chancellor, Chamber of Princes, 1921-4; attended Round Table Conferences, 1930-1; supported All- India Federation.

Bing, Harold Frederick (1897-1975). Teacher, lecturer, pacifist; head, National Committee and Youth Section, No More War Movement, 1933-7; International Advisory Council, War Resisters 'International', 1925-75; sponsor, Peace Pledge Union, 1937-75; associate of Fenner Brockway, Reginald Reynolds, Carl Heath, Wilfred Wellock etc., supporter of Gandhi.

Birdwood, William, Riddell (1865-1951). Field-marshal; served in India, 1885-99, South Africa, 1899-1902; assistant military secretary, 1902-4; military secretary, 1905-9; commanded Northern Army, India, 1920-4; commander-in-chief, India, 1925-30; field-marshal, 1925.

Birkenhead, Frederick Edwin Smith, first earl, (1874-1930). Conservative MP 1906-19; attorney-general, 1915-19; lord chancellor, 1919-22; secretary of state for India, 1924-8.

Birla, G.D. (1894-1983). Indian commercial and industrial magnate; president, Federation of Indian Chambers of Commerce and Industry, 1929-31; on good terms with many Congress leaders; close associate of Gandhi.

Blatchford, Robert Peel Glanville (1851-1943). Unconventional and independent socialist; believed in the inevitability of the evolution of socialism; denounced religion as a barrier to social progress; unusual phenomenon in British socialist movement.

Boothby, Robert John Graham, (1900). Conservative politician; MP, 1924-50, 1950-58 when he was created Baron Boothby; parliamentary private secretary to Winston, 1926-29;

parliamentary secretary to ministry of food, 1940-41; British delegate to council of Europe at Strasbourg, 1949-55; etc.

Bose, Subhas Chandra (1897-1945). Educated in Cuttack, Calcutta and Cambridge: qualified for the I.C.S. but resigned in 1921; detained or exiled for long terms; president of the Congress 1938 and 1939; resigned in 1939; escaped to Germany 1941; organized the Indian National Army in South East Asia; died in an aircraft accident August 1945.

Brailsford, H.N. (1873-1958). British radical journalist and committed socialist; editor, *New Leader,* 1922-6; wrote regularly in *New Statesman and Nation.*

Braithwaite, Joseph Gurney (1895-1958). Served in World War I; parliamentary secretary, ministry of transport, 1951-4; Conservative MP, 1931-5, 1939-55.

Brelvi, S.A. (1891-1949). Bombay nationalist; editor, *Bombay Chronicle,* 1924-49.

Bridgeman, Reginald Francis Orlando (1884-1968). Socialist, anti-imperialist, well travelled journalist and diplomat; interested in Persia and India; visited India on several occasions; involved in the 'Hands off China' committee; made a few intensive studies of illiteracy, poverty and working class of other countries.

Brittain, Vera Mary (1893-1970). Author, pacifist and feminist in the 1920s worked both for the Liberal and Labour parties; joined Womens' International League for Peace and Freedom; in 1937 became a sponsor of the Peace Pledge Union.

Brockway, Archibald Fenner (1888-1990). Labour politician; socialist; journalist; editor, *Labour Leader,* 1912-17, *New Leader,* 1926-9, 1931-46; secretary, ILP, 1923; chairman, ILP, 1931; general secretary, ILP, 1934-8; Labour MP, 1929- 31, 1946-64; chairman, Congress of Peoples Against Imperialism 1948, etc.

Brown, Herbert Runham (1879-1949). Chairman, Enfield branch, No Conscription Fellowship, 1915-19; No-More-War movement, 1921-36; honorary secretary, War Resisters' International, 1923-49; Christian pacifist.

Brown, William John (1894-1960). Author; journalist; Labour MP, 1929-31; ILP MP, March 1931-October 1931; independent MP, 1942-50.

Butler, Spencer Harcourt (1869-1938). I.C.S.; secretary, foreign department, 1907-10; in charge of education, 1910-15; lieutenant-governor, United Provinces, 1918-21; governor, United Provinces, 1921-23.

Carson, Edward Henry, Baron Carson (1854-1935). Leader, Irish unionists in the Commons; MP, 1918-21 passionate speaker, fearless advocate, etc.

Castle, Barbara (1911-). Labour MP for Blackburn since 1945; cabinet minister in 1964-70 Labour government.

Cavendish, Victor Christian William, ninth duke of Devenshire and Marquess of Hartington (1868-1938). Unionist MP, 1891-1908; financial secretary to treasury, 1903-5; governor-general of Canada, 1916-21; colonial secretary, 1922-4, active in preparations for British Empire Exhibition of 1924.

Chamberlain, (Arthur) Neville (1869-1940). Conservative Statesman; outstanding figure in Birmingham industrial life; Conservative MP for Birmingham, 1918-40; chancellor of the exchequer, 1923-24; minister of health, 1923-29; prime minister, 1937-40, etc.

Chamberlain, Sir (Joseph) Austen (1863-1937). Statesman; liberal unionist MP, 1892-1914, 1914-37; civil lord of admiralty, 1895-1900; secretary of state for India, 1915; member of war cabinet, 1919-21; conservative leader, 1921; foreign secretary,

1924-9; first lord of admiralty in National government, August-October 1931; Nobel peace prize, 1925.

Chatterjee, Sir Atul Chandra (1874-1955). Indian civil servant; educated at Calcutta and Cambridge; high commissioner, London, 1925-31; on India Council, 1931-6; represented India at International Labour Conferences and at League Assembly, 1925, etc.

Chattopadhyaya, Birendranath (Chatto) (d. 1946). Revolutionary; communist; brother of Sarojini Naidu; had close relation with C.R. Pillay, Raja Mahendra Pratap, Madam Cama, Lala Hardayal, Bhupendra Nath Dutta, M.L. Dhingra, Syamaji Krishnavarma; came into contact with Trotsky and Lenin; worked for Communist International.

Chelmsford, Thesiger Frederick John Napier, first viscount (1863-1933). Called to the bar, 1893; governor of Queensland, 1905-9; governor of New South Wales, 1909-13; viceroy of India, 1916-21.

Chetwode, Philip Walhouse, first baron Chetwode (1869-1950). Field-marshal; active services in Burma, 1892-3; South Africa, 1899-1902; in France in 1915-16; in Egypt, 1916-17; Jerusalem, 1917-18; at War office, 1919-20; chief of general staff, India, 1928-30; commander-in-chief, 1930-5; field marshal, 1933.

Chintamani, C.Y. (1880-1941). Famous journalist, almost the maker of the *Leader* of Allahabad and its editor, 1909-23, 1926-41.

Churchill, Winston L.S. (1874-1965). Conservative leader; prime minister, 1940-5, 1951-5; organized British victory in World War II; die-hard imperialist; opposed to concession to India.

Clark, George Sydenham (1848-1933). Civil servant and administrator; on the staff of Royal Indian Engineering College,

1871-80; secretary, Colonial Defence Committee, 1885-93; governor of Victoria, Australia, 1901-4; of Bombay, 1907-13; member, executive committee of Indian Empire Society, 1930.

Clifton Brown, Douglas (1879-1958). Conservative politician; MP, 1918-51; speaker of the House of Commons, 1943-51; viscount, 1951; active member of executive committee, Indian Empire Society.

Clynes, John Robert (1869-1949). Labour leader; on Labour Party national executive, 1909-39; Labour MP, 1906-31, 1935-45; home secretary, 1929-31; refused party leadership, 1931.

Cole, George Douglas Howard (1889-1959). University teacher, writer and socialist; joined Fabian Society and ILP; advocate of guild socialism; chairman, Fabian Society, 1939-46, 1948-50; chairman, *New Statesman,* 1956.

Corbett, Geoffrey Lotham (1886-1957). ICS; assistant commissioner, C.P. 1905-9; deputy secretary, government of India, 1919-21; secretary, commerce department.

Cooper, Alfred Duff (1890-1952). Conservative politician; MP, 1924-29 and 1931-45; financial secretary to the war office, 1928-29 and 1931-34, secretary of state for war, 1935-37; first level of the admiralty, 1937-1938 when he resigned over the Munich agreement, minister of information, May 1940-July 1941; ambassador in Paris, 1944-47.

Craddock, Reginald Henry (1864-1937). Indian civil servant; chief commissioner, Central Provinces, 1907-12; home member, viceroy's council, 1912-17; lieutenant governor, Burma, 1917-22; Conservative MP, 1931-7.

Creech Jones, Arthur (1891-1964). Trade unionist; national secretary, transport workers' union, 1919-29; Labour MP, 1935-50 and 1954-64; parliamentary under-secretary of state for colonies, 1945-46 etc; chairman, Labour Party advisory committee on imperial questions, 1940-45.

Cripps, Sir Stafford (1889-1952). Solicitor-General in the Labour government, 1930-1; expelled from the Labour Party for advocating united front, 1939; visited India after the outbreak of war, 1939; British ambassador in Moscow, 1940-2; member of war cabinet and deputed by it to India, 1942; minister of aircraft production, 1942-5; president, board of trade, 1945-7; member of cabinet mission to India, 1946; chancellor of the exchequer, 1947-50.

Croft, Henry Page (1881-1947). British politician; formed a strong imperialist National Party, 1917-22; returning to Conservative fold agitated for tariffs and against Indian self-government; joint parliamentary under-secretary, 1940- 5.

Crozier, William Percival (1879-1944). Journalist; joined *Manchester Guardian;* editor, 1932-44; had extensive contact with Indian Liberals through B. Shiva Rao.

Culverwell, Cyril Tom (1895-1963). Conservative politician; MP, 1928-48; member of Bristol city council, 1924-30.

Curtis, Lionel George (1872-1955). Public servant; in South Africa, 1899-1909; a founder of the *Round Table,* 1907-9; Bait lecturer on colonial history, Oxford, 1912, studied Commonwealth problems, 1911-16; joined constitutional discussions in India, 1916-17; published *Dyarchy,* 1920; and *Civitas* Dei (3 vols, 1934-7; brought about the foundation of Royal Institute of International Affairs, 1920-1.

Das, Chitta Ranjan (1870-1925). Leading barrister of Calcutta; joined Congress in 1906; formed with Motilal Nehru the Swaraj party within the Congress in 1922; president of Congress, 1922.

Desai, Mahadev (1892-1942), Gandhi's Private Secretary and close associate.

Desai, Bhulabhai (1877-1946), Advocate and nationalist leader; joined Annie Besant's Home Rule League; member, Liberal party; assisted the official committee to look into the peasant's grievances after Bardoli satyagraha; participated in the civil disobedience movement; elected to the central assembly, 1934; defended the I.N.A. prisoners.

de Valera, Eamon (1882-1975). American-born Irish statesman; took part in Dublin rising, 1916; republican leader, 1917-26; head of government, 1932-48, 1951-4, 1957-9; president of the Eire, 1959-73.

Elliot, Water Elliot (1888-1958). Conservative politician; MP, 1918-23, 1924-45, 1946-50, and 1950-58; under-secretary of state for Scotland, 1923-24, to 1924-26; under-secretary of state for Scotland, 1926-1929; secretary of state for Scotland 1936-38; etc.

Ellis, Henry Havelock (1859-1939). Pioneer in the scientific study of sex; thinker; critic; essayist and editor; saw search for scientific truth as the source of artistic satisfaction and study of sex as his life-work; publications include *Studies in the Psychology of Sex,* 7 volumes (1897-1928).

Emerson, Sir Herbert (1881-1962). Administrator; ICS, 1905; home secretary, 1930-3; governor of the Punjab, 1933-8.

Fazlul Huq, A.K. (1873-1962). Indian nationalist, lawyer of Calcutta; member, Bengal legislative council, 1913-20; president, Muslim League, 1916-21; chief minister of Bengal, 1937-43.

Fitzalan, first viscount of Derwent (1855-1947). Conservative MP, 1899-1902; 1854-1921; joint parliamentary secretary, 1915-21; viceroy of Ireland, 1921-2; etc.

Foot, Michael Mackintosh (1913-). Journalist, author and Labour statesman; editor, *Evening Standard,* 1942-3; political columnist, *Daily Herald,* 1944-64; managing director, *Tribune,* until

1974; member of the national executive committee, Labour Party, 1948-50 and from 1970; Labour MP, 1945-55, 1960-90; biographer of Aneurin Bevan, H.G. Wells, co-author of *Guilty Men* (1940), etc.

Forster, Edward Morgan (1879-1970). British novelist and man of letters; one of the Bloomsbury group; visited India, 1912 and 1921; worked out in his *A Passage to India* the rubric of personal relationships between human beings irrespective of political and social differences.

Freeman, Peter (1888-1956). Labour MP, 1929-31, 1945-56; chairman, Theosophical Society in Wales, 1922-44.

Fry, John P. (1864-1957). Member, Society of Friends; did much to forge the society's reputation for business acumen and financial integrity.

Gallacher, William (1881-1965). British communist politician; intimately involved with British working class movement; Communist MP, 1935-50.

Gandhi, Mohandas Karamchand (1869-1948). Indian national leader; organized non-violent movements against British imperialism; insisted on the supremacy of means over ends.

Garvin, James Louis (1868-1957). Journalist; joined *Newcastle Chronicle,* 1891; *Daily Telegraph,* 1899; wrote in *Fortnightly Review;* edited *Outlook,* 1905-6; *Pall Mall Gazette,* 1912-15; *Observer,* 1918-42; established remarkable personal influence; also wrote for *Sunday Express,* 1942-5 and for *Daily Telegraph,* 1945-51, etc.

Gibson, Arthur Lumis (1899-1959). Labour leader and trade unionist; an official of the National Union of Clerks and Administrative Workers; elected to the Birmingham city council.

Gollancz, Victor (1893-1967). Teacher, publisher, author and public campaigner; founded Left-Book Club, Save Europe Now and the Campaign against Capital Punishment.

Greenwood, Arthur (1880-1954). Teacher; researcher; Labour MP 1922-31, 1932-54; junior minister, second Labour government; deputy leader, Labour Party, 1935; member, war cabinet, 1940-2; lord privy seal, 1945-47.

Grenfell, D.R. (1881-1968). Coalminer; trade unionist; Labour MP, 1922-59.

Haig, Sir Harry (1881-1956). Indian civil service, 1905-40; secretary to the home department, Government of India, 1926-30; home member, viceroy's executive council, 1932-34; governor, UP 1934-9.

Hailey, Sir Malcolm (1872-1969). Indian civil service 1895-1930; member, viceroy's executive council, 1919-24; governor of Punjab 1924-28, and of UP 1928-30 and again 1931-34; director, African research survey, 1935-38.

Haldane, John Burdon Sanderson (1904-64). Geneticst; Fullerian professor of physiology, 1930-2; professor of genetics, University College, London, 1933-57; chairman, editorial board, *Daily Worker,* 1940-50; member, Biometry Research Unit, Indian Statistical Institute, Calcutta, 1957; became Indian citizen, 1961.

Hale, Leslie (1902-). Solicitor; Liberal parliamentary candidate, 1929; Labour MP, 1945-68.

Hales, Harold Keates (1868-1942). Shipper and merchant; founder of the firm of Hales Brothers; Conservative MP, 1931-35.

Hallett, Maurice Garnier (1883-1969). Entered ICS 1907; chief-secretary, Bihar and Orissa 1930-32; home secretary 1932-36; governor of Bihar 1937-9; governor of U.P. 1939-45.

Hankey, Sir Maurice (1877-1963). Naval officer and civil servant; secretary, committee of imperial defence, 1912-38; secretary, imperial war cabinet, 1917-18; secretary to the cabinet, 1919-38.

Harrison, Agatha (1883-1954). Member, Society of Friends; worked for C.F. Andrews and Gandhi; became secretary, India Conciliation group with Carl Heath as chairman, Alexander Wilson as treasurer, Henry Polak, William Paton, Dr Harold Mann, Grace Lankester and several ex-missionaries as active members; became the group's driving force till 1947. India and Gandhi were central to her concerns for two decades.

Haycock, Alexander Wilkinson Frederick (1882-39). Labour politician; MP, 1923-4, 1929-31; barrister-at-law.

Heath, Carl (1869-1950). Connected with the ecumenical movement since 1927; took part in the second World Conference on Faith and Order at Edinburgh; important member of India Conciliation Group.

Hewett, Sir John Prescott (1854-1941). ICS; secretary, Indian home department, 1895-1902; lieut.-governor, United Provinces, 1907-12; conservative MP, 1922-3; active member, Indian Empire Society.

Hicks, Ernest George (1879-1954). Trade unionist and labour leader; general secretary of Amalgamated Union of Building Trade Workers, 1921-41; president of Trades Union Congress, 1927, National Federation of Building Trade Operations, 1919-37; Labour MP, 1931-50.

Hoare, Sir Samuel, later viscount Templewood (1880-1959). Conservative MP, 1910-44; secretary of state for air, 1922- 3, 1924-9; secretary of state for India, 1931-5; foreign secretary, 1935; home secretary, 1937-9; lord privy seal, 1939-40; British ambassador in Spain, 1940-4.

Holmes, John Haynes (1879-1964). American clergyman; one of the foremost figures of the Social Gospel movement in 20th century American protestantism; an advocate of pacifist socialism; made Gandhi known in the United States; travelled widely; prolific writer; one of the founders of the National Association for the Advancement of Coloured People.

Horniman, B.G. (1873-1948). Politician and journalist; editor of *Bombay Chronicle;* deported from India, April 1919; returned, 1926.

Horrabin, James Francis (1883-1962). Artist, lecturer, cartoonist, cartographer, left-wing socialist; advocate of guild socialism; first editor of *Plebs;* Labour MP, 1929-31; chairman, Fabian Colonial Bureau, 1945-50.

Housman, Lawrence (1865-1959). Writer; art critic; playwright; pioneer feminist; pacifist socialist and Gandhian.

Hunter, John Mark Somers (1865-1932). Made his career in the Indian educational service; director of public instruction, Burma; knighted, 1923; secretary, Indian Empire Society, 1930.

Husain, Sir Fazl-i (1877-1936). A lawyer of the Punjab; chief organizer of the Unionist party; member of viceroy's council, 1930-5.

Hutchinson, Hugh Lester (1904-1968). British politician of strong leftist leanings; elected from Manchester as a Labour candidate, 1945-50.

Huxley, Aldous Leonard (1894-1963). British writer and man of letters; works include essays, fictions and travel books.

Iqbal, Sir Mohamed (1876-1938). An influential Islamic philosopher and poet in Persian and Urdu.

Irwin, Baron, Edward Frederick Lindley, later Earl Halifax

(1881-1959). British statesman; under-secretary for colonies, 1921-2; president of the board of education, 1922-4, 1932-5; minister of agriculture, 1924-5; viceroy of India, 1926-31; foreign secretary, 1938-40; British ambassador in Washington, 1941-6; applauded for an attempt at 'reconciliation' with India.

Iyengar, A. Rangaswami (1877-1934). Journalist, parliamentarian, constitutionalist, publicist; Swarajist; editor of *The Hindu,* January 1928-34; attend the 2nd RTC.

Jacob, Claud William (1863-1948). Field-marshal; served in the Indian army; chief of general staff, 1920-4; general, 1920; commander-in-chief, 1925; secretary, military department, India Office, 1926-30.

Jagger, John (1872-1942). Labour politician; trade unionist; private secretary to Herbert Morrison, 1940; Labour MP, 1935-40.

Jayakar, M.R. (1873-1959). Barrister and judge; leader of the Liberal Party; worked closely with Tej Bahadur Sapru.

Jehangir, Sir Cowasji. Bombay Parsi industrialist and Liberal politician.

Jinnah, M.A. (1876-1948). Barrister; president, Muslim League 1916, 1920 and from 1934 till his death; campaigned for the creation of Pakistan; governor-general of Pakistan, 1947-8.

Jones, Thomas Isaac Mardy (1879-70). Labour activist; gave much attention to Wales Miners' Federation and to questions of local government and India; economist; Labour MP, 1922-31, etc.

Jones, Morgan (1885-39). Teacher; imprisoned as a conscientious objector during World War I; ILP leader, 1920-1; Labour whip, 1922; parliamentary secretary, board of education, 1924, 1929-31; chairman, public accounts committee,

1931-8, etc.; Labour MP, 1921-39; member, national executive, Labour party, 1931-9.

Joshi, N.M. (1879-1955). Father of the Trade Union movement in India and pioneer in labour legislation; joined Servants of India Society, 1909; started a sister organization, Social Service League, 1911; started All India Trade Union Congress, 1921, its secretary till 1929; started the Trade Union Federation, 1929; between 1922 to 1929 often nominated to represent Indian Labour at I.L.O.; government nominee in the RTC; on the joint parliamentary committee; member of the Royal Commission on Indian Labour, 1929-30; belonged to the liberal school of politics.

Kelkar, Narasimha Chintamani (1872-1947). Maharashtrian journalist; politician; follower of Tilak; editor of *Mahratta,* 1896-1918; Puna municipal councillor, 1896-1924.

Kemal, Mustapha (1880-1938). Architect of modern Turkey; adopted the name Kemal Ataturk; a distinguished commander, organized a successful revolution in 1919; abolished the sultanate in 1922, the Caliphate in 1924; set up Turkish republic, 1923; secularized state, encouraged Western lifestyle.

Kenworthy, Joseph Montague (1886-1953). Liberal MP, 1919-26; Labour MP, 1926-31; succeeded to peerage as Baron Strabolgi, 1934; chief Labour Party whip in the house of lords, 1938-42.

Keonen, Wilhelm. German communist leader; lived in exile in England with Nazi ascendancy from 1933; formed the German cultural group in Britain, 1938; belonged to German communist group of USSR; one of the 'Willi Munzenberg boys'.

Keynes, John Maynard (1883-1946). Economist; fellow, King's College, Cambridge; his *The Economic Consequences of the Peace* (1919) became centre of controversy in European countries; made significant contributions in contemporary budgetary policy.

Khan, Abdul Ghaffar (1891-1989). Congress leader of NWFP; founded the 'Red Shirt' volunteer organization in 1929; supporter of Congress upto 1947.; adherent of non-violence; known as Frontier Gandhi.

Khandalkar, G.L.; Communist leader and associate of B.T. Ranadive; president, Girni Kamagar Union; favoured cooperation with Congress in 1930-2.

Kipling, Joseph Rudyard (1865-1935). Author; born in Bombay; cousin of Stanley Baldwin, wrote especially of the imperial race doing justice and upholding law; became known through stories, verse, novels and as the principal exponent of imperial ethics; entertained an authoritarian political faith; awarded nobel prize for literature, 1907.

Kitchlew, Saifuddin (1886-1963). Indian nationalist leader; led the anti-Rowlatt Act agitation 1919; president, the All India Khilafat Committee, 1924; opposed the partition of India; following Indian independence severed links with the Congress party and was drawn towards communism.

Klugmann, James (1912-72). Played a leading role in the international student movement in the 1930s having joined the CP in 1933; served in the army in the Middle East and Yugoslavia during World War II; worked for the party as lecturer, editor and writer; editor, *Marxism Today,* 1962-72; wrote two volumes of the history of CPGB, *Formation and Early Years, 1918-1924* (1968) and *The General Strike, 1925- 1926* (1969).

Knight, George Wilford Holford (1877-1936). Barrister-at-Law; Labour MP, 1931-5; engaged in London municipal government.

Kunzru, Hriday Nath (1887-1978). Indian nationalist; actively associated with Congress until the Liberals seceded in 1918;

member, United Provinces Legislative Council, 1921- 3; MLA, 1927-30; prominent in Servants of India Society.

Lansbury, George (1859-1940). Christian socialist and pacifist of Britain; led the Labour Party after the formation of MacDonald's national government; resigned in 1935 on the question of sanctions against Italy for its invasion of Ethiopia.

Laski, Harold Joseph (1893-1950). British political theorist; professor of political science, LSE, University of London, 1925-50; rejected the pluralist theory of state and moved closer to Marxism in 1930-1; chairman of the Labour Party and chief target of the Conservative election campaign in 1945.

Laski, Frieda (1885-) Committed suffragist; involved in workers' birth control and abortion movement, law reform association, Fabian women's group and India League; a committed socialist and unconventional feminist; married to Harold Laski.

Lawson, Harry Lawson Webster Levy, Viscount Burnham (1862-1933). Liberal MP, 1985-92; served on Indian statutory committee 1927-30; managing proprietor of *Daily Telegraph,* 1903-28, etc.

Lee, Jennie (1904-89). Writer, lecturer, director of the *Tribune;* Labour MP, 1929-31, 1945-70; member, national executive committee of Labour Party, 1958-70; chairman, 1967-8; created Baroness Lee, 1970.

Lenin, V.I. [Vladimir Ilyich Ulyanov] (1870-1924). Russian communist revolutionary; lived in exile until World War I; re-entered Russia and headed Bolshevik revolution, 1917; president of council of Soviet Union till 1922.

Lester, Muriel (1883-1968). Christian associate of Gandhi; pacifist; met Gandhi at Sabarmati *ashram* in 1925; founded the

Kingsley Community Hall in East End, London, on principles much in common with those of Gandhi's *ashrams;* took up the cause of prohibition in England on the initiative of Gandhi; became a spokesman of Gandhi in England; in 1938 joined the Indian Fellowship of Reconciliation; known as the great fellow-traveller of Gandhi; author of many works, including, *Entertaining Gandhi,* (1932), *Gandhi's Signature* (1932), *Everlasting Gandhi* (1932), *It Occurred to Me,* (1937), *It So Happened* (1947), *My Host, the Hindu* (1949).

Lindsay, Alexander Dunlop (1875-1952). Educationist; fellow and classical tutor. Balliol College, Oxford, 1906-22; master of Balliol, 1924-49; welcomed opening of Oxford to wider social classes; his democratic theories were based on his Christian beliefs and they made him a national figure; adviser on education to Labour Party and trade unions; chairman, committee on work of Christian colleges in India 1930; vice-chancellor, Oxford University, 1935-8; etc.

Lloyd, Sir George, later Lord Lloyd (1879-1941). Conservative MP, 1910-18; governor of Bombay, 1918-23; secretary of state for colonies, 1940-1.

Lloyd George, David (1863-1945). British Liberal politician; MP, 1890-1945; controversial chancellor of the exchequer of the 'peoples' budget' fame, 1909; introduced first war budget, 1914; secretary of state for war, 1916; prime minister in coalition government, 1916-22.

Locker-Lampson, Oliver Stillingfleet (1880-1954). Conservative M.P. 1910-45; private secretary to Asten Chamberlain; proprietor of *Peterborough Standard, Huntingdonshire Post* and *Empire Review.*

Lohia, Ram Manohar (1910-1967). Scholar, thinker, socialist, nationalist; member, executive committee of the Congress Socialist party (1934); editor, the Congress Socialist; left the congress to from the Socialist Party; editor, Mankind, 1956; prolific writer and sought to define the contours of socialism in Indian context.

Longden, Fred (1886-1952). Member of Union of Democratic Control and conscientious objector during World War I; lecturer and author; Labour MP, 1929-31, 1945-50.

Lothian, (Philip Kerr), eleventh marquis, Lord (1882-1940). Editor, *Round Table,* 1910-16; secretary to Lloyd George, 1916-21; parliamentary under-secretary for India 1931-2; chairman, Indian franchise committee, 1932; British ambassador in Washington, 1939-40.

MacDonald, Ramsay (1866-1937). British Labour leader; joined the ILP in 1894; chairman, 1906-9; led the parliamentary Labour Party, 1911-14; prime minister, 1924, 1929-31; prime minister in the National government, 1931-5.

MacDonald, Malcolm John (1901-1981). Son of Ramsay MacDonald; Labour MP, 1929-31, 1931-5, 1936-45; parliamentary under-secretary for dominions, 1931-5; British high commissioner in India, 1955-60.

Mackay, James Lyle, first earl of Inchcape (1852-1932). Shipowner; senior partner of Mackinnon, Mackenzie and Co, Calcutta, 1974; served on Bengal legislative council, 1891-3; chairman and director of numerous shipping and banking companies, served on council of India, 1897-1911, Imperial defence committee, 1917, Geddes economy committee, 1921-2; ardent free trader, crossed from Liberal to Conservative benches, 1926.

Macmillan, Maurice Harold (1894-). Conservative statesman; Conservative MP, 1924-29, 1931-1945 and 1945-64 aid-de-camp to the duke of Devonshire, governor general of Canada, 1919-20; parliamentary under secretary of state for the colonies, 1942;

minister of housing and local governments, 1951-54; minister of defence 1954-55; foreign secretary, 1955; CHANCELLOR OF EXCHEQUER, 1955-57; prime minister and FIRST LORD OF THE TREASURY 1957-1963.

Mahmud, Syed (1889-1971). Lawyer of Patna and personal friend of Jawaharlal Nehru and his wife; minister in Bihar 1937-9 and 1946-52.

Malaviya, Madan Mohan (1861-1946). One of the founders of the Banaras Hindu University; attended the second RTC with Gandhi; developed Hindu orientation in politics; founded All-India Hindu Mahasabha, 1906; president of Mahasabha 1923, 1924, 1926; president of Congress, 1909, 1918, 1932and 1933; vice-chancellor of Banaras University, 1919-38.

Mann, Tomas (Tom) (1856-1941). Trade unionist and communist; founded Social Democratic Federation, 1885; helped London dock strike, 1889; president, Dockers' Union, 1889-93; ILP, 1894-7; founder member, British Communist Party, 1920; chairman, National Minority movement, 1924-32; general secretary, Amalgamated Society of Engineers, 1919-20 and Amalgamated Engineering Union, 1920-21.

Marley, James (1920-54). Teacher; Labour MP, 1923-4, 1929-31; founder and joint secretary, Teachers' Labour League.

Martin, Basil Kingsley (1897-1969). British journalist and editor; lead-writer, *Manchester Guardian,* 1927-30; editor, *New Statesman* and *New Statesman and Nation,* 1931-60; cofounder with W.H. Robson of the *Political Quarterly.*

Masani, M.R. (1905- 199). Indian politician; educated at Elphinston College, Bombay and London School of Economics; founder secretary, Congress Socialist Party, 1934-39; mayor or Bombay, 1943-44; member, the Central Assembly, 1945-47;

Indian ambassador to Brazil, 1948-49; M.P. 1949-53; one of the founders of the Swatantra Party.

Maxton, James (1885-1946). Politician, teacher and persuasive platform orator; organizer, ILP, 1919; chairman, 1926-31, 1934-9; MP, 1922-46.

McElwee, Andrew. Labour MP, 1923-4; 1929-31; active till 1932.

Meherally, Yusuf Jaffar (1903-1950). Socialist activist; educated in Calcutta and Bombay; organized Bombay Youth League, 1928; demonstrated against Simon Commission; in 1929 started the *Vanguard*; the civil disobedience movement was run by this formidable youth force ater the arrest of the leaders; in 1934 imprisoned for two years; one of the founding members of the CSP; in 1938 travelled to Europe, England and the USA arrested in 1940, presided over the All India Students' Conference in Patna, 1941; arrested during 1942.

Mehta, Ashok (1911-1985). Indian socialist activist; believed in social justice individual freedom and dignity, democratic values and economic egalitarianism; in 1934 founded CSP; edited the *Congress Socialist* weekly in 1934-39; founder and first secretary of the Hind Mazdoor Sabha; elected twice to the Lok Sabha, became the deputy chairman, Planning Commission, minister of the union cabinet.

Meston, James (1865-1943). ICS; lieutenant-governor, United Provinces, 1912-18; associate of Lionel Curtis and his group.

Milne, Charles Black (1879-1960). Advocate and Conservative politician; MP, 1929-35.

Mirabehn (Madeleine Slade) (1892-1982). Daughter of Admiral Sir Edmond Slade; Romain Rolland introduced her to Gandhi who gave her the name of Mira; became a close associate of Gandhi; accompanied Gandhi to the second RTC in 1932 as his interpreter; imprisoned in India thrice, etc.

Mody, H.P. (1886-1969). Advocate, businessman, philanthropist, writer etc.

Mohammed Ali, Maulana (1878-1931). Pan-Islamist, Indian nationalist politician and journalist; founder of *Comrade* and *Hamdard;* interned in 1915-19; a leader of the Khilafat agitation; in jail for sedition, 1921-3; president of Congress, 1923; thereafter drifted away from the Congress.

Mond, Alfred Moritz, first baron Melchet (1868-1930). Industrialist, financier and politician; successfully advocated and worked for principles of coordination and cooperation as basis of industrial enterprise.

Montagu, E.S. (1879-1924). Secretary of state for India, 1917-22; visited India in 1918 and, with the viceroy, Chelmsford, made proposals which formed the basis of the reforms of 1919.

Moonje, Balakrishna Shivaram, 1872-1946. Doctor of medicine; went to South Africa during the Boer War; lived with Gandhi for a week; started practising at Nagpur, 1921; came in close contact with Tilak, accepted Tilak as guru; entered the Swadeshi movement; joined the swaraj party; and then Hindu Mahasabha; president of the Sabha in 1926, resigned from Congress 1920. The years since 1937 he devoted to promote his Military School.

Morgan, John Hartman (1876-1955). lawyer; leader writer for *Manchester Guardian,* 1904-5; professor of constitutional law, University College, London, 1923-41; legal adviser to American war crimes commission, 1947-9; etc.

Morrison, Herbert (1888-1965). Labour MP, 1923-24, 1929-31; 1935-39; junior minister in second Labour government, member, Churchill's war cabinet; deputy PM, 1945-51; secretary of state for foreign affairs, 1951.

Mosley, Oswald (b.1896). Conservative MP, 1918-22; independent MP, 1922-24; Labour MP, 1926-31; formed the New Party, 1931; Leader of the Fascist movement in Britain.

Munzenberg, Willi (1889-1940). Communist publisher of Berlin; a genius at organization and publicity; worked for Communist International; created the concept of fellow-traveller.

Murray, George Gilbert Aimé (1866-1957). Renowned classical scholar and internationalist; regius professor of Greek, Oxford, 1908-36; founder of the League of Nations Union and chairman of its executive council, 1923-38.

Naidu, Sarojini (1879-1949). Poet and politician; president of Congress, 1925; governor of Uttar Pradesh, 1947-9.

Nambooripad, E.M.S. (1909-2001). Indian communist leader; at an early age influenced by Gokhale, Tilak and Gandhi; joined the civil disobedience movement in 1932; arrested for 3 years; became a socialist in jail; one of the founders of CSP at Patna in 1934; in 1937 elected to Madras legislative assembly; in 1940 joined the Communist Party of India; member of the bureau, till 1964; joined CPIM; first communist chief minister, Kerala, 1957; the principal contribution was to build communist movement.

Narayan, Jayaprakash, 1902-1977. Social politician and nationalist activist; educated in Patna, Benaras and Wisconsin, USA; studied radical social studies, Harkishan and the works of M.N. Roy; joined the civil disobedience movement; met at Nasik jail, Achyut Patwardhan and Minoo Masani; formed the CSP in 1934; became a firm advocate of *purna swaraj* and *socialism,* etc.

Narendra, Deva (Acharya), 1889-1956. Socialist leader and educationist; as a young man came under the influence of Swami Ram Tirtha and Madam Mohan Malaviya; attended the Congress session at Lucknow in 1899; as a student at Allahabad came under the spell of Tilak, Lajpat Rai, Bipin Pal, Aurobindo Ghosh; established a live contact with Sachindranath Sanyal and through him to several other revolutionaries; joined Kashi Vidyapith at Banaras in 1981; deeply studied scientific socialism and Buddhism; associated with Gandhian movements; president, CSP 1934; accepted Gandhi's leadership; courted arrest, 1940 and 1942; in 1946 elected to UP Legislative assembly in 1948 CSP seceded from the Congress; vice-chancellor, Lucknow University, 1947-51; vice-chancellor, Banaras Hindu University, 1951-53.

Natesan, G.A. (1873-1949). Liberal nationalist; publisher; established a monthly journal called *Indian Politics* and then, the *Indian Review,* 1910; first secretary of Indian Liberal Federation; humanitarian; for about 50 years publicized the nationalist cause.

Nehru, Motilal (1861-1931). Lawyer of Allahabad; president of Congress, 1919, 1928; founder with C.R. Das of the Swaraj party and leader of the party in the Central Assembly, 1924- 6.

Nehru, Rameshwari (Mrs Brijlal Nehru) (1886-1966). Indian nationalist; devoted to women's upliftment in Allahabad, 1908-28; following Lahore session of Congress in 1929, engaged herself in mobilizing women to join the nationalist movement; went to England in the early 1930s and became chairman, Women's Committee, CIL, April, 1931; remained in England during second RTC as an activist of the League; went to Geneva on the invitation of the League of Nations, 1933; president, All India Women's Conference, 1940; imprisoned during the Quit India movement; undertook relief work during Bengal famines, 1943-4; associate of Sarojini Naidu, Aruna Asaf Ali etc; devoted herself to the rehabilitation of refugees, Harijan upliftment, promotion of Afro-Asian solidarity and nuclear disarmament, 1949-66.

Nehru, Jawaharlal (1889-1964). Son of Motilal Nehru; barrister and politician; entered politics as supporter of Gandhi; proponent of *purna swaraj* and socialist cause; president of Congress, 1929, 1936, 1937, 1946, 1951-4; prime minister of India, 1947-64.

Noel-Baker, Philip John (1889-1978). Professor of International Relations, London, 1924-9; secretary, League of Nations, 1919-22; parliamentary private secretary to foreign secretary, 1929-31; secretary of state for air, 1946-7; secretary of state for commonwealth relations, 1947- 50; Nobel peace prize, 1959; Labour MP, 1929-31, 1936-70; member, national executive committee, Labour Party, 1937-48; chairman, 1946-7.

O'Dwyer, Michael Francis (1864-1940). ICS, 1865; revenue commissioner, NWFP, 1901-8; acting resident, Hyderabad, 1908-9; viceroy's agent in Central India, 1910-12; knighted, 1913; lieutenant-governor, Punjab, 1913-19; responsible for the massacre of Amritsar; active member of Indian Empire Society, 1930-5; assassinated in London by Udham Singh, 1940.

Ormsby-Gore, George Arthur (1885-1964). Conservative politician; MP, 1910-1938, when he succeeded to peerage; under-secretary of state for colonies, 1922-24, 1924-29; secretary of state for colonies, 1936-38; high commissioner to South Africa, 1941-44, chairman, Midland Bank, 1952-57.

Palme-Dutt, R. (1896-1974). Significant Marxist theoretician; member of executive committee of British Communist Party, 1922-65; editor, *Labour Monthly,* from 1921 till his death.

Pankhurst, Sylvia (1882-1960). Leading suffragette; socialist; wrote the influential *The History of the Women's Suffrage Movement* (1911); politically moved to left of ILP; edited *The Women's Dreadnought,* a weekly for working-class women; joined CP to be expelled soon; wrote *India and the Earthly Paradise* (1926); known as an artist and a crusader for justice and freedom.

Patel, Vallabhbhai (1875-1950). Congressman of Ahmedabad; organized no-rent campaign in Bardoli, 1928; president of Congress, 1931; member of interim government, 1946-7; deputy prime minister, 1947-50.

Patel, Vithalbhai, 1873-1933. Indian nationalist; barrister; associated with Dadabhai Naoroji, entered legislative council, 1912; piloted the primary education bill; member, imperial legislative assembly; 1916-21; resigned to joined satyagraha; entered Indian legislative assembly, 1924-26; reelected 1927; refused to insisted Simon to the assembly Chambi; etc. died in Europe.

Paton, John (1886-1976). Labour leader; general secretary, ILP, 1927-33; editor, *New Leader* and *Penal Reformer;* Labour MP, 1945-50, 1950-64.

Paton, William (1886-1943). British Presbyterian minister and secretary of International Missionary Council; secretary, National Christian Council of India, Burma and Ceylon, 1921-7; editor, *International Review of Missions,* 1927-43; member, India Conciliation Group.

Peel, Lord (1867-1937). Conservative secretary of state for India, 1922-4, 1928-9.

Pethick-Lawrence, Emmeline (1867-1954). Suffragette; socialist; in 1907 along with her husband launched *Votes for Women,* a journal of the WSPU, until 1912; in 1926, president of the feminist Freedom League; World War II shook her long-standing faith in pacifism; distinguished by a desire for justice which was at the root of both her socialism and feminism.

Pethick-Lawrence, Frederick Williams, first baron (1871-1961). Labour MP, 1923-31, 1935-45; secretary of state for India, 1945-7; member of cabinet mission to India, 1946.

Picton-Turbervill, Edith (1872-1960). Social worker; interested in evangelical work; trained missionary; closely connected with YWCA; visited India several times; worked for women's suffrage; Labour MP, 1929-31.

Platts-Mills, John Faithful Fortescue (1906-1993). Left- wing Labour; a 'Bevan boy', 1944-5; member, Finsbury borough council, 1945-53; Labour MP, 1945-50; expelled from Labour Party, 1948; member of Labour Independent Group, 1949-50; QC, 1964; an India League activist.

Polak, H.S.L. (1882-1959). Solicitor; spent early years in South Africa, where he became a friend of Gandhi; active in the Commonwealth of India League in the nineteen-twenties; member, India Conciliation group; member, Labour Party's special committee on colonial issues.

Pole, David Graham (1877-1952). Solicitor; Labour politician; served in France retiring with rank of Major, 1914-18; treasurer, National Labour Club, 1919-30; vice-chairman, Machinery of government committee, Labour Party, 1920-30; honorary secretary, British Committee on Indian Affairs, 1916-30; Labour M.P., 1929-31.

Pollitt, Harry (1890-1960). British communist leader; active in voicing opposition to World War I; participated in 'Hands off Russia' movement; founder member of CPGB; general secretary of CPGB, 1929-56, with a short break; responsible for CP's publication, *The British Road to Socialism* (1951).

Prasad, Rajendra (1884-1963). Lawyer of Patna who joined Mahatma Gandhi in 1917; president of the Congress 1934, 1939 and 1947-8; president of the constituent assembly, 1946-50; President of India, 1950-62.

Pritt, Denis Nowell (1887-1972). Lawyer; in his youth worked for the conservatives in Bromley; joined in turn the Liberal

Party and then the Labour Party; elected in 1935 a Labour M.P.; expelled in 1939 from the Labour Party; an anti-fascist activist; turned to a definite Marxist-Leninist approach; anti-colonial advocate; among his most notable political cases was the defence of Jomo Kenyatta in 1952.

Purcell, Albert Arthur William (1872-1935). Trade unionist; leading member of general strike committee, 1926; president, International Federation of Trade Unions, 1924-7; Labour MP, 1923-4.

Rajagopalachari, C., (1878-1972). A lawyer from Salem in Madras who joined the non-cooperation movement in 1919; member of the working committee of Congress 1922-42, 1946-7 and 1951-4; chief minister of Madras 1937-9 and 1952-4; left the Congress in 1942 but rejoined in 1946; governor of West Bengal, 1947-8; governor-general of India, 1948-50; union minister without portfolio and then her home affairs, 1950-51; founder of the conservative Swatantra party.

Rangachariar, T. (1865-1945). Teacher, lawyer, politician; one of the general secretaries of Congress during the 1914 session at Madras; ardent Congressman; social reformer and writer.

Rao, Nageswar (1867-1938). Gandhian politician and social worker; participated in salt-*satyagraha;* philanthropist.

Rathbone, Eleanor Florence (1872-1946). Writer on economic, sociological and industrial questions; member, Liverpool city council, 1909-35; Labour MP, 1929-1946.

Reading, Rufus Isaacs, first marquis (1860-1935). Jewish Conservative politician; solicitor-general, 1910; attorney-general, 1910-13; lord chief justice, 1913-21; ambassador in Washington, 1918; viceroy of India, 1921-6; foreign secretary, 1931.

Reddy, Muthulakshmi (1886-1968). Educationist; social worker given to political and social upliftment of women; associated with the Sarada Home, Madras Seva Sadan, and Society of the Indian Ladies' Samaj, etc.; member of Madras legislative council, 1926-30; M.L.C., 1952-7, etc.

Redfern, Thomas Harwood. Joint secretary, Commonwealth of India group and then, Commonwealth of India League, 1929-31; in charge of its northern chapter.

Reynolds, Reginald (1905-58). Non-conformist Quaker; worked for India's freedom; stayed in 1930-1 in Gandhi's *ashram* at Sabarmati; enjoyed Gandhi's confidence and became an exponent of Gandhi's philosophy; wrote profusely; works include *Gandhi's Fast: Its Causes and Significance* (1935) and *India, Gandhi and World Peace* (1930); worked as confidant of Gandhi, Alexander and Irwin.

Rolland, Romain (1866-1944). French novelist and sociological writer; committed fighter against war; votary of human freedom.

Rothermere, Harold Sidney Harmsworth, viscount (1868-1940). Newspaper proprietor; British secretary for air, 1914-18; director of propaganda to neutral countries, 1918; took over *Daily Mail* on his brother's death (1927).

Roy, M.N. (1890-1954). Left India in 1915; participated in revolutionary movements in Mexico and Europe; attended second world congress of Comintern, 1920; representative of the Comintern in China, 1927; differed from the Comintern, 1928; arrested on his return to India in 1930 and sentenced to six years imprisonment; supported the British government during World War II.

Royden, (Agnes) Maude (1876-1956). Preacher; suffragist; edited *Common Cause,* 1913-14; undertook preaching tours to the United States, Australia, New Zealand, India and China.

Russell, Bertrand Arthur William, third earl (1872-1970). Philosopher and social reformer; prolific writer; teacher at various universities; Nobel prize for literature, 1950; campaigned aginst nuclear weapons; great advocate of various rational and progressive movements and scientific outlook.

Sahajananda Saraswati, 1889-1950; Indian nationalist and peasant leader; born in backward rural environment in Uttar Pradesh; renounced home in 1906; studied grammar and philosophy for eight years; plunged into the Bhumihar - Brahmin movement; came under the influence of Gandhi; turned a militant nationalist; joined non-cooperation movement; arrested on 2 July 1922 and underwent a spell of rigorous imprisonment; activities for the promotion of Khadi and prohibition, 1924-28; joined civil disobedience, 1930; from 1928 to the end of his life, worked against feudal oppression and for the emancipation of the oppressed peasantry; worked for building the Kisan movement and organizing the Kisan Sabha; the programme of the intensification of class struggle led to the rupture with Congress; he worked henceforth as an independent Leftist with Marxist inclination; in 1929 the Provincial Kisan Sabha was founded; in 1939, sided with Subhas Bose, associated with Patna university.

Sahni, Ruchi Ram, 1863-1949. Nationalist, social activist; influenced by some of the ideas of Guru Dutt, the Arya Samajist leader; also influenced by Shiv Narain Agnihotri, a professional teacher of science advocated western education, member of the Panjab legislative council, 1926 associated with Dayal Singh Majithia, the Dayal; Singh College at Lahore, Dayal Singh Library, Indian National Congress; non-cooperation movement, Gurdwara Reform movement including Guru ka Bagh Morcha, founded Punjab Science Institute, Indian Association, All India Social Conference, 1929, the Punjab University 1929, founding member of the Brahmo Samaj in Punjab.

Saklatvala, Shapurji Dorabji (1874-1936). Communist politician; once a member of Home Rule League of Annie Besant; founded Workers' Welfare League, 1916; worked among Indian seamen in London; became agent of AITUC in 1921; by mid-1920s identified Workers' Welfare League with communist left; during both his tenures in the House of Commons, 1923 and 1924-9, worked closely with the left-wing Scottish ILPers and made it his particular concern to emphasize the demands of workers and peasants in colonial countries, above all, in India.

Sampurnanand (1889-1969). Nationalist, editor and socialist; started career as editor, Maryada; joined active politics in 1921; elected to AICC, 1922; chief minister, UP; wrote many books.

Sankey, John (1866-1948). British statesman; Labour leader; lord chancellor, 1929-35; member of the National government of MacDonald; chairman, imperial relations committee and of federal structure committee, 1931-2.

Sapru, Tej Bahadur (1875-1949). Prominent advocate of Allahabad; leading Liberal leader; member, UP legislative council, 1913-16; member, central legislative council, 1916- 20; law member of governor-general's executive council, 1920-30; attended the RTC.

Sasmal, Birendranath, 1881-1934. Nationalist leader of Bengal; barrister; participated in Swadeshi movement; attended the Nagpur session of the Congress and joined the non-cooperation movement; secretary Bengal provincial Congress; helped Deshbandhu organize the Bengal Swarajya party; one of the directors of *Forward;* president, Krishnagar session of Bengal Congress; appointed a member of the non-official enquiry committee to go into the cases of atrocities in Midnapur during civil disobedience movement.

Sastri, V.S. Srinivasa (1869-1946). Politician; joined Servants of India Society, 1907; president of the society, 1915-27; member of viceroy's legislative council, 1916-20; privy councillor, 1925; represented India as agent of Government of India in South Africa, 1927-9; member, royal commission on labour, 1929.

Satyamurthi, S. (1896-1943). Advocate and Congressman of Madras; member of Madras legislative council, 1923-30 and of central legislative assembly, 1935-43; served several terms of imprisonment in the non-cooperation campaign.

Schuster, George Ernst (1869-1936). British politician; finance member, viceroy's executive council, 1928-38; Liberal M.P., 1940-44.

Scott, Charles Prestwick (1846-1932). Editor, *Manchester Guardian,* 1872-1929; gave the paper serious standing as critic of arts and letters and raised it to a leading place as a moral force in world politics.

Setalvad, Chimanlal Harilal (1866-1947). Advocate; moderate and liberal nationalist; advocated peaceful and constitutional method to achieve national freedom; played an important part in the first and second Round Table Conferences.

Setna, Pheroze Cursetjee (1866-1938). Businessman; member of insurance experts' committee, 1936; member of Bombay port trust, city improvement trust, Bombay municipality, Bombay legislative assembly, Sir Ratan Tata charities, N.M. Petit charities, Indian Sandhurst committee, etc.; attended the three RTCs.

Shafi, Sir Muhammad (1869-1934). Punjabi politician; president, All-India Muslim League, 1913; president, All India Muslim Educational Conference, 1909-12; education member of governor-general's council, 1919-22.

Shaukat Ali, Maulana (1873-1938). Elder brother of Mohammad Ali; Pan-Islamist, journalist and politician; helped to found Anjuman-i-Khuddam-i-Ka'aba, 1913; interned, 1915-19, 1921; Khilafat leader; drifted away from Congress.

Shaw, George Bernard (1856-1950). Irish playwright; socialist; joined Fabian Society, 1884; controversial dramatist; Nobel prize in literature, 1925; political works include *Common Sense about the War* (1914), *The Intelligent Women's Guide to Socialism and Capitalism* (1928) and *Everybody's Political What's What?* (1944); a heathen mystic; his socialism was prompted by a desire for an orderly community and a conviction that poverty, ignorance and ill health must be abolished.

Shelvankar, Krishnarao, Shivarao (1906-96). Indian writer, journalist and diplomat; close associate of Krishna Menon and India League activist since 1928; his professional association with the *Hindu* (Madras) lasted, with brief interruptions, for a quarter of a century; press adviser of Jawaharlal Nehru, 1947-51; following the 1962 war with China was recalled to Delhi to help Government of India with its press and public relations; associated with *India Weekly,* London since its reception in 1964; ambassador to Soviet Union, 1972-74, and to Norway, 1974-78; author of the celebrated volume, *Situation in India,* 1936.

Shinwell, Emmanuel (b.1884). Labour MP, 1922-24, 1928-31, 1935-70; junior ministers in Labour governments; secretary of state for war, 1947-50; life pear, 1970.

Shiva Rao, Benegal (1891-1967). Indian politician; influenced by Annie Besant; teacher at Central Hindu School at Banaras, 1910; joined Besant's *New India,* 1917; associated with Madras Labour Union of Textile Workers; devoted trade unionist; helped Tej Bahadur Sapru in the preparatory work of the Commonwealth of India Bill; accompanied Besant to England in 1925-6; associated with Sapru, N.M. Joshi; attended R.T.C.; Delhi correspondent of *Manchester Guardian,* 1936-53 and of the *Hindu,* etc.

Silverman, Julius (1905-1996). Barrister-at-Law and Labour politician; member, Birmingham city council 1934-45, Labour MP, 1945-55, 1955-74, 1974-90.

Simon, Sir John (1873-1954). Liberal politician and lawyer; chairman, Indian Statutory Commission, 1927-30.

Sinha, Sachinananda (1871-1950). Nationalist, editor and advocate; worked as a volunteer in Dadabhai Naoroji's election campaign in England; editor, Beharee; started, Search Light, 1918; became an executive councilor of Bihar, 1926; non-official vice-chancellor, Patna University, 1936-44; elected to Patna Legislative Council, 1944; member, constituent assembly.

Smith, Rennie (1888-1962). Teacher, labour leader and Labour MP, 1924-31; secretary, Friends of Europe, 1938; joint editor, *Central Europe as Observer,* 1940-6.

Smith, Francis Samuel (1854-1940). Labour MP, 1929-31; member, London county council, 1892-1910; secretary of confederation of engineering and shipbuilding trades for 20 years.

Smuts, Jan Christian (1870-1950). South African statesman; educated at Cambridge; participated in negotiations leading to peace settlement in South Africa, 1902; minister of education under Louis Botha (1907-10); formed South African Defence Force; deputy prime minister, 1933-9; formed the United South African National Party, 1934; prime minister, 1939-48; field-marshal, 1941; frequently consulted by British statesmen.

Snell, Harry (d.1944). Self-educated; active in secular and rationalist movement; member ILP; Labour MP, 1922-31, parliamentary under secretary of state for India, 1931.

Snowden, Philip, Viscount (1864-1937). Prominent member of ILP; chancellor of the exchequer, 1924, 1929-31; lord privy seal, 1931-2.

Sorabji, Cornelia (1866-1954). Indian barrister and social activist; born in Bombay presidency; adviser in court of wards, Bengal, Bihar and Orissa, 1904-22; practised as barrister in India, 1924-9; settled in London, 1929.

Sorensen, Reginald William (1891-1971). Labour MP, 1929-31, 1936-1950, 1950-64; government whip in the House of lords, December 1964 - April 1968; chairman, National Peace Council, India League, World Congress of Faiths, Gandhi Memorial Fund, Tagore India Centre, London Brahmo Samaj; etc.

Stanley, Oliver Frederick (1905-79). Conservative MP, 1924-45; parliamentary under-secretary of state, home office, 1931-3; minister of transport, 1933-4; minister of labour, 1934-5, president, board of education, 1935-7; president, board of trade, 1935-7; etc.

Stephens, Ian Melville (1903-1980). Public servant, journalist and academic; deputy director, bureau of public information, Government of India, 1930-35; editor, *The Stateman*, 1937-1951; coronation medal, 1927; life-fellow, Kings College, Cambridge.

Strachey, (Evelyn) John St. Loc (1901-63). Politician and writer; joined Labour Party, 1923; editor, *Socialist Review* and *Miner;* Labour MP, 1929-31, 1945-50, 1950-63; between 1931-40 supported the Communist party; assisted Victor Gollancz in founding the Left Book Club, 1936; wrote for *Left News;* secretary of state for war, 1950-1; etc.

Stuart, Louis (1870-1949). ICS, 1891-1930; held important and responsible positions in the judicial service in India including judicial secretary to Government of India, 1910- 12; judge, Allahabad high court 1922-5; chief judge, Oudh chief court, 1925-30; joint secretary, Indian Empire Society, 1931-8; editor, *Indian Empire Review,* 1932.

Bibliography

A. Manuscript Sources

1. Nehru Memorial Museum and Library, Delhi

V. K. Krishna Menon Papers

The volume is based round the papers of V.K. Krishna Menon. They are kept in the Nehru Memorial Museum and Library (Teen Murti House) at New Delhi. I am grateful to the late Indira Gandhi for giving me permission to study and examine these papers. The papers of the period after September 1946 are still to be opened to the scholars. The collection is rich and rewarding.

Horace Alexander Papers

Balakrishna Shivaram Moonji Papers

2. National Archive of India, Delhi

M. R. Jayakar Papess

3. India Office Library, London

Halifax (Irwin) Papers
Templewood (Hoare) Papers
Zetland Papers
Graham Pole Papers
Saklatvala Papers
S.K. Dutt Papers
Malcolm Hailey Papers
Cornelia Sorabji Papers

4. University Library, Cambridge

Templewood (Hoare) Papers

5. **Churchill College, Cambridge**

Page Croft Papers
Noel-Baker Papers
Bevin Papers
Fenner Brockway Papers
Lord Lloyd Papers
A.V. Alexander Papers
Patrick Gordon-Walker Papers

6. **South Asia Centre Archives, Cambridge**

Benthall Papers

7. **Trinity College, Cambridge**

Pethic-Lawrence Papers

8. **Bodleian Library, Oxford**

Louis Stuart Papers
Lionel Curtis Papers

9. **Nuffield College Library, Oxford**

Stafford Cripps Papers

10. **Rhodes House, Oxford**

Arthur Creech Jones Papers
Papers of Fabian Colonial Bureau
R. Coupland Papers

11. **University Library, Hull**

Winifred Horrabin Papers
Reginald Bridgeman Papers
Harold Laski Papers
Union of Democratic Control Papers

National Council of Civil Liberties Papers

12. **University Library, York**

Graham Pole Papers

13. **National Museum of Labour History, Manchester**

Papers of Advisory Committee on Imperial Question
William Gillies Papers

14. **Communist Party Archives, London**

Rajni Palme Dutt Papers
Ben Bradley papers

15. **Friends House, London**

Indian Conciliation Group Papers
Agatha Harrison Papers
Horace Alexander Papers

16. **Friends House, 40 Bull Street, Birmingham**

Minutes of meetings of various centres

17. **Woodbrook, Selly Oak**

Horace Alexander Papers
Gandhi's visit at Selly Oak

18. **British Library of Political and Economic Science, London**

George Lansbury Papers

19. **Sussex University Library, Brighton**

Kingsley Martin Papers

20. **House of Lords Records Room**

Wedgwood Benn (First Viscount Stansgate) Papers
Sorensen Papers

21. **Theosophical Society, Adyar, Madras**

Annie Besant Papers

22. **Institute of Working Class History, Berlin, Germany**

P. C. Joshi Collection
Wilhelm Koenen Papers

B. Official Rcords

National Archives of India, New Delhi

Home Department, Political Branch, Proceedings (Home [Pol.])
Political Department Procedings

India Office Library, London

Private Office Papers (L/PO)
Scotland Yard Papers
External Department Collection (L/P & S 12)
Private Secretary to the Viceroy Papers (R//3/1)

C. Newspapers and Journals

The Bombay Chronicle (Bombay)
The Hindu (Madras)
The Hindustan Times (Delhi)
The Leader (Allahabad)
The Congress Socialist (Bombay)
The Tribune (Lahore)
Manchester Guardian (Manchester)

Daily Mail (London)
Daily Express (London)
The Times (London)

Journals

The Plebs
The Twentieth Century, (London)
The New Statesman and Nation, (London)
The Spectator, (London)
The Contemporary Review, (London)
The Round Table, (London)
The Nineteenth Century, (London)
The Quarterly Review, (London)
The Political Quarterly, (London)
The Fortnightly Review, (London)
The Anti-Imperialist Review, (Berlin)
New Left Review, (London)
The Indian Review, (Madras)
The Modern Review, (Calcutta)
Presidency College Magazine and Calendar, (Madras)

D. Pamphlets

Daily Mail

1. *Save India for the Empire,* London 1934

Indian Empire Society

1. Price, G. Ward, *Face the Facts in India,* London, 1934
2. _____. *Why Lose India?* London, 1930
3. Lord Sydenham, *A Warning,* London, 1931
4. _____, *All India Federation, A Dangerous Illusion,* London 1931
5. Anon, *Facts - The Indian Empire Society,* London, 1933.
6. Fisher, F. Victor, *The Threatened Indian Chaos,* London, 1933
7. Anon, *Policy Recommended by the Indian Empire Society,* London, 1933

8. Lymington, Viscount, *Our Duty to India,* London, 1934

9. E.P.J., *The White Paper Proposals with Regard to Law and Order,* London, 1933

10. Lovett, Verney, *The Present Extent of Terrorism in India,* London, 1933

11. Anon, *Alas The Poor Indians: A Sidelight on the White Paper,* London, 1933

12. Harrison, J.H.C., *Has Socialism Shaped Our India Policy?* London, 1933

13. Lovett, Verney, *The Present Extent of Terrorism in India,* London, 1933

14. British Raj, *The White Paper Plan,* London, 1933

15. Sydenham, Lord. *The Tragedy of India: Retrospect and Prospect,* London, 1932

16. Lalkaka, K.K., *The Parsees in India,* London, 1932

17. _____. *Some Points: A Sympathetic Briton Ought to Know,* London, 1934

18. Harrison, J.H.C., *What has Gone Wrong with the British Raj?* London, 1935

Defence of India League

1. Blair, Hamish, *India-The Eleventh Hour,* London, 1934

2. Anon, *The Pledges We Gave to India,* London, 1934

3. Anon, *Report of Joint Select Committee,* London, 1934

4. O'Dwyer, Michael, *The Indian States and Federation,* London, 1934

5. _____., *The Indian Report: A Minority View,* 1934

6. Morgan, J.H., *The Dangers of Federalism,* London, 1933

7. Fitzalan and Wolmer, *The Indian Crisis,* London, 1933

8. K.K. Lalkaka, *Britain's Plain Duty towards India,* London, 1934

9. Anon, *The British and the Scheduled Castes,* London, 1934

10. Zeta, *The White Paper and the Indian Judicature,* London, 1934

11. Sumnar, Viscount, *Looking Forward,* London, 1931

12. O'Dwyer, Michael, *Lord Sankey and the Third Round Table Conference,* London, 1932

13. _____. *The Provision of Safeguards under the Federal Constitution,* London, 1932

14 J.A. Tassie, *Future Prospects for Britishers in India,* London, 1935

Union of Britain and India

1. *The White Paper: What India Thinks: An MP's Impressions,* London, 1934

2. Thompson, John Perronet, *India: The White Paper,* London, 1933

3. Hailey, Malcolm, *Six Crucial Aspects of Reform,* London, 1933

4. Thompson, John, *The Reform Prospects and Their Reasons,* London, 1933

5. _____. *Effects of Civil Disobedience and Boycott Movement in India,* London, 1934

Labour Party

1. *Labour Problems after the War,* 1917

2. Brockway, Fenner, *India and its Government,* 1991

3. Buxton, Charles Roden, *The Black Man's Rights,* 1995

4. Anon, *Labour Problems after the War,* 1918

5. Anon, *Report of the First British Commonwealth Labour Conference,* 1925

6. Anon, *Labour and Empire,* 1926

7. Anon, *Labour and the Nation,* 1929

8. Anon, *The Colonies,* 1933

9. Horrabin, J.F., *The Break with Imperialism,* 1934

Commonwealth of India League and the India League

1. Commonwealth of India League, *Indian National Demand,* 1928

2. Puncell, A.A., *The English Trade Union Report on Industrial India,* 1928

3. _____, *Report on Indian Labour Conditions,* 1928

4. Besant, Annie, *India Bonded or Free?* 1926

5. Menon, V. K. Krishna, *India's Demand,* 1929

6. Shiva Rao, B., *Plantation Labour in India,* 1929

7. _____, *The Trade Union Movement in India,* 1929

8. _____, *Indian Labour and Self-Government,* 1929

9. Freeman, Peter, *Parable of a Conquered State,* 1930

10. Bristol Branch, *The Pearl in India,* Bristol 1930

11. Gandhi, M.K. *India and the National Congress,* 1932

12. Menon, V. K. Krishna, *Notes on Gandhi,* 1931

13. _____, *India at the Cross Roads,* 1934

14. _____, *The Ordinance Rule,* London, 1933

15. _____, *The Village under Ordinance,* London, 1933

16. _____, *Police Raj in Action,* London, 1933

17. _____, *Law and Prisons in India,* London, 1933

18. _____, *White Paper Examined,* London, 1933

19. _____, *Circular on Fascism,* London, 1933

20. _____, *Terrorism by Ordinance,* London, 1939

21. _____, *Indian View on the White Paper,* London, 1933

22. _____, *Chittagong: Facts and Fictions,* London, 1932

23. _____, *Indian Labour and Self-Government,* London, 1934

24. _____. *India Speaks,* London, 1934

25. _____, *Chittagong and Hijli,* London, 1933

26. Russell, Bertrand, *Know the Facts,* London, 1932

National Minority Movement

1. *British Imperialism: An Outline of Workers' Condition in the Colonies,* 1928

Communist Party of India

1. *Imperialism and Labour: The Meaning of British Policy in India. An Appeal to the Workers of Great Britain,* Bombay, 1925

2. *Manifesto on the Round Table Conference,* Bombay, 1931.

League Against Imperialism and for National Independence

1. *Introduction to Communist International, Theses on the National and Colonial Question,* London, 1921

2. Burnes, Emile, *Imperialism: An Outline Course,* London, 1927

Communist Party Great Britain

1. Johnston, Thomas and John F. Sime, *Exploitation in India,* Dundee, 1927

2. *Class Against Class: The General Election Programme,* London, 1929

3. Page, Arnot Robin, *How Britain Rules in India,* London 1929

4. Rust, W., *India's Fight for Separation and Independence,* London, 1932

5. *Tenth Congress Report,* London, 1929

6. *Resolutions adopted by the Executive Committee,* London, 1929

7. *Is India Different? Class Struggle in India, Saklatvala-Gandhi Correspondence,* London, 1927

8. *Storm over India,* London, 1930

9. *India and the Round Table Conference,* London, 1932

Meerut Conspiracy Case

1. Bridgeman, R., *The Meerut Conspiracy Case, Open Letter to the Delegates to 31st Annual Conference of the Labour Party at Scarborough, 5-9 October 1931,* London, 1931

2. CPGB, *Meerut Conspiracy Trial: Open Letter to the Delegates to the 64th Annual Meeting of the Trades Union Congress, Newcastle,* London, 1932

3. Glading, Percy, *The Meerut Conspiracy Case,* London, 1933

4. Meerut Prisoners' Defence Committee, *The Meerut Trial: Facts of the Case,* London, 1933

5. Dutt, Clemens, *Conspiracy Against the King,* London, 1930

6. League Against Imperialism and for National Independence, *The Mutiny in Meerut Jail: Memorial of the Meerut Prisoners,* London, 1932

7. Bridgeman, R., *Memorandum on the Meerut Case,* London, 1931

8. CPGB, *Terror in Meerut,* London, 1931

E. Oral Testimony

Names of those who agreed to grant interviews to the author.

Mulk Raj Anand, 26 October 1987

Michael Foot, 6 April 1991, 9 May 1995

P.N. Haksar, 18, 19, 20 and 21 June 1995

V.R. Krishna Iyer, 18, 20, 21 April 1996

John Faithful Fortescue Platts-Mills, 20 May 1991

Emily Polak, 16, 18 May 1992

Dr Krishna Shelvankar, 6 and 7 May 1992

Mary Shelvankar, 8 May 1992

Julius Silverman, 28 April 1992

T.Z. (Zeff) Carrasco, 6 April 1992

Narayani Chatterjee, 29 May 1992

Pam Cullen, 2 May 1992

Narayan Menon, 20 September 1988

F. Selected Books

Adams, William Wheen Scovell. *Edwardian Portraits.* London, 1957.

Ahmad, Aziz. *Islamic Modernism in India and Pakistan, 1857-1964.* London, 1967.

Andrews, C.F. *The Renaissance in India.* London, 1912.

_____, *India and Britain: A Moral Challenge.* London, 1931.

_____, ed. *Mahatma Gandhi at work.* London, 1931.

Anon. *A Great Humanist: Dr George Arundale: A Biography.* Madras, 1978.

Arora, K.C. *V.K. Krishna Menon, A Biography.* New Delhi, 1998.

Arundale, G.S. *Home Rule for India.* Adyar, 1916.

Attlee, Clement. *The Labour Party in Perspective.* London, 1937.

Baden-Powell, R.S.S. *The Scoutmaster's Training Course.* London, 1912.

_____, *To Scouters Overseas.* London, 1912.

Balabushevich and Dayaker (ed.), *A Contemporary History of India.* New Delhi, 1964.

Ball, Stuart. *Baldwin and the Conservative Party, The Crisis of 1929-1931.* London, 1988.

Banerjea, Surendranath. *Nation in Making.* Bombay, 1925.

Barraclough, Geoffrey. *An Introduction to Contemporary History.* London, 1964.

Beauchamps, John. *British Imperialism and India.* London, 1960 (ed)

Beer, Max. *The League on Trial.* London, 1940.

Bellamy, Joycee M. and John Saville. *Dictionary of Labour Biography.* 7 vols., London, 1972-87.

Benewick, R. *Public Violence and Public Order.* London, 1972.

Bergere, Marie-Claire. *The Golden Age of Chinese Bourgeoisie,*

1911 -1937. Cambridge, 1989.

Besant, Annie. *The Birth of New Nation.* Adyar, 1917.

_____, *Gandhian Non-Cooperation or Shall India Commit Suicide?* Madras, 1920.

_____, *Lectures on Political Science.* Adyar, 1922.

_____, *The Future of Indian Politics.* Adyar, 1922.

_____, *England, India and Afghanistan.* London, 1925.

_____, *Shall India Live or Die?* Madras, 1925.

_____, *The Commonwealth of India Bill.* Adyar, 1927.

_____, *Why India Wants Home Rule.* London, 1927.

Blackburn, Robin, ed. *Ideology in Social Science.* London, 1972.

Blair, Hamish. *Governor Hardy.* London, 1931.

Blythe, Ronald. *The Age of Illusion, England in the Twenties and Thirties, 1919-40.* London, 1963.

Bolitho, H. *Jinnah, Creator of Pakistan.* London, 1954.

Bose, S.C., *The Indian Struggle.* London, 1935.

Bramsted, Ernest, K. *Goebbels and National Socialist Propaganda.* London, 1965.

Branson, Noreen and Margot Heinemann. *Britain in the Nineteen Thirties.* London, 1956.

Branson, Noreen. *Poplarism, 1919-1925.* London, 1979.

Brecher, Michael. *Nehru: A Political Biography.* Oxford, 1968.

_____, *India and World Politics.* Oxford, 1968.

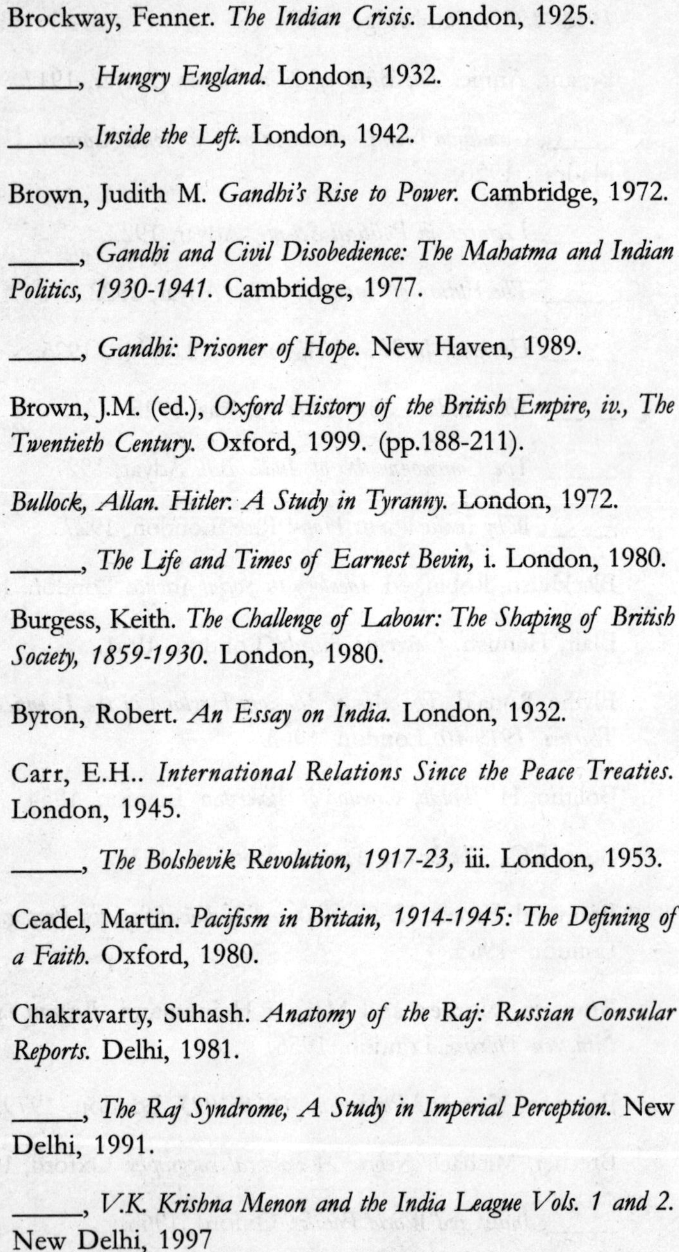

Brockway, Fenner. *The Indian Crisis.* London, 1925.

_____, *Hungry England.* London, 1932.

_____, *Inside the Left.* London, 1942.

Brown, Judith M. *Gandhi's Rise to Power.* Cambridge, 1972.

_____, *Gandhi and Civil Disobedience: The Mahatma and Indian Politics, 1930-1941.* Cambridge, 1977.

_____, *Gandhi: Prisoner of Hope.* New Haven, 1989.

Brown, J.M. (ed.), *Oxford History of the British Empire, iv., The Twentieth Century.* Oxford, 1999. (pp.188-211).

Bullock, Allan. Hitler: A Study in Tyranny. London, 1972.

_____, *The Life and Times of Earnest Bevin,* i. London, 1980.

Burgess, Keith. *The Challenge of Labour: The Shaping of British Society, 1859-1930.* London, 1980.

Byron, Robert. *An Essay on India.* London, 1932.

Carr, E.H.. *International Relations Since the Peace Treaties.* London, 1945.

_____, *The Bolshevik Revolution, 1917-23,* iii. London, 1953.

Ceadel, Martin. *Pacifism in Britain, 1914-1945: The Defining of a Faith.* Oxford, 1980.

Chakravarty, Suhash. *Anatomy of the Raj: Russian Consular Reports.* Delhi, 1981.

_____, *The Raj Syndrome, A Study in Imperial Perception.* New Delhi, 1991.

_____, *V.K. Krishna Menon and the India League Vols. 1 and 2.* New Delhi, 1997

_____, (ed.), *India League's Condition of India.* Delhi, 1998.

Chandra, Bipan, *The Indian Capitalist Class and Imperialism before 1947.* Delhi, 1972.

_____, *Elements of Continuity and Change in Early Nationalist Activity.* Indian History Congress Proceedings, 1972.

_____, *Communalism in Modern India.* New Delhi, 1979.

_____, *Nationalism and Colonialism in Modern India.* Delhi, 1979.

_____, (ed.) *The Indian Left,*

Chandra, Bipan, Mridula Mukherjee, Aditya Mukherjee, K.N. Panikkar and Sucheta Mahajan. *India's Struggle for Independence.* New Delhi, 1988.

Chow-tse-tung. *The May Fourth Movement.* Cambridge, 1960.

Clarke, Peter. *Stafford Cripps.* London, 2002.

Cripps, Stafford. *Can Socialism Come by Constitutional Method?* London, 1933.

Cross, J.A. *Sir Samuel Hoare, A Political Biography.* London, 1979.

Cross, C. *The Fascists in Britain.* London 1961.

Cunningham, Valentine. *British Writers of the Thirties.* Oxford, 1989.

Das, Sisir Kumar. *The English Writing of Rabindranath Tagore* iii. New Delhi, 1996.

_____, *A History of Indian Literature, 1911-1956, Struggle for Freedom: Triumph and Tragedy.* New Delhi, 1995.

Desai, A.R. *Peasant Struggle in India.* Delhi 1978 (ed)

Deutscher, Isaac.: *The Great Contest, Russia and the West.* London, 1960.

_____, *The Prophet Outcast.* London 1963.

Dev, Acharya Narendra. *Socialism and National Revolution.* Bombay, 1946.

Dimotrov, Georgi. *United Front of the Working Class against Fascism.* Calcutta, 1969 (edn).

Donaldson, E. *Edward VIII.* London, 1975.

Dutt, Romesh Chandra. *Economic History of British India under Early British Rule from the Rise of the British Power in 1757 to the Accession of Queen Victoria in 1837.* London, 1902.

Dutt, R.P. *Modern India.* London, 1927.

Edwards, R.D. *Victor Gollancz: A Biography.* London, 1987.

Foot, Michael. *Aneurin Bevan: A Biography.* London, 1962.

French, Patrick. *Liberty or Death.* London, 1997.

Gallacher, W. *Revolt on the Clyde.* London, 1936.

Gandhi, M.K. *Hind Swaraj or Indian Home Rule.* Rev. edn., Ahmedabad, 1938.

_____, *An Autobiography, My Experiments with Truth.* London, 1949.

Gathy, Vera. *Nehru, A Portrait.* Budapest, 1989.

Gedye, G.E.R. *Betrayal in Central Europe.* London, 1939.

George, T.J.S. *Krishna Menon: A Biography.* London, 1964.

Gilbert, Martin. *Winston S. Churchill,* v, Companion part 2.

Kramnick, Isaac and Barry Sheerman. *Harold Laski: A Life on the Left.* London, 1993.

Kumar, Ravinder, and Haridev, Sharma. *Selected Works of Motilal Nehru,* vi. Delhi, 1995.

Kutty, Madhavan. *V.K. Krishna Menon.* New Delhi, 1988.

Labour Party Annual Conference Reports. London, 1924-36.

Laquer, Walter. *Fascism: A Reader's Guide.* London, 1972.

Laquer, W. Z. *Communism and Nationalism in the Middle East.* London, 1957.

Laski, Harold. *Authority in the Modern State.* London, 1919.

_____, *Foundation of Sovereignty and Other Essays.* London, 1921.

_____, *A Grammar of Politics.* London, 1925.

_____, *Politics.* London, 1931.

Lazitch, Branko and Milorad M. Drachkovitch. *Biographical Dictionary of the Commintern.* California, 1986.

League against Imperialism and for National Independence. *The Colonies and Oppressed Nations in the Struggle for Freedom.* Berlin, 1931.

Lenezowski, G. *The Middle East in World Affairs.* Ithaca, 1952.

Lengyel, Emil. *Krishna Menon.* New York, 1976 (ed).

Lerner, Daniel, et.al. *The Nazi Elite.* London, 1951.

Lichtheim, George. *A Short History of Socialism.* London, 1969.

Lindsay, A.D. (ed.). *Report of the Commission on Christian*

Education in India. London, 1931.

Low, D.A. (ed.) *Soundings in Modern South Asian History.* London, 1968.

Lucas, Jack. *The 1930s: The Challenge to Orthodoxy.* London, 1978.

Mackenzie, N. (ed.). *The Letters of Sidney and Beatrice Webb,* iii. London, 1978.

Mackenzie, R.T. *British Political Parties.* London, 1968.

MacKenzie, John (ed.). *Propaganda and Empire: The Manipulation of British Public Opinion, 1880-1960.* Manchester, 1984.

Macmillan, Harold, *Winds of Change.* London, 1966.

Mahon, John. *Harry Pollitt, A Biography.* London, 1976.

Manuel, F.E. *The Politics of Modern Spain.* London, 1938.

Manwell, R. and H. Frankel. *Herman Goering.* London, 1962.

_____, *Himler.* London, 1965.

Marquand, David. *Ramsay MacDonald.* London, 1977.

Martin, Kingsley. *Father Figures: A Volume of Autobiography.* London, 1966.

_____, *Editor.* London, 1968.

Marwick, Arthur. *The Deluge: British Society and the First World War.* London, 1965.

_____, *Britain in the Century of Total War.* London, 1968.

_____, *Britain in Our Century.* London, 1984.

McNair, John. *James Maxton, The Beloved Rebel.* London, 1953.

Mehrotra, S.R. *India and the Commonwealth, 1885-1929.* London, 1965.

Memmi, Albert. *The Colonizer and the Colonized.* Boston, 1967.

Menon, S. *Social and Cultural History of Kerala.* New Delhi, 1979.

Menon, V.K. Krishna (ed.). *Young Oxford and War.* London, 1933.

Menon, A. Sreedhara. *A Survey of Kerala History.* Kottayam, 1967.

Middlemas, R.K. *The Clydesiders.* London, 1965.

Middlemas, Keith and John Barnes. *Baldwin.* London, 1969.

Miliband, Ralph. *Capitalist Democracy in Britain.* Oxford, 1982.

Minkin, L. *The Labour Party Conference.* London, 1978.

Moore, R.J. *The Crisis of Indian Unity, 1917-1940.* Delhi, 1974.

_____, *Escape from Empire: The Attlee Government and the Indian Problem.* Oxford, 1983.

Morgan, K.O. *Keir Hardie.* London, 1975.

Moss, George, L. *Towards the Final Solution, A Bistory of European Racism.* New York, 1978.

Mowat, C.L. *Britain between the Wars.* London, 1955.

Muggeridge, Malcolm. *The Thirties.* London, 1967.

Munzenberg, Willi. *From Demonstration to Organization.* Brussels, 1927.

Namboodiripad, E.M.S. *Kerala, Yesterday, Today and Tomorrow.* Calcutta, 1967.

Nanda, B.R., *The Nehrus,* London, 1962.

_____, *Gokhale, The Indian Moderates and the British Raj*. Delhi, 1977.

_____, ed. *Mahatma Gandhi, 125 Years.* Delhi, 1995.

Nehru, J. *Soviet Russia.* Allahabad, 1933.

_____, *Whither India?* Allahabad, 1933.

_____, *Letters from a Father to His Daughter.* Allahabad, 1933.

_____, *Glimpses of World History* (2 vol. edition). Allahabad, 1934.

Neumann, Franz. *Behemoth: The Structure and Practice of National Socialism.* London, 1944.

Newman, Michael. *Harold Laski, A Political Biography.* London, 1993.

Pearce, Robert. *Attlee.* London, 1997.

Peele, Gillian and Chris Cook. *The Politics of Reappraisal, 1918-1939.* London, 1995.

Phadnis, Urmila. *Towards the Integration of Indian States, 1919-47.* Bombay, 1968.

Phillips, G.A. *The General Strike.* London, 1976.

Pilgrim Trust *Men without Work.* London, 1938.

Polak, H.S.L. *Hon'ble Mr. Gokhale in South Africa.* Puna, 1912.

Portar, B. *Critics of Empire.* London, 1968.

Priestley, J.B. *English Journey.* London, 1933.

Pritt, D.N. *From Right to Left.* London, 1965.

Pugh, Martin. *The Making of Modern British Politics, 1867- 1939.* Oxford, 1982.

Ram, Janaki. *V.K. Krishna Menon: A Personal Memoir.* Delhi, 1977.

Rao, B. Shiva. *Indian Labour and Self-Government.* London, 1929.

_____, *The Trade Union Movement in India.* London, 1929.

Reynolds, Reginald. *My Life and Crimes.* London, 1956.

Rieff, P. (ed.). *On Intellectual, Theoretical Studies.* Garden City, 1969.

Robbins, Lord. *Autobiography of an Economist.* Glasgow, 1971.

Roth, Jack, J. ed. *World War I: A Turning Point in Modern History.* New York, 1967.

Rothermund, Dietmar. *India in the Great Depression, 1929-1939.* Delhi, 1992.

Ruthnaswamy, M. *The Political Theory of the Government of India.* Madras, 1928.

Saklatvala, Sehri. *The Fifth Commandment.* Salford, 1991.

Samuel, Raphael, Ewan MacColl, and Stuart Cosgrove. *Theatres of the Left, 1880-1935.* London, 1985.

Samuel, Bernard. *Imperialism and Social Reform.* London, 1960.

Sanyal, Hirendra Kumar. *Parichaer Kuri Bachar O Anyanya Smritichitra* (in Bengal). Calcutta, 1977.

Sarkar, Sumit. *Writing Social History.* Delhi, 1998.

Savarkar, Vinayak Damodar. *Hindutva: Who is a Hindu?*

Bombay, 1923.

Schwartz, Benjamin, ed. *Reflection on the May Fourth Movement: A Symposium.* Cambridge, Mass., 1972.

Searle, *Eugenics and Politics in Britain, 1900-1914.* Leiden, 1976.

Sen, Sukomal, *Working Class of India, History of Emergence and Movement, 1830-1970.* Calcutta, 1977.

Setalvad, C.H. *Recollection and Reflection: An Autobiography.* Bombay, n.d.

Seton, Marie. *Panditji: A Portrait of Jawaharlal Nehru.* New Delhi, 1967.

Seton-Watson, H. *Eastern Europe between the Wars, 1918-41.* London, 1945.

Shankar, Girija, *Socialist Trend in Indian National Movement.* Meerut, 1987.

Shaw, George Bernard, ed. *Fabianism and Empire.* London, 1900.

Shirer, William L. *The Rise and Fall of the Third Reich.* London, 1977.

Sinha, Aruna. *Lord Reading: Viceroy of India.* Delhi, 1985.

Skidelsky, Robert. *Oswald Mosley.* London, 1975.

Spector, I. *The First Russian Revolution: Its Impact on Asia.* Englewood Cliff, 1962.

Squires, Mike. *Saklatvala, A Political Biography.* London, 1990.

Srinivasa Sastri, V.S. *Life of Gopal Krishna Gokhale.* Bangalore, 1937.

Stevenson, John and Chris Cook. *The Slump: Society and Politics during the Depression.* London, 1977.

Strachey, John. *The Menace of Fascism.* London, 1933.

_____, *The Nature of Capitalist Crisis.* London, 1935.

Stuart, C. (ed.). *The Reith Diaries.* London, 1975.

Taylor, A.J.P. *English History, 1914-1945.* London, 1965.

_____, *Beaverbrook.* London, 1972.

Taylor, Miles. *The Decline of British Radicalism, 1847-60.* Oxford, 1995.

Taylor and Jon Lawrence (eds.). *Party, State and Society.: Electoral Behaviour in Britain since 1820.* Aldershot, 1997.

Tegart, Charles. *Terrorism in India.* London, 1933.

Templewood, Viscount. *Nine Troubled Years.* London, 1954.

Tendulkar, D.G. *Mahatma,* 8 vols. Bombay, 1951-4.

The World Committee for the Relief of the Victims of German Fascism, *The Brown Book of Hitler Terror.* London, 1933.

Thompson, Edward, *An Indian Day.* 1927.

_____, *The Reconstruction of India.* London, 1930.

_____, *A Letter from India.* 1932.

Thompson, E.P. *William Morris, Romantic to Revolutionary.* London, 1977.

Thompson, Lawrence. *Robert Blatchford: Portrait of an Englishman.* London, 1931.

Thomson, D. *Democracy in France: The Third and Fourth Republics.* London, 1958.

Thurston, E. *Caste and Tribes in Southern India.* London, 1965.

Trivedi, Harish. *Colonial Transactions.* Manchester, 1993.

Tyson, Geoffrey. *Danger in India.* London, 1931.

Union of Democratic Control. *The Secret International.* London, 1932.

_____, *Patriotism Ltd.* London, 1933.

Utley, Freda. *Lancashire and Far East.* London, 1929.

Verghese, T.C. *Agrarian Crisis and Economic Consequences: Land Tenure in Kerala, 1850-1960.* Calcutta, 1970.

Wells, H.G. *Imperialism and People.* London, 1929.

Werskey, Gary. *The Visible College.* London, 1978.

Wessinger, Catherine Lowman. *Annie Besant and Progressive Messianism, 1847-1933.* Queenston, 1969.

William, Joyce. *Fascism and India.* London, 1933.

Williamson, Philip. *National Crisis and National Government: British Politics, Economics and Empire, 1926-32.* Cambridge, 1992.

Wolpert, Stanley. *Tilak and Gokhale, Revolution and Reform in the Making of Modern India.* Berkeley, 1962.

_____, *Jinnah of Pakistan.* Delhi, 1985.

Woodcock, G. *Kerala: A Portrait of the Malabar Coast.* London, 1976.

Woolf, Leonard. *Downhill all the Way, An Autobiography of the*

Years 1919-1939. London, 1967.

Young, G.M. *Stanley Baldwin*. London, 1952.

Zacharias, H.C.E. *Renascent India: From Rammohan Roy to Mahatma Gandhi*. London, 1933.

Zetland, Marquess of *Essayez*. London, 1956.

Index